Law, Policy, and International Justice

Law, Policy, and International Justice

*Essays in Honour of
Maxwell Cohen*

Edited by
WILLIAM KAPLAN
AND DONALD McRAE

McGill-Queen's University Press
Montreal & Kingston • London • Buffalo

© McGill-Queen's University Press 1993
ISBN 0-7735-1114-8

Legal deposit fourth quarter 1993
Bibliothèque nationale du Québec

Printed in Canada on acid-free paper

Publication of this book has been made possible by generous donations from the Faculty of Law, McGill University; the Faculty of Law, University of Ottawa; and the Law Foundation of Ontario.

Canadian Cataloguing in Publication Data

Main entry under title:
　Law, policy and international justice: essays in honour of Maxwell Cohen
　Includes bibliographical references.
　ISBN 0-7735-1114-8
　1. International law. 2. Civil rights – Canada.
　3. Habeas corpus – History. 4. Law – Study and teaching – Canada. 5. Cohen, Maxwell, 1910– Bibliography. I. Kaplan, William, 1957– .
　II. McRae, D.M. (Donald Malcolm), 1944– .
　III. Cohen, Maxwell, 1910– .
　K160.L39 1993   340   C93-090335-8

Typeset in Baskerville 10/12 by
Caractéra production graphique inc., Quebec City.

Contents

Contributors   ix

Foreword   xi
The Right Honourable BRIAN DICKSON

Preface   xiii

INTERNATIONAL LAW

Legal Aspects of the Gulf War of 1991 and Its Aftermath   5
OSCAR SCHACHTER

The Agent in Litigation in the International Court of Justice   41
SHABTAI ROSENNE

The Case for an Arctic Region Council and a Treaty Proposal   69
DONAT PHARAND

International Human Rights Law in Canadian Courts   107
ANNE F. BAYEFSKY

Free Trade in Criminals: Canadian-American Extradition before 1890   144
DALE GIBSON

International Dispute Settlement under the Canada–United States Free Trade Agreement 186
DONALD McRAE

PUBLIC LAW

Maxwell Cohen's Perspective on Human Rights in Canada: The Entrenchment of the Charter and the Enactment of the Emergencies Act 207
ANNEMIEKE HOLTHUIS

Maxwell Cohen and the Report of the Special Committee on Hate Propaganda 243
WILLIAM KAPLAN

The Right to Protection against Group-Vilifying Speech: Towards a Model Factum in Support of Anti-Hate Legislation 275
IRWIN COTLER

The Charter of Rights and Freedoms and Positive Obligations 298
WILLIAM W. BLACK

Language and Canadian Public Law 320
JULIUS GREY

LEGAL HISTORY

The Writ of Habeas Corpus in Early Modern England: A View from Within 365
LOUIS A. KNAFLA

Habeas Corpus and the Case of the Man Who Escaped from Devil's Island 385
ROBERT J. SHARPE

LEGAL EDUCATION

Dreaming the Impossible Dream: Maxwell Cohen and McGill's National Law Programme 409
RODERICK A. MACDONALD

Anglophone Quebec and the Quiet Revolution: Maxwell Cohen at McGill University 431
EDWARD McWHINNEY

Maxwell Cohen and the Theory and Practice of
Canadian Legal Education   440
J.P.S. McLAREN

The Role of the Canadian Institute for the
Administration of Justice in the Development of Judicial
Education in Canada   455
DAVID C. McDONALD

The Founding of the Canadian Judicial Centre   481
WILLIAM STEVENSON

Bibliography
Maxwell Cohen: An Overview of His Publications   493
ANNEMIEKE HOLTHUIS

Contributors

ANNE F. BAYEFSKY is a professor of law at the University of Ottawa. The author of numerous articles and books, she was recently awarded the Bora Laskin Fellowship in Human Rights.

WILLIAM W. BLACK is director of the Human Rights Centre at the University of Ottawa. His interests include constitutional law and human rights.

IRWIN COTLER is a professor of law at McGill University and chair of InterAmicus, the McGill-based human rights advocacy centre. Professor Cotler was recently appointed to the Order of Canada, where he was cited for his "extraordinary contribution to the cause of civil rights."

DALE GIBSON is Bowker Professor of Law at the University of Alberta. He has published widely in Canadian constitutional law, torts, and legal history.

JULIUS GREY teaches at the Faculty of Law at McGill University. He has represented linguistic minorities in several well-known cases and is a past president of the Canadian Human Rights Foundation.

ANNEMIEKE HOLTHUIS is counsel, Human Rights Law Section at the Department of Justice, Ottawa. She provides advice on the Canadian Charter of Rights and Freedoms, the Canadian Human Rights Act, and international human rights instruments.

WILLIAM KAPLAN teaches at the Faculty of Law of the University of Ottawa. His books include *Everything That Floats: Pat Sullivan, Hal*

Banks and the Seamen's Unions of Canada and *State and Salvation: The Jehovah's Witnesses and Their Fight for Civil Rights*.

LOUIS A. KNAFLA specializes in English and Canadian legal history, and is currently engaged in a multi-volume study of litigation in the county of Kent in the early seventeenth century.

DAVID C. McDONALD is a judge of the Alberta Court of Queen's Bench. He was the first president of the Canadian Institute for the Administration of Justice.

RODERICK A. MACDONALD is a professor of law at McGill University. He was dean of the faculty between 1984 and 1989, and is currently director at the Law and Society Programme of the Canadian Institute of Advanced Research.

J.P.S. McLAREN is the Lansdowne professor of law at the University of Victoria. He has written on the history of legal education, the legal regulation of prostitution, and the history of racism and the law.

DONALD McRAE is dean of the Faculty of Law of the University of Ottawa. He has served on several Canada–United States free trade dispute resolution panels.

EDWARD McWHINNEY teaches constitutional and international law at Simon Fraser University. He is a member of l'Institut de Droit International, l'Institut Grand-Ducal (Luxembourg), and an associate member of l'Académie Internationale de Droit Comparé.

DONAT PHARAND is professor of law emeritus at the University of Ottawa. He has written three books and numerous articles on the law of the sea and the Arctic regions.

SHABTAI ROSENNE is a former ambassador of Israel who also served as a member of the International Law Commission. He is the author of numerous articles and books.

OSCAR SCHACHTER is the Hamilton Fish Professor Emeritus of International Law and Diplomacy at Columbia University. He is also a past president of the American Society of International Law, and the author of numerous articles and books.

ROBERT J. SHARPE is dean and professor of law at the Faculty of Law of the University of Toronto. His published works include *The Law of Habeas Corpus*.

WILLIAM STEVENSON is a retired judge of the Supreme Court of Canada and past president of the Canadian Institute for the Administration of Justice.

Foreword

This volume of essays honours a great Canadian jurist, and it is a special privilege for me to contribute the foreword. The range of topics covered by the distinguished contributors to this volume corresponds to Maxwell Cohen's remarkably varied career.

Cohen commenced his academic career at a time when few in Canada devoted themselves full-time to research, writing, and teaching. He is rightly seen as an academic pioneer. A perusal of the bibliography of his public work indicates the diverse range of intellectual interests, from legal history to international and constitutional law, human rights, and legal education. A reading of his work reveals the powerful combination of a careful, thorough method with an incisive, imaginative spirit of inquiry.

Cohen is one of Canada's leading exponents of international law. His work in that sphere has earned him a worldwide reputation and a string of appointments to a variety of international bodies and commissions, culminating in membership as a judge ad hoc at the International Court of Justice.

As a practitioner and man of action, he served his country during times of peace and war in a number of capacities as a military officer, legal counsel, diplomat, commissioner, and special government adviser. His work as chair of the Special Committee on Hate Propaganda is still cited as the leading study on that controversial subject, and it is but one of a long list of reports he wrote and royal commissions on which he served.

Cohen is also a teacher and academic administrator of great renown. He has lectured on a wide variety of subjects at universities in Canada and around the world. He served as dean of one of this country's great law schools, McGill, where he fostered the vision of the National Law Programme, an academic monument to Canada's bijuridical legal culture. More recently, he has been scholar-in-residence at the Faculty of Law at the University of Ottawa.

Of his many remarkable achievements, there is one that remains permanently in my mind. During the five years in which he presided over the Canada–United States International Joint Commission, every judgment was unanimous, even where bitter boundary disputes had existed. At the Supreme Court of Canada the best we have been able to do has been unanimity in 75 per cent of cases.

Maxwell Cohen's vital contribution to the Canadian and international legal communities has inspired the editors and authors responsible for this collection. Their work constitutes a fitting tribute to a great Canadian and an admirable friend.

THE RIGHT HONOURABLE BRIAN DICKSON

Preface

As a law professor, dean, and scholar, and in Canadian and international public service, Maxwell Cohen has made an indelible mark on the law and on legal institutions. His contribution ranges through writings in the public press, books, articles in scholarly journals, reports to government, speeches, and lectures. When we began gathering papers for a volume of essays in honour of Maxwell Cohen in 1990, our chief difficulty lay in choosing topics that would reflect the remarkable contribution of a man who has been prolific in output and wide-ranging in interests and tastes.

Born in Winnipeg in 1910, and educated at the University of Manitoba,[1] Maxwell Cohen's interest in legal education and legal scholarship was forged by his studies at Northwestern University and at Harvard in the 1930s, where he experienced the teaching and the works of John Henry Wigmore, Walter Wheeler Cook, Roscoe Pound, Thomas Reed Powell, Manley O. Hudson, and Felix Frankfurter. As a student and throughout his career, Cohen contributed to public knowledge and debate – in student newspapers, the *Christian Science Monitor*, the *Atlantic Monthly*, *Saturday Night*, the daily press, and, of course, learned journals. His interest in public policy and government regulation, particularly in the economic sphere, was whetted by his studies and by the first position he held after graduation – lawyer for the Combines Investigation Commission of the Department of Labour. In 1938 he wrote one of the first analytical treatments of Canadian anti-trust law.

Cohen's interest in international affairs, inspired in part by his role as a wartime correspondent and by service in the Canadian Army, became specifically focused on international law when, in 1946, he was hired to teach a course on that subject at McGill. He began an association with a field of scholarship and an institution that was to be both long and productive. Cohen shaped legal education at McGill for the next forty years, and he set an exemplary standard of scholarship and service to the field for international and domestic lawyers in Canada. As chair of royal commissions and the Canada–United States International Joint Commission, as adviser to governments, and as judge ad hoc at the International Court of Justice, Maxwell Cohen has brought a powerful intellect, a creative and imaginative mind, a world view, and a deep-seated concern for humanity to the myriad of problems of social order and organization with which he has been confronted.

The articles in this book are intended to reflect in a broad way the key areas of Maxwell Cohen's interest over his career: international law, public law, legal history, and legal education. The problem of selecting from within these fields was compounded by the difficulty of choosing among the potential contributors. Over the course of his career, Cohen had many colleagues, influenced several generations of students, and won the admiration of those who came into contact with him and his work. There was no shortage of interest in contributing to this volume. The difficulty was one of ensuring that the volume did not become too large.

All the articles reflect Cohen's interest in issues of contemporary concern and are linked to issues he himself has pursued. They are written by people who were associated with Cohen in some way or who have been influenced by what he has written or done. These contributors have made important achievements in their own fields and, like Cohen's, their contributions have broken new ground.

The articles in part one of this collection relate to the field of international law. Reflecting Cohen's abiding interest in issues of peace and security, Oscar Schachter begins the section by analysing the United Nations and the Gulf War. Another longstanding colleague and distinguished international lawyer, Shabtai Rosenne, contributes a study on the agent in litigation before the International Court of Justice. Canada's leading authority on the law of the Arctic, Donat Pharand, makes the case for an arctic region council, a proposal first made by Cohen himself in 1971. Anne Bayefsky, who has written jointly with Cohen on the subject, considers the reception of international human rights law by Canadian courts. Dale Gibson looks at Canadian-American relations through a study of extradition between the two countries one hundred years ago. Relations along the forty-ninth parallel have been a continuing interest of Cohen's, and part one concludes with a study by Donald McRae on dispute settlement in the relations of Canada and the United States, focusing on the dispute settlement mechanism under the Canada–United States Free Trade Agreement.

The articles in part two are in the field of public law, with a particular emphasis on the protection of rights. Annemieke Holthuis begins with a paper on Maxwell Cohen's perspective on human rights in Canada as seen through a case study of the entrenchment of the Charter of Rights and Freedoms and the enactment of the Emergencies Act. William Kaplan examines the work of the Special Committee on Hate Propaganda which Maxwell Cohen chaired, and which led to the passage of the hate propaganda provisions of the Canadian Criminal Code. Irwin Cotler follows with a discussion of key Canadian hate propaganda cases and the presentation of a model factum for the prosecution of hate propaganda anywhere in the world. William Black discusses the "positive obligations" created by the entrenchment of the Charter, while Julius Grey analyses language and Canadian public law, particularly as applied to the contemporary situation in Quebec.

Habeas corpus was the subject of Cohen's dissertation at Northwestern, and two articles on this issue are included in part three, on legal history. Louis Knafla considers the writ of habeas corpus in early modern England, and Robert Sharpe tells the engrossing and exciting tale of habeas corpus and the man who escaped from Devil's Island.

Part four contains articles on legal education. A generation ago, Maxwell Cohen founded the National Law Programme at McGill, and Roderick Macdonald's paper deals with this topic specifically and with legal education at McGill more generally. Edward McWhinney considers anglophone Quebec and the Quiet Revolution from the portals of the McGill Law School during the time that Cohen was a professor and later dean. J.P.S. McLaren takes a broader look at Cohen's contribution to legal education. The final two articles in the volume consider the growth of judicial education in Canada. David McDonald provides a history of the Canadian Institute for the Administration of Justice and William Stevenson tells the story of the Canadian Judicial Centre. These institutions are products of the enormous changes that have taken place in Canadian legal education, changes in which Maxwell Cohen has played an important role.

A selected bibliography of Cohen's published work completes the volume.

This work celebrates a man who, as teacher, scholar, judge, and administrator, has made a vital contribution to the law, to learning, to Canada, and to the world. As colleagues of Maxwell Cohen, we have been influenced by his work and inspired by his example, his vision, and his commitment.

At the University of Ottawa, we were assisted by Lise Fraser, Barbara Main, and Maureen Martyn. Madeleine Glazer handled all the administrative arrangements with her usual efficiency and goodwill.

At McGill-Queen's University Press, it has been a pleasure to work again with Philip Cercone and Joan McGilvray. Cercone indicated his interest in this project from the outset and has shown strong support at every stage. In copy editing the text, Rosemary Shipton made many improvements, and we would also like to thank Kathleen Fraser and Lydia Wakulowsky for reading the proof.

WILLIAM KAPLAN and DONALD McRAE

NOTE

1 For a full biography of Maxwell Cohen see R. St J. Macdonald, "Maxwell Cohen at Eighty: International Lawyer, Educator and Judge" (1989), 27 *Canadian Yearbook of International Law* 3.

PART ONE
International Law

Legal Aspects of the Gulf War of 1991 and Its Aftermath

OSCAR SCHACHTER

It is a special pleasure for me to contribute to a volume honouring Maxwell Cohen. His wit, learning, and exuberance have enhanced countless professional meetings in the four decades I have known him. His wide interests and intellectual energy have made him a man for all seasons, a reminder that cross-fertilization of ideas may be more valuable than narrow specialization. United Nations law was one of his many interests that combined the scholarly and the practical. As the Canadian representative on the Legal Committee of the UN General Assembly, he took an active part in furthering UN peacekeeping in the framework of the Charter, construed as a developing constitutional instrument.

Peacekeeping was one the many fields he dealt with in his professional writings. All manifested his inveterate idealism and hopefulness, tempered by his sense of political reality and human resistance. It seems fitting to bear these views in mind as we reflect on the recent efforts to develop an effective system of collective security.

The invasion of Kuwait by Iraq in 1990 and the Gulf War that followed opened up a new chapter in contemporary international law. The unparalleled collective response to aggression under the aegis of the United Nations was widely hailed as a vindication of international law and of the principle of collective security. It dramatically marked an end to the impasse created by the Cold War that had rendered the United Nations nearly impotent to suppress acts of aggression. A "new world order" based on the rule of law was proclaimed by the president of the United States and echoed throughout the world. On the level of action, decisions were taken by the United Nations and by states involving the provisions of the Charter and general international law. The law that unfolded grew more complicated, as new problems arose. Political differences produced ambiguity, "creative" or otherwise. The expulsion of Iraq from Kuwait and the cessation of active warfare did not bring an end to UN involvement and to legal controversy. Novel legal issues came up amid political uncertainties. As of mid 1992 (when this article was written), the relations between the UN and Iraq remain problematical and new legal developments can be expected. My aim in this article is to analyse the main legal issues that arose up to July 1992 and to consider some of the implications for future collective measures.

In addressing the legal issues, one should not lose sight of the policial context in which they arose. The Security Council and governments in general do not behave like courts; rather, the positions they take on legal questions generally serve their political ends. That the law is treated as instrumental does not mean that it lacks significance. Governments with diverse interests generally recognize that common action requires an agreed frame of reference and that their basic compact, the UN Charter, along with general principles of international law, provides that frame of reference. In practical political terms, this understanding was vital in obtaining the support of many governments as well as their domestic constituencies, as was shown by the debates in several national legislative bodies. Yet the role of law must be seen in the light of the broad grant of authority given to the Security Council and its member states in responding to aggression and in maintaining peace and security. Their sphere of discretion is very wide; the chief requirement is the agreement of the governments concerned. This process involves mainly political and practical considerations rather than legal concerns. Yet, as we shall see, the decisions taken did fit into a legal framework, and they raised issues concerning legal authority and responsibility with important policy implications. In sum, law was part of the political process – but it had a distinctive role that looked beyond the immediate necessities to maintaining a structure for collective action to keep the peace.

In pointing this out, I do not mean to slight the important differences that arose in both policy and law. The exuberant optimism about a "new world order" and the triumph of collective security was far from unanimous. True, the condemnation of Iraqi aggression was almost universally applauded, but differences arose from the outset about the means and goals of international action. There was wide-

7 Legal Aspects of the Gulf War of 1991 and Its Aftermath

spread concern about both the necessity and the proportionality of military action, particularly in comparison with economic sanctions. And there was much criticism of the dominant role taken by the United States and of the failure of the Security Council to exercise full control of the military action. As the war went on, the devastation of civilian life, especially in Iraq, and the suffering of displaced people within and outside Iraq, gave rise to more criticism. Even the apparent decisive military defeat of the aggressor was not wholly satisfactory, since the Iraqi regime and Saddam Hussein remain in power and as a potential menace. On the more general philosophic level, political "realists" warned of the illusion of collective security and stressed the national interest. On the other side, proponents of the rule of law and of United Nations authority expressed their misgivings that the Charter was not applied as envisaged and that a genuine United Nations military force was not employed.

As we shall see, these critical views were reflected in the legal issues that arose. In addition, many of the legal questions were produced simply by the complexities of the situations. Even if all had been in agreement on the main issue, numerous questions had to be faced in implementing the extraordinary number of actions required of the international bodies and governments. It is likely that no previous international action has been so productive of legal issues. The summary that follows will discuss the major issues – and touch on others – but it is far from complete. A full study would require a book.

THE CONDEMNATION OF AGGRESSION AND ITS LEGAL EFFECT

On 2 August 1990 the UN Security Council was faced with the massive Iraqi invasion of Kuwait and the purported annexation. This was the first time since the founding of the United Nations that the entire territory of a member state was forcibly annexed. It was not the first time that a state used force to seek recovery of territory it claimed as its own.

The council acted with unanimity to condemn the invasion. It referred expressly to Articles 39 and 40 of the Charter, bringing the matter under chapter VII and the power of the council to impose mandatory measures. The resolution demanded the immediate and unconditional withdrawal of Iraqi forces.[1] It also called on both countries to begin "intensive negotiations" to resolve their differences. The resolution did not specify what those differences were, but presumably they included the territorial and financial claims. Considering that Iraq was asserting its sovereignty over the entire territory of Kuwait, the council resolution might have seemed to be calling on Kuwait to "negotiate" a claim to its extinction. This twist was surely not intended, but it is a reminder of the problem faced by the council in seeking a peaceful solution to a conflict. At that stage, the council would normally wish to avoid legal judgments and leave room for negotiations.

It is surprising, however, that the council did not condemn the invasion as a violation of Article 2(4) and an act of aggression. Clearly, it was both. Yet council Resolution 660 determined only that a breach of the peace had occurred, a finding sufficient to apply measures under chapter VII. Why was there not a finding of a violation of Article 2(4) or explicit reference to aggression? Even the second resolution,[2] adopted four days after the first, did not explicitly refer to Article 2(4) or aggression, although it did refer to the right of self-defence as applicable in response to the Iraqi attack. It also imposed sanctions under Article 41. To be sure, the statements made in the council by government representatives and those made by political leaders left no doubt that they considered Iraq's action as aggression and a violation of Article 2(4). I would not attribute any legal significance to the omission of these conclusions from the resolutions. The omission may only have reflected the hope of some members of the council that Iraq would be more likely to negotiate if it were not expressly condemned for the "supreme crime" of aggression. This omission may also have facilitated the decision-making process in the Security Council.

Iraq's claim to Kuwait as "lost" Iraqi territory was not regarded by any member of the council as a legal justification for the invasion. This point is significant, since other invading states have justified their use of force as legal on the ground that the territory invaded was their own. For example, India said in 1961 that there was "no legal frontier" between it and Goa because the latter territory had been under the "illegal domination" of Portugal for 450 years. Consequently, the armed takeover by Indian troops was legal.[3] Similarly, Argentina had long claimed that the Malvinas (Falklands) were its territory, despite British control for 150 years, and therefore that its use of force in 1982 to "recover" the islands was "self-defence."[4] Although the Argentine position was not accepted by the Security Council, it received support from several states, especially those with active territorial claims.

In view of the persistence of irredentist claims, the council's unequivocal rejection of Iraq's claim is likely to be recalled in the future. It affirms that armed force may not be used to change the existing boundary of a state even if that boundary was established unjustly

9 Legal Aspects of the Gulf War of 1991 and Its Aftermath

or by conquest. The unanimity on this issue of principle strengthens its force as an interpretation of Article 2(4). The council underlined its position in this regard by its decision in a later resolution "to guarantee the inviolability" of the international boundary between Iraq and Kuwait, which had been agreed to by the two states in 1963.[5]

A further consequence of Iraq's aggression under general international law is that it gives rise to an obligation on Iraq's part to make restitution and reparation. The Security Council noted this obligation in a resolution adopted a few weeks after the invasion in which it declared Iraq liable under international law to pay compensation for any damage or loss suffered by Kuwait or other countries (see below).

NON-MILITARY SANCTIONS UNDER ARTICLE 41

The Security Council acted with unprecedented speed to impose a trade and financial embargo on a defiant Iraq. Only four days after the demand for immediate withdrawal, the council, noting Iraq's failure to comply, decided to require mandatory sanctions of a comprehensive character.[6] There was never any question of its legal authority to do so. Article 41, though not mentioned in the resolution, clearly empowered the council to take measures not involving the use of force to give effect to its decisions and to call on all members to apply such measures. The council decision (not simply a recommendation) was legally binding under Article 25 of the Charter. Article 41 is open ended; it does not list all the measures that the council may take under its authority. It does mention the complete interruption of economic relations and of air, sea, and other means of communication. The council acted accordingly. Resolution 661 required all states (not only member states) to ban imports to, and exports from, Iraq and Kuwait. It barred the transfer of funds to Iraq and Kuwait and, in effect, required a freeze on the bank accounts affected. These sweeping sanctions were required notwithstanding any prior contract or licence. Exceptions were made to provide for medical supplies and foodstuffs in strictly humanitarian circumstances.

A committee of the council was set up to monitor the implementation of the resolution through reports from states on actions they had taken. A few weeks after the embargo resolution, the council found that Iraqi vessels were still being used to export oil. Alarmed, the council called on the states "co-operating with the Government of Kuwait" that had maritime forces in the area to use such measures as might be necessary "to halt all inward and outward maritime shipping in order to inspect and verify their cargoes and destinations and to ensure strict implementation" of the embargo decision.[7] This resolution was understood to authorize states to use naval force to halt the shipping in question. Only once before had the council authorized the use of force in regard to an embargo: in 1966 the United Kingdom was given specific authorization to use naval force to block a particular vessel from delivering oil to Mozambique, oil that was destined for Southern Rhodesia in violation of the embargo against that territory's regime.[8]

The council's embargo of Iraqi trade was later augmented by Resolution 670, which ordered all states to deny permission to any aircraft destined for Iraq or Kuwait to overfly their territory except where the United Nations had given prior approval. The resolution also included provisions to strengthen compliance with the economic sanctions. It authorized the council's sanctions committee to continue monitoring the air embargo and also to continue gathering information from all members on the trade and financial aspects of the embargo.[9]

In connection with the embargo, the council took account of Article 50 of the Charter.[10] This article provides that any state which finds itself confronted with special economic problems arising from preventive or enforcement measures taken by the Security Council shall have a right to consult the council regarding a solution of those problems. This "relief" provision was invoked by twenty-one states that had suffered from the trade embargo.[11] They included oil-importing countries dependent on Iraqi oil, and countries that made substantial exports to Iraq and Kuwait. It also was invoked by countries that had many migrant workers in Kuwait and were heavily dependent on them for financial remittances. Recommendations of the council's committee on sanctions urged states to increase financial and development assistance to the countries injured by the embargo. The UN specialized agencies and other international organizations were also asked to increase their aid to those countries. The council did not arrange for any direct financial reimbursement to the claimant countries, but it declared that Iraq is liable to pay compensation for damage to Kuwait and other countries in connection with the invasion and occupation.[12] As a condition of the cease-fire, Iraq accepted in principle its liability, as required by the council.[13]

After the first two months, it was evident that the embargo was largely effective, particularly in stopping Iraq's oil exports and in cutting off the supply of significant imports of a technical and military nature. There appeared to be little doubt that the Iraqi economy was substantially damaged. However, it was much less clear whether such damage, even if continued, would bring about the demanded change in policy on the part of the Iraqi leadership, and, if so, when. The United States government concluded by November 1990 that military action would probably be required to compel Iraq to withdraw from Kuwait. It persuaded most of the other council members to support a resolution authorizing the states cooperating with Kuwait to take the necessary means to uphold and implement the prior resolutions and to restore peace and security in the area.[14] This authorization was to be effective on 16 January 1991, if Iraq did not comply by that date. The two members of the council opposed to the resolution (Cuba and Yemen) questioned its validity on the ground that the council had authorized the use of force without determining that the Article 41 sanctions would be inadequate. In their view, that determination was required when force was authorized under the terms of Article 42.[15]

There were two possible answers to this point. One is that Article 42 was not being applied; this issue is examined below. The other is that even if Article 42 was applied, several members considered that the economic sanctions would not be adequate to achieve the withdrawal of Iraq. Whether this supposition was well founded can only be a matter of speculation, since armed force was used on 16 January 1991.

The end of the hostilities and the Iraqi withdrawal did not bring an immediate end to the sanctions under Article 41. The Security Council decided to maintain a selective embargo to ensure compliance by Iraq with all the conditions in the resolutions. The resolution adopted by the council in April 1991 called for the acceptance by Iraq of a great number of conditions imposed by the council as a basis for a formal cease-fire.[16] The sanctions under Article 41 were modified to a limited extent, in particular to allow the import of food and material for certain essential civilian needs and humanitarian purposes. The export of petroleum and petroleum products would be permitted to the extent necessary to meet claims on Iraq and the cost of imports.

The conditions imposed on Iraq in the resolution fell broadly into three categories. One related to Iraq's military capabilities, and another, to the liability of Iraq for loss and damage to foreign governments, nationals, and corporations as a result of the invasion and occupation of Kuwait (see below). A third category of items in the resolution related to the boundary between Iraq and Kuwait (see above) and to the deployment of a UN observer unit to establish conditions for the withdrawal of the coalition forces from Iraq. Other provisions in the resolution related to the repatriation of Kuwaiti and third-country nationals and to a commitment against terrorism.

The April 1991 resolution is probably the most complex decision ever adopted by the council. Its implementation required a number of administrative and institutional measures by the UN secretary-general as well as by national governments and international bodies. Enforcement extended beyond repelling aggression or ending hostilities. Iraq accepted the conditions while protesting that the sanctions were illegal and unfair.[17] The Iraqi contention was not persuasive to the council. Article 41 expressly allows for sanctions to give effect to the council's decisions taken under chapter VII. Such decisions must of course fall within the terms of Article 39 and therefore within the broad aim of maintaining or restoring peace and security. In this case, the council's decisions rested in part on the premise that the measures taken serve to maintain the peace by reducing the military capabilities of a state that has been guilty of aggression and may be a continuing threat to international peace and security. Other provisions, particularly those on compensation for loss, are measures reasonably related to the establishment of a just peace in keeping with international law. While those measures go beyond the original demands for Iraqi withdrawal, the council had ample reason to take such action as part of the restoration of peace and security in the area. It is hard to take seriously the claim of an aggressor that its sovereign rights are violated by restraints on its military capability or by requiring it to pay for damage it caused.

COLLECTIVE SELF-DEFENCE UNDER ARTICLE 51

The legal concept of collective self-defence was invoked in the Gulf conflict almost immediately after the invasion by Iraq. Kuwait requested the aid of other countries, and the United States, the United Kingdom, and Saudi Arabia took steps to lend assistance. The Security Council in its Resolution 661, which, as we saw, adopted sanctions under Article 41, also included in its preamble a paragraph that affirmed "the inherent right of individual or collective self-defence in response to the armed attack by Iraq against Kuwait."[18]

This was the first time the council recognized in a resolution that the right of collective self-defence applied in a particular situation. It is interesting that the council did so in the same resolution in which it adopted economic sanctions. Presumably, the members did not consider at the time that measures of self-defence were inconsistent with, or terminated by, the council's nonforcible sanctions (see below).

13 Legal Aspects of the Gulf War of 1991 and Its Aftermath

In affirming the applicability of collective self-defence in the Gulf situation, the council recognized (again by implication) that third states had the right to use force to aid Kuwait, even though those states themselves had not been attacked and had no treaty or other special links with Kuwait. The point has some importance because earlier legal commentary by respected scholars such as Bowett and Kelsen had suggested a contrary position.[19] The council's affirmation supports the position that any state may come to the aid of a state that has been illegally attacked. However, the council took no position on whether such aid must have been requested by the victim state, as held by the International Court of Justice in the *Nicaragua* case of 1986.[20] That question was not an issue in the Iraq-Kuwait case since Kuwait had expressed its desire for assistance.

While the council's affirmation of the right of collective self-defence was not legally required, it served to bolster the case for naval action against Iraq to enforce the embargo. It also supported the contention that it would be legitimate for the third states to use force, if necessary, against Iraq to compel its withdrawal. Since there had been an armed attack, the only additional requirements would be the conditions imposed by general international law – that the self-defence measures would be necessary and proportional to the end sought.[21] The determination of those conditions would be left, in the first instance, to the states resorting to self-defence, but the council could, if it so decided, order termination of the self-defence measures.

The right of collective self-defence, however, came into question a few weeks after the United Nations imposed the sanctions under Article 41. The perception that such sanctions were not likely to bring about an Iraqi withdrawal had led to proposals for military action. The United States, the United Kingdom, and some other governments considered that such action would be permissible collective self-defence, based on the necessity to compel the aggressor to withdraw unconditionally. Against this position, other governments and some international lawyers argued that the right of self-defence no longer applied when the Security Council had adopted measures it considered necessary to repel the armed attack. This argument rested on the language of Article 51, which safeguarded the right of self-defence "until the Council has taken measures necessary to maintain international peace and security." If these words are taken literally, the right of self-defence would be overridden whenever the Security Council adopted measures considered necessary in case of an armed attack on a state. This would be an implausible – indeed, absurd – interpretation. A council decision that calls on an invader to withdraw and to cease hostilities is certainly a necessary measure, but it could not be intended to deprive the victim state of its right to defend itself when the invader has not complied with the council's order. A reasonable construction of the provision in Article 51 would recognize that the council has the authority to adopt a measure that would require armed action to cease even if that action was undertaken in self-defence. However, this would not mean that any measure would preempt self-defence. The intent of the council as expressed in its decision would determine whether the right to use force in self-defence had been suspended by the council.

In the Iraq-Kuwait case, the principal argument that collective self-defence was superseded by council action relied on the fact that the council had adopted mandatory economic sanctions under Article 41. It was obvious that such economic sanctions were adopted in the hope they would be effective in bringing about the withdrawal of Iraqi forces. While this was the hope, the resolutions contained no indication that self-defence rights were meant to be terminated by the adoption of sanctions. Indeed, Resolution 661, which first adopted the economic sanctions, included the preambular paragraph referred to above, affirming rights of individual and collective self-defence. The adoption of sanctions and the simultaneous affirmation of self-defence are surely inconsistent with an intention to bring an end to self-defence measures. It is, however, fair to say that discussions showed that the council members desired economic sanctions to be used in lieu of military measures. At the same time, some participating states, notably the United States and the United Kingdom, made it clear that the failure of economic sanctions might make it necessary to resort to armed force under Article 51. In their view, no further authorization by the council was required if collective self-defence proved to be necessary.

Significantly, no government contested the ultimate right of the council to prohibit all military action by a state, even if defensive. Article 51 is entirely clear that self-defence claims are subject to the council's authority. The council may order a claimant to cease military action even if that action was legitimate defence. However, a decision of that character would need the unanimous concurrence of the permanent members; hence, it could not be adopted over the objection of one or more of those members. In the Gulf case, the council would not have been able to adopt a resolution terminating or suspending the right of self-defence as long as a permanent member opposed that proposal.[22]

The controversy over preemption ended when the Security Council adopted Resolution 678 on 29 November 1990, authorizing the states cooperating with Kuwait to use "all necessary means to uphold and

15   Legal Aspects of the Gulf War of 1991 and Its Aftermath

implement" the council's resolutions if Iraq did not unconditionally withdraw on or before 15 January 1991.[23] It was amply clear that necessary means included the use of armed force to bring about Iraq's withdrawal and compliance with other provisions of the twelve resolutions adopted between 2 August and 29 November. As of 16 January, Resolution 678 was treated as the legal basis of the large-scale military action by the coalition of states that brought about the defeat of Iraq at the end of February 1991 and its withdrawal from Kuwait.

The precise Charter basis of Resolution 678 was not specified. The resolution declared that the council was acting under chapter VII, but it did not identify which article of chapter VII. It thus left several possibilities open to conjecture. One was that chapter VII in general provided an adequate legal basis. Another view was that a resolution authorizing armed force necessarily came within Article 42 and had to meet the requirements of that article. Still a third position was that the authorization came properly within the scope of collective self-defence and that the council was exercising its authority under Article 51 (which is also in chapter VII).

A good case can be made for this latter position. I will comment on it here and leave for later discussion the applicability of Articles 42, 48, and 43. One reason for treating Resolution 678 as falling within Article 51 is that it authorized the group of states identified as cooperating with Kuwait in resisting the invasion to take the necessary means to achieve the objectives previously declared by the council and, in addition, to restore peace and security in the area. It is significant in this respect that the council did not decide that the armed forces of the cooperating states were to be placed at the disposal or under the control of the Security Council. No United Nations command was set up; no reference was made to a United Nations force or to use of the UN flag. These were features of the UN authorized force in Korea; their omission here is further evidence that the Security Council intended to leave the choice of means, timing, command, and control to the participating states.

It may be asked why a new resolution was required when the council had already affirmed the right of collective self-defence soon after the invasion. Moreover, collective self-defence action did not require council approval or authorization; member states were free to use force against the aggressor within the limits of self-defence. However, the resolution served the policial purpose of underlining the general support of the United Nations for the military measures if Iraq did not withdraw before 16 January 1991.[24] In addition, the resolution, supported by all the cooperating states committed to collective action, clarified the objectives of the collective defence action.

Considering the action of the United Nations and the coalition as legally within collective self-defence calls for some further comment. To characterize the military action as collective self-defence rather than as a United Nations action does not imply that the use of force was wholly a matter of discretion for the cooperating states, nor does it mean that the council lacked authority to place limits on the military action. Article 51 expressly recognizes that, in cases of self-defence, the council retains the authority and responsibility to take such action as it deems necessary to restore international peace and security. This language makes it clear that the council may decide on the limits and objectives of the military action authorized as collective self-defence.

The many resolutions adopted by the council in the Iraq-Kuwait conflict and especially its aftermath show that the members of the council recognized the continuing responsibilities of the council, particularly in regard to the objectives of the collective action and in some respects the means used. True, there was no disposition on the part of the major actors to turn over the direction and command of the coalition forces to the council or any UN body. Secretary-General Perez de Cuellar recognized this political reality, but he observed at one point that "the Council needs to exercise guidance, supervision or control with respect to the actions authorized by it." He specifically suggested the need for a "more institutionalized mechanism for reporting by the concerned states."[25]

The implication of his suggestion is that an authorization by the council is not merely an endorsement or green light; it also imposes a degree of responsibility on the council and calls for procedures to carry out such responsibility. Of course, this conception of UN responsibility for "authorized" collective self-defence differs significantly from the centralized mechanism envisaged by Articles 43–7 of the Charter. However, in cases where concerned governments are not ready to accept direct control by the council of military measures against an aggressor but are willing to turn to the council for its approval of the collective measures and relevant objectives, it makes sense for the council to take steps to carry out its responsibility in an effective manner.[26] A council that appears to be merely a "rubber stamp" rather than a responsible body for policy discussions will lose its value as an authorizing and legitimizing organ.

Resort to collective self-defence (*jus ad bellum*) is also subject to requirements of necessity and proportionality, even though these conditions are not expressly stated in Article 51. Both requirements were discussed in the Security Council and by the governments concerned for several months. Indeed, the length and intensity of the

17 Legal Aspects of the Gulf War of 1991 and Its Aftermath

open debates on these issues are without precedent in international bodies. One important issue – already noted – was whether economic sanctions would be effective enough to make military action unnecessary or excessively costly in human lives and material. Though these issues were (and remain) controversial, the conclusions reached by a majority of the council and reflected in its authorization to use armed force may be regarded from the legal standpoint as an authoritative determination of "necessity" by the competent international organ acting on behalf of the entire United Nations.

It is worth noting that the debate in the council and elsewhere on whether the use of force was "necessary" self-defence took a direction rather different from the way the issue had been previously discussed by international lawyers. The argument advanced by opponents of the use of force contended that the economic embargo would prove to be effective in due course; hence, in their view, force was not required as a matter of self-defence. The debate then centred on whether that contention was well founded.

The criterion of necessity thus debated is quite different from the view previously accepted that an illegal armed attack on a large scale is in itself sufficient to meet the requirement of necessity for self-defence. Thus, when the Japanese attacked Pearl Harbor or when the Germans invaded Poland to begin the Second World War, it was taken for granted that armed self-defence by the victim states met the requirement of necessity. The possibility that an economic blockade might cause the aggressors to turn back was not seriously considered to be a legal reason for denying the right of self-defence. Admittedly, there might be prudential reasons for concluding that peaceful means in lieu of armed force would be sufficient to redress the wrong of an armed attack. But to introduce this possibility as a ground for concluding that armed self-defence against an attack or invasion is not "necessary" until peaceful means are sought and found unavailing would radically change the prevailing view of self-defence.[27] It is unlikely that states will move in that direction under existing international conditions.

THE APPLICABILITY OF ARTICLE 42

Prior to the Iraq case it had generally been assumed that the council's authority to apply armed force under chapter VII could only be found in Article 42. This assumption was also evident in statements made by some of the Security Council members. This is not surprising. For one thing, Article 42 is the only provision in the Charter that expressly empowers a UN organ "to take action by air, sea, or land forces" as may be necessary to maintain or restore international peace and security. Moreover, Article 39, the "basic" provision of chapter VII, authorizes the council to "decide what measures shall be taken in accordance with Articles 41 and 42, to maintain or restore international peace and security." A reasonable inference is that if the council decides on measures, they should be under either Article 41 (not involving force) or Article 42 (if military action is taken).[28] Hence, if Resolution 678 is a "measure decided on" by the council involving armed force, Article 42 would necessarily apply.

The argument is not entirely compelling. Although Article 42 is the only Charter article that expressly empowers a UN organ to take action by armed force, it does not follow that other provisions may not also apply. This point was made by the International Court of Justice in its advisory opinion in the *Expenses* case. The court then rejected the argument that the armed force authorized by the United Nations in the Middle East and the Congo had to be based on Article 42. It declared, "The Court cannot accept so limited a view of the powers of the Security Council."[29] The court's Delphic comment does not point to any alternative article, but it suggests that the council could act on a liberal construction of its authority derived from its general powers to maintain and restore international peace and security. On that approach,[30] the reference to chapter VII in Resolution 678 would call for no further specification. As in the case of consensual peacekeeping operations, the council would draw on the broad language of the Charter provisions.

There are, of course, advantages to constitutional interpretation of such flexibility in cases where decisions are generally acceptable. At the same time, invoking UN authority for coercive armed force touches an especially sensitive area, often with far-reaching effects. Confusion or uncertainty about the precise legal basis may well create friction. By avoiding reference in Resolution 678 to any particular article of chapter VII, the council left the matter in doubt, giving rise to questions of authority that may require specific legal grounds. My view, suggested earlier, is that Resolution 678 is more compatible with an authorization of collective self-defence than with a conception of the council as itself taking action by air, sea, or land forces. There is no reason to doubt that the council has authority under Article 51 to express approval of collective defence actions in a particular case. This may not be incompatible with Article 42, since its terms are flexible, allowing for a variety of actions.

To put it in another way, Resolution 678 may be read as consistent with both Articles 51 and 42. In regard to Article 42, the council's resolution is an example of "action" taken by the council involving the use of military force. The word "action" does not have to mean that those armed forces are under the control or command of the council. That such command and control was contemplated under other articles of chapter VII should not be read into Article 42. Recognizing Article 42 as a relevant source of authority, together with Article 51, would not in itself enhance the council's authority over the armed forces. It should not be forgotten that Article 51 gives the council full authority and responsibility in cases of self-defence to take measures to maintain and restore international peace and security.

To be sure, the use of the term "action" in Article 42 may mean "enforcement" in a mandatory sense rather than an authorization. But even if Article 42 allows for mandatory "action," this should embrace the lesser power to recommend or authorize action.[31] It does not make sense to require a mandatory decision where a recommendation or authorization would suffice to achieve the desired action.

If we assume that the council's Resolution 678 is also a form of "action" within the meaning of Article 42, the question arises (as it did in the council) whether the conditions of that article have been met. One such condition is that the council shall have made the determination required in Article 39. The council did so when, in Resolution 660, it found that a breach of the peace had occurred. It also took provisional measures under Article 40 when it ordered withdrawal and negotiation.[32]

Article 42 requires that the council, before acting under that article, "consider that measures provided for in Article 41 would be inadequate or have proved to be inadequate." At least two members of the council argued that the council never did decide that the sanctions under Article 41 would be inadequate; consequently, they questioned the legal validity of Resolution 678. It is true that the council did not formally declare the inadequacy of the economic sanctions under Article 41, but it was at least clear that several members believed that the sanctions would prove to be inadequate to bring about a withdrawal by Iraq. The defiant position taken by the Iraqi regime even after many months of economic sanctions added support to the belief that military action was needed to bring about its compliance. Whether a longer period would have been effective remains conjectural, but there is no doubt that the council had the legal right to decide on the need for military action.

THE APPLICATION OF ARTICLE 48

Another relevant Charter article in chapter VII is Article 48, which imposes an obligation on members to take action required to carry out the decisions of the council, "as the Council may determine."

Article 48 is a key article in chapter VII. It implements the enforcement measures decided on by the council by giving the council the right to impose a duty to act upon some or all member states. It is more specific than Article 25, which provides generally that members have agreed to carry out decisions of the council; Article 48 centralizes within the council the power to determine which members shall take action required by council decisions under chapter VII. Hence, the mandatory decisions by the council in the Gulf conflict are covered by Article 48, whether or not it is mentioned.[33] For example, the sanctions not involving force imposed by Resolution 661 under Article 41 are given obligatory effect by Article 48. Article 48 is particularly applicable where the council requires action by a given state or group of states. Presumably, that is why the council referred expressly to Article 48 (as well as to Article 25) in its Resolution 670, which prescribed action in regard to air transport and freezing of assets by states in a position to take such action.

Article 48 was not applicable, however, to the use of armed force authorized by the council in Resolution 678. It was clear under that resolution (as well as under Resolution 665 on the naval blockade) that the military measures were not required action. Hence, by its terms, Article 48 did not apply to such permissive action, whereas it did apply to the mandatory economic and transportation embargoes required of all members.

Article 48 is also significant as the basis for the binding character of the council's decisions that imposed conditions on Iraq to be carried out after the cease-fire, in particular in Resolution 687, discussed earlier. These conditions were accepted by Iraq, obviously under duress, but they are obligatory by virtue of Articles 48 and 25, irrespective of Iraq's "acceptance."

SPECIAL AGREEMENTS UNDER ARTICLE 43

It has been suggested that the resolution authorizing force is incompatible with the requirement of Article 43 that the Security Council conclude special agreements with member states for the provision of armed forces and facilities to be on call for Security Council action. During the early years of the United Nations, and even recently, it was thought that such agreements were a condition precedent to collective military measures by the Security Council. Article 106 clearly suggests that interpretation.[34] This view was held by the governments at the San Francisco Conference[35] and was often expressed by commentators on the Charter.[36] No explicit language in Article 42 or in Articles 43, 44, and 45 (which refer to the special agreements), however, precludes states from voluntarily making armed forces available to carry out the resolutions of the council adopted under chapter VII.[37] The voluntary response to the resolutions in the Korean action is in point. In that case, sixteen states provided armed forces and military facilities to assist South Korea in repelling the North Korean aggression.[38] They did so in response to a recommendation, and no legal argument was made by any government that a mandatory decision was necessary.

Article 43, though drafted in obligatory language, has never been applied. The Security Council has not taken the initiative to negotiate such special agreements, though Article 43 requires that this be done "as soon as possible." It does not appear that any member state has ever requested such a negotiation. In effect, Article 43 had become a dead letter. Even when a majority of UN members (including the United States) emphasized the need for states to make armed forces available for service under the United Nations aegis, they did not urge recourse to Article 43 agreements. Thus, the General Assembly adopted resolutions during the Korean War that recommended that "each Member maintain within its national armed forces elements so trained, organized and equipped that they could promptly be made available, in accordance with its constitutional processes for service as a United Nations unit, or units upon recommendation by the Security Council or the General Assembly."[39] It is not surprising, of course, that at that time no consideration was given to agreements negotiated by the Security Council, then hopelessly split by the Korean action and more generally by the Cold War. The Collective Measures Committee, set up by the General Assembly in 1950 to consider means of strengthening collective military action, reported on various proposals but did not suggest any use of Article 43.[40] Whatever measures were considered (including stand-by forces and even a "reserve" of individual volunteers) were not linked to the agreements under Article 43. The underlying premise was that if member states supported use of armed force under the United Nations, they would be expected to provide the means without legal compulsion.

The fact that Article 43 agreements have not been concluded and have not been found necessary for military measures in the Gulf conflict does not mean that the article is devoid of present interest. One implication of the article is important. It makes clear that member states cannot be legally bound to provide armed forces unless they have agreed to do so. It thus affirms a limitation on the authority given to the council by Article 42 and by Articles 48 and 49. True, this important point rests on an inference, not express language. However, there is added support in the legislative history of the Charter and in the process of ratification for concluding that the Security Council may not impose an obligation on a member state to make armed forces available unless that state has agreed to do so through a special agreement with the council.[41]

In June 1992, Secretary-General Boutros-Ghali raised the question of Article 43 agreements in a major report, entitled "An Agenda for Peace."[42] He suggested that the long-standing obstacles to such special agreements should no longer prevail. The availability of armed forces on call could serve as a deterrent to aggression and could at least be useful to meet a threat posed by a military force "of a lesser order." He then recommended that the Security Council initiate negotiations under Article 43, supported by the Military Staff Committee, which may be augmented for this purpose. Although this proposal was not immediately taken up by the Security Council, the question of Article 43 may soon be placed on the agenda. Nonetheless, it must still be doubted that most governments will be prepared to commit troops to combat at the Security Council's behest when they would not know against whom and under what circumstances that might be required. Obviously the permanent members of the council are protected in this respect by their veto, but the rest of the membership would lack that safeguard.

THE HUMANITARIAN RULES OF ARMED CONFLICT

An especially tragic aspect of the Gulf War was the extensive destruction of civilian lives and property that resulted from the coalition's aerial bombing and long-distance missiles. Critics of the war, and not only critics, have called attention to apparent violations of the prohibitions in the international law of armed conflict against causing disproportionate and unnecessary suffering to noncombatants. International lawyers, faced with cynicism, are not likely to be comfortable in reviewing the events.

It is worth noting that no government in the coalition and no military commander suggested that the aggressor state or its inhabitants should be denied the protection of the law of armed conflict. Such suggestions have not been lacking in the past. For example, the prosecution in the International Military Tribunal in the case against Nazi leaders at Nuremberg argued that the criminal behaviour of the defendants meant that their actions could not be regarded as legal warfare and therefore must be considered to be common crimes of murder, theft, and the like.[43] This argument was not accepted by the tribunal. From time to time it has been suggested that armed forces resisting aggressors were not fully bound by the requirements of the *jus in bello*. In 1952, during the Korean War, some doubt was expressed by a committee of the American Society of International Law that the laws of war were "fully applicable" to a United Nations force opposing an aggressor.[44] The committee suggested that the United Nations should not feel bound by all laws of war but should select those rules that "fit its purposes."[45] In contrast, the Institut de Droit International concluded in 1971 after some years of study and debate that UN forces engaged in hostilities, even if against an aggressor, must comply in all circumstances with the humanitarian rules of armed conflict, including the rules for protection of civilian persons and property.[46] While this conclusion concerned UN forces, it would surely apply equally to national forces opposing an aggressor.

The coalition forces in the Gulf War expressed no doubt as to the applicability of the rules of armed conflict to their operations. They did charge from time to time that Iraqi actions violated those rules. The Security Council also accused Iraq of grave breaches of the fourth Geneva Convention on protection of civilian persons and property, and the council affirmed the liability of Iraq and of individuals who committed or ordered such grave breaches.[47] However, it was never suggested by any responsible authority that violations by Iraq, however serious, would release the coalition forces from their obligations under the law of armed conflict.

Questions were raised in the council and the media whether the bombing by the coalition forces of Iraqi civilian dwellings and facilities violated the law's proscriptions of indiscriminate or excessive (disproportional) attacks. The military leaders of the coalition responded that only sites of military significance were targeted, but they acknowledged that heavy "collateral damage" affecting civilians had occurred. Some of that damage evidently resulted from inadequate information or error and involved the unintended destruction of noncombatant personnel and civilian dwellings. More important was the strategic bombing aimed at the infrastructure that supports military capacity such as power plants, bridges, roads, communications. Such bombing predictably devastated civilian life. A United Nations survey after hostilities ended found that most means of modern life support in Iraq were destroyed or rendered "tenuous," including food supply, water purification, and other essentials.[48] The enormous devastation that did result from the massive aerial attacks suggests that the legal standards of distinction and proportionality did not have much practical effect.

The international law issues raised by the aerial bombings of Iraq are too complex to be discussed here in any depth. Nonetheless, some observations can be offered. First, the separation of the *jus ad bellum* and the *jus in bello* has been implicitly affirmed in the specific sense that responsibility under the former was not considered to affect the position of the parties under the latter; all are equally bound, aggressor and defender alike. Second, all parties accepted in principle the customary law rule of "distinction" – that is, noncombatant protection.[49] All agreed that armed force may be directed only against military objectives. However, the hostilities revealed how difficult it can be to make a sharp separation between the military targets and civilian objects, especially in an industrial society where their commingling is widespread. The proposed lists of lawful targets, beginning with the 1923 Hague Air Rules and including the more recent enumeration in the authoritative commentary of the International Committee of the Red Cross, mention structures and installations that may serve, in some circumstances, both military and civilian objectives.[50] No matter how "smart" the bombs may be, civilian life is also likely to be profoundly damaged when they destroy a power plant partly serving military needs. The attempt of Protocol 1 of 1977 to prescribe a presumption in favour of considering an object to be "civilian" (Article 52) remains controversial, particularly as the presumption is believed by some to encourage a state to camouflage its military installations.[51]

This possibility also suggests the importance of clarifying the responsibility for violations of the principles of distinction and proportionality in connection with collateral civilian casualties. Here, too, the problem is increased by the commingling of civilian uses and military objectives. In the Gulf War, commanders of the coalition forces maintained they took every reasonable precaution to minimize civilian casualties, but they did not conclude that aerial bombing of legitimate military objectives was prohibited because civilian casualties would result. A relevant provision of Protocol 1 (Article 57) requires that a commander do everything "feasible" to minimize civilian casualties. What is "feasible" is not defined, and it is far from clear that it provides much direction to the commanders in a war situation.[52]

The Gulf War also raised an issue, long debated by experts, in regard to the responsibility of a state subjected to the threat or actuality of aerial bombing. It has been maintained that under customary law, the government in control of an area under attack and of its population has a legal obligation to protect the noncombatant civilians from casualties. Protocol 1 also recognizes that obligation,[53] though critics of the protocol have charged that it is unduly disposed to place responsibility on those engaged in the aerial attack.[54] In the controversy over the bombing of Iraq, the coalition forces charged that Iraq had placed important military facilities in civilian areas in some cases and had also moved civilians close to places of military importance. To what extent these charges were well founded has not been evident in public records, but they do point out the complexity of determining responsibility for collateral damage resulting from aerial warfare. Since it is unlikely that new technology will eliminate such collateral damage, the goal of providing protection to civilian populations remains a daunting task for governments and their military branches.

RESTRICTIONS ON IRAQ'S MILITARY CAPABILITIES

The Security Council imposed a number of conditions on Iraq as a basis for the cease-fire. The most important related to Iraq's military capabilities.[55] Iraq was required to destroy all chemical and biological weapons along with related research and manufacturing facilities. Nuclear weapons and related items were also to be destroyed, and all nuclear-weapons-usable material was to be placed under the control of the International Atomic Energy Agency (IAEA). In addition, all ballistic missiles with a range greater than 150 kilometres were to be destroyed along with related production facilities. Iraq was required to accept these conditions and to pay for their implementation. Verification and control procedures of an unprecedented far-reaching character were also adopted. An international commission was authorized to conduct searches on land or by air and to destroy prohibited weapons and facilities for their manufacture.

Iraq accepted these and related conditions but protested they were unfair and illegal violations of the principle of sovereign equality. At various times, Iraqi officials took steps to obstruct and resist the inspection and control measures of the UN and IAEA.[56] The Security Council condemned these actions as material breaches of the obligations of Iraq and of its undertakings to cooperate with the UN control procedures. The council strengthened the inspection and placed it on a permanent basis.[57] The council also established a demilitarized zone along the border between Iraq and Kuwait and provided for UN monitoring.

These unprecedented measures were legally well founded. They rested not only on Iraq's "acceptance" (obviously under duress) but principally on the broad powers of the council under chapter VII to take measures necessary to maintain peace and security and to give effect to its decisions (Articles 39, 41, and 48). In reaction subsequent to Iraqi obstruction, the question arose whether Resolution 678, authorizing member states to use all necessary means, properly gave such authority to enforce the restrictions imposed on Iraq's military capacity. The United States and some other members considered they were authorized to use armed force, if necessary, to compel Iraq to fulfil its obligations under all council decisions. This position is legally supported insofar as it relates to Iraq's obligations to demilitarize as specified in the council resolutions, for in that regard the individual states would be exercising a continuing right of collective self-defence against a defeated aggressor still potentially dangerous.

The underlying premise must be that Iraq's past conduct, even though checked by its expulsion from Kuwait, remains a threat, at least as long as the same leadership is in power. The council also noted that Iraq was not in compliance with five treaties, three concerned with weapons, one on the boundary with Kuwait, and the fifth on hostages. The implication is that such noncompliance (even if Iraq was *not* a party) could be relevant to a finding that Iraq remained a threat to peace. In a later resolution the council stated that Iraq violated its safeguard agreement with the IAEA. In this resolution, the council acted in a quasi-judicial capacity and relied partly on its finding to demand compliance, backed by an implied threat of force and a strengthened inspection system.[58] This action invites conjecture as to future cases of nonobservance of treaties concerned with arms limitations and possible UN enforcement action.

DUTY TO PAY COMPENSATION AND FOREIGN DEBTS

The Security Council reminded Iraq, not long after its invasion, that it was liable under international law for loss, damage, or injury to Kuwait and other countries and their nationals resulting from the invasion and occupation.[59] It also invited all states to collect information regarding their claims and those of their nationals for restitution or compensation. Later, Iraq was required as a condition of the cease-fire to accept the obligations to make reparations, and member states were authorized to use all necessary means to ensure fulfilment of the obligation.[60]

The obligation to make reparation was broadly stated and expressly included environmental damage and depletion of natural resources. However, the resolution went beyond reparations into Iraq's foreign-debt obligations. It declared that Iraq's repudiation of foreign debts

27   Legal Aspects of the Gulf War of 1991 and Its Aftermath

was null and void and it demanded that Iraq adhere to all its foreign-debt obligations.[61] Since this was part of a mandatory resolution, it was presumably covered by the authority given to the individual states to use all necessary means to bring about compliance.[62] However, it is hard to believe that the members of the Security Council meant to give states the discretionary right to use force to collect contractual debts – a right outlawed by the Hague Convention of 1907 and customary law.[63] A more plausible interpretation would be to regard this outcome as an unintended result of a provision in a complicated resolution that was not adequately considered from a legal standpoint. It is most unlikely that the defaults on foreign debts even by states guilty of acts of aggression can reasonably be accepted as a ground for the use of armed force to compel payment.

To effect payment of the reparations, the council established a Compensation Fund and Compensation Commission. The commission has the responsibility to evaluate losses, the validity of claims, and to resolve disputes over claims.[64] Iraq bears the expenses but has no standing in the commission. The fund is provided mainly from Iraq's oil exports, and the council decided that 30 per cent of such revenues would go to the fund.[65] To avoid the many thousands of individual claims, each government concerned was asked to consolidate all claims of their respective individuals and companies as well as those of the government.[66] However, the report of the secretary-general on the establishment of the commission and fund leaves room for individual claims to be filed in exceptional cases involving very large and complex claims. An important category of claims are those submitted by about fifty governments for damage caused by the trade embargo of Iraq and occupied Kuwait. The claimed losses in this category are substantial; they have been presented by countries in all parts of the world that had prior trade relations with Iraq cut off by the embargo.[67]

Thus far (January 1993), Iraq has resisted full compliance with the compensation scheme and has restricted its oil exports, allowing relatively small amounts to be sold for essential food and medical supplies and for funds to the United Nations for administering the armistice conditions. In the meantime, a vast body of information based on claims is being assembled and procedures are being established.

A legal question to be settled is whether reparation claims would be receivable by domestic courts. To allow such individual claims, especially in countries with Iraqi frozen assets, would introduce a considerable complication with possibilities of unfair and unjust treatment. The most likely solution appears to be that all governments would consolidate claims and seek lump-sum settlements with Iraq through the Compensation Commission. The essential preliminary is that the basic scheme for allocation of Iraq's oil-export revenues be implemented.

Some commentators have raised the issue of "collective punishment" prohibited by the Fourth Geneva Convention and questionable for humanitarian considerations.[68] It is true that substantial reparations along with continuing economic sanctions will exact heavy suffering of the most vulnerable populace – the poor, infirm, women, and children. The suffering of these groups in Iraq has been of international concern and it has been urged that reparations should not be so severe as to add to that suffering. The Security Council had taken this concern into account by allowing 70 per cent of the oil revenues to be used for food and other vital humanitarian needs. The fact that the Iraqi regime refused to allow major oil exports under the UN arrangement – asserting it violated Iraq's sovereignty – added to the hardships of its own vulnerable population. To be sure, the leadership itself and the wealthier section do not seem to have suffered and Baghdad has been substantially reconstructed in spite of the sanctions. It does not appear likely that reparation claims will be paid until the Iraqi regime is changed. Even so, it is estimated that the process will take at least a decade or two to complete, assuming Iraqi cooperation.

PROTECTION OF MINORITIES AND HUMANITARIAN AID

The Security Council resolution setting the conditions for a cease-fire were far-reaching in the restrictions they imposed on Iraq. However, they did not call for the ouster of the Iraq leader or his regime nor did they require any change in the internal structure to the Iraq state. Whether this was wise has been a contentious issue, but there were clearly misgivings about the political feasibility of imposing a new leadership or occupation regime. Viewed from the standpoint of the UN Charter, it may be said that this restraint was in keeping with the right of Iraq to political independence and territorial integrity, and with the basic principle of sovereign equality.

However, the savage repression of dissident minorities by the Iraqi forces after hostilities ended imposed severe strains on the policy of nonintervention in internal affairs. The humanitarian concerns led to demands for United Nations involvement and proposals for military action by the coalition forces. The reluctance of some members of the council to intervene with armed force in an "essentially internal" affair has been attributed to their fear that it would be a precedent for coercive intervention into their countries, which faced ethnic or religious opposition. An added element in the Iraq situation was the large-scale exodus of the Kurdish and Shiite opponents into Turkey and Iran, giving rise to tension between those countries and Iraq. Taking account of that factor, a majority of the council supported a resolution that condemned Iraq's repression of the Kurds and other groups as a threat to international peace and security.[69] The resolution went on to say that the council "insists" that Iraq allow access by international humanitarian organizations to all who need assistance in all parts of Iraq. It also requested that the secretary-general use all means at his disposal to address the critical needs of the displaced population of Iraq. The resolution was understood to provide further ground for continuing economic sanctions, but it did not refer to renewed military action.

Pressure for military protective measures by the coalition forces increased as Iraqi troops continued their attacks on the dissident minority refugees. Safety zones or enclaves were proposed to be guarded by the armed forces of the coalition. Iraq objected on grounds that the internal conflict was a matter for Iraq alone to handle and that its acceptance of the cease-fire terms of the council did not extend to the exercise of authority and police powers by foreign forces in domestic affairs. Initially, the United States, the United Kingdom, and France hesitated to establish such enclaves, mainly because they feared continuing involvement in a civil war that raised difficult issues of a constitutional character. Subsequently, they did take such action over the objections of Iraq and the expressed misgivings of several other governments. But the Security Council was not asked to authorize or endorse the protective measures in the safety zones, presumably because not all the permanent members were prepared to support them. The absence of explicit Security Council endorsement, together with the basic Charter provision against intervention in matters essentially within domestic jurisdiction, was cited by dissenting UN members as grounds for condemning the use of troops in the safety zones as Charter violations of serious import. All states, it was argued, had reason to fear the effect of that precedent.

The legal case in support of the protective enclaves rests in part on the council's finding that Iraq's repression of the minorities constituted a threat to international peace and security. This was a credible proposition in light of the transborder consequences and the resulting tension with neighbouring states. Added to this consideration was the close relation between the plight of the displaced

Iraqis and the war against Iraq. It could not be ignored that the internal strife was in some respects a consequence of the international military action, placing responsibility of a political and humanitarian character on the coalition to prevent massive attacks by Iraqi forces against noncombatants belonging to particular ethnic and religious communities.

A further point of legal significance is that the foreign forces in the enclaves were limited to the necessary protective action for a relatively short period to allow for relief and the eventual return of the refugees. They did not seek to impose an internal regime of autonomy or minority rights. United Nations police forces were expected to replace the coalition forces.

Iraq's acceptance of the UN relief operations, however, did not extend to UN armed forces. The secretary-general concluded that he could not legally send in a UN force unless the Security Council ordered Iraq to accept it or Iraq agreed to do so. However, in May 1991, following Iraqi agreement, the secretary-general did dispatch a small contingent of UN "guards" to perform minimal policing in an area where displaced Kurds were located and UN relief operations were carried out.[70] While the guards were not equipped to defend Kurds from Iraqi military attacks, their presence alone was expected to deter such attacks. The secretary-general's action was not expressly authorized by the Security Council. However, it could reasonably be regarded as implicitly authorized by council Resolution 688 of 5 April 1991, paragraph 5, which requested that the secretary-general "use all the resources at his disposal ... to address urgently the critical needs of the refugees and displaced Iraqi population." No objection was raised in the Security Council to the development of the UN guards.

The impasse drew attention to proposals that UN peacekeeping troops be deployed where internal strife or disorder gave rise to the need for humanitarian assistance. It is unlikely that most governments would approve a broad right of the UN to introduce troops for humanitarian purposes against the wishes of the government. However, developments after the Gulf War showed that the Security Council could invoke chapter VII in cases of humanitarian necessities to call on member states to provide military forces to protect relief operations and to establish a secure environment for such operations. A decision on these lines was adopted by the council in its Resolution 794 (3 December 1992) in regard to the tragic situation in Somalia caused by the breakdown of law and order in that strife-torn country. The absence of governmental authority in Somalia precluded the possibility of obtaining consent of the state. The Security Council went beyond the precedent of the Iraqi-Kuwait case by authorizing the secretary-general and the states concerned to arrange for a unified command and control and to establish mechanisms for coordination with the United Nations. It recognized that the council will have the authority to decide on the transition to peacekeeping operations after hostilities in the country have ended and a cease-fire is in effect throughout the country.

Protection of humanitarian relief in a war-torn area was also undertaken by the UN Security Council in regard to areas of armed conflict in former Yugoslavia, particularly Bosnia. Chapter VII was referred to in the council's resolution as the legal basis for calling on states to provide military units. Unlike Somalia, the resolution had the express approval of the recognized governments directly concerned – Bosnia, Croatia, and the truncated Yugoslavia (Serbia and Montenegro). It was also clear that the UN protective forces would not be used for "enforcement" or disarming of local forces. As this is written (January 1993), the situation in those areas remains problematical, especially because the UN military personnel have been too few and too restricted in their mandate to ensure adequate protection for relief and other humanitarian efforts. Whatever the difficulties, it seems safe to conclude that the UN military intervention to protect humanitarian assistance in grave emergency cases is no longer considered to be barred by the "domestic jurisdiction" restriction of Article 2(7) or by the principle of sovereign equality. True, governments remain reluctant, understandably, to incur the costs and risks of military intervention in areas of serious internal conflict and disorder. Yet the actions taken in respect of the Kurds and later in Somalia and Bosnia are evidence of a sense of moral responsibility that demands common action, even the use of force, to save lives and societies. The United Nations has to serve both a symbolic and a practical role to that end. Its Charter and law have provided a flexible framework for joint action in situations unforeseen by its founders.

COLLECTIVE SECURITY AS IDEAL AND REALITY

The ideal of collective security was often referred to in the debate during the Gulf conflict. The political leaders of the coalition and their representatives in the United Nations proclaimed the necessity of common action against the aggressor in terms reminiscent of statements earlier in the century by Woodrow Wilson, Henry Stimson, Maxim Litvinov, Winston Churchill, and Franklin Roosevelt. One could have gone back three centuries earlier for similar statements by philosophers and public figures. A legal historian could have observed that collective security was given legal effect in 1648 after the Thirty Years' War since the Treaty of Münster (a part of the Peace of Westphalia) declared it to be the common obligation of the states party "to protect each and all" and to aid the victim of aggression with "advice and arms."[71] The aphorism "an attack on one is an attack on all" was much quoted as the way to deter aggression and to "enforce the peace."[72] The nineteenth-century Concert of Europe had elements of the idea, though it was animated more by the idea of balance of power than by the conception of a common responsibility.[73]

The latter conception, put in global perspective, was given legal form in the Covenant of the League of Nations. All league members accepted the legal obligation to act against an aggressor; they were committed to maintaining an indivisible peace and to defending any state attacked.[74] The analogy to criminal law appealed to lawyers: a potential outlaw state would face community sanctions and therefore would be deterred from aggression. This optimistic prospect, deceptively simple, had a powerful appeal. However, it was not universally applauded. Many feared it would sweep their countries into wars that were of no direct interest to them. Some historians and political scientists viewed the idea as illusory, unworkable in a world dominated by national interests and power.[75] The sceptics found confirmation of their views in the failures of the League of Nations to halt the aggressions of Japan, Italy, Germany, and the Soviet Union prior to 1939. In contrast, the Second World War was perceived as a successful collective mobilization of law-abiding states against the fascist aggressors. The victors, especially the United States, moved to place the wartime alliance on a permanent institutional basis that would eventually include all states.

The UN Charter did not expressly refer to "collective security," but it did declare that "collective measures" against aggression and to prevent breaches of the peace were a major aim of the organization. Unlike the Covenant, it did not rely on a self-executing obligation to deter aggression. The responsibility to take collective measures was placed in the Security Council, a political body with wide, almost unlimited, authority to permit, and even compel, action by all member states. The price for that unprecedented grant of authority was the requirement of unanimity of the five permanent members. This ensured that coercive action could not be applied against a major power – or, as it turned out, against any state a permanent member chose to protect. The veto and the Cold War, taken together, operated to bring collective security virtually to the vanishing point.

Understandably, the Gulf conflict and the success of the collective action under UN authority have led to a new perception. That success showed, for one thing, that unanimity of the permanent members is not a will-o'-the-wisp and that a good part of the international community would be prepared to support measures against aggression adopted by the Security Council. It also revealed – though this aspect has not been highlighted – that governments may legitimately give effect to collective security without obtaining the authorization of the Security Council or of any UN body. This is not new. As we saw, the Charter always included collective self-defence as a legal basis for coercion when a state has been attacked and other states are prepared to aid that state by economic sanctions and armed force. Both NATO and the Warsaw Pact, and the earlier Rio Pact, relied on the principle of collective self-defence as the legal ground for commitments to aid the victims of aggression.[76]

Thus, the experience of the Gulf conflict underlined two legal grounds for collective security. It showed that the council was no longer hopelessly thwarted in meeting aggression by the absence of great power unanimity. The council could adopt nonforcible sanctions of a binding character and it could authorize military measures. But the Gulf episode also indicated that council action was not legally required where collective self-defence could provide the legal basis for measures against aggression. On that basis, authorization by the council would not be required as a matter of Charter law. Of course, as mentioned earlier, the council could use its authority to prohibit or terminate collective self-defence measures. However, since this would require a council decision, it could not be accomplished without the support of the five permanent members and the nine required votes. Once again, the veto would impose itself as crucial. In a case of this kind, the veto could be employed, not to impede the collective action but to ensure that such measures would not be barred by the council's decision. To take the example of the Gulf conflict: hypothetically, a majority of the council might have favoured relying solely on the nonmilitary sanctions to compel Iraq to withdraw, whereas (say) at least two of the permanent members might have considered military measures essential. Since the majority could not adopt a decision (in view of the veto) to terminate or prevent military action under Article 51, a collective self-defence action would have been legal under the Charter.

Since collective self-defence may well be the legal basis for future collective security actions, it becomes important to remind states that the conditions for self-defence, collective and individual, are imposed by international law. The states claiming the right to use force in collective self-defence cannot be the final arbiters of its legality.[77] It is for the international community acting through the competent organs of the United Nations or, *faute de mieux*, through the decentralized responses of states, to pass judgment on the legality of the claim to self-defence. Such judgments have in fact been made by the General Assembly (where the veto does not apply) as well as by the Security Council. In its much-discussed judgment, the International Court in the *Nicaragua* case passed on the collective self-defence claim of the United States. The court in that case affirmed the requirements of necessity and proportionality, as well as the necessity of a prior armed attack and a request for aid by the attacked state. The discussion in the Gulf conflict showed sharp differences of opinion over the necessity and proportionality of the military action taken by the coalition. It is likely that such questions will arise whenever collective self-defence measures are taken.

In consequence, UN organs, and especially the Security Council, will have a responsibility under Article 51 to consider issues of legality regarding collective defence actions. In order to do so effectively, the council will need adequate reports on self-defence measures. Such reports should be timely and should give enough information concerning necessity, proportionality, and the ends sought to enable the council to make an informed judgment about the legality of the actions taken. It is doubtful that the reports submitted to the Security Council on the military actions by the coalition in the Gulf conflict were intended to be reviewed by the council. Of course, post audits by the council on compliance with such abstract standards as necessity and proportionality might be unproductive and perhaps even counter to the proper ends of collective self-defence. This suggests the need for further consideration by the council and other appropriate bodies of the requirements of legitimate collective self-defence and of the role of the council under Article 51. As we noted earlier, Secretary-General Perez de Cuellar drew attention to this need in April 1991, but it did not lead to any action by the council.

An obvious question raised by the Iraq case is whether the precedent of collective measures supported by the near unanimity of the Security Council will prove to be a deterrent against acts of aggression, at least against aggression as clear as Iraq's invasion. An expectation that the council will act similarly in future cases has been viewed as a factor that will deter governments with territorial claims or designs against their neighbours. It has been suggested that small and weak states may take comfort from the precedent.

Blatant aggressions such as Iraq's annexation of Kuwait are rare. National interests in taking costly action against a law-violating state may not seem as compelling in other cases. The application of collective security is bound to have a selective and uneven character, and extrapolation from the Gulf conflict is uncertain. A more likely outcome of the Gulf conflict, from an optimistic perspective, would be a sustained effort to strengthen preventive measures through collective action. Among the more obvious steps would be greater use of international peacekeeping forces under United Nations or regional authority to perform monitoring and "trip-wire" functions in threatened regions. The introduction of military confidence-building measures, as suggested for Europe by the Conference on Security and Co-operation in Europe, is also likely to win support as a useful preventive measure. High on an agenda for preventive action in the Middle East and other troubled areas are arms-limitation measures. These would be directed not only to countries in the region but to the supplying states. One principal aim would be to eliminate nonconventional weapons and to cut down on buildups of conventional military capabilities. The obstacles to achieving such restraints are generally recognized, and easy solutions are not expected. The Security Council's resolution on conditions of a cease-fire is but a first step.

The Gulf conflict has also increased an awareness of the economic and social deficiencies that contribute to internal tensions and to interstate conflicts. Economic development and enhanced employment opportunities are now seen as linked to the maintenance of peace. Observance of the internationally recognized human rights and of democratic processes is also given more prominence on the agenda for creating a more stable international order. It remains to be seen how seriously these goals will be taken by governments and to what degree a collective responsibility to maintain peace will be given practical effect. The Gulf conflict, in some respects a great calamity, did demonstrate that many countries recognize a common responsibility to combat aggression, although they remain somewhat ambivalent about meeting the costs in lives and material resources. It may well be utopian to expect that wars will be prevented by a common obligation to "protect each and all," but it is surely realistic for governments to press for the goal of security through preventive measures and the commitment to uphold – and, if necessary, to enforce – the basic law of the UN Charter.

NOTES

The author has drawn on an earlier article, "United Nations Law in the Gulf Conflict" (July 1991), 85 *American Journal of International Law* 452–73, in the preparation of this paper.

1 SC Res. 660 (2 Aug. 1990).
2 SC Res. 661 (6 Aug. 1990).
3 16 UNSCOR 987 meeting, 10–11 (1961). A majority in the Security Council voted in favour of a draft resolution requesting India's withdrawal from Goa, but the USSR vetoed the draft. See Q. Wright, "The Goa Incident" (1962), 56 *American Journal of International Law* 617.
4 Statement of Argentina in UN Doc. A/37 PV51 (2 Nov. 1982).
5 SC Res. 687 (1991), adopted 3 April 1991 after the fighting ceased. The decision guaranteed the inviolability of the boundary that had been accepted by the parties in 1963. For an analysis of the boundary issue see M.H. Mendelson and S. Hulton, "The Iraq-Kuwait Boundary, Legal Aspects" (1990), 92 *Revue Belge de Droit International* 293–332.
6 SC Res. 661 (1990).
7 SC Res. 665 (25 Aug. 1990).
8 SC Res. 221 (1966).
9 SC Res. 670 (25 Sept. 1990), reprinted in 29 *International Legal Materials* at 1334.
10 SC Res. 669 (1990).
11 UN Docs. s/22021 (1990) and s/22193 (1993).
12 SC Res. 674 (1990) (para. 7, 8); Res. 686 (1991).
13 Iraq notified the council in March 1991 of its acceptance of liability in principle as demanded by Resolution 686. UN Doc. s/22456 (6 April 1991). See also the response of the president of the Security Council, UN Doc. s/22485 (11 April 1991), calling the Iraqi statement an "irrevocable and unqualified acceptance." See Section IX below on compensation.
14 SC Res. 678 (1990).
15 Article 42 begins: "Should the Security Council consider that measures provided for in Article 41 would be inadequate or have proved to be inadequate, it may take such action by air, sea or land forces."
16 SC Res. 687 (1991).
17 Iraq's response to Res. 687 is in UN Doc. s/22456 (11 April 1991).
18 SC Res. 661, supra note 2.
19 D. Bowett, *Self-Defence in International Law* (Manchester 1958) 216–18; H. Kelsen, *Law of the United Nations* (New York 1950) 792.
20 ICJ Judgment, Military and Paramilitary Activites in and against Nicaragua, ICJ Rep. 1986, 105 (para. 199).
21 Ibid. at 103 (para. 194).
22 It has been suggested that if a proposed resolution authorizing force such as 678 had been vetoed, collective self-defence action would have been barred. See M.E. O'Connell, "Enforcing the Prohibition on the Use of Force: The UN's Response to Iraq's Invation of Kuwait" (1991), 15 *Southern Illinois University Law Journal* 453. This suggestion is clearly

wrong. It does not make sense to conclude that failure of the council to endorse action by a state should bar that action when it is otherwise permitted by the Charter and international law. A veto can obviously prevent a council decision and therefore block the council from prohibiting action. But a veto of a resolution that would approve or authorize otherwise permissible action cannot have the legal effect of precluding that action.

23 By setting a deadline of 15 January, Resolution 678 implied that military force would not be used prior to that date and that the governments most concerned confirmed the forty-seven-day "period of grace." It is not unreasonable to infer that the right of collective self-defence was suspended for that period even though the council did not expressly ban the use of force. C. Dominicé, "La Sécurité Collective et la Crise du Golfe" (1991), 2 *European Journal of International Law* 85, 104; N. Schrijver, "The United Nations and the Use of Force," in Liber Akkerman, *In- and Outlaws in War* (1992), 255, 262.

24 Many governments supporting action against Iraq regarded it as important for domestic political reasons to have UN authorization. See T. Friedman, "Allies Tell Baker Use of Force Needs UN Backing," *New York Times*, 8 Nov. 1990 at A14, col. 1. The UN resolution authorizing force was probably of decisive importance in obtaining U.S. Congressional approval.

25 UN Press Release SG-SM4560, 24 April 1991.

26 Commentators who have criticized the United States and its allies for avoiding the centralized enforcement mechanism of the Charter in acting against Iraq have tended to ignore the legal authority of the council under Article 51. See, for example, B. Graefrath and M. Mohr, "Legal Consequences of an Act of Aggression: The Case of the Iraqi Invasion and Occupation of Kuwait" (1992), 43 *Austrian Journal of Public International Law* 109, 118–19; B. Weston, "Security Council Resolution 678 and Persian Gulf Decision Making" (1991), 85 *American Journal of International Law* 516, 517.

27 See O. Schachter, "The Right of States to Use Armed Force" (1984), 82 *Michigan Law Review* 1620, 1635; Y. Dinstein, *War, Aggression and Self-Defence* (Cambridge, Eng., 1988), 216.

28 See Kelsen, *Law*, 744ff. See also Russett and Sutterlin, "The U.N. in a New World Order" (1991), 70 *Foreign Affairs* 69 (assumes Article 42 applies to Resolution 678).

29 Certain Expenses of the United Nations, Advisory Opinion, 1962 ICJ Rep. 151, 167.

30 This position was taken by C.A. Fleischauer, legal counsel to the secretary-general of the United Nations, in a panel at the annual meeting of the American Society of International Law on 19 April 1991. In

his statement, Mr Fleischauer also stated that Resolution 678 was not adopted under Article 42 since it did not provide "for a collective enforcement action by the United Nations, let alone under its command"; (1991), 85 *Proceedings,* ASIL at 431.
31 See Kelsen, *Law,* 756.
32 SC Res. 660 (1990).
33 Although Article 48 refers generally to "the action required to carry out the decisions of the Security Council," it must mean "the decisions" that are made under chapter VII involving action that is legally required. It would not apply to all decisions made by the council in the sense of Article 27 (on voting). The important distinction between binding and non-binding decisions is not erased or blurred by Article 48.
34 Article 106 of the Charter supports that interpretation. It reads: "Pending the coming into force of such special agreements referred to in article 43 as in the opinion of the Security Council enable it to begin the exercise of its responsibilities under Article 42."
35 See interpretation in Committee Report in UNCIO Doc. 88/III 3/46 p. 7, quoted by Kelsen, *Law,* 756.
36 See L. Goodrich and A. Simons, *The United Nations and the Maintenance of International Peace and Security* (Washington 1955) 398–405; Kelsen, *Law,* 756; K.P. Saksena, *The United Nations and Collective Security* (Delhi 1975) 93. In 1948 UN Secretary-General Lie also stated that action under Article 42 required the agreements under Article 43. See UN General Assembly Official Rec. 3rd Sess, Part 2, Doc. A/656.
37 See D. Bowett, *United Nations Forces* (London 1964) 277; L. Sohn, "The Authority of the United Nations to Establish and Maintain a Permanent Force" (1958), 52 *American Journal of International Law* 230.
38 See Bowett, *United Nations Forces,* 30–9.
39 General Assembly Res. 377 (V) 1950 (para. 8); General Assembly Res. 503 (VI) 1952 (para. 2).
40 UN Doc. General Assembly Official Rec. 7th Sess., Supp. no. 17 (1952).
41 See UNCIO report, *supra* note 26. See also M. Glennon, "The Constitution and Chapter VII of the United Nations Charter" (1991), 85 *American Journal of International Law* 74; Note, "Congress, the President and the Power to Commit Forces to Combat" (1968), 81 *Harvard Law Review* 1771, 1800.
42 UN Secretary-General, Report "An Agenda for Peace," UN Doc. A/47/277 (17 June 1992), para. 43.
43 See B. Meltzer, "A Note on Some Aspects of the Nuremberg Debate" (1946–7), 14 *University of Chicago Law Review* 455, 461.
44 Report of Committee on Study of Legal Problems of the United Nations, "Should the Law of War Apply to United Nations Enforce-

ment Action" (1952), 46 *Proceedings of the American Society of International Law* 216.
45 Ibid. at 220.
46 Annuaire, (1971) 54 (II) *Institut de Droit International* 465–70.
47 SC Res. 670 and 674 (1990). On violations by Iraq see T. Meron, "Prisoners of War, Civilians and Diplomats in the Gulf Crisis" (1991), 85 *American Journal of International Law* 104. A more detailed report on Iraqi violations was issued by the U.S. Department of Defense in 1992. It is included in an appendix on "The Role of the Law of War" to its general report on the conduct of the Persian Gulf War. See (May 1992), 31 *International Legal Materials* 612.
48 See UN Doc. S/22366 (20 March 1991) (Report of secretary-general's mission to assess humanitarian needs).
49 Article 49 of Protocol I additional to the Geneva Conventions of 1949 provides: "In order to ensure respect for and protection of the civilian population and civilian objects, the Parties to the conflict shall at all times distinguish between the civilian population and combatants and between civilian objects and military objectives and accordingly shall direct their operations only against military objectives." This fundamental principle is generally accepted and regarded as customary law. See T. Meron, *Human Rights and Humanitarian Norms as Customary Law* (Oxford 1989), 62–70.
50 International Committee of the Red Cross, Commentary on the Additional Protocols of 8 June 1977 to the Geneva Conventions of 12 August 1949, 632–3 (1957). For discussion of restrictions on attacks against dams, dikes, and nuclear power stations see G. Aldrich, "Progressive Development of the Law of War" (1986), 26 *Virginia Journal of International Law* 693, 714–16.
51 See W.H. Parks, "Air Law and the Law of War" (1990), 32 *Air Force Law Review* 1, 138–9.
52 Ibid. at 156–8. For a more detailed discussion of targeting, collateral damage, and civilian casualties, see appendix to Department of Defense Report, supra note 47 at 621–7.
53 See, for example, Articles 57 and 58 of Protocol I.
54 See Parks, "Air Law," 157–64.
55 SC Res. 687 (1991), 30 ILM 846 (1991).
56 See, for example, SC Doc. S/23122.
57 SC Res. 707 (1991). Ibid., para V, requiring Iraq to allow flights for all relevant purposes. SC Res. 715 (1991).
58 SC Res. 707.
59 SC Res. 674 (1990), A, para. 8.
60 SC Res. 686 (1991) and 687 (1991), paras. 16–19.
61 Ibid., para. 17.

62 See Graefrath and Mohr, "Legal Consequences," 122–3.
63 The Drago doctrine prohibiting the use of force to collect debts was accepted by a number of countries in the Western Hemisphere and then included in the Hague Convention of 1907. See C. Hyde, *International Law* (rev. ed., Boston 1945) 1008.
64 UN Doc. s/22553.
65 SC Res. 705 (1991), para. 2.
66 UN Doc. s/22559. See also Graefrath and Mohr, "Legal Consequences," 124–7.
67 See section "Non-Military Sanctions under Article 41" above.
68 See Graefrath and Morh, "Legal Consequences," 136: "International sanctions, even if responding to the crime of aggression, cannot have the function of inflicting punishment, neither on the State nor on the people of Iraq. The sanctions' only objective can be to wipe out the aggressor's capacity."
69 SC Res. 668 (1991).
70 The secretary-general emphasized in June 1991 that the UN guards were not a police force but served as "witnesses" to induce the refugees to return to their homes and convince them they will be secure after the withdrawal of the coalition forces. See P. Malanczuk, "The Kurdish Crisis and Allied Intervention in the Aftermath of the Second Gulf War" (1991), 2 *European Journal of International Law* 114, 130. Although the secretary-general relied on the agreement of Iraq to send the UN observers and guards into Iraq, he did not withdraw them when the agreement expired after one year. Whether they will remain in the area without renewed Iraqi agreement remains unsettled as of July 1992.
71 Quoted in G. Mangone, *A Short History of International Organization* (New York 1954), 32.
72 I. Claude, *Power and International Relations* (New York 1962), 106–7.
73 F.H. Hinsley, *Power and the Pursuit of Peace* (Cambridge, Eng., 1963), 225–37.
74 See W. Schiffer, *The Legal Community of Mankind* (New York 1954), 202–23. See also A. Zimmern, *The League of Nations and the Rule of Law* (London 1936), 265.
75 See Claude, *Power*, 153; H. Morgenthau, *Politics among Nations* (1960), 470–1; R. Stromberg, "The Idea of Collective Security" (1965), 17 *Journal of the History of Ideas* 250–63.
76 See Dinstein, *War, Aggression and Self-Defence*, 230–53; M. Virally, "Panorama du Droit International Contemporain" (1983), 183 *Recueil des Cours* 9, 298.
77 O. Schachter, "Self-Defense and the Rule of Law" (1989), 83 *American Journal of International Law* 259.

The Agent in Litigation in the International Court of Justice

SHABTAI ROSENNE

Maxwell Cohen has been a friend and colleague for many years. He has also been a source of wise counsel. In 1964, during the course of a long walk on the grounds of McGill University in Montreal, Cohen came to the rescue when he suggested the title of my book, *The Law and Practice of the International Court*. The problem was to find a title which would express the continuity between the Permanent Court of International Justice and the present International Court of Justice. Cohen's suggestion was a perfect bridge between the two. The publication of this book enables me to express my gratitude to Maxwell Cohen and my appreciation of his friendship on many different, and some difficult, occasions.

Article 8 of the Treaty of Peace and Amity between "His Britannic Majesty and the United States of America" – a curious narration of the parties to the treaty, indicative of the perplexity the establishment of a great republic had on the manners of monarchical diplomacy – the so-called Treaty of Ghent of 24 December 1814,[1] referred to the agents of His Britannic Majesty and of the United States "who may be respectively appointed and authorized to manage the business on behalf of their respective governments." This terse statement in treaty language admirably compresses into a few words the essence of the task for which agents are appointed and duly authorized by their governments in the conduct of international litigation – to manage the business on behalf of their respective governments.

As a perusal of the collections of international arbitrations during the nineteenth century will show, the individual appointed and authorized by a government to manage the business before an international arbitral tribunal was generally, but not invariably, designated "agent." That term is frequently encountered in diplomatic and other official terminology with different technical meanings dependent upon the context, but always with the implied allusion to that person's being "authorized" to perform given acts on behalf and in the name of the appointing government. The *Dictionnaire de la terminologie du Droit international* gives six usages, the sixth reading: "Dans la procédure arbitrale ou judiciaire internationale *a*) Devant un tribunal arbitral: celui qui est chargé par un Gouvernement d'agir pour le compte de celui-ci en demandant ou défendant, le rôle et les pouvoirs de cet agent pouvant varier suivant les dispositions qui régissent ce tribunal ... *b*) Devant la C[our] P[ermanente de] J[ustice] I[nternationale] ou devant la C[our] I[nternationale de] J[ustice], celui qui est chargé par un Gouvernement de le représenter."[2]

Nevertheless, during the nineteenth century the terminology was not consistent or standardized. For instance, the Institute of International Law in its *Règlement* on arbitral procedure adopted during its session at The Hague in 1875 laid down, in Article 13, that "Chacune des parties pourra constituer un ou plusieurs représentants auprès du tribunal arbitral."[3] A leading authority of the nineteenth century, under the curious heading of *Des auxiliaires de la justice internationale*, observed that "auprès des tribunaux internationaux comme auprès des tribunaux ordinaires, les parties sont représentées par des agents spéciaux." That author recalled Article 13 of the institute's *Règlement* and went on to say that in addition to these official representatives, special counsel, professors, jurisconsults, advocates, and even businessmen are added if necessary to assist the principal agent in his mission, to write opinions, compile the documents and evidence, "en un mot de s'occuper des détails de l'affaire sous la surveillance et la responsabilité de l'agent officiel."[4]

The matter was discussed officially for the first time during the first Hague Peace Conference of 1899. That led to Article 37 of The Hague Convention No. 1 on the Pacific Settlement of Disputes of that year.[5] The discussion is best summarized in the Report of the Third Commission at the 1899 conference:

The delegates or special agents of the parties play an important rôle in arbitral procedure: they are the intermediaries between the parties and the tribunal. [After citing Article 13 of the Institute's *Règlement* of 1875, the report continues] The appointment of such representatives exists everywhere in practice. Article 37 sanctions it by making a distinction between these principal official agents and the counsellors and lawyers who are, under different conditions, also aids to arbitral justice. The committee ... expressed the opinion that no member of the [Permanent] Court [of Arbitration] can, during the exercise of his functions as a member of an arbitral tribunal, accept a designation as special agent or attorney before another arbitral tribunal. The committee did not feel itself in a position to go farther in the matter of inconsistencies applicable to all States ... [I]t was stated that the expression "arbitral tribunal" did not designate any tribunal except one formed from the Permanent Court of Arbitration. [Three representatives] were of the opinion that it was important to establish the duties of a member of the Permanent Court of Arbitration as generally inconsistent with those of special agent or attorney before this Court, making an exception only in the case where a member of the Court might represent as attorney or special agent the country which appointed him to the Court.[6]

Article 37 accordingly provides that the parties are entitled to appoint special agents to attend the tribunal to act as intermediaries between themselves and the tribunal. They (the parties) are further authorized to retain counsel or advocates appointed by themselves for the defence of their rights and interests before the tribunal.

Further discussion at the 1907 Conference led to an addition to this provision, which appeared as Article 62 of The Hague Convention No. 1 of 1907.[7] The addition provided that members of the Permanent Court of Arbitration might not act as agents, counsel, or advocates except on behalf of the power that had appointed them members of the court – a provision that has probably remained a dead letter. The considerations underlying that addition appear from the following extract from the Report of the First Commission of the 1907 Conference:

Article 37 of the act of 1899 left to the parties absolute liberty in the choice of agents, counsel or lawyers.

The members of the arbitral tribunal constituted by virtue of the protocols of Washington of May 7, 1903, for the Venezuelan affair,[8] called the attention of the Governments to the possible difficulties of nominating members of the Permanent Court of Arbitration as delegates or counsel before the arbitral tribunal. They requested that the signatory Powers of the Hague Convention should take this question under serious consideration, noting, however, the great difference existing between the case where the functions of agent, counsel, or lawyer are combined with the duties of members of the Permanent Court of Arbitration to the benefit of the State which named him, and the other cases where these duties of agent, counsel, and lawyer are accepted by a member of the Permanent Court for the profit of a foreign State.

Three solutions were possible. (1) The retention of the conditions established by the First Hague Peace Conference, which was preferred by the Belgian and French delegations; (2) the system defended by the British and American delegations and supported by the following amendment of the Russian delegation:

> The members of the Permanent Court of Arbitration have not the right to plead before the Court as counsel or advocates for States in dispute, nor to act as agents.

And (3) the amendment of the German delegation which excepted from this restriction the situation where the agents, counsel, or advocates might exercise their duties on behalf of the Power which nominated them, as members of the Court.

The compromise solution, proposed by the German delegation, was accepted with a slight textual modification.

But it was understood by the Committee that the clauses concerning this disability set forth in the article with which we are dealing, could not deprive any member of the Permanent Court of Arbitration of the right to give legal advice which might be asked of him by the parties litigant.

The article is therefore revised as follows:

Article 62

The parties are entitled to appoint special agents to attend the tribunal to act as intermediaries between themselves and the tribunal.

They are further authorized to commit the defense of their rights and interests before the tribunal to counsel or advocates appointed by them for this purpose.

The members of the Permanent Court may not act as agents, counsel, or advocates except on behalf of the Power which appointed them members of the Court.[9]

This brief survey provides the background to the Statute of the Permanent Court of International Justice.

References to the agent appear in Articles 17, 42, 43, 44, 49, and 54 of the Statute of the present International Court of Justice, all, except Article 42, paragraph 3, taken over from the Statute of the Permanent Court of International Justice.

The major statement of principle is contained in Article 42, which reads:

1. The parties shall be represented by agents.	1. Les parties sont représentées par des agents.
2. They may have the assistance of counsel or advocates before the Court.	2. Elles peuvent se faire assister devant la Cour par des conseils ou des avocats.
3. The agents, counsel and advocates of parties before the Court shall enjoy the privileges and immunities necessary to the independent exercise of their duties.	3. Les agents, conseils et avocats des parties devant la Cour jouiront des privilèges et immunités nécessaires à l'exercice indépendant de leurs fonctions.

Article 17 prohibits any member of the court – that is, an elected judge – from acting as agent, counsel, or advocate in any case.[10] Article 43, paragraph 5, states that the oral proceedings shall consist of the hearing by the court of witnesses, experts, agents, counsel, and advocates. Article 44 deals with the service of all notices upon persons other than the agents, counsel, and advocates, the implication being that the agent is the normal person to whom correspondence and other notices intended for a party and relating to a particular pending case should be addressed. Article 49 empowers the court, even before the hearing begins, to call upon the agents to produce any document or to supply any explanations, adding that formal note shall be taken of any refusal.[11] Article 54 alludes to the presentation of the case by the agents, counsel, and advocates. Taken together, these provisions illustrate the agent's formal and, in the diplomatic sense, representative character.

In the drafting of the Statute of the Permanent Court in 1920, little attention seems to have been paid to the nature of the agent's role and functions. On the basis of nineteenth-century arbitration experience and the decisions of the conferences of 1899 and 1907, the matter appears to have been taken for granted. A draft of a general agenda submitted by the Secretariat of the League of Nations to the Advisory Committee of Jurists of 1920, convened to prepare the Statute of the Permanent Court in accordance with Article 14 of the Covenant of the League of Nations, listed "Agents, Counsel" under the rubric of ordinary procedure.[12] The record of the discussion at the committee's fifteenth meeting shows agreement that there must always be an agent appointed to represent a party, to keep and prepare documents, and to receive communications and the like; that there must always be but one agent for each party, and, as the government is always the *dominus litis*, the agent must be the representative of the government; and that the right of a private individual associated with his government in a suit to have an agent of his own is a domestic question concerning the individual and the government.[13] The only comment appears in the Report of the Advisory Committee, which wrote: "The Committee, in defining the procedure, decided that the parties should be represented by Agents, and assisted by Counsel or Advocates, in accordance with the rules of procedure in arbitration."[14]

At the Third Assembly of the League of Nations (1921), detailed examination of the draft Statute of the Permanent Court in the light of the changes introduced by the Council of the league to the draft submitted by the Advisory Committee was undertaken in a subcommittee of the Third Committee. At the fifth meeting of the subcommittee, what became Article 42 (then Article 40) was adopted in a revised form designed to improve the concordance between the English and the French texts.[15] The subcommittee rejected an amendment by Argentina reading: "The Parties shall be represented by agents. They [the parties] may have counsel or advocates to represent them or to plead before the Court." The chair explained that if the idea of the amendment was to establish that there was no incompatibility between the function of agent and that of advocate, it was unnecessary. If, however, it was intended to state that not only the agents but also the advocates were representatives of the parties, it was inexact. The report of the subcommittee accordingly stressed that only the agent can represent the parties, but that agents may at the same time fill the role of advocates.[16]

In retrospect, it is perhaps curious to find that the initial Rules of Court adopted by the Permanent Court in 1922 do not deal in any depth with the function of the agent, beyond passing references in Article 46 regarding the order of speaking in the oral proceedings; in Article 55 regarding the inclusion of the names of the agents, advocates, and counsel in the minutes of the oral proceedings; and in Article 62 requiring the judgment to contain the names of the agents of the parties.[17]

In the preliminary session of the Permanent Court in 1922, at the fourteenth meeting there was a brief discussion on the categories of persons who should be allowed to plead before the court. It was decided that no rule limiting the right of pleading should be introduced into the Rules of Court. "Any person appointed by a State to represent it should be admitted by the Court."[18] At the twenty-fourth meeting there was a proposal that the names of the agents should be included in an application instituting proceedings or in a special agreement, but no agreement was reached.[19] This omission is not explained, since draft rules proposed by the president of the court, Judge Loder, did suggest that the name and address of the agent should appear in both documents, but the suggestion was not accepted by the Committee on Procedure.[20]

When the first revision of the Rules of Court was undertaken in 1926, the registrar (Åke Hammarskjöld) proposed amending Rule 35, on the institution of proceedings, by requiring the addition of some reference to the agent. He explained that these additions were calculated to remove practical difficulties which had frequently been encountered during past years. The additions proposed included an indication of the names of the agents in the special agreement and a similar reference in the application instituting proceedings. The registrar also proposed that, wherever possible, persons permanently resident at the seat of the court (The Hague) should be selected as agents. He went further: "Parties may be represented before the Court by agents, counsel and advocates. These functions may be performed by the same person or allocated to different persons. The agent who alone is qualified to submit documents and, apart from speeches by counsel, to make statements, must if possible be actually resident at The Hague."[21]

In the course of the discussion, the registrar recognized that it might be rare for the names of the agents to be mentioned in a special agreement. On the question of the residence of the agent, the registrar explained several different cases that had arisen. One was where the agent was on the spot. That presented no difficulty. The second case was where the agent had selected an address at a legation at The Hague,[22] but was not content with the notification of documents to that address and also asked that he should be sent – "sometimes even by telegram" – the same notifications to the place where he was at the time. The third case, "which also happened very frequently," was where the parties confused the functions of agent and advocate and appointed the same person to both. "If the Registrar sent notifications to that representative alone, his government sometimes desired that all documents should also be communicated to the legation." The registrar went on to explain that this sometimes involved considerable delays, and that his real purpose was "to induce governments to follow the very natural procedure of appointing as their agent their Minister or Chargé d'Affaires at the Hague." For countries which did not have a legation at The Hague, they had one in Brussels or London. By a vote the court then adopted a phrase reading: "Wherever possible persons permanently resident at the seat of the Court shall be selected as agents."[23]

That phrase did not survive the drafting committee, however, and in the Revised Rules of Court of 1926, Article 35 was amended in two major respects. In cases brought by special agreement, the special agreement or the document notifying the court of the agreement was to mention (a) the names of the agents appointed by the respective parties for the purposes of the case; and (b) the permanent addresses at the seat of the court to which notices and communications intended for the respective parties were to be sent. In all other cases in which the court has jurisdiction, the application was to include the same information; and in the case of proceedings introduced by application, "the first document sent in reply thereto shall likewise mention the name or names of the agent or agents and the addresses at the seat of the court." Paragraph 1 continued with the following:

Whenever possible, the agents should remain at the seat of the Court pending the trial and determination of the case.	Les agents doivent, autant que possible, résider au siège de la Cour pendant la durée des débats et jusqu'au prononcé de l'arrêt.

At the same time, a new provision was inserted into Article 34, requiring that all documents of the written proceedings submitted to the court be signed by the agent or agents duly appointed; and Article 54 was amended to permit the agents, advocates, or counsel to correct or revise the verbatim record of a hearing, subject to the direction of the court.[24]

That was the first attempt to give formal content to the role of the agent in litigation before the Permanent Court of International Justice.

In 1929 a Committee of Jurists on the Statute of the Permanent Court was convened at Geneva, *inter alia* to consider possible amendments to the Statute. At the committee's tenth meeting on 15 March 1929 a brief exchange took place between Judge Anzilotti, the president of the Permanent Court participating by invitation in the committee's work, and Sir Cecil Hurst, a member of the committee. In that exchange Anzilotti stated that the court had frequently noted a tendency to confuse the duties of agents and of counsel, a fact that might well give rise to certain inconveniences. He nevertheless agreed there was no objection to an agent and a counsel being the same person, but "the Governments should be reminded that the duties of the agent and those of counsel were different."25 No change was made in the relevant texts.

Article 35 of the 1926 rules was retained without change as Article 35 of the rules of 1931. No discussion of Article 35 took place on that occasion.26

Against this background, the general revision of the rules undertaken by the Permanent Court between 1933 and 1936 (following the revision of the Statute in 1929) provided the opportunity for a re-examination of the position of the agent. The basis for this re-examination was supplied in a lengthy report by the registrar of June 1933. In that report the registrar indicated that notwithstanding the provision of Article 35, paragraph 1, the court had in practice recognized applications to be valid when the agent had been appointed not in the body of the document itself but in a covering note, and he suggested extending the terms of the first paragraph to cover the contingency contemplated by the second paragraph. He proposed that if the terms of a special agreement allowed it to be notified to the court by one party acting unilaterally, the document notifying the agreement need only mention the name of the agent of the party making the notification. He went on to explain that the court had admitted documents instituting proceedings even though such documents had not mentioned the appointment of the agent, or even though they had merely announced the future appointment of an agent, "provided always that it has been made clear in the covering note, or otherwise, that the diplomatic representative at The Hague of the interested country is authorized to act provisionally as agent: sometimes the indication of the party's legation at The Hague had been regarded as implying this." As regards the designation of an agent, formal appointment by an authority generally known to be qualified to speak on behalf of the interested government was necessary; the signature by a given person of the document instituting proceedings did not suffice to invest that person with the status of agent. The document instituting the proceedings might, however, be signed by the person appointed as agent in the covering note accompanying the document. Finally, the court had recognized that a person appointed exclusively in the capacity of counsel was not as such empowered to take decisions on questions of procedure binding on the government on whose behalf he appeared: "such powers belong exclusively to the agent."27

Examination of this part of the registrar's report was entrusted in 1933 to the Second Committee, of which Sir Cecil Hurst, now a member of the court, was chairman. That committee submitted two reports. In the first report it proposed an extensive rearrangement of that part of the rules which dealt with procedure, and this would have commenced with a series of "general provisions." A reference to the *Polish Agrarian Reform* case then before the court[28] was sufficient to show the inconvenience that arose if the agents were not appointed at an early stage of the proceedings. The committee also thought that it was equally necessary that interested governments proposing to take part in advisory proceedings should nominate their agents at an early stage of the proceedings and that the rule on the subject should appear in the general provisions, and not only in the rules relating to contentious proceedings. For the committee, the date at which the nomination of the agent is communicated to the court was more important than the mention of the appointment in any particular document. The committee continued:

There seem to be substantial reasons against trying to insist in the Rules of Court on the appointment of the agent or agents being made in the Special Agreement or Application. In the case of a Special Agreement which requires the approval of the legislature, it may be months or even years before the case is submitted to the Court, and there is no need for a government to choose its agent until the case is about to be submitted to the Court. In a case of great importance, the Special Agreement or the Application will probably be prepared by the high legal authorities of a government, whereas the choice of the agent will be made by the executive government.

The committee accordingly proposed a new rule which should provide for the nomination of an agent by each government concerned and for the notification of his name and permanent address at The Hague to the court either in the document submitting a case to the court or in the covering letter, "or in the document in reply to the communication from the Court transmitting to the other government or governments concerned a Special Agreement filed unilaterally or an Application instituting proceedings or a Request for an advisory opinion."[29]

A preliminary examination of this report took place at the meeting of the court on 15 March 1934. Hesitations were expressed over the approach, which would include general provisions applicable to both contentious and advisory proceedings – partly because of the international discussions then taking place in the United States regarding that country's accession to the Protocol of Signature of the Statute of the Permanent Court – but the prevailing feeling was that this road should not be followed. There was also some discussion on whether the failure of a party against whom the application was directed to notify its agent's name should constitute a "defaut," but the president (Sir Cecil Hurst) cut this short by pointing out that that question was outside the scope of the proposed new rule. Other drafting questions were raised.[30]

The Second Committee then submitted a supplementary report in which it removed the references to the advisory proceedings, explaining that the adoption of its proposed new rule in contentious cases would conduce to the better functioning of the court. The new rule also aimed to harmonize the rigidity of the existing rules with the present practice of the court, as it had been explained by the registrar.[31]

The report of the Co-ordination Commission of 14 May 1934[32] *grosso modo* adopted the text proposed by the Second Committee, with some drafting changes, concentrating in a single article the rules regarding the appointment of the agent and related matters. The commission's draft related not only to proceedings introduced by special agreement or by application instituting proceedings, but also to applications for permission to intervene, declarations of intervention, applications for revision or interpretation of a judgment, and, provisionally, advisory proceedings. The report, published only in French, included the following important passage:

La question a été soulevée de savoir si le fait, par une partie, etc., de ne pas se conformer aux dispositions du nouvel article, constituerait un cas de défaut déclenchant la procédure envisagée à l'article 53 du Statut. On a soutenu, d'une part, qu'il conviendrait d'exprimer clairement que tel ne serait pas le cas, le défaut n'étant constitué que par le fait, pour une partie, de ne pas présenter ses pièces de la procédure écrite dans les délais fixés ou de ne pas faire acte de présence lors de la procédure orale; mais il a été maintenu, d'autre part, que le texte de l'article 53 du Statut, à côté du cas où l'une des parties s'abstient de faire valoir ses moyens, vise également le cas où elle ne "se présente" pas.

Dans ces conditions, la Commission a préféré laisser la question ouverte pour le moment, afin que la Cour puisse la trancher en pleine liberté si elle venait à se poser dans un cas concret.[33]

The report of the Co-ordination Commission was discussed at the court's meeting of 19 May 1934, when the decision was finally taken to exclude all reference here to advisory proceedings. In the course of this discussion, Anzilotti proposed including a paragraph to read: "Every proceeding before the Court shall be taken by an agent furnished with legal authority by his government." This attracted some opposition on the ground that the Statute already provided in Article

42 that the parties were to be represented by agents. The registrar observed that, in practice, certain proceedings were normally taken by the diplomatic representatives of interested governments at The Hague; in particular that was so as regards the filing of the document instituting proceedings. "If this were to be regarded as a procedural act, governments would be placed in a somewhat difficult position by the proposed draft," he said. After further discussion, the court adopted the proposed text, subject to re-examination of the wording by the Co-ordination Commission.[34]

In 1935 it was decided to rearrange the articles of the rules, and Article 32 bis became Article 36, later renumbered Article 35.[35] In its final form, Article 35 of the 1936 Rules of Court of the Permanent Court read as follows:

1. When a case is brought before the Court by means of a special agreement, the appointment of the agent or agents of the party or parties lodging the special agreement shall be notified at the same time as the agreement is filed. If the special agreement is filed by only one of the parties, the other party shall, when acknowledging receipt of the communication announcing the filing of the special agreement, or failing this, as soon as possible, inform the Court of the name of its agent.

2. When a case is brought before the Court by means of an application, the application, or the covering letter, shall state the name of the agent of the applicant government.

3. The party against whom the application is directed and to whom it is communicated shall, when acknowledging receipt of the communication, or failing this, as soon as possible, inform the Court of the name of its agent.

4. Applications to intervene under Article 64 of the present Rules, interventions under Article 66 and

1. Lorsqu'une affaire est portée devant la Cour par voie de compromis, la désignation du ou des agents de la partie ou des parties présentant le compromis doit accompagner le dépôt de cet instrument. Si le compromis est déposé par une seule des parties, l'autre partie doit, en accusant réception de la communication relative à ce dépôt, ou sinon le plus tôt possible, faire connaître à la Cour le nom de son agent.

2. Lorsqu'une affaire est portée devant la Cour par requête, celle-ci, ou sinon la lettre d'envoi de ce document, devra faire connaître à la Cour le nom de l'agent du gouvernement requérant.

3. La partie contre laquelle la requête est présentée et à laquelle elle est communiquée doit, en accusant réception de cette communication, ou sinon le plus tôt possible, faire connaître à la Cour le nom de son agent.

4. Les requêtes à fin d'intervention présentées conformément à l'article 64 du Règlement, les déclarations

requests under Article 78 for the revision, or under Article 79 for the interpretation, of a judgment, shall similarly be accompanied by the appointment of an agent.	d'intervention faites conformément à l'article 66, ainsi que les demandes en révision conformément à l'article 78, ou en interprétation d'un arrêt conformément à l'article 79, doivent être accompagnées de la désignation de l'agent.
5. The appointment of an agent must be accompanied by a mention of his permanent address at the seat of the Court to which all communications as to the case are to be sent.	5. La désignation d'un agent doit être accompagnée de l'indication du domicile élu par lui au siège de la Cour et auquel seront adressées toutes les communications relatives à l'affaire en cause.

This was not the only provision in the 1936 rules relative to the agent, although it was the major one. Article 21 (on the duties of the registrar), paragraph 2, contained the sentence that "Communications addressed to the agents of the parties shall be considered as having been addressed to the parties themselves." Article 32, paragraph 3, on the institution of proceedings by means of an application, required that the original of an application should be signed either by the agent of the party submitting it, or by the diplomatic representative of that party at The Hague (in 1946, "at the seat of the Court"), or by a duly authorized person. It went on to require that if the document bore the signature of a person other than the diplomatic representative of that party at The Hague, the signature must be legalized by that diplomatic representative or by the competent authority of the government concerned. By Article 37 the president was empowered to summon the agents to a meeting as soon as they had been appointed for the purpose of ascertaining the views of the parties with regard to questions connected with the procedure. By Article 40, the original of every document of the written proceedings (in 1946, "pleading") was to be signed by the agent, who could also request the registrar to arrange for the printing of a document intended to be filed with the court. By Article 51, the order in which the agents, counsel, or advocates should be called upon to speak would be determined by the court unless there was an agreement between the parties on the subject. By Article 53, witnesses and experts could be examined by the agents, counsel, or advocates of the parties under the control of the president. By Article 59 the minutes of the hearings required by Article 47 of the Statute must include the names of the agents, counsel, or advocates present at each sitting. By Article 74, a judgment had to contain the names of the agents of the parties.

All these provisions were taken over unchanged save for matters of drafting by the International Court of Justice in the Rules of Court of 1946,[36] and later in those of 1972,[37] when the numbering of rules 24 to 85 was altered to 24 to 91. The presentation and rules of law governing the matter were, however, revised in the rules of 1978.[38]

The basic rule now appears in Article 40, which reads:

1. Except in the circumstances contemplated by Article 38, paragraph 5, of these Rules, all steps on behalf of the parties after proceedings have been instituted shall be taken by agents. Agents shall have an address for service at the seat of the Court to which all communications concerning the case are to be sent. Communications addressed to the agents of the parties shall be considered as having been addressed to the parties themselves.

2. When proceedings are instituted by means of an application, the name of the agent for the applicant shall be stated. The respondent, upon receipt of the certified copy of the application, or as soon as possible thereafter, shall inform the Court of the name of its agent.

3. When proceedings are brought by notification of a special agreement, the party making the notification shall state the name of its agent. Any other party to the special agreement, upon receiving from the Registrar a certified copy of such notification, or as soon as possible thereafter, shall inform the Court of the name of its agent if it has not already done so.

1. Sauf dans les circonstances envisagées à l'article 38, paragraphe 5, du présent Règlement, tous les actes accomplis au nom des parties après l'introduction d'une instance le sont par des agents. Ceux-ci doivent avoir au siège de la Cour un domicile élu auquel sont adressées toutes les communications relatives à l'affaire. Les communications envoyées aux agents sont considérées comme ayant été adressées aux parties elles-mêmes.

2. Lorsqu'une instance est introduite par une requête, le nom de l'agent du demandeur est indiqué. Dès la réception de la copie certifiée de la requête ou le plus tôt possible après, le défendeur fait connaître à la Cour le nom de son agent.

3. Lorsqu'une instance est introduite par la notification d'un compromis, la partie procédant à la notification indique le nom de son agent. Toute autre partie au compromis fait connaître à la Cour le nom de son agent dès qu'elle reçoit du Greffier une copie certifiée conforme de la notification ou le plus tôt possible après, si elle ne l'a déjà fait.

Article 31 repeats the earlier provision that the president may summon the agents of the parties to meet him as soon as possible after their appointment to ascertain the views of the parties with regard to questions of procedure: it goes further by permitting him to do this also "whenever necessary thereafter". Article 38 also repeats the earlier provision regarding the signature of an application introducing proceedings. The exception of Article 38, paragraph 5, to which Article 40 refers, relates to the case where the applicant state proposes to found the jurisdiction of the court upon a consent thereto yet to be given or manifested by the state against which an application is made. Article 39 follows the earlier rule regarding proceedings introduced by special agreement. Article 52 requires the original of every pleading to be signed by the agent. Article 61, paragraphs 2 and 3, allow the court, or any judge, to put questions to the agents, counsel, and advocates and ask them for explanations, and they may answer immediately or within a time-limit fixed by the president. By Article 65, witnesses and experts shall be examined by the agents, counsel, or advocates of the parties under the control of the president. The previous provisions regarding the inclusion of the names of the agents of the parties in the minutes of sittings and in the judgment now appear in Articles 71 and 95. In a change of presentation, Articles 81 and 82 require that an application for permission to intervene under Article 62 of the Statute and a declaration of intervention under Article 63 shall state the name of the agent. The reason for this change is probably to be found in the comprehensive codification of all the procedural rules for both types of intervention in one place. The most important provision appears in Article 60, paragraph 2, which provides:

2. At the conclusion of the last statement made by a party at the hearing, its agent, without recapitulation of the arguments, shall read that party's final submissions. A copy of the written text of these, signed by the agent, shall be communicated to the Court and transmitted to the other party.	2. A l'issue du dernier exposé présenté par une partie au cours de la procédure orale, l'agent donne lecture des conclusions finales de cette partie sans récapituler l'argumentation. Copie du texte écrit signée par l'agent est communiquée à la Cour et transmise à la partie adverse.

Two changes are to be noted in this set of rules. The first is the new sentence added to Article 40, emphasising that all steps on behalf of the parties after proceedings have been instituted shall be taken by the agents. The second is the revised version of Article 60, which now makes it clear that the Registry transmits the final conclusions to the adverse party: the previous version, in Article 56 of the 1972 rules, was ambiguous on this score.[39]

Paragraph 3 of Article 42 of the Statute of the present court is new. There was no provision in the Statute of the Permanent Court regarding the privileges and immunities of the agents, counsel, and advocates (or indeed of any other persons) of a party engaged in either contentious or advisory litigation before the court. This absence does not appear to have caused any serious inconvenience – at least the matter is not mentioned in the contemporary literature. However, Judge Hudson, in an important study he prepared during the Second World War, pointed out the inadequacy of Article 19 (on the enjoyment of diplomatic privileges and immunities of the members of the court when engaged on the business of the court) and Article 32, paragraph 8 (on the exemption from all taxation of the salaries, allowances, and compensation of the members of the court and the registrar). "Adequate dealing with the whole problem would assure not only the position of the members and staff of a tribunal, but also that of agents and counsel engaged in presentations before the tribunal," he wrote.[40] Paragraph 3 was added to Article 42 of the Statute at the San Francisco Conference itself.[41]

One of the consequences of the integration of the Statute with the Charter is that the conventional basis for the diplomatic privileges and immunities of the personnel of or connected with the court has been broadened, and as a generality Article 105 of the Charter is applicable in principle to any person having legitimate business with the court, including its members and its staff. Particularly relevant is paragraph 2 of that article, by which the representatives of members of the United Nations and officials of the organization enjoy such privileges and immunities as are necessary for the independent exercise of their functions in connection with the organization.

It is indeed on that basis that the matter has been clarified in relation to all classes of persons belonging to or having business with the court. This was achieved through Resolution 90 (I) of 11 December 1946 of the United Nations General Assembly, to which was annexed an exchange of letters between the president of the court and the minister for foreign affairs of the Netherlands. Paragraph 5 of the appendix to that exchange of letters provides:

5. The assessors of the Court and the agents, counsel and advocates of the Parties, shall be accorded such privileges, immunities and facilities for residence and travel as may be required for the independent exercise of their functions.

Witnesses and experts shall be accorded the immunities and facilities necessary for the fulfilment of their mission.

This has been completed by a recommendation of the General Assembly, in paragraph 5 of the cited Resolution 90 (1), that the agents, counsel, and advocates before the court should be accorded, during the period of their missions, including the time spent on journeys in connection with their missions, the privileges and immunities provided for in Article IV, sections 11, 12, and 13, of the Convention on the Privileges and Immunities of the United Nations of 13 February 1946.[42]

As far as is known, no difficulties have arisen over the implementation of these provisions during the existence of the International Court of Justice. The registrar normally informs the Dutch authorities of the persons entitled to these privileges and immunities.

There is, however, a technical issue to be noted. Article VI, section 30, of the Convention on the Privileges and Immunities of the United Nations provides for a form of judicial settlement through invocation of the contentious or the advisory procedure of differences arising out of the interpretation or application of the Convention.[43] Having regard to the principle *Nemo judex est in causa sua*, should a case involving privileges and immunities of any person connected with the court and coming within the scope of the Convention arise, recourse would probably have to be had to another mode of settlement, as indeed is envisaged in section 30.

A detailed account of the practice of the Permanent Court of International Justice regarding the agent and counsel is contained in Hudson's *The Permanent Court of International Justice 1920–1942*.[44] The International Court of Justice has by and large followed that practice, and no fundamental change was introduced following the revisions of the Rules of Court in 1978. Some further indications of practice may be noted.

The present court has been faced with a relatively new problem, that of the "unwilling respondent," coupled or not, as the case may be, with the "nonappearance" of the respondent, bringing into play Article 53 of the Statute. Connected with that, many states have shown an inclination to accompany their appointment of the agent with an explicit reservation of their right to raise preliminary objections, or an explicit announcement that the appointment of the agent is without prejudice to their right to dispute the jurisdiction of the court. Strictly speaking, a reservation of this nature is unnecessary. The right to dispute the jurisdiction of the court so that the matter will be decided by the court rests on Article 36, paragraph 6, of the Statute, and exists whether or not an agent has been appointed.

Likewise, the fact that an agent has been appointed does not bar a state from refraining from taking further part in the proceedings, a step that again is likely to bring into play Article 53 of the Statute.

In the *Protection of French Nationals in Egypt* case, the court, placing on record the discontinuance of the case, recognized that the appointment of an agent by the respondent was a "step in the proceedings" (*acte de procédure*) for the purposes of Article 69 of the Rules of Court of 1946, in this respect now unchanged as Article 89 of the Rules of Court of 1978.[45] This may be contrasted with the statement in the court's order of discontinuance in the *Pakistani Prisoners of War* case that "Whereas the Government of India, while it has addressed certain communications to the Court through its Ambassador in The Hague, has not yet taken any step in the proceedings."[46] Read together with the revised Article 40, paragraph 1, first sentence, of the 1978 Rules of Court, this strongly suggests that the first "step in the proceedings" on the part of any state against which proceedings are instituted in the International Court is the appointment of the agent, and until that has been done, that state has not taken any step in the proceedings.

The present court has had two instances of joined cases, the *South West Africa* and the *North Sea Continental Shelf* cases. In the *South West Africa* cases each party retained its own agent; at the same time, Ernest Gross was appointed agent by each applicant government, and he conducted the main pleading in this case.[47] In the *North Sea* cases, Denmark and the Netherlands retained their own agents. However, a single individual, Sir Humphrey Waldock, is listed as "Counsel and advocate" for each of the two states, and he made the main pleading on their behalf.[48] After the joinder, correspondence from the court was addressed to the original agents or to the joint agent, according to circumstances. These precedents apply to the situation in which three states are involved. There has been no instance yet of the joining of two separate cases between two different sets of parties.

The present court has followed a precedent established by the Permanent Court and has several times made orders indicating provisional measures of protection in cases in which the respondent had not appointed an agent, whatever other communications it might have sent to the court through the diplomatic channel.[49] Notwithstanding the non-appointment of an agent, however, with the consequence that the respondent state was not represented in the hearings on the application for the indication of provisional measures, the court has taken into consideration communications made to it "informally" through the diplomatic channel. In the revised Rules of Court of 1978, the court may be seen to have endorsed this practice.

Article 74, paragraph 3, requires the court to receive and take into account any observations that may be presented to it before the closure of the oral proceedings.

The court has adopted a similar position in the circumstances of the *Nottebohm* case. Here the respondent did not appoint an agent. It reacted to the receipt of notification of the filing of the application instituting the proceedings by a communication from the minister for foreign affairs, in effect challenging the jurisdiction of the court. The court decided to treat this communication as raising a preliminary objection, and arranged for the applicant to file written observations on it, to be followed by a hearing. At the hearing only the applicant was represented. In its judgment the court rejected the preliminary objection and resumed the proceedings on the merits, for which it fixed new time-limits. In its judgment the court said that "once its jurisdiction has been established by the present Judgment with binding force on the Parties, the difficulty, in which the Government of Guatemala considered that it had been placed, will be removed and there will be nothing to prevent that Government from being represented before the Court in accordance with the provisions of the Statute and Rules."[50]

Care must be taken not to read too much into this case, which expresses a particular situation of fact not easily generalized. A refinement appears in the order of the court fixing the time-limits for the written proceedings in the *U.S. Diplomatic and Consular Staff in Tehran* case. The respondent had not taken any part in the proceedings for the indication of provisional measures of protection and had sent communications to the court denying it had jurisdiction. After the indication of the provisional measures, the court proposed consultations with the parties regarding the time-limits for the written proceedings, but the respondent failed to reply. In those circumstances the court fixed short time-limits for the memorial and for the counter-memorial, but with regard to the latter added that if Iran appointed an agent "for the purpose of appearing before the Court and presenting its observations on the case," it could apply for reconsideration of the time-limit. This is an important indication that the appointment of an agent is the equivalent of appearing before the court, significant for the application of Article 53 of the Statute which distinguishes between appearing before the court and defending a case ("faire valoir ses moyens").[51]

In the *Aerial Incident of 3 July 1988* case, the court was faced with an unprecedented issue. The application instituting these proceedings was filed on 17 May 1989 and was duly communicated to the United States, as respondent. The president convened a meeting of the agents for 17 July, postponed to 20 July, and at that meeting the respondent was represented. The appointment of the agent, however, was not notified to the court until 14 August, and on 1 September the respondent formally notified the court that it was its "present intention" to file preliminary objections before the submission of the applicant's memorial. After further interlocutory proceedings, the court made its initial order fixing the time-limits for the first round of written pleadings. In the course of the interlocutory proceedings the applicant averred that the respondent was estopped and time-barred from raising jurisdictional questions, on the ground that its intention to do so should have been notified to the court ealier, and at the latest with the communication to the court of the name of the agent. In its order the court included the following passage: "whereas the Court is not at the present time seised of a preliminary objection by the United States; and whereas accordingly the Court is not called upon, at the present stage of the proceedings, to pronounce on the questions of preclusion and estoppel raised by Iran, whose views in this respect may be put forward later."[52]

A curious and unexplained incident involving an agent occurred in connection with the attempted intervention by Fiji in the *Nuclear Tests* cases. This application for permission to intervene duly completed with the appointment of an agent was filed on 16 May 1973. On 12 July the court issued its orders deferring consideration of the application for permission to intervene until the court had pronounced upon the questions of the jurisdiction of the court to entertain the dispute and of the admissibility of the application. On 10 September 1974 the agent of Fiji, referring to the pending application for permission to intervene, requested that the written pleadings in the principal cases be made available to his government. Other states had made similar requests, and they had been granted. But here the question which seems to have arisen for the court was not whether but how to reply to that request. The method chosen was unusual. Although the agent of Fiji was in regular communication with the court and the orders of 12 July had been sent directly to him, in this instance the registrar wrote to the permanent representative of Fiji to the United Nations in New York, referring to the agent's letter of 10 September, on 11 October 1974. In his communication the registrar wrote: "the Court, having consulted the Parties to the cases, has decided that the request made by Fiji as a Member of the United Nations should be acceded to. Copies of the pleadings so far filed will therefore be sent to your Government."[53]

There is no instance of the representatives of a state taking part in advisory proceedings being designated "agent," not even when the court, in accordance with Article 68 of the Statute, has recognized that the provisions of the Statute which apply in contentious cases are applicable in the advisory case, for instance as regards the appointment of a judge *ad hoc*.[54]

It is clear that when Article 42 of the Statute employs the word "represented," it is using the word in its accepted diplomatic sense. This is exemplified by the fact that by Article 38, paragraph 3, of the Rules of Court the initial notification to the court of an application instituting proceedings is to carry in one form or another either the signature of the diplomatic representative of the applicant country at the seat of the court or be signed "by the competent authority of the applicant's foreign ministry." That "competent authority" would normally be the minister for foreign affairs or an official of the ministry whose authority is a matter of common knowledge, although in current international practice the head of the state, the head of the government, or the minister for foreign affairs are normally regarded as having this manifest authority. (It is surprising that this requirement is stated formally only with respect to the agent of the applicant government: no such requirement is expressed with regard to the appointment of the agent of the respondent government, or of either party when the case is instituted by notification of a special agreement, although the general practice is similar in both those cases.)

To use the language common at the beginning of the century, the agent[55] is the intermediary between the court and the government appointing him.[56] As far as the court is concerned, the agent has exclusive control over the relations between his government and the court in respect of that particular case. This role is, therefore, essentially of a political character: as has been written, "en matière de procédure et en matière politique, seules les déclarations de l'agent engagent la responsabilité du gouvernement qu'il représente."[57] This is further demonstrated by the refusal of the Permanent Court in 1922 to pose any formal requirements regarding the professional qualifications of the agent, the matter being left to the good taste and the requirements of the appointing government. Although the agent is the intermediary between the government and the court, it does not necessarily follow that the agent is in every case the head of the delegation in the oral proceedings: indeed, in many instances either an official of the permanent diplomatic mission at The Hague (or a nearby capital) or a subordinate member of the staff of the legal adviser of the Ministry for Foreign Affairs is appointed agent to manage the business of the government before the court, the head of the delegation in the oral proceedings being a senior official or a senior member of the national bar or even of some other bar, or a professor of international law. The agent does not have to be a national of the state appointing him or her.

It would appear that the correct classification of the agent in the scale of diplomatic representatives is that the agent represents the appointing party vis-à-vis the court, and only vis-à-vis the court; and that the agent has no formal role in relation to the adverse party, beyond the normal relationships that can exist between representatives of states to the same organ of the United Nations. The appointment or nonappointment of an agent concerns the relations of that party itself towards the court in respect of that particular case, and has nothing directly to do with the relations between the two parties themselves. The appointment of the agent is usually the first step in the proceedings ("acte de procédure") of each party, and for the respondent corresponds to an "appearance" in internal litigation. The nonappointment of an agent may entitle the adverse party to invoke the default procedure of Article 53 of the Statute, but that it not invariable as the cited precedent of the *Nottebohm* case illustrates. Similarly, the appointment of an agent, as a step in the proceedings, is something different from defending the case. However, the appointment of an agent cannot go further than that in so far as concerns the rights and positions of that adverse party. For this reason, notwithstanding the apparently categorical imperative of the English ("shall be") and the French ("sont") versions of Article 42 of the Statute, Article 42 is categorical for the party introducing the proceedings, whether by unilateral application or otherwise, and it is exhortatory for the party or parties against whom the application is directed.[58] Cogent support is to be found in the wording of Article 40, paragraphs 2 and 3 (second sentence), of the Rules of Court of 1978, especially when they are read against the legislative history of that provision as described above. By that provision, the respondent may delay the appointment of its agent until "as soon as possible" – a time qualification incapable of objective and generalized definition.[59] Consequently, that party retains freedom of action whether it will take part in the proceedings or not (Statute, Article 53), and should appoint its agent "as soon as possible," whenever that might be.

The conception found in some legal systems that an attorney is somehow an "officer of the Court" does not attach to the office of agent. What is required of a person exercising this function is that the agent should act in good faith and that his or her personal integrity is never in doubt. That is a general requirement of a

63   The Agent in Litigation

diplomatic agent in all circumstances. The agent of a party in international litigation is no different a position.

NOTES

1 C.I. Bevans, 12 *Treaties and Other International Agreements of the United States of America, 1776–1949,* 41, 44.
2 J. Basdevant, *Dictionnaire de la terminologie du Droit international* 29 (Paris 1960).
3 Institut de Droit international, 1 *Annuaire* 126; H. Wehberg, ed., *Tableau général des Résolutions (1873–1956)* (Basle 1957), 147, 150.
4 A. Mérignhac, *Traité théorique et pratique de l'arbitrage internationale* (Paris 1895), 244.
5 Bevans, 1 *Treaties,* 230; ratified by the United Kingdom in 1900, UK Treaty Series No. 9 (1901) Cd. 798. Canada is listed as participating in the Permanent Court of Arbitration, presumably through that ratification. See 89 *Rapport du Conseil administratif de la Cour permanente d'Arbitrage sur les travaux de la Cour ... 1989* at 4, 18. Neither the Convention of 1899, nor that of 1907 (see note 7 below), is listed in C.L. Wiktor, *Canadian Treaty Calendar* (1982) or in any issue I have seen of the Canadian Treaty Series.
6 J.B. Scott, dir., *The Proceedings of the Hague Peace Conferences, Translation of the Official Texts, the Conference of 1899* (1920), 144.
7 Bevans, *Treaties,* 577. This Convention was ratified by the United Kingdom in 1970. UK Treaty Series No. 6 (1971) Cmnd. 4575.
8 See United Nations, 10 *Reports of International Arbitral Awards* (1960), passim.
9 Scott, dir., *Proceedings; The Conference of 1907,* vol. 1: *Plenary Meetings of the Conference* (1920), 429.
10 It is not clear whether that means "in any case" or "in any case before the Court." Probably the former meaning is intended, but this cannot be established conclusively. As for ad hoc judges, during the pendency of the *Military and Paramilitary Activities In and Against Nicaragua* case, in which Professor Claude-Albert Colliard was appointed judge ad hoc by Nicaragua, he was appearing before the court as counsel for Libya in the *Continental Shelf* (Libya/Malta) case. Indeed, he was already appearing before the court in that capacity before he was chosen as judge ad hoc. See (1984) *International Court of Justice Reports* (ICJ) 4, 6; (1985) ibid., 14, 17. This leaves a feeling of unease, especially as in addition there was one member of the court of French nationality. Through what is probably an oversight, the *qualités* of the 1984

judgment on jurisdiction and admissibility do not place on record his appointment as judge ad hoc in that case: this is left to the *qualités* of the 1986 judgment on the merits, where the customary statement that the court saw no objection to that choice does not appear. (1986) ibid., at 17 (para. 6). There is no known case in which a judge ad hoc served as agent in another case, or vice versa, during the pendency of the case for which he was appointed.

11 For a rare instance see *Corfu Channel* (merits) case, (1949) ibid., 4, 32. In the *Anglo-Iranian Oil Co.* case, the registrar explained that, before the court could invoke Article 49 at the instance of a party, that party would first have had to have appointed its agent. ICJ Pleadings 728, doc. 63.

12 Permanent Court of International Justice, Advisory Committee of Jurists, *Procès-Verbaux of the Proceedings of the Committee* (1920), 39.

13 Ibid., 340. For a recent similar instance note the composition of the delegation of the United States in the *Elettronica Sicula S.p.A.* (ELSI) case, which included a member of the Italian Bar who, in his pleading, referred to matters of fact within his knowledge as an attorney who had acted for the private interests concerned in the case. (1989) ICJ Reports 15, 16, 19 (para. 8).

14 *Procès-Verbaux*, 736.

15 League of Nations, Permanent Court of International Justice, *Documents Concerning the Action Taken by the Council of the League of Nations under Article 14 of the Covenant and the Adoption by the Assembly of the Statute of the Permanent Court of International Justice* (1922), 135.

16 Ibid., 212.

17 International Intermediary Institute, The Hague, *The Permanent Court of International Justice, Statute and Rules*, 73 (the Rules of 1922 were never published officially by the Permanent Court, and this edition was semi-official but authentic).

18 Permanent Court of International Justice (PCIJ), Series D, No. 2, at 79.

19 Ibid., 134.

20 Ibid., 260 (Article 28) and 300 (Article 28).

21 Ibid., Addendum 308 (1926).

22 This was before the current practice of maintaining diplomatic representations at the level of embassy, with rare exceptions. At that epoch, most countries were represented in The Hague by legations.

23 PCIJ, Ser. D, No. 2, Addendum 308 at 73–5.

24 Ibid., passim.

25 League of Nations, Committee of Jurists on the Statute of the Permanent Court of International Justice, *Minutes of the Session Held at Geneva, March 11th–19th, 1929*, doc. C.166.M.66.1929.V., at 64.

65 The Agent in Litigation

26 PCIJ, Ser. D, No. 2, Addendum 2, passim. For the 1931 Rules see Ser. D, No. 1, 2d ed., 23.
27 Ibid., Addendum 3 (1936), 803, 817 (on Article 35).
28 PCIJ, Ser. A/B, No. 58 (1933); Ser. C, No. 71.
29 PCIJ, Ser. D, No. 2, Addendum 3, 763. For the full text of the proposed new Rule 32 bis, see 764.
30 Ibid., 840, 843–6. After the United States had discontinued further participation in the *Military and Paramilitary Activities In and Against Nacaragua* case, it nevertheless sent communications to the court through its deputy agent. (1987) ICJ Reports, 188.
31 PCIJ, Ser. D, No. 2, Addendum 3, 773, 774.
32 Ibid., 857, 866, under Article 32 bis. Comments or amendments were annexed by Judges Baron Rolin-Jaequemyns (at 909) and Fromageot (at 913).
33 Ibid., at 866. On this issue, which has since become a prominent feature in the work of the International Court of Justice, see G. Guyomar, *La défaut des parties à un différend devant les juridictions internationales* (Paris 1960) 191; J.B. Elkind, *Non-Appearance before the International Court of Justice* (Boston 1984) 91; H.W.A. Thirlway, *Non-Appearance before the International Court of Justice* (Cambridge 1985), particularly at 32. In the light of this legislative history it seems that the words "as soon as possible" now appearing in Article 40, paragraphs 2 and 3, of the Rules of Court of 1978, preserve the right of any state other than the applicant to avail itself of Article 53 of the Statute.
34 PCIJ, Ser. D, No. 2, Addendum 3, at 41. For further discussion and adoption of the text at the meeting of 1 June 1934 see ibid., at 143. For the text as adopted by the court see 920 (Article 32 bis).
35 In the revised rules adopted by the court on 10 April 1935 the article was numbered 36. It was adopted as such with a minor drafting change by the court on 4 April 1935. Ibid., 431, 954, 987. The rule was finally adopted by the court at its meetings of 18 February and 11 March 1936. Ibid., 580, 729.
36 International Court of Justice, Acts and Documents concerning the Organization of the Court, No. 1, *Charter of the United Unions, Statute and Rules of Court and Other Constitutional Documents*, 2d ed. (May 1947), 54.
37 Ibid., No. 3 (1972), 91.
38 Ibid., No. 5 (1989), 91. See *Background Note V*, Note by the Registry on the Revised Rules of Court (1978).
39 That provision read: "Written copies of these [final submissions], signed by the agent, shall at the same time be communicated to the Court and to the other party."

40 Manley O. Hudson, *International Tribunals, Past and Future* (New York 1944), 51. See also his *The Permanent Court of International Justice 1920–1942: A Treatise* (New York 1943), 326.

41 13 United Nations Conference on International Organization 208. It was pointed out that this problem might be important because these persons might have to travel through several countries to reach the court, and also because of the possibility that special chambers of the court might sit at places other than The Hague. For the addition of "advocates" see 375. For the report of the Rapporteur of Committee IV/1 see 381 at 389 (where Articles 19 and 42 of the Statute are treated together). The reference to journeys reflects the experience of the Permanent Court in the *Electricity Company of Sofia* case, PCIJ, Ser. A/B, No. 80 (1940), 6. Cf M.O. Hudson, "The Twenty-fourth Year of the World Court" (1946), 40 *American Journal of International Law* 1, 37.

42 1 United Nations Treaty Series 15; 90 ibid., 327 (corrigendum). The Netherlands is a party to this Convention. See also *Staatsblad van het Koninkrijk der Nederlanden* No. H (1947), 79. It may be noted, however, that the Convention has only been included in the court's publication *Charter of the United Nations, Statute and Rules of Court and Other Documents* since its third edition of 1977. Frequently a member of the country's diplomatic mission at The Hague is appointed agent or co-agent (deputy agent) and the mission itself is elected as the place of residence. In those circumstances, it is suggested that the principle underlying Article 75 of the Vienna Convention on the Representation of States in their Relations with International Organizations of a Universal Character, 1975, would be applicable and such persons would retain their privileges and immunities as members of their permanent diplomatic mission in addition to the privileges and immunities accorded by the special arrangements made between the court and the Netherlands government. For that Convention, which is not yet in force, see United Nations Conference on the Representation of States in Their Relations with International Organizations, II *Official Records* 207 (doc. A/CONF.67/16); (1975) *United Nations Juridical Yearbook* 87. The Netherlands has not signed that convention.

43 For an illustration see the *Applicability of Article VI, Section 22, of the Convention on the Privileges and Immunities of the United Nations* advisory opinion, (1989) ICJ Reports 177, particularly at pages 188 and 190 (paras. 29 and 37). That case concerned the applicability of the Convention to a special rapporteur of the Sub-Commission on Prevention of Discrimination and Protection of Minorities of the Commission on Human Rights, considered as an expert performing a mission on behalf of the United Nations. It could be applicable in other circumstances coming within the scope of the Convention.

67   The Agent in Litigation

44 Hudson, *The Permanent Court of International Justice*, 527.
45 (1950) ICJ Reports, 59. And see the statement by the registrar, in transmitting the order to the respondent, specifically noting that the court had deemed the appointment of the agent to be a step in the proceedings. Pleadings, 25, doc. 29.
46 (1973) ICJ Reports 347, 348. This follows the decision of the Permanent Court in the order of discontinuance in the *Treaty of November 2nd, 1865, between China and Belgium* case, PCIJ, Ser. A, No. 18/19, 7, where the court noted that the respondent had never taken any proceeding (*acte de procédure*) in the suit so there was nothing to prevent the unilateral withdrawal of the suit by the applicant government (1929).
47 (1962) ICJ Reports 320, 322; (1966) ibid., 6, 9.
48 (1969) ibid., 3, 4, 8.
49 The cases include *Anglo-Iranian Oil Co.* (1951) ibid., 89; *Fisheries Jurisdiction* (1972) ibid., 12, 30, (1973) ibid., 302, 313; *Nuclear Tests* (1973) ibid., 99, 135; *Aegean Sea Continental Shelf* (1976) ibid., 3; and *United States Diplomatic and Consular Staff in Tehran* (1979) ibid., 7. In all these cases except *Anglo-Iranian Oil Co.*, the respondent never appointed an agent, and the case proceeded on the basis of Article 53 of the Statute.
50 (1953) ibid., 111, 123.
51 (1979) ibid., 23.
52 (1989) ibid., 132, 133.
53 II Pleadings 433, 435, docs. 191, 194. The explanation for this roundabout manner of handling the question is probably to be found in the intricacies of the court's practice and procedure governing applications for permission to intervene.
54 *Western Sahara* case (1975) ICJ Reports 12.
55 Parties may in addition appoint a co-agent, a deputy agent, and an additional agent. (1988–9) 43 ICJ Yearbook 122. On the sickness of the agent in the *South West Africa* cases, the additional agent who had previously been appointed assumed the duties of agent. VIII Pleadings 72, XII ibid., 552, 553 (docs. 65, 67). It is now also recognized that the agent can appoint an acting agent in the event of temporary absence from The Hague, indisposition, or other reasonable cause. In that sense, the general rules regarding the acting head of a delegation to an organ of the United Nations would probably be applied.
56 There have been only two instances, to date, in which a woman has been appointed agent: Ms Joyce Gutteridge, who was agent of the United Kingdom in the *Aerial Incident of 27 July 1955* case, and S.ra Flora Díaz Parrado, agent for the intervening party (Cuba) in the *Haya de la Torre* case.
57 B. Schenk Graf von Stauffenberg, *Statut et règlement de la Cour permanente de Justice internationale, Eléments d'interprétation* (Berlin 1934), 320.

See also R. Monaco, "Représentation et défense des parties devant les instances internationales," in *Festschrift für Rudolf Binschedler*, ed. Emanuel Diez et al. (Berne 1980), 373.

58 Cf Hudson, *The Permanent Court of International Justice*, 527.

59 In one important respect the modern technological advances in communications have affected the functioning of the agent – through the introduction of facsimile transmission of documents. A striking example is provided by the order of 12 June 1990 extending time-limits in the *Aerial Incident of 3 July 1988* case. Iran's request for this extension was made in a letter of 11 June, transmitted to the United States agent through the United States Embassy at The Hague the same day. The reply of the United States was transmitted from Washington by facsimile the next day, together with a notification of the appointment of a new agent. The registrar's acknowledgment of that communication notifying the United States of the order in question was transmitted directly to Washington by facsimile. (1990) ICJ Reports 86. Use of this method of communication stands in sharp contrast to the dismay expressed by the first registrar of the Permanent Court at his having sometimes to communicate with a party "by telegram." See PCIJ, Ser. D, No. 2, Addendum 308 at 73–5. For the initial communication to the court of an application instituting proceedings by facsimile, followed by the document itself, see the application by Chad in the *Chad/Libya Territorial Dispute*, ICJ Communiqué No. 90/14, 4 Sept. 1990.

The Case for an Arctic Region Council and a Treaty Proposal

DONAT PHARAND

In 1971 Maxwell Cohen proposed that a formal system of cooperation should be developed throughout the arctic basin. The idea has now matured to the point where it is time to make concrete treaty proposals. What is needed is an Arctic Region Council, which should be established by way of a treaty. The first part of this article will examine the main areas of cooperation in which an Arctic Region Council would be engaged and the second will present a draft treaty proposal for the creation of an Arctic Council.

ARCTIC COOPERATION AND THE ROLE OF CANADA

Cooperation to save our planet Earth is particularly vital at the regional level where the same ecosystems must be shared. This is especially true of the Arctic, a region of low biological productivity and high vulnerability to pollution and human disturbance. With the second largest arctic territory and situated between Russia and the United States, Canada is well placed to play a leading role in the promotion of cooperation among all eight arctic states (Canada, Denmark, Finland, Iceland, Norway, Sweden, Russia, and the United States). Such a role was envisaged by two American commentators who observed, "not only would this role fit nicely with the image that many Canadians hold regarding the place of Canada in international society and that has energized Canadian efforts in the fields of arms control and peacekeeping, it would also help to assuage Canadian fears about being sandwiched between the great powers in the Far North and about succumbing to American pressures regarding issues of sovereignty and security in the Arctic."[1] Their observation is well based. The Canadian fear of American pressure is of long standing and was probably the main reason for Prime Minister Louis St Laurent and Secretary of State Lester B. Pearson to state, as far back as 1946, that Canada wished to work "not only with the U.S.A., but with the other Arctic countries, Denmark, Norway, and the Soviet Union," in fostering cooperative measures for the economic and communications development of the Arctic.[2]

In 1971 Professor Cohen not only suggested that Canada cooperate with all other arctic states, but also envisaged that this cooperation be formalized in a treaty. He wrote, "the most urgent objective of Canada policy ... is the development of a body of Arctic basin consensus, perhaps an *Arctic basin treaty*."[3] He was convinced that "Canadian Arctic policy ... offers a superb opportunity for Canadian leadership in the development of an *Arctic basin systems approach* having relevance to the polar area as a whole and to the Canadian archipelago and its waters in particular."[4] Cohen's suggestion was made in the context of the emerging new law of the sea, shortly after Canada's adoption of the Arctic Waters Pollution Prevention Act in 1970, but his suggestion is fully applicable today to all other areas of arctic concern.

The concept of an arctic system or council, and the role of Canada in promoting it, remained dormant from 1971 to 1987, when a working group of the National Capital Branch of the Canadian Institute of International Affairs, of which Professor Cohen was a member, discussed the suggestion further. Encouraged by the positive reaction to the idea by the participants at a seminar on the Arctic sponsored by Canada and Norway at Tromso in December of that year,[5] the working group recommended the establishment of an Arctic Council in its report the following year.

The recommendation of the Canadian Institute was well received by the government and, in November 1989, at the time of his visit to the Soviet Union to conclude a number of bilateral agreements on the Arctic, Prime Minister Brian Mulroney asked towards the end of his address at the Arctic and Antarctic Institute in Leningrad, "And why not a council of Arctic countries eventually coming into existence to coordinate and promote cooperation among them?"[6] A few months after the prime minister's question, an independent panel, co-chaired by Franklyn Griffiths and Rosemary Kuptana, was established.[7]

The panel produced a preliminary report, "To Establish an Arctic Basin Council," in March 1990 and, by November of that year, the

71 The Case for an Arctic Region Council

idea had been accepted in principle by the Canadian government. Speaking in Ottawa on 28 November 1990, Joe Clark, secretary of state for external affairs, stated: "The Government believes that now is the time to move forward to establish that Arctic Council. Canada intends to propose an Arctic Council to the seven other Arctic Countries ... We will raise the proposal at a ministerial meeting in Finland next spring on environmental co-operation." As an indication of the seriousness of the proposal, he went on to say that "Canada is willing to host a small secretariat for this Council and contribute to sustaining it from the outset."[8] Heartened by Clark's statement, the Arctic Council panel produced a second, more comprehensive, framework report in January 1991, which was discussed at a roundtable in Ottawa. The report, which was generally well received by the participants, proposed a comprehensive structure in which there would be direct participation by aboriginal peoples and other non-state entities, as well as a broad agenda permitting a discussion of both civil and military matters.[9]

In March 1991 another working group of the National Capital Branch of the Canadian Institute of International Affairs published a report on the arctic environment which urged the government to demonstrate Canada's commitment to the establishment of an Arctic Region Council by outlining its main purposes and composition.[10] Attached to the report was an appendix, "Draft Arctic Treaty: An Arctic Regional Council," prepared by the author.[11]

Taking into account the comments made at the roundtable, the Arctic Council panel published a second framework report in May 1991.[12] The report provides for different types of structure and expresses a preference for a compact structure composed of ten members: eight for the arctic states, one for the Arctic Aboriginal Conference, and one for the Northern Forum.[13]

On the mandate of the council, the report noted that "currently, the arctic States are unanimous in tacit opposition to negotiations among arctic States on confidence-building and arms control measures affecting the region, and would see all such issues treated in non-arctic negotiating forums only."[14] Considering, however, the strong feeling on the part of aboriginal peoples, territorial governments, and others that no major arctic issue or problem should be excluded from consideration, the panel urged that "the mandate of an Arctic Council be an open one that allows for growth in the Council's agenda with the growth of consensus."[15] More specifically, it stated that "no international arctic matter should in principle be barred from discussion or negotiation on Council," adding that "this applies to questions of international peace and security."[16]

More must be done by way of preparatory work to take advantage of the momentum for the creation of such a council. The fourteen draft founding articles included in the report[17] are excellent as general guidelines for the preparation of a founding instrument or document, and that document should be drafted without delay. Otherwise, Canada risks finding itself insufficiently prepared to pursue its own initiative with other arctic states.

The question of an Arctic Council was not a subject for direct discussion at the ministerial conference in Finland in June 1991 on the protection of the arctic environment. The ministers agreed on an Arctic Environmental Protection Strategy[18] and a Declaration on the Protection of the Arctic Environment. The Canadian initiative, however, has since received further support from the president of the Russian Federation. At the time of his visit to Ottawa on 1 February 1992, President Boris Yeltsin and Prime Minister Mulroney signed a Declaration of Friendship and Cooperation in which they affirm their support for an Arctic Council. The declaration states: "Canada and the Russian Federation, as major Arctic states, affirm their support for the creation of an international Arctic Council to protect the Arctic, its peoples and its resources, while fostering prosperity in the region through enhanced cooperation among circumpolar states."[19]

The adoption and signing of declarations, strategies, and action plans have real merits and are evidence of serious intentions, but there is a need for an arctic treaty that would give legally binding effect to the political will of arctic states. A treaty system has worked well for the Antarctic and is being proposed by the European Parliament to replace the ministerial conference system for the Protection of the North Sea that has been in place since 1984.[20] Such a treaty, establishing a council with its own structure and implementation mechanism, would permit a much-needed cooperative and holistic approach for the fulfilment of the various purposes of the council.

ARCTIC COOPERATION FOR THE PROTECTION OF THE ENVIRONMENT

The distribution of pollutants in the Arctic has been increasing at an alarming rate. Those pollutants originate mainly from industrialized areas in lower latitudes and are carried by the atmosphere, rivers, and ocean currents.[21] The resulting damage to the environment manifests itself in a multiplicity of ways, such as the "arctic haze," depletion of the ozone layer, contamination of the food chain, global warming, and pollution of the marine environment and of the environment generally.

73 The Case for an Arctic Region Council

Arctic Haze

The phenomenon known as the arctic haze in the atmosphere is caused by pollutants (mainly soot, hydrocarbons, and sulphates) which originate mostly from the air masses of Europe and Asia. These pollutants travel across the Arctic Ocean "to reach the northern Canadian arctic and Alaska, where they form a persistent low level hazy blanket, from which pollutants are deposited."[22] This hazy blanket could eventually affect weather patterns in the northern hemisphere.

Ozone Layer

The depletion of the ozone layer, which protects the Earth's surface from solar radiation, was discovered over the Antarctic some ten years ago but was detected in the Arctic only in 1986. Scientists believe that the depletion is due to certain chemicals, mainly chlorofluorocarbons (CFCs) and other related substances widely used in industrialized countries all over the world. The result is that "the increase in solar radiation reaching the surface through depleted ozone layer can cause skin cancer and eye cataracts in humans and animals, suppress immune systems, damage shallow-dwelling marine organisms, and inhibit the germination of seeds."[23] In 1985 a Convention for the Protection of the Ozone Layer was signed in Vienna and was followed by a protocol adopted in Montreal in 1987 on "Substances that Deplete the Ozone Layer."[24] Although those instruments commit the parties to reduce the use of chlorofluorocarbons by 50 per cent by the year 2000, they have not yet received the necessary number of ratifications to enter into force. Fortunately, this has not prevented some steps being taken to strengthen the Montreal protocol, and an amendment, adopted in 1990, raised the goal to 100 per cent elimination by the year 2000.[25] These are instruments of general application, but there is also a need for a regional convention for the protection of the atmosphere in the Arctic.

Food Chain

Toxic substances, particularly organochlorides (mainly PCBs), which originate from industrial and agricultural practices have been found in high concentrations in the fatty tissue of animals at the top of the food chain, such as arctic seals, polar bears, and whales. These poisonous substances eventually find their way to the indigenous populations who depend on those local animals for their survival. Dr E.F.

Roots, science adviser emeritus at Environment Canada and a well-known authority on arctic science, reports that, in a native village in the eastern Canadian Arctic, "a significant proportion of the inhabitants have body concentrations of toxic organochlorides significantly higher than the average for Canadians as a whole."[26] Such damaging effect is corroborated by Mary Simon, currently president of the Inuit Circumpolar Conference, who states that "polychlorinated biphenyls (PCBs) and other persistent chemicals are seriously jeopardizing the health of Inuit, our northern environment and our wildlife."[27]

Global Warming

The climate change, which is presently taking place in the form of global warming because of the accumulation of the so-called greenhouse gases in the upper atmosphere, will be particularly felt in the Arctic. In the words of Dr Roots, "the best current estimates suggest that the entire planetary surface will likely warm an average of 1.5 to 4 degrees Celsius in the next fifty years, and that the warming of the arctic regions around 70° N latitude would be 2 to 2.4 times as great as the world average."[28] Some of the environment changes that could result from global warming during the next half-century include increased cloudiness, storm, and snow along arctic coastlines; increased variation of regional climate in the Arctic; increased snow cover on sea ice, resulting in thinning and greater clearing; increased snowfall on glaciers and ice-caps, adding to their size; and changed biogeographic zones and hydrological systems in northern North America and Siberia, causing a northward extension of the tree line and affecting the supply of north-flowing rivers.[29] These possible changes are, of course, far from certain. What is certain, however, is that some changes will occur, the risk of damage is high, and cooperation is necessary at the regional as well as at the global level.

Marine Environment

Special protection is needed for the marine environment in the arctic region. A general recognition of this need with respect to vessel-source pollution is contained in a special provision of the 1982 Convention on the Law of the Sea. Because of the presence of ice and the possibility of major harm and irreversible disturbance of the ecological balance, coastal states are empowered not only to adopt but to enforce protective measures to prevent, reduce, and control marine pollution from vessels.[30] That provision was gratifying to arctic states, particularly to

Canada, which had adopted its Arctic Waters Pollution Prevention Act in 1970 containing such powers. Although the Law of the Sea Convention has not yet come into force, the special arctic clause may be considered as forming part of customary international law because of the degree of acceptance it has received, particularly by arctic states. In 1971 the Soviet Union adopted similar protective measures for its arctic waters, and in 1988 the United States, which had opposed the arctic clause during the Law of the Sea Conference, recognized that its commercial vessels would conform with the provisions of Canada's arctic legislation and, consequently, has impliedly accepted the substance of the arctic clause.

In addition, all the arctic states agreed in 1991 to "apply the principles concerning the protection and preservation of the Marine Environment as reflected in the 1982 United Nations Convention on the Law of the Sea."[31] The provisions of the convention cover marine pollution from all sources: land-based, sea-bed activities, dumping, vessels, and the atmosphere. However, states must still take specific measures individually and collectively to implement those provisions which remain, for the most part, of a general character. For this implementation to take place, close cooperation is necessary both at the bilateral and regional levels.

At the bilateral level, a good beginning has been made with respect to pollution from vessels and sea-bed activities. In 1983 an agreement was concluded between Denmark and Canada relating to the waters between Greenland and the Canadian Arctic Archipelago. The parties agree to consult each other prior to the initiation of works or undertakings which could cause marine pollution damage and to pay compensation for damage caused from installations engaged in exploration or exploitation. Annexes to the agreement establish two joint contingency plans, one for pollution incidents resulting from offshore exploration or exploitation and the other resulting from shipping activities.[32]

On 20 November 1989 a Memorandum of Understanding on Cooperation relating to the Prevention and Control of Arctic Marine Pollution was concluded between Canada and the Soviet Union. The understanding came into force upon signature and is for a period of four years. Both countries having already adopted national legislation to combat marine pollution in their respective arctic waters, this understanding enhances bilateral cooperation to prevent, reduce, and control ship-source pollution in ice-covered areas. It provides for the exchange of information on such topics as environmental legislation, pollution prevention policy, pollution monitoring, pollution incident response capabilities, and research results. Transport Canada and the Merchant Marine of the Soviet Union are responsible for the implementation of the understanding.

At the regional level, the Arctic Environmental Protection Strategy, adopted by the eight arctic states in June 1991, represents an importance step in the right direction. This is particularly so with respect to their agreement to "take measures as soon as possible to adhere to the strictest relevant international standards within the conventions, to which the countries are parties, regarding discharges irrespective of origin."[33] This represents a considerable commitment, in that there are eight general international conventions dealing with the protection of the marine environment.

Environment Generally

Protection of the environment, at both the global and regional levels, was given special impetus at the United Nations in December 1989, when it was decided to hold a Conference on the Environment and Development in Brazil in 1992. The General Assembly resolution reaffirmed the responsibility of states "to ensure that activities within their jurisdiction or control do not cause damage to the environment of other States or of areas beyond the limits of national jurisdiction and to play their due role in preserving and protecting the global and *regional environment* in accordance with their capacities and specific responsibilities."[34] The assembly resolution specified that one of the objectives of the conference is "to examine ways and means further to *improve co-operation* in the field of protection and enhancement of the environment *between neighboring countries*, with a view to eliminating adverse environmental effects."[35]

If states, in any region of the world, should cooperate to ensure that their activities (particularly their resource development activities, both on-shore and off-shore) do not cause transboundary damage to the environment, surely that obligation applies with much greater force in the Arctic. In addition, protection of the delicate arctic environment cannot be assured unless there is an adequate coordination of scientific research.

ARCTIC COOPERATION FOR THE COORDINATION OF SCIENTIFIC RESEARCH

Arctic cooperation must result in an effective coordination of research among all countries concerned and in a high degree of interaction between science and policy-making. Although cooperation has begun, more needs to be done, and Canada has the potential to make a significant contribution to arctic science.

Effectiveness of Coordination

Effective coordination of research presupposes that a number of conditions are met, including equal access to scientific information and data; sharing of current information on environmental effects; comprehensive monitoring and data collection systems; and fuller participation of aboriginal peoples in scientific research.[36] It is also important that scientists from the various countries use internationally comparable methodologies to collect information and data, otherwise adequate coordination of research is difficult. This was found to be the case in the study of the North Sea environment, and a task force was established to prepare a new Quality State Report, using data based on internationally comparable methodologies. "At present," writes Dr Philip Reid, North Sea scientific coordinator at the Department of the Environment of the United Kingdom, "each country has its own North Sea programmes with different emphases and/or scientific methodologies. The Task Force provides a means to ensure the eventual harmonization and co-ordination of these different approaches."[37]

Science and Policy-Making

Close interaction between science and policy-making is also of the utmost importance. Two political scientists at the Fridtjof Nansen Institute in Oslo have studied the role of science in North Sea policy-making and have found a number of deficiencies. They identified the following institutional deficiencies: "co-ordination of research and monitoring is flawed; the awareness of the importance of a clear distinction between science and politics is too low; policy-makers and scientists speak different languages and translation is sparse; the media lack the necessary expertise to involve the public in a rational way."[38]

Beginnings of Coordination

With respect to the coordination of scientific research in the Arctic, a good beginning has been made on a bilateral basis (particularly between Canada and the Soviet Union),[39] but, at the multilateral level, the first important step has only recently been taken. In 1990 an International Arctic Science Committee (IASC) was established, in which the eight arctic countries all participate, as well as the six non-arctic countries that carry out significant research in the Arctic (France, Germany, Japan, the Netherlands, Poland, and the United Kingdom). In the words of the report of the Canadian Institute of International Affairs, "the real challenge for IASC will be to engage the participation of the scientific communities of all countries that can contribute to arctic science, sustain co-operation on an ongoing basis, and, at the same time, facilitate the science which is seen to be in the national interest of member countries."[40]

Canada's Potential Contribution

As for Canada's future contribution to arctic science, the report emphasizes the necessity of improving its arctic research capability: "if Canada is to do its share in contributing to international arctic science, or even obtain the information it needs about the arctic environment to develop its own domestic policies, it will have to *strengthen its indigenous capabilities, and provide means for better co-ordination on ongoing scientific research activities* within the Canadian Scientific community."[41] The creation of the Canadian Polar Commission in 1991, with provision for at least one regional office north of 60° N latitude, is a step in the right direction in eventually making an adequate contribution to international polar science. Canada being a member of the Antarctic Treaty since 1988, although only as a nonconsultative member, the Polar Commission should be able to obtain research information on both polar regions. Along with the other four arctic basin states, which were already members of the Antarctic Treaty, Canada can now contribute to and benefit from the vast amount of scientific research being pursued in the Antarctic in various fields of relevance to the Arctic, such as sea ice structure and behaviour, climate dynamics, and the protection of the marine environment. To attain its objectives, the Polar Commission must receive the necessary funding and it "must not be allowed to become an instrument of government or the tool of a particular department or agency."[42] Unfortunately, it would seem that these dangers are nearly always present.

Antarctic Model

Close cooperation in scientific research within the antarctic treaty system augurs well for similar cooperation in an Arctic Region Council. This is particularly so when one considers that five (the United States, Russia, Norway, Sweden, and Finland) council members are also members of the Scientific Committee for Scientific Research (SCAR) for the Antarctic. Canada has accepted invitations to participate at SCAR conferences and has become involved in some SCAR activities, but has not yet made formal moves to become a member, although it adheres to the parent organization of SCAR, the International Council of Scientific Unions (ICSU).

ARCTIC COOPERATION FOR THE CONSERVATION OF LIVING RESOURCES

The conservation of living resources in the Arctic must involve the participation of aboriginal peoples and take into account their understanding of wildlife and their sustenance practices.

Understanding of Wildlife

As stated by the Inuit Circumpolar Conference in its Comprehensive Arctic Policy, "wildlife is the basis of Inuit life, culture and economy."[43] But, since wildlife does not respect political boundaries, it "cannot be properly managed nor can its habitat be adequately protected in independent jurisdictions without regional, national and international cooperation."[44] Indigenous populations have developed a unique understanding of wildlife and their habitat. They recognize more than anyone that wildlife is a shared resource which must be protected and managed in a manner that maintains the delicate ecological balance of the region, whilst responding to the needs of the people.

Sustenance Practices

Aboriginal sustenance practices must be taken into account, not only because it is a matter of duty to respect the needs and culture of native communities, but also because such practices, if carried out on the scale to which aboriginals have traditionally developed their economy, are in conformity with the concept of sustainability. Aboriginal societies are accustomed to taking from nature only what is necessary for their survival today, so that nature will still be there for them tomorrow. To quote from an Inuit hunter: "I just get enough for my own use the coming year. Next year the animals are going to be there anyway, that's my bank."[45]

The issue of subsistence harvesting was the subject of a statement of principles in June 1991, at the meeting held in Greenland, of the Inuit Circumpolar Conference, an established association of Inuit from Alaska, Canada, and Greenland, with observers from the Saami of the Nordic countries and the native people of the Russian north. The basic principle is expressed as follows: "Subsistence harvesting continues to be essential to the cultural, social and physical well being of the Arctic indigenous peoples. Subsistence is the traditional and direct dependence on renewable resources."[46] The statement goes on to underline that their subsistence is increasingly threatened by the anti-harvesting lobby movement, and concludes by calling on governments to recognize fully their rights to the harvesting of renewable resources and to direct participation in the development and implementation of any measures for the protection and conservation of arctic species and habitats.

Involvement of Aboriginal Peoples

The Inuit realize it is in their long-term interest that wildlife be conserved and its habitat protected, so they have developed and are trying to implement a Regional Conservation Strategy.[47] The direct involvement of all major user groups is necessary for the implementation of that strategy or any international agreement, such as the Agreement on the Conservation of Polar Bears of 1973.[48] This necessity was demonstrated with respect to the polar bear population in the Beaufort Sea crossing the political boundary between the United States and Canada. With different national regulations on each side of that boundary, the coastal population of polar bears was threatened until 1988, when an agreement was concluded between the North Slope Borough and the Inuvialuit Game Council. The Beaufort Sea Polar Bear Management Agreement of 1988 protects bears in dens and females with cubs. It also provides for annual quotas to be allocated to both groups, based on the best scientific evidence.[49]

Beginnings of Cooperation

Aside from the polar bear treaty of 1973, arctic states have yet to conclude regional agreements for the protection of transboundary living resources such as migratory birds, porcupine caribou, and various species of whales and seals. These resources have been the subject of bilateral agreements, but more needs to be done on a regional basis.[50]

At the national level, Canada is to be commended for having adopted an Arctic Marine Conservation Strategy in 1987. Its stated purpose is "to ensure the future health and well-being of Arctic marine ecosystems thereby enabling Canada to fulfill its national responsibilities in the Arctic and to provide for the sustained utilization of Arctic marine resources, in particular, use by Arctic peoples."[51] One of the guiding principles of the strategy is the cooperation with other arctic states. It provides that the "implementation of the strategy should recognize regional seas as broad management units as well as the need for international co-operation."[52]

Realizing the need for cooperation, arctic states might well consider the advantages of concluding a regional agreement for the conservation of vital living resources.[53] Whatever cooperative measures they take, their implementation would be greatly facilitated by the proposed Arctic Region Council in which the indigenous populations would have meaningful participation.

ARCTIC COOPERATION FOR SUSTAINABLE ECONOMIC DEVELOPMENT

The achievement of sustainable economic development in the Arctic presupposes a common understanding of sustainability. It also requires cooperation in the development of nonrenewable resources and in their transportation to markets.

Meaning of Sustainability

The best definition of sustainable development is that given by the World Commission on Environment and Development (the Brundtland Commission) in 1987: "Sustainable development is development that meets the needs of the present without compromising the ability of future generations to meet their own needs."[54] The concept of the development of resources implies a most important limitation: that such development be limited to meeting essential needs so as to leave enough for future generations to meet their own essential needs. In the words of the commission, "a society may in many ways compromise its ability to meet the essential needs of its people in the future – by overexploiting resources, for example. The direction of technological developments may solve some immediate problems but lead to even greater ones. Large sections of the population may be marginalized by ill-considered development."[55] This danger of marginalization is particularly present for the indigenous people of the Arctic who live off the land and whose subsistence depends on the continuing quality of their environment. To quote again from the commission's report, because of its special pertinence to the Arctic: "Sustainable development requires that the adverse impacts on the quality of air, water, and other natural elements are minimized so as to sustain the ecosystem's overall integrity."[56] Considering the special vulnerability of the Arctic and the large increase in population of native people, as well as the damage to the habitat of many northern animals used by these people for food, the achievement of sustainability will be very difficult.

Nonrenewable Resources

With respect to the development of nonrenewable resources, especially petroleum hydrocarbons, Harriet Critchley concludes that the arctic basin states, being dependent on those resources, should seize the opportunity afforded by the present modest level of activity "to explore and develop cooperative institutions and mechanisms for further economic development in the face of pressures that might otherwise promote conflict."[57]

Critchley's suggestion is in line with the overtures made by the Soviet Union in recent years. In his speech at Murmansk in 1987, President Gorbachev stated that "the Soviet Union attaches much importance to peaceful cooperation in developing the resources of the North, the Arctic. Here an exchange of experience and knowledge is extremely important. Through joint efforts it could be possible to work out an overall concept of rational development of northern areas."[58] He added: "We have an interest in inviting, for instance, Canada and Norway to form mixed firms and enterprises for developing oil and gas deposits of the shelf of our northern seas. We are prepared for relevant talks with other States as well."[59] This overture was repeated by Ambassador Rodionov at a conference in Edmonton in 1989, where he stated: "The Soviet Union pays a great deal of attention to cooperation in the development of Arctic resources. It is necessary, in our view, to establish jointly a mechanism for such cooperation in the interests of national development of northern regions."[60] He specified later: "We are interested, for instance, in the participation of Canadian companies in joint ventures for developing oil and gas deposits in the shelf of our northern seas."[61]

Transportation of Resources

Commercial resource development means transportation to southern markets. Except for oil and gas, which may be brought to market by pipeline or tankers, arctic resources must be transported by ships and barges accompanied by ice-breakers. In Russia, all oil and gas production has been on land, mostly from the West Siberian basin in the sub-Arctic, and the production is carried by pipeline.[62] Other

Russian arctic resources, such as timber and mining products, are shipped on its north-flowing rivers to the Northern Sea Route, which is usually open from July to October and links Murmansk to Vladivostok. The Soviet Union has developed an ice-breaker fleet of more than seventy-five ships, sixteen of them being large polar ice-breakers capable of continuously breaking level ice of 1.4 to 2.4 meters in thickness at three knots.[63] By comparison, the United States has only two ice-breakers in this size range, the *Polar Star* and the *Polar Sea*, and Canada has only one, the *Louis St-Laurent*, which has been in the process of refitting for the last several years.

The United States has been shipping its oil from the Beaufort Sea by pipeline, down through Alaska to Valdez and then by tanker along the Canadian coast to the Western American market. It was on the Alaskan coast that the *Exxon Valdez* grounded in March 1989, releasing some 44,000 tonnes of oil. The United States considered using the Northwest Passage in the early 1970s to ship some of its oil from the Beaufort Sea to the American east seaboard, but, to date, this has not yet taken place.

In Canada, a lot of drilling has been done in the Beaufort Sea, but the commercial extraction of oil from its wells has not yet begun. The only oil being shipped from the Arctic is in small quantities from the Bent Horn oilfield in the middle of the Queen Elizabeth Islands, north of the Northwest Passage. Since 1985 the *M.V. Arctic*, a double-hulled class 4 oil bulk ore carrier of 28,000 tonnes, has transported a few shipments of light crude oil each year for transshipment to smaller tankers. These vessels are then escorted by Coast Guard ice-breakers through the ice-covered areas, and the oil is shipped either to Montreal or Europe. In addition, a small quantity of light crude is delivered locally from Bent Horn to Resolute Bay and to Polaris Mine on Little Cornwallis Island.[64] The producers (Esso, Shell, and Gulf) of the Mackenzie Delta gas have received a licence from the National Energy Board to export 9.2 trillion cubic feet over the next twenty years, but environmental approval must still be obtained. The transportation to market would take place by pipeline.

As for the eventual oil shipping from Beaufort Sea wells, it must still be decided if this will take place by pipeline or by tanker. In its final report of 1984, the Beaufort Sea Environmental Assessement Panel expressed a preference for the pipeline method, but concluded that crude oil could be shipped by super tankers if a program of accelerated research established that it could be done without undue negative effect on wildlife and the Inuit traditional way of life.[65] The panel also recommended that one agency only be responsible for oil-spill contingency planning – the Canadian Coast Guard. Consequently, the Coast Guard pressed for and the government eventually approved the construction of a Polar 8 ice-breaker that was "central to the research and spill response recommendations of the Beaufort Sea Panel."[66] Indeed, the *Polar 8* would have been capable of operating year-round in fifteen of the sixteen safety zones of the Canadian Arctic (all zones except M'Clure Strait), and "the vessel would have also provided the first significant national capability to enforce Canada's Arctic pollution regulations year-round."[67] It was to have space on board for up to 150 specially trained personnel. Unfortunately, in 1990, the government decided to rescind its approval for the construction of the *Polar 8*, because of the high cost, and the country is left with very inadequate oil-spill response capability.

In September 1990 the first major finding of a Public Review Panel on Tanker Safety and Marine Spills Response Capability was that "the capability to respond effectively to a spill of any significant magnitude does not presently exist anywhere in Canada."[68] Consequently, the panel made a number of stringent recommendations, some of which apply specifically to the Arctic. It recommended in particular that "it be mandatory for tankers involved in Arctic fuel resupply to be double-hulled";[69] that "the federal government provide a dedicated oil spill monitoring and clean-up vessel for operation during each Arctic shipping season";[70] and that "all Canadian Coast Guard icebreakers operating in the Arctic should have containerized spill clean-up equipment on board, as well as a crew trained in its use."[71] This last recommendation was also made for all tankers and barges.[72]

Signs of Cooperation

s brief review of the experience in resource transportation gained by three of the eight arctic states shows that much would be gained by close cooperation among them all in this important area. Such a recommendation was strongly urged at the International Conference on Arctic Cooperation in Toronto in October 1988 by Dr A. Arikaynen of the All-Union Institute for Systems Studies in Moscow. He went so far as to suggest that arctic states "begin the preparation of a collective monograph on the state-of-the-art and problems of Arctic navigation."[73] Later, at the McGill Conference on Arctic Policy, his compatriot Dr R.V. Varatanov, head of the World Ocean and Environment Section of the Academy of the USSR, went even further in suggesting that the shipping of foreign cargoes on Soviet vessels in the Northern Sea Route could lead to consideration of "the advisability of establishing joint companies engaged in Arctic shipping."[74] This kind of close cooperation in marine transportation between Canada and Russia appears to be materializing. In September 1991 Canarctic Shipping Co. Ltd was reported to have been negotiating with two Russian ship companies in the hope of adding Russian vessels to its fleet of cargo ships operating in the Canadian Arctic. In turn, Canarctic, which has developed an excellent navigation system, hoped to sell navigation and communications equipment to Russia.[75]

Economic cooperation among arctic states seems to be developing at the bilateral level, at least between Canada and Russia, but there is nothing comparable on the multilateral side. The Cold War between the former Soviet Union and the United States having been replaced by manifestations of good will, the development of economic cooperation between all arctic states ought to be promoted through an Arctic Region Council.

ARCTIC COOPERATION FOR THE PROTECTION OF THE HEALTH AND SOCIAL WELL-BEING OF ARCTIC INHABITANTS

The Preamble to the Declaration of the Arctic Indigenous Leaders Summit, signed in June 1991 by the representatives of the three participating organizations (the Inuit Circumpolar Conference (ICC), the Nordic Saami Council, and the Russian Association of Northern Small Peoples), states that they are "deeply concerned for the health, well-being and ultimate survival of our peoples, including recognition of our nutritional needs and the rights of renewable resource harvesters, and for the protection of our Arctic environment, both now and in the future."[76] This affirmation sums up, in essence, what needs to be protected to insure the health and well-being of arctic indigenous peoples. To provide that protection adequately, however, governments of arctic states must understand how those populations perceive their own health and well-being. They wish to continue living in close relationship with their natural environment, of which they properly consider themselves the primary custodians. The Arctic Policy adopted by the General Assembly of the ICC in 1989 specifies the meaning attached to the terms health and well-being, as well as the expectations people have of services from government.

Health Policy

The "Principles and Elements on Health and Social Well-Being" forming part of the Arctic Policy cover six pages of single-spaced typewritten text.[77] What follows is a summary of some of those principles and elements, followed by the relevant paragraph number.

- Health refers to the state of the whole person and has a direct bearing on the development and quality of life of the individual. (1)
- "Spiritual, emotional, psychological and physical well-being are all elements to be considered in striving for good health." (2)
- Arctic governments have a duty to guarantee health and social services to northern peoples. (4)
- Inuit must participate in the health care and social services systems. (5)
- "As a general rule, the socio-cultural impact of health programs in the North should be assessed." (7)
- "If the right to health as a fundamental human right is to have real meaning in the Arctic, a comprehensive strategy must be devised and carried out." (8)
- Increasing health risks are being found in the Arctic environment (9), and "environmental causes of health problems in the Arctic should be carefully studied." (10)
- Because of the overconsumption of alcohol and drugs (12), "state governments ... should provide adequate financing for such problems as alcohol and drug abuse." (13)
- "A comprehensive program to deal with violence in the home should be devised," (14) including counselling for victims, community education, therapy for those perpetrating the assaults, legal advice, training of police officers to deal with family disputes, and legal reforms. (14)
- Community-based health-care systems should be developed, as well as adequate transportation links to deal with emergency cases. (15)
- "Higher education and specialized training are necessary to substantially increase the number of Inuit professionals in health and social services." The acute shortage of medical personnel should be remedied, and non-Arctic personnel should undergo cross-cultural orientation and training. (18)
- A comprehensive health strategy should take into account the benefits of Inuit traditional medicine, as well as the Inuit cultural and religious customs that form an integral part of their healing practices. (22)
- International cooperation in health and social research programs in the North should be encouraged, and research priorities should be determined in consultation with the local communities. (23)
- Arctic states should maintain systems to collect and analyse health and social data pertaining to the North. (24)

- Arctic states are encouraged to recognize traditional Inuit adoption legally. (26)
- Arctic states should give due recognition to Inuit traditions with respect to family planning and treatment of children. (27)
- Inuit women should have the choice of delivering babies in their own community, in the absence of anticipated complications, and be assisted by traditional midwives if they so wish. (28)

Basic Elements

Four basic propositions may be extracted from the above principles and elements on health and social well-being. First, health and well-being encompass the whole of the person: the physical, the psychological, the emotional, and the spiritual. Second, the Inuit are greatly concerned about the increasing health risks in their environment. Third, they wish to acquire a higher level of education to enable them to participate in the planning and delivery of more adequate health care and social services for their people. Fourth, they expect arctic governments to cooperate in health and social research programs so as to help them devise and implement a comprehensive strategy. Two of those four propositions should be commented upon: education and international cooperation.

With respect to the level of education, statistics show that only about 13 per cent of Inuit in Canada graduate from grade twelve and, of those who do graduate, few are in the academic stream. In the period from 1980 to 1985, for instance, only seventeen Inuit graduated in the academic program.[78] This means that even fewer will develop the technical and professional qualifications necessary for a meaningful participation in health-care and social services.

On the question of international cooperation, the indigenous people realize that some institutional machinery will be necessary to foster that goal. In their Declaration of June 1991 they agreed to include as one of three issues to be discussed at their Second Arctic Indigenous Leaders Summit "the mandate and role of existing and future organizations relevant to the Arctic."[79] It is the understanding of this writer that one future organization they had specifically in mind was an Arctic Region Council.

ARCTIC COOPERATION FOR PEACEFUL USES ONLY

"The Arctic is a place for sharing and cooperation, sustenance and *peace*."[80] The aboriginal peoples of the Arctic "are convinced that the time is now to take unequivocal and committed actions to ensure lasting peace and security in the Arctic – actions that will clearly benefit all peoples and all nations."[81] It is also time to bring a wider perspective to the meaning of security and to consider seriously the creation of a zone of peace or a nuclear-free zone, and, eventually, the demilitarization of the Arctic.

Security Interests

Although the main purpose of the Arctic Region Council would be to cooperate in civil matters (environment, scientific research, economic development, and human welfare), cooperation cannot be complete and fully meaningful if all security questions are excluded. Now that the Cold War is finally over, to the point where the United States is leading the way to provide food and other humanitarian aid to the former Soviet republics, there is no more valid reason to exclude eventual discussion of the peaceful uses of the Arctic. Surely it is in the security interests of arctic states and their populations to insure that the gradual delimitarization of Europe does not result in the gradual militarization of the Arctic.

Zone of Peace or Nuclear-Free Zone

The time has come when serious consideration should be given to the arctic zone of peace concept put forth by President Gorbachev in his speech at Murmansk on 1 October 1987.[82] If it is premature to discuss such a zone in the sense of complete demilitarization, it might well be the time to broach the subject of a nuclear-weapons-free zone or a geographically limited demilitarization, accompanied by an agreement on conventional arms control. An Arctic nuclear weapons free zone (hereafter referred to simply as nuclear-free zone), total or partial, has been suggested by numerous people and organizations for nearly thirty years.[83] A demilitarization (total or partial) of the Arctic has also been suggested by a number of people and organizations.[84]

For an arctic nuclear-free zone to be successful, four main points at least would have to be agreed upon: a complete ban of nuclear weapons; the delimitation of the denuclearized area (which should include the Kola Peninsula); a system of verification and control; and the inclusion of all circumpolar states. Since all arctic states have renounced the deployment of nuclear weapons on their territory, except the Soviet Union and the United States, the problem is to convince the two super powers to cooperate. As for the Soviet Union, the 1989 Edmonton Conference on Peace and Security in the Arctic brought a reassuring view from two Soviet participants. In answer to questions by Gwynne Dyer on the inclusion of the Kola Peninsula and the acceptability of a nuclear-free zone, the Soviet ambassador to Canada (Alexei A. Rodionov) assured the audience that "the Soviet Union does not intend to exclude our Kola Peninsula and other points of our Arctic and the North from our efforts in the field of arms control. We are prepared now to discuss the Kola Peninsula as well as other parts of our North as part of a general disarmament dialogue."[85] On the acceptability of a nuclear-free zone in the Arctic, the reply came from a counsellor in the Department of Arms Limitation and Disarmament, Ministry of Foreign Affairs: "If an agreement for a nuclear-free zone in the Arctic is based on the preservation of both mutual security and the existing balance of forces on a minimum level, it is quite acceptable."[86] Since the Soviet republics have become independent, there is nothing to indicate that the answers would now be different.

As for the United States, its traditional position on nuclear-free zones has been negative, perhaps because it perceived the Soviet Union as a threat. This in no longer the case and, since the United States has no nuclear weapons in the Arctic now, there is no need to place any. Even before the dismantling of the Soviet Union, the associate director of the Center for Defense Information in Washington, James T. Bush, who was on nuclear-powered missile-firing submarines for ten years, spoke strongly in favour of an arctic nuclear-free zone. "Why wouldn't we [the United States] sign a treaty making the Arctic a nuclear-free zone?" he asked. And, in answering his own question: "Signing an agreement for nuclear-free zone in the Arctic, I believe, would reduce the threat of nuclear war – as would a South Pacific nuclear-free zone. It is hard for me to understand why the United States opposes this."[87] Allowing himself a facetious comment as to why the United States was against nuclear-free zones, he thought it was related to NIH. "This does not stand for the National Institute for Health," he explained, "but for Not Invented Here. If it isn't an idea that we personally hold, we don't like somebody trying to tell us that this is the way we should go."[88] Be that as it may, the perceived threat of the Soviet Union having disappeared, there would appear to be no longer any reason for the United States to have the same hesitation.

Demilitarization

On the question of demilitarization, serious consideration should be given to suggestions such as those presented by David Cox and Tariq Rauf at the Canada-USSR Conference on Canadian-Soviet Arctic

Cooperation in October 1989.[89] Their suggestion is to establish a Central Arctic Demilitarized Zone beyond the 200 nautical mile exclusive economic zone of arctic basin states, covering the sea-bed and subsoil, the water column and the air space, with a verification system for both the waters (surface and subsurface) and the air space.[90] This demilitarized zone would be accompanied by an "open skies" agreement that would permit parties to fly reconnaissance aircraft within the zone.[91] In addition, there would be aerial confidence-building measures such as the prohibition of simulated bombing missions within the demilitarized zone and of foreign military aircraft into Air Defence Identification Zones.[92] Finally, the report recommends a ban on the deployment of long-range, nuclear-armed sea-launched missiles (SLCMS) and, failing total ban, a ceiling on the number of SLCMS at the lowest possible level.[93] The plan is ambitious and it met with a number of objections at the conference, but the idea of a central demilitarized zone beyond the 200-mile limit remains worthy of serious consideration.

A TREATY PROPOSAL FOR AN ARCTIC REGION COUNCIL

Given this background, what then are the reasons for proposing a treaty? What is the meaning of a "semi-enclosed sea" in relation to the Arctic Ocean? And what is the obligation, if any, to cooperate in certain marine-related activities?

Reasons for a Treaty

The value of ministerial conferences and the adoption of declarations and strategies, to begin the process of cooperation among states, is unquestionable. However, the conclusion of a treaty, with its own implementation mechanism and which gives legally binding effect to the political will of the parties, is eventually necessary to insure the effectiveness of such cooperation. More specifically, there are two reasons to have a treaty: first, the legal status of ministerial declarations is uncertain, and, second, such declarations cannot serve as the founding instrument of an arctic council.

The legal status of ministerial declarations and other similar instruments is uncertain and controversial in international law. Exceptionally, it is possible for such declarations to contain legally binding commitments; indeed, even unilateral declarations have been held on two occasions to create legal obligations: once by a minister of foreign affairs[94] and the other by a head of state.[95] In the first case, the declaration was not the main basis of the court's decision and, in the second, the declaration by the head of state was followed by similar declarations by three of his ministers from which the International Court – albeit a divided one – was able to find an intention to be legally bound. The difficulty in such declarations, whether they are unilateral, joint, or common, is to find the necessary intent to be legally bound, in the sense that a breach of the undertaking contained in those declarations could entail state responsibility. In a recent study on the "Legal Status of International North Sea Conference Declarations," Professor van der Mensbrugghe concludes that "clearly, they are not legally binding instruments: no international responsibility, no resort to the rule of court."[96] True, such declarations have some legal significance, in that they represent an official intention to take certain measures. It could even be argued that, in a concrete case, the doctrine of estoppel could be invoked to render such commitments legally binding. But that doctrine, although often invoked, has seldom, if ever, succeeded in front of an international tribunal as the sole basis for a decision. The conclusion that such declarations do not constitute legally binding undertakings in international law is a valid one.

The second reason to have a treaty is that a ministerial declaration – assuming it would be legally binding – could not serve as a founding instrument or constitution for an international organization, with its own structure, powers, and mechanism of implementation. An Arctic Region Council, which would involve the participation of nonstate entities and international organizations (both governmental and nongovernmental), will necessitate its own constitution. This basic instrument will be meant to endure and, like any constitution, will represent the fundamental law binding the parties. It will have to be negotiated among the governments of arctic states, and nonstate entities and organizations should be involved in the process. The basic document will have to specify the geographical area of the council's activities; the main purposes of the council; the conditions of membership; the main organs of the council and their respective powers and mode of operation; the holding of meetings and the sharing of expenses; the settlement of disputes; the manner of entry into force; and the procedure of amendments and review. Such provisions can only be found in an international agreement governed by international law – a treaty. The draft treaty contained in this article tries to spell out the various matters mentioned above.

A further justification for a treaty may be found in the obligation contained in two provisions of the Law of the Sea Convention of 1982 pertaining to enclosed or semi-enclosed seas.[97] These two provisions are Articles 122 and 123. Article 122 is one of definition and Article 123 provides for cooperation in matters relating to the living resources of the sea, the marine environment, and scientific research. The implementation of those provisions raises the question whether the Arctic Ocean falls within the definition of a semi-enclosed sea and, if it does, whether they impose a legal obligation to cooperate.

Arctic Ocean as Semi-Enclosed Sea

For purposes of the convention, Article 122 states that an "enclosed or semi-enclosed sea" is "a gulf, basin or sea surrounded by two or more States and connected to another sea or the ocean by a narrow outlet or consisting entirely or primarily of the territorial sea and exclusive economic zones of two or more States." Obviously, the definition is a general one and the two requirements are flexible. The first requirement, when applied to the Arctic Ocean, is that the "basin" be "surrounded by two or more States." In fact, the Arctic Basin is surrounded by the eight arctic states and, in the words of *The Times Atlas of the Oceans*, "is almost encircled by land areas."[98] The second requirement, again as applied to the Arctic Ocean, is that it should consist "entirely or primarily of the territorial seas and exclusive economic zones of two or more coastal States." In the present instance, a 200-nautical-mile limit north of the land masses and islands of the five states actually bordering on the Arctic Ocean englobes about 60 per cent of the ocean. On the Soviet Union's side alone, the five marginal seas (Barents, Kara, Laptev, East Siberian, and Chukchi) occupy 36 per cent of the Arctic Ocean.[99]

Obligation to Cooperate

Having concluded that the Arctic Ocean falls within the definition of a semi-enclosed sea, is there a legal obligation on bordering states to cooperate? Article 123 provides that "states bordering an enclosed or semi-enclosed sea should cooperate with each other in the exercise of their rights and in the performance of their duties under this Convention." The use of the word *should*, instead of the usual *shall*, indicates something short of a strict legal obligation. However, it must be noted that the object of the cooperation envisaged is so encompassing that it would be virtually impossible to enforce if a legal obligation really existed. What is important is that the same article does impose a legal obligation on states to attain certain objectives.

It provides that states bordering a semi-enclosed sea "shall endeavour, directly or through an appropriate regional organization":

- to coordinate the management, conservation, exploration and exploitation of the living resources of the sea;
- to coordinate the implementation of their rights and duties with respect to the protection and preservation of the marine environment;
- to coordinate their scientific research policies and undertake where appropriate joint programs of scientific research in the area;
- to invite, as appropriate, other interested states or international organizations to cooperate with them in furtherance of the provisions of this article.

In creating an Arctic Region Council, states bordering the Arctic Ocean would be discharging their obligation to endeavour to coordinate their activities relating to the living resources of the sea, the marine environment, and scientific research. As well, by inviting other interested states to become members of that regional organization, they would fully complete the fulfilment of their obligation under that same provision. Finally, the establishment of a council might allow the Arctic Ocean to be added to the United Nations Regional Seas Program, the main purpose of which is to benefit those regional seas in need of special protection.[100]

DRAFT ARCTIC TREATY, WITH COMMENTARY

PREAMBLE

The Governments of Canada, Denmark, Finland, Iceland, Norway, Sweden, the Russian Federation, and the United States of America,

Recognizing the increasing concern of the indigenous peoples of the Arctic Region for the deterioration of their environment and their traditional way of life;

Realizing the vulnerability of the Arctic Region to climatic and environmental change that can affect the well-being of all northern states;

Noting that, pursuant to the United Nations Convention on the Law of the Sea (Article 123), states bordering an enclosed or semi-enclosed sea have an obligation to endeavour directly or through an appropriate regional organization to coordinate their activities related to scientific research, the protection of the marine environment, and the conservation of the living resources of the sea;

Noting also that their obligation includes the invitation of other interested states or international organizations to cooperate with them in relation to those activities;

Believing that regional cooperation should lead to the use of the Arctic Region for peaceful purposes only;

Affirming that such peaceful uses are in the interest of all humanity and in furtherance of the first purpose of the United Nations, which is to maintain international peace and security;

HAVE AGREED to establish an international organization to be known as the Arctic Region Council.

Commentary. The purpose of the Preamble is only to indicate, in general terms, the reasons for establishing the council. It contains no legal obligation as such.

AREA OF APPLICATION

For the purposes of the present Treaty, the "Arctic Region" means the area north of 60° north latitude, including the Aleutian Islands, Labrador, and the region of northern Quebec known as Nunavik.

Commentary. The expression "Arctic Region" was chosen instead of "Arctic Basin" to permit the inclusion of Iceland, Finland, and Sweden, which do not border on the basin but are within the region as defined. Of the numerous ways to define the Arctic Region, the sixtieth parallel of latitude appears to be the most appropriate. That latitude includes all the land areas covered by the tundra or continuous permafrost, except for parts of northern Quebec and Labrador; hence, their express inclusion in the definition. The land areas north of sixty includes virtually all the permafrost territory of the arctic states: Canada (the Yukon, the Northwest Territories, most of northern Quebec, and the tip of Labrador); Denmark (all of Greenland); Finland (all); Iceland (all); Norway (all of Svalbard and most of mainland Norway); Sweden (most of the territory); Russia (roughly the northern half – counting the archipelagos – of the territory, including the numerous rivers emptying in the Arctic Ocean); and United States (virtually all of Alaska). The Aleutian Islands are included in the area of application, considering they are included by the United States in the definition of the Arctic in its Arctic Research and Policy Act adopted in 1984. The act also includes the entire Bering Sea.

The area of application includes all the Arctic Ocean, the surrounding seas, and the southern limit of sea ice. By contrast, an area delimited by the Arctic Circle would have left out significant bodies of water and large portions of the tundra and the sea ice.

PURPOSES

The main purposes of the Arctic Region Council (hereafter Council) are:
- to facilitate regional cooperation generally among its members;
- to insure that measures are taken for protection of the environment;
- to promote the coordination of scientific research;
- to encourage the conservation and appropriate management of living resources;
- to foster sustainable economic development;
- to further the health and social well-being of the indigenous and other inhabitants of the arctic region;
- to promote the use of the arctic region exclusively for peaceful purposes.

Commentary. The above purposes put the emphasis on civil matters (environment, scientific research, economic development, and human welfare), but they include the military indirectly through the promotion of use for "peaceful purposes." Although this is a loaded expression which has caused considerable difficulty of interpretation, it does appear in certain key treaties (Antarctic, Non-Proliferation, and Law of the Sea) and states have accepted it.

MEMBERSHIP

I: The founding members of the Council shall be the eight states whose territory projects north of the Arctic Circle: Canada, Denmark, Finland, Iceland, Norway, Russia, Sweden, and the United States of America.

Commentary. Because of the geographic location of their territories (bordering the Arctic Ocean or the adjacent seas) and the fact that all indigenous peoples are located on most of those territories, the eight arctic states are founding members and have special interests and responsibilities.

II: The admitted members may be states, governmental and non-governmental organizations (NGOs), and territorial and regional governments. Such states, organizations, and governments are eligible for membership if they have demonstrated a substantial interest in the work of the Council and a capacity to further its purposes. Admission shall be decided by the Assembly on the recommendation of the Commission.

Commentary. To permit participation of all those with sufficient interest, the Council is open to membership of other states (such as France, Germany, Japan, the United Kingdom), organizations of states (such as the European Community), NGOs (such as the Inuit Circumpolar Conference/Arctic Aboriginal Conference) and territorial governments (such as Alaska, the Yukon, the Northwest Territories, and Greenland), and regional governments (such as Chukotski, Nunavik, and the Nordic Sami Council). Admission criteria must be developed to insure a sufficiently wide participation for the Council to attain its basic purposes and yet to insure that members are actively concerned and involved in arctic issues. The admission of new members will depend on a favourable recommendation of the Commission where the founding members form a majority of two-thirds.

ORGANS OF THE COUNCIL

The Council shall be composed of an Assembly and a Commission, as the two main organs, and a Secretariat as a subsidiary organ.

The Assembly

The Assembly shall consist of all members of the Council.

The Assembly may discuss all questions relating to the purposes of the Council and shall establish general policies for the coordination of the activities of the Council and its members. It may make recommendations to the members or to the Commission on measures to be taken for the fulfilment of the purposes of the Council.

The Assembly shall elect the four nonpermanent members of the Commission and appoint the secretary of the Council. It may establish such subsidiary organs as are required to exercise its functions.

A majority of members of the Assembly shall constitute a quorum and its resolutions shall be adopted by consensus. In the absence of a consensus, resolutions shall be adopted by a two-thirds majority. The Assembly shall adopt its own rules of procedure and elect its president.

Commentary. The Assembly, as for all similar plenary bodies, has nearly unlimited powers of discussion and rather limited powers of decision. It should be the forum where the basic purposes and general policies are discussed and agreed upon, but it is too large a body to see to the implementation of specific measures. The Assembly may exercise some indirect control over such implementation, however, through the election of the four nonpermanent members of the Commission.

Since procedure by consensus has now gained a large degree of acceptance (particularly at the United Nations and the Third Law of the Sea Conference), it is suggested here. It seems wise, however, to provide for actual voting if a consensus fails to materialize.

The Commission

The Commission shall consist of twelve members, of which the founding members shall be permanent. The four nonpermanent members shall be elected by the Assembly, on the basis of an equitable representation of the admitted members. The nonpermanent members shall be elected for four years, except for the first election when two shall be elected for two years only.

The Commission shall decide on measures to fulfil the purposes of the Council and on the implementation of such measures. It may establish subsidiary organs required to exercise its functions.

The Commission shall adopt its resolutions by consensus or, in the absence of a consensus, by a vote of eight members. The Commission shall establish its own rules of procedure and elect its president.

Commentary. The Commission is intended to be the governing body where the founding members will have a controlling voice by their number (eight out of twelve) and permanency. They will have no right of veto, however, and the other four members (on a four-year rotating basis) will enjoy equality of status during their term on the Commission.

The Commission will see to the actual taking and implementation of measures, since the member states on the Commission are the ones with the principal means of enforcement and will bear the brunt of any consequent responsibility.

The consensus mode is provided for, but it is prudent to foresee the possibility of actual voting. In such cases, resolutions would be adopted by a two-thirds majority or eight members.

The Secretariat

The Secretariat shall be located on the territory of one of the founding members. It shall comprise a secretary and such staff as may be required. The secretary shall be the administrative officer of the Council and shall be appointed by the Assembly on the recommendation of the Commission. The secretary shall act in that capacity at all meetings of the Assembly and the Commission. The secretary shall make reports to the Assembly on the work of the Council at its regular meetings.

Commentary. The Secretariat is intended to be – certainly at the beginning – a very small organ consisting only of a secretary and a small staff. Of course, it might develop into an important office, depending on the activities of the Council.

MEETINGS

Regular meetings of the Assembly and of the Commission shall be held every other year. Special meetings may be held at such other time and place as each organ may decide. Regular meetings shall be held in the arctic region and under the auspices of one of the founding members in rotation.

Commentary. A meeting every two years should be enough in the early period of operation, with the possibility of special meetings for both the Assembly and the Commission.

The special interests of the founding members is recognized in that they will host the meetings. Canada might volunteer to host the founding meeting.

EXPENSES

Each member shall bear its own expenses, unless otherwise agreed. The expenses of the Secretariat shall be borne by the member on whose territory it is located.

Commentary. The expenses of the Council should be kept at a minimum and each member should defray its own expenses for attending meetings. The expenses of the Secretariat might pose a problem, particularly if it has to produce documents in more than one language. If so, some kind of sharing formula will have to be devised. As for the location of the Secretariat, members might wish to accept the offer by Canada to provide such services to begin the work of the Council, particularly if Canada hosts the founding meeting.

SETTLEMENT OF DISPUTES

Any dispute as to the interpretation or application of this Treaty shall be resolved by negotiation, inquiry, mediation, conciliation, arbitration, judicial settlement, or other peaceful means to which the parties to the dispute agree.

Commentary. This being a delicate subject, it is preferable to go no further than what is already provided for in Article 33 of the Charter of the United Nations.

ENTRY INTO FORCE, AMENDMENTS, AND REVIEW

Entry into Force

The present Treaty shall enter into force upon signature [or after ratification] by all the eight founding arctic states. It shall come into force for each of the other members at the time of their signature [or after their ratification/accession].

Commentary. Depending on their constitutional requirements, ratification might be necessary for some of the states. If so, the Treaty would have to be subject to ratification by states. If not, consent to be bound could be expressed by signature, which would apply to both states and organizations.

Amendments

Amendments to the Treaty shall be adopted by the Assembly on the recommendation of the Commission. Such adoption shall be made by consensus or, failing that, by a vote of two-thirds.

Amendments shall enter into force upon signature [or, after ratification] by two-thirds of the members.

Commentary. Although amendments should not be frequent, they should be possible and should not be blocked by a lack of consensus in the Assembly; hence, their possible adoption by a vote of two-thirds. The entry into force of amendments would be effected in the same way as the entry into force of the Treaty itself.

Review Conference

After the Treaty has been in force for twenty-five years, any member may request a conference to review the operation of the Treaty.

Such conference shall be held on the recommendation of the Commission and approved by the Assembly, either by consensus or by a vote of two-thirds. Any amendment adopted by the conference shall enter into force after signature [or ratification] by all members.

Commentary. Although the whole treaty system should be made to endure, a review might become desirable after a while. Twenty-five years would appear to be a reasonable trial period. It was thirty years for the Antarctic Treaty of 1959, which entered into force in 1961, and it is fifty years for the Antarctic Protocol on Environmental Protection of 1991.

NOTES

The author would like to thank Dr E.F. Roots, science adviser emeritus, Environment Canada, who read the manuscript and made useful suggestions. This article originally appeared in (1992), 23 *Revue Générale du Droit* 163–95.

1 Gail Osherenko and Oran R. Young, *The Age of the Arctic* (Cambridge: Cambridge University Press 1989), 242.
2 Quoted in John Holmes, *The Shaping of Peace: Canada and the Search for World Order, 1943–1957*, vol. 1 (Toronto: University of Toronto Press 1979), 288.
3 Maxwell Cohen, "The Arctic and the National Interest" (1970–1), 21 *International Journal* (emphasis added).
4 Ibid., 81 (emphasis added).
5 *The North and Canada's International Relations* (Ottawa: Canadian Arctic Resources Committee 1988), 58–9. This writer had proposed such a council at the 1987 Tromso seminar. He made the same proposals in 1988 as member of a panel on the Legal Regimes of the Arctic in Washington; see *Proceedings of the American Society of International Law*, 1988, 332–3. He reiterated the proposal, in October 1989, in his address to the Canadian Council on International Law at the award of the John E. Read Medal, as well as in "Les problèmes de droit international de l'Arctique" (1989), 20 *Études internationales* 161–3.
6 *Notes for an Address by the Right Honourable Brian Mulroney*, 24 Nov. 1989.
7 The study made by this panel was sponsored by the Canadian Arctic Resources Committee (CARC), the Inuit Circumpolar Conference, and the Arms Control Center, and was funded by the Walter and Duncan Gordon Charitable Foundation.
8 Address by the Rt-Hon. Joe Clark, "The Changing Soviet Union: Implications for Canada and the World," Ottawa, 28 Nov. 1990.
9 *To Establish an International Arctic Council: A Framework Report* (Ottawa: CARC, Jan. 1991).

10 *The Arctic Environment and Canada's International Relations* (Ottawa: CARC, March 1991), 68–71.
11 Ibid., appendix, A1–A10.
12 *To Establish an International Arctic Council* (Ottawa: CARC, 14 May 1991).
13 Ibid., 19–22.
14 Ibid., 23.
15 Ibid., 26.
16 Ibid.
17 Ibid., 28–9.
18 Reproduced in (Nov. 1991), 30 *International Legal Materials* 1624–69.
19 Para. 6 of the declaration.
20 D. Freestone and Ton Ijlstra, eds., *The North Sea: Perspectives on Regional Co-operation*, special issue of (1990) *International Journal of Estuarine and Coastal Law*, 331.
21 CARC, *The Arctic Environment*, 13.
22 E.F. Roots, *Environmental Concerns and Co-operation in the Arctic*, a paper presented at a conference on Canadian-Soviet Cooperation in the Arctic, Ottawa, 23–26 October 1989, 8.
23 CARC, *The Arctic Environment*, 21.
24 For the texts of the convention and the protocol see (1987) 26 *International Legal Materials* 1516 and 1541.
25 Neither the protocol nor the amendment have received the necessary number of ratifications. However, most of the major industrial producers of chlorofluorocarbons have taken steps to reduce their production in accordance with the amendment.
26 J. Jensen, "Report on Organochlorines," in *The State of the Arctic Environment: Reports*, Arctic Centre Publications No. 2 (Rovaniemi, Finland 1991), 335–84. For the latest report see D. Kinloch, H. Kuhnlein, and D.C.G. Muir, "Inuit Foods and Diet: An Assessment of Benefits and Risks," in *Science of the Total Environment* (in press).
27 Mary Simon, "Security, Peace and the Native Peoples of the Arctic," in Thomas R. Berger et al., *The Arctic: Choices for Peace and Security*, published by the True North Strong and Free Inquiry Society (Edmonton 1989), 34. To the same effect see Karen Twitchell, "The Not-So-Pristine Arctic" (Feb./March 1991), III *Canadian Geographic*, 53–60.
28 Roots, *Environmental Concerns*, 7.
29 CARC, *The Arctic Environment*, 27–9.
30 See Article 234, Law of the Sea Convention, 1982.
31 *Arctic Environmental Strategy*, 14 June 1991, Article 7. It is expected that the government of the Russian Federation will assume the obligations of the former USSR with respect to the Arctic.
32 Agreement for Cooperation relating to the Marine Environment, Canada/Denmark, 26 Aug. 1983, *Canadian Treaty Series*, No. 19.

33 *Arctic Environment Strategy*, Article 7, ii.
34 UN Document A/Res/44/22, 22 Dec. 1989 (emphasis added).
35 Ibid. (emphasis added).
36 On these and other prerequisites see *supra*, note 10, 62–3.
37 Philip C. Reid, "The Work of the North Sea Task Force," in *The North Sea: Perspectives on Regional Environmental Co-operation*, special issue of (1990) *International Journal of Estuarine and Coastal Law* 88; see also a review of this special issue by the present writer in (1991) 36 *McGill Law Journal* 1110–24.
38 Jorgen Wettestad and Steinar Andressen, "Science and North-Sea Policy-Making: Organization and Communications," in *The North Sea*, 121–2.
39 Agreements providing for scientific cooperation were concluded in 1971, 1972, 1984, and 1989. The 1989 Agreement on Arctic Cooperation includes a program in science and technology which covers geology, meteorology, climatology, environmental protection, construction, and arctic marine, land, and air technology. It provides for joint research, joint conferences, and joint publications.
40 CARC, *The Arctic Environment*, 64.
41 Ibid., 65 (emphasis added).
42 Ibid., 66.
43 Inuit Circumpolar Conference, *Principles and Elements for a Comprehensive Arctic Policy* (Ottawa 1989), 53.
44 Ibid.
45 H. Brody, *Living Arctic: Hunters of the Canadian North* (Toronto: Douglas & McIntyre 1987), 78, quoted in Randy Kapaskesit and Murray Klippenstein, "Aboriginal Group Rights and Environmental Protection" (1991), 36 *McGill Law Journal* 930.
46 *Statement on Subsistence, the Traditional and Direct Dependence on Renewable Resources*, 20 June 1991, signed by the leaders of the Inuit Circumpolar Conference, the Nordic Saami Council, and the USSR Association of Northern Small Peoples.
47 In that way, the Inuit have given effect to the *World Conservation Strategy: Living Resource Conservation for Sustainable Development*, prepared by the International Union for Conservation of Nature and Natural Resources (IUCN), with the advice, cooperation, and financial assistance of the United Nations Environmental Program (UNEP) and the World Wildlife Fund (WWF), in collaboration with FAO and UNESCO (Gland, Switzerland 1980). See also *Caring for the Earth: A Strategy for Sustainable Living*, published by IUCN, UNEP, and WWF (Gland, Switzerland 1991).
48 The treaty came into force in 1976, after the ratification by the five Arctic Basin States; see *Canadian Treaty Series*, 1976, No. 24.
49 Leslie Tresedar and Andy Carpenter "Polar Bear Management in the Southern Beaufort Sea" (April 1989), 15, 4 *Information North*, newsletter of the Arctic Institute of North America.

50 See in particular the Convention for the Protection of Migratory Birds of 1916 between Canada and the United States; the Agreement on the Conservation of the Porcupine Caribou Herd of 1987 between Canada and the United States (which is proving very difficult to implement), and the Memorandum of Understanding on the Conservation and Management of Narwhal and Beluga of 1989 between the Fisheries Departments of Canada and Greenland; and the Agreement on Sealing and Conservation of Seal Stocks in the Northwest Atlantic of 1971 between Canada and Norway.
51 Fisheries and Ocean Canada, *Canadian Arctic Marine Conservation Strategy* (Ottawa 1987), 81.
52 Ibid.
53 For a similar recommendation see D.L. Vanderzwaag and C. Lamson, "Ocean Development and Management in the Arctic: Issues in American and Canadian Relations" (1986), 39 *Arctic* 328.
54 The World Commission on Environment and Development, *Our Common Future* (Oxford: Oxford University Press 1987), 42. On the meaning of sustainability see also P.S. Elder, "Sustainability" (1991), 36 *McGill Law Journal* 833–6, and Franklyn Griffiths and Oran R. Young, *Managing the Arctic's Resources*, Impressions of the Co-chairs of a Working Group on Arctic International Relations (1991), 32.
55 World Commission, *Our Common Future*, 44.
56 Ibid., 46.
57 W. Harriet Critchley, "L'importance internationale du développement économique des régions arctiques" 20 *Études internationales* 7, for a summary in English, and 26, in French.
58 Mikhail Gorbachev, *The Speech in Murmansk*, 1 Oct. 1987 (Moscow: Novosti Press Agency Publishing House 1987), 30.
59 Ibid.
60 Simon, "Security," 211.
61 Ibid., 212–13.
62 John Hannigan, "Oil and Gas Activity in the Soviet North" (July–Aug. 1988), 16 *Northern Perspectives* (14–17), published by the Canadian Arctic Resources Committee.
63 Lawson W. Brigham, "Soviet Arctic Marine Transportation" (July–Aug. 1988), 16 *Northern Perspectives* 20–3.
64 Public Review Panel on Tanker Safety and Marine Spills Response Capability, *Protecting Our Waters*, Final Report, Sept. 1990, 166.
65 Federal Environmental Assessment Review Office, *Beaufort Sea Hydrocarbon Production and Transportation*, Final Report of the Environmental Assessment Panel, July 1984, especially 70.
66 Public Review Panel, *Protecting Our Waters*, 171.
67 Ibid., 178.
68 Ibid., i.

69 Recommendation 6–35, ibid., 176.
70 Recommendation 6–39, ibid., 179.
71 Ibid.
72 Recommendation 6–41, ibid.
73 A. Arikaynen, *Exchange of Experience in Arctic Marine Transportation*, 17, paper presented at the International Conference on Arctic Cooperation, 27 Oct. 1988.
74 R.V. Varatanov, *Some Economic, Political and Legal Problems in the Development of Cooperation between States in the Exploitation of Marine Areas of the Arctic*, 11, paper presented at an International Conference on Arctic Policy, Montreal, Dec. 1988.
75 *Ottawa Citizen*, 1 Sept. 1991.
76 Signed at Horsholm, Greenland, on behalf of the ICC, the Nordic Saami Council, and the USSR Association of Northern Small Peoples, 20 June 1991.
77 ICC, *Principles and Elements for a Comprehensive Arctic Policy*, 1989, 75–80.
78 Tom F. Schneider, "Inuit Education: Between Past and Future," chap. 5 in "Inuit Self-Government in the N.W.T.: The Nunavut Proposal," (MA thesis, Queen's University 1988), 103.
79 See above, note 76.
80 Mary Simon, "Militarization and the Aboriginal Peoples," 19, paper presented by the president of the ICC at an International Conference on Arctic Cooperation, Toronto, 26–28 Oct. 1988.
81 Ibid.
82 Gorbachev, *Speech*, 28–31.
83 See in particular Alexander P. Vinogradov, "Arctic Disarmament" (1964), 20 *Bulletin of the Atomic Scientists* 22–3; George Ignatieff, "In Self-Defence," *Maclean's*, 21 April 1980, 6; Hanna Newcombe, "A Proposal for a Nuclear-Free Zone in the Arctic" (1980), 12 *Peace Research* 175–81; Robert Reford, "Our Seat at the Table: A Canadian Menu for Arms Control" (1981), 36 *International Journal* 663–4; Inuit Circumpolar Conference, "Arctic as a Nuclear-Free Zone," resolution 83–01, 1984, 30; Legislative Assembly of the Northwest Territories, "Declaration of a Nuclear-Weapons-Free Zone," *Hansard, June 19, 1986*, 1253–4, as amended at 1259; Consultative Group on Disarmament and Arms Control Affairs, Report on the meeting entitled *Peace and Security in the Arctic: Decisions for Canada*, 12 Nov. 1987, 18–21; James T. Bush, "Maritime Strategy and Nuclear-Free Zone," in Berger et al., *The Arctic*, 227–36 and 237–43.
84 See for example Franklyn Griffiths, *A Northern Foreign Policy* (Toronto: Canadian Institute of International Affairs 1981), 60–2; Ron Purver, *Arms Control in the North* (Kingston: Queen's University Centre for International Relations 1981), 130–7; and "Security and Arms Control

at the Poles" (1984), 39 *International Journal* 903–5; Special Committee of the Senate and House of Commons on Canada's International Relations, *Independence and Internationalism* (Ottawa: Canadian Government Publication Centre 1986), 135; David Cox and Tariq Rauf, *Security Co-operation in the Arctic: A Canadian Response to Gorbachev's Murmansk Initiative*, 6–11, presented at the Canada-USSR Conference on Canadian-Soviet Arctic Cooperation, Ottawa, 24 Oct. 1989.

85 Simon, "Security," 238.
86 Ibid.
87 Ibid., 233.
88 Ibid., 234.
89 Rauf, *Security Co-operation in the Arctic*.
90 Ibid., 6–11.
91 Ibid., 12–18.
92 Ibid., 19–21.
93 Ibid., 22–4.
94 See *Eastern Greenland* case (Denmark v. Norway), 1933, PCIJ, Ser. A/B, No. 53.
95 See *Nuclear Tests* case (Australia, New Zealand v. France), 1973 ICJ Report, 253 and 457.
96 Yves van der Mensbrugghe, "Legal Status of International North Sea Declarations" (1990), *International Journal of Estuarine and Coastal Law* 21 (special issue entitled *The North Sea: Perspectives on Regional Environmental Cooperation*).
97 Although strictly speaking the Law of the Sea Convention has not yet received the necessary number of ratifications for its entry into force, the practice of states has been such that it may be assumed to have legal force and effect for the present purposes.
98 Alastair Couper, *The Times Atlas of the Oceans* (London: Time Books 1983), 62.
99 John E. Sater, *The Arctic Basin* (Washington: Arctic Institute of North America 1969), 14.
100 For additional reading on whether the Arctic Ocean is a semi-enclosed or a regional sea, see Nigel D. Bankes, "Canada and the Natural Resources of the Polar Regions," Proceedings of the Conference on International Law: Critical Choices for Canada 1985–2000 (1986) *Queen's Law Journal* 213; D.M. McRae, "Management of Arctic Marine Transportation: A Canadian Perspective" (1986), 39 *Arctic* 354; J.C. Nelson and R.D. Needham, "The Arctic as a Regional Sea" (spring 1985), 12 *Governmental Conservation* 7–15; Anatoli L. Kolodkin, "Legal Regimes of the Arctic," *Proceedings of the American Society of International Law*, 1988, 319; see also articles by Alain E. Boyle (at 324) and by Donat Pharand (at 332) in the Proceedings; D. Vanderzwaag, J. Donihee,

and M. Faegteborg, "Towards Regional Ocean Management in the Arctic: From Co-existence to Cooperation" (1988), 37 *U.N.B. Law Journal* 22; R.V. Varatonov, "Some Economic, Political and Legal Problems in the Development of Cooperation between States in the Exploitation of Marine Areas in the Arctic," 4, paper presented at an Arctic Policy Conference, McGill University, 1–3 Dec. 1989; A.A. Sagiryan, "The Arctic: Coordination of Approaches," 12, paper presented at an Arctic Policy Conference, McGill University, 1–3 Dec. 1989; Donat Pharand, "Les problèmes de droit international dans l'Arctique" (1989), 20 *Études internationales* 162–3.

International Human Rights Law in Canadian Courts

ANNE F. BAYEFSKY

In 1982 in my second year of teaching at the University of Ottawa, I was honoured by the request of my senior, distinguished colleague, Maxwell Cohen, to co-author an article on the links between public international law and the Canadian Charter of Rights and Freedoms. That collaborative effort was the beginning of a relationship which, for me, has been constantly stimulating and immeasurably satisfying. On one level, Cohen's fascination for the interplay between international and constitutional law has continued to inspire me; that article served in later years as the subject of a much larger work, to which Cohen contributed the foreword. On another level, his wise counsel on all matter of subjects, both personal and scholarly, has in many respects served as the bulwark of my university years. The unfailing generosity of both Max and his wife Isle has acted as a well-spring of encouragement and sustenance for which I have been only one of many fortunate beneficiaries. It is a pleasure to be able to contribute a paper on one of our favourite subjects for this long-deserved Festschrift.

In the field of human rights, international standards are manifold and are proliferating rapidly. Nations are anxious to be perceived as playing a leadership role in expanding the range of subjects covered by international human rights law. Such eagerness dissipates, however, when the issue of implementation arises. This is a problem that divides the international community, well after general agreement on standards is reached.

The consequence of this division has been the establishment of a number of international supervisory bodies with different enforcement tools. The Human Rights Committee set up by the International Covenant on Civil and Political Rights, with additional powers granted by an Optional Protocol, considers individual communications concerning violations of the covenant. The power of individual petition is not available, however, with respect to violations of the Convention on the Elimination of All Forms of Discrimination against Women, signed some fifteen years later. In general, while the pace of standard-setting is increasing almost exponentially, the form of enforcement mechanisms has tended to weaken in the twenty-five years since the Optional Protocol was signed.

Even where more adequate enforcement machinery has been created, it is often inaccessible to individual grievors. Correspondence with an international agency is beyond the reach of many potential clients for a variety of reasons: lack of resources, ignorance of local counsel of international remedies, or failure of national authorities to disseminate information about international human rights obligations of the state.

Consequently, it is imperative to identify other means by which international standards can be enforced. Since the concern of most states in refusing to participate in the creation of significant international machinery is the preservation of national sovereignty, recourse to national enforcement agencies offers a logical alternative.

International agencies readily concede their status as fora of last resort.[1] International human rights treaties which do permit a right of individual petition contain a standard clause requiring grievors to exhaust domestic remedies before coming forward. In other words, there is an initial reliance on national agencies to protect human rights. It would be a natural extension of such reliance to encourage national judicial bodies to enforce international human rights standards.

The appropriation of domestic courts to serve as the missing link between promulgation and realization of international human rights norms can benefit both international law and domestic law. On the one hand, international bodies, whose work tends to be far more interstitial than that of national judicial organs, can benefit from more frequent interpretations of international standards by a variety of national courts. On the other hand, more enlightened interpretations of domestic human rights laws may also be fostered through reference to international law.

Canadian courts are particularly well placed to serve this bridging function. Canada has taken an active role in promulgating international human rights standards and has readily acknowledged the legally binding quality of such rules by ratifying a large number of international human rights treaties. At the same time, Canada's constitutional Bill of Rights was drafted with those international standards clearly in view. There is a significant opportunity for beneficial interaction between Canadian human rights norms and international law.

CUSTOMARY INTERNATIONAL LAW

The Basic Rule

The rules governing the relationship of international law to domestic or municipal law are attempts to reconcile a variety of policies: protection of national sovereignty; protection of the supremacy of Parliament and the legislatures from the powers of the executive; satisfaction of Canada's international obligations; and realization by individuals of the benefits of international norms. Different considerations for harmonizing these policies arise for conventional and customary international law. The result has been that the relationship between international law and municipal law in Canada has historically received a different response in respect of customary international law as compared with conventional international law.

The different ways of reconciling these policies are formulated in two general theories about the relationship between municipal law and international law: the adoption or incorporation theory and the transformation theory. The adoption theory states that international law is part of domestic law automatically – that is, without an act of incorporation – except where it conflicts with statutory law or with well-established rules of the common law. Transformation theory expresses the view that international law is part of domestic law only when it has been incorporated into domestic law.

In general, Canadian case law suggests that the adoption theory governs the relationship between municipal law and customary international law. There is, however, no clear statement to this effect from the Supreme Court.[2] Cases from lower courts tend more clearly to support the adoptionist approach.[3]

Proving Customary International Law

International jurisprudence sets two conditions for the existence of a customary rule of international law: evidence of a sufficient degree of state practice, and a determination that states conceive themselves as acting under a legal obligation.[4] In *Reference Re the Seabed and*

Subsoil of the Continental Shelf Offshore Newfoundland,[5] the Supreme Court applied essentially this definition of customary international law. In the court's words: "[i]n order to constitute a custom there must be substantial uniformity or consistency, and general acceptance."[6]

Articulating customary international law is not a simple task. The International Court of Justice has commented on the difficulty of defining precise rules of customary international law.[7]

The Norms of Customary International Human Rights Law

A limited list of customary international human rights has been identified by national and international bodies. The International Court of Justice in the *Barcelona Traction* case suggested that freedom from slavery and racial discrimination "have entered into the body of general international law."[8]

Untied States courts have also identified certain rights as customary international law, in particular: the right not to be murdered;[9] freedom from torture;[10] standards for the treatment of prisoners embodied in the United Nations Standard Minimum Rules for the Treatment of Prisoners;[11] freedom from arbitrary detention;[12] the right not to be subjected to cruel, inhuman, or degrading treatment or punishment;[13] the right not to be a slave;[14] disappearance, defined as abduction by state officials or their agents followed by official refusals to acknowledge the adduction or to disclose the detainee's fate;[15] loss of consortium.[16]

The Restatement of the Foreign Relations Law of the United States would add to this list the following violations of customary international law: genocide; systematic racial discrimination; and a consistent pattern of gross violations of internationally recognized human rights.[17]

Founding a Right of Action

The actual use which can be made of customary international human rights law by Canadian courts depends on its relationship to the primary source of human rights protection in Canada – the Canadian Charter of Rights and Freedoms. Their interaction indicates two roles for customary human rights law in Canadian courts.

First, customary international human rights law can be directly invoked, as part of the law of the land, to itself provide the basis for a remedy. This right of action has not been affected by the Charter.

According to section 26 of the Charter: "The guarantee in this Charter of certain rights and freedoms shall not be construed as deying the existence of any other rights or freedoms that exist in Canada." Hence, rights or freedoms embodied in customary international law, and which under an adoption theory exist as part of the law of Canada, continue to exist with the enactment of the Charter. This will be relevant with respect to "other" rights embodied in customary international human rights law which bear little or no resemblance to rights and freedoms guaranteed in the Charter.[18] In other words, in human rights areas where the common law has not been settled, and a conclusive statute or constitutional provision does not exist, customary international human rights law can fill in the gaps.

Assistance in Interpreting Canadian Law

A second distinct use that can be made of customary law in Canadian courts is to indicate international standards which are of assistance in interpreting and applying domestic law. In this context, customary law can influence Charter rights themselves.

There is a presumption at common law that Parliament and the legislatures do not intend to act in breach of international law, both customary and conventional.[19] Concomitantly, there is a principle of construction that Canadian law should be interpreted as far as possible consistently with international law. This presumption is applicable in the context of construing the Charter.[20]

The Supreme Court has itself clearly stated that customary law is both useful and relevant in the Charter context. It has done so, however, without making any reference to the presumption as justification. Chief Justice Dickson writing in dissent in *Reference Re Public Service Employee Relations Act*[21] stated:

A body of treaties ... and *customary* norms now constitutes an international law of human rights under which the nations of the world have undertaken to adhere to the standards and principles necessary for ensuring freedom, dignity and social justice for their citizens. The Charter conforms to the spirit of this contemporary international human rights movement, and it incorporates many of the policies and prescriptions of the various international documents pertaining to human rights. The various sources of international human rights law ... *customary* norms – must, in my opinion, be relevant and persuasive sources for interpretation of the Charter's provisions.[22]

Although the majority in this decision came to its conclusion without making any reference to international law, it did not expressly dispute this general rule.

Then in *Davidson v. Slaight Communications*[23], Dickson CJ writing for the majority repeated some of the remarks concerning the relevance of international law in interpreting the Charter he had made in *Reference Re Public Service Employee Relations Act* and added:

> Canada's international human rights obligations should inform not only the interpretation of the content of the rights guaranteed by the *Charter* but also the interpretation of what can constitute pressing and substantial s.1 objectives which may justify restrictions upon those rights. Furthermore, for purposes of this stage of the proportionality inquiry, the fact that a value has the status of an international human right, either in *customary international law* or under a treaty to which Canada is a State Party, should generally be indicative of a high degree of importance attached to that objective.[24]

Dickson CJ again failed to articulate the common-law presumption or to offer any justification for referring to international law. Nevertheless, he makes it quite clear that customary international law is relevant and important in Charter interpretation. This is true both in the context of defining the content of rights and freedoms and the appropriate scope of their limitations.[25]

CONVENTIONAL INTERNATIONAL LAW

The Basic Rule

The use of customary international human rights law by domestic courts will be greater in those states which have ratified few international human rights conventions, such as the United States.[26] Canada has, however, ratified a considerable number of international human rights treaties.[27] Consequently, references to international human rights law in Canadian courts have been almost entirely to conventional law. Given the difficulties of proof and the limited scope of customary human rights law, in addition to the rapidly expanding scope of conventional human rights treaties, this trend will almost certainly continue.

In Canada, treaty-making is an executive act, part of the Royal Prerogative, the residue of authority left in the Crown. In practice it is exercised by the Governor General-in-Council – that is, the governor general of Canada acting on the advice of privy councillors who are ministers of the government. Parliamentary consent is not required for Canada to enter into an international agreement.²⁸ The use domestic courts in Canada make of international conventions will often reflect a policy to protect the authority of Parliament and the legislatures from any attempt by the executive to change the law simply by the exercise of the prerogative.²⁹

Generally speaking, a treaty will only be part of the law of Canada if it is implemented by legislation.³⁰ This principle was stated in the case of *Re Arrow River and Tributaries Slide & Boom Co. Limited.*³¹ It has been reiterated on numerous occasions.³²

A Treaty-Implementing Power

In a federal state, the general rule raises a number of unique issues. Most important, can the federal Parliament legislate in implementation of a treaty on matters that would otherwise be within provincial jurisdiction? This question was answered in the negative in *A.G. Can. v. A.G. Ont. et al. (Labour Conventions* case) decided by the Judicial Committee of the Privy Council.³³ According to the *Labour Conventions* case, although treaty-making is a power of the federal executive, treaty-implementation is distributed between the federal government and the provinces.

The authority of *Labour Conventions* has, however, been eroded. The Supreme Court of Canada has explicitly criticized the case. In *MacDonald v. Vapour Canada Ltd.*³⁴ in *obiter*, the Supreme Court went so far as to say, "the foregoing references would support a reconsideration of the *Labour Conventions* case," and "assuming it was open to Parliament to pass legislation in implementation of an international obligation by Canada under a treaty or Convention (being legislation which it would be otherwise beyond its competence)."³⁵

In *R. v. Crown Zellerbach*,³⁶ the Supreme Court considered the constitutional validity of federal legislation (the Ocean Dumping Control Act) which governed the dumping of substances in the internal waters of a province. The majority opinion found that the Act was enacted to implement Canada's international obligations under the Convention of the Prevention of Marine Pollution by Dumping of Wastes and Other Matter, 1975.³⁷ The court then used international law to assist in finding that the legislation was *intra vires*. More specifically, it held that the legislation was *intra vires* because it fell within the "national concern" doctrine of the peace, order, and good government power of the federal government, and it used the international dimension to find that the requirements of the national concern test were satisfied.³⁸ Although the court does not directly deal with *Labour Conventions*, according to *Labour Conventions*, international obligations of

Canada are irrelevant in determining constitutional validity. *Crown Zellerbach* clearly contradicts this rule.[39] *Labour Conventions* has, therefore, not yet been expressly overruled, but its authority is diminishing.[40]

Defining Implementation or Incorporation

Since international conventional law is not part of the law of Canada unless implemented, it becomes important to discover just when domestic legislation is to be considered as implementing a convention.

In *MacDonald v. Vapour*, Laskin CJ, speaking for four other members of the court, stated that section 7 of the Trade Marks Act did not implement a treaty because there was an "absence of an express declaration ... that ... [it] was enacted in implementation of the obligations of the Convention."[41] This form of implementing legislation was clearly demanded in the context of a potential authorization of federal jurisdiction in an otherwise provincial field. It is therefore possible that such a requirement be confined to this context and not preclude less rigid forms of implementation where federal or provincial governments are acting within their respective spheres in the absence of a treaty.[42]

In *R. v. Crown Zellerbach*, however, the Supreme Court seemed to relax the *MacDonald v. Vapour* standard for implementing legislation. The court found that the Canadian legislation was implementing legislation in the absence of any express declaration in the Canadian legislation to that effect. It inferred this conclusion from the references to the convention in the act, from the similarity in language between the convention and the act, and from the nexus between changes to the convention and subsequent changes to the domestic law.

However, the *MacDonald v. Vapour* case, and to a lesser extent *Crown Zellerbach*, in so far as they require an express reference to the convention in the domestic legislation, are at odds with the Department of External Affairs' own stated methodology for implementing treaties. In a letter of 1 February 1985, the Legal Bureau replied to a Council of Europe questionnaire on the means by which states express their consent to be bound by a treaty. One question asked: "Do treaties to which your country is a party become incorporated into your country's domestic law?" And the Legal Bureau letter responded, "[t]reaties require implementing legislation ... If it is necessary to change domestic law ... to discharge ... treaty obligations this may be done in a number of ways: (a) by enacting the required legislation without express reference to the treaty."[43]

The policy of facilitating Canada's satisfaction of its international obligations will not be met by a narrow conception of when legislation or legislative provisions are aimed to give legal effect in domestic law to a treaty. Express reference to the treaty or an explicit statement that a provision or act is being enacted in order to implement a treaty is an excessive requirement for satisfying the policy that the executive not infringe on the authority of Parliament or the legislatures. Only where there is a possibility that implementing legislation will permit Parliament to trench on provincial jurisdiction is the requirement of explicit reference to the treaty, or of an express statement of the legislative intention to implement a treaty, justifiable.

Are Canada's Human Rights Treaties Incorporated?

Canada's human rights treaties have been incorporated in part into Canadian legislation, including the Charter. This conclusion can be drawn from three factors.

First, the legislative history of the Charter contains frequent references to international human rights law. Throughout the approximately fifteen-year drafting period from 1968 to 1982, the proliferation of international norms was monitored and digested by Canadian constitutional framers. New conventions raised the issue of ratification for Canada. Ratification required consideration of the adequacy of domestic law. The quest for a constitutional bill of rights coincided with increased international participation.[44]

To take but one example, in 1978 the minister of justice, Otto Lang, tabled a paper entitled "Constitutional Reform: Canadian Charter of Rights and Freedoms" at the Federal-Provincial First Ministers Conference in Ottawa.[45] In the course of justifying the need for "constitutional protection of rights and freedoms," it said:

The widespread acknowledgment of the fundamental nature of rights and freedoms, and the importance of their preservation and enhancement is perhaps no better demonstrated than by the several international instruments which have been adopted by the United Nations and subscribed to by many nations, including Canada ... One only need refer to the Universal Declaration of Human Rights (1948), the International Convention on Elimination of All Forms of Racial Discrimination (1965), the International Covenant on Civil and Political Rights (1966) and the International Covenant on Economic, Social and Cultural Rights (1966).[46]

By this date, Canada had ratified all three of the above-mentioned treaties, and their influence on the substance of the government's proposals was clear. The paper made many references to international sources in its later proposals of provisions.

More specifically, one can consider the history of Charter section 15. The Constitutional Amendment Bill (Bill C-60), 1978, contained a section 6, which stated: "It is accordingly declared that, in Canada, every individual shall enjoy and continue to enjoy the following fundamental rights and freedoms ... the right of the individual to equality before the law and to the equal protection of the law."[47] Lang's 1978 paper[48] explained why the words "equal protection of the law" were introduced, the word "equal" being an addition to the Canadian Bill of Rights, section 1 (b).[49] It says: "One finds similar provisions in the Universal Declaration of Human Rights and the U.N. Covenant on Civil and Political Rights."[50]

In the October 1980 Proposed Resolution, the equality rights provision section 15 stated:

(1) Everyone has the right to equality before the law and to the equal protection of the law without discrimination because of race, national or ethnic origin, colour, religion, age or sex.
(2) This section does not preclude any law, program or activity that has as its object the amelioration of conditions of disadvantaged persons or groups.[51]

Many of the groups appearing before the Hays-Joyal Committee in the fall of 1980 criticized this proposal as incorporating a closed list of grounds of discrimination. This criticism was made specifically on the basis of Canada's international treaty obligations.[52]

In January 1981 the minister of justice, Jean Chrétien, indicated that the government was willing to accept a new section 15. Subsection (1) stated: "Every individual is equal before and under the law and has the right to the equal protection and equal benefit of the law without discrimination and, in particular, without discrimination based on race, national or ethnic origin, colour, religion, sex or age."[53] The minister's accompanying statement indicated his view that this new language made section 15(1) "open-ended."[54]

In a Federal-Provincial-Territorial Ministerial Conference on Human Rights of 2–3 February 1981, ministers issued a joint statement which made the following commitment: "Each government undertook to ensure that current and future legislation is compatible with Canada's international obligations."[55] At that same meeting, the ministers considered a document entitled, "Areas of Deficiency Requiring Ministerial Attention with Respect to the International Covenants."[56] That document specifically pointed out that the equality or nondiscrimination provision of the Civil and Political

Covenant, and other provisions in the Economic, Social and Cultural Covenant "prohibit discrimination on grounds of status. This concept is extremely wide and could include discrimination on grounds of physical and mental handicap ... Consideration should, therefore, be given to increasing the number of prohibited grounds of discrimination if Canada is to meet its obligations under the two Covenants."[57] On 17 February 1981 Chrétien moved in the House of Commons a Revised Proposed Resolution to Amend the Constitution, which for the first time included "mental or physical disability."[58]

The legislative history of the Charter indicates, first, that international human rights law was an important motivating factor throughout the fifteen-year effort to constitutionalize a bill of rights. Second, many specific Charter sections are directly indebted in both language and intent to specific international law provisions.[59]

The second factor supporting the conclusion that Canada's international human rights treaties have been incorporated in part into Canadian legislation is that ratification took place only after extensive federal-provincial consultation. The provinces also agreed to implementation in the context of matters within their legislative jurisdiction. The major policy reason for denying that the Charter, or other selected federal and provincial statutes, is implementing legislation in the absence of express reference to international obligations of Canada is that the nature of federalism would be threatened. Provincial legislative authority could be bypassed if treaties could be implemented without provincial participation. This policy is not applicable in the context of Canada's major human rights treaties because they were ratified only after the prior consultation and consent of all Canadian governments.

The third factor is that Canadian diplomats represent the Charter and other statutes as implementing legislation in many international fora. Again, to take but one example, the Human Rights Committee considered Canada's Supplementary Report on the Covenant on Civil and Political Rights in October 1984. Ambassador Beesley, the permanent representative of Canada to the United Nations in Geneva, made a statement highlighting provisions of the Charter and relating them specifically to the covenant. He told the committee:

Section 2 of the Charter ... corresponded generally to the provisions of articles 18, 19, 21 and 22 of the Covenant. Sections 3 to 5 of the Charter ... corresponded to article 25 of the Covenant. Section 6 of the Charter ... [i]ts counterpart in the Covenant was article 12. Sections 7 to 14 of the Charter ... those provisions were comparable to articles 6, 7, 8, 9, 14 and 15 of the Covenant ... Section 15 was the counterpart of article 26 of the Covenant ...

Section 3 of the Charter ... contributed to the implementation of articles 26 and 27 of the Covenant.[60]

Moreover, he stated:

Although it was true that the Charter and the Covenant were not identical in every respect, their differences could not hide the high degree of similarity and complimentarity between them. The Charter gave effect to many of Canada's obligations under the Covenant. Further, the Covenant and the comments made by members of the Committee during their review of Canada's initial report, had contributed to many of the changes to the original draft of the Charter ...

The final version of section 1 of the Charter reflected the requirements found in various provisions of the Covenant that limits on rights must be reasonable and prescribed by law. Moreover, the Charter, like the Covenant, prohibited all types of discrimination in the enjoyment of equality rights. Whereas the original version of the Charter had prohibited discrimination on a specific number of grounds, the current wording of section 15 was based on articles 2 and 26 of the Covenant. Section 28 of the Charter guaranteed Charter rights equally to men and women; one of the reasons for adding that section to the Charter was article 3 of the Covenant. Finally, Canada's obligations under the Covenant had also led to recognize [sic], in section 11 of the Charter, the right to be tried within a reasonable time and to the recognition that retroactive laws must be justified to deal with acts which, at the time of their commission, had been crimes in international law. Those obligations had also resulted in improvements in the Charter provisions relating to search and seizure, detention and arrest, bail and remedies.[61]

Beesley also later stated: "Canada ... must take increasing account of international standards and it was therefore entrenching in the Constitution the fundamental human rights embodied in the Covenant."[62] In other words, a senior representative of the Canadian government testified to an international supervisory body of independent experts that the Charter gives effect to many covenant obligations and that specific changes in the draft of the Charter were made on the basis of the Covenant. This is a clear representation that the Charter implements part of the Covenant on Civil and Political Rights.[63]

Consequently, an absence of express reference to Canada's international human rights treaties either in the Charter or in certain other statutes related to human rights should not be fatal to a determination that they are indeed implementing legislation, or intended to "give effect to" Canada's human rights treaty obligations. On the contrary, the overall policy of facilitating Canada's adherence to its international obligations, without undermining the nature of Canadian federalism, would be adequately served by acknowledging the Department of External Affairs' stated guideline that implementing legislation may be enacted "without express reference to the treaty."[64]

Interpretation of Implementing Legislation

The presumption that Parliament and the legislatures do not intend to act in breach of Canada's international obligations is applicable to conventional international law. In the words of Pigeon J in a concurring judgment in *Daniels v. The Queen*,[65] there is a "rule of construction that Parliament is not presumed to legislate in breach of a treaty or in any manner inconsistent with the comity of nations and the established rules of international law."[66] In the context of implementing legislation, this means that Canadian courts should interpret domestic implementing legislation in conformity with the convention insofar as the domestic legislation permits. The rule has been reiterated on a number of occasions, most recently by the Supreme Court in *American Farm Bureau Federation v. The Canadian Import Tribunal*,[67] in which Gonthier J (speaking for the majority) stated: "where the text of the domestic law lends itself to it, one should also strive to expound an interpretation which is consonant with the relevant international obligations."[68]

At the same time there is no doubt that if the domestic legislation cannot be given a possible meaning in conformity with the treaty, or there is a conflict between the domestic legislation and international law, it is the domestic legislation that will prevail. As Pigeon J also said in *Daniels*: "If a statute is unambiguous, its provisions must be followed even if they are contrary to international law ... the plain words of a statute could not be disregarded in order to observe the comity of nations and established rules of international law."[69]

However, in *Schavernoch v. Foreign Claim Commission et al.*,[70] the Supreme Court suggested that only domestic legislation appearing as ambiguous *prior* to consideration of the treaty will permit consideration of the treaty as an aid to interpretation. In this case the court considered Canadian regulations which implemented an international agreement between Czechoslovakia and Canada. Estey J, speaking for the court, stated: "Because, however, there is in my view no ambiguity arising from the above-quoted excerpt from these Regulations there is no authority and none was drawn to our attention in argument entitling the Court to take recourse ... to an underlying international agreement."[71] He spoke of the intention as indicated international agreement."⁷¹ He spoke of the intention as indicated "within the four corners of the Order-In-Council"⁷² and was concerned to point out that "[n]owhere ... is there any clear principle enunciated that ... international law somehow overrides or imposes its interpretations on validly enacted domestic law."⁷³

The *Schavernoch* idea was adopted by the Federal Court of Appeal in *National Corn Growers Assn. v. Canadian Import Tribunal*.⁷⁴ On appeal, however, the Supreme Court in *American Farm Bureau* rejected the approach of the Federal Court⁷⁵ and stated in contrast: "[I]t is reasonable to make reference to an international agreement at the very outset of the inquiry to determine if there is an ambiguity, even latent, in the domestic legislation ... [T]here is no need to find a patent ambiguity before consultation of the agreement is possible ... [S]uch an international agreement may be used ... at the preliminary stage of determining if an ambiguity exists."⁷⁶

Consequently, in the context of implementing legislation, a Canadian court may have recourse to the underlying international agreement if there is an ambiguity or uncertainty in the implementing legislation. As Gonthier J said in *American Farm Bureau*: "where the domestic legislation is unclear it is reasonable to examine any underlying international agreement. In interpreting legislation which has been enacted with a view towards implementing international obligations ... it is reasonable for a tribunal to examine the domestic law in the context of the relevant agreement to clarify any uncertainty."⁷⁷ And that ambiguity may only be apparent on examination of the implementing legislation in the light of the international agreement.⁷⁸

Interpreting Canadian Law in the Absence of a Finding of Incorporation

If Canadian courts do not expressly find Canada's human rights treaties to be implemented, or with respect to those provisions for which such a conclusion is not possible, the issue arises of the place of unincorporated treaty obligations in Canadian courts. In the absence of implementing legislation, the presumption that Parliament and the legislatures do not intend to legislate in violation of Canada's treaty obligations still operates. Accordingly, wherever possible, statutes are not to be interpreted as violating unimplemented but binding international conventional law.

In practice, prior to the introduction of the Canadian Charter of Rights and Freedoms, there were very few cases even raising the issue of the usefulness of unincorporated treaties in interpreting domestic legislation. In *Capital Cities Communications v. Canadian Radio-television*

Schavernoch, required an ambiguity to be established before considering the treaty.[80] Other cases ignored any benefit which might have been gained from using treaties as aids to statutory interpretation, not explicitly on the grounds that no ambiguity appeared in the legislation, but on the basis that an unincorporated treaty is of no possible legal effect.[81]

After the introduction of the Charter, there was an exponential growth in the number of cases which referred to conventional international human rights law in the course of interpreting domestic law. Today it is the cases which involve international human rights law that are defining the nature of the relationship between conventional international law and domestic law in Canada. These cases, including those of the Supreme Court, have made virtually no effort to consider the issue of whether Canadian human rights treaties have been implemented. They have also tended not to raise the constitutional rule that without implementing legislation the treaty is not part of domestic law.

Between 1982 and 1993 there have been approximately 115 cases that have referred to international human rights treaties ratified by Canada. In about half these cases the reference to international law supported the decision made.

In two non-Charter cases concerning human rights, *Mercure v. A.G. Sask et al.*[82] and *Bell v. Quebec*,[83] the Supreme Court used human rights treaties ratified by Canada as well as the ILO Constitution to support interpretations of domestic law. No justification for introducing international law was given, no requirement of ambiguity mentioned.

The strongest statement of a majority of the Supreme Court of the relevance of international law in interpreting the Charter was made in *Davidson v. Slaight Communications*.[84] The court referred to the right-to-work provision of the International Covenant on Economic, Social and Cultural Rights in concluding that the legislative objective of a provision of the Canada Labour Code was pressing and substantial (in other words, satisfied the requirements of Charter section 1). In coming to this conclusion, Dickson CJ, speaking for the majority, stated:

Especially in light of Canada's ratification of the International Covenant on Economic, Social and Cultural Rights ... and commitment therein to protect, inter alia, the right to work in its various dimensions found in Article 6 of that treaty, it cannot be doubted that the objective in this case is a very important one. In *Reference Re Public Service Employee Relations Act* ... I had occasion to say ... "The content of Canada's international human rights obligations is, in my view, an important indicia of the meaning of the 'full benefit of the Charter's protection.' I believe that the Charter should generally be presumed to provide protection at least as great as that afforded by similar provisions in international human rights documents which Canada has ratified." Given the dual function of s.1 ... Canada's international human rights obligations *should inform* not only the interpretation of the content of the rights guaranteed by the *Charter* but also the interpretation of what can constitute pressing and substantial s.1 objectives which may justify restrictions upon those rights. Furthermore, for purposes of this stage of the proportionality inquiry, the fact that a value has the status of an international human right, either in customary international law or under a treaty to which Canada is a State Party, should generally be indicative of a high degree of importance attached to that objective. This is consistent with the importance that this Court has placed on the protection of employees as a vulnerable group in society.[85]

This statement goes beyond the mere suggestion that international law may be used to an admonition that it should be used, at least to ensure that the Charter provides protection as great as that afforded by Canadian international legal obligations. Dickson CJ refers specifically here to international legal obligations of Canada, ratified treaties as well as customary international law. However, he gives no precise justification – namely, the common-law presumption – for the relevance of this international law. He is nevertheless clear about the use to which these obligations can be put in applying the Charter: interpreting the content of the rights guaranteed and defining the scope of their limitations under section 1. In the latter context, international law can assist in determining the degree of importance of a legislative objective or whether it is pressing and substantial.

In the post-Charter era, the Supreme Court is referring with unprecedented frequency to international treaties of Canada which have not explicitly been found to be incorporated.[86] These judgments are not encumbered by an effort to look for an ambiguity in the legislation prior to referring to a treaty, even in the non-Charter context as illustrated in *Mercure* and *Bell*. At the same time, the justification for referring to international treaties ratified by Canada has never been clearly stated and the necessity for its consideration in a Charter context now emanates from the chief justice's views in *Davidson* rather than the time-worn presumption and resulting admonition to bring Canadian law into conformity with international legal obligations where possible. Consequently, while the legitimacy of introducing international legal obligations of Canada into problems of interpretation of Canadian law is comfortably established, the impact of such law in any given case will apparently depend on the proclivities of a result-oriented decision-maker rather than their inherent usefulness to the interpretative problem at hand.

The absence of a principled use by the Supreme Court of international law, despite the periodic receptivity to such sources, is perhaps most obvious in the freedom of association and equality rights cases. The Supreme Court has defined freedom of association to exclude collective bargaining[87] and the right to strike.[88] This is to ignore completely Canada's many international obligations concerning freedom of association and its essential parameters.[89] In the equality rights context the Supreme Court has strictly limited the prohibited grounds which can come within the constitutional protection of equality,[90] while Canadian international nondiscrimination obligations are open-ended and do not entail such an imposing preliminary hurdle.[91]

Furthermore, in the absence of any general basic justification for referring to international treaties, the *Davidson* comment might be read as applying only to international human rights law and only to the Charter. Human rights cases in Canadian courts might turn out to be *sui generis*, with different rules applicable where the relevant international law is on a different subject. *American Farm Bureau* placed an emphasis on the domestic law's uncertainty or ambiguity which the Supreme Court has not articulated in the Charter context. And in *American Farm Bureau* the court was careful to point out that the Canadian legislation was implementing legislation before turning to international law, while in the Charter context the court has ignored the issue of implementation.[92] Even if the Charter is seen to be a special case, the contrast between *Bell* and *Mercure* on the one hand, and *Capital Cities* on the other, gives some indication that the rules for the relationship between international law (which is either unincorporated or for which the issue of incorporation has been disregarded) and domestic law will differ for human rights as opposed to nonhuman rights issues. This is an illogical result. The policy considerations are identical. The policy of ensuring the executive not infringe on the authority of Parliament or the legislatures by entering into treaties is equally applicable in human rights and nonhuman rights cases. The presumption is not limited to certain subject matters of international law, and the policy behind the presumption – namely, that the judiciary should avoid bringing Canada into violation of its international obligations – remains equally relevant.[93]

INTERNATIONAL LAW TO WHICH CANADA IS NOT A PARTY

The dearth of justification for considering international conventional law to which Canada is a party in the course of interpreting domestic law may explain the contemporaneous multiplication of Canadian cases referring to conventional international law to which Canada is not a party. This essentially post-Charter phenomenon has occured virtually without judicial explanation. The common-law presumption to promote Canada's adherence to its international obligations is irrelevant.

This development is justifiable. First, Canadian courts have traditionally made some reference to nonbinding sources of law from other jurisdictions, such as the United States, for the purpose of formulating informed responses to domestic legal questions. Second, in the case of the Charter, section 1 specifically defines an acceptable limitation upon rights in terms of the requirements of a free and democratic society. In so doing, it invites comparison with the legal responses of other free and democratic societies. Furthermore, in the context of the European Convention on Human Rights and associated jurisprudence (to which 85 per cent of the cases refer), additional justifications can be made, such as the similarity between its provisions and those of the Covenant on Civil and Political Rights, to which Canada is bound.

Unfortunately, such legitimizing principles have rarely been articulated by Canadian courts. Consequently, use of this nonbinding law, while frequent, is again unpredictable and uneven.

Between 1982 and 1993 there have been approximately 175 cases that have referred to international law which does not bind Canada. In about half these cases the reference supported the decision made. For example, in *R. v. Oakes*[94] the Supreme Court held that section 8 of the Narcotic Control Act, which contained a reverse onus clause, was inconsistent with the guarantee to the presumption of innocence in section 11(d) of the Charter. Dickson CJ, writing for the majority, referred to the Universal Declaration of Human Rights as evidence of "the widespread acceptance of the principle of the presumption of innocence."[95] In other words, he used it to reinforce the value already set out in the Charter. He dealt at greater length with the European Convention on Human Rights, examining two early decisions of the European Commission of Human Rights.[96] One of these decisions suggested criteria for examining a reverse onus clause, and it was a factor in the court's articulation of appropriate requirements for constitutionality. No reason was given for referring to the

Universal Declaration, the European Convention, or the jurisprudence of interpreting bodies thereunder.[97]

In none of the opinions of the Supreme Court citing nonbinding international law to support an interpretation of the Charter is any justification given for the reference. At the same time, despite its diminished significance in theory as compared with Canadian international obligations, no mention is made of any ambiguity requirements. In the absence of justification, however, reference to such sources seems to be completely haphazard. Dissenting opinions of the court refer to it in support of their conclusions as many times as do majority opinions. In other words, such international law is apparently invoked where it supports a conclusion already determined. If it suggests any contrary result it is ignored.

This highly casual and disconnected use of nonbinding international conventional law is most obvious in the context of the issue of defining the Charter right in section 11(b) to be tried within a reasonable time. A majority of the Supreme Court has ignored the well-established jurisprudence of the European Court of Human Rights, interpreting similar language. The European Court has said a calculation of delay can include time prior to what is encompassed in a very formal definition of the word "charge" in circumstances where the situation of the suspect is substantially affected.[98]

GOVERNMENT VIEWS OF THE APPROPRIATE JUDICIAL FUNCTION

In unprecedented degrees conventional law, both binding and nonbinding, is now cited in Canadian courts. The legal development is consistent with the representations of Canadian officials both abroad and at home. The governments of Canada have made it clear that it is appropriate for Canadian courts to refer to international law in the course of interpreting domestic law, particularly the Charter.

For example, in 1985 Canadian government officials appeared before the Committee on the Elimination of Discrimination against Women (CEDAW). The committee was considering Canada's First Report on the Convention on the Elimination of All Forms of Discrimination against Women. The Canadian representatives pointed out: "Canadian courts were increasingly taking into account the specific provisions of treaties in order to interpret ... legislation ... It was expected that the Convention, as well as other human rights instruments, would be important instruments in the interpretation of the Charter."[99]

At the same time, government representations about judicial helpfulness in ensuring that Canadian international obligations are met may be exaggerated, and even distorted, in an effort to avoid international embarrassment. When the Second Report of Canada on Articles 6–9 of the International Covenant on Economic, Social and Cultural Rights was reviewed on 10–13 February 1989 in Geneva, Ambassador de Montigny Marchand made a speech that stated: "Members of the Committee may also be interested to know that the courts frequently rely on the provisions of the Covenant in interpreting the relevant provisions of the *Canadian Charter of Rights and Freedoms* and occasionally those of the provincial human rights charters and legislation ... [f]or example, in several cases involving freedom of association, which is guaranteed by section 2(d) of the Charter, the courts have relied on article 8 of the Covenant, which defines trade union rights."[100] On the contrary, the decisions in the Supreme Court cases which had been decided at that time on the issue of freedom of association determined that the right to strike was not entailed in section 2(d), in contrast to the express protection of the International Covenant on Economic, Social and Cultural Rights. The majority opinions made no mention of any international law, let alone this provision of the covenant. Furthermore, the Canadian delegation was later asked by one well-informed member of the committee to single out a few cases in which the actual text of the covenant or of ILO conventions had been discussed; the member also asked specifically about the Supreme Court case involving the right to strike of public employees, which he understood as rejecting the usefulness of ILO conventions.[101] It is not to the credit of the Canadian delegation that the response was as follows: "A recent decision taken by the Supreme Court of Canada relating to some trade-union rights was clearly inspired by the Covenant."[102] The only case from the Supreme Court displaying any inspiration from the covenant did so in the context of the dissenting opinion. The committee could only have been misled by such an answer. The length taken here to cover up Canadian deficiencies at least makes it very obvious that failure by Canadian courts to take account of Canadian international obligations in construing the Charter, or any other domestic legislation where possible, can lead to real international embarrassment.

MISTAKES

While judicial enthusiasm for using international human rights law has grown dramatically since the advent of the Charter, judicial comprehension of public international law has not. The references to international law include many examples of basic errors. Canadian courts have spoken of ratification of General Assembly or ECOSOC Resolutions,[103] and ratification of treaties by provinces.[104] They have misstated the jurisprudence of the European Convention on Human Rights,[105] confused the European Court of Human Rights with the European Court of Justice,[106] and identified Canada as a signatory to the European Convention on Human Rights.[107] In one instance, the Federal Court of Appeal refused to take judicial notice of international human rights law, and associated reference material, both binding and nonbinding upon Canada.[108] They held that public international law was analogous to foreign municipal law and must be specifically pleaded and proved. The Supreme Court itself has referred on a number of occasions to very old and outdated jurisprudence of the European Court of Human Rights.[109] In *Morgentaler*, MacIntyre J argued that "the American Convention on Human Rights ... expressly addres[sed] the question of abortion, [while] the Charter was silent on this point."[110] Consequently, he continued, the Charter could not be construed to protect a constitutional right to an abortion. However, he neglected to articulate what the American Convention actually said. And since it expressly protects the right to life from the moment of conception, the silence of the Charter in contrast to the convention's specificity would lead, if anywhere, to the conclusion that the Charter takes the opposite view and protects a woman's security of the person in the abortion context.

In the Supreme Court case of *Re McKinney and University of Guelph et al.*,[111] the majority opinion of Mr Justice La Forest relied on an old and very general 1973 resolution of the United Nations General Assembly which made no specific statement about mandatory retirement.[112] The opinion completely ignored the more recent World Assembly on Aging, whose Plan of Action was adopted by the General Assembly in 1982. That Plan of Action specifically recommended the abolition of mandatory retirement.[113] In other words, the Supreme Court's majority relied on an international principle which was both obsolete and used to justify an inaccurate account of the international standard on the subject of mandatory retirement. The dissenting opinion in *Kindler v. A.G. Can.*,[114] per Cory J, concluded that to surrender a fugitive who may be subject to the death penalty violates section 12 of the Charter, the right to be free from cruel and unusual treatment. In support of his conclusion, he stated that Canada had given an international commitment to abolishing the death penalty by virtue of having voted in favour of the adoption by the United Nations General Assembly of the Second Optional Protocol to the International Covenant on Civil and Political Rights (on the Death

Penalty).[115] On the contrary, Canada has no international obligations with respect to this treaty, since it has neither signed nor ratified it.

These cases indicate that there remains in Canada widespread unfamiliarity of both bench and bar with international human rights law. Improvement will require at least increased judicial education, expansion of the number of law students reached by related law school courses, and significantly enriched library collections.

CONCLUSION

Although the scope of international human rights standards is increasing dramatically, its quality is undoubtedly deficient. Such standards are drafted in contexts which result in their generally representing a minimum common denominator. Consequently, in many instances, Canadian human right norms will be an improvement on international law. The point is, that where human rights protection is less adequate, it can benefit through informed and selective judicial injection into Canadian law of international rules. At the same time, the inherent limitations of international supervisory bodies can in large measure be overcome by domestic judicial efforts the world over to ensure that domestic law does not violate international human rights standards. Canadian courts must therefore be encouraged to place their articulated goal of strengthening human rights protection through recourse to international law on a firmer foundation.

NOTES

1 The European Court of Human Rights reminds states that international machinery for protecting fundamental rights is subsidiary to national systems of safeguarding rights. The court has stated that the national authorities are in a better position than the international judge to determine the appropriateness of limitations upon rights.
2 Early cases concerning admiralty law noted with approval early British cases (*Triquet v. Bath* (1764), 3 Burr. 1478) supporting an adoption approach (*Dunbar v. Sullivan* (1907), 11 Ex. C.R. 179 at 188). In *Reference Re Power of Municipalities to Levy Rates on Foreign Legations and High Commissioner's Residences* [1943] 2 DLR 481), however, ambiguous statements were made. See Duff CJ at 484 and the confusing use of the word "accepted," or Rinfret J at 502–3 and "acquired validity." Ambiguous comments on the relationship between customary international law and domestic law are found in the Supreme Court case of *Reference*

Re Exemption of U.S. Forces from Canadian Criminal Law ([1943] 4 DLR 11 at 41; [1943] SCR 483 at 517, per Taschereau J). *Pan American World Airways Inc. et al. v. The Queen et al.* ((1982) 129 DLR (3d) 257; [1981] 2 SCR 565) is another example of confusing articulation by the Supreme Court of the relationship between international law and municipal law. See the confused terminology "expressly incorporated" at 258 DLR and at 567 SCR.

3 *Re Alberta Union of Provincial Employees et al. v. The Crown in Right of Alberta* (1981), 120 DLR (3d) 590 (Alb. QB); (1982), 130 DLR (3d) 191 (Alb. CA); *Re Regina and Palacios* (1984), 7 DLR (4th) 112 (Ont. CA); *R. v. Sunila and Solayman* (1986), 26 CCC (3d) 177 (NSCA); *R. v. Alvarez* (Newfoundland Supreme Court – Trial Division, 29 Jan. 1990 (Barry J) [1990] NJ No. 48).

At the same time, a number of Canadian cases have accepted corrollaries of an adoption approach: conflicting statutory rules will modify or prevent the incorporation of customary international law into domestic law (*Gordon v. R. in Right of Canada*, [1980] 5 WWR 668, at 671 (BCSC), (1980), 22 BCLR 17 (CA)); the customary international law relating to diplomatic immunities is part of the law of Canada and operates except in so far as it is contradicted by Canadian statutory law. (*Re Regina & Palacios* (1984), 7 DLR (4th) 112 (Ont. CA)).

The case of *Reference Re the Seabed and Subsoil of the Continental Shelf of Nfld.* (1984), 5 DLR (4th) 385 (SCC); [1984] 1 SCR 86 might also be said to support an adoptionist approach to customary law. The Supreme Court apparently assumed that a determination of the customary international law relating to claims to the continental shelf would govern rights as between the governments of Canada and Newfoundland. (In this case, though, it was the absence of customary international law on the subject in 1949 that determined the right to explore and exploit the continental shelf today.)

4 Article 38 (1) (b) of the Statute of the International Court of Justice states that the court shall apply "international custom, as evidence of a general practice accepted as law"; custom therefore contains two elements, general practice and its acceptance as law.

5 *Supra*, note 3.

6 *Supra*, note 3, at 411 DLR and at 118 SCR.

7 Albeit not in a human rights context, but rather in a case involving the delineation of a maritime boundary between Canada and the United States in the Gulf of Maine, the court stated:

> [a] body of detailed rules is not to be looked for in customary international law which in fact comprises a limited set of norms for ensuring the co-existence and vital cooperation of the members of the international community, together with a set of customary rules whose presence in the *opinio juris*

of States can be tested by induction based on the analysis of a sufficiently extensive and convincing practice, and not by deduction from preconceived ideas. [1984] ICJ Rep. 246, paragraph 111.

A degree of judicial crystallization of a rule embodied in state practice and intentions will often be necessary. But the project is clearly analogous to the familiar task of the Canadian judge in defining the common law.

8 *Case Concerning the Barcelona Traction, Light and Power Co. Ltd.*, [1970] ICJ Rep. 4 at 32, paragraphs 33 and 34.
9 *De Sanchez v. Banco Central de Nicaragua* 770 F. 2d 1385 (5th Cir. 1985) at 1397. *Forti v. Suarez-Mason* 672 F. Supp. 1531 (ND Cal. 1987); Motion to reconsider granted in part and denied in part 694 F. Supp. 707 (ND Cal. 1988).
10 *Filartiga v. Pena-Irala* 630 F. 2d 876 (2nd Cir. 1980); *De Sanchez v. Banco Central de Nicaragua*; *Forti v. Suarez-Mason*.
11 *Lareau v. Manson* 507 F. Supp. 1177 (D. Conn., 1980); Aff'd in part. Modified and remanded in part. 651 F. 2d 96 (2nd Cir. 1981). Only the District Court decision spoke of the Standard Minimum Rules as relevant by way of customary international law.
12 *Rodriguez-Fernandez v. Wilkinson* 654 F. 2d 1382 (10th Cir. 1981); *De Sanchez v. Banco Central de Nicaragua*; *Forti v. Suarez Mason*.
13 *De Sanchez v. Banco Central de Nicaragua*. But see *Forti v. Suarez-Mason* 694 F. Supp. 707 (ND Cal. 1988), which held that "cruel, inhuman or degrading treatment" was not a violation of customary international law.
14 *De Sanchez v. Banco Central de Nicaragua*.
15 *Forti v. Suarez-Mason*, 711.
16 1984 WestLaw 9080 (CD Cal.) (No. CV82–1772–RMT (MCX), 24 Sept. 1984.
17 *Restatement of the Law of the Foreign Relations Law of the United States*, vol. 2, section 702, 161, the American Law Institute, 14 May 1986, c.1987. In total, the Restatement lists the following other rights as having the status of customary international human rights law: slavery or slave trade; the murder or causing the disappearance of individuals; torture or other cruel, inhuman, or degrading treatment or punishment; prolonged arbitrary detention; section 702, 161.

The Restatement is careful to note that customary international human rights law continues to develop, and this list "is not closed" (section 702, Comment a, 161–2). See in general on the use of international human rights law in U.S. courts, A. Bayefsky and J. Fitzpatrick, "International Human Rights Law in United States Courts: A Comparative Perspective" (1992), 14 *Michigan Journal of International Law* 1–89.

18 Examples of acts found in U.S. courts to violate the law of nations (under the Alien Tort Claim Act, 28 USC s.1350 making actionable a "tort ... committed in violation of the law of nations") and which are not reflected in Charter rights and freedoms are the unlawful seizure of a vessel and its disposition as a prize; the seizure of neutral property upon the ship of a belligerent; and the concealment of a child's true nationality coupled with the wrongful inclusion of that child on another's passport. See B.A. Barenblat, "Torture as a Violation of the Law of Nations: An Analysis of 28 U.S.C. §1350" (1981), 16 *Texas International Law Journal* 117.

19 *Bloxam v. Favre* (1883), 8 PD 101, at 197: "Every statute is to be so interpreted and applied, as far as its language is mixed, as not to be inconsistent with the comity of nations or with the established rules of international law"; *Reference Re Power of Municipalities to Levy Rates on Foreign Legations and High Commissioner's Residences*, 502, per Duff CJC. In the context of customary international law, Duff CJ said: "The general language of the enactments imposing the taxation in question must be construed as saving to the privileges of foreign states"; *The Ship "North" v. The King* (1906), 37 SCR 385 at 398: "No prudent sovereign power would willingly, in these modern times, invite conflict with a neighbour by enacting a statute directing that to be done which international law had clearly forbidden or that which had been denied as an inherent right. This statute now in question must be read in light of the well-known, recognized, customary or international law that has preceded it, and is yet in force, and receive interpretation thereby"; *Salomon v. Commissioners of Customs and Excise*, [1967] 2 QB 116. In the context of conventional international law, but expressed in general language, Diplock LJ said: "there is a prima facie presumption that Parliament does not intend to act in breach of international law, including therein specific treaty obligations" (143) and "we ought always to interpret our statutes so as to be in conformity with international law" (141).

20 See Dale Gibson, *The Law of the Charter: General Principles* (Toronto: Carswell 1986) 59–62, for other presumptions applicable to the Charter despite constitutional status.

21 (1987), 38 DLR (4th) 161; [1987] 1 SCR 313.

22 Emphasis added; *supra*, note 21, at 184 DLR and at 348 SCR.

23 (1989), 59 DLR (4th) 416; [1989] 1 SCR 1038.

24 Emphasis added, *supra*, note 23, at 427–8 DLR and at 1056–7 SCR.

25 See section 1, Canadian Charter of Rights and Freedoms.

26 The United States has failed to ratify a significant number of human rights conventions. This is a consequence of the fact that treaties

require, for ratification, the advice and consent of two-thirds of the Senate (United States Constitution requires, Article II, section 2) and, once ratified, if they are self-executing (*Foster v. Neilson* 27 U.S. (2 Pet.) 253 at 314), become part of the law of the United States without the need for legislation. (United States Constitution, Clause 2, Article VI). In other words, ratification is politically more difficult than in Canada, at the same time that its domestic legal implications are much more significant.

27 As of October 1992 Canada had ratified forty-seven principal international treaties on human rights or treaties containing significant human rights components.

28 A form of parliamentary "approval" has, however, become traditional for certain agreements in Canada. The opinion of the Department of External Affairs on this issue is expressed in a letter of the Legal Bureau, dated 1 February 1985 ([1986], 24 *Canadian Yearbook of International Law* 396–402): "There is no legal requirement for Parliamentary approval to enable the Government of Canada to enter into an international agreement. On occasion, however, international agreements may be brought directly to the attention of Parliament and the approval of the House of Commons and the Senate may be sought by joint resolution before Canada commits itself to treaties which involve military or economic sanctions, political or military commitments of a far-reaching character, or the large expenditure of public funds. The decision on whether parliamentary approval should be sought is made, in each instance, by the government of the day. In some instances the government will table a treaty in Parliament to bring it to the attention of the House of Commons and the Senate, before or after the treaty is signed but without seeking formal approval by joint resolution."

29 This is not a concern with respect to customary international law, where obligations arise over time from the consent and practice of nations, not merely an act of executive authority.

30 Exceptions exist with respect to treaties which "give recognition of incidents of sovereignty" or concern "matters in exclusively sovereign aspects," but could probably be described as not extending to matters which "affect the rights of individuals." See *Francis v. The Queen* (1956), 3 DLR (2d) 641 at 647; [1956] SCR 618 at 625; *Secretary of State of Canada v. Alien Property Custodian for the United States*, [1931] SCR 170 at 198; [1931] 1 DLR 890 at 902–3. *Ritcher v. The King*, [1943] Ex. CR 64; *Bitter v. Secretary of Canada as Custodian of Enemy Property*, [1944] Ex. CR 61; *Mastini v. Bell Telephone Canada* (1971), 18 DLR (3d) 215 at 218 (Ex. CR).

31 "The treaty in itself is not equivalent to an Imperial Act and without the sanction of Parliament, the Crown cannot alter the existing law by entering into a contract with a foreign power ... these rights and privi-

leges are, under our law, enforceable by the Courts only where the treaty has been implemented or sanctioned by legislation rendering it binding upon the subject ... In the absence of affirming legislation this provision of the treaty cannot be enforced by any of our Courts whose authority is derived from municipal law." [1932] 2 DLR 250 at 260–1; [1932] SCR 495 at 510–11.

32 *Francis v. The Queen*, per Kerwin J at 621 SCR and at 643 DLR, per Rand J at 626 SCR and at 647 DLR; *A.G. Can v. A.G. Ont. (Labour Conventions Case)*, [1937] 1 DLR 673 at 678 (PC); *Capital Cities Communications v. C.R.T.C.* (1978), 81 DLR (3d) 609 at 631 (SCC); [1978] 2 SCR 141 at 173; *Operation Dismantle Inc. et al v. Canada et al.* (1985), 18 DLR 481 (SCC) at 513; [1985] 1 SCR 441 at 484; *Re Regina and Palacios*, at 119. See also Letter of the Legal Bureau of the Department of External Affairs, 1 Feb. 1985 (1986), 24 *Canadian Yearbook of International Law* 396–402.

33 *Supra*, note 32, at 682–3.

34 (1976), 66 DLR (3d) 1; [1977] 2 SCR 134. The court held that they did not have to consider directly the authority of *Labour Conventions* because the section of the act before them was not enacted in implementation of an international obligation.

35 *Supra*, note 34, at 29 DLR and at 169 SCR. Similarly, in *Schneider v. The Queen*, [1982] 2 SCR 112; (1982), 139 DLR (3d) 417 (SCC), the Supreme Court repeated the dicta of *MacDonald v. Vapour* in relation to the *Labour Conventions* case, but concluded that no federal legislation implementing Canada's international obligations, within whose scope the *Heroin Treatment Act* might have fallen, existed.

36 [1988] 1 SCR 401; (1988), 49 DLR (4th) 161.

37 *Supra*, note 36, at 165 DLR and at 408 SCR.

38 The majority looked to the subject-matter of the convention to determine the purpose of the act – namely, the control of marine pollution (*supra*, note 36 at 174–5 DLR and at 419–20 SCR). Satisfaction of the national concern test required that the subject-matter of the legislation "have a singleness, distinctiveness and indivisibility that clearly distinguishes it from matters of provincial concern and a scale of impact on provincial jurisdiction that is reconcilable with the fundamental distribution of legislative power under the Constitution" (at 184 DLR and at 432 SCR). The court held: "Marine pollution, because of its predominantly extra-provincial as well as international character and implications, is clearly a matter of concern to Canada as a whole" (at 187 DLR and at 436 SCR). Furthermore, "[m]arine pollution by the dumping of substances is clearly treated by the Convention ... as a distinct and separate form of water pollution having its own characteristics and scientific considerations" (at 187 DLR and at 436 SCR). The court also used a

United Nations Report on Marine Pollution to conclude there is an "essential indivisibility of the matter of marine pollution by the dumping of substances" and that marine pollution is "sufficiently distinguishable."

39 There are other cases where Canadian courts, without expressly overruling *Labour Conventions*, have reasoned in a similarly contradictory manner.

In *Reference by the Governor-General-in-Council Concerning the Ownership of and Jurisdiction over Offshore Mineral Rights*, [1967] SCR 792 at 821; (1967), 65 DLR (2d) 353 at 380, the Supreme Court of Canada, in coming to the conclusion that exploitation of the mineral resources of the territorial sea and the continental shelf was within federal jurisdiction, within the Peace, Order and Good Government Power, took into account federal responsibility to the international community for breaches of international obligations under the 1958 Geneva Convention on the Continental Shelf.

See also *Denison Mines v. A.G. Can.* (1973), 32 DLR (3d) 419 at 430 (Ont. HC).

40 For criticism of this development see "L'évolution des rapports entre le droit Canadien et le droit international un demi-siècle après l'affaire des conventions internationales de travail." A.L.C. de Mestral, (1987), 25 *Canadian Yearbook of International Law* 301.

41 *Supra*, note 34, at 30–1 DLR and at 171–2 SCR.

42 In a second opinion concurring in the result, de Grandpré, speaking for two other members of the court, found, upon looking at the convention its purpose as set out in Article 1 and other provisions, that the treaty did not support the constitutionality of the particular provision of the Trade Marks Act because the treaty did not deal with the same matter or direct prohibition of the same acts as did the domestic provision. The implication perhaps is that it was the deficiency in the overlap or similarity between the terms of the convention and the domestic legislation, and not a lack of an express declaration of implementing intent, that prevented an otherwise attractive submission (*supra*, note 34 at 176 SCR and at 34 DLR) that the legislation was in implementation of a treaty from succeeding.

43 The other ways were "(b) by legislation which makes reference to the treaty but without expressly enacting its provisions. This may be done either with or without annexing the text of the treaty ... (c) by incorporating into law the treaty or the relevant provisions" ([1986], 24 *The Canadian Yearbook of International Law* 396–402).

44 The major contemporary international human rights treaties came into force in Canada in the following years, respectively: the International Convention on the Elimination of All Forms of Racial Discrimination

(1970), the Freedom of Association and Protection of the Right to Organize Convention (ILO No. 87) (1973), the International Covenant on Civil and Political Rights (1976), the International Covenant on Economic, Social and Cultural Rights (1976), the Convention on the Elimination of All Forms of Discrimination against Women (1982).

45 A.F. Bayefsky, *Canada's Constitution Act 1982 and Amendments: A Documentary History*, 2 vols (Toronto: McGraw-Hill Ryerson 1989), I, 499.
46 Ibid., I, 500.
47 Ibid., 347–8.
48 Ibid., 499.
49 Ibid., II, 965.
50 Ibid., I, 505.
51 Ibid., II, 748–9.
52 John Humphrey, president of the Canadian Human Rights Foundation, stated: "By this Covenant [Civil and Political] Canada undertakes to respect and to ensure the rights set forth in it without distinction of any kind such as race, colour, sex, language, religion, political or other opinion, property, birth or other status. You will note sir, that the obligation is to respect and to ensure, and that the list of prohibited grounds of discrimination is open-ended, and in particular that it includes several prohibited grounds of discrimination, including language, political or other opinion, property and birth, which are not mentioned in the proposed Canadian Charter of Rights and Freedoms" (Minutes of Proceedings, Issue No. 11, 28, 24 Nov. 1980).

Noel Kinsella, chairman, New Brunswick Human Rights Commission, similarly stated: "[T]he non-discrimination grounds should be indicated the way we have suggested, namely everyone is equal before the law without regard to discrimination on such grounds as ... etc. or other status ... [R]ather than attempt to give complete enumeration and to respond to whoever may be able to get before you and argue that a given ground be added, by following the terminology which I just suggested, which is the terminology of the covenants to which we are already committed ourselves, that many other categories, if you like, or classes of non-discrimination rights by virtue of things like physical disability, etc. can be captured" (Minutes of Proceedings, Issue No. 11, 35–6, 24 Nov. 1980).
53 Bayefsky, *Canada's Constitution Act*, II, 769.
54 "Statement by the Honourable Jean Chrétien, Minister of Justice to the Special Joint Committee on the Constitution," 12 Jan. 1981, 8–9: "I want to make clear that the listing of specified grounds where discrimination is most prohibited does not mean that there are not other grounds where discrimination is prohibited ... [T]he amendment ... does not list certain grounds of discrimination to the exclusion of all

others. Rather, it is open-ended ... I prefer to be open-ended rather than adding some new categories with the risk of excluding others."
55 Joint Statement, Ottawa, 2 and 3 Feb. 1981, Document: 830–89/037, 3 Feb. 1981.
56 Federal, Document: 830–89/008, Ottawa, 2 and 3 Feb. 1981.
57 *Supra*, note 56, at 2 n1, 3.
58 Proposed Resolution for a Joint Address to Her Majesty the Queen Respecting the Constitution of Canada, as Amended by the Committee, Bayefsky, *Canada's Constitution Act*, II, 790.
59 In particular, these are Charter sections 1, 6(1), 8, 11(a), (b), (g), (h), (i), 15, 28.
60 Summary Record of the 558th Meeting, 31 Oct. 1984, CCPR/C/SR.558, at 3–4.
61 *Supra*, note 60, at 4.
62 Summary Record of the 559th Meeting, 31 Oct. 1984, CCPR/C/SR.559, at 4.
63 Overall, Canadian government officials clearly represent, in international as well as domestic fora, a number of provisions of Canadian law to be implementing Canada's international treaty obligations. They include many parts of the Charter; provincial and federal anti-discrimination codes; the Canadian Multiculturalism Act RSC 1985, c. 24 (4th Supp.); the Criminal Code amendments concerning torture RSC 1985, c.10 (3rd Supp.), s.2; the Emergencies Act RSC 1985, c.22 (4th Supp.), ss.1–63.
64 The few Canadian cases which have addressed the issue of implementation and the Charter are inconsistent. For example, a number have found some human rights treaty obligations have been implemented, in part by the Charter. (*Re Public Service Employee Relations Act* (1987), 38 DLR (4th) 161 at 184–5; [1987] 1 SCR 313 at 349–51, per Dickson CJ dissenting. Dickson CJ uses the word "incorporates." *Re Service Employees' International Union, Local 204 and Broadway Manor Nursing Home et al.* (1983), 44 OR (2d) 392 at 439 (Ont. HC). (Appeals allowed in part and dismissed in part (1985), 48 OR (2d) 225 (CA). The Appeal Court did not consider the Charter or international law.) *R. v. Videoflicks* (1984), 14 DLR (4th) 10 at 35 (Ont. CA). *R. v. Finta* (1989), 60 OR (2d) 557 at 569. (Ont. HC) (Note *R. v. Finta* (1992) 73 CCC (3d) 65 (Ont. CA) at 129, per Tarnopolsky J. On appeal to SCC). *Nealy, Wallace, Wasserman, Glaser, Goldberg v. Johnston, Long & Church of Jesus Christ Christian-Aryan Nations*, Canadian Human Rights Tribunal, 25 July 1989, 10 CHRR D/6450 at D/6483, paragraph 45690. (See *Taylor et al. v. Canadian Human Rights Commission* (1990) 75 DLR (4th) 577, upholding constitutionality but not mentioning section as response to international obligations.)

Other courts have stated that Canada's international human rights treaties, or parts thereof, have not been implemented. *R. v. Milne,* [1987] 2 SCR 512 at 527; *Re Warren, Clagsburn, Boyle and Costigan* (1983), 35 CR (3d) 173 at 177 (Ont. HC); *Henry v. The Queen,* [1987] 3 FC 429 at 435 (FCTD); *Penikett et al. v. The Queen et al.* (1987), 43 DLR (4th) 324 at 365. Appeal allowed (but not with respect to the disposition of the international law claim, which was not dealt with by the Court of Appeal) [1988] 2 WWR 481 (YCTA).
65 (1968) 2 DLR (3d) 1; [1968] SCR 517.
66 *Supra,* note 65, at 23 DLR and at 541 SCR. See also the dissenting judgment of Pigeon J in *Ernewein v. M.E.I.* (1979), 103 DLR (3d) 1 at 17, Pigeon J quoted "the important principles stated by Lord Diplock ... in *Post Office v. Estuary Radio Limited* ... 'there is a presumption that the Crown did not intend to break an international treaty (see *Salomon* ...)'."
67 [1990] SCJ No. 110, 8 Nov. 1990 (SCC).
68 *Supra,* note 67, at 27, Wilson J wrote a concurring opinion for three of the seven judges in which she refused to reconsider, on an application for judicial review, the tribunal's interpretation of GATT (at 54).
69 *Supra,* note 65 at 23 DLR and at 541 SCR; in *Capital City Communications et al. v. C.R.T.C., supra,* note 32 at 631 DLR and at 173 SCR, Laskin CJ, speaking for the majority, stated: "certainly the Convention *per se* cannot prevail against the express stipulations of the Act."
70 (1982), 136 DLR (3d) 447; [1982] 1 SCR 1092.
71 *Supra,* note 70, at 452 DLR and at 1098 SCR.
72 *Supra,* note 70, at 454 DLR and at 1101 SCR.
73 *Supra,* note 70, at 454 DLR and at 1101 SCR. However, it is not the case that a prior finding of ambiguity before considering a treaty is necessary to ensure that domestic courts only give effect to the domestic legislation itself, or that they will only formulate an interpretation which the language of the domestic law can reasonably or plausibly bear. See, for example, the very different approach of the English Court of Appeal in *Benin v. Whimster,* [1976] 1 QB 297 at 308–9.
74 (1988), 92 NR 264 (FCA) at 268.
75 "The Court of Appeal's suggestion that recourse to an international treaty is only available where the provision of the domestic legislation is ambiguous on its face is to be rejected." *Supra,* note 71, at 27, per Gonthier J.
76 *Supra,* note 71, at 27–8, per Gonthier J.
77 *Supra,* note 71, at 26–7.
78 Gonthier J maintained such an approach was not inconsistent with *Schavernoch,* which in his view was "not explicit" (*supra,* note 71 at 27).

In any case, *Schavernoch*, as applied by the majority of the Federal Court of Appeal, was unjustifiable, particularly in the context of an explicit effort by legislators to implement treaty obligations.

79 *Supra*, note 32.
80 Laskin CJ wrote, "I do not find any ambiguity that would require resort to the Convention," *supra*, note 32 at 631 DLR and at 173 SCR.
81 As Pigeon J stated in dissent in *Capital Cities*, however, "it is an oversimplification to say that treaties are of no legal effect unless implemented by legislation," *supra*, note 32 at 188 SCR and at 642 DLR. In fact, it is clearly at odds with the presumption that Parliament and the legislatures do not intend to breach Canada's international obligations.
82 [1988] 1 SCR 234 at 268; (1988), 48 DLR (4th) 1 at 57 (SCC).
83 [1988] 1 SCR 749 at 806; (1988), 51 DLR (4th) 161 (SCC) at 203.
84 *Supra*, note 23.
85 Emphasis added; *supra*, note 23, at 427–8 DLR and at 1056–7 SCR.
86 The Supreme Court's other references to international human rights treaties ratified by Canada are as set out below.

The reference is supportive of the outcome in the following cases: *U.S.A. v. Cotroni*, [1989] 1 SCR 1469 at 1481; and *R. v. Brydges*, [1990] 1 SCR 190 at 214–15; *R. v. Keegstra*, [1990] 3 SCR 697 at 749–55, 758; *Canada (Cdn. Human Rights Commn.) v. Taylor* (1990), 75 DLR (4th) 577 (SCC) at 594–5, 598; *Kindler v. A.G. Can*, [1991] 2 SCR 779 at 833–4, per Mr Justice La Forest, and the companion case of *Reference Re Ng Extradition (Can.)*, [1991] 2 SCR 858. (La Forest J uses, *inter alia*, binding international law to establish the lack of international norms in the context of the death penalty, and considers the lacunae to be significant); *R. V. Furtney*, [1991] 3 SCR 89 at 107; *R. v. Butler* (1992), 70 CCC (3d) 129 (SCC) at 160.

In the following instances the references to international law were essentially irrelevant: *Oakes*, [1986] 1 SCR 103 at 120 and at 140–1; (1986), 26 DLR (4th) 200 (SCC) at 213 and 228–9; *Smith v. The Queen* (1987), 40 DLR (4th) 435 at 468; [1987] 1 SCR 1045 at 1061.

In one case, *R. v. Milne*, [1987] 2 SCR 512 at 527, international law was not followed on the grounds that it was inconsistent with a Charter provision. In another case, *R. v. Zundel* (1992), 95 DLR (4th) 202 (SCC) at 268–9, per McLachlin J, the supposed absence of Canadian international obligations was used to strike down legislation as inconsistent with the Charter.

In the following cases the international law reference was made in the context of supporting a dissenting opinion: *R. v. Mills*, [1986] 1 SCR 863 at 881–2 and at 919; (1986), 29 DLR (4th) 161 at 188–9 and at 218; *Reference Re Public Service Employee Relations Act* (1987), 38 DLR (4th) 161 at 184–5; [1987] 1 SCR 313 at 348–50; *Government of*

Saskatchewan et al. v. Retail, Wholesale and Department Store Union (1987), 38 DLR (4th) 277 (SCC) at 295, per Wilson J; *Edmonton Journal v. A.G. Alb. et al.*, (1989), 64 DLR (4th) 577 (SCC) at 598 and at 600–1; [1989] 2 SCR 1326 at 1373–4 and at 1377–8; *Kindler v. A.G. Can*, [1991] 2 SCR 779 at 804–9, 820–3, 826–7, per Mr Justice Cory, and the companion case of *Reference Re Ng Extradition (Can.)*, [1991] 2 SCR 858 at 865; *R. v. Zundel* (1992), 95 DLR (4th) 202 (SCC) at 230–1, 233, per Cory and Iacobucci JJ.

The international law reference was essentially irrelevant to the outcome of the dissenting opinion of Madam Justice Wilson in *Re McKinney and University of Guelph et al.* (1990), 76 DLR (4th) 545 (SCC) at 58.

In two related dissenting opinions the relevance of international law was expressly rejected. *R. v. Keegstra*, [1990] 3 SCR 697 at 820–2, 837–9; *Canada (Cdn. Human Rights Commn.) v. Taylor* (1990), 75 DLR (4th) 577 (SCC) at 619.

87 *Professional Institute of the Public Service of Canada v. Northwest Territories (Commissioner), A.G. Can. and A.G. Ont.* (1990), 72 DLR (4th) 1.
88 *Reference Re Public Service Employee Relations Act, supra*, note 86.
89 Various International Labour Organization conventions (and decisions of the Freedom of Association Committee interpreting the ILO conventions), the International Covenant on Civil and Political Rights, and the International Covenant on Economic, Social and Cultural Rights point in different ways to an interpretation of "freedom of association" which includes protection of collective bargaining. The Freedom of Association Committee jurisprudence on ILO Conventions 87 and 98, and the explicit provision of the International Covenant on Economic, Social and Cultural Rights, add to the meaning of freedom of association the right to strike in limited circumstances. In fact, the Freedom of Association Committee had specifically examined the same Alberta legislation at issue in the *Reference Re Public Service Employees Relations Act* and had decided that it contravened ILO Convention 87, which Canada has ratified (Case No. 1247/Alberta, 241st Report of the Committee on Freedom of Association, GB 231/10/13, 231st Session, Geneva, 11–15 Nov. 1985). This was specifically pointed out by Dickson CJ in his dissent.
90 *The Law Society of B.C. & A.G.B.C. et al. v. Andrews & Kinersly*, [1989] 1 SCR 143; (1989), 56 DLR (4th) 1 (SCC); *Reference Re Validity of ss. 32 & 34 of the Workers Compensation Act, 1983*, [1989] 1 SCR 922; (1989), 56 DLR (4th) 765 (SCC) and *Turpin & Siddiqui v. The Queen*, [1989] 1 SCR 1296. See A.F. Bayefsky, "A Case Comment on the First Three Equality Rights Cases under the Canadian Charter of Rights and Freedoms: Andrews, Workers' Compensation Reference, Turpin" (1990), 1 (2d)

Supreme Court Law Review 503–31. These three cases interpreted section 15 of the Charter to mean that the possible prohibited grounds of discrimination are strictly limited to those which can be said to be analogous to the grounds already enumerated.

91 The legislative history of the Charter makes clear that the language of section 15 was at least intended to implement Article 26 of the Covenant on Civil and Political Rights. The covenant follows the language of the European Convention on Human Rights, Article 14, in this respect. Article 14 has long been interpreted by the European Commission and Court of Human Rights to mean that if a distinction of any kind has been made, the right is engaged and the issue of whether or not it has been violated never turns on whether the given distinction is covered by the section. See A.F. Bayefsky, "The Principle of Equality or Non-Discrimination in International Law" (1990), 11, 1–2, *Human Rights Law Journal* 1.

92 *Supra*, note 67, at 26.

93 In a limited number of instances, judgments of lower courts have been more precise about justifying recourse to Canadian international human rights treaties. See, for example, *Re Federal Republic of Germany and Rauca* (1983), 41 OR (2d) 225 (Ont. CA) at 244, 246; *Re Warren, Clagsburn, Boyle and Costigan, supra*, note 66 at 177; *Re Mitchell and the Queen* (1983), 150 DLR (3d) 449 (Ont. HC) at 461–2; *Re Service Employees' International Union, Local 204 and Broadway Manor Nursing Home et al., supra*, note 64, (1983), 44 OR (2d) 392 (Ont. HC) at 439; *R. v. Videoflicks* (1984), 14 DLR (4th) 10 (Ont. CA) at 35–6. *International Fund for Animal Welfare Inc., Best & Davies v. Minister of Fisheries and Oceans* (1988), 83 NR 303 (FCA).

However laudable, such decisions are isolated and infrequent. Greater consistency throughout the Canadian judicial system will require a statement of principle by the Supreme Court.

94 *Supra*, note 86.
95 *Supra*, note 86, at 334.
96 *Supra*, note 86, at 342–3.
97 The Supreme Court has also used nonbinding international law as support for other decisions: *Schmidt v. The Queen* (1987), 39 DLR (4th) 18 (SCC) at 39; [1987] 1 SCR 500 at 522; *Rahey v. The Queen* (1987), 39 DLR (4th) 481 at 513; [1987] 1 SCR 588 at 633; *B.C. Government Employees' Union v. A.G.B.C.* (1989), 53 DLR (4th) 1 at 17; [1989] 2 SCR 214 at 236–7; *Law Society of B.C. et al. v. Andrews et al., supra*, note 90 at 45 DLR and at 203–4 SCR; *U.S.A. v. Cotroni, supra*, note 86 at 1481; *Tremblay v. Daigle* (1989), 62 DLR (4th) 634 at 661–2 DLR; [1989] 2 SCR 530 at 567–8 SCR; *Re McKinney and University of Guelph et al.* (1990), 76 DLR (4th) 545 (SCC) at 659–60, 665; *R. v. Keegstra*, [1990] 3 SCR 697 at 753–

4; *Canada (Cdn. Human Rights Commn.) v. Taylor* (1990), 75 DLR (4th) 577 (SCC) at 594 (see also *R. v. Andrews*, [1990] 3 SCR 870); *Kindler v. A.G. Can.*, [1991] 2 SCR 779 at 833–4, 839, per Mr Justice La Forest, and the companion case of *Reference Re Ng Extradition (Can.)*, [1991] 2 SCR 858; *Committee for the Commonwealth of Canada v. Canada*, [1991] 1 SCR 139 at 210–11; *R. v. Lippé*, [1991] 2 SCR 114 at 153–5; *R. v. Butler* (1992), 70 CCC (3d) 129 (SCC) at 160, 177; *R. v. Nova Scotia Pharmaceutical Society*, [1992] 2 SCR 606 at 636–7, 639, 641–2, 649, 654–8.

In the following cases the Supreme Court's references to nonbinding international law were essentially irrelevant: *Valente v. The Queen*, [1985] 2 SCR 673 at 686 and at 691–2; (1985), 24 DLR (4th) 161 (SCC) at 170 and at 174; *Beauregard v. Canada*, [1986] 2 SCR 56 at 76; (1986), 30 DLR (4th) 481 at 496; *Smith v. The Queen* (1987), 40 DLR (4th) 435 at 468 (SCC); [1987] 1 SCR 1045 at 1061; *A.G. Que. v. La Chaussure Brown's Inc. et al.* (1988), 54 DLR (4th) 577 at 609 (SCC); [1988] 2 SCR 712 at 754; *A.G. Que. v. Irwin Toy Ltd. et al.*, [1989] 1 SCR 927 at 1003; (1989), 58 DLR (4th) 577 at 633 (SCC); *Reference re Criminal Code ss. 193 & 195.1(1)(c) & Guindon & A.G. Man.*, [1990] 1 SCR 1123 at 1150–1, 1200; *The Queen v. Committee for the Commonwealth of Canada*, [1991] 1 SCR 139 at 210–11; *Lavigne v. Ont. Public Service Employees Union et al.*, (1991), 81 DLR (4th) 545 at 576–7, per Madam Justice Wilson.

In one case, nonbinding international law was clearly not followed because it was inconsistent with a Charter provision. *Law Society of B.C. et al. v. Andrews et al.*, supra, note 90 at 20 DLR and at 177 SCR. In another case, in the opinion of McLachlin J, nonbinding international law was not followed on the grounds it was internally incoherent. *Kindler v. A.G. Can.*, [1991] 2 SCR 779 at 856.

In the following cases the nonbinding international law reference was made in the context of supporting a dissenting opinion: *R. v. Mills*, [1986] 1 SCR 863 at 881–2 and at 931 and 946; (1986), 29 DLR (4th) 161 at 188–9 and at 227 and 239 (SCC); *R. v. Jones* (1986), 31 DLR (4th) 569 (SCC) at 583; [1986] 2 SCR 284 at 319–20; *Morgentaler, Smoling and Scott v. R. & A.G. Can.* (1988), 44 DLR (4th) 385 at 469; [1988] 1 SCR 30 at 143; *R. v. Conway*, [1989] 1 SCR 1659 at 1709; *R. v. Kalanj*, [1989] 1 SCR 1594 at 1618; *Edmonton Journal v. A.G. Alb. et al.*, supra, note 86 at 598, 601 DLR and at 1373, 1378 SCR; *Lavigne v. Ont. Public Service Employees Union et al.* (1991), 81 DLR (4th) 545 at 625, per Mr Justice La Forest (in the minority on the issue in which he used international law, namely, whether s.2(d) of the Charter was violated); *Kindler v. A.G. Can.*, [1991] 2 SCR 779 at 804–9, 820–3, per Mr Justice Cory.

The international law reference was essentially irrelevant to the outcome of a dissenting opinion in *Re McKinney and University of Guelph et al.* (1990), 76 DLR (4th) 545 at 581, per Wilson J.

The dissenting opinion in *R. v. Keegstra*, [1990] 3 SCR 697 at 820–2, rejected the relevance of international law.

98 *Corigliano v. Italy*, European Court of Human Rights, Series A, vol. 57, 10 Dec. 1982, at paragraph 34; *Foti v. Italy*, European Court of Human Rights, Series A, vol. 56, 10 Dec. 1982, at paragraph 52; *Eckle v. Federal Republic of Germany*, European Court of Human Rights, Series A, vol. 51, 15 July 1982, at paragraph 73; *Deweer v. Belgium*, European Court of Human Rights, Series A, vol. 35, 27 Feb. 1980, at paragraph 46.

In marked contrast, *R. v. Kalanj*, *supra*, note 97, held that pre-information delay was not relevant to determining whether a person had been tried within a reasonable time, despite the fact that some eight months earlier the accused had been arrested (and released), told that charges would be laid, and prohibited from leaving the area. The European Court of Human Rights would have considered the clock to start at the point where the situation of the accused had clearly been substantially affected.

99 Summary Record of the Forty-Eighth Meeting, 22 Jan. 1985, CEDAW/C/SR.48, at 2, 3 per Mr Sullivan.

100 Summary record of the Eighth Meeting, 15 Feb. 1989, E/C.12/1989/SR.8, at 5. "Frequently" is somewhat of an exaggeration considering that there had been fewer than ten references to the International Covenant on Economic, Social and Cultural Rights of approximately 150 cases which had, by that time, referred in some way to international human rights law.

101 *Supra*, note 100, at 6, per Mr Alston. (The rights in ILO Convention 87 are specifically affirmed by the provision on trade union rights in the International Covenant on Economic, Social and Cultural Rights.)

102 Summary Record of the Eleventh Meeting, 17 March 1989, E/C.12/1989/SR.11, at 12, per Martin Low.

103 *Collin v. Kaplin* (1982), 1 CCC (3d) 309 at 310 (FCTD); *International Fund for Animal Welfare Inc., Best & Davies v. Minister of Fisheries and Oceans* (1988), 83 NR 303 at 312 (FCTD); *R. v. Thomas McC., Michael L. and Jason H.* (1991), 4 OR (3d) 203 at 219 (Ont. Ct. Prov. Div.).

104 *Re Boyd and Earl & Jennie Lohn Ltd.* (1984), 47 OR (2d) 111 (Ont. HC) at 113. *Parsons v. Styger* (1989), 67 OR 1 (Ont. SC) at 10.

105 *The Queen v. Operation Dismantle* (1983), 3 DLR (4th) 193 (FCA) Appeal, *supra*, note 32; *Dolphin Delivery Ltd. v. Retail, Wholesale and Department Store Union, Local 580 et al.* (1984), 52 BCLR 1 at 13 (BCCA) Appeal; *Re Regina and Carter* (1984), 8 DLR (4th) 156, per Nemetz, CJBC (BCCA).

106 *Borowski v. A.G. Can.* (1987), 39 DLR (4th) 731 (Sask. CA) at 746–7. Appeal dismissed at [1989] 1 SCR 342.

107 *R. v. Robinson & A.G. Can.* (1989), 73 CR (3d) 81 at 110 (Alb. CA).

108 *Re Taylor et al. and Canadian Human Rights Commission* (1987), 37 DLR (4th) 577 at 587–8 (FCA). Note that, in contrast, the Study on the Implementation of Article 4 was appended to a decision of the Ontario Court of Appeal, *R. v. Andrews et al.* (1988), 43 CCC (3d) 193 at 226 (Ont. CA), which used the article to support its conclusion that the same section of the Criminal Code did not violate the Charter.
109 *Rahey v. The Queen*, supra, note 97 at 513 DLR and at 633 SCR; *R. v. Conway*, supra, note 97 at 1709 SCR and at 250 CR. The *Wemhoff* decision is from 1968 and the European Court has had occasion to deal with the subject of when the time period ends (with respect to the right to be tried within a reasonable time) on many subsequent occasions. Reference to more up-to-date material would be more appropriate. See, for example, *Eckle v. Federal Republic of Germany*, supra, note 98 at paragraph 76; *Corigliano v. Italy*, supra, note 98 at paragraph 36.
110 *Supra*, note 97 at 469 DLR and at 143 SCR.
111 (1990), 91 CLLC 17,004.
112 *Supra*, at 16,083, 16,085.
113 Report of the World Assembly on Aging, Vienna, 26 July–6 Aug. 1982, United Nations, UN Doc. A/CONF.113/31, see Recommendations For Action, A.2, para. 44, at 59, Recommendation 36, para 73, and Recommendation 37 at 72; GA Res. 37/51 (1982).
114 [1991] SCJ No. 63.
115 *Supra*, at 52–3, 72.

Free Trade in Criminals: Canadian-American Extradition before 1890

DALE GIBSON

"I shall be glad to see the day when 'free trade' in criminals shall exist."[1]

The following account of early extradition arrangements between Canada and the United States is offered as a token of the author's profound respect for Maxwell Cohen's splendid contributions to amity along the forty-ninth parallel. Professor Cohen's career has straddled many boundaries, geographic as well as intellectual. His work with the International Joint Commission reflected only one aspect – albeit an extremely important one – of his interest in transboundary problems. His first scholarly article, published in 1936, concerned an individual's unsuccessful attempt to resist expulsion from Canada in a deportation proceeding – a situation not unlike that of the extraditees discussed herein. Both that article and three which followed it on the origins and modern law of habeas corpus (the favourite legal tool of extraditees) exhibited Cohen's deep concern for freedom of the person. Much of his subsequent work related to processes for resolving what he once called "undeadly quarrels" in the international arena. This piece examines the evolution of such processes in extradition disputes that came close, on occasion, to being deadly.

INTRODUCTION: EXTRADITION AND THREATS OF WAR

Winter solstice, 1864: the icy core of another northern winter, and one of the darkest periods in Canadian history. The grand new scheme for Confederation of the British North American colonies was snowbound, or worse, in the Atlantic colonies, and the possibility of invasion from south of the undefended forty-ninth parallel by the world's most powerful army was on the minds of many Canadians.

The Reciprocity Treaty with the United States, which had assured freedom of north-south commerce since 1854, was about to expire with no prospect of renewal. More disturbing still, the U.S. secretary of state had recently given Great Britain notice of American intention to terminate in six months' time the Rush-Bagot Treaty of 1817, which had until then ensured that the border between the United States and British North America remained virtually unarmed. The United States Senate had approved the secretary of state's notice, and had at the same time passed a bill calling for an increase in the number of armed patrol vessels on the Great Lakes.

On 17 December the U.S. State Department issued an order requiring all British North Americans entering U.S. territory to carry passports. That was the same day the *Toronto Leader* published the text of a chilling order made by General Dix of the United States Army. The American Civil War was in its final throes, and the desperate South had launched a pair of paramilitary incursions against the North from Canadian territory. Dix had responded by calling on his troops to follow fugitives into British territory if necessary, and not to allow them to be dealt with by British authorities. The normally restrained *New York Times* had expressed a sentiment shared by many Americans when it declared: "We were never in better condition for a war with England."[2]

While the factors leading up to this precarious state of affairs were complex, they had been brought to a head in December 1864 by the decision of a Montreal magistrate to release a group of southern raiders, rather than hold them for extradition. What is especially intriguing for legal historians about that provocative decision is that while it was politically explosive it was legally correct. The fact that higher judicial authorities subsequently helped to disarm the situation with a ruling that was more politically acceptable, but was legally questionable, reveals much about the law of extradition at the time, and perhaps about the legal process generally.

The threat of war was by no means the only factor contributing confusion to nineteenth-century extradition law. To place the cases concerning the Confederate Civil War raids in perspective, it will be necessary to examine Canadian-American extradition experience both before and after the Civil War period.

EARLY ARRANGEMENTS: EXECUTIVE EXTRADITION

Although France led the world in the number of extradition treaties entered into in the eighteenth and early nineteenth centuries,[3] it was in the United States that extradition law and procedure were most thoroughly developed in the early years.[4] The large number of states, each a distinct legal jurisdiction, which made up that country, and the need for an effective process (usually referred to as "rendition") for returning fugitive criminals to the jurisdictions from which they escaped were the reasons behind this development. Because Canada shared an extremely long and easily traversed boundary with the United States, fugitives from justice, both north and south of the boundary, were often tempted to seek refuge on the other side. This fact, together with the exposure of Canadians to American legal ideas, resulted in an earlier and more sophisticated development of extradition law in pre-Confederation Canada than in the mother country or any other British territory.

The early evolution of Canadian extradition law was marked by four interrelated themes: Canada's ever-present anxiety about the reaction that unsatisfactory decisions might produce south of the border; the complications caused by trying to apply normal extradition principles to fugitive slaves brought to Canada from the southern states; Britain's relative lack of interest in Canadian-American extradition unless the issue of slavery was involved; and the constant efforts of Canadian authorities to find a comfortable way to mesh the legal and political components of the process.

This last factor involved especially complex considerations. Politicians and bureaucrats normally tended to favour easy extradition, and to be impatient of legal impediments to swift rendition. Their motives were obvious: to keep the Americans happy, to prevent Canadian criminals eluding justice, and to ensure that Canada would not become a haven for American outlaws. They had also to remain responsive to the opinions of their electorates, however, and there were times when public opinion was strongly opposed to the surrender of particular fugitives, especially in the case of escaped slaves who found their way to Canada from the southern states by means of the increasingly active "underground railway." In those circumstances it was sometimes expedient for the politicians to defer, or appear to defer, to the judiciary. Some judges resented having what they considered to be primarily political questions thrust upon them for decision. Other judges seemed to welcome the opportunity.

The earliest treaty basis for extradition between the United States and British territories was Article 27 of Jay's Treaty, 1794:

Article XXVII. It is further agreed that His Majesty and the United States, on mutual requisitions, by them respectively, or by their respective Ministers or officers authorized to make the same, will deliver up to justice all persons who, being charged with murder or forgery, committed within the jurisdiction of either, shall seek an asylum within any of the countries of the other, provided that this shall only be done on such evidence of criminality as, according to the laws of the place where the fugitive or person so charged shall be found, would justify his apprehension and commitment for trial, if the offence had there been committed. The expense of such apprehension and delivery shall be borne and defrayed by those who make the requisition and receive the fugitive.[5]

The rudimentary and, essentially political, nature of the process contemplated by Article 27 is noteworthy; while "evidence of criminality" was required, it was apparently only executive officers, not judges, who had to be satisfied on that score. There is little indication that this provision was ever much relied upon. Although it was invoked in at least one notorious case,[6] a study of extradition carried out by the Harvard Law School and published in the *American Journal of International Law* in 1935, claimed that "this treaty was never an effective instrument of extradition."[7] In any event, Article 27 expired in 1807, and no treaty replaced it for thirty-five years.

The reason for this hiatus was that first the Americans and then the British found the subject of extradition to be political dynamite. The problems began with the surrender of a man called Robbins to the Canadian authorities by President John Adams in accordance with the terms of Jay's Treaty. This surrender created a political storm in the United States that was thought by some to have contributed to the defeat of the Adams administration.[8] The War of 1812 then intervened, and politicians on both sides were understandably chary about the subject for the next decade or so. By the time sporadic negotiations concerning a possible new extradition treaty finally got under way, the issue of returning fugitive slaves, upon which intense public opinion had become focused in both countries, proved to be an insuperable barrier to British agreement.[9]

The absence of an extradition treaty did not entirely prevent extradition between the United States and the British-American colonies, however. Judicial opinion was expressed on both sides of the border that the executive arm of government had the inherent power to expel fugitives without the authorization of treaty or statute. In the United States, no less illustrious a jurist than Chancellor Kent stated, in the 1819 case of *Re Washburn*: "It is the law and usage of nations, resting on the plainest principles of justice and public utility, to deliver up offenders charged with felony and other high crimes, and fleeing from the country in which the crime was committed into a foreign and friendly jurisdiction."[10] He went on to state that after the expiry of Jay's Treaty, which he conceded might have restricted that general power to the offences covered by the treaty, "the general and more extensive rule of the law of nations prevailed."

The *Washburn* case involved an attempted extradition to Canada which Kent did not allow to proceed. Having ruled that the power to extradite in appropriate circumstances existed independently of treaty or statute, he concluded that there was insufficient evidence of the alleged offence – larceny – to justify extradition in that case, and he granted the prisoner habeas corpus. Eight years later, however, a Lower Canadian judge adopted and acted upon the Kent dictum. In *Re Fisher*,[11] the extradition to Vermont of a man charged there with larceny was ordered. In rejecting Fisher's application for release on habeas corpus, Reid CJ approved Kent's remarks in *Re Washburn*, and added some trenchant observations of his own:

This right of surrender is founded on the principle, that he who has caused an injury is bound to repair it, and he who has infringed the laws of any country is liable to the punishment inflicted by those laws; if we screen him from that punishment, we become parties to his crime – we excite retaliation – we encourage criminals to take refuge among us. We do that as a *nation*, which as *individuals* it would be dishonorable, nay, criminal to do. If, on the contrary, we deliver up the accused to the offended nation, we only fulfil our part of the social compact, which directs that the rights of nations as well as of individuals should be respected, and a good understanding maintained between them; and this is the more requisite among neighboring states, on account of the daily communications which must necessarily subsist between them.

While the views of Chancellor Kent and Chief Justice Reid may have had much to commend them as political policies, they were highly questionable as statements of law. An eminent authority on American extradition law pointed out that the Kent position was contrary to almost all other judicial, academic, and professional opinion of the time, and concluded that extradition without treaty or legislative support was unlawful.[12] In Canada, which was subject to the British position that even treaties require legislative implementation to affect internal law, the absence of statutory authority should have been decisive.[13] It appears that executive extradition was recognized as being unlawful against subjects, and valid only with respect to persons alien to the country of refuge.[14] Fisher was a Prussian. Even that distinction was dubious, however, since English law, which governed Canadian courts, extended rights such as habeas corpus to friendly aliens as well as to subjects.[15]

The unlawfulness of executive extradition was eventually acknowledged in 1833, when the governor of Canada, Lord Aylmer, was requested to surrender to American authorities four men accused of murdering ("barbarously," in the words of one writer[16]) a woman in Champlain, New York, but refused: "It is not competent to the Executive, in the absence of any regulation by treaty or legislative enactment on the subject, to dispense with the provision in the *habeas corpus* Act."[17] If Chief Justice Reid, the Canadian judge who decided *Re Fisher*, had paid greater heed to expediency than to law, Lord Aylmer, a British politician, was willing to give law a higher priority. The paradox was indicative of a confusion between the legal and political roles that was evident for the rest of the period under review. It also illustrated the gulf that often separated Canadian and British attitudes towards extradition.

1833 CANADIAN LEGISLATION

Canadian politicians recognized the need for a Canadian-American extradition process, and they moved swiftly after Lord Aylmer's refusal to replace executive extradition with a statutory scheme. Although it was far from certain that a colonial legislature had jurisdiction over the subject, external affairs being the responsibility of the imperial government, the Canadian legislature enacted, in February 1833, An Act to Provide for the Apprehending of Fugitive Offenders from Foreign Countries and Delivering Them Up to Justice.[18] The key provisions of that enactment read as follows:

the Governor, Lieutenant Governor, or Person Administering the Government of this Province, shall have power, and he is hereby authorized at his discretion, and by and with the advice of the Executive Council, on requisition being made by the Government of any Country, or its Ministers or Officers, authorized to make the same, within the jurisdiction of which Country the crimes hereinafter mentioned shall be charged to have been committed, to deliver up to Justice any person who may have fled to this Province, or who shall seek refuge therein, being charged with Murder, Forgery, Larceny or other crime, committed without the jurisdiction of this Province, which crimes if committed within this Province would by the Laws thereof be punishable by death, corporal punishment, by Pillory, or Whipping, or by confinement at hard labour, to the end that such person may be transported out of this Province to the place where such crime shall have been charged to have been committed; *Provided always*, that this shall only be done upon such evidence of criminality as, according to the Laws of this Province, would, in the opinion of the Governor, Lieutenant Governor, or Person Administering the Government, and of the Executive Council, warrant the apprehension and commitment for trial of such fugitive from Justice, or person so charged, if the offence had been committed within this Province.

And be it further enacted by the authority aforesaid, That for preventing the escape of any person so charged, before any order for his apprehension can be obtained from the Governor, Lieutenant Governor, or Person Administering the Government of this Province, it shall be lawful for any Judge, or for any Justice of the peace in this Province, acting within his jurisdiction, to issue his Warrant for the apprenhension, and for the commitment of any such person charged as aforesaid, in order that he may; be detained in secure custody until application can be made to the Governor, Lieutenant Governor, or Person Administering the Government, under the provisions of this Act, and until an order can be made thereon; which Warrant shall nevertheless only be granted upon such evidence on oath as shall satisfy such Judge or Justice that the person accused stands charged with some crime of the description hereinbefore specified, or that there is good ground to suspect him to have been guilty thereof.

This was a considerably more sophisticated measure than the Jay Treaty extradition article had been. It extended beyond murder and forgery to include "larceny or other crime" for which punishment by at least imprisonment with hard labour was appropriate. And although the final decision to extradite remained a political one, requiring involvement of the governor, lieutenant-governor or administrator, and the Executive Council, the courts were now empowered to order the fugitive held pending that decision. The latter power could be exercised upon evidence that the fugitive had been charged in the home jurisdiction, or even where there was "good ground to suspect him to have been guilty."

It is not clear how much use was made of this Canadian legislation, but it probably functioned effectively until 1842. Sir Edward Clarke stated that "only one question of difficulty seems to have arisen under this Act."[19] That case, which involved a fugitive slave named Gallagher, may have been one of the factors leading to the renewal of treaty-based extradition between the United States and Britain. The primary impetus for treaty negotiations seems, however, to have been the case of *The Creole*, in which British authorities denied, in the absence of treaty or statute, an American request for the extradition of several African slaves, bound from England to the United States, who had seized a ship, murdered a passenger, and sailed to the British Bahamas.[20]

In the *Gallagher* case,[21] an escaping slave was alleged to have stolen a horse in New York to assist his flight to freedom in Canada. American authorities, knowing that running away from slavery would not be accepted as an extraditable offence in Canada, sought his return on larceny charges instead. Governor Sir Charles Bagot refused the request, but there are differing versions of his reasons for doing so. La Forest suggests that he did so on instructions of the British government, which "doubted the validity" of the Canadian extradition legislation.[22] The American author J.B. Moore, upon whom La Forest relied, stated that "doubts arose on the part of the Imperial government as to whether the power of extradition could properly be exercised by the colonial authorities" without sanction from Westminster, and that the governor "had received instructions from the Imperial Government not to surrender fugitives without special permission."[23] This explanation was based on a letter from the secretary of state to the president. However, Moore also referred to a statement made about the matter in the British House of Commons on 19 July 1842 by Colonial Secretary Lord Stanley, a statement that indicated no doubt in Lord Stanley's mind about the validity of the Canadian legislation, which he appeared to consider operative (while demonstrating some ignorance as to its precise terms).[24] This explanation lends credence to the rival account of Sir Edward Clarke, who claimed that the governor had simply been instructed by English Attorney-General Sir John Campbell to deny extradition in the particular case for the reason that "the essential ingredient of the felony, the *animus furandi*, was wanting," presumably because Gallagher had turned back the horse before crossing into Canada.[25] This confusion may not be altogether attributable to the academics; it is not unlikely that politicians, playing a very sensitive game, offered different reasons to different audiences at different times.

Whatever the basis for the *Gallagher* decision, and whatever its effect on the British-American extradition negotiations that were then under way, the 1833 statute under which the extradition request was made in that case was soon supplanted by a new treaty and consequent legislation. The last had not been heard of the 1833 act, however.

ASHBURTON-WEBSTER TREATY, 1842

Desultory negotiations on the subject of extradition had been under way since 1824.[26] The obstacle to agreement was always the question of runaway slaves. The American government, under pressure from the southern states, was primarily interested in establishing a process for the return of persons they termed "fugitives from labour." The British negotiators let it be known privately that while their government was not itself opposed to the rendition of slaves, antipathy to slavery among the British populace was so strong that it would be politically impossible to reach an agreement on that subject. British authorities, prodded no doubt by the Canadians, were at least mildly interested in the extradition of criminals other than slaves, but they clearly did not consider the topic to be one of great urgency.

Finally, however, in 1842, in the afterglow of the *Creole* and *Gallagher* controversies, the lengthy negotiations finally bore fruit. The Ashburton-Webster Treaty of that year, which settled a number of outstanding disagreements between the United States and Great Britain, included a provision, Article x, on the subject of extradition:

It is agreed that Her Britannic Majesty and the United States shall, upon mutual requisitions by them or their Ministers, Officers, or Authorities, respectively made, deliver up to justice all persons who, being charged with the crime of murder, or assault with intent to commit murder, or piracy, or arson, or robbery, or forgery, or the utterance of forged paper, committed within the jurisdiction of either, shall seek an asylum, or shall be found within the territories of the other; provided that this shall only be done upon such evidence of criminality as, according to the laws of the place where the fugitive or person so charged shall be found, would justify his apprehension and commitment for trial if the crime or offence had there been committed; and the respective Judges and other Magistrates of the two Governments shall have power, jurisdiction, and authority, upon complaint made under oath, to issue a warrant for the apprehension of the fugitive or persons so charged, that he may be brought before such Judges or other Magistrates, respectively, to the end that evidence of criminality may be heard and considered; and if, on such hearing, the evidence be deemed sufficient to sustain the charge, it shall be the duty of the examining Judge or Magistrate to certify the same to the proper executive authority, that a warrant may issue for the surrender of such fugitive. The expense of such apprehension and delivery shall be borne and defrayed by the party who makes the requisition and receives the fugitive.[27]

This measure differed from the Canadian statute of 1833 in several respects. The range of crimes covered (murder, assault with intent to murder, piracy, arson, robbery, forgery, and uttering) was narrower. The exclusion of larceny was significant, because it was the charge upon which return of the escaped slave Gallagher had been sought. The judiciary was given a larger role to play than previously, being called upon to determine whether there was sufficient evidence to sustain the charge against the alleged fugitive. The treaty did not, however, sanction committal on the basis of "good grounds to suspect" the person's guilt, without proof of a charge having been laid, which the Canadian statute had permitted.

BRITISH IMPLEMENTING STATUTE, 1843

To implement this treaty, the British Parliament in 1843 enacted a statute setting out the procedures to be followed when a request for extradition was made.[28] This legislation was found inconvenient to apply in Canada, however, because the cumbersomeness of its procedures afforded fugitives ample opportunity to escape. Fortunately, it contemplated that colonial legislatures might prefer to enact alternate implementing procedures, and it provided for the suspension of its own provisions during the currency of any colonial statute that the Queen-in-Council (the British cabinet, in effect) found to be a suitable substitute.[29] The Canadian legislature decided to take advantage of this option by enacting, in 1849, extradition legislation that it considered to be more satisfactory than the imperial statute.[30] The Queen-in-Council approved the Canadian statute in January 1850 and suspended the imperial legislation for the duration of its operation.[31]

CANADIAN IMPLEMENTING STATUTE, 1849

The salient features of the 1849 Canadian enactment were:

- Any superior court judge or justice of the peace could, upon receipt of a sworn or solemnly affirmed complaint that a person was guilty of an extraditable crime in the United States, issue a warrant for the apprehension of that person.[32]
- The judge or justice must then consider "the evidence of criminality," and if "the evidence be deemed sufficient ... to sustain the charge according to the laws of this Province" it "shall be the duty"

of the judge or justice to commit the person to prison and to transmit the decision and a copy of the evidence to the governor or lieutenant-governor.[33]
- The governor or lieutenant-governor was then empowered, upon receipt of a requisition for extradition from appropriate authorities of "the United States or of any such States," to issue a warrant to deliver the person to those authorities.[34]
- If the governor or lieutenant-governor failed to do so within two months, the person could be released by a superior court upon a writ of habeas corpus.[35]

THE JOHN ANDERSON CASE

These procedures remained in effect for more than a decade and appeared to serve tolerably well. They were still in force when an internationally notorious attempt to extradite John Anderson, a fugitive slave from Missouri who had settled in Canada West, exploded under the government of Canada in 1860.[36] During his flight to freedom north of the forty-ninth parallel, Anderson had killed a man who was attempting to capture him. There was evidence that Anderson might have exerted more force than was reasonably necessary to effect his escape. In any event, he had certainly used violence to resist an arrest that was lawful in the state where the incident occurred. When he was finally apprehended in Canada, after several years' peaceful residence there, the justice of the peace before whom he was examined concluded that even though slavery was not lawful in Canada, Anderson's acts constituted murder by Canadian law. He was accordingly detained for extradition.

As knowledge of the committal spread, it became clear that Canadian public opinion was strongly opposed to sending Anderson back to almost certain death in Missouri. Attorney-General John A. Macdonald, never anxious to offend public opinion, delayed requesting the governor to extradite Anderson until a higher court could reconsider the matter in a habeas corpus hearing. Three judges of the Court of Queen's Bench, headed by Chief Justice Sir John Beverley Robinson, convened such a hearing, but they too, by a majority of two to one (McLean J dissenting), found Anderson to be extraditable under both the treaty and the statute.

At this point a British anti-slavery organization intervened. It persuaded the English Court of Queen's Bench to issue a writ of habeas corpus requiring Anderson to be brought before that court to have the validity of his detention re-examined. This development produced consternation in many Canadian quarters, since even if

English courts were legally capable of exercising such priority over their Canadian counterparts, which many lawyers considered a doubtful proposition,[37] it was highly offensive to the authorities of a colony as mature as Canada that they should do so. Fortunately for Anglo-Canadian relations, a showdown was avoided. This was accomplished by a habeas corpus application being made to a second Canadian tribunal: the Court of Common Pleas, before the English writ could be acted upon. While the Common Pleas judges declined to differ from their Queen's Bench brethren on the merits of the substantive law involved, they found a technical error in the drafting of the original warrant of committal, and held that the error justified Anderson's immediate release. Rather than charging Anderson with the extraditable offence of "murder," the warrant had referred only to "wilfully, maliciously and feloniously killing" the man in question. Since such "killing" did not necessarily constitute "murder" in the judges' opinion, and the treaty did not apply to killing other than murder, the warrant was held to be fatally defective.[38]

While it would have been possible to rearrest Anderson on a new, more carefully drafted warrant, that never occurred. This may have been because of the care with which he was subsequently protected by sympathizers in Canada and the United Kingdom, to which he soon travelled; or because American attention was by now diverted by the more momentous events of the war between the states.

1861 AMENDMENTS

Canada's extradition statute was amended in 1861.[39] This was no doubt due, at least in part, to the *Anderson case*. The amendment most readily attributable to *Anderson* removed the possibility of an extradition request coming from a state government, as had occurred in *Anderson*, and required the involvement of federal authorities instead.[40] Although the types of judges who might commit for extradition were extended to include members of the Upper Canada County Court, city recorders, and police or stipendiary magistrates, jurisdiction was removed from justices of the peace (with the exception of certain Lower Canadian police officials).[41] This might also have stemmed from concern about the apparently biased manner in which the *Anderson* case had been handled by the committing JP.[42]

A major amendment was made concerning the authority of the judge or magistrate. Whereas the 1849 legislation had stipulated that "it shall be the duty" of that officer to issue a committal warrant if a case for extradition were made out, the 1861 version stated only that "it shall be lawful" to do so, thus converting a duty to a discretion.[43] This too, was probably a product of the discomfiture experienced by Macdonald and the Canadian government during the *Anderson* controversy. The 1849 act had offered no loophole by which a politically sensitive extradition could be avoided by either the courts or the government. If legal grounds for extradition were established, the examining judge or justice was obliged to commit, the governor had no express power to release the prisoner, and judges of the superior courts could release on habeas corpus only if the detention were shown to be unlawful. Macdonald would not have wanted a direct governmental discretion to release such prisoners, because that would have involved a violation of the Ashburton-Webster Treaty, and would, in any event, have left the decision up to imperial authorities, since the Canadian government had no direct authority over international matters. If the courts were given a discretion as to committal, however, there would be room for behind-the-scenes nudging by Macdonald and his colleagues, without involving the imperial government, and without overtly violating the treaty. Hence the insertion of judicial discretion. It would not be long, however, before John A. Macdonald would have cause to reconsider his faith in judicial wisdom.

An important amendment that does not seem to have been connected to the *Anderson* case clarified the standard of proof required to establish a case for extradition. The 1849 statute had required that "the evidence of criminality ... be heard and considered," and had obliged the judge or justice to commit for extradition "if, on such hearing, the evidence be deemed sufficient by him to sustain the charge according to the laws of this province."[44] A judge or justice could be excused for interpreting this as requiring a decision to be made as to the prisoner's innocence or guilt on the basis of the normal criminal law standard of proof. That was not what the treaty called for. Although it too referred to "evidence ... sufficient ... to sustain the charge," the treaty required only "such evidence of criminality as, according to the laws of the place where the fugitive ... shall be found, would justify his apprehension and *commitment for trial*."[45] Section 1 of the 1861 act was brought into closer alignment with the treaty, making it clearer that the party seeking extradition need only present evidence sufficient to commit for trial, not to convict.[46]

TEMPORARY DISTRACTION

American reaction to Canada's failure to extradite John Anderson was ultimately drowned out by Civil War cannons. This does not mean that American responses, actual and anticipated, were unimportant. There was much interest displayed in the United States when the *Anderson* case first came before the Canadian Court of Queen's Bench, just before the war. With the northern and southern states so sharply split over slavery, and those differences having brought the two parts of the country to the brink of hostilities, it was not surprising that American opinion whether Canada should surrender Anderson had divided largely on north/south lines. Interestingly, though, even much northern opinion acknowledged that the treaty obliged Canadian authorities to order extradition.[47] In late November 1860 the *New York Times* had taken note of Canada's dilemma, and had reported to its readers that Attorney-General Macdonald viewed the situation as one that could, if handled badly, become "a *casus belli* between the two countries."[48]

The Civil War had begun by the time the English Court of Queen's Bench issued its writ of habeas corpus in the *Anderson* case in January 1861, but even then many American newspapers found the space to note the development and, in both north and south, to deplore it.[49] Macdonald's already difficult position had been complicated by this threat to ripening Canadian autonomy. His strategy of delay, entirely characteristic of "Old Tomorrow," had eventually paid off, however. The Court of Common Pleas' ruling that Anderson's warrant was procedurally invalid had come at a time when Americans were completely distracted by the war. Its effect, moreover, was unlikely to offend the anti-slavery forces that ultimately won the war.

Macdonald knew that the respite would be brief. He feared that the United States might treat some perceived snub like the *Anderson* case as an excuse to fulfil its territorial ambitions in British North America. And those ambitions were not difficult to divine; American Secretary of State William Seward would soon announce his view that it was his country's "manifest destiny" to expand westward and northward.[50] For the moment, the Americans were too preoccupied to do anything about that long-range ambition, and Canada had avoided harmful consequences from the *Anderson* challenge. But more perilous extradition adventures lay in store.

By the autumn of 1864 the war was not going well for the South. Confederate forces were driven to desperate measures, which included two daring incursions against the North from Canadian territory: the first a hilarious failure; the other a brilliant success. These raids would subject extradition arrangements, and Canadian-American relations generally, to great stress.

THE BURLEY CASE

The first episode involved piracy on Lake Erie.[51] A Confederate officer named Bennett Burley, dressed in civilian garb, boarded the passenger boat *Philo Parsons* in Detroit on 18 September 1864 and requested that it stop at Sandwich and Amherstburg, on the Canadian side, where a number of his comrades, also posing as civilian passengers, came on board carrying a trunk filled with arms. After the ship was well out on Lake Erie, the soldiers disclosed their identity and took control of the vessel at gunpoint.

Their mission was daring in the extreme: to free a number of southern comrades-in-arms who were being held at a prisoner-of-war camp maintained by the Union army on Johnson's Island in Lake Erie. What transformed the scheme from audacious to ludicrous was the fact that the island was guarded by a large gunboat, which the Confederates planned to disarm by a comic-opera gambit. One of the raiders, disguised as a generous businessman, was to host a champagne dinner for the crew of the gunboat. During the dinner the bogus businessman would administer a drug to everyone and, when the crew was safely insensate, he would signal the *Philo Parsons* pirates that the way was clear to board and seize the gunboat. The Confederate prisoners would then be released, and the commandeered naval vessel would be used to bombard Buffalo and other northern settlements.

The first part of the venture went smoothly enough. After taking over the *Philo Parsons*, the pirates locked the male passengers in the hold, put the female passengers and two crew members ashore on a remote island, and took a quantity of wood from the island as fuel. When a steamer carrying unarmed Union soldiers was encountered at the island, it was seized and scuttled. The *Philo Parsons* then steamed to a position where the all-clear signal from the bogus dinner host aboard the gunboat could be observed. The signal never came. The host had been exposed as a spy, allegedly by a woman to whom he had indiscreetly disclosed his mission after imbibing a little too much of his own champagne before dinner.

When they realized that something had gone awry, the pirates steamed back towards Canadian waters at top speed, defiantly flying the Confederate flag. Passengers and pirates were put ashore (some of the latter appropriating property they found on board) before the vessel was scuttled in the Detroit River off Windsor. Although most members of the expedition escaped, the leader, John Yates Beall, was captured in New York, convicted of sabotage and treason, and executed. Bennett Burley, who had been second-in-command of the pirate operation, was arrested at Guelph, after evading American authorities. He was charged with robbery of property taken from the *Philo Parsons* and was committed for extradition at a hearing before the recorder of Toronto.

Burley then sought a habeas corpus hearing before Chief Justice William Draper of the Upper Canada Court of Queen's Bench.[52] Although fully empowered to decide the matter by himself, Draper requested, because of "the nature of the questions to be determined,"[53] that three colleagues sit with him: Justices Hagarty and Wilson of his own court, and Chief Justice Richards of the Court of Common Pleas. It was not unprecedented for superior courts to sit *en banc* in matters of this kind; in the *Anderson* case, for example, both Canadian superior courts had sat with three judges, and the English Queen's Bench[54] had sat with four. The multiplicity of judges indicated, nevertheless, that the case was considered sensitive, and the highly unusual step of seeking a representative from another court as well probably betrayed an understandable nervousness on Draper's part that the decision could have serious implications for Canada's future relations with the United States.

At least three of the legal questions raised by Burley's counsel were of considerable importance. The answers, given by the four judges, separately expressed but unanimous in substance, were everything a government worried about American reaction would have wanted, and resulted in Burley's extradition:

- Could a British subject, as Glasgow-born Burley was, be extradited from British territory? The judges answered affirmatively, pointing out that neither the treaty nor the statute made any reference to the nationality of fugitives from justice.
- Was extradition possible without a charge having first been laid against the fugitive in the United States, and a request for extradition having been made by American authorities? The judges held that it was. While both the treaty and the statute required that a charge be laid, there was no need for it to be laid in the United States; and while an official American requisition for extradition was also necessary, it did not have to be made before committal for extradition. The fact that neither a formal charge in the United States,[55] nor even an extradition request, had preceded Burley's committal by the Toronto recorder was accordingly of no avail to him.
- Could activities like those of the *Philo Parsons* pirates be considered lawful acts of war, which are immune from extradition? This was Burley's principal defence, and it was a plausible one. In order to ensure the neutrality of countries dealing with belligerent nations, acts of war are not treated as extraditable offences. This defence failed also, however. The prosecution had been careful to charge Burley with only the least "military" of his acts: robbing the owner

of the *Philo Parsons* at gunpoint of a quantity of money. The judges pointed to the possibility, in the light of this and other appropriations of property by the pirates, that "the alleged belligerent enterprise was ... put forward as a pretext to cloak very different designs,"[56] "an expedition for the purposes of plunder."[57]

While the first two rulings are difficult to fault, the judges' rejection of the "belligerent act" defence was questionable. Draper's reasoning was typical of the approach taken by all the judges:

The prisoner ... was a leader in an expedition embarked surreptitiously from a neutral territory ... into the territory of the United States. Thus assuming their intentions to have been what was professed, they deprived the expedition of the character of lawful hostility, and the very commencement and embarkation of their enterprise was a violation of neutral territory and contrary to the letter and spirit of the manifesto produced.[58]

This gives greater reason for carefully enquiring whether, looking at the whole case, the alleged belligerent enterprise was not put forward as a pretext to cloak very different designs.

Taken by themselves, the acts of the prisoner himself clearly establish a prima facie case of robbery with violence – at least according to our law. The matter[s] alleged to deprive the prisoner's acts of this criminal character are necessarily to be set up by way of defence to the charge ... Assuming some act done within our jurisdiction which, unexplained, would amount to robbery – if explanations were offered, and evidence to support them were given at a preliminary investigation, the accused could not be discharged – the case must be submitted to a jury. The case cannot, from its very nature, be investigated before our tribunals, for the act was committed within the jurisdiction of the United States. Whether those facts necessary to rebut the prima facie case can be proved can only be determined by the courts of that country. We are bound to assume that they will try and decide it justly.[59]

Nonsequiturs and improbabilities abound in this key passage. Assuming that it was a violation of British neutrality to board an American ship in Canada peacefully, but carrying clandestine arms for intended warlike use in American waters, how could that render the ensuing events anything other than belligerent acts? Given that President Davis's manifesto endorsing Burley's conduct was signed after Burley was in custody (and presumably with full knowledge of the acts involved, since newspaper coverage of the event was widespread), how could the inclusion of a pious passing reference to neutrality be reasonably construed as a negation of the Confederate government's complete and unequivocal acceptance of responsibility for the raid? And could the judges genuinely have believed that the whole outrageously elaborate scheme was merely aimed at stealing a small quantity of money from the captain?

The oddest aspect of the ruling was the assertion that a jury would be required to determine these questions,[60] and that only the home jurisdiction could provide such a jury. The "belligerent acts" defence is a basis for refusing extradition. If the factual basis for the defence could only be established by a jury in the place where the alleged crime occurred, the defence would never be available. Draper and his colleagues held, in effect, that Burley would have to be extradited in order to determine the validity of his extradition.

If logic was lacking from the judges' decision in the *Burley* case, what was the real explanation of their ruling? There is much evidence in the reasons for judgment of indignation about the use made of Canadian territory by the pirates, as well as about the clandestine, unorthodox (and, one senses, unmanly) nature of the operation. Mr Justice Wilson expressed these feelings most vividly: "We can look with no favour on treachery and fraud. We cannot countenance warfare carried on except on the principles of modern civilization. We must not permit, with the sanction of law, our neutral rights to be invaded, our territory made the base of warlike operations."[61] Was there also something else? Wilson began the paragraph in which the foregoing passage occurred with the words: "The attitude of the United States toward us is no concern of ours."[62] Can he and the other judges really have believed they should be unconcerned about the impact a ruling unsatisfactory to Washington would have on the way Canada was regarded by a nation with an undisguised interest in territorial expansion, and an invincible, soon-to-be-unemployed, army? If so, why did Wilson feel the need to raise the issue of American attitudes at all?

THE ST ALBANS RAIDERS

Mr Justice Wilson did so because the topic of American hostility towards Canada was on everyone's lips. As we have seen, the United States was eager to end the Rush-Bagot disarmament treaty, a passport requirement was about to be imposed on Canadian visitors to the United States, and annexationist sentiments were growing rapidly south of the border. A general of the northern army had, as we have noted, recently ordered his troops to cross the border if they found it necessary to do so.[63]

The Lake Erie piracy had been only partially responsible for these stern measures. A more immediate and provocative cause had been an attack launched from Lower Canada by Confederate soldiers against the little Vermont town of St Albans, and the controversial way the matter was treated by a Canadian judge. The raid occurred 19 October 1864, about a month after the Lake Erie fiasco. In contrast to the earlier incursion, it was highly successful.[64]

During the second week of October 1864, some two dozen young men had drifted into St Albans from north of the border, professing to be members of a Montreal fishing and hunting club on an annual outing. They had seemed more interested in the layout of the town than in the surrounding countryside, however. And some of them spoke with southern accents. They were, in fact, Confederate soldiers under the command of Lieutenant Bennett H. Young.

After assembling in St Albans and reconnoitering the town, the raiders carried out their operation with admirable precision. On 19 October Young stepped out onto the porch of his hotel, produced a pistol, and announced to startled passers-by that he was taking possession of St Albans in the name of the Confederate States of America. At this signal squads of Young's men robbed the town's three banks, rounded up potential defenders, and commandeered enough horses to make their escape. As they galloped away, carrying some $200,000 in plunder, the raiders threw bottles of an inflammable substance known as "Greek fire" at buildings in an apparent attempt, fortunately unsuccessful, to torch the town.

A posse of townsmen set off in hot pursuit, and got close enough to the fleeing Confederates at one point to prevent a planned additional bank robbery at the town of Swanton. Young then decided to head directly for the border, and by setting fire to a hay-filled wagon on a covered bridge he and his men were able to cross into Canada just ahead of their pursuers.

The boundary line did not deter the posse members long. They continued the chase in Canada, and eventually caught Young and a few of his men. A British major intervened at that point, persuading the Americans to surrender their prisoners to Canadian authorities. The Canadians, for their part, undertook to apprehend the remaining fugitives, and by 23 October fourteen of the raiders were in custody, and a considerable sum of stolen money had been seized.

The judicial machinery was then set in motion. Canadian governor Monck ordered Montreal magistrate Charles J. Coursol to commence extradition proceedings, which he promptly did. The hearing proceeded slowly, however, and was eventually adjourned until 13 December to permit defence lawyers to obtain documents from the Confederate government certifying that the raiders had in fact been acting on its behalf. In the meantime, northern American impatience was mounting.

When Coursol reconvened the extradition hearing in Montreal on the morning of 13 December, defence counsel presented him, not with the expected evidence of Confederate government authorization for the belligerent actions, but with a challenge to his jurisdiction:

MR. KERR: I wish to bring under your Honour's notice a question affecting your jurisdiction in this case.
THE JUDGE of the Sessions: As Judge of the Sessions?
MR. KERR: As Judge of the Sessions or in any other capacity in which you may sit.[65]

Although counsel for the United States government objected to Coursol hearing the challenge, and proposed that the evidence at least be heard subject to any concerns about jurisdiction, the magistrate said he was obliged to deal with the defence motion immediately:

THE COURT: The objection cannot be disregarded. I am bound to hear the exceptions to my jurisdiction.

This jurisdictional challenge was based on the fact that the Canadian legislation under which the hearing purported to be conducted had repealed the original 1849 Canadian statute implementing the Ashburton-Webster Treaty. It will be recalled that the British implementing statute of 1843 had authorized colonial legislation to be substituted for it, if approved by the Queen-in-Council, and that the Canadian legislature had enacted such a substitute statute in 1849. The British order-in-council approving that statute had stipulated, in accordance with the British Act, that the latter legislation "be suspended so long as the said provincial Act shall be and continue in force, and no longer."[66] The "said provincial Act" was no longer in force, having been replaced and repealed by the 1861 Canadian statute.[67] Although counsel for the United States government contended that the new statute was simply a continuation of the old, that was not the case; it embodied significant alterations. Since the new act had received no imperial approval as a substitute for the 1843 British implementing statute, it was the latter statute, and not the Canadian legislation, that now governed Canadian-American extradition.

The reason Magistrate Coursol lacked jurisdiction to deal with the St Albans raiders was that the British Act required a warrant to be issued by the governor for the apprehension of fugitives. No such warrant had ever been issued, because the Canadian legislation did not require it. Coursol adjourned the hearing for a couple of hours to consider this bombshell. When he returned to the courtroom, an hour later than announced, he ruled in favour of the defence objections and released the prisoners. Although he was ridiculed, reviled, and temporarily suspended from the bench, when news of this decision spread beyond the shocked courtroom, there can be little doubt that Coursol was legally correct. A subsequent investigation of his conduct exonerated him and resulted in his reinstatement on the bench.

But was the ruling *adjudicatively* correct? Was it the decision a wise, competent, and fair judge, who respected the rule of law, would have rendered in the circumstances? That is a much more difficult question, since there is not, even at this relatively late stage in the evolution of Western jurisprudence, a wide consensus, other than at the level of platitude, about the character of the ideal legal judgment. There certainly was widespread disgust on both sides of the international boundary that the St Albans raiders had been released, and that Anglo-American relations had been jeopardized, on a "technicality." Only when "legal technicalities" appear to serve our sense of justice do we approve of their invocation. "Technicalities" tend, in fact, to transmute into "fundamental principles" when they are perceived to nourish justice.

Coursol could certainly have evaded the inconvenient "technicality" if he had chosen to do so. He was not compelled to rule on the jurisdictional challenge instantaneously; he could have adjourned the hearing overnight, or longer, to give himself an opportunity for fuller consideration of the arguments, or to permit the question to be referred to higher judicial authority for determination. To do so would, of course, have given the authorities time to obtain the requisite warrant from the governor, and thus legitimize the proceedings. In the penultimate paragraph of his closely argued and well-written reasons for judgment (too highly polished to have been prepared during the recess, some thought), Coursol acknowledged the possibility of deferring his jurisdictional ruling, but he asserted that it would be wrong to do so: "If I could have reserved the point for the decision of a higher tribunal, I would most willingly, and I may say cheerfully, have done so, but the objection being one formally directed against my jurisdiction, I came to the conclusion that every judge or magistrate, in a case where the liberty of the person is concerned, should be prepared positively, and in a definite manner, to decide whether he has jurisdiction or not.[68] "I am bound in law, justice and fairness," he concluded, "to order the immediate release of the prisoners from custody."[69]

It is difficult to assess or debate the propriety of Coursol's adjudicative response without knowing what was going on in his head at the time. If, as the transcript appears on its face to represent, the judge was presented with an unexpected, but valid, objection to his jurisdiction, and felt obliged by both law and justice to rule on the objection immediately, without regard for political consequences, the case poses the classic problem of whether judges in socially or politically volatile situations should respond instrumentally, or should allow the legal chips to fall where they may. But it is far from certain that Coursol was truly surprised by the challenge to his jurisdiction. There was an intriguing exchange between the judge and defence counsel a month before the prisoners were released, at the hearing in which the adjournment to obtain southern evidence was sought and eventually granted:

At the opening of the Court at two o'clock,

Judge Coursol said: Now that the voluntary examinations have been closed, I desire to add that I in no way recognise this proceeding as regular or legal, and do not wish that it should be considered as a precedent for the other cases. The voluntary examinations were taken because Mr. Johnson, as representing the Crown, in this case requested it; but I entertain serious doubts as to the necessity of it, and would, therefore, wish it to be understood that I give no legal opinion as to whether the voluntary examination of the accused, under the provisions of the Statute to give effect to the Extradition Treaty, is a proper proceeding or not. Then, coming to the point submitted to me before the recess, I have arrived at the conclusion that it is better to allow the accused a reasonable delay for their defence; but, before according that delay, I must be satisfied that a sufficient reason exists for it, and I therefore call upon the counsel for the defence to state whether they have any preliminary objections to urge as to the proceedings in the St. Albans bank case, as the nature of their objections if there are any may very much affect my course of procedure in granting the delay asked for on the part of the defence. The disposal of these preliminary objections seems to me necessary, with the view to save time, and to dispose of those matters as speedily as possible. Those objections may be of such a nature as to dispense with the necessity of any defence whatever, and upon this point I must be satisfied before I grant a delay for a defence upon the merits. It is necessary, in the interests of the public service, for the peace and tranquillity of the country, that these cases should be proceeded with as speedily as possible, having, of course, due regard to the interests of the accused, and I will do all in my power to see that no unnecessary delay shall arise. At the same time, I shall expect the prosecution, whether a delay be granted or not, to proceed with the other cases, or declare they withdraw them; if the counsel for the defence had any preliminary objections to the proceedings in the St. Albans bank case I am prepared to hear them.

Mr. Abbott said that such a question took them very much by surprise, and that he had not yet scrutinised the proceedings for the purpose of ascertaining whether a preliminary objection was available; but that he would be prepared to answer the question if a little time were given.

Judge Coursol said that the delay to be given to the prisoners for preparing their defence would depend greatly upon the nature of the preliminary objections made.

Mr. Abbott said that surely the fact that the prisoners considered the proceedings informal, and objected to them, could not possibly affect the opinions of the Judge as to the length of time that should reasonably be allowed them for their defence.

Judge Coursol said that it might very materially affect that question.

Mr. Kerr said that the counsel for the prisoners would offer no preliminary objection which they did not feel their duty to their clients compelled them to do; and he trusted that the performance of that duty would not expose their clients to have the time shortened, which would otherwise be considered a reasonable time.

Judge Coursol said he should decide, after hearing the objection, what delay would be reasonable.

Mr. Devlin desired to know what the objections were?

Mr. Abbott said that at this moment he could not say whether any objection would be made or not.

Mr. Rose said he thought the objections should be previously signified to the parties in writing.

Mr. Johnson said he had supervised the proceedings on the part of the Crown, and that he was prepared to sustain them without any previous notice.

Judge Coursol said that to require previous notice was very unusual."[70]

The court then adjourned for the day. When it reconvened, defence counsel, who were still obviously puzzled about what the magistrate had in mind, made a rather unconvincing technical objection to the fact that although the warrant identified the Bank of St Albans as the robbery victim, the court had no formal evidence that such a bank existed as a legal person. Coursol rejected this objection peremptorily, and then, after considering affidavit evidence as to the need for a delay to gather evidence to support a defence on the merits, granted the requested adjournment without further reference to the concerns he had alluded to the previous day.

Although he did not identify the possible objection he had in mind, it seems highly likely that Coursol had already noticed the legislative defect that would ultimately cause him to discharge the prisoners. At the reconvened hearing on 13 December, after ordering the prisoners' release and listening to an outraged response by counsel for the United States government, he was reported to have said that he "knew *from the beginning of this case to the present* that those parties had been arrested without any legal warrant," and that he had been convinced, "as soon as the want of jurisdiction became apparent, after a legal test," that he "had not the shadow of a right to detain the prisoners one minute longer."[71]

While the judge's apparent attempts to alert defence counsel to the jurisdictional problem at the earlier hearing had fallen on uncomprehending ears, the raiders' lawyers were certainly well prepared to argue the matter by the time the hearing resumed on 13 December. Had the magistrate whispered in someone's ear in the meantime? If so, it would have been a one-sided communication, since counsel for both the Crown and the American authorities were unquestionably taken by surprise. Had they been aware of the difficulty they would undoubtedly have arranged for a governor's warrant to be issued.

It seems improbable that there was any direct connivance between the magistrate and counsel for the defence. It is much more likely that the latter ran down the legislative defect themselves after being given the scent by the judge's remarks. That would not necessarily acquit the judge of instrumentalist charges, however. Would not an even-handed judge, concerned about what he perceived to be a possible flaw in his jurisdiction, have drawn his concerns to the attention of all counsel, immediately and simultaneously, rather than simply dropping heavily veiled hints?

Courtroom spectators burst into applause when Coursol pronounced the dramatic words, "Let the prisoners be discharged." One cannot help wondering whether the magistrate shared some of their sympathy for the daring Confederate commandos. Perhaps that is being unfair to Coursol. He did make his original Delphic remarks about jurisdiction in open court, after all, and the Crown could have researched the legislation as easily as the defence did during the interval between the hearings. And if Coursol was indeed acting instrumentally in support of the prisoners, his conclusions at least had a sounder legal basis than those reached by the Upper Canadian judges who would extradite the Lake Erie pirates, for obviously instrumentalist reasons, a short while later.

Coursol's reasoning was also more persuasive than that on which the next judge to become involved in the *St Albans* case was to support his initial conclusions. As soon as the raiders were released, prosecution counsel rushed to the chambers of Mr Justice William Smith, from whom they immediately obtained a new warrant for the released men's arrest. On the authority of that warrant several of the raiders, including Bennett Young, were eventually reapprehended. The Crown had still not taken the precaution of obtaining a governor's warrant in accordance with the British Act, perhaps because the Canadian government preferred, for political reasons, to maintain the stance that extradition was an entirely judicial responsibility. This enabled defence counsel to raise the same jurisdictional objections that had succeeded before Coursol. Smith rejected them, and ruled in a lengthy and unconvincing judgment that the Canadian legislation was still in force.[72]

When the case for extradition was argued before him on its merits in early April 1865, however, Smith ruled in the prisoners' favour. Their incursion had been a belligerent act, he found, to which the extradition treaty had no application:

[T]he attack on St. Albans was a hostile expedition authorized ... by the Confederate States; and carried out by a commissioned officer of their army in command of a party of their soldiers. And therefore ... not act committed in the course of, or as incident to, that attack can be made the ground of extradition under the Ashburton Treaty.

... It is conceded without controversy, by writers and by the courts that extradition laws are to be interpreted by the law of nations ...

...

Now, if the public law of both countries, at the time the extradition Act was passed, recognized the principle of international law that lawful belligerents are entitled to all rights incident to a state of belligerency – that should be regarded as the law governing us, just as much as if it were actually inserted in the Treaty ... The United States themselves, and all civilized countries, make a wide distinction between offences committed during a normal state of things, and those which are incident to political convulsions ... Under this distinction, political offenders have always been held to be excluded from any obligation of the country in which they take refuge ... unless ... the treaty expressly includes them ... Political offenders ... form the most conspicuous instances of exclusion from the operation of extradition law.

...

... I have come to the conclusion that the prisoners cannot be extradited, because I hold that what they have done does not constitute one of the offences mentioned in the Ashburton Treaty, and because I consequently have no jurisdiction over them.[73]

The prosecution lawyers, who had been careful to proceed on only the first of several charges against the prisoners, announced after this ruling that they intended to proceed on the others. They doubtless realized that their chances of success were slight, though, and when Smith reconvened his court the following morning he was informed that an arrangement had been reached to conclude the proceedings. Counsel for the United States government agreed to withdraw the remaining charges in return for the Crown's undertaking to prosecute Young and his colleagues in Canada for violation of neutrality laws.[74]

Before leaving the Coursol and Smith decisions in the *St Albans* case, two postscripts are worth noting. As to the jurisdictional issue, the imperial government soon saw fit to issue a proclamation legitimizing the 1861 Canadian Act.[75] As to the belligerency defence, the British Law Officers of the Crown issued an opinion agreeing with the conclusion of Smith J (and impliedly disagreeing with that of Draper CJ and his colleagues) that the incursion had been an nonextraditable act of war.[76]

The neutrality charges against the St Albans raiders were eventually proceeded with (in Toronto, where anti-American feeling was perhaps less strident than in Montreal), but they were dismissed for insufficiency of evidence.[77] By then, however, it was October 1865, and the political situation was much less volatile. The United States government had withdrawn its proposals to end the Rush-Bagot Treaty and to increase armaments on the Great Lakes.[78]

Several factors had been involved in the reduction of international tensions. For one thing, the Civil War had ended in April, not long after Smith's dismissal of the St Albans extradition proceedings. For another, Canadian authorities, both legal and political, had been striving assiduously to assuage American antagonism ever since the Coursol decision. The questionable extradition of Lake Erie "pirate" Bennett Burley by judges in Upper Canada has already been mentioned, and the legislative and executive arms of the Canadian government had also been most accommodating. An emergency statute called the Alien Act, authorizing the expulsion of aliens involved in hostile acts towards friendly foreign nations, and the punishment of anyone who assisted in the preparation for or execution of such hostile acts, had been enacted in early February.[79] It is said that Governor General Monck rode a horse through high snowdrifts in order to ensure that the measure received early Royal Assent.[80] The Canadian government also promised to compensate for the loss of a portion of the seized St Alban's loot that had been released from official custody by reason of Coursol's discharge order, and that promise was fulfilled in September.[81]

Even before these steps were taken, the Canadian government had established a border police force in November 1864.[82] Stipendiary Magistrate Gilbert McMicken, the head of the Upper Canadian contingent of that force, had supervised the arrangements for returning Burley to American territory after his extradition hearing.[83] Three-and-a-half years later, after the four most prominent British North American colonies had confederated as the Dominion of Canada and American hostility had lessened, but not disappeared, McMicken would find himself responsible, in his judicial capacity, for the first controversial extradition case since the *St Albans* and *Burley* affairs. The task would be made no easier by the fact that he would have to deal with it on the basis of newly revised legislation.

THE 1868 STATUTE

The creation of the Dominion of Canada in 1867 had necessitated the enactment of federal extradition legislation, and the Parliament of Canada passed a statute implementing the Ashburton-Webster Treaty at its first session.[84] Rather than giving the act immediate Royal Assent, the governor general reserved assent for signification of the wishes of Her Majesty (the British government). This is not surprising, given the peril that had attended recent Canadian-American extradition proceedings, the tension that still persisted between the dominion and its neighbour, and the considerable uncertainty that prevailed concerning the respective law-making responsibilities of the federal and provincial legislatures under the new Canadian Constitution. There was no doubt also a desire to ensure that a timely British order-in-council be issued approving the legislation before it came into force, so as to avoid the legal lacuna that had caused the release of the St Albans' raiders. British approval was eventually received, however, and the act was proclaimed in force by the governor general on 8 August 1868.[85]

For the most part, the 1868 statute duplicated the 1849 United Canada legislation and extended its operation to the entire dominion. There were also a few substantive changes, however. The group of persons designated as competent to issue warrants of apprehension of fugitives and commitment for extradition was expanded to include a "commissioner" appointed for that purpose, for example.[86] The two most significant changes sharpened the political responsibility of the governor general and expanded the rights of accused persons.

Section 4, which specified for the first time that the governor general had the discretionary power to release a person committed for extradition, as an alternative to ordering extradition, was perhaps to be expected. Uncertainty as to the existence of such a discretion had arisen in the *Anderson* case, and John A. Macdonald had learned from the Civil War cases that it was not always an advisable tactic to abdicate ultimate responsibility for extradition to the courts. While a political decision to release a prisoner committed for extradition might constitute a violation of the treaty, politicians were better placed than courts to assess the risks of real or perceived treaty violations.

Section 3 was revised to prevent the governor general delivering a prisoner to American authorities until at least seven days after the judicial commitment for extradition. The interval was doubtless to permit time for a habeas corpus application to a higher court. While this fetter on political discretion might seem inconsistent with the augmented responsibility given to the governor by section 4, in reality the safeguard was calculated to protect politicians as well as prisoners, since it provided time for public opinion, the democratic politician's eternal guideline, to take shape.

The fact that political control over the extradition process was somewhat strengthened did not, in law at least, diminish the responsibility of the courts. The week's delay after commitment ensured an opportunity to seek review from a superior court, in fact. Front-line judges still bore the initial burden of weighing the evidence, determining whether such evidence would justify committal for trial in the case of a similar offence committed within the jurisdiction, and, if so, exercising the power to commit the accused for extradition by the governor.[87]

THE RENO CASE

The Reno gang, consisting of brothers John, Frank, William, and Simeon Reno, and assorted associates, was notorious throughout the north-central United States. They had been terrorizing Indiana, Iowa, Ohio, and Missouri with a series of train robberies and other large-scale armed depredations for at least two years before they came to the official attention of Stipendiary Magistrate Gilbert McMicken at Windsor, Ontario, in August 1868.[88]

What occasioned McMicken's involvement with the Reno gang was the apprehension of two of its members, Frank Reno and Charlie Anderson, in Windsor by the Pinkerton Detective Agency. Pinkerton detectives, who represented an express company victimized by a daring Reno gang train robbery in Marshfield, Indiana, three months previously, presented McMicken with a request for the arrest and extradition of Reno and Anderson for that crime. The various escapades of the Reno gang, including this attempt to find refuge in Canada, had attracted widespread interest from newspapers throughout the United States, so McMicken knew he would be watched closely from south of the border. The American public would not be happy if scoundrels as nefarious as Reno and Anderson eluded the clutches of justice.

Although the new extradition statute seemed to require an exercise of independent judgment, an awareness of the calumny that Magistrate Coursol had brought down upon himself by deigning to perform an autonomous judicial role in a sensitive extradition situation could not have failed to affect McMicken's view of his proper function as he dealt with Reno and Anderson. When he subsequently reported his actions in the case to Prime Minister John A. Macdonald, he remarked that he had done what he thought "you would have wished me to do," and expressed the hope that "I brought it to a conclusion at once right and satisfactory to you."[89]

The "conclusion" to which McMicken's letter referred was his decision to commit Reno and Anderson for extradition, and he was probably justified in claiming that, in addition to being satisfactory to the prime minister, the decision was also "right" in a legal sense, at least insofar as issues brought before him at the hearing were concerned. The chief legal question the magistrate had to determine was whether to take account of evidence submitted on behalf of the prisoners that they were somewhere else at the time the crime was committed. McMicken properly ruled that alibi evidence was for the trial court, not the extradition tribunal, to assess. He was upheld in this ruling by Chief Justice Draper of the Ontario Court of Queen's Bench, before whom a subsequent habeas corpus application was brought.[90]

The chief justice also rejected a much more plausible argument by the prisoner's counsel. The original information in the case had alleged that Reno and Anderson "did feloniously *shoot at*" the conductor of the train "with intent to kill and murder," and Magistrate McMicken's committal warrant had employed the same terminology.[91] The treaty and the statute, however, covered only "*assault* with intent to commit murder."[92] This discrepancy had come to McMicken's attention after the habeas corpus application was launched, and he decided to take advantage of a delay in the proceedings caused by the jailer's uncertainty as to how the costs of transporting the prisoners from Sandwich to Toronto for the habeas corpus hearing would be paid to issue an amended committal warrant, conforming to the language of the treaty and statute. Counsel for Reno and Anderson objected to both the failure of the information to allege an offence covered by the legislation and McMicken's attempt to rewrite his warrant. Draper refused to accept either objection, holding that the words used in the information amounted to an allegation of assault with intent to murder, and that even if this were not the case the amended committal warrant would have put things right.[93] While he may have been right on the first point, his reliance on the second warrant as fall-back authority is difficult to understand. Even if McMicken were not *functus officio* after issuing the first warrant, surely any legal defects in the *information* could not be expunged by altering the language of the committal *warrant*. It is difficult to escape the feeling that Draper, like McMicken, was determined to do whatever it took to bring the case to a conclusion "satisfactory" to Macdonald.

The most noteworthy events in the case of *Reno and Anderson* occurred outside the courtroom. One was the dispersal by McMicken of a mob of the prisoners' supporters (whom he described in his report to Macdonald as "fugitive vagabonds from the u.s."[94]) a couple of days before announcing his original decision. Some time before that it had been reported in the press that the magistrate had turned down an offer, conveyed to his son, of $6000 in gold in return for refusing extradition.[95]

Following the unsuccessful habeas corpus bid, Reno and Anderson attempted, again unsuccessfully, to escape from the Sandwich jail by lifting some of the floor planks.[96] Later the same day there was abortive attempt to shoot at a hack carrying Alan Pinkerton, as well as Gilbert McMicken and his son, and, still later, Pinkerton was attacked by a pistol-wielding assailant across the river in Detroit.[97] When the prisoners were eventually conveyed to the United States, under elaborate security arrangements to avoid both potential rescuers and potential lynchers, the ship that carried them collided with another in the Detroit River, and both Pinkerton and his charges were almost drowned.[98] Not long after being taken to New Albany, Indiana, and lodged in prison there with other captured members of the Reno gang, the prisoners were released, beaten, and hanged from the prison porch by a group of masked lynchers thought to have come from the vicinity of the Seymour train robbery.[99] Extradition could be a hazardous business for both extraditors and extraditees.

THE MORTON AND THOMPSON CASE

While Magistrate McMicken was in Toronto for the *Reno and Anderson* habeas corpus hearing, he assumed responsibility for a second extradition proceeding involving fugitive American train robbers.[100] This robbery had occurred in White Plains, New York, several months previously. Two men had boarded a train, bound and gagged the express company's clerk, broken open a safe, and made off with a large quantity of cash and securities. Pinkerton detectives had traced the suspected culprits, Ike Morton and "Piano Charlie" Thompson, to Toronto, where they had been arrested and brought before a police magistrate named McNabb for extradition.

Counsel for the accused had presented Magistrate McNabb with startling defence. One of the prisoners had taken the stand and had brazenly admitted that he and his partner had taken the valuables from the train. However, he claimed, the express clerk had willingly collaborated in the crime. Defence counsel contended that this converted the offence from "robbery," which was covered by the extradition treaty, to "embezzlement," which was not. The argument made sense to McNabb, who released the prisoners.

It did not make sense to Gilbert McMicken, however. He quickly granted the request of Alan Pinkerton for a new arrest warrant, making it returnable before him at Sandwich, where he expected to be, and was, by the time Morton and Thompson were found and rearrested. After a second hearing, McMicken issued a warrant for the prisoners' extradition. As in the *Reno* case, this warrant was challenged in habeas corpus proceedings before a superior court: this time a three-judge panel of the Ontario Court of Common Pleas. Again, McMicken's decision was upheld.[101]

The rulings reported in the superior court's reasons for judgment were not seriously contestable: that an extradition application may be reinstituted before a second magistrate after being dismissed by a first (the principle of double jeopardy not being applicable in the absence of a determination of guilt or innocence); that McMicken's jurisdiction extended throughout Ontario; and that he had not erred in permitting both *viva voce* testimony and written depositions to be admitted at the hearing. More surprising was the absence of any direct reference to the argument that had won the prisoners' release from Magistrate McNabb; that because of the express clerk's connivance, the offence had not been robbery but some nonextraditable crime, such as embezzlement, or inducing breach of trust. The only plausible explanations for this omission would appear to be that:

- the argument was not pressed before McMicken;
- evidence tendered before McMicken indicated that the clerk had not collaborated after all; or
- McMicken and the Court of Common Pleas took the position that such evidence was for the trial court, rather than the extradition court, to consider.

The absence of a full report of the hearing before McMicken prevents confirmation of either the first or the second point. If the third explanation was the reason for not taking account of this argument, it was a questionable reason. While it is true that many kinds of defence evidence – such as the alibi evidence that McMicken and Draper both refused to consider in the *Reno* case – ought not to interest an extradition court, this evidence was of a type highly relevant to the issue of extradition. It concerned not just the guilt or innocence of the accused, but also their *extraditability*. If the clerk had really been in cahoots with the express bandits it would be difficult to characterize their crime as "robbery," the only applicable extraditable offence. And if the determination of that key question were left to the trial court after extradition, it would be too late. While evidentiary conflicts relating to the substance of a criminal charge should certainly be relegated to the ultimate trier of guilt, logic requires that those which relate to the applicability of the extradition treaty must be dealt with by the extradition tribunal.

The reason this distinction was not recognized by the Court of Common Pleas in *Morton and Thompson* may have been the judges' concern about the narrow range of offences for which extradition was available. It was a concern felt by many Canadians. Not long before the *Morton and Thompson* hearing, for example, the *London Free Press* had published an editorial, reprinted in at least one other Canadian newspaper, lamenting the fact that

Canada is ... becoming the recognized refuge for rogues ... [W]e have to harbour and support other peoples' rogues as well as our own ... [T]he existing state of the law ... proclaims a man a villain on the south side of the lines and sets the dogs of justice at his heels; while incoming to this side he is ... encouraged to walk our streets, hoist his legs in our hotels, expectorate profusely on our floors, and wear an unlimited amount of gold chain over his waistcoat. Let us have a little reciprocity for the benefit of morality ... [and] the protection of our homes ... as well as in hay and oats.[102]

In the *Morton and Thompson* case itself, the Common Pleas judges expressed similar sentiments. Chief Justice Hagarty complained that

"The present law of extradition is unfortunately powerless to reach the class of felonies most common in occurrence, to the vast injury of the peace and good order of both the countries interested; and the almost complete impunity enjoyed by fugitive criminals on either side of the lines is a matter of such dangerous significance as probably soon to force itself on the attention of both governments."[103] Wilson J added: "I have but to express the hope that the time will soon come when other offences may safely come within the provisions of a more liberal treaty."[104]

In the absence of "a more liberal treaty," the judges were apparently prepared to stretch existing arrangements to serve what they considered to be the public good. Hagarty acknowledged that "I have always felt disposed to give the fairest and most liberal interpretation to the provisions of an arrangement like this Extradition Treaty, entered into by two nations professing a common civilization, with a thousand miles of coterminous boundary. They properly agree that their respective territories shall not be the asylum for those who commit crimes abhorrent to the laws of both communities."[105]

Their Lordships would undoubtedly have concurred in the hope expressed some years later by Mr Justice Osler that the politicians would one day make it easier to achieve this goal by means of a more sweeping treaty and statute: "I shall be glad to see the day when 'free trade' in criminals shall exist."[106]

EVENTUAL REFORMS

Freer trade in fugitives from justice would eventually come, but not for more than a decade after the *Reno* and *Morton* cases. In the meantime, however, the international tensions that had induced judges to find as much authorization for free trade as they could in existing arrangements gradually eased. The political passions that had complicated Canadian-American extradition in the past were cooling even by the time the *Reno* and *Morton* cases arose, in fact. Annexation fears flared again briefly in 1869–70, in connection with the Red River Rebellion, but they quickly subsided, and once Manitoba and the Northwest Territories were safely within Confederation, international tensions were almost entirely dissipated.

Judges were thereafter under less pressure to engage in juridical contortions when interpreting and applying existing extradition law. So, for example, Mr Justice Osler held, in the case in which his "free trade" remark was made, that the prisoner in question had to be discharged because of the limited range of the treaty and legislation. After expressing his desire for "free trade in criminals," he continued as follows: "but so long as there is an extradition law under which a criminal whose extradition is sought has rights to be observed here he is entitled to have those rights administered in our courts."[107] That ruling was made in 1882, in an international situation vastly different from the nervous days of December 1864 when Magistrate Coursol had been so severely castigated for expressing and acting upon similar sentiments.

The elimination of international tensions did not simplify the state of extradition law. Legal confusion continued to reign for some years to come. The chief source of confusion was a new British statute, the Extradition Act, 1870,[108] which established uniform implementation procedures for all British extradition treaties with foreign countries. It supplanted the earlier legislation implementing the Ashburton-Webster Treaty, as well as all statutes applying to extradition treaties with other countries. The new act was an improvement over the old, in that, like the Canadian legislation, it abolished the need for preliminary formalities before extradition could be sought. Its effect on Canada was unclear, however, because it appeared to abolish the previous approval of Canadian legislation, and the British government refused for the next several years to approve updated implementation legislation enacted by the Parliament of Canada.[109] After several years of uncertainty, it was finally held in *R. v. Browne*[110] that the previous Canadian legislation remained in force, under the authority of an opaque provision of the 1870 imperial statute. In 1882 British authorities finally gave approval to a new Canadian implementing act, passed in 1877.[111] Like the British Act of 1870, the Canadian legislation covered all extradition between Canada and every country with which the United Kingdom had an extradition treaty.

In 1889 the Ashburton-Webster Treaty was finally renegotiated and its range was expanded greatly by supplementary provisions.[112] Several of the new features were clearly products of difficulties faced by the courts in some of the cases discussed above. The attempt of Ike Morton and "Piano Charlie" Thompson to slip through the extradition net by claiming connivance with the express clerk was, for example, doubtless the reason that "Embezzlement, larceny; receiving any money, valuable security, or other property knowing the same to have been embezzled, stolen or fraudulently obtained"[113] was added to the list of extraditable offences. The addition of "piracy by the law of nations"[114] and "Revolt or conspiracy to revolt ... on board a ship on the high seas"[115] (the original treaty covering only "piracy ... within the jurisdiction of either" country) was probably a delayed result of cases like *The Creole*,[116] in which the alleged wrongdoing occurred at sea.

Attempts in the slavery and Civil War cases to extradite fugitives on straw charges, so as to prosecute them for nonextraditable offences after they had been surrendered for extraditable ones, produced an important new provision: "No person surrendered ... shall be triable or be tried for any crime or offence committed prior to his extradition, other than the offence for which he was surrendered, until he shall have had an opportunity of returning to the country from which he was surrendered."[117]

The "political act" defence, which had been merely implicit in the original treaty, was now made explicit: "A fugitive criminal shall not be surrendered if the offence in respect of which his surrender is demanded is one of a political character, or if he proves that the requisition for his surrender has in fact been made with a view to try or punish him for an offence of a political character."[118] And the final determination of "political character" was now clearly left to the government of the sanctuary country: "If any question shall arise as to whether a case comes within the provisions of this Article, the decision of the authorities of the Government in whose jurisdiction the fugitive shall be at the time shall be final."[119] That did not relieve the courts of the uncomfortable responsibility for deciding whether a crime or a prosecution was political, but it did acknowledge that a refusal on political grounds to surrender a fugitive – whether based on a judicial or executive determination – was unchallengeable under the treaty.

CONCLUSION

What morals can be drawn from the efforts of Canadian judges to administer extradition law in the century between Jay's Treaty and the revised Ashburton-Webster Treaty? What can be said, in particular, about judicial attempts to respond to international pressures by giving generous "free trade" interpretations to the narrow provisions of the pre-1889 law?

A gradual recognition that both legal and policy factors are important to effective extradition practice can be seen in the fluctuating emphases placed on the respective roles of courts and politicians during the period reviewed. The focus swung from predominantly political, to predominantly judicial, and then back to a relatively balanced situation towards the end of the period. That fluctuation is hardly surprising. Much more problematical is the confusion of roles caused by the extent to which some of the judges appear to have concerned themselves with policy factors. In the *Burley* case, for example, we observed the cream of Upper Canada's judiciary behaving in a manner that was highly questionable from a legal viewpoint, although highly expedient in terms of the country's welfare. Was that a travesty? Was it an abberation? Or was it the way good judges ought to respond to such situations? If it was an instance of acceptable judicial practice, what does that tell us about the concept of the rule of law?

Before dealing with these questions, we should dispose of a matter that might otherwise confuse the discussion. Most laws confer a degree of discretion, larger or smaller, upon the judges who are charged with their interpretation or application. Laws that impose liability for "unreasonable," "wilful," or "malicious" conduct, for example, give the courts some leeway in determining whether particular conduct is "unreasonable," "wilful," or "malicious." Most other laws have similar built-in pockets of judicial discretion. When exercising the discretion such laws give them, it is unavoidable that judges take account of nonlegal policy considerations that affect the justice of exercising the discretion in one way or another. That normal use of judicial discretion was not what was involved in the *Burley* case, however. There, as we have seen, the judges went well beyond the bounds of law's normal elasticity to reach a conclusion that ignored or defied the dictates of law.

If the *Burley* case stood alone, it could be dismissed as a glitch with which neither jurisprudence nor legal history should be concerned. The decision does not stand alone, however. Scores, perhaps hundreds, of well-known judicial decisions can be identified in which highly competent and sophisticated judges reached conclusions that were legally indefensible, but were sound from the societal point of view and appear to have been reached for societal reasons. Some of those decisions, like *Burley*, involve extradition law; others can be found in every field of law that is capable of affecting the community in crucial ways. In the field of constitutional law, they abound.[120] Should historians condemn such decisions? Many critics do so. They contend that judges should be blind to the policy consequences of their legal rulings except in circumstances where law clearly bestows a policy discretion upon them. Otherwise, they contend, policy factors are for politicians to assess and apply. Judges should hew to the adage that "Justice must be done though the heavens may fall!"

This, perhaps, is what Magistrate Coursol did in the *St Albans* case. If judges do not restrain themselves in this way, it is said, they will dangerously undermine the rule of law, a principle essential to all just societies. Even worse than the fact that law is defied in these situations is the fact that judges themselves do it, thus casting doubt on their sincerity whenever they invoke the rule of law on other occasions.

These are cogent arguments. In many circumstances they deserve to carry the day, but not always. Put yourself in the robes of Chief Justice Draper in the *Burley* case. By law, you know you should release the Lake Erie pirates. You also know, however, that if you do so there is a viable possibility that your decision will trigger armed retaliation against Canada by the most powerful army in the world. You cannot pass the responsibility on to the politicians, because they have no legal role to play at this stage of the extradition process. Your choice, therefore, is to honour the rule of law and thereby put your country at considerable military risk, or to bring down a decision that is politically and militarily a good deal safer, though it carries some risk to the respect with which the rule of law will be regarded in the community. If you opt for the same solution chosen by Draper and his colleagues, you will probably also conclude, as they did, that the rule of law will be damaged less in the public eye if you pretend that your decision was dictated by law, than if you admit that your have circumvented legal norms. That, at least, is what I would have done.

If I am correct in believing that occasional violation of the rule of law by competent and honourable judges is endemic to any legal system, the rule-of-law concept needs to be seen in a new light by lawyers, judges, and the general public. It is not an absolute value, before which all else must yield, as we lawyers usually profess. It is, rather, an ideal towards which we strive whenever possible, knowing that there will be occasions when it must yield to imperatives of higher priority. One of the most important of those higher imperatives is the survival of the nation. Those who are entrusted with the care of the legal system have a duty to keep those occasions to a minimum. When they do periodically occur, however, wise judges accept the inevitable, recognizing that the legal system is at least as flawed as the human beings it serves. Historians can do no less.

NOTES

The research assistance of Lee Gibson, Scott Gibson, and Dana Graves is gratefully acknowledged.

1 Per Osler J in *Re Parker* (1882), 9 PR 332 at 335 (QB).
2 See R.W. Winks, *Canada and the United States: The Civil War Years* (Montreal: Harvest House 1960), 303–4; D. Creighton, *The Road to Confederation* (Toronto: MacMillan 1964), 194–5 and 212–14; P.B. Waite, *The*

181 Free Trade in Criminals

Life and Times of Confederation: 1864–1867 (Toronto: University of Toronto Press 1962), 28–34 and 150–2.
3   Harvard Law School, "Research in International Law – Extradition" (1935), 29 *American Journal of International Law* (Supp.) 41. For other accounts of the history of extradition see J.B. Moore, *A Treatise on Extradition and International Rendition*, vol. 1 (1891), chaps 1, 2, 4, and 20; E.G. Clarke, *A Treatise upon Extradition*, 4th ed. 1903, chaps 2–6; and G.V. La Forest, *Extradition to and from Canada*, 3rd ed. by A.W. La Forest (Aurora: Canada Law Book 1991), chap. 1.
4   Clarke, *Treatise*, 27.
5   Concluded 19 Nov. 1794; ratifications exchanged 28 Oct. 1795; proclaimed 29 Feb. 1796. Reprinted in Moore, *Treatise*, vol. 2, 1095. Article 27 was one of several which, by virtue of Article 28, lapsed twelve years after ratification.
6   Moore, *Treatise*, 90.
7   Ibid., 41.
8   Ibid., 90.
9   Ibid., 90–2.
10 (1819), 4 Johnson's Chancery cases 105, at 107. He expressed similar views in 1 *Kent's Commentaries* 37.
11 (1827), 1 Stuart's Lower Canada cases Rep. 245; 1 RJRQ 238.
12 Moore, *Treatise*, vol. 1, 16–21.
13 See the 1841 case of *The Creole*, discussed in Clarke, *Treatise*, 127–8, in which the American government sought and was denied extradition of a group of African slaves who, en route from England to New Dishonourable, seized the ship, murdered a passenger, and fled to the British port of Nassau. Clarke states that "The law authorities in England were unanimously of opinion upon this case that they could not be given up in the absence of an Act of the English Parliament giving power to the executive."
14 Ibid., 624; La Forest, *Extradition*, 3.
15 *Re Besset* (1844), 8 JP 743; *Shanley v. Harvey* (1762), 2 Eden 126; *R. v. Schiever*, [1759] 97 ER 551 (KB).
16 Clarke, *Treatise*, 93.
17 Ibid., quoting from a letter from Lord Aylmer to New York governor Marcy, 27 May 1833.
18 (1833) 3 Wm IV, c.7.
19 Clarke, *Treatise*, 95.
20 Moore, *Treatise*, vol. 1, 16–21.
21 See Clarke, *Treatise*, 95–6.
22 La Forest, *Extradition*, 3–4.
23 Moore, *Treatise*, 626.
24 *Hansard*, 19 July 1842, 323.

25 Clarke, *Treatise*, 95–6.
26 The negotiations are summarized in Moore, *Treatise*, vol. 1, 890–932.
27 Concluded 9 Aug. 1842; ratifications exchanged 13 Oct. 1842; proclaimed 10 Nov. 1842. Reprinted in Moore, *Treatise*, 1095–6.
28 6 & 7 Vict., c.75 (Imp.). This legislation was revised in 1862: 25 & 26 Vict., c.70 (Imp.).
29 Ibid., s.5.
30 (1849) 12 Vict. 19.
31 The Canadian proclamation bringing the 1849 act into force (1850 *Canada Gazette*, 8295–6) recites the passage of the British order-in-council, 8 Jan. 1850.
32 *Supra*, note 5, s.1.
33 Ibid.
34 Ibid., s.3.
35 Ibid., s.4.
36 The case is exhaustively examined in P. Brode, *The Odyssey of John Anderson* (Toronto: Osgoode Society, 1989).
37 Ibid., 73–5. The result of the controversy was a British statute, enacted in 1862, preventing writs of habeas corpus being issued to Canada by courts of the mother country: ibid., 118.
38 Ibid., 96–7.
39 (1861) Vict. 6. This statute repealed and replaced the first three sections of (1850) Consolidated Statutes of Upper Canada, c.89, which had repealed and replaced the 1849 act, without significant change, as part of a general consolidation of legislation.
40 Compare section 3 of the 1849 act with the amended version.
41 Ibid., s.1.
42 See Brode, *Odyssey*, 22ff. Since the official in question, William Matthews, was described variously as a "justice of the peace" and as a "magistrate," it is not clear whether the amendment would exclude persons in his position.
43 See s.1.
44 *Supra*, note 5, s.1.
45 Note 27 above, emphasis added.
46 Note 39 above, s.1.
47 See Brode, *Odyssey*, 51–3, for a survey of American newspaper coverage of the case just prior to the Civil War.
48 *New York Times*, 29 Nov. 1860.
49 See Brode, *Odyssey*, 83ff.
50 *St Paul Daily Times*, 22 Sept. 1861.
51 Winks, *Canada and the United States*, 287ff.
52 (1865), 1 UCLJ (NS) 34 (QB).
53 Ibid., 44.

54 *Ex Parte Anderson* [1861] 121 ER 525 (QB).
55 There had been a charge of piracy laid against Burley in the United States, but robbery, the sole offence alleged in the extradition proceeding, had not been included.
56 *Supra*, note 27, at 44, per Draper CJ.
57 Ibid., 48, per Richards CJ.
58 The "manifesto" referred to was a document signed by Confederate president Jefferson Davis which certified that the entire escapade had been "a belligerent expedition ordered and undertaken under the authority of the Confederate States of America against the United States of America, and that the government of the Confederate States of America assumes the responsibility of answering for the acts and conduct of any of its officers engaged in the said expedition, and especially of the said Bennett G. Burley, an Acting Master in the Navy of the Confederate States" (ibid., 37–8). Chief Justice Draper's reason for refusing to accept this explicit endorsement as covering Burley's conduct was that the manifesto also stated that the officers involved had been instructed to avoid violating the laws or the neutrality of Britain or Canada.
59 Ibid., 44.
60 And another factual question, somewhat more plausible in the circumstances: Was the act of robbery a separate private act by Burley, unrelated to the public purpose he claimed for the overall raid? Chief Justice Richards mentioned that the prosecution had raised that question (ibid., 48).
61 Ibid., 51.
62 Ibid.
63 Winks, *Canada and the United States*, 303–4.
64 The following account is drawn from ibid., 295ff. Winks's description of the St Albans affair is thorough, discriminating, and well documented.
65 The hearing was reported verbatim in the 14 December 1884 issue of the *Montreal Gazette*, from which the following account is largely taken. An edited version, corrected by judge and counsel, will be found in L.N. Benjamin, *St Albans Raid* (Montreal 1865). This useful compendium also contains the transcripts of earlier and later proceedings in the matter, together with witnesses' depositions and other supporting documentation.
66 Note 31 above.
67 It was also argued that an earlier statute, providing for a consolidation of the laws of Upper Canada, had also repealed the 1849 act, but that contention was somewhat less plausible, given the purely formal nature of "repeal" for the purpose of consolidation.
68 Note 65 above.

69 Ibid.
70 Benjamin, *St Albans Raid*, 104–5. Defence counsel's unsuccessful objection the next day, described next in the text, is reported at 106.
71 *Montreal Gazette*, 14 Dec. 1864, emphasis added. It is interesting to note that in the version of the transcript published in Benjamin, *St Albans Raid*, 128, the passage in question contains some additions, which alter its meaning significantly: "He knew *now*, that from the beginning of this case to the present, that those parties had been arrested without any legal warrant" (emphasis added). Benjamin's preface acknowledges that the transcripts were submitted to "Counsel" for revision before publication. Whether Magistrate Coursol was given a similar opportunity is not stated.
72 Benjamin, *St Albans Raid*, 151–62.
73 Ibid., 469–71.
74 Ibid., 472.
75 Ibid., 477.
76 Ibid., 480.
77 Winks, *Canada and the United States*, 333.
78 Ibid., 330.
79 Statutes of Canada, 1865–6, 28 Vict., c.1: An Act for the Prevention and Repression of Outrages in Violation of the Peace on the Frontier of This Province, and for Other Purposes.
80 Winks, *Canada and the United States*, 319.
81 Ibid., 330.
82 National Archives of Canada, Macdonald Papers, vol. 246, 110637, McMicken to Macdonald, 22 Nov. 1864.
83 Ibid., Macdonald to McMicken, 30 Jan. and 15 Feb. 1865: Letter Books 7, 191 and 235.
84 SC, 1867–8 (31 Vict.), c.94.
85 Proclamation was cited in the published version of the statute, ibid., xi.
86 Ibid., s.1.
87 Ibid. Continued use of the expression "it shall be lawful for such judge" to carry out these duties left open the question of whether they were discretionary rather than mandatory powers.
88 See J.D. Horan, *The Pinkertons: The Detective Agency That Made History* (New York: Crown 1967), 166ff; and D. and L. Gibson, "Railroading and the Train Robbers: Extradition in the Shadow of Annexation," in D. Gibson and W. Pue, eds., *Glimpses of Canadian Legal History* (Winnipeg: University of Manitoba Legal Research Institute 1991). This part of the paper draws heavily on the latter publication.
89 Macdonald Papers, vol. 241, 107547–8, McMicken to Macdonald, 23 Sept. 1868.
90 (1868), 4 PR 281 (QB).

91 Ibid., 284 and 287 (emphasis added).
92 Emphasis added.
93 Note 90 above, at 296.
94 Note 83 above.
95 *New Albany Independent Weekly Ledger*, 26 Aug. 1968, quoted in Horan, *The Pinkertons*, 172.
96 Toronto *Telegraph*, 15 Oct. 1868.
97 Ibid., 19 Oct. 1868.
98 Horan, *The Pinkertons*, 174–5.
99 *Ottawa Citizen*, 18 Dec. 1868.
100 For a fuller account of this case see Gibson, "Railroading."
101 *R. v. Morton and Thompson* (1868) 19 UCCP 9. For a synopsis of the subsequent careers of these two very colourful scoundrels see Gibson, "Railroading."
102 Reprinted in *Ottawa Citizen*, 25 Sept. 1868.
103 Note 101 above, 20–1.
104 Ibid., 25.
105 Ibid., 20.
106 *Re Parker* (1882) 9 PR 332, at 335 (QB).
107 Ibid.
108 33 & 34 Vict. (Imp.), c.52.
109 La Forest, *Extradition*, chap. 1.
110 (1881) 31 UCCP 484, affirmed 6 OAR 386.
111 (1877) 40 Vict., c.25; amended (1882) 40 Vict., c.20. La Forest, *Extradition*, relies on Clarke, *Treatise*, for authority that British approval brought the new Canadian legislation into force in 1882. Apparent residual uncertainty as to the state of affairs caused, according to La Forest, a confirming British order-in-council to be issued on 27 Nov. 1888.
112 *Supplementary Convention between Her Majesty and the United States of America for the Extradition of Criminals*, signed 12 July 1889; ratifications exchanged 11 March 1890.
113 Ibid., Article I(3).
114 Ibid., Article I(8).
115 Ibid., Article I(9).
116 Note 13 above.
117 Note 84 above, Article III.
118 Ibid., Article II.
119 Ibid.
120 D. Gibson, "The Real Laws of the Constitution" (1990), 28 *Alberta Law Review* 358; D. Gibson, "Founding Fathers-in-Law: Judicial Amendment of the Canadian Constitution" (1992), 55 *Law and Contemporary Problems* 261.

International Dispute Settlement under the Canada – United States Free Trade Agreement

DONALD McRAE

Throughout his long and distinguished career, Maxwell Cohen has maintained an active interest in the settlement of international disputes – an intellectual interest as a scholar and as an acute observer of the international system, and a practical interest arising out of his own involvement in international dispute resolution processes. As chair of the International Joint Commission, he played a key role in ensuring the proper management of Canada–United States relations in respect of their shared boundary water resources. In that capacity he was particularly effective in gaining consensus among the commissioners of the two countries. As judge ad hoc in the *Gulf of Maine Maritime Boundary* case,[1] Cohen took on an adjudicative role that he performed most effectively, being part of a majority decision that included both national judges and that provided a solution that was at once creative and pragmatic.

This combination of binational problem-resolving processes and formal international adjudication provides an appropriate starting point for a consideration of the dispute settlement mechanisms of the Canada–United States Free Trade Agreement (FTA).[2] Moreover, since Cohen followed closely both the negotiation of the agreement and its implementation, the topic is particularly appropriate in a collection of articles dedicated to him.

When considering the provisions of the FTA relating to the settlement of disputes, it is useful to recall the state of international dispute settlement generally. Notwithstanding the bursts of enthusiasm for the peaceful settlement of disputes following the two world wars of this century, states have not had the habit of referring their disputes to third parties for binding settlement. They have usually preferred to negotiate their disputes, thereby maintaining control over the outcome.[3]

The history of disputes between Canada and the United States is no exception. Between the Alaska Boundary Arbitration of 1903 and the entry into force of the FTA on 1 January 1989, the two countries had resorted to international arbitration or adjudication of disputes between them on only three occasions.[4]

It is perhaps surprising, then, that a method of third-party dispute settlement between states has evolved in the field of international trade law. Although the provisions of the General Agreement on Tariffs and Trade (GATT) do not provide for a formal mechanism to settle disputes, a procedure for third-party dispute settlement did evolve within the framework of GATT, one that is binding only after acceptance of the solution by the intergovernmental GATT Council.[5] The GATT mechanism is used frequently; it has evolved into a relatively sophisticated process that has been enhanced by the procedural improvements negotiated during the Uruguay Round of Multilateral Trade Negotiations.[6]

One of the objectives Canada had in the negotiation of the FTA was the inclusion of a binding dispute settlement process. In fact, the immediate impetus for the negotiation of the FTA was a well-publicized dispute over the levying by the United States of countervailing duties on Canadian imports of softwood lumber. "Contingent protection" from the application of U.S. laws was an important issue for Canada, and negotiators felt that the removal of disputes from the U.S. domestic legal process into a binding binational third-party settlement system would provide that protection.

Beyond this goal, support for binding dispute settlement is not a surprising position for the side that sees itself as the less powerful party in any relationship. The protection afforded by having differences resolved by an objective third party can be seen as counterbalancing the power of the other party. And while this goal provides some explanation for Canada's position, it also explains in part the attitude of the United States, which did not see binding third-party settlement as an essential or necessary part of a free trade agreement. For the United States, disputes could be negotiated and, where appropriate, recourse could be had to the dispute settlement mechanisms of GATT. To put it simply, whereas Canada wanted a legal, adjudicative mechanism included in the agreement – even an international trade court – the United States was satisfied to leave disputes to a political or intergovernmental process.

The provisions ultimately included in the FTA reflect a compromise between these positions. On the one hand, Canada did achieve the removal of judicial review of decisions on anti-dumping and countervailing duty matters from domestic arenas to a binational body with the power to make rulings that are binding, but it did not achieve the creation of a general dispute settlement mechanism that would be binding on the two states. The process in relation to intergovernmental disputes was to remain one whereby the governments themselves would retain final control over the outcome.

THE DISPUTE SETTLEMENT MECHANISM

There are two different dispute settlement mechanisms under the FTA. One, as mentioned, is a form of judicial review under which determinations by domestic courts and agencies in respect to antidumping and countervailing duty matters can be reviewed by a binational panel established under the provisions of chapter 19 of the FTA.[7] The function of the panel, which replaces the domestic review process, is to decide whether the decision or determination in question "was in accordance with the antidumping or countervailing duty law of the importing Party." A panel,[8] whose decisions are binding on the two governments, "may uphold a final determination or remand it for action not inconsistent with the panel's decision."

Although the chapter 19 process may be initiated by governments, it is a process utilized by private parties in respect of determinations made against them by agencies of the other state. Intergovernmental disputes are dealt with in the procedures set out in chapter 18 of the FTA, and it is on these provisions that this paper will focus.

As in GATT, dispute settlement under chapter 18 of the FTA combines both political and legal processes – notification and consultation between the two states to be followed either by binding arbitration or by a recommendatory third-party procedure. If the recommendatory process is chosen, then ultimately the matter comes back to an intergovernmental organ for a final decision.[9] This interplay of legal and political or intergovernmental decision-making processes was essential for the compromises that led to the inclusion of the dispute settlement provisions in the FTA, and they seem to be essential for the effective working of the chapter 18 system.

In broad terms, chapter 18 covers disputes between Canada and the United States arising out of the trading relationship created by the FTA.[10] It is concerned with disputes that may arise over the interpretation and application of the agreement. The process is also available to try to head off problems before their impact is felt.

Chapter 18 covers concerns by one party about actual or proposed measures of the other party that are or would be inconsistent with obligations under the agreement, or about measures, whether or not they conflict with the agreement, that would nullify or impair a benefit reasonably expected by the complaining party to accrue to it under the agreement.[11]

This last head of jurisdiction parallels the equivalent GATT provision,[12] and it is based on the idea that benefits granted through tariff concessions might well be negated through other, possibly nontariff, measures that are not in themselves in conflict with the agreement. To let such measures go unquestioned, however, would undermine the spirit of GATT or the FTA, and both agreements provide mechanisms for redress in the case of nullification and impairment.

In a certain sense, the process set up under chapter 18 constitutes a mechanism for the continuation of intergovernmental negotiations over disputes, with the addition of an opportunity for the parties to refer the matter to a third party either to resolve the dispute or to provide some assistance in the resolution of the dispute without actually resolving it. In this way the agreement interweaves political and legal processes without being wholly one or the other. While the FTA procedure bears a strong imprint of the GATT dispute settlement, the two parties were conscious of the traditional deficiencies of the GATT system – the delays and the opportunity for a party to a dispute to derail the process or to inhibit the adoption of a panel report. The FTA makes a deliberate effort to avoid these problems.

As a first step in dispute settlement, the agreement seeks to encourage dispute prevention, providing for bilateral consultations between the two governments on matters that might affect the operation of the agreement (Article 1804). Each party is required to notify the other of measures that might "materially affect the operation of the Agreement" (Article 1803). These consultations are designed to give the parties the opportunity to resolve any issue that might arise between them without resorting to more formal mechanisms. After these consultations, however, the formal process can be invoked, and ultimately one party can ensure that the issue is brought to some form of resolution.[13]

After bilateral consultations have taken place, either party can decide to refer a matter to the Canada–United States Trade Commission, a body composed of the representatives of the two countries and with the two senior trade officials as principal representatives. These are the minister for international trade for Canada and the United States trade representative. The commission is given thirty days to resolve any dispute placed before it.

In a sense, the process before the commission replicates what has gone on before, as the individuals constituting the commission may be the very people who were involved in the earlier consultations. Thus, elevation of a dispute to the commission is hardly likely to resolve it. The commission does provide the opportunity for a higher political consideration of a dispute, however, and, as an organ under the FTA with specific responsibility for resolving disputes, it has some incentive to get the job done and to transcend the political interests that motivate each party. Indeed, the commission has the broad role of acting as a watchdog over the agreement as a whole, monitoring trade disputes as they arise and making recommendations to resolve them even before the chapter 18 process has been invoked.

If the commission cannot resolve a dispute that has been formally referred to it, two options arise. It may send the dispute to binding arbitration[14] or, at the request of either party, it may establish a recommendatory panel. The agreement does not say much about binding arbitration. According to Article 1806, binding arbitration is to be on such terms as the commission thinks fit and, unless agreed otherwise, the arbitral body will be established and will operate like a recommendatory panel,[15] except that its conclusions are to be binding. This procedure has yet to be invoked.

A recommendatory panel under chapter 18 is composed of five members, two of whom must be nationals of the United States and two of whom must be nationals of Canada. The fifth, the chair, can be the national of either country or of a third state. Each side chooses its two nominees from a roster of names established in advance for that purpose; the chair is chosen by agreement. In the absence of agreement, which has been the pattern so far, the practice has been to choose by the toss of a coin. The panel has as a secretariat the binational secretariat set up under chapter 19,[16] and it handles chapter 18 cases as well.

The parties have established model rules of procedure for chapter 18 panels. The process involves a written submission by the party requesting the panel, a counter submission by the other party, and an oral hearing at which the panel has the opportunity to put questions and to ask for supplementary material. Following the hearing, the parties file supplementary written arguments.

In many respects the procedure before the panel is similar to that of an arbitration taking place under the domestic law of Canada or the United States. But a panel has no power to compel the parties, it does not take evidence under oath, and it can only call on someone to provide additional information with the consent of both parties. In effect, the process is controlled by the two parties acting in concert.

Thus, the panel has to answer the question put to it on the basis of the material supplied in writing or orally by the parties or from responses to questions that it may put to the parties. The panel has no power to make its own independent inquiry.

The panel is given three months to produce an initial report[17] that should contain findings of fact and a determination of whether the measure is or would be inconsistent with the obligations of the agreement or would cause nullification and impairment. It may also make recommendations for the resolution of the dispute. The parties then have fourteen days to comment on this initial report, and the panel has a further thirty days to consider these comments and issue its final report.

The panel's final report goes to the commission – that is, back into the political arena – and the commission must agree on a resolution of the dispute. According to Article 1807(8), this resolution "normally shall conform with the recommendation of the panel." If the commission cannot agree on any resolution within thirty days, the party that considers that its rights have been impaired by the measure is entitled to retaliate by suspending the "application to the other Party of benefits of equivalent effect" (Article 1807(9)).

The result is a relatively complex process that combines the opportunity for a political resolution of disputes with the opportunity for objective third-party determination of issues. Though that third-party determination is not binding on the parties (unless binding arbitration has been chosen), the agreement provides a strong incentive for the parties to accept the panel's decision. That, at least, was the expectation at the time of drafting the FTA.

THE CHAPTER 18 CASES: SALMON AND HERRING, AND LOBSTERS

Two cases have gone through the chapter 18 process to date.[18] The first involved the Canadian landing requirement for west-coast salmon and herring, the second involved live lobsters exported from Canada to the United States. Under Canadian law, all salmon and herring caught in Canada's 200-mile fishing zone on the west coast have to be landed in Canada for sampling and counting as part of Canada's conservation and management program. In the *Salmon and Herring* case the question was whether this requirement was an export restriction under Article 407 of the FTA that was not justified as a conservation measure under Article 1201 of the FTA. In fact, the issue was an interpretation of GATT, because Article 407 of the FTA simply incorporates directly the prohibition on quantitative restrictions contained in Article XI of GATT, while Article 1201 of the FTA incorporates Article XX of GATT.

The *Lobsters* case involved the interpretation of the same provisions, Article 407 (GATT XI) and Article 1201 (GATT XX). In the United States, the sale of live lobsters caught in Canada that do not meet the minimum catch size for lobsters caught in U.S. waters is prohibited. The question was whether this prohibition was an import restriction under Article 407 that was not justified as a conservation measure under Article 1201.

The panel in the *Salmon and Herring* case concluded that the landing requirement did constitute an export restriction and that, to the extent that it applied to 100 per cent of the catch, it was not justified as a conservation measure under Article 1201. The panel indicated what, in its view, would make the landing requirement a "measure relating to the conservation of an exhaustible natural resource" in accordance with GATT Article XX.[19] The commission neither formally accepted nor rejected the panel's decision but negotiated a resolution of the dispute along the lines set out by the panel, varying the actual percentages of the catch that could be exported without landing.[20]

In the *Lobsters* case, a majority of the panel concluded that the prohibition of the sale of undersized lobsters was not a restriction on importation governed by GATT Article XI, but was rather an internal measure governed by GATT Article III and hence beyond the terms of reference of the panel. The minority concluded that GATT Article XI did apply and that the prohibition on the sale in the United States of live lobsters caught in Canada was a restriction on importation that was not justified as a conservation measure under Article XX. The matter was placed in the hands of the commission, which has been unable to date to negotiate a solution.[21]

THE PANEL PROCESS: AN EVALUATION

In the light of these two panel decisions, some comments can be made about the chapter 18 process. These relate to the choice of panelists, the procedural and evidentiary process of chapter 18 panels, the role of the panel as decision-maker, and the contribution of chapter 18 panels to the resolution of the disputes before them and to the development of the law of the FTA and of international trade law generally.

The Choice of Panelists

The FTA provides little detail about the type of individuals contemplated as panelists for chapter 18 disputes. Article 1807 provides for the drawing up, by the commission, of a roster[22] of potential panelists composed of people who are "chosen strictly on the basis of objectivity, reliability and sound judgment, and where appropriate expertise in the particular matter under consideration."[23] But, the parties are not compelled to choose panelists from the rosters, and have chosen both roster and nonroster panelists for each of the cases to date.[24]

When it comes to the choice of a panel for a particular dispute, each party is to choose two members and then agree on a fifth who is to be the chair. The total composition must include two citizens of Canada and two citizens of the United States. In the two panels to date, all members have been nationals of the two parties.[25] While the agreement provides for the appointed panelists to choose the chair in the event of disagreement between the parties, in practice the parties have resolved this matter themselves and not passed it on to the panelists.

The Expertise of Panelists In the absence of explicit guidance in the agreement itself, the question arises concerning the expertise required for chapter 18 panelists. Under chapter 19 the qualifications are relatively clear. The process constitutes a form of judicial review, an area with which lawyers are familiar and for which they have some expertise. Chapter 19 requires that a majority of the members of a panel must be lawyers in good standing and that the panel chair must be a lawyer.[26] No such provision is found in chapter 18.

The appropriate composition of a panel will depend, presumably, on the nature of the question asked. In so far as the questions involve the interpretation of the FTA, one would assume that skill in the interpretation of international trade agreements would be desirable, and that this might suggest that legal skills would be necessary. In fact, the practice of GATT in its dispute settlement process has been to rely primarily on government representatives to GATT as panel members and not to seek out international trade lawyers for GATT dispute settlement panels.

The FTA practice so far is ambivalent. In the first case under chapter 18, the *Salmon and Herring* case, the panel was composed of two lawyers (one Canadian and one American), two fisheries experts (one Canadian and one American), and one trade policy expert (Canadian). Yet the question put to the panel was one of the interpretation of Articles 407 and 1201 of the FTA[27] and hence of Articles XI and XX of GATT.[28] Ironically, that particular composition could have resulted in a majority of individuals who were not lawyers deciding an issue on which primarily legal expertise was required, and a majority of individuals who were not experts on fisheries deciding an issue on which primarily fisheries expertise was required.

In the *Lobsters* case, the panel was composed of three lawyers (two American and one Canadian) and two trade policy experts (one Canadian and one American). The question put to the panel was again primarily a question of interpretation of Articles 407 and 1201 of the FTA and consequently of Articles XI and XX of GATT.[29] The implication was that the problem in *Salmon and Herring* was one that required fisheries management expertise on the panel, whereas in *Lobsters* the issue was perceived as a more traditional issue of trade policy or the interpretation of an international trade agreement.

The composition of the panel in *Salmon and Herring* raises the question of the way in which a panel can be assured of having both technical and decision-making expertise. There is no provision in the FTA for the panel to appoint technical assessors and the panel can call upon additional persons to provide information only with the consent of the parties.[30] Thus, in a case where a detailed knowledge of the technical aspects of a particular industry is required, the parties must either assume that the panelists will understand all the technical evidence and argument or will appoint persons with that expertise as members of the panel. This approach risks confusion between the technical assessment and the decision-making functions.

The Question of Impartiality   A unique aspect of the dispute settlement processes under chapters 18 and 19 of the FTA is that the panel members are nationals of the two disputing parties – Canada and the United States. Since the chairs of the panels so far have been nationals of the two states as well, one party has had a majority of its nationals on the panel.[31] In the case of chapter 19 panels, where the issue involves judicial review under the domestic law of Canada or the United States, this use of nationals is probably inevitable. But chapter 18 involves issues that are more transnational or international in scope and effect, and they will probably not require the same level of domestic law expertise.

The national composition of panels raises the question of objectivity in panel decision-making. The exclusive involvement of nationals in third-party dispute settlement between states is highly unusual. Indeed, the trend has been against the use of nationals in this way. For example, GATT panels were considered to have made a major advance once the disputing parties had been removed from panel membership.

The composition of panels exclusively of nationals of the two states raises two kinds of concerns. At one level there is a question of perception. If panel members are perceived as having divided consistently along national lines, then the process will lose credibility.³² Thus, the national makeup of the panels puts pressure on all panel members to strive both to be objective and to appear to have been objective, to be perceived as having stood aside from national affiliations and viewed the issue from the perspective of a body that is completely independent.

At another level there are questions about national orientation and assumptions. "Pure" objectivity is, of course, a myth. Panel members are from two countries that differ in important respects, and individual views on economic and trade issues may well be influenced by these differences. Panel members may have different perceptions of the free market system and a liberal trade order, both of which GATT and the FTA serve to promote, and of the role of government in regulating economic activity. They may have differing views about the particular industries to which the trade dispute relates.³³

Such differences were surely anticipated by the FTA negotiators, who nevertheless saw a value in having disputes under the agreement referred to panelists who are part of the societies their decisions will affect and who would reflect those differences in outlook and perspective. In other words, by choosing their own nationals as panel members, the parties were ensuring that in a certain sense the panel members would be taking responsibility for their decisions in a way that those who did not live and work in the two countries might not be expected to do.

Of course, the option of appointing a "neutral" panel member from a third state exists under the agreement. But a so-called neutral chair could change the dynamics of the panel's operation. The chair could be perceived as the real decision-maker, and the national nominees of the two states might view themselves as representatives of their state's position, as union or management nominees might do in a labour arbitration, seeking to draw the chair to one side or the other.³⁴ Such a result would not enhance the dispute settlement process. It would shift the whole emphasis in the panel selection process to the appointment of the chair and defeat the objective of having a panel of five members who are obliged to act independently of their national affiliations.

Procedure and Process under Chapter 18

Apart from the formal requirement for written submissions and an oral hearing, the agreement is generally silent on how the process before a chapter 18 panel is to take place. Accordingly, there is some leeway for the panels to develop their practices over time. GATT panels generally treat the oral hearing as an informal consultation, but there is no guidance on how chapter 18 panels are to proceed. However, the relatively short time limits for these panels indicate they must proceed expeditiously. Thus, the oral hearing has to be efficient and there is little time for reconvening a panel to discuss the matter with the parties a second time. But this need for expedition takes place in an environment where there is no provision for methods of proof, no rules of evidence, no formal examination of witnesses, and no cross-examination. Each side presents the panel with its own view of the facts, its own specialists, and its legal argument, and it is for the panel to determine the relevance and weight of the information and evidence provided.

In this light the question arises how panels will be able to assess complex technical evidence about the nature of the particular industry that has given rise to the trade dispute. In *Salmon and Herring* there was fisheries expertise on the panel, but there is no provision in the FTA or in the model rules of procedure for chapter 18 panels for a panel to acquire additional expertise without first getting the consent of the parties. In these circumstances the parties might give consideration to providing panels as a matter of course with technical advisers, individuals who would be available to the panel for consultation and advice, but would not be voting members.[35]

It is premature to consider whether the chapter 18 process should be surrounded by more formality and be subject to procedural and evidentiary rules. Certainly, this is not the kind of process that the United States had in mind in the negotiation of the FTA. Moreover, it is difficult to see what such formalization would add. In a process of this kind the parties are relying on the good sense, judgment, and technical or legal expertise of panel members and their analytical and problem-solving skills. The panel's task is to give each side a reasonable opportunity to make its case in the best way possible. It is then for the panel to draw its own conclusions. Surrounding the process with procedural rules, with which only lawyers may be comfortable, is unlikely to improve the quality of the decision-making of the panels and would perhaps be inconsistent with the intended relative informality of the FTA panel process.

The Role of the Panel

A panel is expected to make findings of fact and to determine whether the measure in question is or would be inconsistent with the obligations of the party concerned under the FTA, or would cause nullification or impairment.[36] It may make recommendations for the resolution of the dispute.[37] The task of a panel in any particular case will depend on the question put to it by the parties. In both *Salmon and Herring* and *Lobsters* the questions put to the panel were essentially legal – the interpretation of specific provisions of the FTA. Neither case involved nullification and impairment, and although the panel was not asked in either case for recommendations for the resolution of the dispute, that option, presumably, would have been open to the panels.[38]

In *Lobsters*, problems arose with the way the question had been framed by the parties. There the panel had been asked about the consistency of provisions of the Magnuson Fishery Conservation and Management Act of the United States with Articles 407 (GATT Article XI) and 1201 (GATT Article XX) of the FTA. However, the question went on: "It is understood that in agreeing to have the Panel examine the consistency of the Magnuson Act amendment with Article 407, and hence GATT Article XI, the United States is not precluded from arguing that the legislation in question is properly within the terms of and consistent with, the national treatment provisions of the FTA and the GATT." A majority of the panel concluded that the case did in fact involve an internal measure governed by the national treatment provision of Article III of GATT, but that its terms of reference precluded it from dealing with the compatibility of that measure with Article III.

Such a consequence is unfortunate. The objective of the FTA panel process is to provide speedy and effective dispute resolution. This is defeated if a panel does not have jurisdiction to deal with the real issue in dispute, or if it does not exercise a jurisdiction that it has. Care ought to be taken by the parties in framing questions for panels to ensure that the result in the *Lobsters* case does not occur again. Perhaps consideration should be given to establishing standard terms of reference for chapter 18 panels so that uncertainty over the scope of their jurisdiction is minimized.[39]

The ambivalence over the adjudicative and conciliatory roles of chapter 18 panels is illustrated by the requirements that the panel issue an initial report. This report, which contains findings of fact and a determination of whether there has been a violation of the agreement or nullification or impairment, suggests a mediatory or conciliatory function, giving the parties an opportunity not only to ensure that the panel has got its facts right, but also to allow the parties to see in advance where the panel is going and perhaps to take steps to resolve the problem themselves. The initial report procedure under GATT has been a slightly different process. There the parties only get to see a statement of facts. They do not get a chance to preview the final determination of the panel.

The initial report process also gives the panel the opportunity to get reactions to what it has said. Particularly in cases where the panel has made recommendations for the resolution of the dispute, the panel can reconsider whether the direction it has proposed is one that is likely to meet with fundamental objections by one or both of the parties. Again, this emphasizes the mediatory or conciliatory functions of a chapter 18 panel. It must be recalled that the function of a chapter 18 panel is recommendatory only; a panel has no power of binding decision, unless it has been constituted as a binding arbitration panel under chapter 1806. Thus, its authority will depend on the extent to which it can make a case for a resolution of the dispute that has a powerful appeal to both parties.[40]

Acceptance of Panel Decisions

The stipulation in paragraph 8 of Article 1807 that the resolution of the dispute by the parties "normally shall conform with the recommendation of the panel" created an expectation that panel decisions under chapter 18 would effectively become final determinations accepted by the parties. In fact, this has not turned out to be the case, and it has led to some criticism of the chapter 18 process. In neither of the two cases heard so far has the commission been able to adopt *simpliciter* the conclusions of the panel. In each case the commission has entered into negotiations in light of the panel decision to try to resolve the issue. In the case of *Salmon and Herring*, these negotiations were successful, the parties agreeing on a solution not dissimilar to the panel's decision. In the case of *Lobsters*, the parties were unable to reach any conclusion through negotiations.

This resort to negotiations rather than simply adopting the panel decision may be inevitable, at least in the early years of the use of the chapter 18 procedures. The issues that have been placed before panels have been difficult politically. They have reached a panel because neither party has been prepared to concede or to make any compromises. Such issues may be of immense local or national concern, which has made it difficult for the two governments to negotiate a solution. The salmon and herring issue, for example, was characterized in the press as one that could cost hundreds of jobs in British Columbia and have catastrophic effects on the fish-processing industry.

In such circumstances, though a panel can make a determination of a legal issue, it may not produce a result that is acceptable politically to one or both of the parties. Moreover, the type of "yes or no" answer that a legal decision often gives may not practically resolve the dispute. Further negotiations may be necessary, in light of the panel decision to produce a solution. However, the panel's decision may have played a crucial role in directing the ultimate result.

Furthermore, the habit of accepting the results of a third-party determination is still in its infancy as far as states are concerned. It will take some time of familiarization with the process under the FTA before the two governments will get used to the idea that while they will win some cases they will certainly lose some. In effect, the two governments, and the public they represent, will have to come to terms with the idea of losing. Accepting a loss in international dispute settlement is difficult because issues are often seen in nationalistic rather than in substantive terms.

In this regard, the two governments have to consider carefully how they respond publicly to panel decisions. Statements by governments create domestic political expectations that make acceptance of a panel report difficult. These statements can also enhance or diminish the credibility of the dispute settlement process.

The chapter 18 dispute settlement process combines both intergovernmental or political elements with objective third-party determination. The system is a hybrid that is perhaps best suited to the realities of trade disputes between the two states, rather than being cast in a single, inflexible mode.

CONCLUSION

It will take more than the two existing panel decisions before any definitive conclusions can be drawn about the chapter 18 dispute settlement process. In one sense these two cases prove that the process can work – the two governments have established a procedure that appears to be able to do what its limited frame of reference contemplates. Nevertheless, the process does have limitations and its utility should not be overemphasized. In this regard, certain comments and tentative conclusions can be offered.

First, sending difficult political issues to an FTA panel does not diminish their political volatility, although it does provide a third party who can be blamed for an unfavourable result! The two parties have to be realistic about what the chapter 18 process can achieve, and send to panels only those cases to whose resolution a panel can make a positive contribution. A panel proceeding is not an alternative to making difficult political decisions or choices.

Second, a panel is essentially a body that, by its makeup and procedure, can best answer questions of interpretation of the agreement where there is reasonably objective criteria on which a decision can be based. Such questions often fall into the "either-or" or "win-lose" categories. Panels will be less effective in making important trade policy choices, and thus may not be a sufficiently sophisticated mechanism for many of the trade issues that arise under the FTA.

Third, while the use of ad hoc, part-time panelists is an element of the compromise between the Canadian institutionalized dispute settlement ideal and the American negotiation-consultation preference, it has its costs. There are, it is true, definite advantages in the early stages of the development of a procedure of this nature in utilizing many different panelists. Nevertheless, there is a loss in continuity, in the building up of expertise and in institutional memory. In this regard the bilateral secretariat has yet to develop the role played by the GATT secretariat in the GATT dispute settlement process.

Fourth, since trade disputes between states ultimately concern the interests of individuals engaged in or affected by trade, some consideration should be given to a procedure in Canada under which individuals could require the government formally to consider initiating chapter 18 proceedings in response to a complaint. Rights of this nature exist in the United States in respect of GATT violations,[41] and a similar process might be considered for Canada for chapter 18 disputes.

Fifth, international trade law, including the law of GATT and the law of the FTA, is only in a formative stage. Notwithstanding the claims of governments that they are holding to well-established principles to support their case, the field is in the early stages of legal development. This means that panels may well be confronted with issues of interpretation that are essentially issues of first impression and they will have to fashion their solutions with little guidance from past decisions. Thus, the role of a panel is not only to resolve the dispute in the case before it, but also to try to contribute to an orderly development in FTA law and the law of international trade generally. This role is crucial, since the issues before panels can have far-reaching implications. The two chapter 18 panels so far, for example, have been concerned with issues relating to the management of natural resources and the relationship of trade law and environmental regulation, issues that go to the heart of the sovereignty of a state.

Sixth, the overlap between the provisions of the law of the FTA and the law of GATT create new possibilities and opportunities. FTA cases involve interpretations of GATT law, and decisions of GATT panels are critical to the FTA panels' decision-making. This raises the question whether the law of the FTA and the law of GATT on similar issues will develop in parallel or whether they will diverge. Will there be forum shopping between FTA and GATT processes? *Salmon and Herring*, for example, could have been placed before a GATT panel. The appropriate forum and the consistency of the two bodies of law is something that can only be worked out over time.

The dispute settlement process under chapter 18 of the FTA raises new questions and new opportunities for the development of international law. It provides challenges for the two governments as well as for those involved as panelists on specific disputes. They are intellectual and practical challenges of a kind to which Maxwell Cohen has devoted his career, and for which his experience as scholar, practitioner, and judge provides exemplary guidance.

NOTES

An earlier version of this paper was delivered at the Canadian Institute of Advanced Legal Studies, Stanford Lectures, Palo Alto, California, July 1990.

1 [1984] ICJ Rep. 246.
2 27 Int'l Leg. Mat. 281 (1988). The agreement entered into force on 1 January 1989.
3 The current caseload of the International Court of Justice would suggest that this trend is changing; see the statement of the president of the court, Sir Robert Jennings, on the report of the International Court of Justice, UN Doc. A/46/PV.44, 6–23 (1991), reprinted in (1992), 89 *American Journal of International Law* 249.
4 These were the *Trail Smelter* arbitration, the *Gut Dam* arbitration, and the *Gulf of Maine Maritime Boundary* case. The first two were before ad hoc arbitral tribunals, and the last was before a chamber of the International Court of Justice. See, generally, Wang, "Adjudication of Canada–United States Disputes" (1981), 19 *Canadian Yearbook of International Law* 158–228.
5 Robert Hudec, "GATT Dispute Settlement after the Tokyo Round: An Unfinished Business" (1980), 13 *Cornell Journal of International Law* 145; Donald McRae, "Recourse to the GATT for Resolving International Trade Disputes," in Owen Saunders, ed., *Trading Canada's Natural Resources* (Toronto: Carswell 1987), 168–88; Hudec, "The FTA

Provisions on Dispute Settlement: The Lessons of the GATT Experience," in Donald McRae and Debra Steger, eds., *Understanding the Free Trade Agreement* (Halifax: Institute for Research on Public Policy 1988), 31–42.
6 *Understanding on Rules and Procedures Governing the Settlement of Disputes under Articles XXII and XXIII of the General Agreement on Tariffs and Trade*, MTN.TNC/W/FA.
7 This process is intended to be in effect for only five years while the parties negotiate a permanent regime for anti-dumping and countervail. It may be extended for a further two years and then terminated by either party on six months' notice. FTA Article 1906.
8 A panel is composed of five members, a majority of whom must be lawyers, appointed from rosters drawn up by each party. Each party selects two panelists and then they jointly choose a fifth. The chair, who must also be a lawyer, is selected from among the five by the panelists themselves. FTA Annex 1901.2.
9 On these processes see, generally, Legault, "Institutions and Dispute Settlement Procedures under the Canada–U.S. Free Trade Agreement," in McRae and Steger, eds., *Understanding*, 21–9.
10 Chapter 17 on Financial Services is excluded from the scope of the chapter 18 process, as are anti-dumping and countervailing duty disputes which fall under chapter 19.
11 Chapter 1801 provides that the provisions of chapter 18 "shall apply with respect to the avoidance or settlement of all disputes regarding the interpretation or application of the Agreement or whenever a Party considers that an actual or proposed measure of the other Party is or would be inconsistent with the obligations of this Agreement or cause nullification or impairment in the sense of Article 2011, unless the Parties agree to use another procedure in any particular case."
12 GATT Article XXIII.
13 Unlike GATT, under the FTA there is a right to a panel.
14 If the dispute relates to emergency action under chapter 11 of the FTA, the commission must send it to binding arbitration. FTA Article 1806(1).
15 Article 1806(2).
16 Article 1909.
17 Unless the parties agree otherwise, the three months run from the appointment of the chair.
18 *In the Matter of Canada's Landing Requirement for Pacific Coast Salmon and Herring*, 16 Oct. 1989; and *Lobsters from Canada*, 25 May 1990. At the time of writing a third panel had been established under chapter 18, but it had yet to deliver a decision. [Eds note: The decision, *In the Matter of Article 304 and the Definition of Direct Cost of Processing or Direct Cost of Assembling*, was delivered in July 1992.]

19 One panel member did not participate in the decision on Article XI; one member of the panel did not concur fully in the decision on Article XX. For a comment on the decision see Ted McDorman, "Using the Dispute Settlement Regime of the Free Trade Agremeent: The West Coast Salmon and Herring Problem" (1990), 4 *Canada–U.S. Business Law Review* 177.
20 These percentages were to be reviewed after a four-year period. The agreement also contained provisions prohibiting the resale of unprocessed herring from the United States to Japan.
21 For a comment on the decision see Ted McDorman, "Dissecting the Free Trade Agreement Lobster Panel Decision" (1991), 18 *Canadian Business Law Journal* 445.
22 Rosters were in fact drawn up for each country.
23 By contrast, chapter 19 panelists must, in addition, be of good character, high standing, and repute and have general familiarity with international trade law. FTA Annex 1901.2.
24 Article 1807 provides that panelists shall be chosen from the roster "wherever possible."
25 Although it is often assumed that it is only the chair who could be a nonnational, under Article 1807(3) any one of the five panel members could be a nonnational.
26 Annex 1901.2 paras. 2 and 3.
27 The panel was asked whether Canada's landing requirement in respect of salmon and herring caught off its Pacific coast was "incompatible with Article 407 of the FTA and if so, whether the requirement is a measure subject to an exclusion applicable under Article 1201."
28 Article 407 constitutes an incorporation into the FTA of Article XI of GATT, and FTA Article 1201 incorporates GATT Article XX. Moreover, the question put to the panel asked expressly for an interpretation of both GATT Article XI and GATT Article XX.
29 The panel was asked whether section 307(1)(J) of the Magnuson Fishery Conservation and Management Act was inconsistent with the United States obligations under Article 407 of the FTA, and, if so, was it subject to an exception applicable under Article 1201.
30 See "Canada–United States Free Trade Agreement, Model Rules of Procedure for Chapter 18 Panels," *Canada Gazette, Part I*, 14 Jan. 1989, Part III, para. 5.
31 In the *Salmon and Herring* case there was a majority of Canadians, and in *Lobsters* there was a majority of Americans.
32 Panel deliberations are not made public and the decisions so far have not disclosed how panelists have voted. In *Salmon and Herring* a single panelist dissented on each issue; in *Lobsters* there was 3:2 majority on each issue. This was reported in the press as being a decision along national lines.

33 Conflicts of interest in panel members are avoided by a disclosure mechanism administered by the secretariat.
34 This comment is made with respect to a panel composed of two nationals from each party and a fifth nonnational chair. The dynamics of a three-person tribunal where there is only one national of each state and a third nonnational as chair might well differ.
35 Each panel member is entitled to appoint an assistant, but it is unlikely that it was intended that such an individual would provide technical expertise.
36 Article 1807 (5).
37 Ibid.
38 In *Lobsters*, the parties apparently indicated to the panel during the course of the proceedings that "the Panel's assignment did not call for recommendations relating further to the possible resolution of the dispute"; *Lobsters*, para. 5.2. Although it was included as part of its decision and not expressed as a recommendation, the panel in *Salmon and Herring* indicated how the Canadian landing requirement could be brought in line with Article xx of GATT. In fact there is some ambiguity in paragraphs 5 and 8 of Article 1807 over what is the "decision" of the panel and what is a recommendation.
39 The standard terms of reference for GATT panels introduced in the decision of the contracting parties of 12 April 1989 provides that the panel is to examine the issue "in the light of the the relevant GATT provisions." *Improvements to the GATT Dispute Settlement Rules and Procedures* (L/6489).
40 For a critical analysis of the chapter 18 process in the context of the *Salmon and Herring* case see Weiler, "Anatomy of a Trade Dispute: Lessons for Newlywed Trading Partners," paper presented at Canadian Institute of Advanced Legal Studies, Stanford Lectures, July 1990.
41 Section 301 of the U.S. Trade Act.

PART TWO
Public Law

Maxwell Cohen's Perspective on Human Rights in Canada: The Entrenchment of the Charter and the Enactment of the Emergencies Act

ANNEMIEKE HOLTHUIS

Maxwell Cohen is known primarily as an international legal scholar, jurist, and practitioner.[1] However, his contribution to Canadian public law, in particular constitutional and human rights law, has also been significant.[2] From his early work on the origins of the writ of habeas corpus to his chairmanship of the Special Committee on Hate Propaganda in Canada and his later works examining the relationship between international law and the *Canadian Charter of Rights and Freedoms*,[3] Cohen's contribution to human rights scholarship in Canada has largely been informed by his international perspective. Indeed, this article will focus on two features of Cohen's approach to human rights law – his emphasis on the relevance of international law principles in interpreting Canadian human rights law and his view of the law as a practical means of solving political problems. This article applies Cohen's distinctive perspective on Canadian human rights law to two related developments in Canadian law: the constitutional entrenchment of a human rights regime and the reforms to Canada's public emergency regime, the War Measures Act.[4]

COHEN'S APPROACH TO HUMAN RIGHTS LAW: AN INTRODUCTION

Cohen's international law writings emphasize both the relevance of international legal norms to Canadian law and the importance of bringing a Canadian perspective to international law.[5] To Cohen, the relationship between international law and Canada's domestic law, both English Canada's common law and Quebec's civil law, is evident.[6] Indeed, Cohen drew on international norms as a major theme in writing about and in advancing human rights law in Canada.

Cohen was one of a number of Canadians actively following the international community's efforts after the Second World War to formulate a new international order.[7] One of the principal purposes of the new United Nations was to promote "human rights," a term first employed in the UN Charter.[8] Writing in 1968, Cohen suggested that a major impetus for the development of the concept of human rights both in Canada and internationally over the previous two decades had been the "radical change" in consciousness effected by the events of the war. Newly focused on human rights issues, the United Nations established a Commission on Human Rights in 1946 and in 1948 adopted a statement of fundamental rights and freedoms, the Universal Declaration of Human Rights.[9] Later, human rights instruments like the International Covenant on Civil and Political Rights (ICCPR), the International Covenant on Economic, Social and Cultural Rights, and the International Convention on the Elimination of All Forms of Racial Discrimination[10] would represent "nothing less than a re-statement of the role of the individual in international law" in Cohen's view.[11] As will be seen below, a similar trend towards strengthening rights protections for the individual would be reflected in Canadian domestic law after the war.

While the United Nations, its constituent bodies, and member states began to develop a complex constitutional and legal framework to address human rights issues, that framework was subject to significant political pressures. In 1960 Cohen emphasized the challenges posed by the Cold War divisions between East and West, the consequent nuclear arms race, the anti-colonial movements and the emergence of new states in Africa and Asia, the population explosion and the need to redistribute wealth, resources, and technology.[12] In resolving political problems such as these, law and legal language, as well as the techniques and skills of lawyers, are essential for Cohen.[13] This is a second distinctive theme in Cohen's writing.

To Cohen, law is "the active helpmate of statesmanship and diplomacy" and it can be used to give practical effect to political compromises.[14] While the art of diplomacy appears initially to depend on flexibility and the possibility of negotiation, he suggests that "behind it are often positions of great rigidity imposed by the political emotions of the situation."[15] In contrast, he argues that law may appear to be inflexible but is by nature subject to an ongoing process of interpretation, redefinition, and reinterpretation.[16] Cohen contends that law is capable of providing a "durable framework within which lasting settlements arrived at politically can have that degree of permanence which alone can promise security, stability, and opportunities for future peaceful change."[17] In his view, the understanding that law should not be divorced from policy considerations is critical to this durable framework.[18]

In sum, this article applies Cohen's two themes to Canadian human rights law. In particular, the article explores the relevance of international human rights norms to the process of constitutionally entrenching human rights in the Charter and to the reforms to Canada's public emergency legislation, from the War Measures Act to the enactment of the Emergencies Act.[19] As well the article examines how the law attempts to fashion practical legal frameworks to address two sensitive political issues in Canada: the constitutional recognition of human rights and the protection of human rights in states of emergency.

THE DEVELOPMENT OF HUMAN RIGHTS IN CANADA

Towards a Bill of Rights and a Charter

Internationally, the human rights abuses perpetrated during the Second World War served as an impetus for renewed efforts to grapple with human rights issues. This international awareness of the need to protect human rights was mirrored in Canada.[20] After the war, Canadians began to examine more critically the Canadian government's exercise of emergency powers pursuant to the War Measures Act during the two world wars.[21] The extensive administrative powers available to the federal government, in particular the government's reliance on the War Measures Act to deport persons of Japanese origin at the end of the war, led to calls for reforms to the act and for greater protection for human rights.[22]

The postwar awareness of the importance of human rights protections would be a factor pushing Canada towards the constitutionalization of human rights norms. Yet, both prior to and during the Second World War, Canadian concerns about discrimination and the promotion of hatred against identifiable groups were already emerging. In 1934 Manitoba adopted legislation to address the question of hate propaganda.[23] Ontario also adopted legislation prohibiting the public display of discriminatory signs in 1944.[24] Canadians began to criticize what Howe calls the war's "double standard." In his words, "Canadians were fighting abroad against racism, while at home interning Japanese Canadians, discriminating against Jews and blacks in the war industries, denying natives access to veterans' benefits and giving women in the war industries less pay than men for the same work."[25] Following the war, legislation to prohibit various forms of discrimination began to be more widely enacted, beginning with the Saskatchewan Bill of Rights and eventually leading to the present-day forms of human rights legislation.[26]

Internationally, Canadian human rights concerns were reflected in Canada's vote in favour of the adoption of the Universal Declaration in 1948.[27] In 1959 Cohen viewed a Bill of Rights as "a more direct link" to these international human rights standards.[28] John Diefenbaker made the introduction of a proposed Bill of Rights part of his election platform in 1957 and 1958, though several parliamentary committees during the previous Liberal administration had studied such a possibility. The notion of a Bill of Rights was controversial.[29] Cohen noted that its introduction "opened the most widespread debate probably ever held in Canada about general and technical questions of civil liberties and related matters."[30]

To Cohen, several factors contributed to Canadians' desire for a Bill of Rights. First, Canadians were aware of the international developments in the field of human rights. Second, the increase in government intervention during wartime into new areas of social and economic policy and its continuation after the end of the war contributed to the "sense of the impingement of the state on the individual."[31] As well, there was, in Cohen's view, a growing "constitutional-mindedness" in Canada as the country began to develop its self-image as an independent nation and as part of the British Commonwealth.[32] As Canadians considered their standing on the international stage, they also began to examine their domestic human rights record and sought to address issues brought to the fore by the events of the Second World War. In light of these considerations, Cohen concluded the time was right to enact a Bill of Rights.

At the same time, Cohen also felt that there had been little serious consideration of a Bill of Rights' international antecedents or the extent to which international law might inform Canada's approach to a Bill of Rights.[33] A Bill of Rights would, in Cohen's view, draw on a number of different historical traditions. In his 1960 testimony before the Special Committee on Human Rights and Fundamental Freedoms, Cohen elaborated on these traditions. To him, the influences of British constitutional history with the development of the common law, the interplay between Parliament and the common law, and the assertions of rights and privileges in the petitions and Charters of Britain were central to a Bill of Rights.[34] The effects of such

Western legal notions as natural law, positive law, and the concepts of man's inalienable rights were also reflected in a Bill of Rights. Indeed, the judicial efforts in later division of powers cases to formulate an "implied Bill of Rights" were, in Cohen's words, an attempt to develop a "secular natural law" which would bind the federal Parliament.[35] Finally, Cohen noted the importation into the proposed Bill of Rights of both Anglo-American notions of "rights" and the international legal terminology of "human rights" and "fundamental freedoms."[36]

In considering a proposed Bill of Rights, Cohen posed two questions: whether Canada had an obligation under the UN Charter to promote human rights and fundamental freedoms in its domestic law and whether the existence of such an obligation would influence the legal definition of "public policy" in Canada.[37] To Cohen, Articles 55 and 56 of the UN Charter clearly imposed an obligation to promote human rights and fundamental freedoms. In his view it was an obligation to be respected notwithstanding the difficulties posed by Canadian federalism.[38]

Despite the constitutional problems inherent in the implementation of international law in Canada, Cohen clearly favoured the introduction of a Bill of Rights as a symbolic "restatement" of those human rights Canadians wished to protect. In his 1958 examination of international law issues of practical interest to Canadian lawyers, Cohen noted several references by both legislators and courts to the UN Charter and the Universal Declaration, most prominently in the *In Re Drummond Wren* case which struck down a race-based restrictive covenant.[39] To Cohen, a Bill of Rights offered the judiciary a mechanism by which it could rely on the Universal Declaration and its elaboration of the UN Charter's phrase "human rights and fundamental freedoms" in formulating Canadian "public policy" without entering into the debate about the Universal Declaration's legal effect.[40] To Cohen, a Bill of Rights would "add to the total Canadian climate of protection of human rights in general" and would "inevitably influence the manner in which judges may be encouraged to look at *all* statutes whether provincial or federal in origin."[41]

The judiciary's eventual treatment of the Bill of Rights would not live up to Cohen's expectations. The Bill of Rights' primary weakness was that it was a federal statute applicable to federal laws and was treated, at best, as a quasi-constitutional document.[42] The judiciary, apparently uncomfortable with the new role accorded to it, interpreted the Bill of Rights restrictively.[43] In 1968 Cohen outlined a "concrete" human rights program for Canada as a practical solution to the deficiencies of the federal Bill of Rights. He recommended strengthening existing provincial human rights legislation and establishing such legislation where it did not exist. He proposed the establishment of a National Council on Human Rights, composed of representatives of all levels of government as well as non-governmental organizations, to assist in developing human rights policy in Canada. Significantly, Cohen also proposed implementing those international human rights conventions to which Canada was a party, and working towards a constitutionally entrenched Charter of Rights.[44]

While the law-making process in the UN resulted in a wide variety of international instruments, foremost among them the two 1966 covenants, Canada was also beginning another period of constitutional negotiation in the 1960s. Cohen suggests that by the 1960s two main objectives drove the constitutional discussions: first, the desire to patriate the Constitution and devise a Canadian amending formula; and second, the desire to establish a new federal-provincial balance of power while at the same time entrenching certain basic rights, linguistic or otherwise.[45]

The notion of an entrenched Charter of Rights, like the Bill of Rights before it, sparked a fierce and very political debate in Canada. It pitted those who wished to limit parliamentary sovereignty by constitutionalizing certain rights protection, whether they be international human rights norms implemented into Canadian law or Canadian formulations of fundamental rights, against the supporters of a purer notion of parliamentary supremacy.[46] In 1968 Cohen stated that "no one can predict what will come out of the present exercise in constitutional review," though at a minimum "such study may help depoliticize many matters which do tend to be escalated artificially."[47]

It is beyond the scope of this article to consider the negotiations leading up to the adoption of the Charter in any detail.[48] The history of the constitutional conferences throughout the 1960s and 1970s is well known. Unsuccessful attempts were made to reach agreement on a variety of constitutional issues.[49] Suffice to note that a central issue of the debate remained the scope of the Charter's application and the desire of some provinces to limit its application within their spheres of jurisdiction.[50] In the fall of 1980, though federal-provincial talks were again stalled, a proposed constitutional package including a Charter was placed before the House of Commons and Senate and submitted to a parliamentary committee for study.[51] In November 1980 and January 1981 Cohen testified before the Special Joint Committee of the Senate and of the House of Commons on the Constitution both personally and in his capacity as chairman of the

Select Committee on the Constitution of the Canadian Jewish Congress (CJC).

In his testimony, Cohen expressed his clear support for the concept of an entrenched Charter.[52] Indeed, he would have extended the concept of mobility rights to include the concept of property ownership and the movement of capital, goods, and services, subject to reasonable limitations which would preserve the basic economic union of Canada.[53] Cohen was also of the view that issues relating to the economic union of Canada and "the means and institutions for improving provincial input into decision making and federal-provincial co-operation generally" should not be neglected. To him, discussions should have been ongoing on all constitutional reform issues.[54] In the context of the 1991–2 constitutional negotiations, Cohen's remarks seem prescient.

Consistent with his emphasis on the relevance of international human rights norms to Canadian domestic law, it was Cohen's view that entrenching a Charter could assist Canada in fulfilling its international obligations, particularly those imposed by the ICCPR. However, he expressed misgivings about whether the proposed Charter reflected all Canada's important international obligations. In particular, Cohen and the CJC argued that the proposed Charter did not meet all Canada's international obligations relating to states of emergency, hate propaganda, freedom of movement, rights on arrest or detention, international war crimes, among others.[55] Cohen's application of international legal norms to the proposed Charter set high standards for the Special Joint Committee.

In addition to these substantive concerns, Cohen testified before the Special Joint Committee on the constitutional amendment process. Commenting on the references before the Manitoba, Quebec, and Newfoundland Courts of Appeal, Cohen argued that the degree of provincial consent required for the patriation of the Constitution and the entrenchment of an amending formula was both a legal and a political question. Cohen expressed the view that provincial consent to the patriation of the Constitution was not a binding rule of law but was "an issue of considerable political importance."[56] The Supreme Court took a similar position in deciding the *Patriation Reference*. A majority of the court held that the federal government's proposed plan to patriate the constitution unilaterally was legal. Provincial consent was not to be a precondition in law for the United Kingdom's Parliament to exercise its legislative powers. However, a majority of the court held that a substantial degree of provincial agreement was required by virtue of constitutional convention.[57] In this manner, the Supreme Court in the *Patriation Reference* effectively manoeuvred the federal government and the provinces back to the negotiating table to hammer out a deal. The court's approach in the *Patriation Reference* arguably exemplifies Cohen's thesis that the law can serve as a flexible framework for the formulation of practical political settlements.

As is well known, on 5 November 1981 the federal and provincial governments struck a political and constitutional deal which incorporated into the Charter a legislative override applicable to the fundamental freedoms, equality rights, and legal rights.[58] Section 33 was a uniquely Canadian political compromise which combined a measure of parliamentary supremacy with a justiciable bill of rights.[59] The entrenchment of the Charter represents, for many, the culminating event in the gradual constitutionalization of Canadian human rights standards. While this development was influenced in large measure by the impact in Canada of the redefined relationship between the state and the individual at international law,[60] the framework and language of the Charter also represent a practical legal solution to the difficult problem, among others, of reconciling the principle of parliamentary supremacy with an entrenched Charter of Rights.

Interpreting the Charter: The Relevance of International Law

Many of the guaranteed rights, as well as the section 1 limitation clause, derive from or have their equivalents in universal standards of human rights such as the Universal Declaration of Rights and the two covenants.[61] Nevertheless the Charter and section 33 reflect a fundamental Canadian ambivalence. Prior to the Charter's entrenchment, Cohen noted this ambivalence by pointing out that Canadians regarded the international human rights standards reflected in the Charter as highly desirable, yet these standards "were viewed ... with some reserve when Canadians were asked to convert these concepts, ideals and potential rules into Canadian statutory or constitutional obligations."[62] However, the Charter affords Canadian human rights lawyers an opportunity both to appreciate the relevance of international human rights standards and to apply them in a uniquely Canadian context.[63]

Cohen addressed this interpretive challenge in an article entitled "Toward a Paradigm of Theory and Practice: The Canadian Charter of Rights and Freedoms – International Law Influences and Interactions." Stating "[t]he ritual of Canadian interpretation is likely to be performed with more or less classical reliance upon the words and structure of the Charter itself," Cohen asks "how far many [sic] extrinsic materials be used whenever the internal structural approach requires the assistance of history or policy to clarify and what will constitute appropriate extrinsic references"?[64] At the heart of Cohen's question lies the issue of the relationship of international law to domestic law.

As early as 1958, Cohen was of the view that Canadian courts had not adequately addressed either the relationship of customary law to domestic law or the scope of Canadian conventional obligations.[65] In 1958 this may have been attributable to the fact that international law in Canada was a relatively new field of study.[66] Yet, the relationship between international and domestic law was only somewhat clearer when Cohen and Anne F. Bayefsky considered it twenty-five years later. Writing a year after the Charter's entrenchment, Cohen and Bayefsky wrote one of the first analyses of the relationship between international human rights norms and the Charter.[67]

In their examination of domestic law's relationship to international law, Cohen and Bayefsky argue that Canadian case law suggests that unless there is a conflicting statutory provision or common law rule, customary law is incorporated directly into Canadian law.[68] In contrast, they note that conventional or treaty law must generally be implemented in Canada by an intervening legislative act by Parliament or a provincial legislature in order to have the force of law.[69] Even if treaties or conventions have been implemented, some courts refer to international instruments only when the statutes are considered ambiguous.[70] Cohen and Bayefsky acknowledge that the relevance of conventional law to which Canada is not a party may be even more limited. However, they argue that the statutory presumption that a legislature intended to act in a manner consistent with its international obligations may add some persuasive force to conventional law which Canada has ratified but not yet implemented.[71]

Cohen and Bayefsky also consider the relationship between international human rights law and the Charter.[72] They note that the Charter does not expressly state it was enacted to implement Canada's international obligations. Only section 11(g) of the Charter refers directly to international law.[73] Thus, in 1983, Cohen and Bayefsky offered a way to remedy this failure to implement directly Canadian's international obligations in the Charter. They suggest that the language of the Charter and the covenants should be compared. The submissions to and by the drafters of the Charter as well as other extrinsic evidence should be considered in order to determine "whether the purpose of the enactment was to implement" or "give legal effect to" a particular international obligation. Arguably, on a section by section basis, the Charter could be found to implement indirectly some, though not all, of the rights of the two international covenants.[74] Cohen concludes in a later article that "[t]he Charter purports to reflect some but not all Canadian commitments where signature and ratification have taken place, as well as being the basis for an interpretive tilt towards international human rights doctrines that are pervasively influential but not conventional obligations."[75]

A court relying on the traditional requirement of explicit implementation of international obligations would clearly not be satisfied by the above approach to implementation. However, Cohen and Bayefsky argue that the traditional rules governing the relationship between international and Canadian law, in particular the rule regarding requisite ambiguity which limits references to international conventional law, should be applied with less rigour to Charter interpretation.[76] This approach would appear to be consistent with the Supreme Court's approach in certain cases. In *Reference Re Public Service Employee Relations Act*, Dickson CJ, though in dissent, stated "the *Charter* conforms to the spirit of this contemporary international human rights movement."[77] For Dickson, customary and conventional international human rights law, including "declarations, covenants, conventions, judicial and quasi-judicial decisions of international tribunals, customary norms" are "relevant and persuasive" sources of extrinsic evidence for interpreting the rights guarantees of the Charter as well as assessing limitations on those rights under section 1.[78]

Still it remains the case, as Cohen stated in 1987, that the connections between the Charter and international law are relatively unexplored. In his view, Canadian scholarship and jurisprudence on the Charter focuses on the somewhat narrow horizons of "the historical, precedential, and parliamentary record within which the Canadian Charter developed."[79] Cohen recognizes that a degree of uncertainty about the extent to which international human rights norms apply in Canada is inevitable given what he terms "the descending scale of Canadian international compliance, from ratified and implemented treaties to simple UN resolutions" and the corresponding scales of relevance and persuasiveness.[80] Nevertheless, Cohen suggests that the relationship between Canadian and international human rights norms remains a fruitful area of future study.[81] For Cohen, the human rights standards in the UN Charter, the Universal Declaration, and the two international covenants and related enforcement mechanisms, including the Optional Protocol to the ICCPR, are sources of law to which judges and scholars can turn when attempting to interpret the provisions of the Charter in a manner consistent with Canada's international obligations. Scholars such as Bayefsky and Schabas are now taking up Cohen's interpretive challenge.[82]

The Tension between Conscience and Responsibility: Derogations from Human Rights in Public Emergencies

In 1968 Cohen argued that the international community had come to a problematic stage in the development of its human rights norms. On the one hand, states with diverse legal systems had achieved sufficient consensus on the content of human rights norms to create the Charter, the Universal Declaration, the covenants, and other conventions such as the Convention on the Elimination of All Forms of Racial Discrimination. On the other hand, "the reluctance of many states, including Canada, to readily accept as a municipal law obligation, varieties of measures for international implementation and supervision, indicates the ambivalence that continues to operate in this tension between conscience and responsibility."[83] This tension was reflected in Canada in the debate during the entrenchment of the Charter over permissible derogations from human rights in times of emergency. Cohen's contribution to this debate is considered below.

In 1968 Pierre Elliott Trudeau, then minister of justice, canvassed alternatives for protecting human rights in emergencies in a proposal, *A Canadian Charter of Human Rights*. The alternatives included an exemption or notwithstanding clause through which the Charter could be suspended in times of emergency; a clause setting out the rights which could be infringed and the permissible extent of such infringement; and a limitations clause which would permit the judiciary to define the limitation of rights in emergencies.[84] The federal government's 1969 proposals incorporated the first alternative.[85] When the proposed Charter finally reached the Special Joint Committee of the Senate and of the House of Commons over a decade later, it contained only a limitation clause, which provided that Charter rights would be "subject only to such reasonable limits as are generally accepted in a free and democratic society with a parliamentary system of government."[86]

In his testimony before the Special Joint Committee on the Constitution in 1981, Cohen considered the proposed section 1. Though this section may be seen as "an attempt to find some kind of practical, legal, political equilibrium" between the conflicting demands of an entrenched Charter and parliamentary supremacy, Cohen argued, as did the Select Committee of the Canadian Jewish Congress (CJC) which he chaired, that "the way in which Section 1 is now worded makes no serious contribution to the protection of the rights system."[87] He argued that section 1 should be eliminated altogether from the Charter of Rights. In his view, under section 1 as drafted, a government might limit rights in a manner inconsistent with Article 5(1) of the ICCPR.[88]

Cohen argued that a separate express provision would resolve the issue of the limitation of rights in emergencies more frankly.[89] Indeed, the CJC's Select Committee proposed such a provision. It would apply in "war, domestic insurrection or natural calamity threatening the life or safety of the nation or any part thereof."[90] The proposal essentially paralleled Article 4 of the ICCPR, the Covenant's public emergencies provision.[91] The CJC proposal thus indirectly raised the issue of a Charter's relationship to Article 4, in particular the protection for fundamental rights.

The CJC proposal contained certain protection for human rights in emergencies. Emergency measures inconsistent with the Charter as ordinarily interpreted would lapse after twenty days unless extended by a two-thirds vote of Parliament.[92] However, the CJC's proposed approach did not refer to the rights which Article 4(2) of the ICCPR designates as nonderogable rights, including the right to life; the right not to be subject to torture or to cruel, inhuman, or degrading treatment or punishment; the right not to be held in slavery or in servitude; and the right to be free from the retroactive imposition of criminal law.[93] In testimony before the Joint Committee, Cohen stated that a detailed analysis of which rights should be nonderogable in a variety of emergencies was desirable. However, there had not been sufficient time to undertake such an analysis. Another CJC representative, Professor Irwin Cotler of McGill's Faculty of Law, noted that there are a limited number of rights which should never be overridden in emergencies.[94]

The Charter in its final form did not expressly implement Article 4 of the ICCPR governing states of emergency, in particular the guarantees of nonderogable rights.[95] Parliamentary supremacy was accommodated in the Charter by the presence of sections 1 and 33. Reliance on section 33 of the Charter could be of serious concern in emergencies, depending on the governmental action taken and the right to which the override applied. There are few limitations on its use to override any or all of the Charter rights within sections 2 and 7 to 15 other than the political costs associated with its exercise.[96] Even if an override is not invoked, section 1 provides for the reasonable limitation of rights, and the manner in which the judiciary would interpret section 1 emergencies is uncertain. In 1986 Cohen argued that the combined effect of the section 1 limitation clause and the section 33 override was to create a "double override."[97] A potential tension thus persists, as Cohen noted, between conscience and responsibility.

Though Cohen and the CJC were not successful in convincing the Special Joint Committee to remove the limitation clause from the Charter and to add a derogation clause for emergencies, submissions by nongovernmental organizations such as the CJC representing a broad range of interests were critical to the final form and, arguably, the very existence of the Charter. Similarly, the efforts of nongovernmental organizations were crucial to the incorporation of the concept of human rights in the UN Charter in 1945.[98] Indeed, Cohen predicted that nongovernmental organizations would be instrumental in pushing states like Canada to overcome their reluctance to make international human rights norms meaningful in domestic law.[99] Several years later, the work of organizations such as the National Association of Japanese-Canadians would help to develop Canada's new emergency regime, the Emergencies Act. This work in Canada was a continuation of the efforts of nongovernmental organizations like the International Commission of Jurists, the International Law Association, and several UN-appointed rapporteurs to formulate legal frameworks regulating the use of governmental emergency powers in states of emergency.[100]

THE DEVELOPMENT OF CANADA'S PUBLIC EMERGENCIES REGIME: THE EMERGENCIES ACT

The enactment of the Emergencies Act and the process of reform of the War Measures Act which preceded it reveal both of Cohen's themes – namely, the use of law as a practical means of solving political problems and the relevance of international law principles to Canadian domestic law. The Emergencies Act's framework and the safeguards which were eventually incorporated into it are practical responses to the experiences of Canadians in the two world wars and the October Crisis. With the Emergencies Act, Parliament attempted to create a legal framework to manage future emergencies in Canada with greater respect for human rights and less potential for abuse of power than the War Measures Act regime. In doing so, many of the safeguards incorporated in the Emergencies Act to protect individual rights and to guard against potential abuses of emergency powers reflect the international norms governing states of emergency in the ICCPR, though neither the Charter nor the Emergencies Act expressly implement Article 4's obligations in Canada. Arguably, the Emergencies Act must be interpreted with reference to those international norms.

As early as 1960, in his testimony before the Special Committee on Human Rights and Fundamental Freedoms, Cohen argued that a fundamental change in approach to emergencies legislation was necessary in Canada. In his view, emergency legislation in the 1960s must be capable of meeting a wide variety of emergencies, including the threat of nuclear war. To Cohen, such a new "survival Act" would have to control the movements of civilian populations, provide for the establishment of emergency shelters, and control food suppliers and other necessary goods and services.[101] The Emergencies Act and its complementary legislative measure, the Emergency Preparedness Act, would eventually respond to Cohen's suggestions.[102]

Eighteen years after his testimony before the Special Joint Committee, Cohen appeared before the Legislative Committee considering Bill C-77, the proposed emergencies regime.[103] In his testimony, he assessed the various approaches to emergency legislation capable of dealing with a variety of emergencies.[104] It was possible to argue that for security matters the ordinary laws of Canada, including the Criminal Code and the National Defence Act, were sufficient, while for social, economic, or other emergencies, ad hoc legislation could be enacted. Others preferred a single War Measures Act "with few sophisticated shadings to inhibit or encourage appropriate or inappropriate action."[105] Between these two extremes lay Bill C-77. Unlike the War Measures Act, which Cohen described as a "simple, single blunderbuss,"[106] Bill C-77 proposed a more flexible emergency regime covering different categories of emergency. Cohen recognized that more flexible legislation could be invoked more quickly, but he agreed with the enactment of such legislation provided it included sufficient safeguards against the abuse of executive powers.[107]

The desire to accord individual rights a greater degree of protection in emergencies and to tailor government emergency powers according to the nature and severity of the emergency figured prominently in the justification for the Emergencies Act.[108] Just as the events of the Second World War were the impetus for the greater protection of human rights internationally and in Canada, the October Crisis of 1970 and the detention of innocent persons under the War Measures Act spurred the process of reforming the War Measures Act. While much has been written about the first peacetime application of the War Measures Act, it is beyond the scope of this article to consider the October Crisis in great detail.[109] Put simply, the October Crisis clearly revealed that the War Measures Act's broad powers were no longer appropriate in a society infused by a new rights consciousness.

The many differences between the Emergencies Act that came into force in July 1988 and the War Measures Act will provide scholars with material for future study. One significant difference is that unlike the War Measures Act, the Emergencies Act creates four categories of "national" emergencies – namely, public welfare emergencies, public order emergencies, international emergencies, and war emergencies.[110] This approach reflects Cohen's two themes. The Emergencies Act provides a flexible framework for dealing with a variety of emergencies. As well, the Emergencies Act, though resting on constitutional foundations similar to those of the War Measures Act, more closely tracks the requirements of Article 4 of the ICCPR – namely, that states may employ emergency measures which are proportional to the nature and severity of the emergency.[111]

Another aspect of the Emergencies Act which reflects international norms is the act's objective of increasing parliamentary or judicial supervision of executive action. Arguably, the principles which underlie Article 4 of the ICCPR suggest that the degree to which a democratically elected legislative body or the judiciary is able to monitor the exercise of these emergency powers may be linked to the potential for ensuring greater respect for individual rights in emergencies.[112] Cohen advocated enhancing the role of Parliament and the judiciary in emergencies. In his view, the previous applications of the War Measures Act demonstrated the need for these changes.

Enhancing the Role of Parliament

Cohen argued before the Special Committee on Human Rights and Fundamental Freedoms in 1960 that the role of Parliament should be expanded during emergencies in Canada. Indeed, the War Measures Act as enacted in 1914 gave Parliament no specific supervisory role. Cohen noted in his testimony that increasing the degree of parliamentary supervision over the executive's exercise of War Measures Act powers appeared to be one of the proposed Bill of Rights' objectives.[113] He also argued that Parliament should sit throughout the duration of an emergency. In his view, the advantage of this would be that "while the proclamation was in force, [Parliament] would become a daily reviewing body over the curtailment of all phases of our life, including liberty."[114]

The 1960 amendments to the War Measures Act would not reflect Cohen's recommendations in their entirety. The amendments provided that the Governor-in-Council could exercise its emergency powers only on the issuance of an emergency proclamation. The proclamation then had to be laid before Parliament immediately or, if Parliament was not sitting, within fifteen days of Parliament being summoned. Parliament could revoke the declaration of emergency upon approving a motion for revocation signed by ten members of either House of Parliament. If both Houses concurred in the motion, the declaration of emergency would cease to have effect.[115] While an improvement, these changes would not, as Cohen noted prior to their adoption, address the problem of a strong parliamentary majority willing to support the government action or circumstances in which Parliament was not sitting.[116]

In addition to the problems Cohen identified, the amendments to the War Measures Act in 1960 failed to provide mechanisms requiring the executive to provide parliamentarians, and through them the public, with sufficient information for effective parliamentary supervision of executive action in emergencies.[117] This deficiency became apparent during the October Crisis. Members of the House of Commons unsuccessfully proposed a variety of independent commissions to address the government's failure to provide adequate information about matters such as the facts allegedly underlying the apprehended insurrection.[118] Throughout the 1970s sporadic and unsuccessful attempts were made to bring to light the facts underlying the 1970 invocation of the War Measures Act and to secure the new emergency legislation which Prime Minister Trudeau had promised during the crisis itself.[119]

The appropriateness of the actions taken by the Quebec and Canadian governments during the October Crisis continues to be the subject of debate in newspapers, television, and radio more than twenty years later.[120] Recalling the sense of fear, "personal and institutionl, fear for self and fear for society," which permeated Canadian society during the October Crisis, Cohen suggested in 1974 that this debate was not a profitable one. Cohen noted that "while pain inflicted on the innocent can never be wholly compensated, on balance the situations seem to have been handled with the courage and firmness, and a minimum of rough dealing with persons and liberty in an authentic crisis."[121] In 1988, while acknowledging that history would probably conclude that governments overreacted in 1970, Cohen still held the view he had expressed earlier.[122] Whatever one's assessment of the federal government's use of force, better mechanisms for providing Parliament with information and better protection for human rights were desirable.[123]

Always a strong advocate of greater public participation by a variety of consultative mechanisms,[124] Cohen in his 1988 testimony on Bill C-77 proposed that a standing Senate-House committee should at least be consulted prior to a declaration of emergency by the Governor-in-Council.[125] While this particular mechanism of parliamentary supervision did not find its way into the Emergencies Act, the act provides a greater role for Parliament in emergencies by requiring that declarations of emergency be confirmed in both Houses of Parliament.[126] As well, Parliament may revoke a declaration of emergency, in whole or in part, at any time during the crisis.[127] Finally, orders and regulations are subject to parliamentary review and approval.[128]

Given the difficulties Parliament encountered when attempting to discern the nature and degree of information available to the government during the October Crisis, the creation of these mechanisms is a significant improvement enhancing the accountability of the executive to Parliament in ways similar to those advocated by Cohen. Thus the Emergencies Act establishes a legal framework which recognizes the supervisory role of a democratically elected legislature in emergencies which the international community suggests underlies Article 4 of the ICCPR. This framework may ultimately prove to be capable of providing Parliament with the information it requires to review executive action adequately while permitting the executive to address the emergency which confronts it effectively.

Enhancing the Role of the Judiciary

The Emergencies Act has also greatly expanded the role of the judiciary in emergencies,[129] an issue considered both by Cohen in his 1960 testimony on the proposed Bill of Rights and by the McDonald Commission twenty-one years later. Cohen advocated the establishment of a separate court, an Emergency Appeal Court, with jurisdiction over matters of arrest, detention, and expropriation of property during an emergency.[130] To address concerns arising out of the October Crisis, the McDonald Commission proposed the establishment of a Board of Detention Review and an independent compensations tribunal for the loss of property or liberty, "without just cause."[131] The latter proposal was eventually incorporated in the Emergencies Act. Indeed, the act provides for a compensation scheme for individuals who suffer "loss, injury or damage" as a result of the exercise of emergency powers.[132]

In his 1988 testimony on Bill C-77, Cohen again addressed the role of the judiciary. This time, his submissions focused on the importance of protecting fundamental rights in emergencies, particularly the rights in Article 4(2) of the ICCPR from which a state may not derogate in public emergencies.[133] Cohen criticized Bill C-77 for failing to implement these international norms expressly and for not clearly making the section 4(2) rights justiciable in domestic law.[134] He noted that the Background Papers to Bill C-77 supported the principle that at a minimum Article 4(2) rights should never be overridden.[135] In addition to recommending that section 6(5) of the War Measures Act, which insulated action under the act from judicial review on Bill of Rights grounds, be amended, the McDonald Commission recommended that Article 4(2) rights should be expressly protected.[136] In Cohen's opinion, the Gouzenko Royal Commission and the October Crisis demonstrated the necessity for protecting certain fundamental rights.[137]

The Emergencies Act partially addresses these concerns. As a practical response to the experiences of Canadians during the two world wars, particularly those of the Japanese Canadians, the Emergencies Act incorporated section 4(b). It provides that the act cannot be construed so as to confer on the Governor-in-Council the power, by order or regulation, to detain, imprison, or intern Canadian citizens or permanent residents on such grounds as race, national or ethnic origin, colour, religion, sex, age, or mental or physical disability.[138] However, the final form of the Emergencies Act does not expressly implement Article 4, governing states of emergency, or the protection in Article 4(2) for nonderogable rights. Thus, without more, the failure to implement Article 4(2) would be of serious concern. Parliament might have been able to rely on section 33 of the Charter to derogate from those Charter rights in sections 2 and 7 to 15.

However, Parliament did not expressly incorporate a notwithstanding clause in the Emergencies Act. Instead, the Emergencies Act's preamble states that the Governor-in-Council's exercise of emergency powers under the act is subject to the quasi-constitutional and constitutional obligations set out in the Canadian Bill of Rights and the Canadian Charter of Rights and Freedoms. This reference to Canada's constitutional and statutory human rights obligations, strictly speaking unnecessary, highlights the importance Parliament placed on protecting fundamental rights in times of emergency.[139]

The rights guarantees in both the Bill of Rights and the Charter, with its remedial powers in sections 24 and 52, apply to governmental action under the Emergencies Act. Despite the new role of the courts in the Charter era, it is difficult to predict how the courts will avail themselves of these new powers of judicial review. The question of judicial deference to the government and to Parliament will figure most prominently in the court's review of the government's justification under section 1 of the Charter of limits on Charter rights in emergencies. The effect of failing to incorporate expressly the provisions of Article 4(2) of the ICCPR into the Emergencies Act or other clause which designates certain rights as nonderogable may well depend on how courts interpret section 1 of the Charter in emergencies and their assessment of the relevance and persuasiveness of international legal norms.

The Emergencies Act itself is ambivalent in its approach to the norms within Article 4 of the ICCPR. The Emergencies Act's preamble states that the Governor-in-Council "must have regard to the provisions of the International Covenant on Civil and Political Rights." Yet the phrase, to "have regard to," appears to have no significance in international law. At best, the preamble's reference to the ICCPR acknowledges the persuasiveness of ICCPR jurisprudence and the relevance of jurisprudence on the European Convention for the Protection of Human Rights and Fundamental Freedoms and the American Convention on Human Rights in interpreting the Emergencies Act. It may be said that this failure to implement Canada's international obligations expressly into domestic law again reflects the tension Cohen described as the tension between conscience and responsibility. However, it is open to the judiciary to interpret the Emergencies Act, and, more importantly, the government to act in a manner consistent with Canada's international obligations.

CONCLUSION

Following the Second World War, the process of constitutionally entrenching human rights and of reforming the War Measures Act were two important developments in Canadian human rights law. Maxwell Cohen was actively involved in both debates. In his approach to human rights in Canada, Cohen draws on international legal norms in commenting on and advancing human rights in Canada. In particular, the development of international human rights norms is closely linked to the development of both the Bill of Rights and the Canadian Charter of Rights and Freedoms and, Cohen suggests, the interpretation of these instruments should be informed by international norms. With regard to the protection of human rights in emergencies, Canada's Emergencies Act has incorporated many of the international norms in Article 4 of the ICCPR, even though the act does not expressly protect the nonderogable rights.

Cohen's approach to human rights law in Canada is also informed by his emphasis on the role of law as a means of formulating practical solutions to political problems. With respect to the implementation of international human rights norms in domestic law, Canadians, in Cohen's view, have been ambivalent. Some international human rights norms are reflected in Canada in the enactment of the Bill of Rights and the entrenchment of the Charter. However, the Canadian solution to the competing demands of parliamentary supremacy and entrenched rights guarantees resulted in the inclusion of the notwithstanding clauses in both the Bill of Rights and the Charter. The very existence of such broad derogation provisions lends support to Cohen's view that the full impact of international human rights norms has not found its way into Canadian law. Yet the failure to implement Canada's international obligations expressly into domestic law can be overcome. The potential exists for Parliament to review, the judiciary to interpret, and the government to act in a manner consistent with Canada's international obligations.

Arguably, the Emergencies Act fashions a practical legal framework which ensures a degree of executive accountability to Parliament and to the Canadian people as a whole, with respect to the exercise of emergency powers. The act provides a greater role for the judiciary in assessing the reasonableness of declarations of emergencies and, through the application of the Charter and the Bill of Rights, provides greater protection for individual rights. Potential problems remain. Parliament may not avail itself of its opportunities to supervise the government and the judiciary may be unduly deferential to government or to Parliament. Thus it remains to be seen if the entrenchment of the Charter and the enactment of the Emergencies Act will become, in Cohen's terms, practical and durable legal frameworks for resolving the tension between individual rights and emergency powers in Canada.

NOTES

This article is written in the author's personal capacity and does not purport to represent the views of the Department of Justice. In writing this article, the author has relied on research done for her LLM thesis, "The Emergencies Act, the Canadian Charter of Rights and Freedoms and International Law: The Protection of Human Rights in States of Emergency" (LLM thesis, McGill University 1991). The text reflects the law as of 30 March 1992.

1 See generally R. St J. Macdonald, "Maxwell Cohen at Eighty: International Lawyer, Educator and Judge" [1989] *Canadian Yearbook of International Law* 3.
2 On constitutional issues see Maxwell Cohen, *The Dominion Provincial Conference: Some Basic Issues* (Toronto: Ryerson Press 1945); "Some Pending Constitutional Issues" (1945), 17 *Manitoba Bar News* 1; "The New Federalism: Comments in the Dark," in P.A. Crepeau and C.B. MacPherson, eds., *The Future of Canadian Federalism* (Toronto: University of Toronto Press, 1965), 173; "Canada and Quebec in North

America: A Pattern for Fulfilment" (1968), 75 *Queen's Quarterly* 389; and "The Canadian Federal Dilemma" (1968), 14 *McGill Law Journal* 357.

On human rights issues see Maxwell Cohen, "Bill C-60 and International Law – The United Nations Charter – Declaration of Human Rights" (1959), 37 *Canadian Bar Review* 228; "Human Rights: Programme or Catchall? A Canadian Rationale" (1968), 46 *Canadian Bar Review* 554; "Civil Disobedience, Dissent and Violence – A Canadian Perspective" (1969), 10 *William and Mary Law Review* 631; "The Hate Propaganda Amendments: Reflections on a Controversy" (1971), 9 *Alberta Law Review* 103; "Human Rights and Hate Propaganda: A Controversial Canadian Experiment," in Shlomo Shoham, ed., *Of Law and Man: Essays in Honour of Mr. Justice Haim Cohn, Supreme Court of Israel* (Tel Aviv: University of Tel Aviv Press 1971), 59; "Human Rights, the Individual and International Law," in Institut international des Droits de l'Homme, *René Cassin, Amicorum Disciplorumque Liber III: Protections des Droits de l'Homme dans les Rapports entre Personnes Privées* (Paris: Éditions A. Pedone, 1971), 69; "The Individual and International Law" in A. Gotlieb, ed., *Human Rights, Federalism and Minorities* (Toronto: Canadian Institute of International Affairs, 1970), 111; and A.F. Bayefsky, "The Canadian Charter of Rights and Freedoms and Public International Law" (1983), 61 *Canadian Bar Review* 265; "Towards a Paradigm of Theory and Practice: The Canadian Charter of Rights and Freedoms – International Law Influences and Interactions" (1986), 3 *Canadian Human Rights Year Book* 47.

3 Canadian Charter of Rights and Freedoms, Part I of the Constitution Act, 1982, being Schedule B to the Canada Act 1982 (UK), 1982, c.11, preamble [hereafter Charter].

4 RSC 1970, C.W-2.

5 See generally "Some International Law Problems of Interest to Canada and Canadian Lawyers" (1955), 33 *Canadian Bar Review* 389; "International Law and Canadian Practice," in E. McWhinney, ed., *Canadian Jurisprudence: The Civil and Common Law in Canada* (Toronto: Carswell 1958), 355, 358; "Some Main Directions of International Law: A Canadian Perspective" (1963), 1 *Canadian Yearbook of International Law* 17, 18ff; "Canada and the International Legal Order: An Inside Perspective," in R. St. J. Macdonald et al., eds., *Canadian Perspectives on International Law and Organization* (Toronto: University of Toronto Press, 1974), 5; "Towards a Paradigm," 50; "*The Canadian Yearbook* and International Law in Canada after Twenty-five Years" (1987), 25 *Canadian Yearbook of International Law* 3.

6 As dean at McGill's Faculty of Law, Cohen also emphasized the practical importance of a legal education which encompassed knowledge of

both legal regimes. See Maxwell Cohen, "Lawyers and Learning: The Professional and Intellectual Traditions" (1961), 7 *McGill Law Journal* 181, for a more detailed examination of the special comparative nature of Canada's perspective on law.
7 To Cohen, several factors contribute to the interpenetration of the international and domestic legal systems. These include the existence of a complex network of UN organizations, the growing number of member states, and the expansion of international law-making into a wide range of areas including human rights. Cohen, "Toward a Paradigm," 51. See also Maxwell Cohen, "The United States and the United Nations Secretariat: A Preliminary Appraisal" (1953), 1 *McGill Law Journal* 169; "The United Nations Secretariat – Some Constitutional and Administrative Developments" (1955), 49 *American Journal of International Law* 295; "Morals and Majorities: Dilemma of the UN," *Saturday Night*, 2 March 1957, 2; "*The Canadian Yearbook*," 15. See also Canada, Department of External Affairs, *Canada and the United Nations 1945–1975* (Ottawa: Minister of Supply and Services 1977), 2ff, 6–7; William A. Schabas, *International Human Rights Law and the Canadian Charter: A Manual for the Practitioner* (Toronto: Carswell 1991) 2–4.
8 The UN Charter, Can. TS 1945 No. 7, contains seven references to "human rights" – in the preamble, and in Articles 1, 13, 55, 62 para. 2, 68, and 76. See John Humphrey, "Human Rights, the U.N. and 1968" (1968), 9 *Journal of the International Community of Jurists* 2.
9 GA Res. 217 A (III), UN Doc. A/810 at 71 (1948) [hereafter Universal Declaration]. See also "The Draft International Declaration and Covenant on Human Rights" (1948), 26 *Canadian Bar Review* 548; "The Draft International Declaration on Human Rights" (1948), 26 *Canadian Bar Review* 1106.
10 Can. TS 1976 No. 47 (in force for Canada 19 Aug. 1976); Can. TS 1976 No. 46 (in force for Canada 19 Aug. 1976); Can. TS 1970 No. 28 (in force for Canada 13 Nov. 1970).
11 Cohen, "Towards a Paradigm," 52. See Cohen, "International Law and Canadian Practice," 318; Cohen, "*The Canadian Yearbook*," 14. In his article, "'Basic Principles' of International Law – A Revaluation" (1964), 42 *Canadian Bar Review*, Cohen examines the development of international law's "basic principles" as against the backdrop of what he views as the need to develop "a very meaningful approach to the scope of social change and mutual support internationally and to the formation of postulates that provide a framework for such peaceful change and mutual aid" (462).
12 Maxwell Cohen, "The Rule of Law in a Divided World," in *This Divided World*, [1960] Conference on World Affairs, 93–5.
13 Ibid., 92–3.
14 Ibid., 93.

15 Maxwell Cohen, "Reflections on Law and the United Nations System" [1960] American Society of International Law, *Proceedings* 244–5.
16 Ibid.
17 Cohen, "Rule of Law," 98; Cohen, "Reflections on Law," 253. See also Cohen, "Some International Law Problems," 390–1; Cohen, "*The Canadian Yearbook*," 3.
18 Cohen, "*The Canadian Yearbook*," 3.
19 SC 1988, c.29, RS, 1985, c.22 (4th Supp.).
20 Canada, *Minutes of Proceedings and Evidence of the Special Committee on Human Rights and Fundamental Freedoms* No. 5 (21 July 1960), 362 [hereafter *Minutes 1960*]. See also Walter Surma Tarnopolsky, *The Canadian Bill of Rights*, 2d rev. ed. (Toronto: Macmillan 1978), 3–7.
21 5 Geo. v, c.2, SC 1914 (2nd Session), c.2; RSC 1927, c.206. A blunt instrument, the War Measures Act delegated to the Governor-in-Council all emergency powers "necessary and advisable" to address a real or apprehended emergency which the Governor-in-Council deemed to exist. F. Murray Greenwood argues that the full extent of the grant of power to the Governor-in-Council was probably not realized at the time of the War Measures Act's enactment. Greenwood, "The Drafting and Passage of the War Measures Act in 1914 and 1927: Object Lessons in the Need for Vigilance," in W. Wesley Pue and Barry Wright, eds., *Canadian Perspectives on Law & Society Issues in Legal History* (Ottawa: Carleton University Press 1988), 292–3, 294–5.
22 Cohen, "The Canadian Federal Dilemma," 362–3; Tarnopolsky, *The Canadian Bill of Rights*, 3–4, 327–8. See also Canadian Bar Association, "Report of the Committee on Civil Liberties" (1944), 22 *Canadian Bar Review* 598; W. Glen How, "The Case for a Canadian Bill of Rights" (1948), 26 *Canadian Bar Review* 759.

Interestingly, Parliament enacted ad hoc legislation during the Korean War, citing the War Measures Act's vast potential to interfere with fundamental freedoms. While this legislation granted the Governor-in-Council broad emergency powers, section 2(2) of the Emergency Powers Act, SC 1950–1, c.5, contained important limitations on the federal government's powers of arrest, detention, exclusion, or deportation. It also prohibited the censorship, control, or suppression of written materials. Herbert Marx, "The "'Apprehended Insurrection' of October 1970 and the Judicial Function" (1972), 7 *University of British Columbia Law Review* 55, n.3; "The Energy Crisis and the Emergency Power in Canada" (1975), 2 *Dalhousie Law Journal* 450.
23 SM 1934, c.23; RSM 1954, c.185, cited in Cohen, "Human Rights and Hate Propaganda: A Controversial Canadian Experiment," 61.
24 SO 1944, c.51, cited in R. Brian Howe, "The Evolution of Human Rights Policy in Ontario" (1991), 24 *Canadian Journal of Political Science* 788.

25 Ibid., 789.
26 Walter S. Tarnopolsky and William F. Pentney, *Discrimination and the Law* (Don Mills, Ont.: De Boo 1985), 1–6 and chap.2; ss 1947, c.35, cited ibid., 2–3.
27 With the adoption of the Universal Declaration, a Joint Committee of the Senate and House of Commons on Human Rights and Fundamental Freedoms examined Canada's obligations under the United Nations Charter and the Universal Declaration. Tarnopolsky, *The Canadian Bill of Rights*, 12. See "The Joint Committee on Human Rights and Fundamental Freedoms" (1948), 26 *Canadian Bar Review* 706.
28 Cohen, "Bill C-60," 233. See *Minutes 1960*, 375, for Cohen's proposed preamble to the Bill of Rights which clarifies such a link.
29 Tarnopolsky, *The Canadian Bill of Rights*, 7–12.
30 Cohen, "Bill C-60."
31 *Minutes 1960*, 361–2.
32 Cohen, "Canada and the International Legal Order," 7. In 1949 appeals to the Privy Council had been abolished and limited powers of constitutional amendment granted to Canada. British North America (No.2) Act, 1949, 13 Geo. VI, c.81 (UK); repealed by Part VII, s.53 of the Constitution Act, 1982, c.11 (UK). See also Peter W. Hogg, *Constitutional Law of Canada* 2d ed. (Toronto: Carswell 1985), 166–8. As well, there had been constitutional discussions between the federal government and the provinces in 1950 on amendments to the Constitution Act, 1867. *Minutes 1960*, 361.
33 Cohen, "Bill C-60," 228.
34 *Minutes 1960*, 363.
35 Ibid. 369. See also Hogg, *Constitutional Law*, 636–8, citing *Re Alberta Statutes*, [1938] SCR 100, per Cannon J, at 146, per Duff J, at 133–5; *Saumur v. City of Quebec*, [1953] 2 SCR 299, per Rand J, at 331, per Kellock J, at 353–4, per Locke J, at 363, 373–4; *Switzman v. Elbing*, [1957] SCR 285, at 307, 328; and *A.G. Canada and Dupond v. Montreal*, [1978] SCR 770, at 796.
36 *Minutes 1960*, 370.
37 Cohen, "Bill C-60," 230.
38 Ibid., 230–1. A primary difficulty in the domestic implementation of international norms continues to be the Supreme Court's judgment in *Attorney-General for Canada v. Attorney-General for Ontario*, [1937] AC 326 (PC), the *Labour Conventions* case, which divides the power to implement treaties between Parliament and the provinces along the lines of the division of powers in the Constitution. Cohen, "Towards a Paradigm," 54; Cohen and Bayefsky, "The Canadian Charter of Rights," 273.
39 [1945] OR 778 cited in Cohen, "Bill C-60," 231. Cohen, "Some International Law Problems of Interest to Canada and Canadian Lawyers," 419. See also Cohen, "Towards a Paradigm," 55; *Minutes 1960*, 373.

40 Cohen, "Bill C-60," 231.
41 Ibid. 232; Macdonald, "Cohen," 40. See also *Minutes 1960*, 371.
42 Cohen, "Human Rights: Programme," 562; Cohen, "Towards a Paradigm," 55. Canada, *Minutes of Proceedings and Evidence of the Special Joint Committee of the Senate and of the House of Commons on the Constitution of Canada*, No. 34 (8 Jan. 1981), 34: 60 [hereafter *Special Joint Committee*].
43 Tarnopolsky, *The Canadian Bill of Rights*, 14–15, 168ff; Bertha Wilson, "Decision-making in the Supreme Court" (1986), 36 *University of Toronto Law Journal* 245
44 Cohen, "Human Rights: Programme," 561–4.
45 Canada, *Special Joint Committee*, 34:61. See Canada, Department of Justice, *A Canadian Charter of Human Rights* (Ottawa: Queen's Printer 1968) (The Hon. P.-E. Trudeau, minister of justice); Canada, Department of Justice, *The Constitution and the People of Canada* (Ottawa: Queen's Printer 1969) (The Hon. P.-E. Trudeau, minister of justice).
46 Cohen, "Towards a Paradigm," 60. See also Tarnopolsky, *The Canadian Bill of Rights*, 10–11, for similar arguments with respect to the Bill of Rights.
47 Cohen, "Canadian Federal Dilemma," 368–9.
48 See Patrick Monahan, *Politics and the Constitution* (Toronto: Carswell 1987) chap. 8; Anne F. Bayefsky, *Canada's Constitution Act 1982 & Amendments: A Documentary History*, 2 vols. (Toronto: McGraw-Hill Ryerson 1989).
49 *Reference Re Resolution to Amend the Constitution*, [1981] 1 SCR 753, at 893–4, 904, *sub nom. Reference re Amendment of the Constitution of Canada (Nos. 1, 2, 3)*, 125 DLR (3d) 1 [hereafter *Patriation Reference* cited to SCR]. See also Filippo Sabetti, "The Historical Context of Constitutional Change in Canada," in Paul Davenport and Richard H. Leach, eds., *Reshaping Confederation: The 1982 Reform of the Canadian Constitution* (Durham, NC: Duke University Press 1984), 11.
50 Cohen, "Towards a Paradigm," 55–6; Donna Greschner and Ken Norman, "The Courts and Section 33" (1987), 12 *Queen's Law Journal* 160; Anne F. Bayefsky, "The Judicial Function under the Canadian Charter of Rights and Freedoms" (1987), 32 *McGill Law Journal* 812–3; *Patriation Reference*, 897.
51 "Proposed Resolution for a Joint Address to Her Majesty the Queen respecting the Constitution of Canada," tabled in the House of Commons and the Senate, 6 Oct. 1980, in Bayefsky, "The Judicial Function" 743ff. For orders of reference for the establishment of the Special Joint Committee of the Senate and the House of Commons see ibid., 762–4.
52 *Special Joint Committee*, 34:58; No. 7 (18 Nov. 1980) 7:82.
53 Ibid., 34:56–7. Both proposals were included in the federal government's 1991 constitutional reform proposals. See *Shaping Canada's*

Future Together: Proposals (Ottawa: Minister of Supply and Services Canada 1991), 3, 30; Canada, *A Renewed Canada: The Report of the Special Joint Committee of the Senate and of the House of Commons* (Ottawa: Canada Communication Group, 28 Feb. 1992), 35 [hereafter Beaudoin-Dobbie Report].

54 *Special Joint Committee*, 34:73. See ibid., 34:74–5, for Cohen's proposal to create a permanent federal-provincial secretariat.
55 See generally *Submission of the Select Committee on the Constitution of Canada*, Canadian Jewish Congress, November 1980.
56 *Special Joint Committee*, 34:72.
57 *Patriation Reference*, 807–8, 883, 904–9. See also Bayefsky, "The Judicial Functions," 816.
58 Originally the override applied to section 28, the equality of the sexes provision. Given the opposition of womens' groups across the country, the override was later amended by the House of Commons. For a detailed discussion of the history of the override see Bayefsky, "The Judicial Function," 812–17; and Roy Romanow, John Whyte, and Howard Leeson, *Canada ... Notwithstanding* (Toronto: Carswell 1984), 257–8.
59 The idea of a legislative override was not new. Various types of overrides had been canvassed over the years of constitutional negotiation – for example, an override to permit Parliament to override Charter rights in times of emergency, to permit provinces which had opted into the Charter's application to then opt out with respect to certain legislative measures, or to permit a legislature to shield certain legislative measures from the application of the proposed Charter. Bayefsky, "The Judicial Function," 812–13. As well, certain provincial human rights acts, like the Alberta Bill of Rights, SA 1972, C.1, RSA 1980, C.A-16, S.2, and the Quebec Charter of Human Rights and Freedoms, SQ 1975, c.6; RSQ 1977, C. C-12, S.52, contained notwithstanding clauses. See also SS 1979, C.S-24.1, S.44; Human Rights Code, 1981, SO 1981, C.53, s.46(2). Similarly, s.2 of the Bill of Rights permits Parliament to declare expressly that an act of Parliament applies notwithstanding the Bill of Rights. See P.W. Hogg, *Canada Act 1982 Annotated* (Toronto: Carswell 1982), 80.
60 Cohen, "Human Rights, the Individual and International Law."
61 Cohen "Towards a Paradigm," 65–70. See also Anne F. Bayefsky, *International Human Rights Law: Use in Canadian Charter of Rights and Freedoms Litigation* (Toronto: Butterworths 1992), 161ff.
62 Cohen, "Towards a Paradigm," 61.
63 Cohen, "*The Canadian Yearbook*," 19–20; Maxwell Cohen, "The Canadian Legal Profession and International Law" (1983), *Manitoba Law Journal* 204, 207.
64 Cohen, "Towards a Paradigm," 62.

65 Cohen, "International Law and Canadian Practice," 323–4, 331.
66 Ibid. 353.
67 Cohen and Bayefsky, "The Canadian Charter of Rights."
68 Ibid., 275, 279–80.
69 Ibid., 292. Cohen and Bayefsky note that "[e]xceptions exist with respect to treaties which 'give recognition to incidents of sovereignty' or concern 'matters in exclusively sovereign aspects,' but could probably be described as not extending to matters which 'affect the rights of individuals.'" Ibid., 292, n116. Canadian case law is unclear whether a statute must explicitly state that it is implementing a particular international obligation, though Laskin CJ in *Vapour Canada* appeared to suggest that this was the case. Ibid., 294.
70 Ibid. 298.
71 Ibid. 298.
72 See ibid., 280–5, 301–9.
73 Ibid., 302. Section 11(g) of the Charter states, "Any person charged with an offence has the right ... not to be found guilty on account of any act or omission unless, at the time of the act or omission, it constituted an offence under Canadian or international law or was criminal according to the general principles of law recognized by the community of nations." See also Cohen, "Towards a Paradigm," 57, 67; François Chevrette, "Protection upon Arrest or Detention and against Retroactive Penal Law," in G.A. Beaudoin and E. Ratushny, eds., *The Canadian Charter of Rights and Freedoms*, 2d ed. (Toronto: Carswell 1989), 442 ff.
74 Cohen and Bayefsky, "Canadian Charter of Rights," 302–5.
75 Cohen, "*The Canadian Yearbook*," 20.
76 Cohen and Bayefsky, "Canadian Charter of Rights," 305.
77 [1987] 1 SCR 313 at 348 [hereafter *Reference*].
78 *Reference*, 349; *Slaight Communications Inc. v. Davidson*, [1989] 1 SCR 1038, at 1056–7; *R. v. Keegstra*, [1990] 3 SCR 697, at 750. See *Kindler v. Canada (Minister of Justice)* (1991), 67 CCC (3d) 1 (SCC), in which international instruments are relied upon by both the majority and dissenting justices.
79 "*The Canadian Yearbook*," 20.
80 Cohen, "Towards a Paradigm," 65. Interestingly, in 1987 Cohen noted that there was an increasing flexibility within international law as to what constitutes an authoritative source of international law. It had gone from "classically defined and recognizable e.g., the practice of states, general principles ... to the newer forums in their many guises," such as "the immense network of rules and regulations spawned by the specialized agencies or ad hoc groups." Cohen, "*The Canadian Yearbook*," 13.
81 Cohen, "*The Canadian Yearbook*," 20.

82 Bayefsky, *International Human Rights Law*; Schabes, *International Human Rights Law*.
83 Cohen, "Human Rights, the Individual and International Law," 76.
84 Department of Justice, *A Canadian Charter of Human Rights*, 30.
85 Department of Justice, *The Constitution and the People of Canada*, 60.
86 "Proposed Resolution," s.1. See Bayefsky, "The Judicial Function," 813–16.
87 *Special Joint Committee*, 34:79.
88 CJC, *Submission*, 1–2. Article 5(1) of the ICCPR states: "Nothing in the present Covenant may be interpreted as implying for any State, group or person any right to engage in any activity or to perform any act aimed at the destruction of any of the rights or freedoms recognized herein, or at their limitation to a greater extent than is provided for in the present Covenant."
89 The Committee on the Constitution of the Canadian Bar Association and the Pepin-Robarts *Task Force on Canadian Unity* also proposed a separate express emergency power, requiring parliamentary confirmation and providing safeguards for provincial powers and individual rights. Canadian Bar Association, Committee on the Constitution, *Towards a New Canada* (1978), 157–8; Canada, Task Force on Canadian Unity, *A Future Together: Observations and Recommendations* (January 1979), 93, 127.
90 CJC, *Submission*, 15.
91 Article 4 of the ICCPR states:
> 1. In time of public emergency which threatens the life of the nation and the existence of which is officially proclaimed, the States Parties to the present Covenant may take measures derogating from their obligations under the present Covenant to the extent strictly required by the exigencies of the situation, provided that such measures are not inconsistent with their other obligations under international law and do not involve discrimination solely on the ground of race, colour, sex, language, religion, or social origin.
>
> 2. No derogation from articles 6, 7, 8 (paragraphs 1 and 2), 11, 15, 16 and 18 may be made under this provision.
>
> 3. Any State Party to the present Covenant availing itself of the right of derogation shall immediately inform the other States Parties to the present Covenant, through the intermediary of the Secretary-General of the United Nations, of the provision from which it has derogated and of the reasons by which it was actuated. A further communication shall be made, through the same intermediary, on the date on which it terminates such derogation.

As to definitions of the "public emergency," the "threat to the life of the nation," and the "strictly required by the exigencies of the situation" elements in Article 4, see generally Roy Chowdhury, *Rule of Law in a State of Emergency: The Paris Minimum Standard of Human Rights Norms*

235 Maxwell Cohen's Perspective on Human Rights

    in a State of Emergency (New York: St Martin's Press 1989), 12, 12–35, 101–19, 119–28.
92 CJC, *Submission*, 15.
93 States party to the ICCPR may not derogate from the rights in Article 4(2) of the ICCPR in public emergencies. These rights include the right to life (Article 6), the right not to be subject to torture or cruel, inhuman, or degrading treatment or punishment (Article 7), the right not to be held in slavery or in servitude (Article 8 (1), (2)), the right not to be imprisoned for the inability to fulfil a contractual obligation (Article 11), the right to be free from retroactive imposition of criminal law (Article 15), the right to recognition as a person before the law (Article 16), and the right to freedom of thought, conscience, and religion (Article 18).

    Arguably, the rights common to the ICCPR, the European Convention on Human Rights, and the American Convention on Human Rights – namely, the right to life, the prohibition against torture and inhuman or degrading treatment, the prohibition against slavery, and the prohibition against the retroactive imposition of criminal law – are also recognized as nonderogable rights at customary law. "The Siracusa Principles on the Limitation and Derogation Provisions in the International Covenant on Civil and Political Rights" (1985), 7 *Human Rights Quarterly* 11–12, principle 69.
94 *Special Joint Committee*, 7:109–10.
95 Indeed, the incorporation of section 33 into the Charter with a redrafted section 1 limitation clause may have further complicated the relationship between the Charter and Article 4, in particular the guarantees of nonderogable rights.
96 Section 33 requires that Parliament or the provincial legislature which wishes to rely on the override must expressly declare or must state its intention to override Charter rights in an act of Parliament or a legislature. It must state generally which rights are being overridden. Finally, a section 33 override is effective for five years or less if so stated and must then be renewed. As well, the Supreme Court held in *Ford v. Quebec*, [1988] 2 SCR 712, that judicial review would be limited to ensuring that these procedural requirements are met. However, the federal government, in *Shaping the Future Together*, 4, proposed that the simple majority needed to invoke the section 33 override be changed to 60 per cent of the members of parliament or of a provincial legislature. See also Beaudoin-Dobbie Report, 36.
97 Cohen, "Towards a Paradigm," 65. In contrast, Weinrib argues that the Charter as judicially interpreted constitutes "an intricate set of institutional arrangements." Weinrib suggests that the Charter, with its interplay between section 1 and section 33, entrenches an ongoing

dialogue between the courts and Parliament as to the content of and permissible limits on Charter rights, a dialogue which enhances their respective roles. Lorraine Weinrib, "Learning to Live with the Override" (1990), 35 *McGill Law Journal* 568, 570.

98 John P. Humphrey, *Human Rights and the United Nations: A Great Adventure* (Dobbs Ferry, NY: Transnational Publishers 1984), 12.

99 Cohen, "Human Rights, the Individual and International Law," 76.

100 See International Law Association, Committee of the Enforcement of Human Rights Law, *Report of the Committee, Minimum Standards of Human Rights Norms in a State of Exception*, in *Report of the Sixty-First Conference Held at Paris, August 26th to September 1, 1984* (International Law Association: Great Britain, 1985), 56; Commission on Human Rights, Sub-Commission on Prevention of Discrimination and Protection of Minorities, Special Rapporteur Erica-Irene A. Daes, *The Individual's Duties to the Community and the Limitations on Human Rights and Freedoms Under Article 29 of the Universal Declaration of Human Rights*, UN Doc. E/CN.4/Sub.2/432/Rev.2 (1983); Commission on Human Rights, Sub-Commission on Prevention of Discrimination and Protection of Minorities, Special Rapporteur N. Questiaux, *Study of the Implications for Human Rights of Recent Developments Concerning Situations Known as States of Siege or Emergency*, UN Doc. E/CN.4/Sub.2/1982/15 (1982); Chowdhury, *Rule of Law*; Commission of Jurists, *States of Emergency: Their Impact on Human Rights* (1983); "The Siracusa Principles."

101 *Minutes 1960*, 395.

102 Emergencies Act, SC 1988, c.29, RS, 1985, c.22 (4th Supp.). See also Emergency Preparedness Act, SC 1988, c.11, RS, 1985 (4th Supp.), c.6.

103 See Bill C-77, An Act to Authorize the Taking of Special Temporary Measures to Ensure Safety and Security during National Emergencies and to Amend Other Acts in Consequence Thereof, 2d Sess., 33d Parl., 1986–7.

104 Canada, *Minutes of Proceedings and Evidence of the Legislative Committee on Bill C-77*, No. 6 (10 March 1988), 6:9–11 [hereafter *Leg. Comm. Bill C-77*]. The author should note that she assisted Judge Cohen in the preparation of his expert testimony to the committee.

105 The McDonald Commission established to examine, among other things, the RCMP's involvement in the October Crisis, recommended in its 1981 report that the War Measures Act be amended, not repealed. In its view, emergencies, other than real or apprehended war, invasion, and insurrection, should have been dealt with by ad hoc legislation. Canada, Commission of Inquiry Concerning Certain Activities of the Royal Canadian Mounted Police. *Freedom and Security under the Law*, Second Report, vol. 2 (Ottawa: Supply and Services 1981) 921 [here-

after McDonald Commission]. See Commissioner Gilbert's minority report, 1063–4.
106 *Leg. Comm. Bill* C-77, 6:9.
107 Ibid., 6:10.
108 Canada, Department of National Defence, *Challenge and Commitment: A Defence Policy for Canada* (June 1987), 73. House of Commons Debates, 16 Nov. 1987, 10809, per the Hon. Perrin Beatty, minister responsible for emergency preparedness.
109 See Jean François Duchaîne, *Rapport sur les événements d'octobre 1970* (Gouvernement du Québec 1981); Denis Smith, *Bleeding Hearts ... Bleeding Country – Canada and the Quebec Crisis* (Edmonton: Hurtig 1971); Ron Haggart and Aubrey E. Golden, *Rumours of War* (Toronto: New Press 1971); Germaine Dion, *Une tornade de 60 jours* (Hull, Que.: Editions Asticons 1985); Fernand Dumont, *The Vigil of Quebec* (Toronto: University of Toronto Press 1974); J.N. Lyon, "Constitutional Validity of Sections 3 and 4 of the Public Order Regulations, 1970" (1983), 18 *McGill Law Journal* 136; Herbert Marx, "The Emergency Power and Civil Liberties in Canada" (1970), 16 *McGill Law Journal* 39; Douglas A. Schmeiser, "Control of Apprehended Insurrection: Emergency Measures vs. The Criminal Code" (1971), 4 *Manitoba Law Journal* 359; Guy Tremblay, "Les Libertés Publiques en Temps de Crise" (1972), 13 *Cahiers de Droit* 306; Tarnopolsky, *The Canadian Bill of Rights*, 331–48.
110 Emergencies Act, section 3. Under the Emergencies Act, a "national emergency" is a critical and urgent situation which seriously endangers Canadians' lives, health, or safety and exceeds a province's capacity or authority to deal with it, or which seriously threatens the Government of Canada's ability to preserve its sovereignty, security, and territorial integrity. As well, the emergency must by definition be temporary. It must also not be capable of being effectively dealt with by any other Canadian law. It should be noted that while four categories of emergency are delineated, economic emergencies are left to be addressed by ad hoc legislation.

Public welfare emergencies include natural disasters, epidemics, or environmental disasters. Ibid., section 5.

Public order emergencies include crises arising from "threats to the securities of Canada" as defined in section 2 of the Canadian Security and Intelligence Service Act, RS, 1985, c.c-23, including espionage or sabotage, threat or use of acts of serious volence against persons or property for political purpose, and activities leading to the violent overthrow of Canada's constitutionally established system of government in Canada, but not lawful advocacy, protest, or dissent. Ibid., section 16.

International emergencies are emergencies "involving Canada and one or more other countries that arises from acts of intimidation or coercion or the real or imminent use of serious force or violence and that is so serious as to be a national emergency." Ibid., section 27.

War emergencies include "war or other armed conflict, real or imminent, involving Canada or any of its allies that is so serious as to be a national emergency." Ibid., section 37.

111 The War Measures Act's constitutionality was upheld on the basis of Parliament's residual power within the "Peace, Order and Good Government of Canada" (POGG) clause in section 91 of the Constitution Act, 1867. See *In Re Gray* (1918), 57 SCR 150, and *Fort Frances Pulp and Power Company Ltd. v. Manitoba Free Press Company Ltd.*, [1923] AC695 (PC) [hereafter *Fort Frances*]. These cases relied on the emergency doctrine, pursuant to which Parliament could encroach on areas of provincial jurisdiction in temporary crises affecting the peace, order, and good government of Canada. The constitutionality of applying the War Measures Act to peacetime emergencies, for example the 1970 October Crisis, was never seriously considered in the case law arising out of the crisis. See *Gagnon and Vallières v The Queen* (1971), 14 CRNS 321 (Que. CA), 17 CCC (2d) 375; and *Chartrand v. The Queen* (1971) 21 CRNS 49 (Que. CA). In *Reference re Anti-Inflation Act*, [1976] 2 SCR 373, the Supreme Court appears to extend the emergency doctrine's application to all emergencies affecting the peace, order, and good government of Canada, including peacetime emergencies. The Emergencies Act applies to both wartime and peacetime emergencies. The act must rest on the above constitutional foundations. See note 91. Under the Emergencies Act, declarations of emergency are of a limited duration: for public welfare emergencies – 90 days; public order emergencies – 30 days; international emergencies – 60 days; and war emergencies – 120 days. Ibid., sections 7(2), 18(2), 29(2), and 39(2). Declarations of emergency may, however, be renewed. Ibid., sections 12(1), 23(1), 34(1), and 43(1).

As well, a declaration of a public welfare or public order emergency may have a limited geographic application. Such a declaration of emergency may be revoked in part so as to no longer apply to a particular part of Canada. As well, the application of the emergency declaration can be extended. Ibid., sections 11, 13, 22, 24.

Finally, for each category of emergency, the Emergencies Act attempts to delegate the Governor-in-Council emergency powers proportional to the seriousness of emergency. For available powers, see ibid., sections 8(1), 19(1), 30(1), and 40. For limitations on those powers see ibid., sections 8(2), (3), 9; 19(2)(3), 20; 30(2), 31; and 40(1.1), (3).

112 The extent of international consensus on these principles is arguable, but see International Law Association, note 100 above, 60–1; "The Siracusa Principles," 9–10; Daes, *The Individual's Duties*, 193–5; Chowdhury, *Rule of Law*, 55–62; Commission on Human Rights, Sub-Commission on Prevention of Discrimination and Protection of Minorities, Special Rapporteur Mr Leandro Despouy, *Third Annual Report and List of States which, since 1 January 1985, Have Proclaimed, Extended or Terminated a State of Emergency*, UN Doc. E/CN.4/Sub.2/1989/30/rev. 2 (18 Dec. 1990), 13.
113 *Minutes 1960*, 372.
114 Ibid., 395–6.
115 *Canadian Bill of Rights*, SC 1960, c.44; RSC 1970, Appendix III, s.6; War Measures Act, sections 6(2), (3), (4).
116 *Minutes 1960*, 395.
117 In an article surveying national security issues in the postwar period, Cohen noted that several controversies during the Second World War – for example, the use of the Canadian Expeditionary Force in Hong Kong – resulted in the appointment of royal commissions during wartime. See Maxwell Cohen, "Secrecy in Law and Policy: The Canadian Experience and International Relations," in T.M. Frank and E. Weisband, eds., *Secrecy and Foreign Policy* (New York: Oxford University Press 1974), 359–60, 374–5.
118 House of Commons, *Debates*, 28 Oct. 1970, 656; 26 Nov. 1970, 1496. Other commissions were proposed to supervise the application of the regulations, to avoid abuses of emergency powers, to review detentions, to evaluate police effectiveness, and to inquire into charges of police brutality. Ibid., 21 Oct. 1970, 422; 26 Oct. 1970, 545–6; 4 Nov. 1970, 872; 16 Nov. 1970, 1184; 25 Nov. 1970, 1467. See also ibid., 28 Oct. 1970, 645.

Another factor contributing to Parliament's lack of information was the fact that the provinces, in particular the attorneys-general, had the constitutional responsibility for implementing and administering the regulations under the War Measures Act. Thus the federal government referred to the provinces questions about the number of detainees; their right to counsel, if any; and whether these persons were permitted contact with families. House of Commons, *Debates*, 16 Oct. 1970, 217, 553; 21 Oct. 1970, 422; 28 Oct. 1970, 653.
119 See Canada, Commission of Inquiry Concerning Certain Activities of the Royal Canadian Mounted Police, *Parliament and Security Matters*, by C.E.S. Franks (Hull: Supply and Services 1980), 54–6; McDonald Commission, 920. See House of Commons, *Debates*, 3 Nov. 1970, 819; 4 Nov. 1970, 882; 11 Jan. 1971, 2255; 27 June 1975, 7134; 28 July 1975,

7979; 28 Oct. 1975, 8613; 29 Oct. 1975, 8657; 27 Nov. 1975, 9509; 8 Dec. 1975, 9796; 5 April 1978, 4156. See House of Commons, *Debates*, 17 May 1977, cited in *Emergency Planning Canada, Safety and Security in Emergencies: Background Papers*, Studies in Various Aspects of Emergency Legislation (Ottawa: Emergency Planning Canada, 1985), 70 [hereafter *Background Papers*].

120 Hubert Bauch, "Was the Crisis a Put-Up Job by the Federal Government," Montreal *Gazette*, 29 Sept.1990, B4; "We Were Romantics Going Off to War," *Gazette*, 29 Sept. 1990, B5; André Bellemare, "Un geste sans précédent ... " Ottawa *Le Droit*, 9 Oct. 1990, 4; Miro Cernetig, "Don't Forget the FLQ Crisis, Clark Warns Meech Critics," *Globe and Mail*, 19 March 1990, 1; Norman Delisle, "Le cadavre reposait sur une couverture et des oreillers," *Le Droit*, 9 Oct. 1990, 10; François Gagnon, "Une opération difficile à oublier," Ottawa *Le Droit*, 9; Michel Gauthier, "A jamais gravé dans leur mémoire," Ottawa *Le Droit*, 9 Oct. 1990, 6; Charles Gordon, "Another October: What Exactly Was It that We Learned," *Ottawa Citizen*, 9 Oct. 1990; Robert McKenzie, "Laporte Was a Poor Subject for Myth," Toronto *Star*, 9 Oct. 1990, A11; Michèle Ouimet, "Un détenu d'Octobre accuse: Trudeau l'a voulu ... " *La Presse*, 9 Oct. 1990, B1; John Ward, "A Loss of Innocence: October Crisis Woke Up Canadians to the Reality of Canada," *Ottawa Citizen*, 6 Oct. 1990, B4–5; Norman Webster, "October Crisis Loses Its Aura," *Gazette*, 9 Oct. 1990, B3; "Pierre Laporte est le grand oublié de la Crise d'Octobre," *La Presse*, 9 Oct. 1990, A2.

121 Cohen, "Secrecy in Law and Policy," 363. See also *Special Joint Committee*, 7:108.

122 *Leg. Comm. Bill C-77*, 6:17.

123 Franks, *Parliament and Security Matters*, 54.

124 Canada, *Minutes of Proceedings and Evidence of the Special Committee on Regulatory Reform*, No. 25 (14 Nov. 1980), 25:10, 18, cited in Macdonald, "Maxwell Cohen," 41–2. Cohen himself served as president of Quebec's Advisory Council on the Administration of Justice and headed numerous royal commissions and inquiries. See Maxwell Cohen, "The Quebec Advisory Council on the Administration of Justice: Le Conseil Consultatif de Justice" (1973), 1 *Dalhousie Law Journal* 349.

125 *Leg. Comm. Bill C-77*, 6:8,15.

126 Instead, a Parliamentary Review Committee was establish to review and report on the executive's exercise of emergency powers regularly. Emergencies Act, sections 61(2); 62, 63; 58. It may be noted that the act provides circumstances in which Parliament is dissolved, prorogued, or adjourned. The confirmation procedures require the government to set out the reasons for the declaration and report on the required consul-

tation with the provinces prior to confirmation. The degree of consultation required differs according to the nature of the emergency. As well, further confirmation procedures apply when declarations of emergency are sought to be renewed.

127 Ibid., sections 10, 21, 32, 41, and 59.
128 The process for amending or revoking an order or regulation is more difficult than for amending or revoking the initial declaration of emergency. The concurrence of both Houses of Parliament is necessary to amend or revoke an order or regulation under the Emergencies Act. See ibid., section 61.
129 Under the War Measures Act, the courts were clearly reluctant to second-guess Parliament's determination that a state of emergency existed or that particular emergency measures were required. The War Measures Act, section 2, itself sent the courts a clear message: the Governor-in-Council's proclamation was conclusive evidence that war, invasion, or insurrection, real or apprehended, existed. Only where a court had before it "very clear evidence that an emergency has not arisen, or that the emergency no longer exists" would it exercise its powers of judicial review. *Fort Frances*, 705–6 (JCPC); *Co-operative Committee on Japanese Canadians v. Attorney-General for Canada*, [1947] AC 87 at 101–2.

In a significant departure from judicial deference in reviewing action under the War Measures Act, the Emergencies Act incorporates several objective "on reasonable grounds" tests. These permit the judiciary to review the reasonableness of Parliament's determination that a state of emergency exists or that particular emergency measures are required. For example, an emergency can only be declared when the Governor-in-Council believes, on reasonable grounds, that a particular class of emergency exists. Emergencies Act, sections 6(1), 17(1), 28(1), and 38(1).
130 *Minutes 1960*, 395. It should be noted that the McDonald Commission did not believe that the War Measures Act provided the authority to create new courts – for example, to deal with matters arising out of an emergency. McDonald Commission, 925.
131 McDonald Commission, 927. Under the War Measures Act, section 7, compensation was limited to covering the appropriation or use of property pursuant to the exercise of emergency powers.
132 *Emergencies Act*, sections 46–56.
133 See note 93 above.
134 Other witnesses before the Legislative Committee expressed views similar to Cohen's. *Leg. Comm. Bill C-77*, 6:41–2 (10 March 1988), per Mr Istvanney, La Ligue des droits et libertés; ibid., No. 7 at 7A:86

(5 March 1988) per Law Union of Ontario; ibid., No. 2 (25 Feb. 1988) at 2:5–6 per Mr Victor Paisley, QC, chairman, Legislation and Law Reform Standing Committee, Canadian Bar Association.
135 Ibid., 6:8–9,15. The *Background Papers* proposed additional nonderogable rights. These included freedom of thought, conscience, and religion; the right not to be subjected to cruel or inhuman punishment; the presumption of innocence; the right to instruct counsel without delay; the principle of nonretroactivity of penal legislation; the right of a citizen not to be deported, exiled, or denaturalized, and the right not to be discriminated against solely on the ground of race, colour, sex, language, religion, or social origin. *Background Papers*, 81–2.
136 Section 6(5) of the War Measures Act deemed actions taken pursuant to the act "not to be an abrogation, abridgment or infringement of any right or freedom recognized by the *Canadian Bill of Rights*." The Public Order (Temporary Measures) Act, SC 1970–71–72, c.2, which later replaced the War Measures Act, relied on section 6(5) to exempt action under the act from certain rights in the Bill of Rights. See Tarnopolsky, *The Canadian Bill of Rights*, 11–14; Charles F. Scott Jr, "The War Measures Act, s. 6(5) and The Canadian Bill of Rights" (1970–1), 13 *Criminal Law Quarterly* 342. The commission was of the view that section 6(5) should be amended such that powers to be exercised, notwithstanding the Bill of Rights, should be expressly identified. McDonald Commission, 927. The commission recommended that other rights, such as the right of a Canadian citizen not to be exiled, deported, or denaturalized, and procedural safeguards such as the nonretroactivity of criminal laws and a maximum limit on detentions before charge, should be incorporated in the War Measures Act. McDonald Commission, 923–4, 927.
137 *Leg. Comm. Bill C-77*, 6:15.
138 Similarly, senators, some of whom had likely experienced first hand the conscription crises during the two world wars, added section 40(1.1) to the Emergencies Act. This limitation provides that the power of the Governor-in-Council "to enact orders and regulations may not be exercised for the purpose of requiring persons to serve in the Canadian Forces." Thus, conscription may not be effected by order or regulation under the Emergencies Act. See *Reference re Canada Assistance Plan*, [1991] 2 SCR 525 at 551.
139 Of course, Parliament may amend the Emergencies Act to include a section 33 override. It is perhaps more likely that Parliament might enact ad hoc emergency legislation to deal with a specific incident and incorporate a section 33 override within that legislation.

Maxwell Cohen and the Report of the Special Committee on Hate Propaganda

WILLIAM KAPLAN

In 1966 the Special Committee on Hate Propaganda, chaired by Dean Maxwell Cohen, presented its report, unanimously recommending amendments to the Criminal Code which would make unlawful the advocacy of genocide, the public incitement of hatred, and the wilful promotion of hatred against identifiable groups.[1] Shortly thereafter the House of Commons was informed that a bill based on the Cohen Committee Report would be referred to a special joint committee of the House of Commons and Senate. As the result, the Parliament and public of Canada became engaged in a debate which ran, off and on, for the next five years, culminating in the passage, on 13 April 1970, of a group defamation concept entirely new to Canadian criminal law.[2]

Soon after the new law came into force, Cohen wrote a short article in the *Alberta Law Review* in which he evaluated the new legislation.[3] He asked five questions, and it is these questions which form the subject matter of this article. First, what gave rise to the demand that such legislation be enacted? Second, what were the means used by the Government of Canada to determine the need for the legislation and the scope of possible amendments to the Criminal Code? Third, how did Parliament approach the problem of deciding upon the legislation as it was finally enacted? Fourth, does the legislation, in the overall, serve a constructive democratic purpose? And fifth, what are the unknowns which all civil libertarians may conscientiously be concerned about now that the legislation has been enacted? Cohen's questions, reconsidered some twenty-five years after the release of his committee's report, provide an opportunity for review and reflection in the context of a short history of the committee and its work. Almost all commissions of inquiry make recommendations. Cohen's special committee led to the passage of a law; one which to the present day raises important questions about the limits to freedom in Canadian society.

THE DEMAND FOR LEGISLATION

The proximate cause of the passage of hate propaganda legislation in Canada is the report of the Special Committee on Hate Propaganda (hereafter the Cohen Committee). However, demands for legislation of this kind predated the establishment of the Cohen Committee. It is fair to say that the Canadian Jewish Congress (CJC) was the leader in bringing the problem of hate propaganda, particularly anti-Semitic literature largely originating in the United States, to the attention of government authorities and in requesting remedial legislation. The CJC was convinced, following a careful analysis of existing Criminal Code provisions, that there was no legal basis to fight hate propaganda in the criminal courts, and for years, beginning in the early 1950s, it had been lobbying for legislative reform.[4]

A careful review of a number of Criminal Code provisions such as sedition, public mischief, mailing obscene or scurrilous material, defamatory libel, intimidation, and spreading false news led the CJC to the conclusion that a prosecution directed against hate propaganda alleging one of these offences would not succeed.[5] While the sedition offence, for example, had once been put to use against the Jehovah's Witnesses for their attack against Roman Catholicism, as a result of the Supreme Court of Canada's decision in *Boucher*,[6] it was no longer available to combat offending words and publications. Simply put, under the law as it then was, even if the hate propaganda in question could be shown to promote feelings of ill will towards Jews (or any other group for that matter), that was not enough to make out a criminal offence. Moreoever, the law of tort offered little prospect for success should a group defamation action be filed, for the law required a plaintiff to show harm to himself or herself as an individual and thus actions alleging harm to a group were difficult, if not impossible, to maintain. Obviously, both the criminal and civil standards established onerous if not insurmountable legal tests. The difficulties in bringing a successful group defamation action meant that if the law was to be effective in challenging the scourge of hate propaganda, Parliament was going to have to use its criminal law jurisdiction to enact a new offence.

The Special Committee on Hate Propaganda

Beginning in the 1950s and carrying into the 1960s, the CJC studied the problem of hate propaganda and made various representations to federal and provincial authorities. Concerns about this issue, and the related requests for government legislative intervention, were hardly unique. Across Canada a growing human rights movement had mobilized and attracted considerable public support for the passage of all sorts of remedial legislation to combat discrimination of various kinds.[7] Human rights commissions were established in many Canadian jurisdictions, and most provincial legislatures passed fair-housing and fair-employment practices acts. Internationally, numerous conventions were signed committing signatory states to the protection of basic human rights, and a number of foreign states had turned their attention to the problem of hate propaganda.[8] The British Parliament, for instance, was seriously considering enacting legislation outlawing the defamation of racial and ethnic groups, and in October 1965 the Race Relations Act came into force.[9] In the United States, concerns about a growth in hate mail were also rising. A number of states passed group defamation statutes (which enjoyed, at best, limited success), while across that country Americans began to grapple with the issue and to debate what should be done.[10]

In Canada, there was a growing belief that the dissemination of hate propaganda was on the rise. The mass dissemination of vituperative materials appeared to accelerate in early 1964, and in March of that year the *Toronto Star* editorialized about the "stream of violently anti-Semitic and anti-Negro material ... circulating through the mails in Toronto," including the notorious Nazi newspaper *Der Sturmer* containing an account of "Jewish ritual murder."[11] From across the country came demands from organizations as diverse as the Manitoba Bar Association, the Canadian Federation of University Women, and the National Convention of the Royal Canadian Legion for government action to halt the attacks.[12] Some commentators called for a "test case" to deal with the use by hate propagandists of the mails. In the meantime, neo-Nazis, their friends, and the curious began to gather in Toronto's Allan Gardens to hear the good news.[13]

The *Star* editorial called for amendments to the law of libel allowing for members of groups to take both civil and criminal action in response to defamation against their group. In the *Star*'s view, libel against a group was a criminal offence and the Criminal Code should be amended to reflect that fact.[14] Several days later, a *Telegram* editorial concurred, as did other Canadian newspapers.[15] In April 1964 Opposition leader John Diefenbaker, in a speech to a Montreal audience, called for curbs on hate literature, stating the "distribution of anti-Jewish and anti-Negro literature is of an outrageous and offensive nature that cannot be justified as an exercise of freedom of speech."[16] In Ontario, Mr Justice Wells of the Court of Appeal began an inquiry on 23 November 1964 into the alleged illegal use of mails by some American neo-Nazis in the National States' Right Party and their Canadian friends. In December 1964 the retired chief justice of the Federal Court, J.T. Thorson, gave a speech in Ottawa in which he recommended that the federal government amend the Criminal Code to stamp out the spread of hate literature in Canada.

In Ottawa, bills were introduced in the House of Commons by Montreal MP Milton Klein and the member from Winnipeg North, David Orlikow. Klein's Bill C-21, which received first reading on 20 February 1964, prescribed the death penalty for anyone who, with genocide in mind, killed a member of a group, as well as a mandatory ten-year prison sentence for anyone who, with genocide in mind, caused bodily or mental harm to a member of group, or deliberately inflicted on a group, or a member of a group, conditions of life calculated to bring about the physical destruction of the group. The Orlikow bill was more modest in scope. It proposed an amendment to the Post Office Act making it an offence to use the mails for the distribution of hate propaganda. In late October 1964, at the suggestion of the government, both bills were sent to the House External Affairs Committee for study, indicating a growing parliamentary interest in the subject and reflecting the growing public interest.

Referring the matter to a parliamentary committee was useful, but so too was the internal review that was already underway at the Department of Justice. Indeed, that department had been looking at the issue, on and off, for years, and as recently as 1962 the minister of justice had asked the Conference of Commissioners on the Uniformity of Legislation (made up of provincial attorneys-general) to consider whether the Criminal Code should be amended to outlaw hate propaganda. The commissioners replied that "while the objective sought was eminently desirable, no recommendation to amend the criminal law was made because no formula had been devised which would deal adequately with the problem without simultaneously affecting the general freedom of expression of opinion in an adverse way."[17]

The evidence was incontrovertible that hate propaganda of various forms was being distributed. Department of Justice files are filled with examples of pamphlets and periodicals sent to Ottawa with calls for action. The propaganda was hardly benign. One publication, originating from the National White Americans Party based in

Georgia, which received a fairly wide distribution throughout major metropolitan centres in Canada, made the following observations:

We believe in sending all negroes back to Africa whence they came. The negro races have never developed a civilization, discovered any new invention, written a great symphony, or even originated an alphabet. They are on a much lower level to the whites.

On the Jewish question our policy is much stricter. We demand the arrest of all Jews involved in communist or zionist plots, public trials and executions. All other Jews would be immediately sterilized so that they could not breed more Jews. This is vital because the Jews are criminals as a race, who have been active in anti-Christian plots throughout their entire history.[18]

The offensive nature of this type of literature was self-evident and its actual presentation replete with stereotypical drawings of the members of the target groups made it even more so. However, while it was true enough that the distribution of hate literature was on the rise, what was questionable was by how much. Nevertheless, it was the perception of a growing crisis which mattered, and slowly but surely a momentum for action emerged.[19]

In Parliament there were repeated and increasing calls for action against hate propaganda in general and, in particular, the use of the mails to distribute it.[20] In the meantime, Cohen was active behind the scenes, and he met with the minister of justice, the Honourable Guy Favreau, on 17 October 1964. Also attending was Michael Garber, president of the CJC, and Saul Hayes, CJC executive vice-president. Cohen and the CJC proposed the establishment of a small working committee to "study in depth the problem of possible effective legislation to control or eliminate the publication and distribution of 'hate' materials."[21]. Cohen suggested that the committee provide the minister and the Department of Justice with a fresh perspective on how to deal with the hate propaganda problem in a manner "that balanced the need to suppress the malice and poison of such publications with the need to keep open all proper lines of free expression in a democratic society."[22]

The suggestion was warmly received, and in early November 1964 Justice Minister Favreau, in a speech to a B'Nai B'Rith Lodge meeting in Montreal, announced the forthcoming appointment of a "special committee of experts to study the problem."[23] Favreau told the packed meeting at the Sheraton Mount Royal Hotel that the government did not intend to allow the challenge to civilization of hate propaganda to "stand without answer." The answer, the minister of justice declared to a standing ovation, would "have to protect all of our peoples against flagrant defamation, without hampering dangerously the freedom of speech which is the cornerstone of our society."[24] Cohen and Hayes were the first two experts appointed. On 10 January 1965 the minister of justice announced the other members of the committee: Dr James A. Corry, principal of Queen's University, Father Gérard Dion, professor of industrial relations at Université Laval, Dr Mark MacGuigan, professor of law at the University of Toronto, Shane MacKay, executive editor of the *Winnipeg Free Press*, and Professor Pierre-Elliott Trudeau of the Faculty of Law of the Université de Montréal. The committee was blue chip, later described by the chief justice of Canada "as particularly strong."[25] The job of the Cohen Committee was to consider and report on whether legislative intervention was required and, if so, to make recommendations as to the scope of possible amendments to the Criminal Code. From the start, Cohen was determined that his committee should study and recommend. To do the latter without the former would be useless.[26]

LEGISLATION AND AMENDMENTS TO THE CRIMINAL CODE

While the Parliament of Canada obviously made its own decision about the need for and content of hate propaganda legislation, it is fair to say that the report of the Cohen Committee was extremely influential. Its influence is reflected in the fact that the legislation initially introduced was virtually identical to that recommended by the committee in its report. Moreover, the committee had given obvious care and attention to its study of the problem, and its findings were both credible and persuasive.

Before beginning its work, the committee had some problems to work out. The House External Affairs Committee under the chairmanship of John Matheson was also studying the problem, and, in appointing the Cohen Committee, Favreau wished to ensure that parliamentary feathers were not ruffled. Cohen took care of that by inviting Matheson, Klein, and Orlikow out to lunch. The purpose of the luncheon was to explain that there was no competition in the work. Matheson, in fact, told Cohen that he regarded Cohen's committee as the main organ of research on the problem, while he saw the House of Commons Committee as a sounding board of opinion.[27]

Cohen invited Justice Department officials to assist in drafting the terms of reference for the committee, and Deputy Minister Elmer Driedger and Assistant Deputy Minister T.D. MacDonald came to the first committee meeting on 29 January 1965 in Montreal. The minutes of that meeting indicate that Cohen, and some of his committee members, had one idea about the scope and mandate of their committee, while Driedger and MacDonald, along with other committee members, had another.

MacDonald opened the meeting with the observation that the Department of Justice did not wish to tell the committee what to do. The department did want a compact exercise, however, and there was no need for sociological or comparative research. Cohen demurred. In his view it would be a "disservice to the scientific underpinnings of a research committee to ignore research of a sociological and comparative kind."[28]

Hayes expressed scepticism about the need for a sociologist. "Surely," he said, "we can take judicial notice of the fact that this is a serious problem."[29] Corry agreed. MacGuigan, however, was in favour of multi-disciplinary research: "A sound factual basis for our work is absolutely essential," he told the group, adding that the committee's job was not an exercise in absolutes but in balancing interests. "We can do this only if we fully understand the weight of the interests being balanced," he said. "Without a factual basis our report might be sophisticated but not expert and informed."[30] For his part, Dion argued that a factual survey was indispensable. "We must have a factual survey," he said, noting that "the Canadian Jewish Congress asserts that there is a great problem but we cannot simply take the contention of one of the interested parties as conclusive without further investigation of the facts."[31] Finally, after much discussion, it was agreed that while there was a need for someone competent to gather and collate the factual material, that person did not need to be a sociologist. It was also agreed that Cohen could have access to departmental records, which, along with the records of the CJC, provided the committee with considerable assistance as it began its work. The first meeting ended with most committee members assigned different research tasks.

Harvey Yarosky, a young criminal lawyer and former student of Cohen's, acted as the chairman's assistant and researcher. He completed his assignment first, a review of Department of Justice files. Yarosky was looking for two things: factual information in the files indicating the nature and extent of the hate propaganda problem in Canada, and legal opinions as to the adequacy or inadequacy of existing legislation in dealing with the hate propaganda problem.

Two broad conclusions emerged from Yarosky's review. First, there was enough information on record to indicate that a sufficient quantity of hate propaganda had been disseminated in Canada during the past several years to disturb significant numbers of Canadians, as well as to contribute "to a poisoning of the social and political atmosphere to the extent that in the minds of a considerable number of representative individuals and organizations in all areas of Canada it represents a problem that the federal government must come to grips with in one way or another."[32] Second, Yarosky determined there was virtually unanimous consensus that the existing provisions of the Criminal Code and other statutes and regulations did not apply to the great bulk of hate propaganda being distributed, and that Canadian law provided no legal power to public or private persons who might wish to take measures to curb the spread of hate propaganda. This second conclusion merely reflected what CJC lawyers and others had been telling the government for years.

In particular, while Yarosky found there was no study or factual analysis on file delineating the precise nature and extent of the hate propaganda problem, Justice Department files indicated that a considerable quantity of this material had been disseminated in Canada and that the large part of this material was in written form. "Hate literature" had been found across Canada, and it was generally anti-Semitic, anti-Negro, and neo-Nazi in character. Much of the literature originated in the United States from organizations such as the National White Americans Party. There was only limited evidence of public or quasi-public meetings directed at disseminating hate ideas, and it appeared that the main means of communication was through the distribution of hate literature rather than through the spoken word.[33]

Yarosky also noted that many members of parliament, other public officials, and hundreds of private individuals had written to Ottawa complaining about hate propaganda and requesting legislation to do something about it. He said that many of the organizations and individuals requesting legislation indicated an awareness of the need to protect freedom of speech, but at the same time expressed the belief that a formula could be found for new legislation that would check hate propaganda while preserving this fundamental freedom.

For his part, MacKay wrote to sixty of his fellow editors and publishers across Canada asking their opinion about the hate propaganda problem and possible legislative remedies. Many replied and, with few exceptions, the view was expressed that hate literature generally defeats itself – the only thing worse would be a new law infringing the traditional freedoms of opinion and expression.[34] Hayes had also surveyed editorial opinion in Canada, and he reported that an analysis of forty-two editorials in Ontario newspapers revealed that twenty-seven were in favour of hate propaganda legislation while fifteen were opposed. These findings were discussed when the committee next met in Ottawa on 5 March 1965. Cohen observed that most editors and publishers who expressed concern about new legislation did so on the ground that it would be difficult to draft a law that would not interfere with freedom of expression. The concerns might evaporate, Cohen noted, if this drafting problem could be overcome.

After discussing a number of administrative matters, the committee met privately with Postmaster-General René Tremblay and his deputy. The committee was given a copy of Mr Justice Wells's Report of the Board of Review on the National States Rights Party, which had previously been tabled in the House of Commons. This was the first Post Office prohibitory order directed against hate propaganda; all the others had been used to suppress lotteries and the dissemination of obscene materials. Section 7 of the Post Office Act gave the Post Office the power to remove mailing privileges, both sending and receiving, of violators. It was a potentially powerful tool in the fight against hate propaganda, except for one thing: the Post Office had no power to open first-class mail, and if no return address was indicated on an envelope it would be difficult, if not impossible, to determine who had sent it. The deputy postmaster estimated that the chances of detecting even 10 per cent of hate literature sent through the mail was small.[35] Exacerbating the problem was the fact that the Post Office did not know what percentage of hate mail originated in the United States. What the postmaster and his deputy did know was that the vast majority of hate mail, perhaps as much as 90 per cent, was sent by bulk mail. While the Post Office was entitled to inspect bulk mail, most hate mail appeared to be sent in relatively small batches, making detection difficult. One administrative change which might facilitate detection would be to require bulk mailers to indicate return addresses on their mail.

Andrew Stewart, chairman of the Board of Broadcast Governors, also appeared before the committee. The Radio Broadcasting Regulations prohibited abusive comment directed at race or religion, while the Television Regulations contained prohibitions against abusive comments directed at race, religion, or creed. In general, Stewart told the committee, the Board of Broadcast Governors was reluctant to use its legal power because it did not wish to "be too much out of step with other communications media."[36] Moreover, there had been only a few incidents in recent years, the most publicized of which was when a Vancouver "hot-line" host attacked North American Indians as "dirty, indolent and no good." In that case, the Board of Broadcast Governors secured a legal opinion from a Vancouver lawyer that a prosecution under the Radio Regulations could succeed. No prosecution was instituted, however because the radio station's licence was up for renewal, and the matter was to be considered in the context of that application. Indeed, in the six years that the regulations in question were on the books there had never been a prosecution with respect to them. Stewart indicated that he would like to see a precise definition of "hate propaganda" in the Criminal Code so that he might have greater guidance in interpreting the Regulations.

On the night of 5 March, the committee went to a local television station where they viewed clips of interviews with noted American and Canadian neo-Nazis, including George Lincoln Rockwell, the star of a recent episode of *This Hour Has Seven Days*. The following morning, the deputy minister of national revenue, Raymond Labarge, appeared and addressed the committee. In his view, Canadian Customs had no legal authority with respect to hate propaganda since there was nothing in the law or regulations covering the importation of these materials. Moreover, Labarge continued, there had only been one complaint about these materials in the last two years, and, prior to it, there were no complaints at all. While Customs did have the authority to refuse entry to indecent and immoral materials, Labarge advised that these terms had been narrowly interpreted by the courts and, in that result, did not give Customs much discretion in deciding what to let in and what to keep out. Very simply, Labarge told the committee that his department felt "no responsibility with regard to the control of hate propaganda."[37] In the discussion that followed, Trudeau expressed the opinion that it should not be up to government departments to use any discretion in prohibition. "Rather," he argued, "it is for Parliament to decide and state in the Criminal Code what is indecent, obscene, scurrilous or abusive – and then the Departments should deal with material, by means of regulations or otherwise, on the basis of the principles set out in the Criminal Code."[38]

In the afternoon, the committee met with J. Alphonse Ouimet, president of the Canadian Broadcasting Corporation (CBC), who expressed the view that there was no problem with hate propaganda insofar as radio and television broadcasting was concerned. Referring to the recent television program about "Commander" George Lincoln Rockwell, Ouimet told the committee that the decision to broadcast this show had been carefully considered. Rockwell was a "phenomenon" and "it is a function of the CBC to put the facts before the public."[39] In broadcasting a show about him, the CBC had been informing the public about a problem and Ouimet stated that the

253   The Special Committee on Hate Propaganda

directors of the CBC felt both before and after the program that it was justified. Notwithstanding the fact that certain groups may have felt hurt by this kind of program, in which Rockwell announced his intention of "gassing queers and liberals" and sending "American Negroes back to Africa from whence they came," Ouimet was of the view that the "presentation of such programs constitutes a public service for the country as a whole."[40]

"The real and only issue," according to Ouimet, was "whether or not there are enough 'nuts' in Canada who would be adversely affected by programs such as the one on Rockwell to overbalance the large number of people who are informed by such a program and who are turned against people like Rockwell as a result of being exposed to the repulsive nature of Rockwell and his propaganda as it is shown on television."[41] In Ouimet's view, the positive value of the Rockwell program greatly outweighed whatever negative effect it might have had on the "nuts." After Ouimet spoke, the committee divided up its future research and adjourned. It was to meet next in Montreal at the end of April.

In the meantime, Professor Harry Kaufman of the University of Toronto's psychology department was retained to do a survey of the literature summarizing recent research on intergroup hatred, incitement, and defamation. He was also asked to consider and report to the committee on what further research, if any might be required. A first-class collection of research materials relating to hate propaganda in North America and indeed from around the world was assembled. MacGuigan prepared and circulated an exhaustive and scholarly review of the law of seditious libel. He later provided committee members with research papers on breach of peace at public meetings and on group libel legislation. Yarosky gathered research materials from the United States and Europe and compiled a book of domestic and international legislation and legislative proposals. For his part, Cohen consulted widely (and privately) with law enforcement organizations, community groups, and others. He also received considerable unsolicited correspondence in the form of hate mail attacking him, personally, and Jews, generally.

When the committee reassembled in Montreal at the beginning of May, representatives of the RCMP, Ontario Provincial Police, and Metropolitan Toronto Police told the committee about their experiences in dealing with hate propaganda and hate propagandists. It was suggested to the committee that the police be given the power to seize literature similar to the powers they already enjoyed with respect to obscene material.[42] Later the Quebec Provincial Police and the Montreal Police,[43] and some members of the RCMP Security Intelligence

Branch based in Quebec, met with the committee and a general discussion ensued about the nature and extent of the problem.

Some general conclusions began to emerge and, at the beginning of June, Cohen wrote his committee members setting out the five questions the committee faced. First, did Canadian legislation provide enough controls over the handling of hate propaganda? Second, if present legislation was not adequate, did it nevertheless provide a basis upon which, with limited additions, the problem of hate propaganda could be addressed? Third, did the hate propaganda problem require new legislation beyond simple amendments to existing law? Fourth, would supplementary criminal law be sufficient to deal with the problem, or would civil measures also be required? And, fifth, was there a role for the community in building a larger sense of public disapproval for hate propaganda?[44]

These issues were discussed in a preliminary way at a three-day meeting beginning on 24 June in Montreal. Cohen declared that the time to attempt to formulate a consensus was approaching, and, as the committee went about its meeting, it was clear that in many respects the members were in general agreement that the committee should recommend some restrictions on hate propaganda that incites violence. Most of the committee members were asked to draft different sections of the report, the final contents of which were to be agreed upon at another meeting in mid-July at a Laurentian resort.

That meeting, which started on 9 July and lasted until the 13th, began with a visit from W.H. Kelly of the Security and Intelligence Branch of the RCMP. Chief Superintendent Kelly told the committee members that the bulk of the hate propaganda in Canada came from the United States and that there was one Canadian behind most of its distribution, a person he identified. Kelly also told the committee members that distribution of hate materials was related to the financial strength of the Canadian distributors; when these distributors had more money they distributed more propaganda. The actual amount of literature distributed changed over time, he said, describing it as an ebb and flow.[45] Kelly subsequently provided the committee with a written report naming other individuals and organizations behind the distribution of hate propaganda. Kelly's written report confirmed what he had previously told the committee. There were only a handful of people involved in the distribution of hate propaganda, and at best one or two "masterminds" promoting the agenda of the "master-race." RCMP intelligence indicated that the different individuals and groups were interconnected.

After Kelly left, committee members began to work their way through a proposed draft of the report, with the different members bringing forward their assigned work. As they did so, a lively discussion about the limits of any hate propaganda legislation emerged. Trudeau led off. He told the committee that at first he was inclined to think that the problem of hate propaganda was not great enough to justify tinkering with the Criminal Code and creating new offences: "However," he said, "I have changed my thinking somewhat. I am not as certain now that the sheer size of the problem is the crucial consideration. We must consider the effects of hate propaganda on those people who are being insulted. Even if there are fewer people affected than we might have thought, this still might be something significant to be dealt with by law."[46]

In general, committee members were in agreement that there should be some legislation to deal with the problem, but that the legislation should be no broader than absolutely necessary. For the next three days, the committee worked through various drafts and had many discussions, including a prolonged one about the implications of including "truth" as a defence. What unanimity had been reached was threatened by disagreement over this point. Some committee members were concerned about the "relativity of truth and by the difficulty of deciding what truth really is." However, some committee members were concerned that if truth was "allowed as a defence," it would "open the door to all kinds of weird and undesirable discussion and attempts at evidence in court proceedings." Whether an exculpatory clause would give hatemongers a forum in which they could allege "truth" was the question others asked, while for his part Hayes quite forcefully argued for the exclusion of "truth" as a defence. MacGuigan, however, insisted that "truth" be recognized as a defence, and he told the other committee members that if it was not, he would not sign the report. In the end, Cohen had a solution: the committee would recommend an exculpatory clause providing a defence of truth or of belief in truth on reasonable grounds coupled with public benefit, with the onus being on the accused. In Cohen's words, "this would have the virtue of not providing explicitly that truth can exist side by side with gross abuse."[47]

Spirited discussions were held on other aspects of the proposed legislation, including whether to recommend criminalizing group defamation which did not reach the plateau of incitement. By the end of the four days, agreement about the scope of the recommended legislation had been reached.[48] It was not all hard work at the Laurentian resort: between discussions, Trudeau entertained other committee members with an exhibition of his skill on waterskis. While a general consensus was reached, the report itself still had to be hammered out. By 20 August, with the help of MacGuigan and Yarosky, Cohen was able to send all the committee members a final draft, which they all signed.

Even before the Cohen Report was released, the government signalled its intention to introduce legislation. Mitchell Sharp, minister of trade, announced in a speech in Winnipeg at the end of October 1965 that the cabinet was looking closely at the problem and that something would likely be done; any curbs that were introduced, however, would not "interfere with the fundamental freedom of the press and the individual."[49] On 9 November 1965 the report was completed and delivered to Lucien Cardin, who had succeeded the scandal-plagued Guy Favreau as minister of justice. It was sent to translation, and on 4 April 1966 it was released.

THE REPORT

One of the most interesting things about the Cohen Report is that it was unanimous.[50] There were no concurrences and no dissents. Everyone agreed. Another interesting aspect of the report is the integration of the work of other disciplines. It was not a strictly legal report because it sought to situate the discussion and the recommendations in the contemporary legal and social context. The decision to obtain and consider social science research made an important and discernable contribution to the work and the conclusions of the committee.

The substance of the report began with the committee's findings about the activities of hate propagandists and the extent of hate propaganda in Canada. There were, the committee found, only a small number of individuals and organizations involved in the dissemination of hate propaganda. Nevertheless, the committee concluded that there was a serious problem which needed to be addressed: "however limited may be the number of persons involved, or the political and administrative significance or effectiveness of many of the organizations responsible for the printing and distribution of hate materials, it would be very unwise, in the Committee's opinion, to ignore them ... it would be a mistake to ignore the potential of prejudice developed by these groups and their continuing 'hate' activities."[51]

To illustrate this point, a number of examples of hate propaganda were reproduced in the report. This propaganda, along with a detailed list of incidents involving distribution of this kind of material, led the committee to conclude that there "exists in Canada a small number of persons and a somewhat larger number of organizations, extremist in outlook and dedicated to the preaching and spreading of hatred and contempt against certain identifiable minority groups."[52]

The committee concluded that the small size of the number of distributors was no reason for them or the problem to be ignored, for as was illustrated in Europe in the 1930s, such materials and ideas can play a significant role in the creation of a climate of malice. There was, the committee found, a potential danger that must be met: "the 'hate' situation in Canada, although not alarming, clearly is serious enough to require action. It is far better for Canadians to come to grips with this problem now, before it attains unmanageable proportions, rather than deal with it at some future date in an atmosphere of urgency, of fear and perhaps even crisis. The Canadian community has a duty, not merely the right, to protect itself from the corrosive effects of propaganda that tends to undermine the confidence that various groups in a multicultural society must have in each other. The Committee therefore concludes that action by Government is necessary."[53]

Before turning to its specific recommendations, the committee discussed some of its findings on the social and psychological effects of hate propaganda and on the role of law and education as controls. The committee was convinced "that a potentially dangerous problem does exist, that the damage which hate propaganda can cause is not necessarily related to its volume, that many normally sensible and decent people are susceptible to it, and that the materials now circulating in this country are deeply hurtful to the minority groups at which they are aimed ... hate propaganda, even in its more irrational forms, can and does have a deleterious effect on society, and ... it has a tendency to encourage other discriminatory social practices."[54]

While the committee recognized that there were a variety of non-legislative measures which could be relied upon to counter hate propaganda (and it discussed some of them in the report), it concluded that legislation was required. Very simply, minority groups were entitled to expect protection from society, and, in its review of existing legislation, the committee found insufficient protection in the laws of the land: "What seems to us significant about the study of legal controls is the wide recognition that there exists a problem for which the older concepts of law and administration are no longer adequate and that newer concepts of law and regulation are justified."[55] Law was, the committee concluded, "a solution," and it recommended that there be new legislation in Canada so as to forbid the advocacy of genocide, the incitement to hatred of groups that is likely to occasion breach of the peace, and group defamation. The committee also concluded that the legislation should be drafted so as to permit maximum freedom of expression consistent with the purpose of the legislation and the needs of a free society.[56]

The committee recommended passage of the following provision:

1) Every one who advocates or promotes genocide is guilty of an indictable offence and is liable to imprisonment for five years.
2) Every one who, by communicating statements in any public place, incites hatred or contempt against any identifiable group, where such incitement is likely to lead to a breach of peace, is guilty of (a) an indictable offence and is liable to imprisonment for two years, or (b) an offence punishable on summary conviction.
3) Every one who, by communicating statements, wilfully promotes hatred or contempt against any identifiable group is guilty of (a) an indictable offence and is liable to imprisonment for two years or (b) an offence punishable on summary conviction.
4) No person shall be convicted of an offence under subsection 3 (a) where he proves that the statements communicated were true, or (b) where he proves that they were relevant to any subject of public interest, the public discussion of which was for the public benefit, and that on reasonable grounds he believed them to be true.
5) In this section
(a) "Genocide" means any of the following acts committed with intent to destroy in whole or in part, any identifiable group: (i) killing members of such a group, (ii) deliberately inflicting on such a group conditions of life calculated to bring about its physical destruction, (iii) deliberately imposing measures intended to prevent births within such a group.
(b) "Public place" includes any place to which the public have access as of right or by invitation, expressed or implied.
(c) "Identifiable group" means any section of the public distinguished by religion, colour, race, language, ethnic or national origin.
(d) "Statements" include words either spoken or written, gestures, signs or other visible representations.[57]

Among the committee's supplementary recommendations was a suggestion that consideration be given to the matter of the seizure of hate materials and their confiscation after conviction.

REACTION TO THE REPORT

Reaction to the report was predictably mixed. The CJC, the Canadian Labour Congress, and various human rights organizations and community groups declared themselves in agreement with the general thrust of the recommendations. The Canadian Civil Liberties Association, however, announced its opposition. Editorial opinion was also divided. The *Winnipeg Free Press* declared itself in favour, but the *Globe and Mail* was opposed. In a May 1966 editorial the *Globe* explained why: "What it comes down to is that truth and freedom are fashioned, always and forever, in a furnace of controversy. Someone is always uttering something to incite somebody to hatred and contempt against some group or other, and sometimes it serves the public good and sometimes it does not. Therefore, if we create a law to stop the mouths of the ugly little neo-Nazis we create a law that sometime, somewhere may be used to stop other mouths, and those other mouths may belong to the prophets and redeemers. In the past, they often have."[58]

Alan Mewett, writing in the *Criminal Law Quarterly*, was critical of the committee itself. The Cohen Committee, he wrote, was "high-powered" indeed. There was, however, an important caveat: "[I]n view of the fact that its entire recommendations boiled down to some tampering with the Criminal Code, [the committee] was perhaps somewhat deficient in criminal lawyers. This may, of course, be explicable on the ground that virtually every criminal lawyer in the country was tied up in various committees and Royal Commissions."[59] That editorial observation aside, Mewett argued that the committee had missed the real point of criminal-law legislation, arguing among other things that the factual information presented in the report itself did not establish that there was, as the report stated, "a serious problem." Even if there was, however, it was far from clear, to Mewett in any case, that "[t]here Ought to Be a Law."[60] Supporters and critics of the proposed legislation had no shortage of opportunity to present their views as the recommended legislation began a marathon trek through Parliament.

ENACTMENT OF THE LEGISLATION

On 7 November 1966 Bill s-49, based almost entirely on the recommendation in the Cohen Committee Report, was introduced as a government measure, and on 20 March 1967 it received second reading in the Senate.[61] Thus began a somewhat tortured legislative process which would go on and off for the next three years. After second reading, Bill s-49 was referred to a special joint committee of the Senate and House of Commons for consideration. However, the parliamentary session ended on 8 May 1967, and so too did consideration of this bill. Subsequently, the government introduced s-5, which was identical to s-49, and it received second reading on

8 November 1967. This bill was referred to a Senate special committee, and some meetings of that committee were held. However, Parliament was prorogued on 23 April 1968, before the deliberations of the Senate committee were completed. In the meantime, one of the Cohen Committee members, Pierre Trudeau, had been elected leader of the Liberal Party and became prime minister of Canada, while another committee member had also joined the government benches; Mark MacGuigan now represented Windsor-Walkerville in the House of Commons. In 1969, in the first session of the new Parliament, the bill was again introduced, this time as Bill s-21. It was given first and second reading, and then sent to the Senate Standing Committee on Legal and Constitutional Affairs, which heard thirty-two witnesses and received representations from almost twenty organizations. There was no shortage of both supporters and critics, and the debate in Parliament centred on whether the proposed legislation was necessary, whether there were alternatives to the criminal-law power available, and whether a hate propaganda law constituted an undue infringement on freedom of speech. Concerns were also raised about the burden of proof and the requirements that an individual show there was some justification for the hate speech being complained about.[62]

One of Canada's noted civil libertarians, Harry Arthurs of Osgoode Hall Law School, appeared before the Senate Committee. Noting that the Cohen Committee did not find a "crisis" insofar as the dissemination of hate propaganda was concerned, Arthurs observed that the "trickle" of hate propaganda of the mid 1960s had shrunk to the point "where it is no more than a residual and putrid puddle."[63] In his view, in the absence of a demonstrable problem there was no justification for legislation inhibiting freedom of speech. Arthurs also warned that the legislation would have unintended and undesirable effects, most notably in that it would provide hatemongers with "an opportunity, publicly sanctioned, to conduct [their] defence by a further propagation of [their] perverted ideas."[64] It was not the job of the law to silence hatemongers; Arthurs contended that that obligation rested upon the citizenry: "What I propose is that within the limits of our resources, we bend every effort towards eliminating real injustices, towards ... stimulating respect for individuals and their differences and for the use of orderly processes for the resolution of grievances."[65] All a criminal law would do, Arthurs concluded, would be to create the illusion that something had been done.

Cohen naturally appeared in defence of the proposed legislation and he was not at all reluctant to answer its critics. The committee knew what it was doing:

261 The Special Committee on Hate Propaganda

Given the Committee's views on the state of the law and its enforcement possibilities; given the character of the psychological effects, with their individual and social damage to target groups not merely in the eyes of the public but in the tragic self-image often created for such target groups themselves by such propaganda; and given the Committee's conviction that no freedom is absolute ... the Committee inevitably concluded that it was justified not only in making its findings but in recommending that the criminal law be altered accordingly.

Finally, the Committee took into account the important criticism aimed generally at any such controls, namely that such legislation cannot change the human heart and that fundamentally change must come from within and that the most formidable enemy of prejudice was education and not punitive criminal law. As a general proposition, the Committee accepted this broad concept of the role of the educational process, and of the social environment in general, as the more desirable framework within which to alter and control "patterns of prejudice." But it could not reject the double conclusion to which it came, namely that many of the community's most important self-educating values were enshrined in statements of criminal law and these in turn, once so enacted, had a continuing educational effect by their very formulation.[66]

Following extended discussions and a number of significant amendments, the Senate Committee published its report, which was adopted on 17 June 1969. That day, Bill s-21 received third reading in the Senate. The bill that was passed reflected the spirit of the Cohen Committee recommendations, but it did not make it to the House of Commons because Parliament adjourned. It was reintroduced, however, as a government bill in the House of Commons when Parliament returned, and on 17 November 1969 Justice Minister John Turner moved second reading:

I am of course fully aware of the significant objections that have been taken against this bill by a number of very prominent persons who are as vitally concerned as the Prime Minister and I are with the problem of civil rights. Some of these persons have said that the bill is not necessary and that the criminal law process should not be used for this purpose. In the alternative, they say that the provisions of the Criminal Code are sufficient to deal with the problems as they now stand.

Notwithstanding the very cogent arguments which have been advanced against the bill both in the Senate and publicly, the government, after a good deal of analysis, accepts as sound the conclusions of the special committee under the chairmanship of Dean Cohen regarding the present inadequate state of the criminal law in Canada ... In the circumstances, the bill is intended to deal with a special problem which can arise in our society because of excessive reactions to identifiable groups within our community. It is my belief that the present bill treads wisely and warily in this difficult and frequently controversial area of human relations.[67]

In the second-reading debate that followed, numerous concerns were raised about some of the implications of the proposed legislation. While there was considerable agreement about the desirability of outlawing the advocacy of genocide, serious reservations were expressed about the threat to freedom of speech and expression raised by other aspects of the bill. One important amendment was proposed by David Lewis, and it modified the bill so as eliminate private conversations from its scope.

The only issue that almost every member could agree on was that this type of law would never, in and of itself, solve the problem of hate propaganda. The debate was never about an issue as simple as that, and the minister of justice indicated as much:

What this bill hopes and seeks to articulate is that we condemn the social evil of the deliberate, wilful dissemination of racial hatred in this country and elsewhere. We consider it to be a poison in a civilized society. We consider it to be contrary to the collective moral sense and total integrity of the Canadian community. We consider in the global village in which we are living, which is almost claustrophobic, that the exploitation of hostility in man and the skilful promotion of hatred must be combatted. As such, in its ultimate sense the criminal law sanction, and in this context the bill outlawing the dissemination of hate – and I make no prediction as to how successful this legislation is going to be; I would be a fool to try to do it and so would any other member – is a conscientious attempt on the part of the government, and I hope of Parliament itself, to outlaw as an articulation of the total integrity of the Canadian community the dissemination of hate in this country and throughout the world, proclaiming our commitment to humanity, humanism and to the rule of law.[68]

Justice Minister Turner's spirited defence of the legislation at second reading was repeated when the bill went to the Standing Committee on Justice and Legal Affairs.

In the end, the bill did not easily pass through the House of Commons, and the concerns raised there, and in the Standing Committee that studied the measure, mirrored those raised in the upper house. On the one hand, some members wished to protect the target groups from hate propaganda. On the other hand, some parliamentarians were concerned about the threat the legislation posed to free expression in Canada, and, in general, these members rejected without reservation the idea that the law could somehow legislate a better and brighter morality.[69] Moreover, these members criticized proponents of the legislation for passing a law where no need could be said to exist. The only crisis, they claimed, would occur as a result of the legislation, for if it were passed freedom of speech would cease to exist.[70] At the end of the day, however, the bill passed by a vote of 89 to 45, with the majority of members voting in favour because, on balance, they felt that the new law would not be an unreasonable invasion into freedom of expression and speech.[71] There were 127 abstentions, indicating the ambivalence many members felt about the principle of the proposed legislation. In general, it was the legislation with respect to group defamation that caused the most controversy, for these provisions placed limits on "freedom of speech."[72]

After passage by the Commons, the bill was sent to the Senate, where an attempt was made to have it referred prior to enactment to the Supreme Court for a ruling on its constitutionality – in particular, whether it conflicted with "that fundamental statute, the Bill of Rights."[73] The attempt failed, and the bill passed, again with crossed party lines, by a vote of 39 to 24. Section 281.1(1) of the Criminal Code was proclaimed law in 1970 and provides:

Every one who advocates or promotes genocide is guilty of an indictable offence and is liable to imprisonment for five years.
(2) In this section, "genocide" means any of the following acts committed with intent to destroy in whole or in part any identifiable group, namely:
(a) killing members of the group, or
(b) deliberately inflicting on the group conditions of life calculated to bring about its physical destruction.
Prosecutions for this offence require the consent of the Attorney General.[74]

Section 282.2(1) of the Criminal Code is entitled "public incitement of hatred" and provides:

Every one who, by communicating statements in any public place, incites hatred against any identifiable group where such incitement is likely to lead to a breach of the peace, is guilty of
(a) an indictable offence and is liable to imprisonment for two years; or
(b) an offence punishable on summary conviction.
"Public place" is defined as "any place to which the public have access as of right or by invitation, express or implied."

Section 281.2(2) deals with "wilful promotion of hatred" and provides:

Every one who, by communicating statements, other than in private conversation, wilfully promotes hatred against any identifiable group is guilty of
(a) an indictable offence and is liable to imprisonment for two years; or
(b) an offence punishable on summary conviction.

This offence does not require the activity in question to lead to a breach of the peace, and would cover, for instance, the mere distribution of hate propaganda. Parliament attempted to ensure that this provision maximized freedom of speech by providing in section 281.2(2) that the person who wilfully promotes hatred shall not be convicted:

(a) if he establishes that the statements communicated were true;
(b) if, in good faith, he expressed or attempted to establish by argument an opinion upon a religious subject;
(c) if the statements were relevant to any subject of public interest, discussion of which was for the public benefit, and if on reasonable grounds he believed them to be true; or
(d) if, in good faith, he intended to point out, for the purpose of removal, matters producing or tending to produce feelings of hatred towards an identifiable group in Canada.

The permission of the attorney-general became a prerequisite to any prosecution for wilfully promoting hatred, a restriction that was intended to avoid spurious prosecutions. Section 281.3 created *in rem* proceedings for the seizure and forfeiture of hate propaganda.

DOES THE LEGISLATION SERVE A DEMOCRATIC PURPOSE?

In the aftermath of the release of the Cohen Committee Report, and throughout the extended parliamentary debate, many Canadians adopted the view of the Cohen Committee that the issue was not the amount of hate propaganda but its effects. To be sure, there was no answering the critics' claims that the amount of hate propaganda appeared to subside in the same way that, at the time of the appointment of the Cohen Committee, it had appeared to have increased. There was really no empirical way of knowing how much hate propaganda was being distributed. What could be said, and Cohen and others said it, was that by criminalizing this offence one of the moral standards of Canadian society was reflected in law, and that, in the overall, this was a greater good than any theoretical loss of freedom of speech. Not surprisingly, this was the position of the CJC, which had been lobbying for the legislation for years:

[T]he general purpose of the Criminal Code makes it eminently proper that it be the vehicle to express the national concern for the harmonious co-existence of different ethnic, racial and religious groups in Canada and that it underscore this concern by properly drafted provisions looking to the elimination of acts and practices which produce or promote injurious discord. The Canadian Jewish Congress is fully aware that any such provisions must be consistent with protection of the democratic character of our society which holds sacred the maximum freedom of speech, of assembly, of association, and of religious worship, consistent with the common weal – and in our context, the common weal is seriously affected by attacks on and incitement against racial, religious and ethnic groups and their members. The Jewish people of Canada share with the rest of the Canadian people a determination to preserve those freedoms which are deeply rooted in the traditions of our country, and for the maintenance of which our country, in alliance with all like-minded nations, fought and sacrificed. However, we do not believe, nor do we think that other Canadians believe, that the preservation and maintenance of these essential freedoms requires us to give licence to those who would arouse hostility between different racial, religious or ethnic groups of our people or to those who by publication of malicious falsehoods would drive wedges between such groups. Conduct of this character undermines democratic rights, sabotages the national welfare and destroys national unity. It exploits our democracy for evil ends. Canada, of all nations, depends for its full development upon unity among its constituent groups, and any activity which in any appreciable degree jeopardizes this objective must be eschewed.[75]

Cohen was also satisfied that democracy had been advanced. In his opinion,

the legislation provides abundant protection both in the definition of the offences, and in the permission required from the Attorneys General in several instances, to render unlikely either harassing prosecutions or easy convictions. The weight, indeed, seems to be on the other side, namely, that the legislation is so seriously concerned to protect freedom from any serious limitations that it may prove very difficult to obtain prosecutions or convictions – except in the case of "advocating genocide." Even here the offence is limited to "advocacy" and "promotion ... " It is obvious that the advocacy will have to be very clear from the evidence before a conviction is successful, limited again by the definition of "genocide" itself.

The most controversial aspects of the legislation are those surrounding the new offence of "group defamation." But here, too, the defences both in the Report and in the legislation as finally enacted, as well as the role of the Attorney General, will make it very difficult for courts ever to have before them frivolous prosecutions or fact situations that really involve serious debate over responsible questions relating to inter-group tensions or political party conflict, no matter how tough or abusive the language used.[76]

Cohen believed that principle was more important than the fact that hate propaganda had an ebb and flow. He was convinced that the legislation was justified: "Not every abuse of human communication can or should be controlled by law or custom. But every society from time to time draws lines at the point where the intolerable and the impermissible coincide."[77] There was, Cohen acknowledged, a bias in favour of free speech, whatever the costs and consequences. But that bias must step aside where there is injury to the community itself and to individual members or identifiable groups innocently caught in a "war of words" that goes beyond legitimate debate.[78] Whether this legislation struck an appropriate balance remained to be seen, but concerns about it would not disappear over time.

CIVIL LIBERTARIAN CONCERNS ABOUT THE LEGISLATION

Whether the legislation would work headed the list of unknowns when the amendments received Royal Assent in the summer of 1970. Equally problematic was whether prosecutions under the amendments would give a forum to hatemongers. Moreover, also left unanswered was the question of the effects of the legislation on freedom of speech. Would the provision be misused to silence democratic dissent? How wide could the net be cast? To these unknowns, a further question had later to be asked – whether the legislation could be justified under section 1 of the Charter of Rights and Freedoms, there being little question that it imposed limits on freedom of speech. Would the courts find that hate propaganda legislation was not a reasonable limit as can be demonstrably justified in a free and democratic society? Each of these questions would be answered in turn.

AFTERMATH OF THE COHEN REPORT

If number of prosecutions and convictions is the standard used for assessment, the legislation has clearly failed.[79] Prosecutions have been few and far between, coming in waves in the same way that hate propaganda appears. Arguably, by requiring the consent of the attorney-general for a prosecution, the provisions have been rendered inaccessible and therefore useless. If, however, the purpose of the legislation is more broadly conceived, then it has been a success, enshrining as it does a standard of tolerance and fair play, and setting out limits on the speech and activities of enemies of the social fabric. Nevertheless, those few prosecutions that have taken place have clearly become a forum for hatemongers, and recognized by them (and everyone else) as such. Ironically, given the key role played by the CJC in persuading the government to establish the Cohen Committee, the "truth" of the Holocaust has been effectively put on trial, and those accused have succeeded to some considerable extent in raising on their own behalf real concerns about the threat the legislation poses to freedom of speech.

The legislation has, of course, come under Charter attack, and the Supreme Court has been called upon several times to review the constitutionality of these provisions. What can be said here is that the questions faced by the courts about the appropriate limits, if any, to freedom of speech are really no different from those considered by the Cohen Committee, and by Parliament, more than twenty years ago. It can also be said that the legislation has not, as feared by some parliamentarians, sounded the death knell for free speech in Canada. By and large, Canadians continue to say what they wish.

CONCLUSION

The Cohen Committee recommended legislation because it became convinced, notwithstanding the fact that the number of distributors of hate propaganda was small, and notwithstanding the fact that hate propaganda had its own peculiar ebb and flow, that something needed to be done and no one was doing it. The Post Office, the RCMP, Customs, provincial and municipal police, the Board of Broadcast Governors, and the CBC all indicated they were powerless to prevent the dissemination of hate materials. Private individuals and organizations were equally helpless, given the state of the civil and criminal law and the almost impossible legal tests that had to be met for prosecutions to succeed. The Cohen Committee quite consciously decided to recommend legislation, knowing at the time that it was not the size of the problem that mattered as much as the effect of the problem on individuals, on groups, and on the community. In this way, the Cohen Committee recognized, as would a later generation of feminist and critical legal scholars, that the impact of "propaganda," whether it be "hate" or, in the later debate, "pornographic," on its victims should not be ignored. Committee members also knew there was a possibility that hate propaganda trials would turn out to be media events for the propagandists and their friends. On balance, however, they believed that this was a risk worth taking. It was important to them, and ultimately to Parliament, that the values articulated in a hate propaganda law be made part of the values of our system of criminal law.[80] In part, this was preaching to the converted; however, by recommending the criminalization of this conduct the committee sought to articulate social values more generally and in a way that recognized and promoted the maximum freedom of speech. This balancing of interests was, of course, anticipatory of section 1 of the Charter of Rights and Freedoms, and it reflected the fact that there was, and is, no easy answer to where the line should be drawn.

Cohen was under no illusion that legislation would end hate propaganda. He did think, however, that it would assist in achieving that objective, and that the limitations on freedom of speech could be justified by a narrowly written law with this goal in mind. Writing privately, Cohen set out some of his personal views: "None of us pretend to be absolutely certain that the recommendations of the kind we made do much more than scratch the surface of the problem of the human heart. But that is the history of all law, which is much more of an educator than it is a mirror or deterrent. Once standards are put into law, they for the most part affect the climate of opinion and behaviour, whether enforcement takes place or not. Personally, I can see no reason why anyone should be allowed to vilify any identifiable group. The whole history of free speech has been one of balancing freedom with many restraints ... There is nothing new in the principles we put forward, for they are only extensions of the social-legal tradition we have developed in our law."[81]

NOTES

I would like to acknowledge, with thanks, a generous financial contribution from the Human Rights Law Fund of the Department of Justice, which funded the research of this article. I would also like to acknowledge the helpful comments of a number of colleagues and friends, including Jamie Benidickson, Stanley Cohen, Rosemary Cairns-Way, Martha Jackman, and David Paciocco. Judy Chan, Celia Henslowe, Michelle Moro, and Roxanne Noel provided much-appreciated research assistance.

1 *Report of the Special Committee on Hate Propaganda in Canada* (Ottawa: Queen's Printer 1966) (chair: M. Cohen) [hereafter Cohen Report].

2 *An Act to Amend the Criminal Code*, RSC 1970, c.11 (1st Supp.), s.1.
3 M. Cohen, "The Hate Propaganda Amendments: Reflections on a Controversy" (1971), 9 *Alberta Law Review* 103.
4 See National Archives of Canada (NA), Cohen Papers, MG 31, E 24, vol. 124, file Hate Literature: J.J. Robinette to S.M. Harris, 1 May 1964: "[I]t is my view that the present sections of the Criminal Code are inadequate to deal with this problem, and I do not think that prosecutions under any of the above sections with reference to the distribution of the 'hate literature' ... would be successful." For a concurring opinion see Arthur Maloney to S.M. Harris, 28 May 1964. In early 1953 the federal government actually considered some draft legislation. However, the consideration was brief, and the decision was made not to proceed. See NA, RG 13, box 29, ACC 89–90/067, file 165533: F.P. Varcoe to minister of justice, 17 Jan. 1953. See also Department of Justice Papers, A.A. Wishart to Guy Favreau, 27 July 1964: "All the evidence which we have so far been able to obtain would, in the opinion of my law officers, indicate that no prosecution under any of the relevant sections of the Criminal Code of Canada would be successful with respect to any of the various forms of literature which have been distributed."
5 Criminal Code, SC 1953–4, c.51, ss.60–2; Ibid., sections 120, 153, 248, 366, and 166.
6 *Boucher v. R.*, [1951] SCR 265. See also W. Kaplan, *State and Salvation: The Jehovah's Witnesses and Their Fight for Civil Rights* (Toronto: University of Toronto Press 1987).
7 In April 1964, for example, a delegation from the Canadian Labour Congress met with the minister of justice and asked for legislation outlawing hate propaganda. See House of Commons, *Debates*, 16 Oct. 1964, 9157.
8 For a review of the state of group defamation law internationally see (1964), 13 *Cleveland Marshall Law Review* 1–117. On the American situation see Z. Chafee Jr, *Government and Mass Communications: A Report from the Commission on Freedom of the Press*, vol. 1 (Chicago: University of Chicago Press), 116–30 and 801–2, which unanimously opposed the enactment of group libel legislation.
9 Race Relations Act 1965 (UK), 1965, c.73.
10 See generally, E.S. Newman, *The Hate Reader* (Dobbs Ferry, NY: Oceana Publications 1964).
11 "Antidotes for Poison," Toronto *Star*, 4 March 1964, 6.
12 See M. Fenson, "Group Defamation: Is the Cure Too Costly?" (1964–5), 1 *Manitoba Law Review* 256–81. The Municipality of Metropolitan Toronto, for instance, passed a resolution on 11 March 1964 condemning the distribution of hate literature and calling for action from

270 William Kaplan

federal authorities. See also Department of Justice Papers, United Church Press Release, 21 Feb. 1964, Anglican Diocese of Toronto, press release, 27 Feb. 1954.
13 See M.R. MacGuigan, "Hate Control and Freedom of Assembly" (1966) 31 *Saskatchewan Bar Review* 232–50.
14 "Antidotes for Poison."
15 "Outlaw Hate Sheets," Toronto *Telegram*, 7 March 1964, 6.
16 "Need Test Case on Hate Tracts, PC Leader Says," Toronto *Globe and Mail*, 22 April 1964, 3.
17 See House of Commons, *Debates*, 24 Feb. 1964, 132–3.
18 Ibid., 16 Oct. 1964, 9156.
19 For example, in a speech given on 4 October 1964 in Montreal, Quebec attorney-general Claude Wagner indicated that he would favour legislation provided that any new law be drafted so "as to offer the maximum protection, with the least possible infringement upon freedom of speech." Cohen Papers, vol. 127, Wagner speech.
20 In 1964 the matter was raised more than 20 times. See eg, House of Commons, *Debates*, 9 March 1964, 687; 10 March 1964, 732; 11 March 1964, 795; 12 March 1964, 818; 13 March 1964, 867 and 873; 17 March 1964, 1158; 5 May 1964, 2927; 11 May 1964, 3116; 2 June 1964, 3834; 5 June 1964, 3971 and 3976; 11 June 1964, 4182; 16 July 1964, 5540; 21 July 1964, 5744; 26 Aug. 1964, 7289; 31 Aug. 1964, 7464; 10 Sept. 1964, 7822; 15 Sept. 1964, 8023; and 21 Oct. 1964, 9278.
21 See Cohen Papers, Cohen to Guy Favreau, 9 Nov. 1964.
22 Ibid.
23 "Favreau Assures Jews of Drive on Hate Mail," *Montreal Star*, 11 Nov. 1964, 30.
24 Ibid.
25 *R. v. Keegstra*, [1990] 3 SCR 697, at 724–5.
26 Cohen Papers, vol. 126, file Hate Committee Documents, 1–32 inclusive: confidential memorandum, 17 Jan. 1965.
27 Ibid., file 109: Minutes of Meeting, 5 March 1965, 2.
28 Ibid., vol. 124: Advisory Committee on Hate Propaganda, McGill University, 29 Jan. 1965, 3.
29 Ibid.
30 Ibid.
31 Ibid., 4.
32 Ibid., file Hate Propaganda: Memorandum to Dean Cohen, 1 March 1965, 2.
33 An appendix to Yarosky's memorandum described the various types of propaganda he had found as well as the numerous representations and requests for action.

271   The Special Committee on Hate Propaganda

34 Cohen Papers, vol. 124: "Survey of Opinion among Newspaper Editors and Publishers," 2 March 1965.
35 Ibid., Special Committee on Hate Propaganda, Minutes of Meeting Held at Justice Building on 5 March 1965, 13.
36 Ibid., 16.
37 Ibid., Minutes of Meeting, Saturday, 6 March 1965, 24.
38 Ibid., 23.
39 Ibid., 31.
40 Ibid.
41 Ibid., 32.
42 Ibid., vol. 127, file Documents: Minutes of Meeting held at McGill University, 1 May 1965, 4.
43 Apparently, the Quebec police brought some examples of "hate propaganda" to share with the committee. It was not, however, what the committee was looking for, as the examples provided were copies of letters of complaint against the police!
44 Cohen Papers, vol. 125, file Correspondence III: Cohen to Committee Members, 9 June 1965.
45 Ibid., vol. 128, file Hate Literature Documents: Minutes of Meeting held at Esterel, 9–13 July 1965, 1–4.
46 Ibid., 17–18.
47 Ibid., 39.
48 J.A. Corry, *My Life & Work: A Happy Partnership* (Kingston: Queen's University Press 1967), 134.
49 "Sharp Pledges Drive against Hate Letters," *Winnipeg Free Press*, 30 Oct. 1965, 3.
50 Well almost. The following appears in a footnote to the recommendations: "Mr. Hayes, while agreeing with these conclusions and recommendations, would have wished the recommendations to go further by excluding truth as a defence." Cohen Report, n17.
51 Ibid., 14.
52 Ibid., 24.
53 Ibid., 25. In the conclusion to the report, the committee stated: "The amount of hate propaganda presently being disseminated and its measurable effects probably are not sufficient to justify a description of the problem as one of crisis or near crisis proportions. Nevertheless, the problem is a serious one. We believe that, given a certain set of socio-economic circumstances, such as a deepening of the emotional tensions or the setting in of a severe business recession, public susceptibility might well increase significantly. Moreover, the potential psychological and social damage of hate propaganda, both to a desensitized majority and to sensitive minority target groups, is incalculable. As Mr. Justice Jackson of the United States Supreme Court wrote in *Beauharnais v.*

Illinois such 'sinister abuses of our freedom of expression ... can tear apart a society, brutalize its dominant elements, and persecute even to extermination, its minorities.'" Ibid., 59.
54 Ibid., 27.
55 Ibid., 58.
56 Ibid., 60–1.
57 Ibid., 69–70.
58 "A Stick for the Neo-Nazi is a Stick for All," *Globe and Mail*, 18 May 1966, 6.
59 A.W. Mewett, "Some Reflections on the Report of The Special Committee on Hate Propaganda" (1966) *Criminal Law Quarterly* 16.
60 Ibid., 17. Cohen later wrote Mewett about his piece: "I have just run across your editorial note in the September, 1966, issue of the Criminal Law Quarterly. I think you are surprisingly harsh in your judgment in what I think was a very serious as well as quite constructive effort to deal with a difficult but by no means unimportant problem. It surely must be of some professional and technical significance that whatever you may think of the criminal law experience and capacities of the members of our Committee, the actual language of our recommendations was almost wholly adopted in the draft Bill presented to the Senate [and also] appealed to the very experienced and hard-nosed members of the Department of Justice. Their concern for the arts of draftsmanship and the problems of practical administration of the results surely cannot be ignored ... When I get more time I shall probably write a counter-irritant, but I hope with more awareness of the professional competence on the part of our critics than perhaps was suggested in your note as to the competence of the authors of the report. We really were not all that ignorant." Cohen Papers, Cohen to Mewett, 16 March 1967. Moreover, Yarosky was a criminal lawyer who worked in one of Montreal's leading criminal law firms. See also R.E. Hage, "The Propaganda Amendment to the Criminal Code" (1970), 28 *University of Toronto Faculty of Law Review* 63.
61 The decision to introduce the measure in the Senate was deliberate. It was thought that review in the other place would be more thorough and expeditous. See House of Commons, *Debates*, 3 Nov. 1966, 9471.
62 There is a considerable amount of literature debating the pros and cons of the legislation and also subjecting the Cohen Report, and the various bills brought before Parliament, to legal scrutiny. This paper does not deal with that aspect of the law, but for further information see, for example, W.S. Tarnopolsky, "Freedom of Expression v. Right to Equal Treatment" (1967) *University of British Columbia Law Review/ Cahiers de Droit* 43, and M.R. MacGuigan, "Proposed Anti-hate Legislation" (1967), 15 *Chitty's Law Journal* 302.

273 The Special Committee on Hate Propaganda

63 Harry Arthurs's presentation to the Senate Committee is reproduced in H. Arthurs, "Hate Propaganda – An Argument against Attempts to Stop It by Legislation" (1970), 18 *Chitty's Law Journal* 1.
64 Ibid., 3.
65 Ibid., 5.
66 Cohen, "The Hate Propaganda Amendments," 109.
67 House of Commons, *Debates*, 17 Nov. 1969, 882–3.
68 Ibid., 6 April 1970, 5557–8. See also ibid., 5610, where Lincoln Alexander, member for Hamilton West, said: "This bill offers hope in that it is an indication that someone is aware of the problem that actually exists, that someone is aware that inciting hatred is unacceptable." David Lewis, leader of the New Democratic Party, agreed with this approach: "I suggest that legislation on the statute books will tell those otherwise decent and law-abiding citizens who have been sold a bill of goods that what they have been doing is contrary to the moral sense of the society in which they live, and is against the law. Many of these people will simply quit because it is against the law, and that is what the law is for. That is the first obvious consequence which is desirable in any society. The second thing is that those who have no regard for the law, and those who will not be influenced by an appeal to morals in our society, will have the dissemination of this literature stopped by law. The third and equally important result of legislation like this is what several members ... pointed out, namely, the educative value of the presence of the law on the statute books of the country." Ibid., 17 Nov. 1969, 817.
69 Ibid., 13 April 1970, 5644.
70 Ibid. See also 7 April 1970, 5612, where Lincoln Alexander said: "What we are doing here is creating an atmosphere not out of crisis but out of a new awareness of what hatred could do to Canada."
71 Ibid., 13 April 1970, 5807.
72 According to Corry, "many Canadians found it easy to support the provisions against incitement to genocide, but hard to balance protection of freedom of speech and protection of minorities. In the course of the thorough and detailed canvassing of the bill in Parliament, a number of amendments were proposed and accepted by the government ... When the politicians thought of the number of groups about whom they might sometimes want to speak contemptuously, they became cautious. Also, the defaming of groups in private conversations as distinguished from open attacks in public was put beyond the reach of the law. And defence against group defamation was provided to protect those who, in good faith, published controversial opinions or arguments on religious subjects. In sum, these hedgings on the draft bill presented by the Committee were thought to be desirable limits on a

measure that did not draw a general consensus. Subject to these limitations, what the Committee argued for became law." Corry, *My Life & Work*, 135–6.
73 Senate, *Debates*, 23 April 1970, 930. See also ibid., 1030.
74 Needless to say, requiring the consent of the attorney-general is also problematic. It may ensure that no frivolous prosecutions take place, but it raises the spectre of selective and political prosecutions.
75 Cohen Papers, vol. 124: Canadian Jewish Congress, Saul Hayes to National Executive Committee, 6 April 1965.
76 Cohen, "The Hate Propaganda Amendments," 112.
77 Cohen Report, preface.
78 Ibid.
79 *Equality Now!: Report of the Special Committee on Visible Minorities in Canadian Society* (Hull: Supply and Services 1984) (chair: B. Doudlin), made a number of recommendations with respect to the hate propaganda provisions of the Criminal Code, all of which had as their objective the facilitation of prosecutions under these provisions. See also Law Reform Commission of Canada, *Hate Propaganda*, Working Paper 50 (Ottawa: Law Reform Commission of Canada 1986).
80 In this way the Committee recognized that some of society's most fundamental values are enshrined in criminal law. See Law Reform Commission of Canada, *Our Criminal Law* (Hull: Supply and Services 1976).
81 Cohen Papers, vol. 125, Cohen to E.M. Howse, 24 Nov. 1966.

The Right to Protection against Group-Vilifying Speech: Towards a Model Factum in Support of Anti-Hate Legislation

IRWIN COTLER

Like many others, I was – and remain – the beneficiary of Maxwell Cohen's scholarship, deanship, counsel. Most important, perhaps, he was – in the very best sense of the word – teacher, mentor, inspiration, and friend. Cohen used to say of Professor Myres MacDougal – that great and legendary teacher of law at Yale – that he had not only students, but disciples. Like MacDougal, Cohen has his disciples – and not only disciples but devotees – and I would be honoured to count myself among them.

Just as MacDougal, together with Harold Lasswell, founded the policy-oriented school of jurisprudence, so did Maxwell Cohen impart a "Gestalt" view of law and society, with society itself as the lawyer's client. For Professor, Dean, Judge, Me Cohen, law was not only a technical body of rules, but articulated the values that men and women should seek to live by; law was not only an agency of social control, but an organizing principle for the reconfiguration of society – with respect for human dignity at its core.

It is this Gestalt Theory that has inspired not only my thinking about law but my involvement in human rights. This paper reflects that interest and is anchored in perspectives of a criminal, constitutional, international, and comparative law approach – a Gestalt approach inspired directly by the thinking of Max Cohen and his chef d'œuvre, the Cohen Committee. For the errors and omissions, however, I alone am responsible.

In December 1989 three cases involving incitement to racial hatred – including anti-Semitic hate propaganda – were joined for hearing before the Supreme Court of Canada.[1] The hearings revolved around challenges to the constitutionality of Canada's anti-hate legislation as being an unconstitutional infringement of the freedom-of-expression guarantee under section 2(b) of the Canadian Charter of Rights and Freedoms, which guarantees everyone "freedom of thought, opinion, belief and expression, including freedom of the press and other media of communication." The trilogy has become the most celebrated litigation involving incitement to racial hatred and the law in the history of Canadian jurisprudence.

In each of these cases there were two central issues before the court, which are both reflective – if not also instructive – of the central concerns of a court in a democratic society called upon to decide a racial-incitement case: first, whether the incitement to racial hatred is protected speech in a free and democratic society like Canada; and, second, even assuming that such racial incitement is *prima facie* protected speech, whether it can nonetheless be subject to "reasonable limitations, prescribed by law, as can be demonstrably justified in a free and democratic society," in the words of the section 1 "balancing principle" in the Charter.

An appreciation of this array of litigation reveals a little-known but significant social/legal phenomenon: that Canada has become an international centre for racist/hate propaganda litigation in general and Holocaust denial litigation in particular. The Canadian experience has generated one of the most compelling and instructive sets of legal precedents respecting this "genre" of litigation in the world. First, there exists a dynamic and dialectical encounter between the rise in hate speech, on the one hand, and the emergence in Canada of a comprehensive legal regime to combat it on the other, coupled with a Rights Charter invoked by both the hatemongers and the victims. Second, the Supreme Court of Canada has articulated a series of principles and perspectives which may help to pour content into what First Amendment scholar Fred Schauer has called the "multiple tests, rules and principles" reflecting "the [extraordinary] diversity of communication experiences."[2]

These judgments – and their respective principles and perspectives – could not have come at a more propitious time, for the period since the cases were joined for hearing before the Supreme Court of Canada has witnessed an almost unprecedented explosion of racial and religious incitement against vulnerable minorities in democratic societies in Europe, Canada, the United States, Latin America, and Asia. Moreover, the legal remedies invoked to combat such incitement have been the object of constitutional challenges in regions around the world, triggering a series of *cause-célèbres* this past year: the *Le Pen* case in France, the *Radio Islam* case in Sweden, the *Smirnov-Ostashvilli* case in the former Soviet Union, the Minnesota "*Cross Burning*" case in the United States, and the historic trilogy in Canada – for which *Keegstra* is a metaphor and message – to name but a few.

What follows is a suggested model factum – or legal argument – in support of the right of members of disadvantaged minorities to be protected against group vilification, and the validity of anti-hate legislation to combat it. "Cantonia" is the generic term for democratic societies that have been experiencing a wave of racial and religious incitement against targeted minorities in their midst. "Petitioner" is counsel submitting arguments on Cantonia's behalf in support of its anti-hate legislation that has been challenged.

The factum is organized around the interpretive principles and perspectives as developed by the Supreme Court of Canada in this trilogy, particularly the *Keegstra* case, while drawing also upon the principles and perspectives of the Special Committee on Hate Propaganda, otherwise known as the Cohen Committee. It is hoped that such a factum – or set of principles and perspectives – may prove useful to scholars, advocates, and judges in appreciating the considerations that ought to be adduced or factored into any analysis of the competing values of freedom of expression on the one hand, and the right of disadvantaged minorities to protection from group-vilifying speech on the other.

FACTUM OF LEGAL ARGUMENT OF
PETITIONER (CANTONIA)

Principle One: Freedom of Expression – The "Lifeblood of Democracy"

1. Petitioner acknowledges and supports the significance and scope of the principle of freedom of expression, and regards it as a "fundamental" principle underlying free and democratic societies such as Cantonia. In a word, Petitioner shares with freedom-of-expression adherents – such as First Amendment scholar Alan Dershowitz[3] in the United States, or Alan Borovoy[4] in Canada – the notion of freedom of expression as "the lifeblood of democracy." Indeed, as the Supreme Court itself acknowledged in the *Keegstra* case, "[the notion] that freedom to express oneself openly and fully is of crucial importance in a free and democratic society was recognized by Canadian Courts prior to the enactment of the *Charter* ... [f]reedom of expression was seen as an essential value of Canadian Parliamentary democracy."[5]

2. In a word, freedom of expression was regarded as a "core" right even before the advent of the Charter, a perspective that ought to be instructive for societies without a constitutionally entrenched Bill of Rights.

3. Admittedly, the rights and freedoms generated by a Charter, such as freedom of expression, are to be given a "generous and liberal interpretation," as befits constitutionally entrenched rights. In the words of the Supreme Court, quoting Professor Paul Freund, "the Constitution should not read like a last will and testament, lest it become one";[6] and what the Canadian experience demonstrates is that a constitutionally entrenched Charter of Rights invites "a more careful and generous study of the values informing the freedom,"[7] and therefore commends itself to those concerned with a more enhanced promotion and protection of human rights generally. But this does not mean that the Canadian experience is inappropriate or irrelevant to societies that do not have an entrenched Bill of Rights, or relevant only to those that do. For even in the absence of a Charter of Rights, freedom of expression remains a fundamental freedom and may well be invoked and applied as if it were a constitutional principle.

Principle Two: Freedom of Expression – Fundamental – but Not an Absolute Right

4. It is submitted that freedom of expression, as Professor Abraham Goldstein put it, "is not absolute, however much so many persist in talking as if it is."[8] Indeed, in every free and democratic society certain forms and categories of expression are clearly regarded as being outside the ambit of protected speech. Even in the United States, certain categories of speech – obscenity, personal libel, and "fighting words" – are not protected by the First Amendment; such utterances, said the U.S. Supreme Court in *Chaplinsky*, "are no essential part of any explosion of ideas, and are of such slight social value as a step to the truth that any benefit ... is clearly outweighed by the social interest in order and morality";[9] some American scholars argue that *Beauharnais v. Illinois*,[10] which upheld the constitutionality of a group libel ordinance, is still good law.

5. In a word, all free and democratic societies have recognized limitations on freedom of expression in the interest of national security, such as prohibitions against treasonable speech; limitations in the interest of public order and good morals, such as prohibitions against obscenity, pornography, or disturbing the public peace; limitations in the interest of privacy and reputation, such as prohibitions

respecting libel and defamation; limitations in the interest of consumer protection, such as prohibitions respecting misleading advertising; and the like.

Principle Three: Freedom of Expression and the "Purposive" Theory of Interpretation

6. Petitioner submits that, in the view of Supreme Court Charter jurisprudence, the proper approach to determining the ambit of freedom of expression – and the "pressing and substantial concerns" that may authorize its limitation – is a purposive one. This principle of interpretation was set forth by Chief Justice Dickson (as he then was) in the *Big M. Drug Mart Ltd.* case as follows: "The meaning of a right or a freedom guaranteed by the Charter was to be ascertained by an analysis of the purpose of such a guarantee; it was to be understood, in other words, in the light of the interests it was meant to protect."[11]

7. In the *Keegstra* case, the Supreme Court reiterated the three-pronged rationale for freedom of expression that had earlier been summarized in *Irwin Toy* as follows: "(1) seeking and attaining truth is an inherently good activity; (2) participation in social and political decision-making is to be fostered and encouraged; and (3) diversity in forms of individual self-fulfilment and human flourishing ought to be cultivated in a tolerant and welcoming environment for the sake of both those who convey a meaning and those to whom a meaning is conveyed."[12]

8. More importantly, as determined by the Ontario Court of Appeal, in *R. v. Andrews and Smith*,[13] and as affirmed by the majority of the Supreme Court in *Keegstra*, it is submitted that "hatemongering" constitutes an assault on these very values and interests sought to be protected by freedom of expression as follows:

> a) First, such hatemongering is not only incompatible with a "competitive marketplace of ideas which will enhance the search for truth," but represents the very antithesis of the search for truth in a marketplace of ideas.[14] It seeks not to inform, but to incite; not to discuss, but to degrade; not to debate, but to defame; not to enlighten through "uninhibited, robust, and wide-open"[15] exchange of ideas – however unpopular or unpalatable – but to diminish, if not deny, through an incipiently violent expression (incitement to racial hatred) the search for any truth at all. Indeed, the only "truth" conveyed is the degradation of the target group and its members, the whole destructive not only of truth, but of the multicultural society itself.

b) Second, it is not only antithetical to participation in democratic self-government, but it constitutes "a destructive assault on that democratic self-government."[16]

c) Third, it is utterly incompatible with a claim to "personal growth and self-realization"; rather it is analogous to the claim that one is "fulfilled" by expressing oneself "violently" (the example given by the Supreme Court in the *Irwin Toy* case). Indeed, such incitement to racial hatred constitutes an assault on the very "self-realization" of the target group and its members. It is not surprising, then, that the Supreme Court in *Keegstra* took judicial notice of, and anchored its reasons for judgment in, the "catastrophic effects of racism," while citing studies showing that victims of group vilification may suffer loss of self-esteem and experience self-abasement rather than self-realization.

Principle Four: Freedom of Expression and the "Contextual" Principle

9. Petitioner submits that a fourth principle of interpretation – or "building block"[17] as Madam Justice Bertha Wilson characterized it – is that of the "contextual" principle. In a word, just as the purposive principle is relevant both in the interpretation of the ambit of a right and the assessment of the validity of legislation to limit it, so is the contextual principle relevant both in the interpretation of the right in the context of the particular facts and circumstances of the case at bar, as well as the assessment of the validity of the legislation to limit the right.

As the Supreme Court put it in *Keegstra*, "it is important not to lose sight of factual circumstances in undertaking an analysis of freedom of expression and hate propaganda, for these shape a court's view of both the right or freedom at stake and the limit proposed by the state; neither can be surveyed in the abstract."[18] As Wilson J (as she then was) said in *Edmonton Journal*, referring to what she termed the "contextual approach" to Charter interpretation:

a particular right or freedom may have a different value depending on the context. It may be, for example, that freedom of expression has greater value in a political context than it does in the context of disclosure of the details of a matrimonial dispute. The contextual approach attempts to bring into sharp relief the aspect of the right or freedom which is truly at stake in the case as well as the relevant aspects of any values in competition with it. It seems to be more sensitive to the reality of the dilemma posed by the particular facts and therefore more conducive to finding a fair and just compromise between ... competing values.[19]

In a recent retrospective on the case, Justice Wilson commented that "there was, for example, no point in assessing the value of freedom of speech for balancing purposes in the context of our political institutions if it had come before the court in the context of advertising aimed at children."[20]

10. One might equally argue – as will be seen through the prism of the principles below – that it makes all the difference in the world if the freedom-of-expression principle at issue comes before the court in the context of political speech, or in the context of hate speech aimed at disadvantaged minorities. As Justice Wilson concluded on this point, "a contextual as well as purposive interpretation of the right was required for purposes of Section 1 balancing."[21] In the matter of hatemongering, then, whether the principle of interpretation adopted is the purposive or the contextual one, both interpretations tend to converge in favour of the right of disadvantaged minorities to be protected against group vilification, while maintaining an "expansive" and "liberal" view of freedom of expression itself as a core right.

Principle Five: Freedom of Expression in a Free and Democratic Society

11. Petitioner submits that according to Supreme Court doctrine, the interpretation of freedom of expression must involve not only resort to the purposive character of freedom of expression (section 2(b)), but "to the values and principles of a free and democratic society." This phrase, as the court put it, "requires more than an incantation ... [but] requires some definition ... an elucidation as to the values and principles that [the phrase] invokes."[22]

12. Such principles, said the court, are not only the genesis of rights and freedoms under the Charter generally, but also underlie freedom of expression (section 2b) in particular. These values and principles include "respect for the inherent dignity of the human person ... [and] respect for cultural and group identity";[23] accordingly, anti-hate legislation is not so much an infringement of free speech as it is promotive and protective of the values and principles of a free and democratic society.

Principle Six: Freedom of Expression in Comparative Perspective

13. Petitioner submits that in determining whether incitement to racial hatred is a protected form of expression, resort may be had not only to the values and principles of a free and democratic society such as Canada, but to the legislative experience of other free and democratic societies. An examination of the legislative experience of such other free and democratic societies clearly and consistently supports the position that such racist hate speech is not entitled to constitutional protection.[24]

14. Indeed, by 1966, the Cohen Committee on hate propaganda had already recorded the existence of legislation in a number of countries which sought to proscribe incitement to group hatred. The countries concerned were demonstrably "free and democratic."[25]

15. Moreover, the legislative pattern since 1966 in these and other free and democratic societies supports the view that not only is such legislation representative of free and democratic societies, but its very purpose is to ensure that such societies remain free and democratic. Indeed, free and democratic societies in every region of the world have now enacted similar legislation, including countries in Asia, the Middle East, and Latin America, as well as the countries of Scandinavia and Western Europe. Such legislation can also be found in the countries of Eastern Europe and the former Soviet Union. These free and democratic societies and those of Eastern Europe and the former Soviet Union that have adopted such legislation include the following:

Austria
Penal Code, Article 283

Belgium
Law on Suppression of Certain Acts Prompted by Racism and Xenophobia, 30 July 1981

Bulgaria
Constitution of 1971, Article 35(4)
Penal Code, Article 162

Czechoslovakia
Penal Code, sections 196, 198

Federal Republic of Germany
Penal Code, Articles 130, 131

Finland
Penal Code, Chap. 13, Article 5

France
Act 72–546 of 1 July 1972

German Democratic Republic
Constitution of 1974, Article 6(5)
Penal Code, Article 140

Greece
Law 927–1979: Concerning the Prohibition of Actions Aiming at Racial Discrimination

Hungary
Penal Code, Act 4 of 1978, as amended in 1989

Iceland
Penal Code of 1973

India
Penal Code, as amended in 1972, sections 153–A and 153–B

Israel
Basic Law: The Knesset, section 7A
Penal Law, as amended in 1986, sections 144a to 144e

Italy
Law No. 654 of 1975, Article 3

Luxembourg
Criminal Code, Article 455, as amended in 1980

Netherlands
Criminal Code, Article 137 (c) (d) (e)

New Zealand
Race Relations Act, 1971, RS, vol. 14, section 25

Norway
Penal Code of 1902, as amended in 1970 and 1981, Article 135A

Romania
Constitution of 1974, Article 17(3)
Penal Code of 1969, Article 317

Sweden
Penal Code, Chap. 16, section 8, as amended in 1982

United Kingdom
Public Order Act, 1986, Part 3, entitled "Racial Hatred"

Uruguay
Criminal Code – Article 149
Decree-Law No. 10,279 of November 1942, Article 6
Law No. 16,048 of 6 June 1989; amendment to Criminal Code

USSR
Constitution of 1977, Article 36(3)
Criminal Code of 1979, Article 74

Yugoslavia
Constitution of 1974, Chap. 3, Article 170
Criminal Code, Article 134

Principle Seven: Freedom of Expression, Hate Propaganda, and the American "First Amendment" Doctrine

16. It is clear that those who challenge the constitutionality of anti-hate legislation anchor their attack in the First Amendment Doctrine, as American constitutional jurisprudence tends to consider such anti-hate legislation a violation of the American Bill of Rights.[26]

17. Petitioner acknowledges that "the [American] practical and theoretical experience is immense, and should not be overlooked by Canadian courts"[27] or indeed courts of any democratic society. "On the other hand," as the Supreme Court put it in *Keegstra*, "we must examine American constitutional law with a critical eye, and in this respect La Forest J has noted in *R. v. Rahey*, [1987] 1 SCR 588 at 639: 'While it is natural and even desirable for Canadian courts to refer to American constitutional jurisprudence in seeking to elucidate the meaning of *Charter* guarantees that have counterparts in the United States Constitution, they should be wary of drawing too ready a parallel between constitutions born to different countries in different ages and in very different circumstances.'"[28]

18. Accordingly, it is submitted that the American Constitutional jurisprudence is less relevant and persuasive for Canada than comparable experience in other free and democratic societies for the following reasons:

i) It is not clear that *Beauharnais* is no longer good law, while it is clear that it has never been expressly overruled. Indeed, credible arguments have been made that later United States Supreme Court cases have not undermined its legitimacy.[29]

ii) As the Supreme Court further noted in *Keegstra*,[30] there is a growing body of academic writing in the United States which focuses "upon the way in which hate propaganda can undermine the very values which free speech is said to protect." This body of writing is receptive to the idea that, were the issue addressed from this new perspective, First Amendment doctrine might be able to accommodate statutes prohibiting hate propaganda.[31]

iii) That feature of the First Amendment doctrine that is most incompatible with anti-hate legislation is the doctrine's seeming antipathy to content-based regulation of expression. Yet, as Chief Justice Dickson (as he then was) put it: "I am somewhat sceptical, however, as to whether this view of free speech in the United States is entirely accurate."[32] Rather, as the chief justice pointed out, in rejecting the extreme position that would provide an absolute guarantee of free speech in the Bill of Rights, the Supreme Court of the United States has developed a number of tests and theories by which protected speech can be identified and the legitimacy of government regulation assessed. What is often required, even with the First Amendment doctrine, is a content-based categorization of the expression under examination.[33]

In short, as the Supreme Court observed in *Keegstra*, "a decision to place expressive activity in a category which either merits reduced protection or falls entirely outside the First Amendment's ambit at least impliedly involves assessing the content of the activity in light of free speech values."[34]

iv) The legislatures and courts of the United States are not bound by international treaties to prohibit hatemongering; in particular, the United States, unlike Canada or other Commonwealth countries and the European states, has not ratified the International Covenant on the Elimination of Racial Discrimination or the International Covenant on Civil and Political Rights. Accordingly, it is not bound to enact legislative measures to implement the anti-hate provisions of those treaties, or to interpret the First Amendment in the light of international human rights law, or to abide by decisions of judicial and quasi-judicial international tribunals.

v) The textual reference to speech in the United States Constitution differs from that of section 2(b) of the Canadian Charter, as do the *travaux préparatoires* bearing on the respective provisions.

vi) The United States Constitution does not contain a limitations clause as do the Canadian Charter, the European Convention, and the International Human Rights Treaties. The two-stage analytical construct of Canadian Charter jurisprudence has no United States parallel.

vii) The United States Constitution contains no section 27 provision directing American courts to interpret the First Amendment in a manner consistent with the preservation and enhancement of the multicultural heritage of the United States.

viii) The historical development and doctrinal underpinning of the First Amendment doctrine – including the "political speech" metaphor and the Meikeljohn influence – are less relevant to a Canadian multicultural society whose enduring *jus gentium*, reflected in the *Report of the Special Committee on Hate Propaganda*, has been the entitlement of vulnerable identifiable groups to protection against deliberate and incipiently malevolent incitement to racial hatred.

ix) The United States Constitution, unlike its Canadian counterpart, has not developed interpretive principles whereby the First Amendment Doctrine will be read in the light of the other rights and freedoms in the United States Constitution, as section 2(b) is read in the light of other Charter rights – for example, equality; on the contrary, the First Amendment Doctrine has always enjoyed a "preferred" status in the hierarchy of rights and freedoms, whereas, in Canada, section 2(b) cannot be insulated from the other associated rights and freedoms.

x) The American Constitution, unlike its Canadian counterpart, has no theory of protection for group rights, and no corresponding ethos of group libel legislation.

Principle Eight: Freedom of Expression in the Light of "Other Rights and Freedoms"

19. It is submitted that the Supreme Court has also determined that the principle of freedom of expression must be interpreted in the light of other rights and freedoms sought to be protected by a democracy like Canada. In the words of the court: "The purpose of the right or freedom in question [freedom of expression] is to be sought by reference to ... the meaning and purpose of the other specific rights and freedoms with which it is associated."[35]

20. It should be noted that the purpose, if not also the effect, of hate speech is to diminish, if not deny, other rights and freedoms, or the rights and freedoms of others; indeed, such hatemongering is the very antithesis of the values and principles underlying these rights and freedoms. Accordingly, any reading of freedom of expression in the light of other rights and freedoms admits of no other interpretation than that such hate speech is outside the ambit of protected expression.

Principle Nine: Freedom of Expression and the Principle of Equality: Hate Propaganda as a Discriminatory Practice

21. Petitioner submits that, as a corollary, if freedom of expression is to be interpreted in the light of other rights and freedoms, a core – and underlying – associated principle is that of equality. The denial of other rights and freedoms – or the rights and freedoms of "the other" – makes freedom of expression, or group defamation, not just a speech issue, but an equality issue. In the words of Professor Kathleen Mahoney: "In this trilogy of cases, the majority of the Supreme Court of Canada articulated perspectives on freedom of expression that are more inclusive than exclusive, more communitarian than individualistic, and more aware of the actual impacts of speech on the disadvantaged members of society than has ever before been articulated in a freedom of expression case. The Court advanced an equality approach using a harm-based rationale to support the regulation of hate propaganda as a practice of inequality."[36]

Principle Ten: Freedom of Expression, Group Libel, and the "Harms-Based" Rationale

22. It is submitted that the concern resulting from the existence of such hatemongering is not, as the Supreme Court of Canada recently observed, "simply the product of its offensiveness, but stems from the very real harm which it causes."[37] This judicial finding of "very real harm" from hatemongering is not only the most recent finding on record by a high court, but may be considered a relevant and persuasive authority for other democratic societies. The following excerpt from the *Keegstra* case is particularly instructive in this regard, while anchored in the analysis and findings of the Cohen Committee:

Essentially, there are two sorts of injury caused by the hate propaganda. First, there is harm done to members of the target group. It is indisputable that the emotional damage caused by words may be of grave psychological and social consequence ...

In the context of sexual harassment, for example, this court has found that words can in themselves constitute harassment (*Janzen v. Platy Ent. Ltd.*, [1989] 1 S.C.R 1252, 4 W.W.R 39, 25 C.C.E.L. 1, 10 C.H.R.R. D/6205, 59 D.L.R (4th) 352, 47 C.R.R 274, 89 C.L.L.C. 17,011, 58 Man. R. (2d) 1, 95 N.R. 81 (sub nom. *Janzen v. Pharos Restaurant*)). In a similar manner, words and writings that wilfully promote hatred can constitute a serious attack on persons belonging to a racial or religious group, and in this regard the Cohen Committee noted that these persons are humiliated and degraded (p. 214).

In my opinion, a response of humiliation and degradation from an individual targeted by hate propaganda is to be expected. A person's sense of human dignity and belonging to the community at large is closely linked to the concern and respect accorded the groups to which he or she belongs (see Isaiah Berlin, "Two Concepts of Liberty," in Four Essays on Liberty (1969), p. 118, at p. 155). The derision, hostility and abuse encouraged by hate propaganda therefore have a severely negative impact on the individual's sense of self-worth and acceptance ...

A second harmful effect of hate propaganda which is of pressing and substantial concern is its influence upon society at large. The Cohen Committee noted that individuals can be persuaded to believe "almost anything" (p. 30) if information or ideas are communicated using the right technique and in the proper circumstances (at p. 8):

In the words of the Cohen Committee:

"[W]e are less confident in the 20th century that the critical faculties of individuals will be brought to bear on the speech and writing which is directed at them. In the 18th and 19th centuries, there was a widespread belief that man was a rational creature, and that if his mind was trained and liberated from superstition by education, he would always distinguish truth from falsehood, good from evil. So Milton, who said 'let truth and falsehood grapple: who ever knew truth put out the worse in a free and open encounter.'

"We cannot share this faith today in such a simple form. While holding that over the long run, the human mind is repelled by blatant falsehood and seeks the good, it is too often true, in the short run, that emotion displaces reason and individuals perversely reject the demonstrations of truth put before them and forsake the good they know. The successes of modern advertising, the triumphs of impudent propaganda such as Hitler's, have qualified sharply our belief in the rationality of man. We know that under the strain and pressure in times of irritation and frustration, the individual is swayed and even swept away by hysterical, emotional appeals. We act irresponsibly if we ignore the way in which emotion can drive reason from the field."[38]

23. It is submitted that the Supreme Court's conclusion on this point – relying as it does on the conclusions of the Cohen Committee itself – is particularly relevant today. In the words of the court:

The threat to self-dignity of target group members is thus matched by the possibility that prejudiced messages will gain some credence, with the attendant result of discrimination, and perhaps even violence, against minority groups in Canadian society. With these dangers in mind, the Cohen Committee made clear in its conclusions that the presence of hate propaganda existed as a baleful and pernicious element, and hence a serious problem, in Canada.[39]

Again, in the words of the Cohen Committee as quoted by the Supreme Court of Canada:

The amount of hate propaganda presently being disseminated [is] probably not sufficient to justify a description of the problem as one of crisis or near crisis proportion. Nevertheless the problem is a serious one. We believe that, given a certain set of socio-economic circumstances, such as a deepening of the emotional tensions or the setting in of a severe business recession, public susceptibility might well increase significantly. Moreover, the potential psychological and social damage of hate propaganda, both to a desensitized majority and to sensitive minority target groups, is incalculable. As Mr. Justice Jackson of the United States Supreme Court wrote in *Beauharnais v. Illinois*, such "sinister abuses of our freedom of expression ... can tear apart a society, brutalize its dominant elements, and persecute even to extermination, its minorities."[40]

Principle Eleven: Freedom of Expression, Hate Propaganda, and International Law

24. It is submitted that, as in the words of the Supreme Court, international law may be regarded as "a relevant and persuasive source"[41] for the interpretation of rights and freedoms under the Charter. Moreover, as Chief Justice Dickson (as he then was) wrote in *Keegstra*, "no aspect of international human rights has been given attention greater than that focused upon discrimination ... this high concern regarding discrimination has led to the presence in two international human rights documents of articles forbidding the dissemination of hate propaganda."[42]

25. Accordingly, it is submitted that reading the freedom-of-expression principle in the light of international human rights law generally, and under these two international human rights treaties in particular,⁴³ requires that such racial incitement be excluded from the protective ambit of freedom of expression. As such, any legislative remedy prohibiting the promotion of hatred or contempt against identifiable groups on grounds of their race, religion, colour, or ethnic origin would be in compliance with Cantonia's international obligations, and indeed have the effect of implementing these international obligations.

26. It is submitted that, to paraphrase a recent opinion by the Supreme Court of Canada, and which reflects the jurisprudential position in countries like Cantonia, "the *content* of [Canada's] International Human Rights obligations are an important *indicia* of the content of rights and freedoms under the *Charter* [of Canada]."⁴⁴ Indeed, as the court put it, "these international human rights obligations should inform not only the content [of freedom of speech], but also the interpretation of what can constitute a pressing and substantial objective which may justify a restriction on the right."⁴⁵

27. As for these two specific human rights treaties, the International Convention on the Elimination of All Forms of Racial Discrimination (CERD) and the International Covenant on Civil and Political Rights (ICCPR), it should be noted that in 1965 the United Nations adopted CERD and that more than 150 countries are now parties to the convention.⁴⁶ Article 4(a) of the convention calls upon state parties to the convention, *inter alia*, to "undertake to adopt immediate and positive measures designed to eradicate all incitement to, or acts of, discrimination ... [and] to declare an offence punishable by law all dissemination of ideas based on racial superiority or hatred, incitement to racial discrimination."

28. In May 1983 the Study of a Special Rapporteur on the Implementation of Article 4 of this convention recorded the concerted measures taken by the states parties to this convention to enact legislation in accordance with Article 4 under the convention.⁴⁷ In the context of racial incitement and freedom of expression, this record of implementation indicates what is considered not only justifiable in an overwhelming number of free and democratic societies, but is also representative of the general principles of law recognized by the community of nations. As such, it would oblige a country like Cantonia to enact legislation to implement such a convention if it has not yet done so.

29. In 1966 the United Nations adopted the International Covenant on Civil and Political Rights. Articles 19 and 20 of the covenant are directly relevant to the definition and scope of freedom of expression. In particular, Article 20(2) provides that "Any advocacy of national, racial or religious hatred that constitutes incitement to discrimination,

hostility or violence shall be prohibited by law." It should be noted that during its nineteenth session (457th meeting on 25 July 1983), the United Nations Human Rights Committee adopted a general comment relating to Article 20(2), which concluded, *inter alia*, that "State Parties are obliged to adopt the necessary legislative measures prohibiting actions referred to therein ... and that these required prohibitions are fully compatible with the right of freedom of expression as contained in Article 19."[48]

30. It is respectfully submitted that if a democratic society like Cantonia has not enacted legislation to prohibit incitement to racism, it would now be obliged to do so; and if it has enacted such legislation, it would find itself in default of its international obligations if such legislation were set aside. Indeed, even in the absence of such domestic legislation, the interpretation of freedom of speech in accordance with Cantonia's obligations under international human rights law would require the exclusion of racist incitement from the ambit of protected speech.

31. It should also be noted that, within Western Europe, twenty-one states are parties to the European Convention for the Protection of Human Rights and Fundamental Freedoms.[49] Section 10 of the convention protects freedom of expression in the following terms:

i) Everyone has the right to freedom of expression. This right shall include freedom to hold opinions and to receive and impart information and ideas without interference by public authority and regardless of frontiers. This article shall not prevent States from requiring the licensing of broadcasting, television or cinema enterprises.

ii) The exercise of these freedoms, since it carries with it duties and responsibilities, may be subject to such formalities, conditions, restrictions, or penalties as are prescribed by law and are necessary in a democratic society, in the interests of national security, territorial integrity or public safety, for the prevention of disorder or crime, for the protection of health or morals, for the protection of the reputation or rights of others, for prescribing the disclosure of information received in confidence, or for maintaining the authority and impartiality of the judiciary.

32. The European Commission of Human Rights, whose role it is, *inter alia*, to determine whether an application for relief under this convention is admissible, has considered whether restrictions on incitement to racism violate Article 10 of the European Convention. In a series of cases, it has decided that such restrictions do not violate Article 10.[50]

33. It is therefore submitted that paragraph 10(2) of this convention permits legislation by the member states which limits incitement to racial hatred. Indeed, in these cases both the national courts, and the European Commission of Human Rights, upheld limitations on racially inciteful speech of the genre of that communicated in Cantonia. Such case law, together with the European Convention of Human Rights, informs us as to what ought to be excluded from the ambit of protected speech in Cantonia; or, if racial incitement is nonetheless to be regarded as *prima facie* protected speech, any limitation prohibiting racial incitement would be demonstrably justified, even necessary, in a society like Cantonia.

34. Accordingly, reasoned the Supreme Court in *Keegstra*, after a review of international human rights law and jurisprudence, "it appears that the protection provided freedom of expression by CERD and ICCPR does not extend to cover communications advocating racial or religious hatred";[51] and, it concluded, and of crucial importance, in assessing the interpretive importance of international human rights law, "CERD and ICCPR demonstrate that prohibition of hate-promoting expression is considered to be not only compatible with a signatory nation's guarantee of human rights, but is as well an obligatory aspect of this guarantee."[52]

Principle Twelve: Freedom of Expression and the Multicultural Principle

35. It is submitted that freedom of expression in Cantonia must be read in light of Cantonia as a multicultural democracy; accordingly, it should be interpreted, to paraphrase section 27 of the Canadian Charter of Rights and Freedoms, "in a manner consistent with the preservation and enhancement of the multicultural heritage of [Cantonians]."[53]

In a word, this interpretive principle admits of no other reading than that such hatemongering is not only an assault on the members of the target group singled out on grounds of their identifiable race or religion, but it is destructive of a multicultural society as a whole; as such, it falls outside the protection of freedom of speech. Conversely, and again to paraphrase Mr Justice Cory in *Smith and Andrews*, anti-hate legislation is designed not only "to protect identifiable groups in a multicultural society from publicly made statements which wilfully promote hatred against them," as Justice Cory observed, but are designed to "prevent the destruction of our multicultural society."[54]

Principle Thirteen: Freedom of Expression and the Principle of "Abhorrent Speech"

36. It is important that one distinguish between political speech – where the government, its institutions, and public officials are the target of offensive speech – and abhorrent, racist speech, intended to promote hatred and contempt of vulnerable and targeted minorities. The hatemongering at issue in *Keegstra* – and in analogous cases – is not the libel of public officials as in the *Sullivan* case[55]; or directed against "the world at large" as in the *Cohen* case;[56] but it is hatemongering wilfully promoted against disadvantaged minorities with intent to degrade, diminish, vilify. In a word, this is not a case of a government legislating in its own self-interest regarding its political agenda, but an affirmative responsibility of governments to protect the inherent human dignity – and equal standing – of all its citizens.

Principle Fourteen: Freedom of Expression and the "Criminalization" of Hate Speech[57]

37. Petitioner acknowledges and appreciates the criminal law maxim that only acts (or conduct) can be punishable; that such acts must be contrasted with thoughts, which are not punishable; and that since speech is "merely" expressive of thought, it is itself not subject to criminalization.

38. Petitioner submits, however, that expression – words – are more than "merely" a thought; rather, they are acts that give expression to thought. And words, as we know, can injure, maim, wound – ignite the world. Words do matter.

39. Accordingly, Petitioner submits that certain words, or expression, may be criminalized if the legislature concludes, as in the "harms-based" rationale set forth above, that these words are sufficiently dangerous to deserve punishment. In a word, assaultive words may be treated as comparable to assaultive acts; and just as treasonable words may be punished, so the very utterance of some words – i.e., the wilful promotion of hatred – may be deemed dangerous enough to justify criminalization.

Principle Fifteen: Freedom of Expression and the "Slippery Slope"

40. It is submitted that those who reject anti-hate legislation, on the grounds that such group libel legislation leads us inevitably down the "slippery slope" to censorship, ignore a different "slippery slope" –

"a swift slide into a marketplace of ideas in which bad ideas flourish and good ones die."[58] In a word, it is submitted that the more that hateful speech is tolerated, the more likely it is to occur. As Karl Popper put it, the "paradox of tolerance" is that it breeds more intolerance – so that the tolerance of hateful speech results in more, not less, hate speech; in more, not less, harm; and in more, not less, hateful actions. For tolerance of hate speech risks legitimizing such speech on the grounds that "it can't be all bad if it is not being prohibited." The slippery slope is there, but it may lead not in the direction of more censorship, which the Canadian experience does not demonstrate, but in the direction of more hate, which it does.

Conclusion

41. Petitioner submits that the wilful promotion of hatred may be said to be composed of a number of characteristics whose collection is itself representative, if not determinative of, a genre of expression that is beyond the ambit of protected speech. These characteristics, taken together, provide a set of indices warranting the exclusion from the ambit of protected speech of such a genre of expression; or if such expression is to be considered *prima facie* protected speech, then such anti-hate legislation as is designed to combat it should be regarded as a reasonable limit prescribed by the law as can be demonstrably justified in a free and democratic society. These indices are:

(a) Where the genre of expression involves not only the communication of hatred – "one of the most extreme emotions known to humankind"[59] – but the wilful promotion of such hatred against an identifiable group, an incipiently malevolent and violent act constituting an assault on the inherent dignity of the human person.
(b) Where it involves not only an assault on the inherent dignity and worth of the human person, but on the equal worth of all human beings in society. For the systematic, public promotion of hatred against an identifiable group has the effect of reducing the standing and respect of that group and its members in society as a whole, while resulting in the self-abasement of each.
(c) Where such hatemongering not only does not preserve, let alone enhance, a multicultural society such as Cantonia, but is destructive of it. In the words of Cory J and applicable to Cantonia, "what a strange and perverse contradiction it would be if the *Charter* of Rights was to be used and interpreted so as to strike down a law aimed at preserving our multicultural heritage."[60]

(d) Where the constitutionalization of the wilful promotion of hatred would not only constitute a standing breach of Cantonia's international obligations under treaties to which it is a party, but a standing breach of its obligation to implement domestic legislation to prohibit such expression. To paraphrase Justice Cory, "what a strange and perverse contradiction it would be if freedom of expression was to be used and interpreted so as to undermine Cantonia's conformity with international human rights law."

(e) Where such hatemongering is not only destructive of the values and principles of a free and democratic society – and opposite to the legislative experience of other free and democratic societies – but constitutes a standing assault on the values and interests, and the purposive rationale, underlying protected speech.

(f) Where the hatemongering not only constitutes an assault on the very values and interests underlying freedom of expression, but is destructive of the entitlement of the target group to protection from group defamation.

(g) Where the hatemongering not only lays the basis for discrimination against, and debasement of, members of the target group, but engenders, if not encourages, racial and religious discord, while causing injury to the community as a whole.

(h) Where such hatemongering not only does not partake in the conveyance of ideas or meaning of any kind, but is utterly without any redeeming value whatever.

NOTES

1 *R. v. Keegstra* [1991] 2 WWR 1 (SCC); *R. v. Andrews and Smith*, [1990] 3 SCR 870; *Human Rights Commission v. Taylor* [1990] 3 SCR 892.
2 F. Schauer, book review, (1989), 56 *University of Chicago Law Review* 397, 410.
3 See, for example, the 1990 Human Rights Lectureship delivered by Alan Dershowitz at McGill Law School on "Rights in Collision: Freedom of Speech and Hate Propaganda."
4 A. Borovoy, "Freedom of Expression: Some Recurring Impediments," in Rosalie Abella and Melvin Rothman, eds., *Justice Beyond Orwell* (Montreal: Yvon Blais 1985), 141.
5 *Keegstra*, 27.
6 *Hunter v. Southam*, [1984] 2 SCR 145, 155.
7 *Keegstra*, 27.
8 Abraham Goldstein, "Group Libel and Criminal Law: Walking on the Slippery Slope." Paper presented at the International Legal Colloquium

295   The Right to Protection against Group-Vilifying Speech

on Racial and Religious Hatred and Group Libel, Tel Aviv University, 1991, 3.
9 *Chaplinsky v. New Hampshire* (1942), 315 US 568, 571–2.
10 *Beauharnais v. Illinois* (1952), 343 US 250.
11 *R. v. Big M Drug Mart Ltd.*, [1985] 1 SCR 295.
12 *Keegstra*, 28.
13 *R. v. Zundel* (1987), 580 R (2d) 129 at 155–6, and quoted with approval on this point in *R. v. Andrews and Smith* (1988) 20 OAC 161, to the effect that "the wilful promotion of hatred is entirely antithetical to our very system of freedom."
14 *R. v. Andrews and Smith*, ibid., per Grange J.A. at 181–4.
15 *New York Times v. Sullivan* (1964), 376 US 254 at 279–80.
16 *R. v. Andrews and Smith*, 161.
17 See Justice B. Wilson, "Building the Charter Edifice: The First Ten Years," conference paper, Tenth Anniversary of the Charter (Ottawa, April 1992), 6.
18 *Keegstra*, 35.
19 *Edmonton Journal v. Alta.* (AG), [1989] 2 SCR 1326 at 1355–6.
20 Supra, Note 14, *R. v. Andrews and Smith*, 6.
21 Ibid.
22 *Keegstra*, 34.
23 *R. v. Oakes* (1986), 24 CCC (3d) 321 (SCC) at 346.
24 See, for example, the *Study on the Implementation of Article 4 of the International Convention on the Elimination of All Forms of Racial Discrimination* (a report on the United Nations Committee on the Elimination of Racial Discrimination, submitted in May 1983) A/CONF. 119/10 18 May 1983.
25 *Report of the Special Committee on Hate Propaganda* (Ottawa: Queen's Printer 1966), 277–88.
26 See, for example, L. Tribe, *American Constitutional Law*, 2d ed. (1988), 861 n2; K. Greenawalt, "Insult and Epithets: Are They Protected Speech?" (1990), 42 *Rutgers Law Review* 304.
27 *Keegstra*, 37.
28 Ibid.
29 Ibid., 38. See, for example, Kenneth Lasson, "Racial Defamation as Free Speech: Abusing the First Amendment" (1985), 17 *Columbia Human Rights Law Review* 11.
30 Ibid.
31 See, for example, Richard Delgado, "Words That Wound: A Tort Action for Racial Insults, Epithets, and Name-Calling" (1982), 17 *Harvard Civil Rights – Civil Liberties Law Review* 133; Irving Horowitz, "Skokie, the ACLU and the Endurance of Democratic Theory" (1979), 43 *Law and Contemporary Problems* 328; Lasson, "Racial Defamation,"

2030; Mari Matsuda, "Public Response to Racist Speech: Considering the Victim's Story" (1989), 87 *Michigan Law Review* 2348; "*Doe v. University of Michigan:* First Amendment – Racist and Sexist Expression on Campus – Court Strikes Down University Limits on Hate Speech" (1990), 103 *Harvard Law Review* 1397.

32 *Keegstra*, 37.
33 As the Supreme Court points out by way of example, obscenity is not protected because of its content (see, for example, *Roth v. U.S.*, 354 US 476, 1 L. Ed. 2d 1498, 77 S. Ct. 1304 (1957)) and laws proscribing child pornography have been scrutinized under a less than strict First Amendment standard even where they extend to expression beyond the realm of the obscene (see *New York v. Ferber*, 458 US 747, 73 L. Ed. 2d 1113, 102 S. Ct. 3348 (1982)). Similarly, the vigorous protection of free speech relaxes significantly when commercial expression is scrutinized (see, for example, *Posadas de Puerto Rico Assoc. v. Tourism Co. of Puerto Rico*, 478 US 328, 92 L. Ed. 2d 266, 106 S. Ct. 2968 (1968)), and it is permissible to restrict government employees in their exercise of the right to engage in political activity (*Cornelius v. N.A.A.C.P. Legal Defense & Educ. Fund Inc.*, 473 US 788, 87 L. Ed. 2d 567, 105 S. Ct. 3439 (1985)).
34 *Keegstra*, 39.
35 *R.W.D.S.U. v. Dolphin Delivery Ltd.*, [1986] 2 SCR 573, per McIntyre, J at 583.
36 Kathleen Mahoney, "*R. v. Keegstra*: A Rationale for Regulating Pornography?" (1992), 37 *McGill Law Journal* 242.
37 *Keegstra*, 42.
38 Ibid., 43.
39 Ibid.
40 Ibid., 44.
41 *Reference re Public Service Employees Act* (Alta) (Dickson CJC dissenting, but not on this point) (1987) 1 SCR 313 per Dickson CJ at 349. See also *R. v. Videoflicks*, (1984) 14 DLR (4th) 10 (Ont. CA) at 35–6.
42 *Keegstra*, 45.
43 *International Convention on the Elimination of All Forms of Racial Discrimination.* See especially Article 4 (a) of the convention; and International Covenant on Civil and Political Rights. See especially Article 20(2) of the convention.
44 *Reference re Public Service Employees Act* (1987), 1 SCR 313 per Dickson CJ at 349.
45 *Slaight Communications Inc. v. Davidson* (1989), 1 SCR 1038 per Dickson CJ at 1056–7, applied in *Keegstra*.
46 Done at New York, 24 Aug. 1966.

47 Study on the Implementation of Article 4 of the International Convention on the Elimination of All Forms of Racial Discrimination, A/CONF. 119/10, 18 May 1983.
48 General Comment 11 [19] HRC 1983 report, Annex VI, 109ff.
49 Done at Rome, 4 Nov. 1950, 213 United Nations Treaty Series 221.
50 *Glimmerveen and Hagenbeck v. The Netherlands* (1979), 4 EHRR 260 (European Commission of Human Rights) at 266–8; *Felderer v. Sweden* (1986), 8 EHRR 91 at 92 (European Commission of Human Rights); *X. v. The Federal Republic of Germany*, European Commission of Human Rights: Decisions and Reports, (1982), vol. 29, 194; *Lowes v. U.K.*, application No. 13214/87, 9 Dec. 1988 (unreported).
51 *Keegstra*, 46.
52 Ibid., 48.
53 Section 27 of the Canadian Charter of Rights and Freedoms.
54 *R. v. Andrews and Smith* (1988), 43 CCC (3d) 193 (Ont. CAO at 211).
55 *New York Times v. Sullivan.*
56 *Cohen v. California* (1971), 403 US 15.
57 This principle and perspective find expression in Goldstein, "Group Libel," 8.
58 Ibid., 33.
59 *R. v. Andrews and Smith* (1988) 20 OAC 161 (Ont. CA), per Cory J at 178.
60 Ibid., 176.

The Charter of Rights and Freedoms and Positive Obligations

WILLIAM W. BLACK

Maxwell Cohen said the adoption of the Canadian Charter of Rights and Freedoms was "perhaps the most far-reaching change to take place in the Canadian legal-political system since Confederation itself."[1] He described it as a bridge between domestic law and international law. In particular, he noted the influence of the complex of international instruments developed by the United Nations since the Second World War to protect a wide variety of human rights.

Though Cohen has identified the potential of this melding of international and domestic law, he has also concluded that these developments will require us to resolve tensions created by apparent conflicts in our legal principles and to reassess traditional ways of thinking about the relationship between domestic and international law. He cited the ambivalent compromise between the principle of parliamentary supremacy – which requires that international norms be incorporated only by specific legislative enactment – and the incorporation of general principles of international law by the courts, through the use of adoption or incorporation theories.[2]

Another factor cited by Cohen is the tendency to recognize traditional civil libertarian norms more readily than economic, social, and cultural rights when considering the application of international standards to domestic issues. He attributes this tendency to the influence of liberal thought on our legal system, and also to habit, ideology, and suspicion of new ideas. He notes that this propensity is counterbalanced by our growing recognition of the essential contradictions in the laissez-faire liberal philosophy of the last half of the nineteenth century and by "the rightful place of economic, social and cultural rights in any domestic Canadian human rights program."[3]

These issues are important in considering the relation between the Charter and international law, but they have also had a more general effect on Charter interpretation. This article deals with the question whether the philosophical influence of liberalism and the principle of parliamentary supremacy preclude recognition of positive obligations under the Charter, particularly with respect to social, economic, and cultural matters.

Those who argue against the recognition of positive obligations assert that such obligations are the sole responsibility of the legislative branch, just as the domestic recognition of international obligations is said to be a legislative responsibility. Some critics argue on the basis of liberal principles that the only legitimate function of the Charter is to control the excessive use of government power.[4] Critics on the left see the need for positive social and economic programs, but they join with critics on the right in arguing that the Charter is not meant to require such programs and that, in any event, the courts are not capable of enforcing positive rights.[5]

I would suggest that the Canadian Charter of Rights and Freedoms clearly imposes positive obligations on governments, and the only matter now open to debate is the extent of these obligations. It is true that the tensions described by Cohen must be taken into account. The democratic values reflected in the principle of parliamentary supremacy are obviously an important part of our governmental system. Liberal values also continue to have a role to play. While these principles and values are among the factors that should be considered in determining the scope of positive obligations, I do not think they are always determinative. They must take their place among other values of our governmental system. Cohen has persuasively shown that the principle of national sovereignty must be reconsidered in light of the complex of international human rights protections. That conclusion reflects the view that no legal principle can be taken as sacrosanct. Similarly, domestic developments require us to reconsider the immunity of governments from liability for failure to act.

In my opinion, the recognition of positive obligations under the Charter is consistent with the historical Canadian view about the role of government in society. It also reflects the affirmative nature of the rights incorporated in the Charter. Positive remedies requiring the extension of government benefits and programs are essential if we are to adhere to the principle that governments should not be allowed to act with impunity in an unconstitutional manner. It is also possible that the Charter sometimes requires the adoption of entirely new programs and activities to implement the rights it contains, though this result is more speculative.

This article does not canvas all the decisions to date on this subject, nor does it examine in detail the exact scope of positive duties under the various sections of the Charter.[6] Rather, it makes the more general point that the Charter cannot be limited to purely negative restrictions on government. Throughout, the primary emphasis is on section 15, the equality rights section.

THE CHARTER'S PHILOSOPHICAL UNDERPINNINGS

If the Charter were a pure reflection of eighteenth-century liberalism, it would be hard to argue that it was a source of positive obligations. Classical liberalism states that the paramount goal is to maximize the liberty of each individual, consistent with the liberty of other individuals. The primary threat to liberty is government, and fundamental rights define the perimeters of legitimate government activity.[7]

The United States Bill of Rights, as originally enacted, was founded upon classical liberal theory.[8] However, there is strong evidence that the Charter has more disparate philosophical influences. Much had changed in the almost two centuries separating the adoption of the United States Bill of Rights and the Charter. It would be surprising indeed if a document enacted in 1982 were a pure reflection of liberal thinkers such as Locke and Jefferson.

We have learned that government programs and activities can play a role in preserving rights. For example, it is almost inconceivable that democratic rights could continue to flourish in the absence of a public education system. Moreover, individual liberty is no longer presumed to be the only interest protected by charters of rights.[9] It is far from clear that the protection of interests such as equality can be achieved simply by limiting governmental activity.

In addition, the belief that government activities should be limited to a narrow range has never been as strong in Canada as in the United States. We have tended to view government as having a nation-building role that goes beyond the narrow function of preserving common-law rights and ensuring public morals and safety.[10] Even in the nineteenth century, the Terms of Union admitting British Columbia into Confederation included a constitutional obligation to build a railway, for example.[11] More recently, the concept of a social safety net has become an important part of our political thought.[12]

Of course the tenets of classsical liberalism have also had a significant influence on Canadian law, but that doctrine is one of many influences rather than the sole focus of the Charter. As Professor Martha Jackman has stated: "Canadians not only recognize that there is no necessary contradiction between individual freedom and state power, but expect governments to act affirmatively to support and maintain individual freedom, by providing the means for its exercise."[13]

One could add that Canadians historically have placed importance on values such as community and cultural preservation that often point in the direction of positive measures. As Patrick Monahan has shown, the goal of preserving communities is the most plausible explanation for a number of sections of the Charter, notably the language-rights sections and sections 25, 27, and 29.[14] Again, these values distinguish the Charter from its U.S. counterpart and belie the supposition that liberalism is its single philosophical reference point.

The status of human rights legislation in our legal system is a reflection of the positive role of government in protecting fundamental rights. Human rights statutes provide governmental resources to protect individuals and groups from discrimination in both the public and private sector. Courts have interpreted the legislation in a way that gives human rights agencies the necessary leeway to act, and the Supreme Court of Canada has held that human rights statutes have quasi-constitutional status.[15] In addition, the court has treated the equality rights in the Charter and the statutory protection against discrimination as a single body of law.[16] It seems unlikely that the need for positive protection was recognized in one sphere and not the other.

CHARTER CONTEXT: OVERVIEW

The nature of the rights set out in the Charter refutes the claim that constitutional charters must necessarily take the form of negative restrictions on government. Some sections of the Charter explicitly impose positive obligations on government. Other sections impose positive obligations as soon as a government embarks on core functions such as law enforcement. Some of the positive duties require minimal effort, but other Charter obligations require extensive activity and resources.

Perhaps the most explicit positive obligation is contained in section 23, which requires governments to provide primary and secondary education in both official languages. In *Mahé* the Supreme Court of Canada said, "Section 23 of the *Charter* imposes on provincial Legislatures the positive obligation of enacting precise legislative schemes providing for minority language instruction and educational facilities where numbers warrant."[17] Sections 16 through 20 provide a number of other positive obligations such as the duty to print the statutes, records, and journals of Parliament and the New Brunswick legislature in both official languages, and the right to receive certain services of the federal or New Brunswick governments in either official language.[18]

A number of other sections impose similar positive obligations. Section 10 requires those arresting or detaining a person to inform that person of the reasons therefore and of the right to counsel. It has been held that this duty includes the obligation to provide facilities such as a telephone to contact counsel.[19] Section 11(a) imposes a similar duty to supply information. Section 14 provides an affirmative right to the assistance of an interpreter.

It is true that the government could avoid these obligations by never arresting, charging, or trying anyone. But law enforcement is so clearly a core function of government activity that this possibility is purely hypothetical. Therefore, in any realistic sense, these sections must be seen as imposing positive obligations on government. Also, it may be possible to reconcile the existence of positive obligations connected with the criminal process with liberal theory. However, that reconciliation tends to undermine the liberal notion that liberty can be preserved simply by restricting governmental activity.

In the previous examples, the positive obligations are explicit. But other sections of the Charter impose similar obligations by necessary implication. The right to vote requires the expenditure of funds to hold an election (section 3). The right to habeas corpus means that resources must be provided for a hearing (section 10(c)).[20] The rights to a fair hearing and to a trial by jury also necessitate the expenditure of funds (section 11(d) and (f)).[21]

These examples negate the idea that the Charter's only function is to restrict government. Provisions such as the minority language education rights cannot be explained on the basis of classical liberal objectives. The only question concerns the extent of positive obligations under the Charter, not their existence. However, there have been suggestions that although some rights clearly impose positive obligations, others such as fundamental freedoms set out in section 2 can be interpreted in a way that conforms strictly to classical liberal objectives and that precludes the existence of any positive obligations. Though such an interpretation may be possible, there is no reason to bifurcate the Charter in this way.

Nothing in the wording of most of the remaining rights precludes the existence of positive obligations.[22] For example, freedom of expression can be interpreted as imposing a duty to facilitate the means of expression; freedom of peaceful assembly can be seen as imposing an obligation to protect a group from attack; and mobility rights might be interpreted as requiring the government to provide some accessible public means of travel.

Section 7 has been discussed extensively elsewhere.[23] Briefly, the procedural safeguards built into the section sometimes require affirmative steps similar to those demanded by section 11.[24] It is quite plausible that the substantive rights built into section 7 also create a duty to afford services and programs in certain circumstances. The argument for such an interpretation has been set out in detail by Jackman.[25] She states that a positive conception of liberty is consistent with Canadian political and philosophical traditions and concludes: "A failure by the state to extend welfare protection to an individual who is unable to satisfy his or her fundamental needs thereby constitutes a deprivation of his or her constitutional right to life and liberty."[26]

Jackman finds that the phrase "security of the person" is an even stronger source for a right to programs and services. She traces the development of a network of government social benefits and services since the 1930s and argues that this social safety net has become a fundamental aspect of our governmental system. She says that "security of the person" must be interpreted against this backdrop and that it incorporates a right to a minimum of welfare protection.[27]

SECTION 15

The wording of section 15 provides strong hints as to the existence of positive obligations. Section 15(2) recognizes that positive programs and activities are a means of affording equality rights, though that subsection stops short of making the laws, programs, and activities it describes mandatory. The fact that section 15(1) contains a right to the equal benefit of the law is also indicative. That right means at the very least that discriminatory restrictions cannot be placed on governmental laws and activities.[28] Admittedly, however, it is grammatically possible to read the section as invalidating discriminatory programs rather than as requiring that such programs be expanded or that new services be initiated.

Though the wording is not determinative by itself, I believe that the trend of recent cases supports a broad interpretation incorporating a positive obligation on governments to provide services and programs in certain circumstances. At a minimum, the effect may sometimes be to expand existing programs or services. Moreover, the concept of equality rights adopted by the courts is consistent with an obligation to develop entirely new programs, though no case has yet decided such a claim.

The first notable case in the series is *Re Blainey and Ontario Hockey Association*, which has been cited with approval by the Supreme Court of Canada.[29] *Blainey* concerned a limitation in the Ontario Human Rights Code excluding protection with respect to athletic activities that are restricted to members of one sex. The Ontario Court of Appeal held that this limitation on the protection afforded by the code violated section 15 and was not saved by section 1. The effect of the ruling was to extend the jurisdiction of the Ontario Human Rights Commission into an area that had explicitly been exempted by the legislature, refuting the claim that section 15 can never result in the expansion of government activity.

Two arguments have been made to limit the significance of *Blainey*. One points out that the court did not explicitly order the government to spend money not appropriated by the legislature. The second notes that the extension in *Blainey* was achieved by striking down an exemption in the statute. Though the scope of the statute was extended, this result was achieved by declaring a part of the statute inoperative. It is argued that different considerations would come into play if a court were to extend the scope of a law by itself stating that the law applied to a new area.

Neither argument is convincing. It seems strange that the scope of a constitutional remedy would depend on accidents of statutory drafting. If the fundamental issue is the relationship between judicial review and parliamentary supremacy, why should the form of the statute make any difference? A law excluding noncitizens from a benefit might say, "Every citizen shall enjoy the following benefit" or "Everyone shall enjoy the following benefit ... except that this provision does not apply to non-citizens." If challenged under section 15, surely both laws would be found equally discriminatory, and if it were an intrusion on parliamentary supremacy to extend the former law by affirmative judicial declaration, it would also be an intrusion to extend the latter by striking the exemption.

The fact that *Blainey* did not directly order an expenditure unauthorized by the legislature seems an even less defensible limitation. The result was to require that Ms Blainey's case be investigated, and that inevitably would require that the budget of the Human Rights Commission be used in a way that fell outside the legislative appropriation.

In any event, later cases have undermined both arguments for limiting *Blainey*. The view that a Charter remedy cannot require the expenditure of funds for a purpose outside that appropriated by the legislature is inconsistent with *Tétreault-Gadoury*. That case concerned a limitation in section 31 of the Unemployment Insurance Act that prohibited the granting of regular unemployment insurance benefits to applicants over the age of sixty-five. The Supreme Court of Canada found that the age limitation violated section 15 of the Charter and was not saved by section 1. The result was to make the respondent eligible for regular benefits.[30]

Unlike *Blainey*, the result in *Tétreault-Gadoury* was to require explicitly that the government make a payment that falls outside any legislative appropriation. In applying section 1, La Forest found that the objective of the act was to provide temporary support for those wishing to remain active in the labour force but unable to find employment, and he added: "The inquiry, therefore, should be whether that objective is furthered in any way by denying benefits to individuals over sixty-five, and whether that denial is compensated for by the provision of other acts. As Lacombe J. properly notes ... there was no evidence put forth to show that the government could not afford to extend benefits to those over sixty-five ... The most unfortunate aspect of s. 31 is that it has the effect of denying unemployment benefits precisely to those who need them most."[31] This quotation shows clearly that the court was aware of the financial consequences to the government. It also characterizes the evil as the denial of benefits to those who need them most. That evil would in no way be cured by a denial of benefits to others as well. Therefore, if the purpose of section 15 is to protect disadvantaged groups in our society,[32] the extension of benefits to Ms Tétreault-Gadoury was the only remedy consistent with that purpose.

Tétreaut-Gadoury, like *Blainey*, extended a social benefit by means of striking down a statutory limitation. Without the limitation, the statute covered the excluded group by its terms. Thus, the case does not consider whether a court can extend a statutory benefit by means other than excising an offending limitation. What if words would have to be read into the statute to cure the constitutional infirmity?

The decision of the Federal Court of Appeal in *Schachter* suggests that the form of the statute should not play a crucial role in defining the scope of constitutional rights.[33] *Schachter* considered the appropriate remedy where the granting of certain child-care benefits to adoptive parents, but not to biological parents, under the Unemployment Insurance Act had been held to violate section 15.[34]

The statute was worded so as to give a specific entitlement to adoptive parents, rather than providing a general grant to all parents and a limitation excluding biological parents. Thus, the approach taken in *Blainey* and *Tétreault-Gadoury* was not available.[35] However, a majority of the court held that the appropriate remedy was to extend the benefit to biological parents.

Heald JA noted that the granting of benefits to adoptive parents was a constitutional governmental activity; it was the exclusion of biological parents from the benefits that violated the Charter. He found that the positive right to equality expressed by section 15 could only be protected by a positive remedy extending the law. He accepted the argument of the intervenor Women's Legal Education and Action Fund (LEAF) that the denial of benefits to adoptive parents would produce only sameness, not equality.

In dissent, Mahoney JA agreed that the extension of benefits to biological parents would best fulfil a purposive approach in applying section 15. However, he found that the remedy of extension would intrude on the power to legislate vested in Parliament, because that result could not be accomplished by striking a portion of the statute. His principal basis for this conclusion was that judicial extension would conflict with the exclusive constitutional power of Parliament to appropriate moneys. As noted above, the later decision of the Supreme Court of Canada in *Tétreault-Gadoury* seems clearly to have decided otherwise.

A decision of the British Columbia Supreme Court lends support to the reasoning of the majority of the Court of Appeal in *Schachter*. *Knodel v. The Queen* concerned regulations under the British Columbia Medical Services Act which allow a person to enrol a spouse on his or her medical plan.[36] The court concluded that the word spouse in itself, and the statutory definition of "spouse," did not include a gay or lesbian couple as a matter of statutory interpretation. The petitioner alleged that as so interpreted, the regulations violated the equality rights in section 15 of the Charter.

The court agreed. Rowles J granted a declaration that same-sex couples are covered by the act, despite her conclusion that, as enacted, the wording of the act would not support this result. In dealing with the argument that this result intruded on the law-making power of the legislature, she said: "In the present case, it would clearly be far more intrusive to strike the legislation and deny the benefits to the individuals receiving them, then it would be to extend the benefits to the small minority who demonstrated their entitlement to them."[37]

THE EFFECT OF SECTION 52

Both *Schachter* and *Knodel* considered the argument that section 52 precludes a court from extending a statutory benefit except by means of striking an exemption. Section 52(1) provides that "any law that is inconsistent with the provisions of the Constitution is, to the extent of the inconsistency, of no force and effect." The argument is that this provision makes any law inconsistent with the Charter automatically ineffective. Where the problem is an "underinclusive" law providing benefits to an unconstitutionally narrow class of persons, the law is simply invalid. Thus, there is no benefit to extend to the excluded group. Similarly, it is argued, there is no inequality to correct since the benefit provided by the law is automatically denied to everyone.

If section 52 required such a result, it would constitute a serious defect in our constitutional system. With regard to section 15, it would largely nullify the right to the equal benefit of the law. Claims to equal benefit will usually be made by a group that has been excluded from the statutory benefit. If there were no remedy that would provide this group any advantage, the right would mean very little.

That result would be lamentable, but such an interpretation of section 52 would have even more widespread consequences. It would undermine one of the most fundamental principles of our legal system – the principle that governments cannot act in an unconstitutional fashion with impunity.

In the past, the Supreme Court of Canada has taken pains to ensure that unconstitutional behaviour is subject to judicial review, both in theory and in practice. For example, in *Crevier v. A.G. Quebec*, the court decided that a privative clause cannot immunize an administrative tribunal when it acts beyond its juridiction.[38] The point is made even more clearly in the cases concerning standing to raise constitutional challenges. Thus, in *Thorson*, Laskin J said: "It is not the alleged waste of public funds alone that will support standing but rather the right of the citizenry to constitutional behaviour by Parliament where the issue in such behaviour is justiciable as a legal question."[39]

Borowski also liberalized the rules of standing to ensure that judicial review was available.[40] Mr Borowski was allowed to challenge the provisions of the Criminal Code allowing abortions in certain circumstances even though he was not personally affected by the provision. Applying earlier cases, the court determined that he had standing because there was no class of persons directly affected or exceptionally prejudiced by the law who would have the motivation and the ability to contest the law. It noted that most of those affected would have no motive to challenge the legislation. It rejected the proposition that the husband of a pregnant woman might bring a challenge, saying that the "progress of the pregnancy would not await the inevitable lengthy lapse of time involved in Court proceedings leading to a final judgment."[41] Thus, the test was whether there was a practical likelihood that someone would be in a position to challenge the legislation, not whether such a challenge was a theoretical possibility.[42] Where those most directly implicated would not have the incentive to bring an action or would not be in a realistic position to do so, standing would be afforded to a party who was not directly affected to ensure that an avenue existed to bring the issue before the courts.

If the only remedy for underinclusive legislation were to declare it of no force and effect, the principle that unconstitutional behaviour should be subject to challenge would be jeopardized in a similar way. Obviously, the group that benefits from the legislation has no reason to challenge it, nor does the government that enacted it. The group excluded from the benefit would stand to gain nothing, even if successful.[43] The only possible motive to litigate for a Schachter or Knodel would be to deny a social benefit to those receiving it. It would be a grave flaw in our constitutional system if the rule of law depended on litigants motivated solely by the desire to hurt someone else.[44] Therefore, it seems wrong to interpret section 52 in this way if another interpretation is possible.

There is an alternative. Section 52 states that a law is "to the extent of the inconsistency, of no force and effect." If one thinks of a law as a series of words on paper, arguably the only choice under section 52 is to strike out some or all of those words, even if the result is to invalidate programs or benefits that are perfectly constitutional except for the fact that they are unduly restricted. If, however, one thinks of a law not as words on paper but as a legal concept or norm, a different result is possible. One can then say that the unconstitutional feature of that norm is the exclusion of a group from the benefits provided and to treat that aspect of the initiative as of no force and effect. In other words, the unconstitutional feature of the laws at issue in *Schachter* and *Knodel* would be the exclusion of certain groups, and that feature would be declared of no force and effect. The result would be to broaden the benefits, just as they were broadened in *Blainey* and *Tétreault-Gadoury*. The form in which the restriction is stated would not control the result.

That was what happened in *Schachter* and *Knodel*.[45] Once one accepts that the effect of a remedy can be to extend a law, as in *Blainey*, there is no principled reason to stop short of judicial extension. The contrary position must be based on the contention that the words of section 52 cannot support an extension of benefits by means other than striking an exemption. This interpretation is insufficiently convincing to justify an otherwise unjustifiable limitation on the available remedies.

WHEN SHOULD A REMEDY EXTEND AN EXISTING PROGRAM?

The fact that the Charter allows courts to order expansion of an existing program does not mean that this is always the appropriate remedy.[46] The remedial provisions of the Charter afford some leeway to the courts since there may be a number of ways to cure the constitutional defect. Therefore, it will be necessary to identify criteria for determining the most appropriate result.

The factors that deserve consideration have been canvassed by Professors Duclos and Roach.[47] They reject the view that the only choice is between automatic invalidation and automatic extension. They also reject the idea that a court can never impose a remedy that requires the expenditure of money. A third possibility – that a court should try to achieve the result the legislature would have intended – is also rejected. They conclude that it is usually impossible to determine what the legislative intent would have been and that a court should not be bound to select a harmful outcome because the court guesses that the legislature would have desired that response.[48]

I agree with the first two points but am less certain that a court should never consider the presumed legislative intent. Admittedly, legislative intent is an artificial concept that is often difficult to apply. That is especially true if, as here, one must ask the hypothetical question of what the legislature would have intended if it had known that its preferred choice was unconstitutional. Nevertheless, this option has the attraction of trying to respect the legislative role as far as is possible. It might at least sometimes serve as one of several criteria to consider.

Duclos and Roach argue persuasively against assigning undue importance to the relative costs of the various possible remedies. They point out that this approach neglects complex questions of fairness, including the relative impact of the different options on the groups affected. They also note the difficulty of accurately assessing costs in a judicial proceeding, particularly where some of the costs are not easily quantifiable in monetary terms.[49]

They propose that a court take guidance from the larger constitutional context. Thus, even when there is a choice between extending a benefit or invalidating it, the Constitution may provide indications of which is the preferred result. If, for example, a law furthers certain constitutional values and is invalid simply because it excludes certain groups from these benefits, there would be strong grounds to extend the law even if striking it would be constitutionally permissible. They cite as an example *R. v. Hebb*, which considered statutory provisions restricting the power to incarcerate persons between the ages of sixteen and twenty-two for failure to pay a fine.[50] The age restriction was held to violate section 15. However, the fact that the law helps to implement rights incorporated in sections 7 and 9 of the Charter provided grounds for extending it so as to provide the same protection to those over the age of twenty-two.[51]

This approach seems promising. Of course, it will not always provide a clear answer, and I think there will be circumstances in which extension might be justified on other grounds, such as a finding that extension was more likely to reflect the legislative intent. One should also take account of the value of ensuring that there is a practical means to challenge unconstitutional behaviour, and the need to preserve the rule of law may justifiably tip the balance in favour of extension in some circumstances. However, the approach suggested by Duclos and Roach will frequently be of considerable assistance in identifying the correct solution. It will also help counter the argument that the choice of remedy should not be purely a matter of judicial discretion.

DOES THE CHARTER REQUIRE NEW PROGRAMS?

The previous discussion dealt with the extension of existing benefits. Another question concerns the creation of new programs. Some sections of the Charter clearly have this effect, most notably section 23. One must ask whether other parts of the Charter, such as section 15, can have a comparable effect.

Admittedly, the case law is not yet well developed, and it is too early to reach firm conclusions. However, there are indications that section 15 can sometimes require the implementation of new programs. My objective is to describe the general framework of the argument, not to analyse the subject in detail or to determine the scope of the duty to develop such programs.[52]

Critics of this kind of positive role for section 15 argue that a right to equality cannot be a source of substantive benefits. They say that section 15 is violated only if a particular law or activity creates a comparative advantage for a protected group. If one starts from a viewpoint that takes account of the relative effects on different groups of each law or activity of government, that conclusion has a certain plausibility.

There are indications in recent cases, however, that such a viewpoint is too narrow. While the Supreme Court of Canada has not ruled on the point. Wilson J left open the possibility of such positive obligations in the *McKinney* case, saying, "It is not self-evident to me that the government could not be found to be in breach of the Charter by failing to act."[53]

Moreover, the theory of equality the court has adopted has an underlying logic that supports the existence of positive obligations. The court has found that the purpose of section 15 is to remedy the persistent disadvantage that certain groups have experienced in Canadian society. In *Andrews*, McIntyre J stated that the "enumerated or analogous grounds" approach most closely accords with the purposes of section 15, noting that this approach focuses the section on questions of disadvantage and of prejudice.[54] He also said: "The promotion of equality entails the promotion of a society in which all are secure in the knowledge that they are recognized at law as human beings equally deserving of concern, respect and consideration. It has a large remedial component."[55] He adopted the view that "s. 15(1) read as a whole constitutes a compendious expression of a positive right to equality in both the substance and the administration of the law."[56]

The judgment of Wilson J noted that noncitizens lack political power and are "vulnerable to have their interests overlooked and their rights to equal concern and respect violated." She added that they are among "those groups in society to whose needs and wishes elected officials have no apparent interest in attending."[57] She went on to say that the determination of what constitutes an analogous group "is not to be made only in the context of the law which is subject to challenge but rather in the context of the place of the group in the entire social, political and legal fabric of our society."[58]

Wilson J's judgment for a unanimous court in *R. v. Turpin* continued this theme. She again emphasized the need to move beyond the particular law under challenge to the broader social, political, and legal context. She added:

A finding that there is discrimination will, I think, in most but perhaps not all cases, necessarily entail a search for disadvantage that exists apart from and independent of the particular legal distinction being challenged.

...

... A determination as to whether or not discrimination is taking place, if based exclusively on an analysis of the law under challenge is likely, in my view, to result in the same kind of circularity which characterized the similarly situated similarly treated test clearly rejected by this court in *Andrews*.[59]

These cases did not raise the issue of the creation of a new program or benefit. However, the need for positive programs would seem to emanate from the approach to equality that has been adopted. The purpose of section 15, we are told, is to deal with historical disadvantage. This disadvantage is to be measured in the larger societal context, not just the law or activity under challenge. Section 15 incorporates a positive right to equality that requires equal concern, respect, and consideration. If the goal is to remedy existing social disadvantage, it seems to follow that positive action will sometimes be required.

The argument is especially strong where the absence of a program operates in the broader context of government activity to cause disadvantage. For example, if child-custody cases are not covered by legal aid, that omission will have a disproportionate effect on women because of the pattern of income distribution in our society. If most men have the resources to retain counsel, and a disproportionate number of women do not, the legal machinery of the state will be skewed to the advantage of men. It does not seem at all far-fetched in such circumstances to say that equality demands that affirmative steps be take to ensure that both parties have comparable resources.

A similar argument could be made in the employment context. Assume that the government hires persons based on a fair assessment of ability to perform the work, but the result excludes a disproportionate percentage of people of aboriginal origin, because they do not have the skills necessary to perform the work. In addition, assume that the training necessary to develop these skills is provided through private training programs that are generally not available to people of aboriginal origin. Arguably, the hiring process does not in itself violate equality rights, since it is based on a fair assessment of job qualifications. In addition, the Charter does not apply to the private training programs, because it is limited to governmental activity.[60] Yet one could argue that the failure to provide public training facilities leads to employment inequality that can be attributed to government. Thus, a duty to provide government training may arise.

Clearly, positive obligations under section 15 to develop new programs and initiatives are subject to limitations. The courts will not attempt single-handedly to set the social agenda for the nation. One can only speculate at this point about the way in which the limitations might be defined. For example, courts might limit the obligation to certain government programs such as education that are the foundation for equality in other spheres of activity. They might alternatively define minimum standards in each area of government activity, leaving to the legislature the decision whether to exceed the constitutional minimum. They might apply the Duclos and Roach concept of constitutional hints. While the nature of the limitations remains unclear, the task is a manageable one, though undoubtedly it will present challenges.

CONCLUSION

The theme of this article is that positive obligations under the Charter are quite common, and that the recognition of positive obligations under sections such as sections 2, 7, and 15 are far from an anomaly. Such obligations conform to traditional Canadian conceptions of the role of government. While the relationship between the judiciary and the other branches of government is a legitimate consideration, it should shape the nature and scope of positive obligations but should not be understood as precluding such obligations. The task of further defining the positive obligations under the Charter is thus a rich area for further research.

In a different context, Maxwell Cohen cited the need for judicial activity to take adequate account of the general North American social ambience and the French-English relationship. He added: "This opportunity, however, was not always taken full advantage of by tribunals unwilling to take novel risks by identifying or creating new rights."[61] In many respects, the courts have taken advantage of the adoption of the Charter to adapt our legal system creatively. One hopes that the approach to positive obligations and positive remedies will be similarly creative and will not reflect timidity such as that which Judge Cohen described.

ADDENDUM

After this article was completed, the Supreme Court of Canada released its decision in *Schachter v. Canada*.[62] The court found section 52 of the Constitution Act 1982 permits the technique of "reading in" so as to expand the scope of a statute. It concluded, however, that an extension of the law was not appropriate in the circumstances of the case.

An addendum is not the place for an extensive case comment. The general message of the case was that the courts should proceed, but with caution. The court set out a fairly lengthy set of criteria for deciding whether it is appropriate to strike down a law, to sever the offending portion, or to "read down" or "read in" provisions so as to cure the defect. It also described guidelines for determining whether a remedy should be temporarily suspended.

Inevitably, the criteria used by the court are general and open to interpretation. Chief Justice Lamer says at one point that reading in will be warranted only in the clearest of cases, but other passages suggest a more flexible approach, and the court cites with approval decisions that have extended the scope of the law.

In light of the more cautious passages, it is fair to ask whether the court established a standard that would make extension an option that is perpetually just out of reach. Fortunately, the first case to apply the *Schachter* guidelines suggests not. In *Haig v. Canada*, the Ontario Court of Appeal held that the Canadian Human Rights Act must be interpreted, applied, and administered as though it contained "sexual orientation" as a prohibited ground of discrimination.[63] Krever JA concluded that striking down the Human Rights Act would be "a gratuitous insult to Parliament."

We still have much to learn about the scope of the remedy of extension. It is now clear, however, that the remedy is sometimes available, and the *Haig* case suggests that it is a useful tool rather than a rare curiosity. Therefore, there are signs that we have the means to implement the positive rights contained in the Charter.

NOTES

1 M. Cohen and A. Bayefsky, "The Canadian Charter of Rights and Freedoms and Public International Law" (1983), 61 *Canadian Bar Review* 266.
2 M. Cohen, "Towards a Paradigm of Theory and Practice: The Canadian Charter of Rights and Freedoms – International Law Influences and Interactions" [1986] *Canadian Human Rights Yearbook* 49.
3 Ibid., 49–56.
4 Cf *McKinney v. University of Guelph*, [1990] 3 SCR 229, at 261, for this point of view.
5 See A. Petter, "The Immaculate Deception" (1987) 45 *Advocate* 857.
6 For a helpful compilation see I. Morrison, "Security of the Person: Is There a Duty on the State?" in the proceedings of the Department of Justice, *Third Annual Conference on Human Rights and the Charter* (Ottawa 1991).
7 See N. Duclos and K. Roach, "Constitutional Remedies as 'Constitutional Hints': A Comment on *R. v. Schachter*" (1991), 36 *McGill Law Journal* 4.
8 For a discussion of how this narrow view of government influenced US history see L. Tribe, *American Constitutional Law*, (2d ed. Mineola: Foundation PRSS 1988), 560–86. Even in the United States, later

315 The Charter of Rights and Freedoms

amendments, particularly the Civil War amendments, may be seen as reflecting other philosophical views.
9 M. Jackman, "The Protection of Welfare Rights under the Charter" (1988), 20 *Ottawa Law Review* 259–66. See also R. Dworkin, *Taking Rights Seriously* (Cambridge: Harvard University Press 1977), 266–78. While I would not entirely subscribe to Dworkin's argument, I would agree to the extent that it shows that freedom from government intervention is not the only basis for fundamental rights.
10 See Tribe, *American Constitutional Law*. Admittedly, the United States found ways to justify activity that went beyond this narrow vision on occasion, but the vision formed the philosophical basis for mainstream political thought in the United States at the time.
11 BC Terms of Union (1871), schedule, s.11; see also s.4, providing vessels for mail, freight, and passenger services to San Francisco and Olympia.
12 This theme was developed in some detail by Wilson J in *McKinney v. University of Guelph*, 352–7.
13 Jackman, "Protection," 262.
14 P. Monahan, *Politics and the Constitution* (Carswell: Toronto 1987), 111–15.
15 Regarding liberal interpretation see *Cdn. National Railway Co. v. Canada (Cdn. Human Rights Commission)*, [1987] 1 SCR 1114. Regarding quasi-constitutional status, see *Winnipeg School Dist. Div. no. 1 v. Craton*, [1985] 2 SCR 150.
16 See, eg, *Andrews v. Law Society of B.C.*, [1989] 1 SCR 143, at 173–4, 36 CRR 193, at 226–7, citing *Ontario Human Rights Commn. v. Simpsons-Sears*, [1985] 2 SCR 536, and *Can. National Ry. Co. v. Canada (Cdn. Human Rights Commn.)*, [1987] 1 SCR 1114; in turn *Brooks v. Canada Safeway*, [1989] 1 SCR 1219, at 1233, cited *Andrews v. Law Society of B.C.*
17 *Mahé v. Alberta*, [1990] 1 SCR 342, at 393, 46 CRR 193, at 233. The court's declaration was in terms of the rights that were due, rather than the exact legislation that must be enacted, because, as the court noted, there was some leeway in selecting the means of complying with these positive obligations. That leeway in no way undermines the recognition that positive steps are required by section 23.
18 Section 133 of the Constitution Act, 1867, imposes similar obligations on Quebec.
19 *R. v. Manninen*, [1987] 1 SCR 1233, at 1241–2, 58 CR (3d) 97, at 103–4.
20 The right to be tried within a reasonable time may in practice require allocation of certain resources, as many governments will currently attest. See *R. v. Askov*, [1990] 2 SCR 1199. Of course, the need for additional resources could be eliminated by charging fewer people or, perhaps, by changes to the criminal process to make it more efficient.

But the right at least means that as long as government continues its core role of criminal prosecution, the Charter will require that some minimum of resources be dedicated to this task.

21 Again, some of these obligations could be avoided by abandoning all law enforcement, but that fact demonstrates how unrealistic it is to think of these as simply limits on government activity.

22 There are exceptions. For example, the right in section 11(c) not to be compelled to testify, and the section 13 privilege against self-incrimination, seem not to give rise to a positive obligation. But the fact that the implementation of certain rights does not call for positive action provides little support for the contention that rights must generally be restricted to negative prohibitions or that positive programs cannot be demanded where necessary to give effect to a right.

23 See, in particular, Jackman, "Protection"; Morrison, "Security."

24 See, e.g., *Singh v. Min. of Employment & Immigration*, [1985] 1 SCR 177.

25 Jackman, "Protection," 322–8.

26 Ibid., 266.

27 Ibid., 267–83.

28 See A. Bayefsky, "Defining Equality Rights," in A. Bayefsky and M. Eberts, *Equality Rights and the Canadian Charter of Rights and Freedoms* (Toronto: Carswell 1985), 21–5.

29 *Re Blainey and Ont. Hockey Assn.* (1986), 54 OR (2d) 513 (Ont. CA); cited with approval in *Canada Employment and Immigration Commission v. Tétreault-Gadoury*, [1991] 2 SCR 21, at 44.

30 The case was sent to the umpire for adjudication consistent with the principles the Supreme Court had set forth. Technically, the *ratio decidendi* of the decision was that the Federal Court of Appeal did not have jurisdiction to consider the matter on a section 28 review from a decision of the Board of Referees; instead, the question should have been raised before the umpire under the act. However, the court went on to rule on the equality challenge and treated its own ruling as authoritative.

31 *Canada Employment and Immigration Commission v. Tétreault-Gadoury*, at 46.

32 See *R. v. Turpin* [1989] 1 SCR 1296, at 1331–2, 48 CCC (3d) 8, at 34.

33 *Schachter v. Canada*, [1990] 2 FC 129, 66 DLR (4th) 635 (FCA).

34 The appellant did not appeal Strayer J's determination that section 15 was violated; only the remedy was at issue before the Court of Appeal.

35 Even here, however, a highly creative excision of particular words from the statutory provisions might have grammatically covered biological parents. For example, section 32(1) refers to "the placement with that claimant of one or more children for the purpose of adoption." Excising the phrase "for the purpose of adoption" arguably would cover biological parents. At best, this approach would have been awk-

ward and artificial (in particular the interpretation of the word "placement"). However, the fact that the possibility exists at all shows how problematic the result would be if constitutional remedies were held to turn on the form in which a statute was written.
36 *Knodel v. The Queen*, [1991] 6 WWR 728.
37 Ibid., 763. I do not think it would be appropriate to refuse to extend benefits merely because the group denied the benefits were large. For example, the right of women to equal benefit of the law would be severely eroded if a benefit excluding women could not be extended. But Rowles J is correct in rejecting the idea that invalidating a law should be presumed to be more consistent with parliamentary supremacy than extending the law.
38 *Crevier v. A.G. Quebec*, [1981] 2 SCR 220, 127 DLR (3d) 588.
39 *Thorson v. A.G. Canada*, [1975] 2 SCR 138, at 163, 43 DLR (3d) 1, at 19.
40 *Min. of Justice (Can.) v. Borowski*, [1981] 2 SCR 575, 130 DLR (3d) 588, see also *Canadian Council of Churches v. Canada (Minister of Employment and Immigration)*, [1992] 1 SCR 236, at 251.
41 Ibid., 596–7 (SCC), 605 (DLR). I should note that since the issue at this point was standing, it would be wrong to interpret this passage as suggesting in any way that a husband should have the right to determine the course of the pregnancy.
42 See also *Nova Scotia Bd. of Censors v. McNeil*, [1975] 2 SCR 265, at 271, 55 DLR (3d) 632, at 637, where the court said that "there appears to be no other way, *practically speaking*, to subject the challenged act to judicial review ... " (emphasis added). It should be noted than in all of the standing cases, the attorney-general was in a position to bring an action for a declaration or a reference, but the court took account of the fact that such a proceeding would not in practice be brought by a government representative.
43 Indeed, such a litigant might well have to rely on the special standing rules of *Borowski* to commence the litigation, since that person would not be directly affected by the outcome.
44 Cf *Canadian Council of Churches v. Canada (Minister of Employment and Immigration)*, [1992] 1 SCR 236, at 250–1. In some situations, one could attribute nobler motives than spite to litigants, particularly where the limitation built into the law was based on prejudice and was an affront to the feelings as well as the pocket-books of the excluded group. Even then, the foundation for the rule of law is shaky if there is no possibility that a victory will be more than symbolic. Moreover, in facts such as *Schachter*, and perhaps *Tétreault-Gadoury*, it is not obvious that an affront to dignity would be sufficient to motivate litigation.

Where a statute requires a private person or organization to provide an underinclusive benefit, the provider of the benefit has a motive to litigate the issue, since striking the legislation would save money. See.

C. Kovacic, "Remedying Underinclusive Statutes" (1986) 33 *Wayne Law Review* 39, at 42. For example, an employer might seek to strike a statutory obligation to provide a benefit to certain workers on the ground that the law discriminated by excluding others from the benefit. However, this option is unsatisfactory. The idea that we should rely on such organizations to protect the interests of disadvantaged groups is offensive. Such a challenge will almost always be brought for the motive of saving money, and one cannot assume that the interests of the groups affected will be adequately represented. Moreover, a system which, in effect, excluded disadvantaged groups from an important class of equality rights cases, and which did so on the ground that the relevant interests were adequately represented by service providers who were motivated by self-interest, would be unacceptable from the point of view of equal participation in our political system.

45 *Schachter v. Canada*, at 135–40 (FC), 639–51 (DLR); *Knodel v. The Queen*, at 759–63.

46 But see Kovacic, "Remedying," 88–95, arguing that extension should be the remedy unless the legislature has explicitly addressed the issue of underinclusiveness. If the court thinks there is a substantial likelihood that the legislature would choose to repeal a law, Kovacic proposed that the court should stay the extension.

47 Duclos and Roach, "Constitutional Remedies."

48 Ibid., 17–19.

49 I note, however, that if any consideration is given to presumed legislative intent, that may open the way to some consideration of costs. In that case it would be important to try not to ignore the nonquantifiable costs nor to assume that the legislature would always prefer the result with the lowest monetary cost, as Duclos and Roach point out.

50 *R. v. Hebb* (1989), 69 CR (3d) 1 (NSSCTD).

51 See Duclos and Roach, "Constitutional Remedies," 26–7. The authors also discuss a number of other examples, including *Schachter* and *R. v. Morgentaler*, [1988] 1 SCR 30.

52 Though I focus on section 15, similar arguments can be made with respect to other sections. For example, a number of writers have concluded that the rights incorporated in section 7 sometimes require implementation of positive programs. See Morrison, "Security," 2. A noteworthy example is Jackman's thorough article arguing that section 7 incorporates a right to the level of welfare protection which is necessary to achieve a minimum social standard of decency. Jackman, "Protection," 322–8.

53 *McKinney v. University of Guelph* (1990), 76 DLR (4th) 545, at 624.

54 *Andrews v. Law Society of B.C.*, at 180–1 (SCR), 232–3 (CRR). McIntyre went on to find that noncitizens were a "discrete and insular minority,"

319 The Charter of Rights and Freedoms

citing *U.S. v. Carolene Products Co.*, 304 US 144, at 152–3 n.4 (1938). That phrase has also been used in other cases. It obviously cannot be taken literally. Sex is enumerated in section 15, but women are not a numerical minority, nor are they an insular group in society. It seems clear that the phrase is meant to refer to groups who have experienced persistent discrimination.

55 Ibid., 171 (SCC), 225 (CRR).
56 Ibid., citing the dissenting decision of Robins JA in *Reference re Act to Amend the Education Act* (1986), 53 OR (2d) 513, at 554 (Ont. CA).
57 Ibid., 152 (SCR), 201 (CRR), quoting J.H. Ely, *Democracy and Distrust* (Cambridge: Harvard University Press 1980), 151.
58 Ibid., 152 (SCR), 202 (CRR).
59 *R. v. Turpin*, at 1332 (SCR), 34 (CCC).
60 See *Retail, Wholesale and Department Store Union Local 580 v. Dolphin Delivery Ltd.*, [1986] 2 SCR 73.
61 Cohen, "Towards a Paradigm," 59.
62 *Schachter v. Canada* (1992), 93 DLR (4th) 1 (SCC). Four other members of the court concurred in the judgment of Lamer, CJ. La Forest (L'Heureux-Dubé concurring) concurred with the result and said that he does not "fundamentally disagree" with the guidelines that are established. However, he preferred to decide the case on narrower grounds because of the unsatisfactory state of the record presented to the court. For a discussion of the Federal Court of Appeal judgment, see the text accompanying notes 33–5.
63 *Haig v. Canada* (1992), 9 OR (3d) 495 (CA).

Language and Canadian Public Law

JULIUS GREY

Maxwell Cohen was a giant figure for me during my years at McGill. He admitted me to the Faculty of Law, and he taught me Government Control of Business, a course which, several years later, I had the honour to teach with him.

Those were heady times. The Quiet Revolution in Quebec, the student revolution across the continent, the massive expansion of social services, and the adoption of Canadian official bilingualism created an atmosphere of excitement and ferment. But there were also signs of danger. After the unexpected Union Nationale victory in 1966, the Quiet Revolution was highjacked by narrow nationalists with an anti-English agenda. The student revolution was often represented by anti-academic extremists and became associated with them. Bilingualism attracted some irrational, red-neck opposition in the English-speaking provinces.

Maxwell Cohen never swerved from his support of the goals of the Quiet Revolution and of bilingualism. The National Law Programme was one way of bridging the gap between Quebec and the rest of Canada. The extension of French-language teaching was another. But at all times, Max knew the importance of supporting the French minority in the rest of Canada and the English minority in Quebec. McGill, for instance, was to remain a basically English but totally open institution, an advertisement for Canadian unity and a great asset for Quebec.

The article I have written restates the basic theme, so important for Cohen, of supporting both the French and English minorities in

Canada and of putting first, ahead of any collective interests, notions of individual rights and common decency. Cohen always believed and still believes that each of our official languages is a treasure which should be cherished by all Canadians. I hope this article contributes in some way to the dissemination of this view in an epoch where politicians on both sides have attempted to challenge it.

Canada was the product of bilingualism from the start. It would be anachronistic to try to work modern ideas of bilingualism, multiculturalism, or constitutional law into historical developments of the eighteenth or nineteenth century, but it must be admitted that the existence of the French language and population was important in preventing the absorption of Canada into the United States during the American Revolution. Subsequently, the English governor and the imperial authorities frequently favoured the French group, enabling it to survive the crucial years until 1840.[1]

History, of course, is not an exact science. Those who attended English schools in Quebec thirty years ago learned of gallant and generous conquerors like General Murray who saved a forlorn, conquered nation. Those who attended French schools learned of a valiant nation which, for a hundred years, resisted an oppressive and often cruel occupier. One gets different viewpoints from Canadian nationalists like Donald Creighton, Quebec moderates like François-Xavier Garneau, Quebec nationalists like Lionel Groulx and Michel Brunet, and outside observers like Francis Parkman.[2] That is as it should be. Each generation and each political tendency must reinvent history, not to falsify the facts but to rearrange them.[3] One of the fundamental facts that has permitted Canada to survive – even if, at times, it weakened its internal unity – was the presence of both languages, both inside and outside Quebec.

The years of crisis, 1840–67 – which began with the one clear attempt to destroy Quebec, the Durham Report,[4] and ended with Confederation – consecrated forever the French nature of Quebec and the bilingualism of all Canada. Other basic features of modern Canada have been added since – for instance, multiculturalism, the Charter, and the social programs – but no one can seriously dispute the linguistic duality as one of the anchors of Canadian distinctiveness.[5]

This point was made by as strong a Quebec nationalist as Henri Bourassa. In "The French Language and the Future of Our Race," he said: "Not only does the maintaining of the French language offer no danger to the religious and national unity of the country but I am sure that the preservation and expansion of the French language in each of the English provinces in Canada is the only positive moral guarantee of both the unity of the Canadian confederation and the maintaining of the British institutions in Canada."[6] He went on: "There are some Anglo-Canadians who honestly believe that since the English language is the language of the mother country, it should also be the colony's. They seem to forget this very important fact: that the English language is the language not only of England, *but also of the United States*" (emphasis added).[7]

The presence of French throughout the country, its predominance in Quebec, and its absolute equality in federal institutions are unconditional requirements for Canada's continued independent existence from the United States. Without the French fact, the other nine provinces will slide imperceptibly into the United States.[8] Quebec would become a closed, narrow society, similar to that desired by Groulx,[9] which will be forced by economic difficulties to give up much of its social progress of the last fifty years. If one is to prevent this triumph of old-fashioned nationalism, it is essential to preserve not only French in the rest of Canada, but English in Quebec. The French but partly English nature of Quebec society is one of the best guarantees against a successful attempt to revise the traditional xenophobic Quebec nationalism. It follows that there are three major pillars of Canadian language policy and therefore language law:

- the bilingualism of federal institutions;
- the preservation and promotion of French outside Quebec; and
- the preservation and promotion of English in Quebec.

THE BILINGUALISM OF FEDERAL INSTITUTIONS

Section 133 and Similar Provisions

The British North America Act of 1867 contained only a limited guarantee of bilingualism in section 133:

Either the English or the French Language may be used by any Person in the Debates of the Houses of the Parliament of Canada and of the Houses of the Legislature of Quebec; and both those Languages shall be used in the respective Records and Journals of the Houses; and either of those languages may be used by any Person or in any Pleading or Process in or issuing from any Court of Canada established under this Act and in or from all or any of the Court of Quebec.

The Acts of the Parliament of Canada and of the Legislature of Quebec shall be printed and published in both those Languages.

Because of the confusion in the minds of many Quebeckers among language, culture, and religion, the guarantees of religious education in section 93 were seen by many as language guarantees. They were indeed in Quebec, both because of the economic position of the English minority and because all Protestants tended to be English.[10] In the rest of the country, this "guarantee" turned out to be a cruel illusion.[11] The Manitoba Act contained guarantees similar to section 133. They were repealed by the English majority less than thirty years later,[12] and then reinstated by the Supreme Court of Canada in recent years[13] when it was too late to restore effective bilingualism to the province. No guarantees were given to the large Acadian population of New Brunswick, but the 1982 amendments to the Constitution did promulgate total bilingualism for the province and, at least in large portions of New Brunswick, they have proved to be effective.[14]

The protection of French was thus quite limited in 1867, although the creation of the province of Quebec with a massive French majority went a long way to overcoming the constitutional weakness. Even in Parliament and in the Supreme Court in its early years, the use of French was far less widespread than it is today.[15] In part, this may have been because of the closed, religious nature of Quebec society which was little interested in the world outside. But the main reason was undoubtedly the dominance of English in Quebec's cities and economic life. For instance, Quebec City at Confederation was 40 per cent English.[16] Montreal had an English majority.[17] Thus, while section 133 continued the use of French in the federal apparatus, it was not nearly as effective as it was in protecting the English language in Quebec. Mallory was right when he wrote: "It needs to be remembered that the BNA Act has never been a very effective protector of the rights deemed necessary by French-speaking Canadians for their survival as a distinct group."[18] He went on to use the example of the withdrawal of rights in Manitoba[19] to illustrate the fragility of French rights in the first century of Canada's existence.

It is easy to attempt to lay the blame entirely on the country's English majority. However, one must keep in mind the fluid and sensible nature of history[20] to avoid simplistic generalization. The lack of a French industrial or commercial base can be viewed in many different ways. Certainly no one can blame the English for living in large numbers in Quebec's largest cities. Orange and imperialist sentiment was undeniably present.[21] Individual historians will have to interpret the weakness of the protection of French in their own way. Today, the protection has been rendered effective by a new vigour in the interpretation of section 133;[22] by the adoption in 1969 of an Official Languages Act, creating equality for the two languages in federal institutions; and by the new constitutional guarantees of 1982.

The courts have declared null and void Quebec's attempt to do away with section 133.[23] It follows that the federal government would be powerless to take away protection from French or English. The Supreme Court has stated that every part of a statute, including citations and annexes, must be bilingual.[24] The Constitution was applied to every enactment of a truly public nature, including subordinate legislation,[25] but it does not apply to more private subordinate legislation (eg, municipal by-laws). It follows that in the federal sphere, all governmental regulations have to be bilingual.

With respect to courts, it is not necessary for every procedure to be bilingual. That would be cumbersome beyond belief.[26] Bilingualism simply means that every person is entitled to speak or write either language before federal or Quebec courts and is presumed to be understood.[27] For administrative reasons, the Federal Court has required, in certain cities, that a lawyer wishing to speak French give advance notice. The *enforcement* of that rule (i.e., ordering the lawyer to proceed in English in the absence of advance notice) would be flagrantly unconstitutional.[28]

With the exception, perhaps, of the rule excluding municipal by-laws, the courts have interpreted section 133 wisely, on the one hand guarding against subtle encroachments and, on the other, refusing to turn it into an obstacle to legal process.[29] The notion of what is connected to "government regulation" can certainly give rise to debate as to detail, but no area of law can ever be codified so as to be entirely free of ambiguity; a constant level of discussion is probably a healthy sign. However, it can no longer be argued that section 133 is an empty shell and does not provide protection. It is by and large effective both with respect to English in Quebec and French in the rest of the country.[30]

A minor problem affecting the application of section 133 arises with respect to the weight of the English and the French versions of laws. Under federal law, they are unquestionably equal, as they are in situations where no mention is made of any distinction.[31] In such circumstances, if the two versions differ, one interprets so as to effect the intent of the legislator best or, more felicitously, so as to bring about a greater degree of justice and harmony with basic laws, such as the Charter.[32]

But what if the legislator specifically gives priority to one language? This is what happened in Quebec in 1974 when the Interpretation Act was amended to include section 40.1, which directs the use of the French version in cases of irreconcilable discrepancies. The scope of this amendment is narrow. Not only must there be a discrepancy but all the other rules of reconciling the texts must fail. Nevertheless, it appears to be a back-door attempt to dilute section 133. It relegates the English text to auxiliary status, always suspect if it in any way differs from the French. As Côté commented on section 40.1:

> The constitutional validity of this enactment is questionable, considering the requirement of equality of the two languages stated in section 133 of the *Constitution Act, 1867*. Furthermore, the provision is not as absolute as it may appear, and should be read in conjunction with section 1 of the *Interpretation Act*. It is applicable only if the purpose, the context or the provisions of the statute being construed do not conflict with the application of section 40.1. Practically speaking, its weight is comparable to that of a presumption of intent, and it should only be relied upon when ordinary rules of interpretation are unable to provide an acceptable solution to differences in the French and English versions.[33]

While Côté's solution – favouring the version closest to the previous law – appears unduly conservative,[34] there is little doubt that his constitutional doubts are sound.

Unfortunately, in *Gagnon v. Southam Inc.*,[35] Mailhot JA said: "Il faut se méfier du titre de la version anglaise de la loi sur lequel semble s'être reposé le juge de première instance, parce qu'il contient les mots '*public inquiries*,' qui n'apparaissent nulle part dans le texte de loi, soit français, soit anglais. Vu ces circonstances, y aurait-il ambiguïté qu'il y aurait lieu évidemment d'appliquer l'article 40.1 de la *Loi d'interprétation* et de donner préséance au texte français."[36] The explanation of this seemingly sweeping approval unclouded by any doubt whatsoever may be that notice of a constitutional contestation was not given under section 95 of the Code of Civil Procedure. In any case, the decision cannot be seen as in any way convincing. No argument is advanced, indeed the problems are not mentioned. There is apparent inconsistency with the Supreme Court's Manitoba decisions.[37] Either we assume Mailhot JA properly applied the presumption of validity to the absence of contestation and thus set no precedent, or she decided an important question *per incuriam*. The issue remains open, with invalidation as the likely result.[38]

Apart from this decision and from minor disputes around regulating instruments, the effect of section 133 is generally settled and generally satisfactory.[39]

A curious dispute arose recently with respect to section 133 and section 530.1e in the Criminal Code guaranteeing a trial in English or in French if the accused so chooses. If a trial is chosen in English, may the crown prosecutor speak French as part of his or her rights under section 133, so long as the accused is provided with an interpreter? Mr Justice Benjamin Greenberg said the prosecutor can in *The Queen v. Cross*.[40] A few weeks later, Mr Justice Tannenbaum came to the opposite conclusion in *The Queen v. Montour*.[41] While both judgments are well researched and cogent, this writer agrees strongly with Tannenbaum J for several reasons. First, it is difficult to see the Crown, which is equally French and English, as claiming language rights. Second, the right to an interpreter is one which belongs to any accused, including one who speaks a language totally foreign to Canada. Surely, a right to a trial in English or in French must mean somewhat more than that. Third, the result of Mr Justice Greenberg's judgment would be that the English or French *accused* would have fewer rights in Quebec, New Brunswick, and Manitoba, precisely where language rights were most protected, than in other parts of Canada where section 133 or its equivalent is not in force. It would follow that the prosecutor's convenience must yield before the accused's rights.[42]

The Official Languages Act

Because section 133 applies only to Parliament and the courts, it is not sufficient to protect French in the federal government. French was largely ignored for the first hundred years of Canada's existence. In 1970, Sabourin writes:

Si on a toujours parlé de bilinguisme au Canada, ce n'est que depuis une dizaine d'années que la notion de biculturalisme est fort répandue. L'insatisfaction générale des Canadiens français résultant du peu d'importance accordé à la langue française avec les institutions fédérales et dans les provinces anglophones n'est pas non plus un phénomène nouveau. Mais la "révolution tranquille au Québec" et une prise de conscience généralisée des Canadiens français face à une assimilation grandissante à une immigration qui avait joué implacablement en faveur de l'élément anglophone, de même que le désir d'un plus grand nombre de Canadiens anglais de miser sur le caractère biculturel du pays afin de mieux résister à l'américanisation et finalement le souci de nombreux leaders d'assurer une forme de parité entre les "deux peuples fondateurs" dans la vie politique canadienne ont poussé (Ottawa) quelques provinces, en particulier l'Ontario et le Nouveau Brunswick et les partis politiques à s'intéresser d'avantage aux problèmes créés par la dualité culturelle.[43]

The institutions of the government of Canada were until the 1960s foreign territory to French-speaking Canadians,[44] despite having the right since 1882 to sit public service examinations in French[45] and the presence at all times of a few francophones in the federal service.

The Official Languages Act, passed in 1969, did not make Canada totally bilingual. Indeed it only applied to matters within the federal powers and had no constitutional character. What it did do was make English and French completely equal as Canada's official languages and guaranteed, to some extent, bilingual services for the population.

The law was consistent with the Trudeau government's ideology of building a bilingual country. The reason why total bilingualism even in federal services was not immediately possible was a practical one. Who was to dispense these services? And for whom? The policy was adopted to expand the use of French across Canada, and especially in Ottawa, but the initial targets were "bilingual districts" where at least 10 per cent of the population belonged primarily to the minority language.

In 1988 a new act extended the right to services, but still stopped short of total bilingualism, although it spelled out the need to promote as well as maintain the minority languages. It also reinforced the powers of the commissioner of official languages and provided a remedy in the Federal Court to those who do not get redress through the commissioner's office.

The first Official Languages Act was challenged by the former president of the Exchequer Court, Mr Justice Thorson, and by Mayor Leonard Jones of Moncton. After winning an important victory on *locus standi*,[46] the attackers were soundly defeated on the merits.[47] The validity of the decision to grant equal status to French was now beyond all doubt.

The Official Languages Act did not immediately receive the type of generous interpretation intended by the Trudeau government. Despite a good start in *Joyal v. Air Canada*,[48] a more cautious view, strongly coloured by fear of impractical results, emerged in the Federal Court in the politically seminal case of *Association des gens de l'air*.⁴⁹ Nevertheless, the spirit of the enactment did lead to some judicial victories for those pursuing a vigorous promotion of bilingualism.⁵⁰

Far more significant was the practical effect of this law. One can be fully satisfied or not with the results of the Trudeau policy,⁵¹ but it is impossible to doubt that the public service, at least in Ottawa, has become substantially bilingual and open to francophones.⁵² Indeed, a distressing English backlash against bilingualism has been gaining ground during the Mulroney years. It is seen in the growth of the Reform Party, the CORE Party in New Brunswick, the pronouncements of many politicians, notably Alberta's former premier, Donald Getty, and in strident criticism of the new Official Languages Act. This backlash is proof of the considerable success of the Trudeau-era policy of making the federal institution functionally bilingual. It also shows how much remains undone.

The Charter

The Official Languages Act was a tremendous achievement, but it was still not enough. First, it was not constitutional and could be revoked at any time. Second, it could be interpreted in the narrow way pioneered by the Federal Court.⁵³

The protection of minority languages⁵⁴ was further enhanced by the adoption of sections 16–22 of the Canadian Charter of Rights and Freedoms. Apart from extending protection to New Brunswick, this change guaranteed constitutionally the original equality of English and French, and extended the notion of progress towards true equality. Finally, the principle of bilingual services was enshrined, though still within limits related to demand. Fortunately, section 33 permitting legislative derogation from the Charter did not apply to these provisions.

One would think that inclusion in the Charter would open language rights to the generous interpretation of constitutional rights applicable in constitutional matters.⁵⁵ Many judges have thought so.⁵⁶

Foucher wrote, speaking of section 23:

Il est maintenant établi que la *Charte canadienne des droits et libertés*, dans son ensemble, doit recevoir une interprétation large et libérale, généreuse, reflétant cette primauté que doit avoir le texte constitutionnel et le souci de ne pas se limiter à la lettre de la loi. En matière de droits linguistiques, en général, la Cour suprême a fait connaître sa position dans le *Renvoi sur les droits linguistiques au Manitoba* lorsqu'elle a relié clairement les droits linguistiques à la dignité humaine et aux besoins de la vie en société, à l'égalité d'accès des francophones et des anglophones aux lois, aux tribunaux et aux corps législatifs. Elle a aussi affirmé le devoir impérieux des tribunaux de faire respecter ces garanties. En ce qui a trait à l'article 23 de la *Charte canadienne des droits et libertés* en particulier, tant la Cour supérieure du Québec que la Cour d'appel de l'Ontario et la Cour de Banc de la Reine de l'Alberta ont adopté cette approche libérale et généreuse. Une interprétation libérale de l'article 23, dans ce contexte, ne signifie pas qu'il faille étendre sa portée pour y voir un désir de protection des droits de la majorité; elle indique qu'il faut lui faire jouer un rôle véritable de garantie des droits des minorités.

Une lecture littérale, tâtillonne et restrictive pourrait certes favoriser les compromis qui ont cours dans certaines provinces: francophones à l'immersion française, classes bilingues dans des écoles mixtes négation de toute forme de gestion autre que par voie du comité consultatif. Ces compromis ne s'accordent pas avec l'interprétation qui doit être celle de l'article 23. Les diverses limites et les appels à la raison venant des gouvernements provinciaux ne peuvent venir réduire l'article 23 à de plates banalités. Sinon, les minorités qui tentent désespérément de survivre, surtout dans les régions où elles sont les plus faibles, seront en droit de douter de la valeur réelle des garanties constitutionnelles, qui ne représenteront pour elles que des illusions.[57]

In an article written with Tremblay, however, Bastarache expressed apprehensions about Supreme Court jurisprudence in the period 1985–6.[58]

The *MacDonald*[59] and *Bilodeau*[60] cases can be explained by common sense. The limitations on language rights in these cases appear sensible and rational. The serious problem is Mr Justice Beetz's decision of *Société des Acadiens*.[61] After quoting *MacDonald* to the effect that language rights are not fundamental but are based on a political compromise, he states the following:

This essential difference between the two types of rights dictates a distinct judicial approach with respect to each. More particularly, the courts should pause before they decide to act as instruments of change with respect to language rights. This is not to say that language rights provisions are cast in stone and should remain immune altogether from judicial interpretation. But, in my opinion, the courts should approach them with more restraint than they would in construing legal rights.

Such an attitude of judicial restraint is in my view compatible with s. 16 of the *Charter*, the introductory section of the part entitled "Official Languages of Canada."[62]

In a concurring judgment, Chief Justice Dickson adopts the new liberal policy of interpretation. Therefore, the restrictive remarks of Beetz J were not necessary for the decision.

The negative side of Beetz's judgment cannot be downplayed. In *Language Rights in the Supreme Court of Canada*, Marc M. Monnin writes:

> Me Bastarache singled out for particular criticism the subsequent decisions of the Supreme Court of Canada in *Société des Acadiens and MacDonald v. Montreal*, referring to them as "a shocking reversal in the reasoning of the Court." He noted with a certain amount of apprehension the remarks of Mr. Justice Beetz for the majority in that decision that language rights are not as important as legal rights. A strong dissent was expressed by Mr. Justice Dickson and Madam Justice Wilson in *Société des Acadiens* constituted a reversal of the more liberal interpretations taken in previous language rights decisions.[63]

Michel Bastarache writes in the same issue:

> A shocking reversal in the reasoning of the Court occurred however in 1986 in the *McDonald v. Ville de Montreal* and *Société des Acadiens de Nouveau-Brunswick v. Association of Parents for Fairness in Education* decisions. In the majority decisions delivered by Mr. Justice Beetz, the Court declared that section 16(1) of the *Charter* does not establish a right to equality of official languages, but rather provides for a goal which is to be reached through the provisions of sections 17 to 20 of the *Charter* and especially through new language rights to be introduced by provincial legislatures. It is true that the Court did not deal in a definitive way with the scope of section 16(1) in these cases. It did, nevertheless, refuse to make use of section 16(1) to further the rights described in section 19(3), which deals with the right to use the language of one's choice before the courts of New Brunswick. Mr. Justice Beetz held that the right to use the French or the English language in all proceedings which is based on section 19(2) is identical to that found in section 133 of the *Constitution Act, 1867*, and that it is a right which belongs to the individual but creates no corresponding obligation on the state or anyone else to whom these proceedings are addressed. This it seems to me is contrary to the findings in *Blaikie (#2)* that rules of Court must be bilingual to ensure equal access to the Courts in both French and English.[64]

Subsequent judgments have reverted to the generous interpretation, at least of section 23.[65] One must therefore conclude either that section 23 is to be interpreted generously, but not sections 16–22, or that *Société des Acadiens*, or at least its dicta on interpretation, constituted an unfortunate error and should be considered a minority view. The last possibility is far more attractive.

It is true that services in English and French are not quite as universal as values as are freedom of expression or association. But in the Canadian context, they are as fundamental. If the Charter had brought in total, immediate equality, then some limitations in unilingual areas might have been attractive for practical reasons. But the Charter is so limited in scope that any doubt should be resolved in favour of the minority. *Société des Acadiens* was altogether too cautious and too timorous.

In conclusion, the Charter provides a number of protections, notably security against repeal of the Official Languages Act. In terms of services, it could prove to be a significant catalyst provided that Beetz J is not followed. There is reason to think he will not be.[66]

The total effect of section 133, the Official Languages Act, and the Charter is to provide a limited but effective bilingualism in federal institutions. The pariah state of French in the first century of our country is definitely behind us, even if some work remains to be done and if a backlash must be defused.

PROMOTION AND PRESERVATION OF FRENCH OUTSIDE QUEBEC

One of the most shameful episodes in Canadian history is the attempt to destroy French-speaking communities outside Quebec. Starting with the harsh treatment of the Acadians in the 1750s, a series of measures was undertaken with an idea to making Canada outside Quebec English only.

Once again, one-sided interpretations of history are dangerous. The Supreme Court, in the *Manitoba Reference*,[67] drew attention to the legal cases that had invalidated the 1890 act which revoked French rights in 1892 and 1909. The temper of the times was such that these laws were simply ignored.[68]

After losing the Manitoba battles, in practice if not in theory, the focus of the battle for French shifted to Ontario. There a long and tragic confrontation occurred over Resolution 17, which abolished French Catholic schools.[69] The entire history of Ontario law is found in *Re Education Act*.[70] The history is not as one-sided as many Quebec nationalists would have it. For instance, speaking of Egerton Ryerson,[71] the court said:

During his tenure, he proposed no restriction on the language of instruction. Indeed, he went further and, in 1851, arranged the passage of a regulation allowing for "the exclusive use of French (or German) in any of the schools of Upper Canada." In 1857, he stated in a letter dated April; 24th, " ... that as French is the recognized language of the country, as well as English, it is quite proper and lawful for the trustees to allow both languages to be taught in their school to children whose parents may desire them to learn both." *French Language Public Secondary Schools in Ontario*, Report from Cultural and Educational Subcommittee of the Ontario Advisory Committee on Confederation, October, 1967, as quoted in the *Bériault Report*: app. "c," A.C.F.O., No. 3; N.D.P., No. 1.[72]

However, the court went on to note "the severe setbacks" suffered by French in the period 1880–1920.[73] The culmination came just before the First World War:

In 1912–13, Reg. 17 was passed. Pursuant to its terms, English was to be the only language of instruction after grades 1 and 2. French might be taught in the later grades, but for no more than one hour per day. This Draconian measure represented the lowest ebb of French language education in Ontario. Officially, it remained in force until 1944 although, in practice, it was circumvented in various ways after 1920 (app. "c," A.C.F.O., No. 16), following an unsuccessful constitutional challenge which reached the Privy Council; *Ottawa Separate School Trustees v. Mackell* (1916), 32 D.L.R. 1, [1917] A.C. 62.[74]

The situation only improved in the 1960s,[75] an improvement noted by Sabourin.[76] It has continued since.

The improvement reached its highest level in New Brunswick which is now constitutionally bilingual, with total equality at least before the law.[77] Although Ontario legislated substantially to improve the lot of French in the administration, schools, and courts,[78] it stopped short of total bilingualism.[79]

Other provinces also legislated with respect to French schools, often in reaction to the Charter.[80] There was also some legislation intended to cut down the effect of court judgments.[81] French rights, at least for someone accused of an offence, were substantially improved by the federal Official Languages Act.[82]

Undoubtedly the most important achievement was section 23 of the Charter.[83] If French had been waning in Canada prior to the revival of the 1960s, it was largely for lack of educational opportunities.[84]

It was essential that section 23 be generously interpreted and that the "numbers permitting" limit be restricted to true cases of lack of demand. This has in fact happened.[85] In *Re Education Act* we read: "This Court has recognized that the Charter must be given a broad and liberal interpretation. It has stated that the Charter should not be stultified 'by narrow technical literal interpretations without regard to its background and purpose': *Re Southam Inc. and The Queen (No. 1)* (1983) 41 O.R. (2d) 113 at p. 123, 146 D.L.R. (3d) 408 at p. 418, 3 C.C.C. (3d) 515. Section 23 of the Charter particularly must be given such a liberal interpretation for it enacts new rights and in effect creates a code which establishes minority language education rights for the nation."[86]

In getting away from the restrictiveness of *La Société des Acadiens*, Chief Justice Dickson said in *Mahé*: "I do not believe that these words support the proposition that s. 23 should be given a particularly narrow construction, or that its remedial purposes should be ignored."[87] What this implies, in practice, is the failure of any schemes to set too high a requirement for "numbers permitting." It also has prevented delegating to school boards the discretion to determine arbitrarily when the numbers permit French instruction.[88] The latter case, as well as the Ontario defence,[89] make it clear that the minority groups are entitled to participate and to some extent control their institution.

Mahé shows that the "numbers permit" test applies separately to different issues of degree of control. Chief Justice Dickson left the greatest possible degree of flexibility with the following remarks:

It is not possible to give an exact description of what is required in every case in order to ensure that the minority language group has control over those aspects of minority language education which pertain to or have an effect upon minority language and culture. Imposing a specific form of educational system in the multitude of different circumstances which exist across Canada would be unrealistic and self-defeating. The problems with mandating "specific modalities" have been recognized by all of the courts in Canada which have considered s. 23. At this stage of early development of s. 23 jurisprudence, the appropriate response for the courts is to describe in general terms the requirements mandated. It is up to the public authorities to satisfy these general requirements. Where there are alternative ways of satisfying the requirements, the public authorities may choose the means of fulfilling their duties. In some instances this approach may result in further litigation to determine whether the general requirements mandated by the court have been implemented. I see no way to avoid this result, as the alternative of a uniform detailed order runs the real risk of imposing impractical solutions. Section 23 is a new type of legal right in Canada and thus requires new responses from the courts.

In arriving at a general description of the sort of management and control mandated by s. 23, I have borrowed heavily from the statements of Purvis J. and Kerans J.A. in the Alberta courts as well as from statements by the

Ontario Court of Appeal in *Reference Re Education Act of Ontario, supra*. The views of these courts show an appreciation of the various considerations involved in ensuring that the minority language group has control over the aspects of minority language education which pertain to or have an effect upon minority language and culture.

In my view, the measure of management and control required by s. 23 of the *Charter* may, depending on the number of students to be served, warrant an independent school board. Where numbers do not warrant granting this maximum level of management and control, however, they may nonetheless be sufficient to require linguistic minority representation on an existing school board.[90]

The expression "sliding scale of rights"[91] illustrates the absence of dogma or any form of rigidity.

The courts have also wisely held that section 23 rights are individual rights[92] and have eschewed any collectivist vision.[93] The purpose of the Charter is to help members of minority language groups, not to classify citizens in language corporations. For instance, it is clear that many citizens will have rights to education in both languages under section 23.[94]

On a different note, francophones have also benefited substantially from the growing bilingualism of federal institutions. This has brought French broadcasting and services to areas where they would normally not have penetrated.

The conclusion is that, while much remains to be done, there has been substantial improvement in facilities available in French across the country. Trudeau's idea of a bilingual Canada has not been realized,[95] but the progress is solid and nothing justifies the apparent desertion of the ideal by many Canadians during the Mulroney years.[96]

THE PROBLEM OF ENGLISH IN QUEBEC

The Issues

Quebec nationalists never tire of describing the conditions of the "best-treated minority in the world." Undoubtedly, the English minority does have institutional facilities, such as hospitals, schools, and universities, unavailable to francophones outside Quebec. Does this make the minority the best-treated in Canada, let alone the world?

In another article, this author expressed his views as follows:

Quebec nationalists frequently boast that the English-speaking community is the world's "best treated minority" and that the claims of injustice toward it are both preposterous and presumptuous.

This type of assertion is always suspect. Generosity is more convincing when the recipients rather than the dispensers proclaim it. It is also very difficult to establish which of the countless minorities in the world is the best-treated.

The very word "generosity" suggests a problem when applied to citizens who are supposed to be equal in every way. However, even with these initial doubts, the nationalists' assertion deserves some analysis. As soon as one begins to consider it, one sees that it is partly defensible and partly not.

What is unquestionably true is that institutionally, English Quebec is better equipped than most minorities and certainly better than any other in Canada. It has three universities, numerous hospitals, constitutionally guaranteed school boards, newspapers, radio, television, and so on. It is easier to be unilingual English in Quebec and survive than to be unilingual French anywhere in the country with the possible exception of parts of New Brunswick.

One point which mitigates Quebec's merit is that these institutions are not the fruit of a conscious act of tolerance. They were established by the minority at a time when it was the dominant force and was, for a long period, the majority in Montreal.

Nor can present-day grants to English institutions be credited to the majority. The minority pays taxes like everyone else. Giving it a portion of the services is justice and not generosity.

Most devastating for Quebec's claim of generosity is its 20-year battle to diminish the role and scope of the English institutions.

English universities are always more hurt than others by financial cutbacks. Bill 191 closed access to English schools to many persons, including anglophones from other provinces, and it took the Canadian *Charter* to restore the rights of most Canadians.

Despite all of this and despite the very serious questions which can be raised as to Quebec's future intentions, it is clear that the institutional structures of the English community are indeed good and that, at best, the minority would be justified in lobbying to keep them but not in complaining about them.

Where individual rights are concerned, the picture is starkly different. Not only is the English minority not the best-treated in the world but, it can be argued, all minorities in Quebec are, on the whole, worse treated than minorities elsewhere in Canada.[97]

A similar view is expressed by historian Ramsay Cook in reviewing Mordecai Richler's book, *Oh Canada! Oh Quebec!* for the Montreal *Gazette*.

Though the English-speaking minority in Quebec continues to enjoy rights that are the envy of most francophone minorities outside Quebec, those rights have been restricted. Who would not be uneasy in a province with a premier who boasted that he had taken away civil rights of some citizens in overriding the Supreme Court's decision that the Quebec Charter protected outdoor commercial signs in English? Here Richler is on solid ground: the main consequence of restrictive language laws is the depressing exodus of young, often bilingual, non-francophones from the province. Does that benefit Quebec? Had Richler paid less attention to anti-semitism and more to Bills 101 and 178, his indictment would have been more effective, forcing his critics into defending the language laws rather than arguing about the relevance of Groulx's name on a Métro station. Even those who have conceded that Richler was at least partly right about Bill 178 have stopped short of urging changes. The negative response to Gretta Chamber's recommentations about admission of English-speaking immigrants to English-language schools is a sad case in point.[98]

Richler himself makes similar points, in the language of the writer rather than the historian.[99]

Exactly the same doubt about the happy state of the English minority, in appropriately sober tone, is found in the Supreme Court judgment of *Association of Protestant School Boards*:

Although the fate reserved to the English language as a language of instruction had generally been more advantageous in Quebec than the fate reserved to the French language in the other provinces, Quebec seems nevertheless to have been the only province where there was then this tendency to limit the benefits conferred on the language of the minority. In the other provinces at the time, either the earlier situation had remained unchanged, at least so far as legislation was concerned, as in Newfoundland and British Columbia which have no legislation on the language of instruction, or else relatively recent statutes had been adopted improving the situation of the linguistic minority, as in New Brunswick, Nova Scotia and Prince Edward Island.[100]

It appears beyond doubt that in the period 1760–1960 the English minority set up an unusually good network of institutions,[101] many of which have been publicly funded or underfunded since 1960. Quebec, or at least Montreal, also functioned in a bilingual fashion until the early 1970s. However, it is important to remember that Montreal was majority English or half English for a large part of the nineteenth century[102] and that even today more than a third of the urban community is non-French. Despite Quebec's attempts to make it French only, Montreal is still functionally bilingual.

The view of many minority members that the period prior to 1974 was a golden age of bilingualism is difficult to justify. Section 133 applied then as it does now, and the two societies were not so much bilingual as separate.[103] The majority of francophones lived in French-speaking groups and encountered English, if at all, only at work. The English minority lived as though its main areas of concentration were in Ontario, not Quebec. This state of affairs was made easy by the fact that the language groups lived in different areas of Montreal.

The Quiet Revolution started in the 1940s rather than in the 1960s, with the growth of a French urban intelligentsia and a corresponding fall in the birth rate.[104] This led to some concern that all immigrants tended to join the English minority. This writer has already conceded some rationality to this argument:

The second, more serious, nationalist argument is based on immigration. Unlike Spain or eastern Europe, Canada is a land of immigration. In the first half of the century, almost all immigrants adopted English as their Canadian language. Once Quebec's birthrate fell to normal, modern standards in the 1960s, it could be argued that, in the long run, French Quebecers could become a minority.

This argument has some merit. That is why the one aspect of Quebec's legislation that can be rationally justified is imposing French school on immigrants. This does not justify the restriction on the teaching of English in French schools, or the attempt to limit the freedom of Canadian citizens, both French and English. However, there is little doubt that a law could have been drafted which would have been compelling and would have placed immigrants in French schools, at least until their naturalization.[105]

After the initial reforms of the Quiet Revolution, which were welcomed by many anglophones as much as by francophones, the revolution turned away from reform and towards classic nationalism. In this situation, the career of novelist Gabrielle Roy's Jean Lévesque,[106] for instance, was advanced over his English or immigrant counterparts through nationalist legislation and even more nationalist attitudes.

The result has been a proliferation of language laws, fundamentally Bill 22, Bill 101, and Bill 178, along with the legislation and subordinate legislation designed to give them effect. Another result, less amenable to legal analysis, has been the exclusion of English-speakers from the public sector[107] and the tendency for many of them to leave Quebec.[108] The classic nationalist response has been to deny or to blame the minority for this phenomenon.[109]

Under growing pressure, Quebec set up a taskforce on English education, headed by Montreal journalist and McGill chancellor Gretta Chambers. The report of the taskforce confirmed the weakness of the minority, its decline, and its lack of representation.[110] Although some of the report's less controversial proposals might bear fruit, the major suggestion – the dilution of the clearly unnecessary restrictions of Bill 101 with respect to access to English school – has been endorsed by almost no francophones.

While opposition to Bill 178 – prohibiting English commercial signs – is common among all segments of the population,[111] changing the law also appears to be extremely difficult. Any weakening of the language legislation immediately arouses a loud lobby which, in the face of all evidence, persists in seeing English as dominant and French as threatened.[112]

It is thus evident that, for political reasons, only the courts can assist the minority. Most political ventures are not viable in a system where politicians study polls and always fear potential majority reactions more than minority ones.[113] The situation is similar to that in the field of civil rights in the United States forty years ago.[114] Purely majoritarian political theory, weak as it is in any case, is simply inapplicable to situations where emotions like nationalism or racism are present. The political process helps one or the other side.[115] Courts necessarily play the role of arbiter and protector. It is in that context that one must evaluate what the courts have done since 1974.[116]

The Laws and the Jurisprudence

Bill 22 of 1971 had as its effect the creation of a unilingual French state, with certain exceptions and within a bilingual federal structure. The constitutional validity of this outcome cannot be questioned since *La Chaussure Brown's* and *Devine*.[117] These cases decided, on the one hand, that the language legislation was valid, from the point of view of purely constitutional law – that is, the division of powers – but, on the other hand, that the prohibition of English commercial signs violated freedom of expression and the right to equality under the Canadian and Quebec Charters. In the Court of Appeal,[118] a minority composed of Paré and Montgomery JJA had suggested that language, not being a power given to the province under section 92 of the BNA Act, was not properly a provincial field of legislation at all, save in certain cases ancillary to section 92 powers. The majority and the Supreme Court refused to accept this idea, and this position is no longer arguable.[119] It is established that Quebec has lawfully declared French to be its official language and that no way exists to obtain a blanket annulment of Bill 101.

Bill 22 restricted access to English schools and made the use of French compulsory, though not exclusive, in many areas of public and even private life.[120] Bill 101 restricted more drastically access to English schools, attempted to do away with section 133 in Quebec courts, and made French the exclusive language of municipalities and commercial advertising, and, to a large extent, of labour relations and the professions. It created vague obligations to offer services in French at all levels – for instance, in stores and restaurants (section 5). In both cases, regulations were authorized to supply many of the details which the legislation did not spell out.

Bill 178 essentially exempted from the operation of the Canadian and Quebec charters the public-sign portions of the law in answer to *La Chaussure Brown's*. It also offered some insignificant expansion of the right to use English in certain cases.[121]

Many Quebec nationalists have complained about the minority's successes before the courts and have even blamed section 96 of the Constitution Act, which provides for federal nomination of judges.[122] In fact, Quebec won the major constitutional battle.[123] The courts have been even-handed in accordance with their duty. However, the one-sidedness of Quebec (a characteristic of nationalism everywhere) has pushed it into policies that naturally attracted judicial review, and the minority has indeed won a number of cases.

The issues that have arisen have been of several types: purely constitutional; Charter; interpretation of the law; and administrative law.

Purely Constitutional Cases. The only purely constitutional case won by the minority was *Blaikie*.[124] This case invalidated Quebec's attempt in Bill 101 to make its system of justice function entirely in French despite explicit bilingualism created by section 133 of the Constitution Act. A fair reading of the constitution could lead to no other result and it is difficult to understand any of the recriminations which followed this innocuous and obvious decision.

Pure constitutional law would also apply to any attempt to restrain the use of trademarks or names of federal corporations, or the operation of purely federal types of enterprises.[125]

Charter Cases. Constitutional law in the form of the Charter is obviously involved whenever legislation as sweeping as Bill 22 or, even more, Bill 101, attempts to limit individual freedom. The obvious lines of defence for civil libertarians are freedom of expression and the rules prohibiting discrimination. Both of these basic principles were held to be violated by Bill 101 in *La Chaussure Brown's*.

On freedom of expression, the court refused to limit the concept to political discourse and held that it applied to commercial expression. This was subsequently reiterated several times.[126] There could be nothing more dangerous than the making of this kind of distinction, which would make any repression of free expression save in direct politics at least arguably legitimate. The court concluded:

> Given the earlier pronouncements of this Court to the effect that the rights and freedoms guaranteed in the Canadian *Charter* should be given a large and liberal interpretation, there is no sound basis on which commercial expression can be excluded from the protection of s.2(b) of the *Charter*. It is worth noting that the courts below applied a similar generous and broad interpretation to include commercial expression within the protection of freedom of expression contained in s.3 of the Quebec *Charter*. Over and above its intrinsic value as expression, commercial expression which, as has been pointed out, protects listeners as well as speakers plays a significant role in enabling individuals to make informed economic choices, an important aspect of individual self-fulfilment and personal autonomy. The Court accordingly rejects the view that commercial expression serves no individual or societal value in a free and democratic society and for this reason is undeserving of any constitutional protection.[127]

On the subject of the section 1 justification,[128] the court also concluded against the government:

> Thus, whereas requiring the predominant display of the French language, even its marked predominance, would be proportional to the goal of promoting and maintaining a French *"visage linguistique"* in Quebec and therefore justified under the Quebec *Charter* and the Canadian *Charter*, requiring the exclusive use of French has not been so justified. French could be required in addition to any other language or it could be required to have greater visibility than that accorded to other languages. Such measures would ensure that the *"visage linguistique"* reflected the demography of Quebec: the predominant language is French. This reality should be communicated to all citizens and non-citizens alike, irrespective of their mother tongue. But exclusivity for the French language has not survived the scrutiny of a proportionality test and does not reflect the reality of Quebec society. Accordingly, we are of the view that the limit imposed on freedom of expression by s. 58 of the *Charter of the French Language* respecting the exclusive use of French on public signs and posters and in commercial advertising is not justified under s. 9.1 of the Quebec *Charter*. In like measure, the limit imposed on freedom of expression by s. 69 of the *Charter of the French*

Language respecting the exclusive use of the French version of a firm name is not justified under either s. 9.1 of the Quebec *Charter* or s.1 of the Canadian *Charter*.[129]

The issue of discrimination was more delicate. Bill 101 applies to everyone, francophones as much as anglophones. Under a strictly formalistic view of discrimination it would not qualify.[130] However, under the Charter, formalism has not been in fashion.[131] The court said:

With these observations in mind, we turn to the question whether s.58 infringes s.10. It purports, as was said by the Superior Court and the Court of Appeal, to apply to everyone, regardless of their language of use, the requirement of the exclusive use of French. It has the effect, however, of impinging differentially on different classes of persons according to their language of use. Francophones are permitted to use their language of use while anglophones and other non-francophones are prohibited from doing so. Does this differential effect constitute a distinction based on language within the meaning of s.10 of the Quebec *Charter*? In this Court's opinion it does. Section 58 of the *Charter of the French Language*, because of its differential effect or impact on persons according to their language of use, creates a distinction between such persons based on language of use. It is then necessary to consider whether this distinction has the effect of nullifying or impairing the right to full and equal recognition and exercise of a human right of freedom recognized by the Quebec *Charter*. The human right or freedom in issue in this case is the freedom to express oneself in the language of one's choice, which has been held to be recognized by s.3 of the Quebec *Charter*. In this case the limit imposed on that right was not a justifiable one under s. 9.1 of the Quebec *Charter*. The distinction based on language of use created by s. 58 of the *Charter of the French Language* thus has the effect of nullifying the right to full and equal recognition and exercise of this freedom. Section 58 is therefore also of no force or effect as infringing s. 10 of the Quebec *Charter*.[132]

The decision was formally decided under the Quebec Charter of Rights and Freedoms, even though the court noted that both Charters were applicable. Although the provincial Charter can be modified at any time, so long as it subsists the effects are similar to that of the Canadian Charter. The Supreme Court has enunciated rules of generous interpretation rather like the ones applicable to the Charter.[133]

The Quebec Charter of Rights specifically prohibits discrimination as to language. Although on the facts of the case Quebec won *Forget v. A.G. Quebec*,[134] all the dicta on the law in the judgment of

Lamer J were favourable to the minority in giving a generous interpretation to linguistic discrimination. Further, *City of Lachine v. Burton*[135] confirmed the principle of generosity to members of the minority in interpreting the Quebec Charter. It would make sense that when a Charter of Rights is adopted and is publicized as particularly far-reaching and avant-garde in its effects, as the Quebec Charter was, courts should be activist in using it.

Quebec's main hope in restraining the use of the Charter was to characterize language rights as "collective" rather than individual. It is irrational to view freedom of expression or equal treatment as collective. However, if any area of the law could be characterized in this way, it was section 23. This was the thrust of Quebec's defence in *Quebec Association of Protestant School Boards*. The courts rightly rejected this approach as a negation of the concept of individual rights.[136] In the first judgment,[137] Deschênes CJ compared this type of theory to Soviet collective agriculture. It is certain that no easier way exists to render the Charter useless and to open the door to group claims to rights or to protection from rights under section 1 otherwise.[138]

Once the "collective rights" heresy is resolved, the predominance of the Canadian Charter over Bill 101 cannot be seen as any more controversial than the upholding of section 133.[139] The court was not unfair to Quebec. It would have had to engage in truly sophistic legal gymnastics to allow Quebec to triumph.

Interpretation of Bill 101. The area of law where there has been the most hesitation is in interpreting language legislation. Should it be given a generous reading[140] or should it be read restrictively as a law that limits freedom? It may be that a single answer is not possible, given the varied nature of the dispositions of the law, the different periods of time in which these dispositions have to be determined, and the radically evolving concept of the judicial role. Nevertheless, this author makes a plea for a restrictive reading.

First, while in 1974 it was possible to argue about the relative strength of the parties, it is now amply clear that these laws are ones promulgated by a powerful majority against an ever-weakening and declining minority. This in itself justifies a narrow interpretation.

Second, it is clear that the restrictions on basic rights are quite fundamental and that the majority is prepared to go to the length of using the notwithstanding clause even after all the levels of court have held that bilingual signs represent no danger to French and that it is legitimate to legislate not only the use but the marked predominance of French so long as there is no prohibition.[141] It is very difficult to feel protective about the language law in such circumstances.

Third, some, though not all of the dispositions of the ban, are marred by patent absurdity.[142] This applies particularly to the "sign law" and to Bill 178. Other portions of the law (eg, contracts) would be patently absurd unless narrowly interpreted to exclude any hint of prohibition or absolute nullity in case of inobservance.

While absurdity is not a ground on which courts may annul laws, as opposed to regulations and other subordinate legislation,[143] it is not impermissible to use interpretation rules to avoid both absurdity and injustice as much as possible.[144] Therefore, a narrow reading of Bills 101 and 178 appear indicated.[145]

This was not always apparent. In the initial enthusiasm of Bill 22, which was perceived by many as an affirmative-action measure to redress past injustice, Deschênes CJ wrote:

On conçoit dès lors, la difficulté de donner aux exceptions stipulées à l'article 73 une connotation large: ce serait trahir l'intention de l'Assemblée nationale suivant qu'elle appert du préambule de la *Charte*, des énoncés de principe qui la fondent et des dispositions rigoureuses qui y entourent l'extension de l'enseignement en anglais dans les écoles du Québec (e.g. art. 79).

C'est donc dans cet esprit que la Cour aborde le problème d'interprétation que pose le paragraphe a) de l'article 73 de la Charte: cette exception qui, par dérogation au principe de base de la loi 101, permet l'enseignement en anglais doit être interprétée strictement et être rigoureusement limitée au cas qu'elle prévoit: si elle est susceptible de deux interprétations, celle qui favorise l'enseignement en français doit prévaloir.[146]

This view cannot be seen as authoritative in any way. First, the Court of Appeal specifically rejected the appeal on procedural grounds and suggested Deschênes CJ was wrong in considering the issue at all.[147] Moreover, Montgomery JA appeared to favour a "middle-of-the-road" approach to interpreting Bill 22, and certainly not Deschênes's way.

Equally significant is Deschênes CJ's own reversal of position in later cases. In *Wang-Woo et al. v. A.G. Quebec, Mak v. A.G. Quebec, Orman v. A.G. Quebec*, and *Toma v. A.G. Quebec*,[148] the question arose whether persons whose permits were reversed, or who only had one or two years of English education, were protected by section 23 of the Charter.

In *Mak* we read:

Cependant le Procureur Général du Québec persiste dans sa contestation car, dit-il, le fils du requérant n'a pas droit à l'enseignement en anglais même sous la *Charte* canadienne, car c'est illégalement qu'il a suivi des cours en anglais au Québec; et le Procureur Général demande à la Cour de sous-entendre le mot "légalement" dans l'article 23(2) de la *Charte* canadienne, qui se lit comme suit:

> "(2) Les citoyens canadiens dont un enfant a reçu ou reçoit son instruction, au niveau primaire ou secondaire, en français ou en anglais au Canada ont le droit de faire instruire tous leurs enfants, aux niveaux primaire et secondaire, dans la langue de cette instruction."

La Cour n'a pas besoin de résoudre ce problème d'interprétation. En effet le Ministre de l'éducation possédait deux remèdes en vertu de la *Charte* de la langue française, que prévoient les articles 77 et 78 de la *Charte*:

> "77. Une déclaration d'admissibilité obtenue par fraude ou sur le fondement d'une fausse représentation est nulle.
> 78. Le ministre de l'éducation peut annuler une déclaration d'admissibilité délivrée par erreur."

Le Ministre s'est expressément prévalu de la seconde de ces dispositions. La Cour, respectant cette décision, ne croit pas qu'il faille cependant lui donner un effet rétroactif. Le requérant satisfait donc aux conditions prévues par l'article 23(2) de la *Charte* canadienne.[149]

While abstaining from deciding the thorny problem of illegals, Deschênes refuses to interpret Bill 101 in the broadest (ie, retroactive) way. In *Wang-Woo* he adds: "Dans la présente requête, il existe un motif additionnel concernant le requérant Fong: l'enfant de celui-ci fréquente en effet l'école de langue anglaise à Ottawa, en Ontario depuis 1980. L'article 23(2) de la *Charte* canadienne des droits et libertés trouve donc dans cette situation un motif additionnel d'application."[150]

Thus, two years suffice for rights to be established.[154] While this could be explained on a generous reading of section 23 of the Charter, which could theoretically be compatible with *Campisi*,[152] the *Mak* case and especially the tone of Deschênes's main judgment, highly critical of Bill 101, makes obvious his change of heart. The language legislation was now helping Goliath against David and could not, save in the eyes of true believers, be seen as protecting the weak.

The tendency to restrict Bill 101 to its express terms can be seen in numerous subsequent judgments.[153] *Lagacé v. Union des Employés*[154] is a particularly significant decision. The issue was whether a union whose constitutive documentation was in English only, contrary to section 48 of Bill 101, can be seen as a total nullity. The Tribunal du Travail had answered in the positive. Both the Superior Court and the Court of Appeal agreed that the tribunal's decision could not stand.

While the Court of Appeal judgment is drafted in very moderate language, it clearly restricted the effect of Bill 101. It approved the following passage of Mr Justice Melançon's Superior Court judgment:

> Il est acquis qu'on ne doit interpréter qu'au cas d'ambiguïté. Avec respect pour l'opinion contraire, et toute séduisante et originale que soit l'argumentation élaborée, le Tribunal ne saurait accepter. Cet article 49 de la Charte de la langue française ne vise que les communications et échanges avec les membres au sens de correspondance, avis, affiches, etc. Il faut, selon la règle bien connue, donner aux mots leur sens courant et conforme à ce qui est visé par le texte. Il n'y a lieu à interprétation qu'au cas d'ambiguïté, que le soussigné ne peut déceler dans le texte sous étude.
>
> En fait, c'est son opinion que par l'interprétation qu'il propose, le savant juge du Tribunal du travail a ajouté au texte de l'article 49 au chapitre 6 de la Charte une disposition que le législateur n'y a pas incluse. Ce dernier d'ailleurs n'a pas voulu, quant à la langue de travail, autre chose qu'en faire " ... la langue normale et habituelle de travail", termes qui impliquent clairement, pour reprendre un mot qui fut à la mode, un "étapisme" évident, et donc qui ne peut que limiter à ce qui est prévu l'obligation de l'utilisation de la langue officielle, dans le respect des règles classiques d'interprétation.
>
> L'on pourrait aussi souligner un autre argument. La langue de travail visée par la Charte a trait, dans chacune des situations visées, au véhicule oral ou écrit de communication à l'occasion de l'exercice des fonctions ou des actes juridiques les entourant et non tout ce qui par extension s'y greffe comme les associations de travailleurs. On ne vise pas la langue des associations, ni en général, ni des associations de travailleurs, sauf pour l'exception qu'on mentionne les communications écrites. La Charte ne comporte pas de clause exigeant par exemple la tenue des livres de minutes des corporations dans la langue officielle, même si plusieurs articles imposent aux corporations l'usage de la langue officielle dans leurs contrats, publicité et autres documents.[155]

With respect to Bill 178, a restrictive interpretation is the natural consequence of the rule that derogation from the Charter must be as limited as possible.[156] A recent case attempted to establish this interpretation, and did to some extent in that the two-year grace period provided by Bill 178 was given a broad and generous interpretation by Madam Justice Dubreuil. However, this precise issue can never arise again, because the grace period has expired, and the case is no more than an indication that the courts will not show zeal in applying this law.[157]

It is perhaps not necessary to jump to the conclusion that language laws will always receive a narrow reading. As we have seen, *La Société des Acadiens* put this too strongly[158] and the law is far more nuanced. In particular, legislation which gives rights as opposed to suppressing them (which is generally limited to Quebec, although once it was the other way around) should be read generously. It is only when individual freedom is attacked that courts should adopt a wary attitude.

Moreover, the Quebec laws will not always receive the narrowest possible reading. The courts have usually appeared moderate on these issues, even when deciding for the minority.[159] Where the intention and the meaning of a section of Bill 101 is clear, the courts need not search for way of restricting it.[160] But, on the whole, the protection of freedom will be a more urgent goal than the broad application of language laws.

Administrative Law. Language law is public law and ordinary administrative law rules apply to it. In *Lagacé* it was decided that Bill 101, being an act of general application, could not be misinterpreted with impunity by an arbitrator or lower tribunal. On the principle of *McLeod v. Egan*,[161] no judicial deference is due to such decisions and the Superior Court may intervene. The only reason that the administrative law cases on Bill 101 are at all special is that they generate excitement whenever they are decided even on the most orthodox grounds.

Sheftel v. Commission d'Appel sur la langue d'enseignement[162] reaffirms the principle that a regulation cannot restrict minority rights granted in the law.[163] *Alliance Quebec v. Rosemere* orders the Office de la langue française to observe the duty to act fairly, to respect legitimate expectations, and to make decisions on relevant consideration only. All of this is, of course, eminently orthodox.

Far more questionable was Viau J's view that a unilingual French employee had the right to work as a social aid worker to a unilingual English older lady.[164] It would seem that common sense requires that such services be delivered in English.

On the whole, of course, judicial review under Bill 101 has favoured the individual against the state. It helps maintain the rule of law in an emotionally charged area of endeavour and, as such, must be viewed in a positive light.

Conclusion on Quebec Legislation

It is clear that courts have tried hard to maintain strict neutrality, but the exuberance and intolerance of Quebec has forced them to intervene on several occasions. Quebec has won a few battles, but lost most – in all cases for very solid reasons. It is difficult to accept as objective the complaints from nationalists about the court's role. Yet even they offer or confirm the court's fairness towards the French minorities outside Quebec. For instance, Luc Huppé writes:

> On retient de ces jugements une imperméabilité presque absolue de la Cour à l'égard des intérêts des francophones du Québec. Alors, qu'elle peut être généreuse jusqu'à l'audace pour soutenir les minorités francophones des autres provinces, on doit attendre *La Chaussure Brown's Inc.* pour qu'elle analyse la vulnérabilité de la langue française au Québec: elle ne mentionne pas même cet aspect du problème dans *Blaikie et Quebec Association of Protestant School Board*. Et encore, elle le fait avec une telle retenue: une cour disposée à faire prévaloir sur la protection de la langue française, un droit constitutionnel de rédiger une quittance ou d'utiliser une raison sociale en anglais, ou la possibilité pour un marchand d'annoncer ses spéciaux de la semaine dans "la langue de son choix" est une cour qu'on n'a ni véritablement convaincue que la langue française soit vulnérable dans le contexte nord-américain, ni suffisamment sensibilisée à l'humiliation que peut ressentir un individu à ce qu'on ne daigne pas s'adresser à lui dans la langue qu'il partage avec une large majorité d'autres individus.[165]

Clearly, Huppé would like French favoured in all situations, minority or majority. He does not consider each case outside that ideological position. The court, necessarily, had to be less partial.

There are several possible court battles ahead. First, a Huntington funeral director, Gordon McIntyre, has obtained leave to appeal Bill 178 to the United Nations under the Optional Protocol.[166] This forum may provide the Quebec authorities with a face-saving way of repealing their odious use of the notwithstanding clause.

Second, the issue of "illegals" under section 23 has not been resolved. Mr Justice Deschênes specifically declined to settle it in *Wang Woo et al*. On this point, it is impossible to predict the result with any certitude.

Third, no one knows what the right to service in French (section 3 of Bill 101) means. Here, a broad interpretation would spell the ruin of many English and ethnic small businessmen, and it is to be hoped that no obligation incumbent on any person (as opposed to institution) to serve in French will be read into this law.

Fourth, no one has yet stated what level of knowledge of French is "appropriate" for any profession.[167] Certainly the exclusion of graduates of professional faculties in English Quebec institutions from the right to seek a temporary permit, while those from institutions outside Quebec may get one, appear to be direct discrimination against the minority. Bill 101 is still subject to contestation in professional law. However, this contestation is not of a fundamental nature.

Fifth, no one has challenged Quebec's cinema laws, which subject the right to show English films to the availability of a French version, with certain exceptions. While the law has been made more bearable recently by allowing films subtitled in French to be counted as a French version, it still constitutes a clear and unnecessary violation of freedom of expression.

However, a few larger questions loom with respect to discrimination. It is clear that Bill 101 discriminates against immigrants and against the majority by forcing them into the mould the nationalists consider desirable. As Magnuson wrote in his *Brief History of Quebec Education*:

The combination of a declining religion and the politics of linguistic nationalism meant that by the late 1970s Quebec schools were, in practice, divided along language lines. In spite of the fact that public schools were still officially designated as Catholic or Protestant, language not religion had become the decisive element in defining the Quebec school population. Viewed unfavourably, religious parochialism had given way to linguistic parochialism in education. As we have seen, the development of a *de facto* language-based school system was undertaken with the express purpose of expanding the Francophone population by channelling immigrants and other newcomers into French schools. The policy also halted the flow of educational traffic from French to English schools, which in the long run may do serious harm to the French-Canadian cause. By "imprisoning" French pupils in their own schools, the arrangement deprives young French Canadians of the opportunity of profiting from an English education, which has always been the hallmark of Quebec's elite. Perhaps the increased number of Francophone students attending Quebec's English-language universities in recent years is an outgrowth of that phenomenon.[168]

The desirability or feasibility of coercing members of ethnic or linguistic groups to remain inside them is an issue which is never far from the surface.[169] Quebec once protected itself with rules against mixed marriage,[170] but this would not pass muster today. Perhaps the methods of the worst parts of Bill 101 will also disappear, especially once more and more francophones realize that the danger to French is partly fictitious and partly manageable in less invasive ways.[171]

In the meantime, the future of the English minority and its institutions is uncertain. There are too many complex issues – possible separation, strong nationalism, a potential and refreshing new French pluralism.[172] No prediction can amount to more than the expression of hope or fear.

The Canadian and Quebec experience do not suggest that protection of minority language is illegitimate and that linguistic laissez-faire is the only road. What they do show is the injustice of repressive language laws, in Manitoba, Ontario, and Quebec. One can promote without prohibiting and coercing.[173]

It appears that many Quebec commentators have lost all hope for a bilingual Canada.[174] Pierre Patenaude said: "La jurisprudence des tribunaux suisses a d'ailleurs reconnu clairement qu'on ne pouvait garantir le maintien des langues nationales sans leur assurer un territoire propre. On a donc confié aux cantons la responsabilité de la protection de leur spécificité linguistique à titre de corollaire au fait que 'l'existence de langues menacées est mieux garantie par la conservation de territoires linguistiques distincts et homogènes.'"[175] The Swiss example is only apt if one applies it to units as small as cantons and not to Canadian provinces. Even then it is a narrow, ungenerous solution. It would, despite the best intentions in the world, totally eliminate English in Quebec and French in the rest of the country.[176] Even the predominance of English in the rest of the continent could do nothing for the beleaguered minority.[177]

The understanding that promotion of minority languages and the broadening of opportunities are the answer will put Canada back on the right path. Undoubtedly, Bill 101 and Bill 178 will one day become as discredited as the law that deprived the French minority of its rights in Ontario and Manitoba. One can only hope this happens in time to save the country and the minority.[178]

ANNEX

It is not fair to criticize Quebec's language legislation without offering an alternative – an alternative that achieves those objectives of the law which are desirable.

First, French should be obligatory on commercial signs. Prior to 1974 it was difficult to find any French signs in Montreal. Therefore, it is a good idea to make certain that no reversion takes place. The prohibition on English and the totally inexcusable use of the "notwithstanding clause," however, must be repealed forthwith. This is necessary for Quebec's international image, and also as a condition of any lessening of linguistic tension. Further, any attempt to legislate "marked predominance"[179] will involve the government in the measuring and evaluation of signs – preoccupations that are absurb and unworthy. The fact that French and no other language will be obligatory will provide sufficient predominance.[180]

On the school issue, the task-force report should be at least partly implemented.[181] The ultimate optimal result will surely be freedom of choice for all Canadian citizens. Immigrants from countries that are not English will be sent to French schools, but will also acquire freedom of choice with citizenship.[182] All persons will then have a chance to have *some* of their education in each language. However, this goal cannot be achieved in the immediate future.

The school issue can be made less confrontational by a requirement of considerable English instruction in French schools and vice versa, going well beyond second-language teaching.[183] The attendance at English or French school will thus become a matter of degree.[184] One could then hope to address the salutary recognition of the right of each person to receive an education which enables him or her to become functionally bilingual, both for career reasons and for personal culture.

Municipalities should be free to declare themselves bilingual without having an English majority. French services should nevertheless remain obligatory, but so should English services where there is sufficient demand.

Tests for professionals and public servants should become an alternative to courses after admission or hiring. Further, where appropriate (eg, Montreal police or public servants, lawyers, and teachers), English should also be tested or taught. It is totally unrealistic to imagine that one can practise law or be a police officer in Montreal without either language. This will give members of the various minorities an equal chance at getting public sector jobs and will eliminate the growing suspicion that the law's purpose is not to promote the French language, but "French Canadians" in the narrow sense of the word.

Much of the rest of the law and its expensive, unnecessary bureaucracy should be phased out. Thus money can be more effectively spent on education and on improving the quality of French rather than policing its predominance.

A number of laws, notably dealing with cinema, interpretation of statutes, education, and immigration, should be stripped of their linguistic colouring. There is no evidence that greater freedom will harm French. It will certainly improve morale and social cohesion in Quebec.

Finally, the Quebec Charter of Rights and Freedoms should be amended to incorporate at least section 23 (1) (6) and 23 (2) of the Canadian Charter as well as the right of all citizens for an adequate training in both languages. Social services in English should also be entrenched.

Those Quebec reforms should be synchronized with a move towards legal bilingualism in Ontario and with an increase in French rights in every province. All Canadians must get the opportunity to learn the other language thoroughly.[185] Justice and social services must, to a perceptible extent, be available in both languages across the country.

A great step forward was taken in the years 1968–84. It is now fashionable to consider as a failure an experiment that was merely incomplete. No serious person can deny the progress made by French, the growth of French immersion, and the francization of the public services in these years. It is now time to resume and complete the bilingual experiment in the entire country, including Quebec. And for the experiment to have a fair chance of success, it must be backed up by laws promoting the minority language, not ones repressing any language on the basis of any social theory or ideology.

Since the writing of this article, the writer has modified some of his views, not so much on questions of principle as of methodology. It is clear that French must remain the official language of Quebec and must be protected in certain ways, or the danger to it, which is now rather far-fetched, will become real. It is also clear that the English language must be accepted as an important and valuable part of Quebec's culture and that Quebec must continue its evolution towards a self-definition which is not tied to the ethnic notion of Quebeckers *de vieille souche* (of old stock). It would appear that the society is ready for a fair compromise. This compromise would deal with some of the more pressing concerns with the language laws but would legitimize the rest in everyone's eyes. It would also lead to a general reconciliation and would end the rut of twenty years on both sides. These ideas were expressed by this writer and Josée Legault in *Le Devoir* in January 1993.[186] The compromise was evolving but not yet crystallized when the rest of the present article was written.

NOTES

1 This view can be seen not only in mainstream works like Mason Wade, *The French Canadians 1760–1967* (Toronto: Macmillan 1968), but also in rabid nationalist works like those of Abbé Groulx, who credits not so much the English as Providence with sparing Quebec from the social revolutions of America and France.
2 Parkman, one of the great historians of Quebec, writing from the vantage point of Boston, combines admiration for French Canada with an understanding of the weakness and retrograde nature of New France and the economic advantages of the Conquest.
3 See R. Douglas Francis, Richard Jones, and Donald Smith, *Origins: Canadian History to Confederation* (Toronto: Holt Rinehart and Winston 1988), 252–3.
4 See Fitz Stern, ed. *The Varieties of History* (New York: Meridian Books 1960).
5 There is now a current of English-Canadian consciousness which believes that English Canada could flourish as a separate identity without Quebec – a current epitomized by the Reform Party. This author cannot accept this proposition.
6 Henri Bourassa, "The French Language and the Future of Our Race," in Ramsay Cook, ed., *French Canadian Nationalism* (Toronto: Macmillan 1975), 141. The reference to "British institutions" sounds archaic today. This entry was written in 1912.
7 Ibid., 141.
8 At least for the foreseeable future, this threat means extreme economic liberalism, which is anathema to most Canadians.
9 It is interesting to note that in his essay extolling Quebec nationhood, "And Our Distressed Brethren" in Cook, ed., *French Canadian Nationalism*, J.M.R. Villeneuve starts with the notion of a "French and Catholic state" and compares it to Poland, Tyrol, Trentino, Latvia, Croatia, or the Balkans (213). It is not hard to see that such a state could be a less open society than today's Quebec. Nor can many serious Quebeckers wish their land to resemble those listed.
10 This was so despite the definition of "Protestant" as every religion save the Roman Catholic. See *Hirsch v. Protestant School Board*, [1928] AC 200.
11 See Wade, *The French Canadians*, 73.
12 See Official Language Act 1890.
13 *Reference re Sec. 23 of the Manitoba Act*, [1985] 1 SCR 721; *Bilodeau v. A.G. Manitoba*, [1986] 1 SCR 449. See also *Mercure v. The Queen*, [1988] 48 DLR 4th 1 (SCC) for the situation in Saskatchewan.

353 Language and Canadian Public Law

14 It has produced an ugly backlash, shown by the success of the anti-French CORE party, which became the official opposition after the 1991 elections.
15 It is difficult to find judgments on subjects other than pure civil law drafted in French in the early days of the court.
16 Wade, *The French Canadians*, 333.
17 Ibid., 334.
18 J.R. Mallory, *The Structure of Canadian Government* (Toronto: Macmillan 1971), 397.
19 Official Languages Act 1890.
20 Francis, Jones, and Smith, *Origins*.
21 Wade, *The French Canadians*, says of the Ontario School crisis: "Dr. J.W. Edwards of Toronto, a Conservative Orangeman, argued that the French language be driven out of Ontario" (636).
22 Developed by the courts in response to Quebec's attempt to limit the section's operation in Quebec.
23 *A.G. Quebec v. Blaikie et al.*, [1979] 2 SCR 1016.
24 *A.G. Quebec v. Collier* (1990), 66 DLR (4th) 474. See confirming 23 DLR (4th) 339 (Que. CA).
25 *A.G. Quebec v. Blaikie no. 2*, [1981] 1 SCR 312.
26 In *MacDonald v. City of Montreal*, [1986] 1 SCR 460, the Supreme Court wisely held that a traffic ticket in Montreal did not have to be bilingual.
27 Must there be bilingual judges or is an interpreter sufficient? This issue arises more with respect to the right to a trial in French than with section 133, which simply authorizes the use of either language. For instance, nothing forces a Speaker of the House to speak a language other than his own even when dealing with members speaking the other language. However, the new *Official Languages Act* modifies this considerably. See below, notes 40, 41, 42.
28 If the court could not proceed, it would have to adjourn to another date.
29 This does not mean that bilingualism must give way to economy. There is no doubt that bilingualism entails some expense and that most of it (eg, translation of all Supreme Court and Federal Court judgments, simultaneous interpreters at the Supreme Court) is amply justified. What one must avoid is needless or foolish expense which benefits no one or which gives purely formal and unnecessary protection to very doubtful rights. Such expense would provide ammunition for opponents of bilingualism.
30 See *Beaupré Interprétation de la législation bilingue* Montreal, 1980, which illustrates the now-established equality between the two languages in

legislation. However, see note 35 below about the threat to that equality from Quebec rules of interpretation giving priority to French.
31 For example, Quebec during the first century of the Civil Code.
32 See *Beaupré*.
33 Pierre-André Côté, *Interpretations of Legislation in Canada*, 3d ed. (Montreal: Yvon Blais 1992), 274.
34 This author prefers the solutions most consistent with justice and fundamental principles of law.
35 *Gagnon v. Southam Inc.*, [1989] RJQ 1145.
36 Ibid., 1152.
37 Especially *Re Sec. 23 of the Manitoba Act*.
38 An example of the desirable attitude is to be found in *Nima (Oriental Rug Bazaar) v. McInnes*, [1989] 2 WWR 634 (BCSC).
39 This right is found also in the new *Official Languages Act*.
40 *The Queen v. Cross et al.*, [1991] RJQ 1430.
41 *The Queen v. Montour*, [1991] RJQ 1470.
42 However, a judge may render judgment in the language of his choice: *Pilotte v. Corporation de l'Hôpital de Bellechasse*, [1988] RJQ 380 aff'd JE 89–1438. This is a reasonable result because the decision no longer involves statements the accused may wish to challenge, save in appeal, and a translation can be prepared in plenty of time for an appeal. It appears also that the right to a trial in French or in English may be compromised if two accused, of a different language, are tried together. The trial is then bilingual. See *La Reine v. Castillo Garcia*, [1990] RJQ 2312 (Que. SC). This outcome remains highly arguable.
43 Louis Sabourin, dir. *Le système politique du Canada* (Ottawa: Editions de l'Université d'Ottawa 1970), 417.
44 See D. Kwavnick, "French Canadians and the Civil Service of Canada" (1968), *Canadian Public Administration* 97.
45 Mallory, *The Structure of Canadian Government*, 176.
46 *Thorson v. A.G. Canada*, [1975] 1 SCR 138.
47 *Jones v. A.G. New Brunswick*, [1975] 2 SCR 182.
48 *Joyal v. Air Canada*, [1976] CS 1211. Deschênes CJ.
49 *Association des gens de l'air de Québec Inc. v. Lang*, [1977] 2 FC 22 affd [1978] 2 FC 371. The struggle for the use of French in air traffic control mobilized nationalist opinion in Quebec and contributed to the PQ victory in 1976.
50 See, for instance, *Gingras v. The Queen*, [1990] 2 FC 68 (FCTD). The constitutional arguments failed in that case, and only the administrative ones succeeded.
51 This author is among the satisfied group.
52 See articles by Lysianne Gagnon in *La Presse*.
53 See *Association des gens de l'air*.

54 Usually French, but sometimes English in Quebec.
55 *Minister of Home Affairs v. Fisher*, [1979] 3 All ER 21 (PC); *Edwards v. A.G. Canada*, [1930] AC 124 (PC).
56 See *Reference re Sec. 23; Quebec Association of Protestant School Boards v. A.G. Que.*, [1984] 2 SCR 6.
57 Pierre Foucher, "Les Droits linguistiques en matière scolaire", in Michel Bastarache et al., *Les droits linguistiques au Canada* (Montreal: Yvon Blais 1986), 277–8.
58 Tremblay and Bastarache "Les droits linguistiques", in Gérald-A. Beaudoin et Edward Ratushny, *Charte Canadienne des Droits et Libertés*, 2e éd (Montreal: Wilson and Lafleur 1989), 737.
59 *MacDonald v. City of Montreal*.
60 *Bilodeau v. A.G. Manitoba*.
61 *Société des Acadiens de Nouveau Brunswick v. Association of Parents*, [1986] 1 SCR 549.
62 *Société des Acadiens*, 578.
63 Marc Monnin, "Language Rights in the Supreme Court of Canada: A Comment" (1991), 20 *Manitoba Law Journal* 408.
64 Michel Bastarache, "Language Rights in the Supreme Court of Canada: The Perspective of Chief Justice Dickson" ibid., 396–7. This writer is less critical of *McDonald* but considers *Société des Acadiens* unacceptable. Unlike Bastarache, however, he believes that Beetz J's remarks are outdated and are not part of the current law.

For a strong criticism of the "incoherence" of Beetz J's judgment in *Société des Acadiens* see A. Prujiner, "Les enjeux politiques de l'intervention juridique en matière linguistique," in Paul Pupier et José Woehrling, eds., *Langue et Droit/Language and Law* (Montreal: Wilson and Lafleur 1989), 103. Several other authors were cited there to the same effect. This writer hesitates to accept Prujiner's description of language law as having a "nature sociale, collective." There are such elements in it, but individual rights are the more important element.

See also B. De Witte, "Des droits fondamentaux et protection de la diversité linguistique," in Pupier et Woehrling, *Langue et Droit*, 85.
65 *Reference re Minority Language Educational Rights* (1988), 49 DLR (4th) 499 (PEI CA); *Reference re Public Schools Act* (1990), 67 DLR (4th) (Man. CA) affd SCC 1992; *Mahé et al v. The Queen*, [1990] 1 SCR 342.
66 See Tremblay and Bastarache, "Les droits linguistiques," 742–4, and Bastarache, "Language Rights," with this writer's comment.
67 *Reference re Sec. 23*, 732–4.
68 An interesting analogy arises with the infamous article 127 of the Quebec Code of Civil Procedures, which prohibited marriage between persons of different religions. In *Despatie v. Tremblay*, [1921] 1 AC 702,

the Privy Council interpreted this article in an innocuous way. The strength of the ultra-Catholic party was such in Quebec that this decision was ignored until the 1970s.
69 Wade, *The French Canadians*, 11.
70 *Re Education Act* (1984), 10 DLR (4th) 491 (Ont. CA) at 506–17.
71 Superintendent of schools, 1844–76.
72 *Re Education Act*, 509.
73 Ibid., 510–11.
74 Ibid., 511.
75 Ibid., 512ff.
76 Sabourin, *Le système politique*.
77 See sections 16–22 of the Charter. New Brunswick is the only fully bilingual province.
78 See Ontario Statutes. Michael Wood, "Chronique de la législation. Le bilinguisme législatif en Ontario: La situation actuelle (1990), 21 *Revue Générale de Droit* 139.
79 Both the Liberals and especially the NDP, when in opposition, had evoked the possibility of official bilingualism. However, the political pressure proved too strong when these parties took office. Nevertheless, this author persists in the belief that a declaration of bilingualism in Ontario would go a long way in defusing the constitutional crisis.
80 *Reference re Public Schools Act; Reference re School Act (PEI)*, (1988) 69 Nfld 2 PEIR 236 (PEI CA), also in 49 DLR (4th) 499.
81 This happened in Manitoba and Saskatchewan.
82 See section 104 and following.
83 Section 23 reads as follows:
   (1) [Language of instruction.] Citizens of Canada.
   (a) whose first language learned and still understood is that of the English or French linguistique minority population of the province in which they reside, or
   (b) who have received their primary school instruction in Canada in English or French and reside in a province where the language in which they received that instruction is the language of the English or French linguistic minority population of the province,
   have the right to have their children receive primary and secondary school instruction in that language in that province.
   (2) [Continuity of language instruction.]
   Citizens of Canada of whom any child has received or is receiving primary or secondary school instruction in English or French in Canada, have the right to have all their children receive primary and secondary school instruction in the same language.

(3) [Application where numbers warrant.]
The right of citizens of Canada under subsections (1) and (2) to have their children receive primary and secondary school instruction in the language of the English or French linguistic minority population of a province
(a) applies wherever in the province the number of children of citizens who have such a right is sufficient to warrant the provision to them out of public funds of minority language instruction; and
(b) includes, where the number of those children so warrants, the right to have them receive that instruction in minority language educational facilities provided out of public funds.
Note that section 23 (1a) is not in force in Quebec.
84 See Julius Grey, "French Is in No Danger in Quebec," *Policy Options*, September 1991, for this writer's view that once a free and compulsory education system is in place, a language is quite secure unless it faces direct persecution.
85 Foucher, "Les droits linguistiques."
86 *Re Education Act*, 518.
87 *Mahé*, 364. See also *Laurie v. A.G. Nova Scotia*, [1989] 91 NSR (2d) 184 (NS CA).
88 *The Reference Re School Act (PEI)* is particularly clear.
89 *Re Education Act*.
90 *Mahé*, 376–7.
91 Ibid., 365–7.
92 *A.G. Quebec v. Quebec Association of Protestant School Boards*, [1984] 2 SCR 66.
93 For this writer's negative views of any concept of collective rights see Grey, "Equality Rights: An Analysis" (1988), 19, *Revue de Droit de l'Université de Sherbrooke* 183.
94 Mixed couples; persons with English native language but French education and vice versa; persons educated in a fully bilingual way. This last part is presently under advisement in Quebec in *Paparelli v. A.G. Quebec* 500–05–011542–881. It is to be hoped that a generous ruling is made.
95 And it still faces angry, rednecked opposition.
96 It is, of course, true that French-speaking Canadians outside Quebec must know English for a successful career. However, this cannot be seen as either unjust or unduly demanding. Many English Quebeckers who face the fact that knowing French, while less essential, still does not give them full equality because they are not "pure laine" could legitimately feel that their situation is worse.
97 Grey, "Anglos as the Best-Treated Minority Doesn't Add Up," *Gazette*, 3 Oct. 1989.

98 *Gazette*, 21 March 1992.
99 Richler, *Oh Canada! Oh Quebec!* (Toronto: Penguin 1992). It is, of course, necessary to separate satire from strict reporting in the work and to downplay the somewhat exaggerated stress on anti-Semitism. The major points made by Richler are very persuasive.
100 A.G. *Quebec v. Quebec Protestant School Boards*, 81–2.
101 Except for CEGEPs (junior colleges) established in the 1960s for all Quebec, it is difficult to find English institutions created by the majority.
102 Wade, *The French Canadians*.
103 Article 127 of the Civil Code even restricted marriage to a certain extent between persons of different religion.
104 The character of Jean Lévesque in Gabrielle Roy's *Bonheur d'Occasion* is a harbinger of the 1960s and 1970s.
105 Grey, "French Is No Danger," 18.
106 A particularly powerful scene is one describing Jean Lévesque's mixture of envy, hate, and desire for English Westmount.
107 Before 1960, the Quebec public sector was also almost totally French but it was insignificant as a portion of the economy. At that time the English had a clear advantage in the public sector. Now the private sector has been opened to the francophones who were, through the various laws, given an opportunity to succeed. This was viewed as justifiable by past injustice, and no doubt was, but the corresponding opening of the expanding public sector to the minority was not part of the program.
108 In *Quebec Association of Protestant School Boards*, at all levels of the courts, the government exhibits were unusually frank in showing that some of the diminution was desired.
109 See Jean-Pierre Proulx, "L'exode des jeunes anglophones," *Le Devoir*, 22 Jan. 1992. Although Proulx admits the bilingualism of young anglophones, he still cannot see the majority's role in creating the disadvantages under which young anglophones live. See also the *Gazette*'s scathing report on minorities in the employ of Montreal and Montreal's urban community. *Gazette*, 16 Nov. 1991.
110 *Report of the Taskforce on English Education*, 12 Feb. 1992.
111 *La Presse* editorialists have been clear and forceful about this opposition.
112 It is ironic that anyone can seriously view the battered and declining minority as a threat to anyone. Its lack of clout has been evident at all levels of constitutional debate.
113 Unless, like the Charter of Rights and Freedoms of 1982, they originate in Ottawa.
114 Though not nearly as drastic.
115 Where there is universal suffrage – the majority.

116 This is the proper function for judges in this type of conjuncture, and it follows that those who complain about judges frustrating the elected assemblies in such circumstances are wrong.
117 *A.G. Quebec v. La Chaussure Brown's Inc.*, [1988] 2 SCR 712; *Devine v. A.G. Quebec*, [1988] 2 SCR 790.
118 *A.G. Quebec v. La Chaussure Brown's*, [1987] RJQ 80.
119 The minority opinion proposes an attractive result and a quick end to Quebec's language battles, but it could not succeed politically. Courts can protect minorities and frustrate majorities, but they cannot, without risking their prestige and their ability to provide redress, take positions totally out of line with social realities.
120 Contracts of adhesion, public signs.
121 Evidently, the Liberal government was attempting to sell its law as a compromise. The subsequent successes of the Equality Party showed that no one was deceived.
122 Quebec's insistence on input into nominations to the Supreme Court as one of its constitutional objectives is a clear manifestation. See below, note 165, for an example of nationalist criticism of the court.
123 See notes 117 and 118, where the legality of language legislation in principle is established.
124 *A.G. Quebec v. Blaikie* no. 1. The subsequent cases dealing with the limits of section 133 were also constitutional.
125 Federal, not by incorporation, but because of the nature of the activities.
126 *Irwin Toys v. A.G. Quebec*, [1989] 1 SCR 927; *Rocket v. Royal College of Dentists of Ontario*, [1990] 2 SCR 232.
127 *La Chaussure Brown's*, supra, 766–7.
128 The most frequently cited precedent is *R v. Oakes* [1986] 1 SCR 103.
129 *La Chaussure Brown's*, 780.
130 The lower courts had not applied discrimination provisions.
131 See *R v. Hayden* (1983), 3 DLR (Man. CA) (4th) 361; *Andrews v. Law Society of British Columbia*, [1989] 1 SCR 143.
132 *La Chaussure Brown's*, 787.
133 *Action Travail Femmes v. CNR*, [1987] 1 SCR 1114, esp. 1133–4; *Re Winnipeg School Division no. 1 v. Craton*, [1985] 2 SCR 150; *Commission des Droits de la Personne v. Ville de Brossard*, [1988] 2 SCR 279.
134 *Forget v. A.G. Quebec*, [1988] 2 SCR 90.
135 *City of Lachine v. Commission des Droits de la Personne et al.*, [1989] RJQ 17 (Que. CA).
136 See Grey, "Equality Rights," 190–201.
137 [1982], CS 673.
138 The Quebec attorney-general's factum in *Quebec Association of Protestant School Boards* is interesting reading on collective rights. The authorities

cited are often from countries we would not see as models for minority protection (eg, India, African countries, Israel).
139 *Blaikie* no. 1.
140 Subject to a generous reading of the Charter of Rights.
141 *La Chaussure Brown's.*
142 See Richler, *Oh Canada! Oh Quebec!* 255–6: "To return briefly to Ms. Bissonnette: Le Devoir editorial writer seems to be of the opinion that I was writing satire in the *New Yorker.* This is flattering, but honesty compels me to protest that no living satirist could improve on what has been happening here ... whenever I have described Quebec's sign laws at dinner parties, whether in Canada or New York, the other guests have accused me of inventing details. They also have warned me never to put it in a novel – nobody would believe anything so patently absurd."
143 *Bell v. R*, [1979] 2 SCR 212.
144 P.B. Maxwell, *On the Interpretation of Statutes*, 12th ed. (London: Sweet and Maxwell 1969).
145 For instance, it would be patently absurd and unjust to annul a contract between two English-speaking persons because of inobservance of Bill 101.
146 *Campisi v. Procureur Général*, [1977] CS 1067 at 1075.
147 *Campisi v. A.G. Quebec*, [1978] CA 520.
148 These are all cases pleaded together with *Quebec Association of Protestant School Boards*. The court numbers are Wang Woo 500–05–007361–825; Mak 500–05–006960–823; Orman 500–05–007362–823; and Toma 500–05–009572–825.
149 *Mak*, 3–4.
150 *Wang-Woo*, 4. *Orman* and *Toma* allow even one year.
151 *Wang-Woo.*
152 Both Bill 101 and the Charter would be generously interpreted and, in a conflict, the Charter would prevail.
153 See, for instance, *McKenna Inc v. Office de la langue française et al.* reported in Deschênes, *Ainsi Parlèrent les Tribunaux*, vol. 11 (Montreal: Jules Deschênes 1985), 234. *Handy Andy Inc. v. Beaudry*, District Court of Sudbury, in Deschênes, *Ainsi Parlèrent les Tribunaux*, vol. 11, 176.
154 *Lagacé v. Union des Employés*, [1988] RJQ 1791 (Que. CA).
155 [1987] RJQ 569.
156 The principle of narrow derogation is stated (on section 33) in *La Chaussure Brown's*, 744–5.
157 *Office de la Langue Française v. Pâtisserie Suisse Viennoise Inc.* 500–27–008519–904.
158 Though, even if correct, it would only apply to sections 16–22 of the Charter.

159 *La Chaussure Brown's*. The strongest judgment was Deschênes's opinion in *Quebec Protestant School Board*.
160 For instance, in *Alliance for Language Communities in Quebec v. A.G. Quebec*, [1990] RJQ 2622, Reeves J refused to interpret Bill 101 so as to prevent revocation of bilingual status of municipalities. He went on to quash the particular revocation on other grounds. It is submitted that he was possibly incorrect in permitting revocation and that this issue should be brought to the Court of Appeal if Quebec ever attempts it again.
161 *McLeod v. Egan*, [1975] 1 SCR 517.
162 *Sheftel v. Commission d'Appel sur la langue d'enseignement*, [1988] RJQ 341 (Steinberg J).
163 In a subsequent case, *Sheftel v. Commission d'Appel*, [1990] RJQ 164, Viau J refused to annul a second unmotivated, negative decision. It is submitted that this decision is sectarian, hasty, and wrong. In any case, we shall never know because the matter was settled favourably to Appellant before it came up in the Court of Appeal.
164 *Centre de Services Sociaux Ville-Marie v. Dufault et al.*, [1990] RJQ 2893. This decision was based on Article 42 of Bill 101.
165 Luc Huppé, "Martyre de la législation linguistique" (1989) 49 *Revue de Bureau* 866. He concludes on the same page: "On ne voudrait pas être obligé de constater le caractère hautement politique de ces décisions, accentué par la discrétion considérable que confère maintenant à la Cour son rôle de protecteur des droits fondamentaux." It is rather Mc Huppé who appears "hautement politique."
166 The case has passed the "first stage of receivability." The United Nations committee determined in April 1993 that Bill 178 does not meet international standards.
167 The issue was raised in *Bernadelli v. A.G. Quebec* 500–05–017128917, but the case was dropped when the subject passed his test.
168 Roger Magnuson, *A Brief History of Quebec Education: From New France to Parti Québécois* (Montreal: Harvest House 1980), 129–30.
169 What if minorities (eg, Jews or blacks) asked for compulsory communal education of their children? Surely this would not be acceptable to anyone.
170 Former Article 127, Civil Code.
171 Grey, "French Is in No Danger."
172 The articles of Lysianne Gagnon in *La Presse* over the last two years are a striking example of openness and tolerance.
173 It is surprising that Quebec, so concerned about culture and language, has been cutting budgetary provisions for both culture and education. The repression of English appears to be a substitute for social spending to improve education and the quality of French.

174 See Pierre Patenaude, "Les droits linguistiques au Canada: de l'intolérance à l'Utopie," paper delivered to a conference on language rights on the 200th anniversary of the founding of the Law Faculty at the University of New Brunswick, 20 Feb. 1992. On different types of language regimes see Luzius Wildhaber, "Le Droit à l'auto-détermination et les droits des minorités linguistiques en droit international," in Pupier and Woehrling, eds., *Langue et Droit*, 117.
175 Patenaude, "Les droits linguistiques," 5.
176 Save, perhaps, in New Brunswick.
177 One often forgets that use of English for business reasons has nothing to do with daily life in English. Then, even if Quebec businessmen continued to use some English, the minority's decline would not necessarily be countered.
178 For general analysis of the conception of language law see Joseph Turi, "Le droit linguistique et les droits linguistiques" (1990), 31 *Cahiers de Droit* 621. See also Turi, "Introduction au droit linguistique," in Pupier and Woehrling, eds., *Langue et Droit*, 55.
179 As the Supreme Court found presumably in *La Chaussure Brown's*.
180 Abolition of the prohibition will allow us to eliminate the inspectors who have acquired the name "language police" among the anglophones and who have strengthened the impression of absurdity created by the law.
181 *Report of the Taskforce*. This report recommends that anglophones from any country be admitted to English schools. There is no reason why the English minorities should not be able to expand as long as English does not absorb all immigrants.
182 The majority will then have "first crack," but will have to win them with an appropriate welcome if it wants to keep them.
183 This implies abolishing the obscurantist rules prohibiting the teaching of English in the first few years of French elementary school while encouraging the teaching of French in English schools. The government is unwittingly creating a bilingual privileged class of anglophones.
184 One of the symptoms of intolerance in recent years has been an attempt to force children in French schools to speak only French in the school-yard. This attempt has not been turned into general policy, but the raising of such an issue is highly disturbing.
185 It is hard to conceive of any disadvantage. Of course, all areas of Canada will never be functionally bilingual, but knowledge of the other language can still be widespread, much as knowledge of English is widespread in Holland or Denmark.
186 Josée Legault and Julius H. Grey, "La guerre Yes Sir!" *Le Devoir*, 26 Jan. 1993.

PART THREE

Legal History

The Writ of Habeas Corpus in Early Modern England: A View from Within

LOUIS A. KNAFLA

Maxwell Cohen's series of articles in the *Canadian Bar Review* on the history of the writ of habeas corpus in English law from its medieval origins to the Habeas Corpus Act of 1679, drawn from his Master of Laws thesis at Northwestern University in 1936, pointed to several new directions in the historiography of habeas corpus. While previous literature had tried to see the origins and development of the writ of habeas corpus as a means to avoid imprisonment and a procedural tool in the evolution of the concept of liberty, Cohen saw it as a device which served a much wider variety of administrative and judicial purposes, and which contributed not to a concept of liberty, but to a concept of the royal prerogative in extending the king's authority over local and special courts and jurisdictions. The basis of Cohen's thesis was formed from a thorough examination of printed treatises and law reports, and made in the spirit of context: the intellectual influences of Teutonic and Roman-canonical law, and the practical influences of administrative necessity in the high courts of justice.

The writ of habeas corpus has had a history of two functions. One, as a device to secure the appearance before the courts at Westminster of those held in detention elsewhere, transferring them to the custody of a court which had issued the writ in order to challenge their original detention. And, two, as a device of mesne process to secure the appearance of parties and jurors who remained at liberty and were required to appear before the court. While most of the historical research and literature has been on the former use of the writ, Cohen sought to bridge the gap between these two functions and illustrate how an understanding of the latter could lead to a more accurate portrayal of the former.

The purpose of this article will be to re-examine the use of habeas corpus in the manner that Cohen did half a century ago, beginning with the major legal treatises. Believing, like Cohen, that context is instrumental in the examination of any historical-legal subject, I will use as context the local courts and special jurisdictions which Cohen referred to as the victims of habeas corpus at the hands of the central courts in the critical era of the expansion of the writ's usage from the 1540s to the Petition of Right, *Selden's* case and *Eliot's* case of 1629–30. Since most of the scholarly literature on habeas corpus since the 1930s has focused on the Petition of Right, the acts of 1641 and 1679, and later developments in England and America, a reassessment of its use in the local courts during the earlier, critical phase may be appropriate.

COHEN'S TYPOLOGY OF HABEAS CORPUS IN THE CENTRAL COURTS

Cohen's initial study of the history of habeas corpus began with an examination of the origins and development of the writ in the thirteenth century along some of the lines noted by the contemporary treatise ascribed to Henry Bracton.[1] The writ was provided in personal actions as part of mesne process to compel the attendance of defendants where force was not alleged. It was also ostensibly provided in criminal actions "to have the body" of the defendant. Cohen held that both of these processes were done in the name of the monarch in order to exercise royal authority over local and franchise jurisdictions to bring defendants before the royal courts. The writ declined in use in the fourteenth and fifteenth centuries. Then the writ of *capias* (arrest) became more effective in these instances, leading to the development of the writ of *habeas corpus ad respondendum*.

Cohen's second study continued the typology of the writ's development in the early modern period, from the 1500s through the 1620s.[2] He perceived the origins of *habeas corpus cum causa* in the early fourteenth century from *ad respondendum*, adding the cause of arrest and detention to merely having the body. The *causa* writ was also used to release debtors from being imprisoned by local courts, and was restricted by statute in the mid sixteenth century to protect the interests of creditors. It also lost its independence when it became associated with writs of *privilege* to release "privileged" individuals, and writs of *certiorari* to enable appeals to the royal courts. The other late medieval development, in the later fourteenth century, was the *sicut alias habeas corpora* to summon jurors into court. This, like other *sicut alias* writs, was used more frequently in the fifteenth and sixteenth centuries with the rise of jury trials in common-law actions when sheriffs had failed to execute the first writ.

The major development of the sixteenth century was the use of the *causa* writ by parties who wished to escape imprisonment by the conciliar courts. Cohen contended that the *causa* writ had come to operate independently of *privilege* and *certiorari*, and he used a wide array of published law reports and books of entry to demonstrate the contention. By the mid sixteenth century, he stated, *habeas corpus cum causa* (having the body with cause) had become *habeas corpus ad faciendum et recipiendum* (having the body to do and receive as the court shall command). And this branch of the writ developed in the next eighty years in the court of King's Bench with three, but not always operationally distinct, endings: *ad faciendum* (to do), *ad recipiendum* (to receive), and *ad subjiciendum* (to submit or undergo).

Therefore, the typology of uses of habeas corpus as outlined by Cohen had, by the early seventeenth century, come to include the following: without cause to bring parties into court; without cause to bring jurors into court; in association with *certiorari* and *privilege*; to test the validity of detentions by other courts; and – in perhaps the majority of cases – simply to do and receive as the court shall command. Finally, he held that by the 1620s the King's Bench had established the precedent that habeas corpus was a prerogative writ that ran everywhere, including against detentions by individual members of the Privy Council. When the issuance of the writ failed against imprisonment by the monarch in 1627 (*Darnell's* case), Parliament included habeas corpus in the Petition of Right, holding that no one could be imprisoned without bail if no cause was given. Confirmed by *Selden's* case (1629), the writ had also become ensconced in English criminal procedure.

The Habeas Corpus Act of 1641, and later amendments, gave final definition to the use of the writ in criminal proceedings. Such statutes empowered the King's Bench to issue the writ out of term, define acceptable causes for detention, determine if the cause was "just" or "legal," specify the time for process to elapse, and fix damages. Thus the writ had moved from one concerned with "having the body" to concern for commitment without cause. But even here there were defects, uncorrected by amendments (until the statutes of 1803–16), which excluded civil imprisonments, allowed judicial abuse, and failed to proscribe arrests by Parliament or the Privy Council. In the end, "having the body to do and receive as the court shall command" remained the major use of the writ in the other central courts, thereby enforcing the interpretation of the writ as primarily one of administrative process – a procedural device to serve the ordinary course of judicial business.

Several facets of Cohen's general overview have undergone revision with research in the records of the central courts. First, the use of habeas corpus in mesne process to compel the attendance of defendants in personal actions had dropped out of the standard mesne process by the mid 1240s. Second, it never became part of the process in criminal actions, where the forms of initial process on appeals were "attachment by the body" for homicide and "attachment by gage and pledges" for other types of appeal. Third, it was already in frequent use as the second stage of mesne process (after *venire facias*) against defaulting jurors by the mid thirteenth century. Fourth, the beginnings of the use of *capias* also goes back to the same period. Fifth, such process writs could be seen not as exercising royal authority over local and franchise jurisdictions, but as a standard stage in the long process of securing a defendant's appearance in court. Finally, there does not seem to be much evidence that habeas corpus was later used to bring parties into court without cause, or that the writ was a prerogative one running everywhere in all its forms except as *ad subjiciendum*.[3]

THE TYPOLOGY OF HABEAS CORPUS IN EARLY MODERN JURISPRUDENCE

Despite its evolution, jurists of the sixteenth and early seventeenth centuries were not much concerned with the writ of habeas corpus in any of its forms.[4] John Spelman gave it some interest in his report of *Serjeant Browne's* case (1540), suggesting that judges could use it to review the cause of imprisonment.[5] But some of the later commentators on the criminal law, such as William Lambard and Ferdinando Pulton,[6] and common-law jurists, such as Sir John Doddridge and Sir Henry Finch,[7] never referred to, let alone discussed it in their works. One of the first authors of the era to identify habeas corpus was Michael Dalton, who, in writing about justices of the peace committing persons upon informations for indictments, refers to it simply as a process to have the body of the prisoner removed to the King's Bench.[8]

The major change in jurisprudence occurred in the stormy political years of the 1620s, and dated from King Charles's arrests for nonpayment of forced loans which resulted in the *Five Knights* case (or *Darnell's* case) in 1626. The ruling by the King's Bench that imprisonment without trial was part of the law of the land led Sir Edward Coke and Sir John Eliot to launch the "rights of subjects" phrase in the parliamentary debates of 1627, linking imprisonment without indictment to the Magna Carta.[9] While Coke in 1625 had assisted the passage of a statute restricting applications for the writ of habeas corpus, in 1627 he attempted to give it the status of a great writ guaranteeing freedom of arrest without lawful cause. But Coke and Eliot did not have the last word. The resolution in the Petition of Right (1629) was watered down, its legal status cast in doubt; *Eliot's* case (1630) was seen as a victory for both parties – king and subject.[10] Whether a royal official could imprison a subject without specifying the charge, or whether a person so committed could be bailed by a writ of habeas corpus, were two questions still unresolved.[11] But Coke, in writing his *Institutes*, penned for posterity the view that the cause of detention must be shown in all forms of habeas corpus issued by a court official, and that this was *Per Legem Terrae* (by the law of the land).[12] Thus, as the story goes, the era 1627–79 brought the modern writ into English jurisprudence as well as an end to its normative development.

Giles Jacob, writing early in the next century, ignored the problems of the seventeenth-century legislation on habeas corpus and expanded upon Coke's account. He stated that the writ was intended to meet the injustices caused by JPs and gaolers, and could be brought before the lord chancellor or any judge. He also specified forfeitures of £100–£500 for denying the privilege of the writ, and concluded with a bold phrase: "The Subjects of England are entitled to Liberty ... Tis therefore both our Common and Statute Laws, have given us the Benefit of the *Habeas Corpus* Writ."[13] This plank resumed the long-held but emotional link between the Magna Carta and habeas corpus that would be cemented by William Blackstone and enshrined in the American Constitution.[14] The link lasted until it was disestablished in the twentieth century by W.S. McKechnie, Faith Thompson, and J.C. Holt,[15] the new tradition in which Cohen worked.[16] While *habeas corpus ad subjiciendum* was not created by the Magna Carta, its provision for imprisonment by "the law of the land" gave an underpinning to the use of habeas corpus as a remedy for reviewing executive detentions.

The fullest summary of the sixteenth and seventeenth developments after the act of 1679 was contained in Jacob's *Law Dictionary*. While waxing prosaic on the subject of habeas corpus and liberty, he also went to great lengths to discuss all the various forms of the writ, in addition to the intricacies of their processes. The "Great Writ" received four long columns of discussion, but the normative writ was still there for the law profession to learn and use. Its forms included *Habeas Corpora* – a general writ for bringing in jurors who refused to appear on a *venire facias* for the trial of a cause; *Habeas Corpora Juratorum* – a writ serving the same purpose in the Court of Common Pleas; and *Distringas Juratores* – a writ for the same purpose in the King's Bench. In addition, he defined the forms *ad prosequendum, ad faciendum et recipiendum, ad respondendum* and *ad satisfaciendum*.[17]

THE QUESTION OF HABEAS CORPUS IN THE LOCAL COURTS

If we take to heart a thesis that has been propounded by the doyen of modern English legal history – that the common law emanated from local custom[18] – then it may well repay us to look at the local courts in order to see if legal processes which developed there can shed any light on those processes which have been identified by Cohen and other scholars in the central courts. What makes this task difficult is that virtually nothing has been written about habeas corpus in the county and borough quarter sessions or the local courts. Almost all our knowledge of the subject in the sixteenth and seventeenth centuries stems from the central common-law courts.

Since the writ of habeas corpus in its *ad subjiciendum* form was used primarily on the criminal side of the law, one might expect to find it in the criminal assizes for gaol delivery. But such is not the case. In a survey of the ten volumes of criminal indictments for the Home Counties, 1558–1625, not a single usage of the writ can be found.[19] The absence of its existence at the assizes confirms this form of the writ as a specifically King's Bench writ associated with the wide review functions which obtained there. It also gives further substance to Cohen's view that the writ in its general forms was largely administrative in nature – in having the body to do and receive, as the court shall command.

This leaves us with the quarter and borough sessions in the counties: those major local jurisdictions which exercised common-law process in the early modern period, and whose deliberations were considered – at least by the early seventeenth century – as part of the custom of the common law.[20] Unfortunately, the recent popularity of English local legal history has not reached to matters of legal process. In the two major studies of county jurisdictions to date in this period, neither of them discusses, or refers to, habeas corpus.[21] That is not to say, however, that the ground is barren. Many series of quarter and borough-sessions court records have been edited and published. But most of them have consisted of minute or order books, which recorded respectively, minutes of the matters heard before the JPs and their orders in resolving disputes.

The published order books for the counties of Surrey, Warwickshire, and Middlesex, for example, provide a case in point. The Surrey volumes comprise an edition of order books and sessions rolls calendared "in some fullness."[22] And the Warwickshire volumes are a virtual transcription of the originals.[23] In neither record is there any mention of habeas corpus, including specimen forms of all writs. But legal process which occurred during the course of a case, and writs issued outside of sessions, would not be included in these record groups. More relevant, therefore, is the published calendar of sessions indictments and court rolls for the county of Middlesex.

The Middlesex Sessions records contain several references to writs of habeas corpus, but they are usually with, or within the meaning of, *certiorari*: requesting the body of a Middlesex suspect gaoled in another county, without bail, to be delivered for trial in Middlesex.[24] Middlesex, however, has also been one of the great anomalies in English legal history. Its use of habeas corpus for matters concerning jurisdiction may not have been unlike that of the King's Bench use of the writ of *latitat*;[25] a possible example of Cohen's "mixed-use" theory of the writ in the central common-law courts.

Other counties, however, where all classes of legal records for more traditional courts survive, offer better opportunities to search for the history of the writ of habeas corpus. The legal records for the county of Kent are a case in point.[26] Virtually all record groups are extant for the years of 1593–1617. These records include the prominent Sessions Rolls – the plea rolls of the county quarter sessions, of borough courts such as Dover, and of courts of liberties such as Romney Marsh. In addition, the supporting record groups of indictments, jury, hundred, and constables rolls, judicial writs, depositions, sessions papers, and recognizances all survive for the period. An examination of these records for legal process reveals that the writ of habeas corpus was a major legal instrument in the county. The study of its uses enables us not only to develop a typology of the writ at the local level, but also to fill in the meaning and interpretation of habeas corpus that has occupied legal historians and commentators since the seventeenth century.

THE TYPOLOGY OF HABEAS CORPUS IN THE COUNTY OF KENT

A number of the borough and franchise courts in Kent whose records are extant do not reveal any use of the writ of habeas corpus. Some of this omission is due to the fact that records which would contain such references do not survive. But some of it must also stem from the fact that not all courts used the writ for administrative processes when other writs sufficed. The Canterbury Sessions of the Peace of Gaol Delivery, for example, held before the mayor and aldermen of the city, has a complete order book. But the entries are brief, and little process is noted.[27] A similar record exists for the Folkestone Sessions of the Peace, with the same result.[28] The borough of Lydd's Hundred Sessions, however, has a roll of all its judicial business extant,[29] together with a collection of miscellaneous legal documents such as writs, presentments, and depositions[30] and a series of plea books marked "curia."[31] None of these records contain a single example of habeas corpus. The same comment can be made for the records of the town and port of Sandwich, whose year book contains minutes of cases, orders, and dispositions.[32]

In other local and county jurisdictions, habeas corpus is found in the traditional manner that has been discussed above. While it was not found in the minutes and legal papers of Rochester's Court of Quarter Sessions,[33] it was found occasionally in the records of its Court of Port Mote – a court of civil actions held before the mayor and jurats.[34] Like many other local plea rolls, this book format contained one page or folio for each case. The court met once every two weeks, and when a plea was entered at the top of a page, that page would be reserved for further entries in the case. Each entry would begin with the date and contain a summary of the proceeding on that day. A typical case that eventually goes to trial would include the following items. The plaintiff comes by his attorney and pleads, and the defendant requests a copy. The defendant does not come, essoins himself, and requests another day (repeated for several sessions). The defendant then comes by his attorney and narrates into the record of the court. The plaintiff requests another day (and either party may request the same on several occasions). Both parties then come by their attorneys and request a writ of *venire facias* for twelve jurors. The jurors do not come, and thus a habeas corpus. The jurors still do not come, and thus a *distringas*. The parties and jurors come, the verdict is given, costs and damages assessed, and the parties are quit.

A similar pattern existed in Hythe's Court of the Queen, but not in its Sessions of the Peace of Gaol Delivery.[35] This latter court, like the Canterbury Sessions, appeared not to have used habeas corpus. The court that did use it, however, was the Court of the Queen, whose jurisdiction extended – like that of Rochester's Court of Port Mote – to civil actions before the mayor and jurats. Hythe's Court of the Queen had a plea book similar to that of Rochester's Port Mote, and habeas corpus was used in the same limited manner.[36] But judicial procedure in Hythe was more complex than in Rochester, and its cases endured for a longer time before coming to trial. Thus in *Thomas Crud vs Peter Knight* for trespass on the case, which began on 21 September 1601, the defendant delayed for over four months before answering. He essoined three times, requested several pre-emptory days and a copy of the plea, was in the mercy three times, eventually condemned for his default, and appeared on 17 April 1602 to pay the award of £3 10s and costs of 10s 5d.[37] The important point here is that this is the kind of case, settled with or without trial by jury, that would use habeas corpus in some instances and not in others.

More distinct patterns of usage can be found in busier courts, and the County of Kent Quarter Sessions was one of the busiest. The records of the court come down to us in numerous record groups which, unfortunately, were created when the Maidstone Museum split up the files extant for c.1593–1617 and reorganized them into different groups. Comprising minute books, rolls, writs, indictments, recognizances, informations and depositions, orders and correspondence, the two record groups relevant to this study are Sessions and Constables Rolls. The Sessions Rolls were organized like the plea books discussed above, with membranes tied together instead of pages or folios, and spaces left for the notation of process.[38] Since the majority of cases heard at quarter sessions went to trial, the Sessions Rolls contain a large number of trials where the use of habeas corpus would be integral to judicial process.

William Hogben of Elham, husbandman, prosecuted for allowing blood and refuse to spill into the highway on 12 January 1602, put himself upon the country. There was a *venire facias* for the jury to come to the April sessions at Maidstone. They did not come to that sessions, or to the next two. For the first two of these sessions, the sheriff did nothing but ask the jurors to appear next time. For the third one, he asked for sureties for their appearance. They came the fourth time (a year later) and gave their verdict of not guilty.[39] In this case, as in many others like it, when jurors did not come there was no writ of habeas corpus to have their bodies. Instead, they were simply called several times, and finally bound to sureties in order to guarantee their appearance.

Judith and Joan Austin escaped custody by being rescued by their husbands Robert and Benjamin on 9 April 1602. The sheriff could not find them and issued writs of *capias* and *pluries capias* in successive sessions of the court to take their bodies, and returns of *cepit corpus*. Apprehending Benjamin Austin, the others could not be found and writs of *exigent* were issued against them.⁴⁰ In this instance the prisoners and culprits faced a set of writs complementary to habeas corpus, except the distinction between "have" and "take" and a process leading to distraint rather than to outlawry. A similar alternative process was used for persons presented for failing to maintain roads, highways, bridges, banks, and cuts. While a *venire facias* was issued for their appearance, a *distringas* instead of a habeas corpus was issued for their non-appearance – the seizure of their goods instead of their bodies.⁴¹ In other cases, however, writs of habeas corpus were used, but only for the nonappearance of jurors.⁴²

The effectiveness of these writs can be seen in the series of Constables Rolls which survive for the county.⁴³ The rolls comprise entries of writs summoning the jurors of hundreds to make presentments of all felonies, trespasses, and misdemeanors to the county quarter sessions, together with the jury panels and calendars of stewards, bailiffs, and constables. Most interesting are the process notes which have been penned to the entries. For some jury panels the annotation is simply that the jurors did not appear, and thus they were remanded.⁴⁴ For other panels, the jurors were remanded, and then a *distringas* was issued.⁴⁵ Writs of habeas corpus were ordered for a number of jurors who failed to appear, but this was not done in any regular manner.⁴⁶ One possible reason for the failure to apply this process uniformly is that often the sheriff or other official returned that the persons named had no goods or chattels to be attached in their bailiwicks.⁴⁷ This problem also existed for culprits or defendants. A partial series of Jury Lists recording the hundred jurors who were sworn for trials at quarter sessions contains notes of defendants having nothing to attach in their bailiwicks, as well as jurors.⁴⁸ Therefore, it appears that at both the county and the local level, habeas corpus was not used in a significant manner and was one of several different administrative devices to cope with the problem of nonappearance, especially in civil causes.

HABEAS CORPUS AS A LEGAL FICTION

The direction in which the writ of habeas corpus was headed is revealed, perhaps, in the records of four local jurisdictions: the Cinque Port boroughs of Dover, Faversham, and New Romney, and the liberty of Romney Marsh. The Dover Hundred Court had a book of pleas that was similar to those of Rochester, Lydd, and Hythe discussed above.⁴⁹ This court, having the jurisdiction of civil pleas, used writs of criminal and civil process without distinction. The prominent ones used to enforce nonappearance and the satisfaction of judgments were *decem tales* (to complete the jury), *capias* (arrest), *capias corpus* (arrest the body), and habeas corpus (have the body). Like the Hythe Court of the Queen, most cases had a long history, and each of the writs noted above was found in the large majority of cases.

For *George and Christiana Hambrock vs Thomas Browser* in trespass on the case, after the initial pleading and sparring there was a *venire facias* for the jury, a *decem tales*, an adjournment, and then the jury came and gave its verdict. But the defendant did not come to satisfy it, and thus the court issued a *capias corpus* instead of a habeas corpus in order to bring the defendant into court for payment.[50] For *Abraham Marlton vs William Wood* in trespass and assault, after the initial sparing there was a *venire facias*, a *decem tales*, and then for the next five months a mixture of requests for another day for the parties and for *sext tales* and habeas corpus for the jurors, until the parties agreed.[51] Clearly it was questionable whether the jurors were really being called to these bimonthly sessions.

The Romney Marsh Quarter Sessions had a Book of Entries that was also similar to the plea books discussed above.[52] Cases before this court were long-lived too, and writs were used as profusely as they were at Dover. In a number of instances, the parties would spend months sparring over pleas and adjournments, and then there would follow a *venire facias* for the jurors, a habeas corpus to have their bodies, a *distringas* to distrain their goods, a trial, judgment, and either satisfaction or an attachment to secure the same. Thus in *Philip Gibbon vs Gilbert Cutlove* in detinue, the parties pleaded from 18 March to 20 May 1602; had adjournments and preemptory days to 23 September; the plaintiff requested a *venire facias* for a jury on 4 and 15 November, 16 December, and 27 January 1603; the defendant requested a habeas corpus for the jurors on 17 February and a *distringas* for them on 10 March; but the jury did not appear to give a verdict until 12 May. Judgment was given for the plaintiff, but the defendant could not be attached. Thus a writ of *fieri facias* was sent to the sheriff to attach the defendant's pledges.[53] The Gibbon case was not unusual for the Romney Marsh Court of Quarter Sessions.[54] Of those parties who went to trial, 54 per cent had a habeas corpus, and 39 per cent a *distringas*. But as with the situation in Hythe, there is some doubt that writs such as habeas corpus and *distringas* were actually being issued.

The situation in the borough of New Romney was similar. New Romney had a Court of Quarter Sessions, but only a book of orders and minutes survives which does not contain any entries of pleas or court process.[55] A precedent book of "Articles of Inquiry for Every

Quarter Sessions" exists for the same period, but it is presented in a textbook manner that suggests it is derivative of the published literature.[56] Of more interest is the Order and Decree Book of the mayor and jurats of the borough's Assembly Court.[57] This 'book' is organized differently from other local plea books. The proceedings before each session are noted together, with one or two lines per case. Thus to follow a case from beginning to end requires a search of the plaintiff's and defendant's surnames in order to establish the entries for a particular case from the first to last date.

Cases in New Romney's Assembly Court tend to have a different profile from those examined in other jurisdictions. Most cases are short-lived, and process is sparse. But on a few occasions, when a case was not settled or abandoned and put to trial, the cause was a long one. For example, *Richard Jorden vs John Geere* in a plea of trespass on the case began on 28 June 1602. The parties appeared by their attorneys, the plaintiff essoined, then pleaded, and was in mercy for a further three sessions. The parties' attorneys came for a further three sessions to speak, and then the defendant put himself upon the country. A *venire facias* was requested for the jurors, but they did not come and were given another day. They still did not come, and a habeas corpus was issued for their bodies, followed by giving them another day. Then on 20 December 1602 Robert Symons, serjeant-at-mace, said that the writ of habeas corpus would not come to his hands quickly and thus the jurors were given another day. There was another habeas corpus on 10 January 1603, followed by four more. Finally, the parties came on 14 March and the defendant paid the plaintiff's award of 30 shillings plus court costs.[58] It is doubtful in these circumstances if the jurors were ever summoned to appear. Since the cost of a single writ of habeas corpus in most borough courts was 2s 4d, which was not much more than the values at issue in many of these cases, one can also doubt if the costs of the alleged issuances of the writs were ever presented for collection. Clearly, court process was suspect.

THE ROLE OF LEGAL PROCESS IN FAVERSHAM

The Cinque Port town of Faversham had three major courts. The Sessions of the Peace, with largely criminal jurisdiction, had numerous grand and trial juries. Juries were summoned by *venire facias*, yet there is not a single reference to a habeas corpus or *distringas* for jurors who did not appear. Parties, as well as jurors, were simply bound over to sureties for their appearance and fined if they defaulted.⁵⁹ The court for withernams, which were suits filed by parties from other Cinque Port towns, summoned many juries for civil actions and for the determination of damages. These cases were quickly disposed of. Yet when jurors did not come, the process issued for their appearance varied from *cepi corpus* to habeas corpus.⁶⁰ On one occasion, both processes were used.⁶¹ But perhaps the most intriguing source for the study of habeas corpus and other related matters of legal process at the turn of the century is the plea book of the town's Court of Port Mote, held before the mayor and jurats at the Guildhall.⁶² This source, it is suggested, contains the answer to the puzzle of habeas corpus and other similar writs which has been posed in this study.

Two occasional plea book entries for cases which could have been recorded before any local court were *William Harrys vs Elizabeth Braynes* for trespass on the case and *William Keeler vs Mary Cowland*, administrators for Edward Payne, for the same. In the Harrys case, after the plaintiff pleaded by his attorney, either the defendant requested another day or the matter was adjourned for nine more sessions, when the entries end.⁶³ In the Keeler case, the same course lasted for sixteen sessions, with both parties requesting additional days. In this case, however, the defendant, over the last seven sessions, requested another day to decide on a demurrer.⁶⁴ Similar patterns existed for other cases, involving fourteen to twenty sessions before the cause was actually brought to an end with a jury trial and judgment.⁶⁵ There were also cases which endured for long periods of time in the manner described above, but which went to trial after some difficulty in obtaining a jury. In these cases, the *venire facias* for the jurors did not meet success, and there were one or two such writs followed by one or more habeas corpus before the jury finally came and gave its verdict.⁶⁶

Patterns such as these, however, did not cover the majority of case entries in the plea book. *George Awnsell vs Edward Lewse* in trespass, for example, had a *venire facias* for twelve jurors issued for seven consecutive sessions before the jurors came and gave their verdict.⁶⁷ And *Jarman Waighte vs Edward Wylson* in trespass on the case had a *venire facias* issued for nine consecutive sessions, with no further entries.⁶⁸ Why was there no habeas corpus or *distringas* issued? In some cases further process was issued: *John Coles vs Thomas Studd*, three writs to have the bodies of the jurors;⁶⁹ *Thomas Saunders vs George Munge*, five writs for the same;⁷⁰ and *John Hallett vs Hugh Whitlocke*, eight writs.⁷¹ Obviously, a strict interpretation of these entries would suggest that the officials were having great difficulty in securing the appearance of jurors even with writs of habeas corpus. Other cases, however, question such an interpretation. In *John Powell vs Elizabeth Philpott*, such writs were allegedly issued for twelve consecutive sessions;[72] in *Edward Amyars vs Simon Trytton*, for thirteen consecutive sessions;[73] and in *Sir Michael Sandes vs Richard Custen*, for twenty-six consecutive sessions.[74] All the causes were in trespass on the case.

The length of the *Sandes* case, involving weekly to bimonthly sessions for more than a year, was not exceptional in the Faversham Port Mote. Neither was the repetition of individual procedural devices. *Reginald Abraham vs Stephen Harper*, in trespass on the case, recorded eighteen preemptory or additional days on the behalf of the defendant, followed by a *venire facias*, a habeas corpus, and three *distringas*, without going to trial.[75] *John Wilye vs John Deaken*, in a plea of debt, recorded fifteen preemptory or additional days on behalf of the defendant, two *venire facias* for jurors, three habeas corpus for their bodies, and a trial and verdict.[76] And *George Mountioye vs Thomas Whyte*, in trespass on the case, recorded three preemptory days on the behalf of the defendant, four writs of *venire facias* for jurors, and eighteen writs of habeas corpus for their bodies.[77] On the last recorded entry, the plaintiff did not prosecute and thus the cause was discontinued.

CONCLUSION

Cohen's thesis that the writ of habeas corpus had become a largely administrative writ in the years from the 1550s to the 1620s is certainly borne out by an examination of the records of the local courts in Kent. The typology he has set out could be concluded as follows. First, the local court records reveal that habeas corpus was used only occasionally in criminal actions to have the body, had been relegated to a secondary role behind that of *capias*, and had all but disappeared with regards to questions of jurisdiction which were now handled through *certiorari*. Second, with regard to civil actions, the records confirm that the main purpose of habeas corpus was to bring parties, who were largely defendants, and juries into court "to do and receive as the court shall command." Third, the records reflect that the writ had acquired in more general terms a "mixed-use" typology that approximated its role in the central courts. This might have been occasioned in part by the central courts reducing their supervision of lower courts to a more narrow legal basis.[78]

There were also, however, some important changes which occurred in the legal process of the local courts that provide a different perspective on the meaning of the writ in the local jurisdictions. It is apparent, for example, that the writ was developing similar functions in both civil and criminal litigation, and that it was dropping the various operational endings (as *ad respondendum*) which had characterized its earlier history. For example, with regard to the use of habeas corpus for securing the bodies of jurors, the *ad faciendum juratam illam* clause is seldom noted.[79] In addition, it is suggested that the writ was being used in the same manner as a *venire facias* to summon jurors, and that both of these writs were taking on the role of a legal fiction to encourage parties to settle out of court and not take their cause to trial.

There are a few additional fragments of evidence to demonstrate this thesis. In a few lines in the plea book of the Faversham Court of Port Mote, the Latin reads not a habeas corpus for the jurors, but "the jurors were not sent, thus a habeas corpus."[80] When a phrase such as this is repeated in entries for consecutive court sessions, the interpretation of the entry is that the jurors were never sent for, and thus the writ was not issued. The cost alone of such multiple issuances would have been prohibitive to the parties. Thus one could conjecture that the writ was being used as a threat to encourage parties to settle their differences without calling a jury. In this sense the writ had become an administrative device *par excellence*.

The use of *venire facias*, habeas corpus, and *certiorari* in these local courts to further the process of dispute resolution also has some statutory support. Parliament, in the year of 1601, enacted a statute that precluded the central courts from using habeas corpus to remove any suit depending in a local court where a jury had been summoned.[81] The statute acknowledged that defendants were using the writ to get juries sworn and plaintiffs to provide testimony, witnesses, and proof before exercising the benefit of the writ. This may well be an instance where the two functions of the writ touched. It also leads to the suggestion that, in the debates on the Petition of Right in 1628, when some MPs from the Kent and Cinque Port boroughs spoke in defence of the writ of habeas corpus, they intended the function not only of the "Great Writ", but also of the normative one that had become part of legal process as well as of legal fiction in the commercial communities of the county.

The local court records which have been discussed above confirm a number of other suggestions that can be pieced together from various scholars in recent years concerning the history of trial by jury, and by scholars whose views have been – both generally and specifically – in dispute among themselves. These suggestions are as follows: that jury service was not popular in the period and the number of qualified jurors was in short supply;[82] that the jury's discretionary influence in making law was passing as judges assumed more of their shared division of power;[83] that jury services were becoming increasingly independent at the local level;[84] and that the definition of the work of the jury was being set by the local community.[85] Thus one could argue that the patterns in the role of the jury in criminal actions may not be as contradictory as they have been portrayed, and that the study of legal process and the jury in civil litigation can shed light on the working both of the institution of the jury and of litigation as a whole.

NOTES

I wish to thank Dr Paul Brand and Janice Erion for their criticisms and suggestions on the first draft of the article; and the participants of the North American Conference on British Studies at Boulder, Colorado, 10 October, 1992 – particularly John Kenyon, Lee Beier, and Marjorie McIntosh – where a second draft was read. All errors and misunderstandings remain my own responsibility.

1 Maxwell Cohen, "Habeas Corpus Cum Causa – The Emergence of the Modern Writ: I" (1940), 18 *Canadian Bar Review* 10–42.
2 Maxwell Cohen, "Habeas Corpus Cum Causa – The Emergence of the Modern Writ: II" (1940), 18 *Canadian Bar Review* 172–99, here and in the paragraph below.
3 Particularly Donald Sutherland, "Mesne Process upon Personal Actions in the Early Common Law" (1966), 82 *Law Quarterly Review* 482–96; Robert Walker, *The Constitutional and Legal Development of Habeas Corpus* (Norman: Oklahoma University Press 1960); William Duker, "The English Origins of the Writ of Habeas Corpus: A Peculiar Path to Fame," (1978), 53 *New York University Law Review* 983–1054; and Paul Brand, *The Origins of the English Law Profession* (Oxford: Clarendon Press 1992).
4 By legal writers I am excluding the law reports, books of entries, and registers of writs which have been explored by Cohen and others.
5 *The Reports of Sir John Selden*, edited by J.H. Baker (London: Selden Society 1977), vol. 93, 183–4.
6 William Lambard, *Eirenarcha: or the Office of the Justices of the Peace* (London 1581), and *Archion: or a Commentary upon the High Courts of Justice in England* (London 1635); and Ferdinando Pulton, *De Pace Regis et Regni* (London 1609).
7 Sir John Doddridge, *The English Lawyer* (London 1631), and Sir Henry Finch, *Law, or a Discourse Thereof* (London 1613).
8 Michael Dalton, *The Covntrey Ivstice* (London 1618), 284–5.

9 See Daniel John Meador, *Habeas Corpus and Magna Carta* (Charlottesville: University of Virginia Press 1966); and Stephen D. White, *Sir Edward Coke and 'The Grievances of the Commonwealth,' 1621–1628* (Chapel Hill: North Carolina University Press 1979), 65–7, 193, 223, 235–56, 240–1.
10 Harold Hulme, *The Life of Sir John Eliot 1592–1632* (London: George Allen and Unwin 1957), 322–38.
11 Paul Christianson, "John Selden, The Five Knights Case, and Discretionary Imprisonment in Early Stuart England" (1985), 6 *Criminal Justice History* 65–88; and Linda S. Popofsky, "Habeas Corpus and 'Liberty of the Subject': Legal Arguments for the Petition of Right in the Parliament of 1628" (1979), 41 *Historian* 257–75.
12 Sir Edward Coke, *Second Part of the Institutes of the Lawes of England* (London 1642), 50–5.
13 Giles Jacob, *The Student's Companion: or, the Reason of the Laws of England* (London 1725), 75–6.
14 The research of Robert S. Walker has demonstrated that the link in fact never existed; that "to have the body" predated the Magna Carta, and is found in the records of the courts at Westminster in the late twelfth century: *The Constitutional and Legal Development of Habeas Corpus as the Writ of Liberty* (Norman: Oaklahoma University Press 1960), 7–16.
15 W.S. McKechnie, *Magna Carta: A Commentary on the Great Charter of King John* (Glasgow: University Press 1914); Faith Thompson, *Magna Carta: Its Role in the Making of the English Constitution, 1300–1629* (Minneapolis: University of Minnesota Press 1948); and J.C. Holt, *Magna Carta* (Cambridge: University Press 1965).
16 For the historiography, there are three useful essays which were published as pamphlets around the 750th anniversary of Magna Carta: Maurice Ashley, *Magna Carta in the Seventeenth Century* (Charlottesville: University of Virginia Press 1965); Daniel John Meador, *Habeas Corpus and Magna Carta* (Charlottesville: University of Virginia Press 1966); and Sir Herbert Butterfield, *Magna Carta in the Historiography of the Sixteenth and Seventeenth Centuries* (Reading: University Press 1969).
17 Giles Jacob, *Law Dictionary* (London 1729), which underwent ten editions in the next forty-five years.
18 S.F.C. Milsom, *Historical Foundations of the Common Law* (London: Buttersworth 1969).
19 *Calendar of Assize Records*, edited by J.S. Cockburn (London: Her Majesty's Stationery Office 1975–90): individual volumes for each of the Home Counties of Essex, Hertfordshire, Kent, Surrey, and Sussex in each of the reigns of Elizabeth I (1558–1603) and James I (1603–25).
20 Louis A. Knafla, "Common Law and Custom in Tudor England: or, 'The Best State of a Commonwealth,'" in *Law, Literature, and the Settlement of*

Regimes, edited by Gordon J. Schochet (Washington, DC: Folger Shakespeare Library 1990), 171–86.
21 J.A. Sharpe, *Crime in Seventeenth-Century England* (Cambridge: University Press 1983); and Cynthia B. Herrup, *The Common Peace: Participation and the Criminal Law in Seventeenth-Century England* (Cambridge: University Press 1987).
22 *Surrey Quarter Sessions Records*, edited by Dorothy L. Powell and Hilary Jenkinson; vol. I (*1659–1661*), vol. II (*1661–1663*), and vol. III (*1663–1666*) (Surrey Record Society, vols. 35, 36, 39 for 1934, 1935, 1938).
23 *Warwick County Records*, edited by S.C. Ratcliff and H.C. Johnson; vol. I (*1625–1637*), and vol. II (*1637–1650*) (Warwick 1935–6).
24 For example, *County of Middlesex: Calendar to the Sessions Records*, edited by William le Hardy, vol. I (*1612–14*) (London 1935), 56. Thomas Edes, committed by the sheriff of Kent, was sought to be removed by habeas corpus on 25 March 1613.
25 Marjorie Blatcher, *The Court of King's Bench 1450–1550* (London: Athlone Press 1978).
26 L. Knafla, "'Sin of all sorts swarmeth': Criminal Litigation in an English County in the Early Seventeenth Century," in *Law, Litigants and the Legal Profession*," edited by E.W. Ives and A.H. Manchester (London: Royal Historical Society 1983), 50–67.
27 Canterbury Cathedral Library, JQ 401/7, volume for 1601–3.
28 Folkestone Public Library and Museum, Fo/AM 1/1, volume for 1604–35.
29 Lydd Town Hall, Lydd JQ s/1, volume for 1601–4.
30 Ibid., Lydd JQ b/1, papers for 1566–1604.
31 Ibid., Lydd JB 6 (volume for 1584–90), and JQ s/2 (volume for 1605–10).
32 CKS (Centre for Kent Studies, alias Kent County Archives), Sa/AC 6.
33 Rochester Town Hall, JQb 1, book and papers for 1606–8.
34 Ibid., JBS 4/A, plea roll book for 1595–1602.
35 Hythe Town Hall, MS 30, volume for 1573–4. A similar situation was found in the town's Court of Guildhall: Hythe MS 32, volume for 1610–24.
36 Hythe Town Hall, MS 31, volume for 1571–1603.
37 Ibid., fol. 172r. A similar case with a habeas corpus for the jurors was *Thomas Amye vs Richard Topcliff*, fol. 173r.
38 For example, CKS, Q/SR 2–4, rolls for 1600–4.
39 Q/SR 3, mem. 2d.
40 Ibid., mem. 4.
41 Ibid., mem. 10d.
42 Ibid., mem. 6d, 13.

43 CKS, QM/SRO 24–28, for 1601–3.
44 For example, QM/SRO 24(2,4); QM/SRO 27 (18,20); QM/SRO 28(2,6).
45 QM/SRO 24(3).
46 QM/SRO 25(1,6); QM/SRO 26(5); QM/SRO 27(17,21); QM/SRO 27(5).
47 QM/SRO 25(14,20).
48 CKS, QM/SP 12, for example, for 1601–4.
49 CKS, QM/Md 110.
50 Ibid., fol. 241r.
51 Ibid., fol. 242r, 25 June–6 Dec. 1602.
52 CKS, RM/JR 2, volume for 1600–5.
53 Ibid., fol. 121r.
54 For example, Loddell vs Swain at fol. 123v, and Stafford vs Alcock at fol. 135r, and Symon vs Lull at fol. 140r.
55 CKS, NR/Z Paa 4/9, "The Session for ye peace" for 1577–1625.
56 CKS, NR/JQZ.
57 CKS, NR/AC 1–2, volumes for 1590–1605.
58 Ibid., AC 1, fols 196v-203r; and AC 2, fols 2r-11v.
59 CKS, Fa/JQs 40–42, volumes for 1598–1603.
60 CKS, Fa/JBW 49, volume for 1600–2.
61 Ibid., mem. 20: Barth Ellwyn for trespass upon the case, 10 Aug. 1601.
62 CKS, Fa/JBS 28, volume for 1601–3.
63 Fa/JBS 28, fol. 58 (2 Oct. 1601–1 June 1602).
64 Fa/JBS 28, fol. 115v (25 Nov. 1602–8 Aug. 1603).
65 Fa/JBS 28, fols 27r (*Robert Collwell vs John Allen*), 27v (*William Beale vs Richard Pease*), and 109v (*William Tomlyn vs George Greenstreet*), all trespass on the case.
66 Fa/JBS 28, fols 8v (*Thomas Tasssell vs Edward Wylson*), 82v (*John Taylor vs Stephen Goodwin*), 94v (*John Swayton vs William Dennys*), all in trespass on the case, and 112r (*John Bissock vs Ann and Philip Peterson* in debt).
67 Fa/JBS 28, fol. 62r (30 Oct. 1601–10 Aug. 1602).
68 Ibid., fol. 9r (19 Dec. 1601–24 July 1602).
69 Ibid., fol. 86v (11 April–1 Sept. 1602).
70 Ibid., fol. 64r (30 Oct. 1601–29 March 1602).
71 Ibid., fol. 84v (20 March–10 Sept. 1602).
72 Ibid., fol. 36v (7 July 1601–12 Feb. 1602).
73 Ibid., fol. 63r (12 Jan.–10 Aug. 1602).
74 Ibid., fol. 45r (14 Aug. 1601–7 Sept. 1602). The prevalence of trespass cases for such process was noted for the earlier period by Sutherland, "Mesne Process," 486–8.
75 Fa/JBS 28, fol. 40r (14 July 1601–23 July 1602).
76 Ibid., fol. 12v (20 Jan.–4 Dec. 1601).

77 Ibid., fol. 25v (20 March 1601–29 March 1602).
78 M.K. McIntosh, "Central Court Supervision of the Ancient Demesne Manor Court of Havering: 1200–1625," in *Law, Litigants and the Legal Profession*, ed. Ives and Manchester, 87–93.
79 *Early Registers of Writs*, edited by Elsa de Haas and G.D.G. Hall (London: Selden Society 1970), vol. 87, 312–34, where the forms of the judicial writs are available.
80 CKS, Fa/JBS 28, fol. 45r, *Sir Michael Sandes vs Richard Custen*.
81 43 Elizabeth I (1601), c. 5.
82 J.S. Cockburn, "Twelve Silly Men? The Trial Jury at Assizes, 1650–1670," in J.S. Cockburn and T.A. Green, eds., *Twelve Good Men and True: The Criminal Trial Jury in England, 1200–1800* (Princeton: University Press 1988), 158–63.
83 Thomas Andrew Green, *Verdict According to Conscience: Perspectives on the English Criminal Trial Jury, 1200–1800* (Chicago: University Press, 1985), 148–50.
84 P.G. Lawson, "Lawless Juries? The Composition and Behaviour of Hertfordshire Juries, 1573–1624," in Green and Cockburn, eds. *Twelve Good Men and True*, 133–7.
85 Cynthia Herrup, "Law and Morality in Seventeenth-Century England" (1985), 106 *Past and Present* 102–23.

Habeas Corpus and the Case of the Man Who Escaped from Devil's Island

ROBERT J. SHARPE

Among Maxwell Cohen's first scholarly work is a series of three articles on the history of habeas corpus.[1] Together, they made up his Master of Laws thesis at Northwestern University. Remarkably well researched and clearly written, these articles remain a leading source on the history of the great writ. I feel a close affinity to this early product of Cohen's insightful scholarship, as my own graduate work was also devoted to a study of habeas corpus. I relied heavily on Cohen's articles in my introductory historical chapter, and, more generally, I drew inspiration from the careful and dedicated scholarship his work demonstrated.

My contribution to this book of essays in Maxwell Cohen's honour follows a principal theme of his historical account of the origins of habeas corpus. After completing his exhaustive review of the available early sources on habeas corpus, Cohen concluded: "the writ in the modern form, upon which rests its fame and utility, was the product of a purely procedural device employed by the courts in the ordinary course of their business, and that chance and a host of social and political considerations, combined with its singular adaptability to a variety of purposes, rather than any special principle or deliberate creation, made it the eminently useful weapon it became in English law."[2] While my subject is later in time and my research is based on archival and other nontraditional legal sources, the underlying thesis is similar. The case of the man who escaped from Devil's Island is merely a more recent example of the phenomenon Cohen described.

THE GUERIN CASE

The decision of the English King's Bench Division in 1907[3] to grant habeas corpus in favour of Eddie Guerin, a notorious criminal widely known as the man who escaped from Devil's Island, attracted attention at the time in the popular press but has been largely ignored by lawyers. The judgment of the court was brief and the issue decided appeared to be entirely factual. Yet the case was a remarkable one from a legal perspective and merits further attention. It deals with a difficult and crucially important legal point – the burden of proof and the resolution of issues of disputed fact on habeas corpus – in a most unusual and intriguing way.

Almost twenty years before, in 1888, Guerin had been committed for extradition at the request of the French government. He lost a habeas corpus application challenging the legality of his detention, was returned to France, convicted, and sentenced to a lengthy term. Shortly after his release, he was involved in a daring robbery and, this time, sentenced by a French court to penal servitude for life at Devil's Island. He made a dramatic escape from the notorious French penal colony and ultimately returned to England, only to face in 1907 further extradition proceedings. Once again he was committed for extradition, and once again he brought a habeas corpus application. This time he succeeded. In 1888 and in 1907 precisely the same issue arose on habeas corpus, and in both cases the courts demonstrated remarkable procedural flexibility and willingness to engage in a highly complex factual inquiry. However, the courts reached completely opposite and contradictory results, ostensibly because of differing views on the burden of proof. The judge who decided the 1907 case, Lord Alverstone, Lord Chief Justice of England, was no stranger to Guerin. In 1888 he had been the attorney-general and had successfully argued against Guerin precisely the same point he decided nearly twenty years later in the prisoner's favour.

This article, based on archival and contemporary sources, revisits the Guerin case to see what light it sheds on the law and practice of habeas corpus. It also considers why the courts reached such different conclusions on the same issue.

THE 1888 PROCEEDINGS

It may be useful to begin with a word about Guerin himself. He was born in 1860, but the place of his birth and the precise details of his upbringing are matters of considerable doubt. By adolescence, however, he had embarked on a life of crime, and at the age of twenty-eight, at the time of his first habeas corpus case, he had a long record of convictions in England and the United States. Guerin's memoirs, published in 1928 under the title *The Autobiography of a Crook* in England and Canada and *I Was a Bandit* in the United States, record his own highly romantic version of criminal exploits in America, England, and France, and give vivid descriptions of life in the penal institutions of all three countries.[4]

When arrested in 1888 on an extradition warrant issued at the request of France on a charge of larceny from a Bank in Lyons, Guerin was advised that the extradition treaty between the United Kingdom and France precluded the surrender of "native born or naturalized subjects."[5] Guerin claimed status as a British subject and decided to resist extradition on that ground, as well as challenging the sufficiency of the evidence against him. Charles F. Gill, then a rising young barrister,[6] was retained. He fought the extradition proceedings before the Bow Street magistrate tenaciously but unsuccessfully. After nine days of evidence, four of which were devoted to Guerin's claim to status as a British subject, an order for his extradition was made.

Gill immediately launched a habeas corpus application. First, he contended that the magistrate who had committed Guerin had acted without jurisdiction since he had not heard all the evidence, the hearing having been started by another magistrate. Second, Gill argued that the magistrate had erred in failing to find that Guerin was a British subject and therefore not liable to extradition under the treaty between England and France. On Gill's advice, Guerin retained Harry Poland, a barrister well known in the criminal courts for his forceful conduct of prosecution briefs.[7] Gill appeared as junior counsel.

The matter first came before Pollock B and Manisty J of the Queen's Bench Division on 6 November 1888 as an *ex parte* application for habeas corpus.[8] The judges were intrigued by the first point and quickly held that it warranted a full hearing. The court made an order in the form of a *rule nisi* requiring that the appropriate authorities be served and called upon to justify the legality of the proceedings that led to Guerin's extradition.

The issue of Guerin's nationality evoked less interest. Poland conceded that as some evidence had been called before the magistrate to show that Guerin had been born in the United States, "it must be taken, of course, that the Magistrate was satisfied of that,"[9] but he contended that although Guerin had been born in the United States, his parents were Irish and he could claim status as a British subject on that account. That point had not been taken before the magistrate, and the court agreed that a *rule nisi* should be given to permit it to be argued as well.[10]

The matter was argued as a contested motion a week later in the Queen's Bench Division before Wills and Grantham JJ.[11] It was apparent that the English government took the case seriously and was anxious to be rid of Guerin. The attorney-general, Sir Richard E. Webster, QC, led. Webster, a highly successful barrister perhaps known more for hard work than brilliance, served as attorney-general in the years 1885–6, 1886–92, and 1895–1900.[12] With Webster was R.S. Wright, junior Treasury counsel, a fine lawyer who would be appointed a high court judge two years later.[13] The Bank of France briefed its own counsel, but available accounts of the proceedings indicate that Webster and Wright carried the argument. Guerin was represented by Poland and Gill.

At first the argument focused on whether the magistrate, not having heard all the evidence, had jurisdiction to commit, but it became apparent that the evidence he had heard himself was sufficient to warrant the committal.[14] Poland next argued that it was open to Guerin to challenge the magistrate's finding on nationality since the fact was crucial to the magistrate's jurisdiction: if Guerin was a British subject, there was no lawful authority to extradite him. The judgment of Wills J accepting this argument is one of the clearest statements of the jurisdictional fact doctrine on habeas corpus: "where a matter of fact which is cardinal to the existence of a magistrate's jurisdiction is collateral to the subject of inquiry, the decision of the magistrate is not final, and the court has the right to inquire into the sufficiency of the evidence upon which the magistrate acted, as being a matter on which his jurisdiction to hear the case at all is based."[15]

There was conflicting evidence, however, and disputed issues of fact are not readily dealt with on habeas corpus. Indeed, the law of habeas corpus is often said to be riddled with technical rules which preclude entertaining disputed questions of fact. I have argued elsewhere that despite the arcane "rule against controverting the return," complex factual issues can be dealt with on habeas corpus,[16] and the Guerin case provides a good example. Wills asked whether the best course would be to direct that the issue of nationality be tried separately, if necessary, before a jury. R.S. Wright agreed.[17] Wills had no doubt about the court's power: "As there are contradictory affidavits it will be necessary, if the point is to be considered, for the court to order an issue to be tried to determine whether the prisoner is entitled to the status of a native born subject or not. As to our jurisdiction to do this, I have no doubt that it is the only means at the disposal of this court by which it can inform itself upon such a matter of fact."[18] The trial of the issue would take place in two months and the verdict of the jury would be reported back to the Divisional Court so that the habeas corpus application could be determined in the light of the factual findings.[19] Almost as an aside, Wills stated: "The onus lies on any person claiming exemption to prove that he comes within the exemption."[20] No further thought was given to the question of onus of proof – certainly Poland does not seem to have argued the point.

On the same day that the order was made, 16 November 1888, the French ambassador wrote to the foreign secretary[21] explaining that the French government considered Guerin's extradition to be a particularly important matter since it involved the security of the Bank of France. The Treasury solicitor observed that as the attorney-general thought important points of law might arise, the services of the law officers would be made available.[22] The Treasury insisted, however, that the preparation of the case be undertaken by and at the expense of the Bank of France. The French authorities were not all happy with this state of affairs. The French ambassador pleaded with the English to assume more responsibility.[23] The cost of the proceedings was going to be considerable since it seemed clear that witnesses as to Guerin's origins would have to be brought from the United States. The French were also concerned about fighting the case in front of a jury without the Crown appearing as a principal protagonist. Guerin's counsel, they feared, would exploit this situation to their disadvantage. The bank was being put in an awkward position, having, as the ambassador put it, "l'obligation de supporter à elle seule tout le poids moral et pécuniaire" of the case. The bank was not fighting this matter in the expectation of any gain, and had already incurred enormous expense: "elle lutte actuellement pour la sauvegarde d'intérêts d'un ordre général et de principes de haute morale publique, qu'il importe à tous les Gouvernements de voir respecter."[24] The Home Office and Treasury remained firm in the view that while law officers would be provided to argue the case, the bank should bear full responsibility for its preparation. The court itself had styled the case as an issue between the bank and Guerin.

Poland's opening statement at the trial before Huddleston B and a jury made it clear that Guerin's case would rest on the claim he had been born in England.[25] Guerin contended that his parents had come to England in 1859 from America to live with the Walker family at 29 Robert Street, Hoxton, and that he was born there in 1860. Poland called as witnesses members of the Walker family, but decided not to call Guerin as a witness. Poland was concerned that Guerin's long criminal record would be revealed and, perhaps more important, that if he called Guerin as a witness, he would expose him to cross-examination on the issue of his involvement in the robbery in France. He had already called direct evidence which, he thought, made out a *prima facie* case on the nationality point. Poland accordingly rested his case.

The solicitor-general, Sir Edward G. Clarke, QC, "one of the most eminent, if not the most eminent, of the leaders of the Common Law bar"[26] and author of the leading text on extradition law,[27] joined the attorney-general to argue the case against Guerin. Clarke lost no time in commenting on Guerin's failure to testify. The main witness called against the prisoner was Michael M'Mahon, a Chicago policeman who had known the Guerin family since 1854. He swore that Eddie, like his older brother and younger sister, was born in Chicago. On cross-examination, M'Mahon testified that Guerin's father was an Irishman who had deserted from the British Army during the Crimean War and had been naturalized as an American citizen. Residents from Robert Street, Hoxton, were called as witnesses to state they had never heard of a child called Eddie being born at the Walker house, and had never heard of the Guerins. No registration of Eddie Guerin's birth could be found nor did there appear to be any record of his baptism, although it was said that his parents were Roman Catholics. A Scotland Yard detective swore that Guerin spoke with a distinct American accent and that, when arrested, Guerin was in possession of a substantial amount of money, £460 sterling and $1444, which, although less than the £10,000 allegedly stolen from the bank in France, was a suspicious sum.

Guerin's case was hardly an attractive one to put before the jury. He was clearly a suspicious character and he had not testified on his own behalf. Taking his case at its best, Guerin might have been born in England, although even that seemed questionable, and, in any event, he had certainly grown up in Chicago, which made him culturally, if not legally, more American than British. The alternative claim to status as a British subject through an Irish father who had deserted from the British Army in time of war would hardly appeal to an English jury, particularly when the question of Home Rule for Ireland was a matter of hot debate. Gladstone's first Home Rule Bill had been defeated two years before, splitting the Liberal Party and leading to the formation of the Unionist government under Lord Salisbury (who had appointed Webster and Clarke as law officers of the Crown). Both Webster and Clarke were staunch opponents of Irish Home Rule.[28]

In addition, although proof of Guerin's status as a British subject would provide a solid legal basis for refusing extradition, it was not a point likely to attract a great deal of sympathy in an English court. Failure to extradite nationals sits uneasily with English law's concept of territorial jurisdiction, since the combination of the two rules inevitably produces situations where offenders will escape prosecution.[29]

Huddleston B conferred with counsel as to the precise issue to be put to the jury. No argument was presented on the issue of burden of proof. Poland must have assumed that Guerin had to bear the onus, perhaps because he was described as the plaintiff in the order directing the trial, or, alternatively, because he was claiming an exception under the treaty. It occurred to no one to argue that, as the case arose on habeas corpus and involved the liberty of the subject, any doubt on a point of fact should be resolved in Guerin's favour.[30] (In fairness it should be pointed out that it was not until 1935 that such a rule was firmly established in criminal law.)[31] The judge settled upon two questions: "Has the plaintiff Guerin proved to your satisfaction that he was born in Robert Street, Hoxton; secondly, was the plaintiff's father a natural-born subject not naturalized?"[32] Huddleston carefully summarized the evidence, but his direction to the jury was unfavourable to Guerin. He commented adversely on Guerin's failure to testify, and told the jury the issue was whether the prisoner should be sent to France to be tried or be able to stay in England and "defy the law."[33]

The jury returned within twenty minutes with a verdict. It was, to the judge's surprise, uncertain. To the first question, the jury answered that it had "no satisfactory proof that the plaintiff was born in Robert Street, Hoxton," and, to the second, the response was "that they were not satisfied as to nationality of the plaintiff's father."[34] It seemed clear that the matter of onus was crucial.

The verdict had to be referred back to the court that had directed the trial. Clarke moved to have the habeas corpus application dismissed.[35] Poland and Gill countered with an application for a new trial: the jury's verdict was unsatisfactory, they contended. The jury had not positively rejected Guerin's claim to status as a British subject but had only been prepared to say that his place of birth and his father's nationality had not been proved to their satisfaction.

The case came on for final resolution four days later before the Divisional Court, this time constituted by Lord Coleridge CJ and Hawkins J. Poland made relatively little of the contention that Guerin had been born in England. Perhaps he felt that the evidence was weak on that point or that the prosecution's witnesses had discredited his own. The point he pressed was that of Guerin's father's Irish birth. But was there satisfactory evidence that his father was Irish, asked Hawkins J. The recollection of the police officer of an Irish accent would hardly be enough. Why had not the prisoner himself been called as a witness before the jury? He would recollect where his early years were spent and perhaps his father's country of origin. It became apparent that Poland's failure to call Guerin as a witness was going to be the central issue. Poland explained that calling Guerin would have been dangerous. He contended that Guerin might have been asked questions relating to the offence with which he was charged, and, in any case, there was no need to call him since Huddleston B himself had stated in summing up to the jury on the evidence that "the evidence was all one way as to the prisoner's father being an Irishman." But Lord Coleridge was not convinced: "Have you shown more than that the prisoner's father lived in America and spoke with an Irish accent?"[36] Poland, perhaps by now frustrated at being stalled on the point, asserted: "The plain truth is that the verdict went upon prejudice."[37] There was no doubt at the trial, he contended, that the prisoner's father was an Irishman, no real proof that he had been naturalized, but the jury were told the prisoner was charged with a serious offence and left with a choice of sending him to France to face justice or allowing him to stay in England "to defy the law." But neither Lord Coleridge nor Hawkins J was prepared to reverse the finding unless there was something more. Lord Coleridge challenged Poland: "Suppose we should think that, upon the whole, the trial was unsatisfactory, will you undertake upon a new trial to call the prisoner?"[38] Guerin's evidence could be crucial. Even if he had a bad character, he might still be believed. Hawkins J observed that as there appeared to be no other evidence, there could be no point in sending the issue for a new trial unless Guerin was to be called.

The prosecution relied heavily on the burden of proof. Clarke argued that the onus rested on Guerin, who had asserted facts to exempt himself from the treaty, and, since the jury was uncertain, the result had to go against him. The prisoner, he reiterated, had not testified, and to make matters even more uncomfortable for Poland, Clarke asserted that, if called, Guerin could not be cross-examined as to his guilt with respect to the events charged.

Lord Coleridge turned to Poland. The court, he said, was prepared to hear Guerin right then and there to avoid further delay and expense. The judge directed that the prisoner, who had not been in court, should be sent for at once. Poland tried to find a way out. Guerin, he contended, could not testify: in 1888 an accused person was neither compellable not competent.[39] But Hawkins J observed that Guerin already was a witness; he had sworn the affidavit upon which the habeas corpus application was based. Poland finally conceded that he was not prepared to put Guerin into the witness box. He gave no explanation and one can only speculate why he came to this decision. One possibility, of course, is that Poland did not call Guerin because he knew his client would commit perjury.

After a short recess, Lord Coleridge gave judgment. He briefly reviewed the facts and concluded: "The prisoner, therefore, had failed on the evidence before the Court to satisfy the onus which rested upon him. He had failed to satisfy the jury, and he had failed to satisfy the Court; the verdict, therefore, had properly been entered for the prosecutors."[40]

THE 1907 PROCEEDINGS

Following the dismissal of his habeas corpus application in 1888, Guerin was extradited, sent to France, convicted, and given a ten-year prison term. When he was released from prison in June 1899, the French wasted no time in deporting him to England.[41] He made his way back to France where he was convicted in June 1902 of yet another robbery, this time of the American Express office in Paris. This led to his conviction and sentence to the penal colony in French Guyana, a group of island and mainland prison camps known collectively as "Devil's Island" (although Guerin never actually set foot on the island called "Ile du Diable"). In 1905 Guerin escaped and made his way back to England via the United States. All these exploits are described in graphic detail, perhaps with considerable embellishment, in Guerin's memoirs.

The French were anxious to have Guerin back. A warrant for his arrest on the information of the French government was issued by the Bow Street Magistrates' Court on 21 April 1906, and Guerin was arrested shortly thereafter. At the hearing, Guerin went into the witness box to testify that he had been born in Hoxton of Irish parents and that he had always regarded himself as an Irishman.[42] He admitted that the question of nationality had been dealt with by the courts on previous occasions but contended that the jury had been prejudiced by evidence which, Guerin contended, was completely untrue – namely, that his father had been in the British Army and that he had deserted. Guerin also complained bitterly about the way he had been treated in France, but the magistrate was unmoved and committed him for extradition.

Guerin immediately brought a habeas corpus application, again based on the contention that he was a British subject. Counsel briefed by the director of public prosecutions consented to an order which was remarkable, given the supposed reluctance to deal with contested issues of fact on habeas corpus. In effect, it provided for a procedure to enable Guerin to gather the evidence he would need to establish his nationality:

copies of all Affidavits made in America shall be sent to the Agent at Chicago of the Solicitor for the Affairs of His Majesty's Treasury and that the deponents shall on reasonable notice from the said Agent attend before His Britannic Majesty's Consul at Chicago or before a Commissioner for Oaths or other Officer having power in that behalf elsewhere near the residence of any deponents not living in or near Chicago and answer all such questions as may be put then by or on behalf of such Agent and verify a transcript of the short-hand notes of such answers by Affidavit to be filed with the first mentioned Affidavits. Such deponents may in like manner [answer] any questions put by a representative of the Applicant and verify such answers.[43]

The director of public prosecutions retained a firm of lawyers in Chicago, and one of the department's principal clerks fully acquainted with the Guerin matter, who was going to Chicago on personal business, briefed the British consul and the Chicago law firm. As in 1888, everyone's attention was focused on the expense, but this time the Treasury was willing to risk having to bear the cost of gathering the necessary evidence, even if that meant Guerin would succeed.[44] The matter was reviewed in both the Foreign Office and the Home Office. Article xv of the United Kingdom–France extradition treaty contemplated that the French government would bear the costs, but it was plainly awkward to ask them to cover expenses incurred to establish that the prisoner should not be extradited. The matter was raised at the ministerial level, and Home Secretary Gladstone agreed with Foreign Secretary Grey's proposal that the matter should be left in abeyance until the court had made its decision. If Guerin were extradited, then the French could be asked to pay. Should he succeed, the Treasury would have to bear the cost.[45]

Guerin's affidavit explained that the basis of his claim for citizenship was that his father was born in County Limerick, Ireland, and had never changed nationality. He concluded with a plea that his habeas corpus application be allowed so that he not be "handed over to France and from there taken to a penal settlement for the rest of my life where I shall not even see a person speaking my own language."[46] His solicitor, W.T. Ricketts, was very active in preparing the case. He went to great lengths, collecting evidence in England, Ireland, and in the United States. Most of the evidence came from Chicago; in accordance with the procedure contemplated by the court's order, affidavits were prepared on the part of each deponent, who was then examined under the authority of the British consul. The affidavits survive and are contained in the court file.[47] Transcripts of subsequent examinations of the deponents were also filed, but these were not traced.[48] Most of the evidence related to the nationality of Guerin's father. It was anything but conclusive. Several family members swore affidavits on Guerin's behalf, as did a number of Guerin's friends. Several of them were politicians. Joseph J. Duffy, involved in Chicago politics all his life, stated that he had "extraordinary means for knowing the party connections of persons living within his congressional district"[49] and that neither Eddie nor his father Edmund had ever voted, owing to their British status. The affidavits disclosed that after his escape from Devil's Island, Eddie had returned to Chicago; when the French obtained an extradition warrant in the United States, he had consulted several of these political figures, hoping they could pull some strings. Guerin also consulted a lawyer, who advised him that as he was a British subject he could not resist extradition in the United States.

The Chicago lawyers retained by the Treasury found cross-examining the deponents to be a frustrating exercise. They reported that they had done "the best that could be accomplished with these witnesses under the circumstances. It must be remembered that the witnesses were with one or two exceptions, Irish, friendly to the Defendant or his family and willing to do everything in their power to assist. The most noticeable feature of most of this testimony is its indefiniteness." The only witness who had ever seen Guerin's father in Ireland was his sister, Margaret Daley, and she was "wheezing with asthma, so that it was almost impossible to examine her." Her testimony, according to the Chicago lawyer, was "not only indefinite and unsatisfactory, but improbable."[50]

Evidence collected from Ireland was hardly more conclusive. William Lundon, the member of parliament for East Limerick, Ireland, swore that he knew the Guerin family well and that they had emigrated to the United States because of the agricultural depression. His knowledge of Guerin's father, however, was not first-hand. "Almost 40 years ago or thereabouts" while in New Jersey he had been introduced to Edward Guerin who, according to Lundon, strongly resembled his brother Patrick Guerin and his nephew Phillip, who still lived in Ireland. Lundon had visited Eddie in Brixton Prison and swore that he also bore a "strong facial resemblance to the said Phillip and Patrick Guerin."[51]

The prosecution was busy as well. Pinkertons, the American detective agency, was retained to investigate. A census return was uncovered indicating that the Guerins were in Chicago in 1870 with eight children, but that no election records could be found. Authentic election records in Chicago did not commence until 1885, ten years after the father's death, so it was impossible to show that he had voted. Nor were reliable naturalization records available, all records prior to 1871 having been destroyed in the great Chicago fire. City directories showed that the Guerins had been in Chicago during the early 1860s, which tended to cast considerable doubt on Guerin's contention that he was born elsewhere than in Chicago. Again, however, nothing definitive could be found. The Chicago lawyer reported: "[W]e have exhausted every source of information that we can conceive of in an endeavour to ascertain the truth regarding Eddie Guerin's citizenship, and we are free to confess that we are nearly as much in doubt now as when we commenced. The evidence taken is pertinent almost as much for what it does not show as for what it does." All in all, the Chicago lawyer felt that many of the important facts could have been cleared up by the defence if they wanted and that their failure to do so tended to discredit their own case. The family members, he complained, had "slunk under cover of ignorance when anything important was asked."[52]

Even the record of Guerin's habeas corpus proceeding in 1888 was inadequate. The Chicago police officer who had testified against Guerin had since died. There was no transcript of the evidence, and nothing more than the report that appeared in *The Times* and a transcript of the shorthand notes of the judge's summing up. It was not seriously argued that Guerin should be bound by the result reached almost twenty years earlier. Judgment on habeas corpus does not fall within the rule of *res judicata*, and in 1907 the practice was still to allow successive applications for the writ before different judges.[53]

The matter came before the King's Bench Division on 14 June 1907, Lord Alverstone CJ (formerly Richard Webster) presiding.[54] After twelve years as attorney-general, Webster had been appointed Master of the Rolls and then, within a few months, Lord Chief Justice, an office he held from 1900 until his retirement in 1913. It seems highly unusual, at least by the standards of today, that he should have sat on the case in 1907 since he had taken the brief against Guerin in 1888 on precisely the point at issue.[55]

The attorney-general, Sir Robert Finlay, KC, appeared to oppose the application for habeas corpus. Richard D. Muir, a leading member of the criminal bar, appeared on Guerin's behalf.[56] Muir "had been thrilled to the core"[57] at the story of Guerin's escape from the French penal colony and took the case for a nominal fee. He was convinced that his client could not legally be extradited and thought Guerin had already suffered enough at the hands of the French.[58] Muir opened the case by giving a detailed account of the evidence, setting out the facts with respect to Guerin's birth, his father's birth, and the 1888 habeas corpus proceedings. Muir relied mainly on the father's place of birth having been Ireland, indicating that he did not press the case that Guerin had been born in England, the principal witness on that issue not wishing to be "harried" any further. The onus, he submitted, was on the Crown to show that Guerin's father had changed his nationality, and there was in fact no evidence to that effect.

The attorney-general did little to resist Guerin's case. He left it to the court to decide whether that evidence should be accepted, conceding that there was a strong body of evidence that the prisoner's father refused to vote.

The court's judgment was delivered immediately upon conclusion of the argument. Lord Alverstone gave judgment. It rested with the Crown to prove the prisoner's father had become a naturalized American and "as there was not satisfactory proof to the contrary, the prisoner must be deemed a British subject." That meant that, pursuant to the treaty, the court had no choice but to make the rule for habeas corpus absolute, and Guerin was released.[59]

Guerin's case plainly turned on the burden of proof. The evidence was uncertain. He lost in 1888 because he had failed to prove he was British. He won in 1907 because the prosecution failed to prove he was not.[60] The Guerin cases of 1888 and 1907 foreshadowed a continuing ambivalence by the courts on this important issue in the law of habeas corpus.[61] A Privy Council decision in 1931 appeared to place the burden of proof on the party seeking to uphold the detention.[62] but a wartime case went the opposite way.[63] In an immigration case in 1969 the Divisional Court held that the burden of proof rested with the authorities.[64] This result was reversed by a much-criticized decision of the House of Lords in 1980,[65] that in turn was overruled by the House of Lords only four years later.[66] The law now appears to be settled that, where there are disputed issues of fact, the burden rests with the party seeking to uphold the detention. The Guerin case, then, was not the last in which the burden of proof on habeas corpus caused difficulty, but it may be unique in that completely different results were reached on the same facts and between the same parties.

Guerin was convinced that everyone, even the judges who heard his case, was influenced by the Dreyfus affair – the infamous case involving the wrongful conviction of a French army officer for treason. The prolonged debate over Dreyfus shook the French judicial and penal system to the core.[67] Dreyfus, like Guerin, had been sentenced to Devil's Island, and Guerin noted that everyone "had read all about the treatment to which Dreyfus had been subjected [and agreed that] whatever I had done it was not sufficiently bad to condemn me to a poisonous hole where men rotted away and were never heard of for ever more."[68] The Dreyfus case was current in the public mind when Guerin was apprehended in 1906, and it presented the French justice and penal system in the worst possible light.[69] In 1888, two years after the emotionally charged debate on the Irish Home Rule Bill, Guerin was a man claiming to be a British subject through an Irish father who had deserted from the British Army. In 1907, he was presented as the man who had the courage to escape the same filthy penal colony in which Dreyfus had suffered. A man who had escaped from the horrors of Devil's Island was bound to attract public sympathy. One hardly need adhere to the realist or the critical legal studies schools of jurisprudence to suggest that these factors might tip the balance in an area where the law was uncertain.

Perhaps on a more positive note, *Guerin* demonstrates that there is considerably more scope for the determination of issues of disputed fact on habeas corpus than is sometimes suggested.[70] Both in 1888 and in 1907 the courts adapted procedures to meet the exigencies of the case, on neither occasion doubting for a moment the power to delve fully into disputed factual issues crucial to the validity of the applicant's detention.

THE TREATY AMENDED

The exclusion of nationals from extradition is probably based on a fear of the injustice that might result to the requested state's subjects under an alien and unfamiliar judicial system. At the time of the Guerin cases, approximately half the United Kingdom's treaties followed the pattern of the treaty with France and excluded nationals from extradition, while an equal number made extradition of nationals optional, giving the requested state a discretion.[71] As already noted, refusal to extradite nationals leaves an enormous gap: nationality alone does not constitute a basis for the assumption of jurisdiction in English criminal law,[72] and the modern tendency has been to permit extradition of nationals.[73]

Guerin's release led directly to the amendment of the United Kingdom-France extradition treaty. Officials of the Home Office and the Foreign Office quickly decided to turn Guerin's victory to their advantage. Shortly after the judgment, the undersecretary at the

Home Office wrote to his counterpart in the Foreign Office conveying Gladstone's view that "the inability of His Majesty's Government to surrender Guerin to France is a matter for great regret, and that the present would seem to be a favourable opportunity for proposing to the French Government such a modification of the Treaty as would give to both Governments the option of surrendering their own subjects if they thought it desirable to do so."[74] Gladstone recognized that the French government was unlikely to accept a law making surrender of nationals compulsory, but suggested that it should accept a clause permitting either party to surrender its own nationals if it chose to do so. The Foreign Office undersecretary, W. Maycock, agreed that "it undoubtedly was a calamity that Guerin could not be extradited because he had succeeded in establishing his British status" and, adding a bit of colour, noted: "He is a *most dangerous* criminal and I am told rejoices in the possession of the scalps of two policemen."[75] The Foreign Office was not optimistic that the French would agree to amending the treaty. If they did agree, the French would insist on the right to refuse to surrender their own citizens. An optional provision would in practice be unilateral, but, as Maycock put it, at least "it would have enabled us to shed Guerin."[76]

Instructions were duly conveyed to the British ambassador in Paris, Francis Bertie, to commence discussions, noting that "the existence of this Article has prevented our surrendering to France one of the most dangerous criminals who ever lived, one Guerin, who escaped from Devil's Island."[77] Bertie was not to press the French to change their own practice, but the British wanted to have the option for themselves "so that men of the Guerin type should not be allowed to escape justice simply because we are bound by Treaty."[78] Bertie agreed the Guerin case provided a suitable opportunity to raise the issue, and, although concerned about including an optional clause in the treaty,[79] he proceeded with the negotiations. A memorandum focusing on Guerin's case was delivered to the French authorities. The French responded that extradition of their own nationals was unthinkable, but that perhaps the British proposal was worth considering. Drafts were prepared and discussions ensued. By March 1908 the French had accepted an amendment that would allow for the extradition of nationals, all the while emphasizing that this would not involve reciprocity on their part. On learning this outcome, Maycock expressed satisfaction: "We shall be no longer stopped from giving back such desparate characters as Guerin who escaped from Devil's Island."[80]

CONCLUSION

Within a few days of his release in 1907, Guerin was mentioned in the papers again, this time on account of an attempt on his life near Russell Square.[81] A notorious woman known as "Chicago May" Churchill and an accomplice were charged and eventually convicted of attempted murder after what was described as "one of the most remarkable cases that Lord Darling was ever called upon to try at the Old Bailey" and "the sensation of the year."[82] Chicago May had been convicted in France as a confederate with Guerin for the American Express robbery which led to his being sent to Devil's Island. She and Guerin had been lovers, and it was her betrayal that led to Guerin's arrest in 1906 and her jealousy that led her to make an attempt on his life a year later.

Guerin continued to attract public attention on account of his criminal exploits for the next thirty years. Almost invariably described as the man who had escaped from Devil's Island, his name appeared regularly in the police-court columns.[83] Finally, on 5 December 1940 *The Times* recorded: "Eddie Guerin, the man who escaped from Devil's island, has died at Bury, Lancashire."

The Guerin habeas corpus cases of 1888 and 1907 demonstrate that in actual practice the law of habeas corpus is less rigid than is sometimes supposed. Arcane legal rules which may appear to preclude review of factual issues should not stand in the way of a full inquiry. Allocating the burden of proof may be decisive, and the Guerin cases provide stark illustration of the manner in which the courts have wavered on the appropriate rule. But the conflict in the result reached in 1907 with that of 1888 also suggests that the courts' appreciation and evaluation of the facts may on occasion be influenced, if not determined, by matters extraneous to the legal rules.

NOTES

This article first appeared as "Habeas Corpus, Extradition and the Burden of Proof. The Case of the Man Who Escaped From Devil's Island" (1990), 10 *Cambridge Law Journal* 10; I am grateful to the editor for permission to publish in the present form. I also wish to thank Martin Friedland, Kent Roach, Stephen Waddams, and Graham Zellick, who read an earlier draft and provided many helpful comments.

1 "Some Considerations on the Origins of Habeas Corpus" (1937), 16 *Canadian Bar Review* 405; "Habeas Corpus Cum Causa – The

Emergence of the Modern Writ: I" (1940), 18 *Canadian Bar Review* 10; "Habeas Corpus Cum Causa – The Emergence of the Modern Writ: II" (1940), 18 *Canadian Bar Review* 172.

2 "Habeas Corpus I," 197.

3 *R. v. Governor of Brixton Prison, ex p. Guerin* (1907) 51 *Solicitors' Journal* 571; *The Times*, 15 June 1907.

4 In England, Murray 1928. In Canada, Ryerson Press 1928, under the title, *Crime: The Autobiography of a Crook*. In the United States, Doubleday 1929.

5 Article II of the United Kingdom–France treaty (14 Aug. 1876) provided as follows: "Native-born or naturalized subjects of either country are excepted from extradition. In the case, however, of a person who, since the commission of the crime or offence of which he is accused, or for which he has been convicted, has become naturalized in the country whence the surrender is sought, such naturalization shall not prevent the pursuit, arrest, and extradition of such person, in conformity with the stipulations of the present Treaty." Extradition of prisoners to France was a matter of routine. Foreign Office records indicate that, in 1888, there were twenty-seven active files. London, Public Record Office (PRO) Kew, FO 802, vol. 216.

6 Gill, then thirty-seven, went on to establish a reputation as a first-rate counsel, particularly in the criminal courts: "he deserves to be remembered with the great advocates of his generation." *The Times*, 23 Feb. 1923. Guerin described Gill as "one of the greatest criminal lawyers England has ever known ... a man who never had a superior in the defence of prisoners." Guerin, *I Was a Bandit*, 107.

7 See M.L. Friedland, *The Trials of Israel Lispski* (Toronto: Macmillan 1984), esp. 29.

8 *The Times*, 7 Nov. 1888.

9 Ibid.

10 The formal order of the court, however, did not limit Guerin to any specific points or follow the usual practice of being directed to the gaoler. It was, rather, framed as an order to the "French Consulate General and the Bank of France to show cause why a writ of habeas corpus should not issue directed to the Gaoler of Her Majesty's Prison at Holloway in the County of Middlesex commanding him to have the body of the said Eddie Guerin before this court immediately after their receipt of the said Writ together with the day and cause of his being taken and detained by whatsoever name he may be called therein and then and there to undergo and receive all and singular such matters and things as the said court shall then and there consider of concerning in this behalf." PRO Ch. Lane, J74/88, 41. While the order required that notice be given to the Treasury solicitor, the matter was

seen as being essentially one between Guerin, on the one hand, and the French authorities and the Bank of France, on the other.

11 60 LT 538; 58 LJMC 42; 37 WR 269; 53 JP; 16 Cox CC 596; *The Times*, 14 Nov. 1888.

12 Lord Alverstone [Richard Webster], *Recollections of Bar and Bench* (London: Arnold 1914); *Dictionary of National Biography* (DNB) 1912–1921 (London: Oxford University Press 1927), 562–3; *The Times*, 16 Dec. 1915.

13 M.L. Friedland, "R.S. Wright's Model Penal Code: A Forgotten Chapter in the History of the Criminal Law" (1981), 1 *Oxford Journal of Legal Studies* 307.

14 Poland more or less conceded that the evidence actually heard by the committing magistrate was sufficient: see Stephenson to Lushington, 16 Nov. 1888, PRO Kew, HO 144/476. Wills J had taken the extraordinary step of communicating with the magistrate, who had assured him "that he had acted on the French depositions and the evidence before him only, and had not looked at the depositions taken before Sir James Ingham" (60 LT 540). The judgment of the court dismissed the application on the first point, but held that a second magistrate could not act on evidence received by the first (60 LT 540–1): "It is contrary to all my ideas and experience of justice for depositions taken before one magistrate to be considered by another magistrate sufficient evidence to commit a prisoner upon without having seen the demeanor of the witness when they were giving their evidence, and so being in a position to judge for himself of the truth of their statements."

15 60 LT 541; R.J. Sharpe, *The Law of Habeas Corpus*, 2d ed. (Oxford: Clarendon Press 1989), 73–4.

16 Sharpe, *The Law of Habeas Corpus*, 64–91.

17 Indeed, it would seem that Wright was ready for the point as he cited an early case, *Re Andrews* (1873), LR 8 QBD 153, where a similar practice had been followed.

18 60 LT 540. While the *Guerin* case presents one of the best examples of the technique of directing the trial of an issue, it has been resorted to in other cases. See Sharpe, *The Law of Habeas Corpus*, 78–9, 157–9.

19 The formal order of the court followed the earlier order, which framed the issue as one between Guerin and the Bank of France. The court enlarged the time within which cause was to be shown why a writ of habeas corpus should not issue until 27 December 1888, and further ordered: "that in the meantime an issue be tried to ascertain whether the said Eddie Guerin is a native born British subject within the meaning of the Treaty between Her Majesty The Queen and the French Republic concluded on the 14th day of August, 1876 for the mutual Extradition of Fugitive Criminals and the said Eddie Guerin

shall be plaintiff and the said Bank of France the defendants in the said issue" (PRO Ch. Lane J74/88, 52).
20 60 LT 540.
21 Waddington to Lord Salisbury, 16 Nov. 1888, PRO Kew, HO 144/476.
22 23 Nov. 1888, HO 144/476.
23 11 Dec. 1888, HO 144/476.
24 Ibid.
25 (1888), 5 TLR 160.
26 DNB 1931–1940 (1949), 179; Edward Clarke, *The Story of My Life* (London: John Murray 1918); D. Walker-Smith and E. Clarke, *The Life of Sir Edward Clarke* (London: Thornton Butterworth 1939).
27 Edward Clarke, *Treatise on the Law of Extradition* (London: Stevens and Haynes, first published in 1866 with subsequent editions in 1874, 1888, and 1903), contains a lengthy reference to the Guerin case, 179–82.
28 Clarke, *The Story of My Life*, 265. Webster described Clarke's noted speech in response to Gladstone's second Home Rule Bill as "one of the most magnificent efforts I ever listened to." Alverstone, *Recollections of Bar and Bench*, 164.
29 A Royal Commission on Extradition in 1878 had deprecated treaty clauses restricting the extradition of nationals: see Clarke, *Extradition* (4th ed., 1903), 259. The matter had also received adverse judicial comment: In *R. v. Wilson* (1877), 3 QBD 42 at 44–5, Lord Cockburn CJ stated: "[T]his blot upon the law should be removed, so as to prevent an Englishman who commits an offence in a foreign country from escaping with impunity."
30 For discussion of the way the law has developed on the point see below.
31 *Woolmington v. D.P.P.*, [1935] AC 462.
32 5 TLR 162.
33 Ibid., 190.
34 Ibid., 162.
35 Ibid., 188; *The Times*, 18 Jan. 1889.
36 5 TLR 189.
37 Ibid., 190.
38 Ibid.
39 Evidence Act, 1851 (14 & 15 Vict., c.XCIX), s.3.
40 5 TLR 192.
41 Guerin was put on board the ss *Dora* at Le Havre, bound for Southampton, on 6 June, along with his confederate, Frank Denning. The French authorities must have warned the English that Guerin had been shipped back. The assistant commissioner of police advised the Home Office of Guerin's arrival, pointing out that Guerin and Denning had criminal records and that "both of these men are dangerous criminals

and will probably be heard of again in connection with some crime" (7 June 1899, PRO Kew, HO 144/476).

The Home Office was annoyed at having Guerin back, but felt that nothing could be done. The minute on Guerin in the Home Office file reads as follows: "The French government, of course, know perfectly well that these men are American subjects: Guerin fought his extradition alleging that he was a British subject, without success (Denning wished to go). But I do not think it would be of any use to protest: they were in the UK last and they were arrested here. If they had been deported to the US there would have been no means of preventing them from coming back to England" (15 June 1899, ibid.).

42 *The Times*, 23 June 1906.
43 A copy of the formal order is to be found in PRO Kew, FO 372/10.
44 Dysart, director of public prosecutions, noted: "What has occurred in this case will probably lead to expenditure which is quite unusual in an extradition case and may be not inconsiderable – I do not know whether in the circumstances the French Government would make any contribution to the cost which is being incurred to check a claim which if established will lead to the discharge of the accused to whose surrender they as I understand attach considerable importance" (7 Aug. 1906, ibid.).
45 Letter from Home Office to the Foreign Office, 23 Aug. 1906, ibid.
46 5 July 1906, PRO Ch.Lane, KB 1 347/1 no. 277.
47 1 Oct. 1906, ibid., KB 1 347/2 no. 365.
48 PRO Ch. Lane Index Entry KB 39/31 refers to a bundle of twenty-two documents having been filed 14 June 1907, but these are said to be missing at the time of transfer and may well be the transcripts.
49 1 Oct. 1906, PRO Ch. Lane, KB 1 347/2 no. 365.
50 Letter from Bulkley, Gray and More, Chicago, to the director of public prosecutions, 6 Dec. 1906, PRO Kew, FO 272/10.
51 5 Oct. 1906, PRO Ch. Lane, KB 1 347/2 no. 367.
52 See note 49.
53 For discussion, see Sharpe, *The Law of Habeas Corpus*, 201–12. Successive applications were eliminated by *Re Hastings (No. 2)*, [1959] 1 QB 358. See also *R. v. Governor of Winson Green Prison, Birmingham, ex p. Littlejohn*, [1975] 1 WLR 893, where the applicant lost a habeas corpus application, was sent to Ireland for trial, escaped, and when again arrested in England launched another habeas corpus application on the same grounds as the first. The court considered the application on the merits, but on the ground that fresh material had been presented.
54 The other members of the court were Darling and Lawrence JJ.
55 No mention is made of the Guerin cases in his memoirs, *Recollections of Bar and Bench*, nor did Guerin mention the fact that Lord Alverstone

405 The Case of the Man Who Escaped from Devil's Island

cJ had appeared against him in the earlier case. However, Guerin was relieved to learn that Sir Edward Clarke would not appear again to oppose his application. Guerin, *I Was a Bandit*, 267.

56 Guerin credited his success in 1907 in part to the determination of his counsel, Richard Muir, "who for eight months, tooth and nail, fought the extradition proceedings like a terrier. He won in the end because he would not be beaten." Guerin, *I Was a Bandit*, 264.

57 S.T. Felstead, *Sir Richard Muir: A Memoir of a Public Prosecutor* (London: Lane 1927), 321.

58 For Muir's view of the case see ibid., 318–23.

59 (1907), 51 Sol. J. 571; *The Times*, 15 June 1907.

60 Text writers have tended to ignore the 1907 decision and continue to cite the 1888 decision as authority for the proposition that the burden of proving nationality as an exemption rests with the prisoner: see F. Piggott, *Extradition* (London: Butterworth 1910), 67–8 (criticizing the 1907 decision); V.E. Hartley Booth, *British Extradition Law and Procedure*, vol. 1 (Sijthoff & Noordhoff 1980), 73; I. Stanbrook, *The Law and Practice of Extradition* (London: Barry Rose 1980), 4 (citing both the 1888 and 1907 decisions for this proposition); G.V. La Forest, *Extradition to and from Canada*, 2d ed. (Toronto: Canada Law Book 1977), 78.

61 For a detailed discussion see Sharpe, *The Law of Habeas Corpus*, 85–91.

62 *Eshugbayi Eleko v. Officer Administering the Government of Nigeria*, [1931] AC 662.

63 *Greene v. Secretary of State for Home Affairs*, [1942] AC 284.

64 *R. v. Governor of Brixton Prison, ex p. Ahsan*, [1969] 2 QB 222.

65 *Zamir v. Secretary of State for the Home Department*, [1980] AC 930.

66 *Khawaja v. Secretary of State for the Home Department*, [1984] AC 74.

67 The literature on the Dreyfus case is vast. For a lively and detailed recent account see J.-D. Bredin, *L'Affaire* (Paris: Julliard 1983), translated as *The Affair: The Case of Alfred Dreyfus* (Firefly 1986).

68 Guerin, *I Was a Bandit*, 248.

69 On the same day Guerin's *ex parte* application for habeas corpus was reported in *The Times*, there was also an account of the argument before the Court de Cassation in proceedings to review Dreyfus's conviction: 6 July 1906.

70 Sharpe, *The Law of Habeas Corpus*, 64–91.

71 See Clarke, *Extradition* (4th ed., 1903), for the texts of the treaties. The treaties with Luxembourg, Spain, and Switzerland provided for the extradition of British subjects, but not nationals of the other state.

72 See note 29 above.

73 Most modern treaties give the requested state discretion: see Hartley Booth, *British Extradition Law*, 69–73, 299. The extradition of nationals has been upheld under the Canadian Charter of Rights and Freedoms,

s.1, as a reasonable limit on the s.6 right of "every citizen of Canada ... to enter, remain in and leave Canada." *Re Federal Republic of Germany and Rauca* (1983), 145 DLR (3d) 638 (Ont. CA); *United States of America v. Cotroni; United States v. El Zein*, [1989] 1 SCR 1469.
74 6 Aug. 1907, PRO Kew, FO 372/50.
75 Minute, 8 Aug. 1907, ibid.
76 Ibid.
77 Maycock to Bertie, 12 Aug. 1907, ibid.
78 Ibid.
79 Bertie to Campbell, 28 Aug. 1907, PRO Kew, FO 372/10: "The crime of which a British subject might be accused might be on the borderland between common and political crime. If we surrendered him, there would be an outcry in England; if we refused to give him up there might be an outcry in France with political inconvenience to us."
80 Minute, 16 March 1908, PRO Kew, FO 372/103.
81 *The Times*, 17 June 1907.
82 D. Barker, *Lord Darling's Famous Cases* (London: Hutchinson 1936), 45; *The Times*, 26 July 1907.
83 See, for example, *The Times*, 10 April 1908; 22–24 Jan. 1912; 25 April 1913; 8 July 1918; 30 Sept. 1920; 7 Jan. 1924; 29 May 1928; 10 April 1931; 25 Nov. 1932; 31 Dec. 1934; 10 Oct. 1935; 2 Feb. and 14 March 1938; 29 May 1939.

PART FOUR
Legal Education

Dreaming the Impossible Dream: Maxwell Cohen and McGill's National Law Programme

RODERICK A. MACDONALD

INTRODUCTION: MAXWELL COHEN
THE DREAMER

Among Max Cohen's many abilities as a legal educator, two are emblazoned on my mind: his almost unlimited capacity for "dreaming" and his silver-tongued eloquence and enthusiasm. The former led to several rounds of undergraduate curricular reform at McGill from the 1940s through the late 1950s, to the reinvigoration of the Institute of Air and Space Law in the early 1960s, to the establishment of the Institute of Foreign and Comparative Law in 1965, to the reorientation of the Bachelor of Civil Law (BCL) tuition in the mid 1960s, and finally to the launching of the faculty's National Programme in 1968.[1] The latter served to attract and enthuse generations of students, alumni, aspiring law teachers, and young colleagues about the "mission" of Canadian legal education and McGill's special role in achieving that mission.[2]

I have first-hand experience with both of these talents. Shortly after I was nominated as dean of the Faculty of Law in 1984 I received a brief visit from Max in which he sketched, in the most convincing terms, both the joys of deaning and a dozen or more projects that I absolutely had to undertake in the ensuing five years. Whether I actually achieved any of the goals he set for me then I leave to his judgment; that I am deeply indebted to him for his encouragement and counsel is incontrovertible. For this reason, I am delighted to offer this reflection on McGill's National Programme as a tribute to Max Cohen.³

Other essayists have noted Cohen's contribution to chronicling the sorry state of Canadian legal education in the postwar period and to shaking the law-teaching establishment from its intellectual torpor.⁴ Those commentators have tended to focus on his influence in three particular areas: the relationship of the universities to the legal professions in the general pedagogical orientation of law faculties; the reorientation of the upper-year curriculum to promote student research and writing through an expansion of the number of optional courses and specialized seminars; and the role of the law teacher as scholar and public servant. In these ways, as in so many others, Cohen is rightly remembered in common-law Canada as having had a national impact.

But what is much less well known is Cohen's role, over the two decades from his appointment as a professor in 1946 until the end of his deanship in 1969, in modernizing (indeed transforming) the curriculum of Canada's only Englgh-language civil-law institution – the Faculty of Law at McGill University. As John Brierley has observed, despite a venerable tradition of university-based legal education dating from the 1840s, the challenges that faced Quebec's law faculties in the postwar period were no less daunting than those encountered elsewhere.⁵ How Cohen, an outsider to McGill and to Quebec, was able to meet those challenges and overcome seemingly insurmountable obstacles in his plan to develop an undergraduate National Programme of civil-, common-, and public-law studies at McGill is the story told here.

THE DREAM CONCEIVED: CHALLENGES OF CANADIAN LEGAL EDUCATION IN THE 1950S AND 1960S

Formally, the story begins in the late 1940s with Cohen's recruitment to McGill. The first Jewish member of the full-time teaching staff, the faculty's second Canadian common lawyer (the first having been Ira Mackay, a Dalhousie graduate who held a professorial position from 1921 to 1924), and the first of McGill full-time professors to have taken extensive graduate training in the United States, Cohen quickly began to shake up his adoptive institution.⁶ From his insistence on the introduction of a pioneering seminar in jurisprudence (1948), to his rewriting of the faculty's annual announcement to include the statement that the program was designed to provide "a liberal education in legal principles and theory" (1949), to his demand that the faculty create upper-year elective courses as a counterweight to the Quebec Bar's imposition of a fourth-year of "practical training" on the undergraduate curriculum (1950), to his championing of the creation of the graduate Institute of International Air Law (1951), to his enthusiasm for the establishment of the *McGill Law Journal* (1952), to his promotion of Canada's first interdisciplinary law-school course – Government Control of Business (1953) – the pattern is clear.[7] Legal education at McGill was insubstantial and could benefit from a healthy injection of ideas from below the forth-ninth parallel.[8]

Not surprisingly, the reaction of the older members of the faculty (Dean W.J.C. Meredith, Stuart Lemesurier, and Frank Scott), of Quebec's professional corporations (Bar and Board of Notaries), and of the university administration was less than enthusiastic. Most of Cohen's elder colleagues were McGill-trained civil lawyers whose intellectual affiliations were either with the United Kingdom or with France. The leadership of the bar and notarial profession during the Duplessis era had a view of university law teaching not dissimilar to that of the more conservative elements of the Law Society of Upper Canada. And the university saw legal education as peripheral to its principal mission, with the result that it was not prepared to invest the resources necessary to build up an American-style Faculty of Law. For much of the 1950s, then, Cohen's overall view of the faculty's role, and especially his "policy-oriented" conception of law teaching, was neither widely shared nor generally acted upon. But this is not to say that none of Cohen's ideas (or ideas of others which Cohen whole-heartedly embraced) was adopted. The faculty did impose a 10,000-word senior essay-writing requirement on students. It also expanded the number of upper-year options offered to undergraduates, again began to teach a few courses and seminars in the French language, and put into place the rudiments of a comparative private law curriculum. The professoriate (throughout the period a modest six full-timers) published some dozen books and fifty articles during the decade, and both Scott and Cohen were key players in the ongoing conflict about legal education in Ontario.[9] Nevertheless, despite Cohen's urgings, the self-image of the faculty throughout the 1950s remained primarily that of a professional school rather than that of a typical university faculty.[10]

All that began to change in 1960 when Cohen was named acting dean of the faculty following the sudden death of W.J.C. Meredith. As acting dean, Cohen established an ad hoc Curriculum Review Committee with a view to enlarging further the number of upper-year optional seminars, lobbying the legal professions to reduce the number of obligatory undergraduate courses, and, by implication, levering additional professorial positions out of the university administration.[11] This ad hoc committee was allowed to expire, however, when Scott returned from an overseas research leave and assumed the deanship of the faculty the following year. But parts of Cohen's initiative survived. Scott – by this time no ally of Cohen generally – put the issue insofar as McGill was concerned very well in his Annual Report as dean for 1961–2:

Part of the problem lies in the conflicting ideas about the function of the McGill Law Faculty. It may be viewed as a technical school primarily designed to train English-speaking members for the legal and notarial professions in Quebec ... Or it may be seen as both a professional school and a university Faculty in the sense that its students are soundly trained in basic principles of law as well as professional skills, and are brought to appreciate what is meant by saying that the law is a learned profession ... Both these images concentrate upon the Faculty as existing for law students only ... Both exclude the concept of the law school as a live centre of legal research and writing, and of the professor as an obvious partner in the legal order with the lawyer and judge ...

As put by Professor Cohen in his Report as Acting-Dean for 1960–61, "It is the high duty of law schools that have had full-time teaching staffs for a sufficient length of time to create a scholarly research and teaching tradition, to further that tradition, to expand it and to continue performing their deeply social and public role" ... [T]he McGill Law Faculty is a place where the research programme is concentrated in those areas where by position and tradition the Faculty is particularly endowed, namely Comparative Law, Air and Space Law, and in the training of leaders for the Bar, for government and business in Canada who are bilingual and conversant with the culture and outlook of the main ethnic groups that make up the country's population.[12]

It was precisely the challenges implied by this conception of the faculty that preoccupied Max Cohen for the rest of the decade, in his administrative capacities as director of the renamed Institute of Air and Space Law from 1961 through 1965 and as dean of the faculty from 1964 through 1969.

When Cohen assumed the directorship of the Institute of Air and Space Law it had lost much of its initial momentum. That inertia was due in part to a rapid turnover in directors (he was the fourth in five years, but the first to have previously held a full-time academic appointment at McGill), in part to its increasingly professional rather than scholarly and research vocation, and largely to its precarious financial position.[13] Cohen immediately set about to remedy those problems, seeing the institute as a good laboratory for putting into practice some of his ideas about legal education and scholarship. He first attacked the problem of funding and, in that initial year, devoted substantial energy to raising money from the American Ford Foundation. With the $250,000 over five years that he was granted by the foundation in 1962, Cohen was able to launch a *Yearbook of Air and Space Law* and to organize a first International Conference on the Law of Outer Space. Ford Foundation money was also used to offer graduate fellowships to international students, and to recruit a number of air and space law scholars as research fellows and professors – Ivan Vlasic, Peter Sand, and Geoffrey Pratt in 1962 alone.

During the period of his directorship Cohen constantly pressed for the transformation of the teaching curriculum, both at the graduate and undergraduate levels. He set out to rejuvenate the Doctor of Civil Law (DCL) program, which had been more or less dormant since the turn of the century. By 1966 he had obtained Senate approval for a new set of graduate regulations for the doctoral degree. Furthermore, even though the 1960–1 ad hoc Curriculum Review Committee was disbanded in 1962 without having filed a report, Cohen continued to proselytize about the challenges facing undergraduate legal education at McGill and in Canada generally.[14] But little changed until 1964, when Scott retired as dean and Cohen was named to succeed him.[15] While remaining director of the Institute of Air and Space Law, Cohen directed most of his attention to remaking the faculty's BCL curriculum. Ideas which lay behind the creation of the ad hoc curriculum committee during his acting-deanship quickly resurfaced, often to be implemented in the absence of prior consultation or committee study within the faculty.

In 1964–5, without seeking the approval of the Quebec Bar, which even then retained strict control of the entrance requirements for legal study and the content of the undergraduate curriculum through its Professional Education Regulations, Cohen launched a substantial renovation of the BCL teaching program. New (and to many, esoteric) third-year options were introduced: Criminology, Principles of Soviet Law, and Theories of Civil Responsibility. The following year, again without approval from the profession, six electives and five other seminars primarily in the fields of public law, regulatory law, international law, and legal theory were added to the curriculum, and the BCL degree regulations were modified so as to permit students to take courses in the Faculty of Arts. Moreover, all undergraduates were required to take at least one of the elective courses and one "perspectives" seminar. Of course, there is nothing particularly novel or transformative about any of those changes to the curriculum if one takes a North American perspective. But they were a first in Canada and, what is more, they were undertaken in a jurisdiction where the Quebec Bar insisted not only on controlling the minutest details of legal education, but also on imposing a predominantly private law and professional cast on the curriculum.[16]

The principal graduate curricular initiative of Cohen's early deanship was even more ambitious. Another funding application to the Ford Foundation in 1965 resulted in a grant of $425,000 over five years to establish a second specialized teaching and research unit – the Institute of Foreign and Comparative Law. As his first annual report as dean makes clear, in Cohen's mind the institute was to be the vehicle by which McGill finally adopted the nonprofessional view of its mission that he had long preached and thereby rejoined the vanguard of North American legal education.[17] By December 1965, however, most professors realized that Cohen was not just tinkering with the graduate teaching program. In two memoranda circulated to all professors the following spring, the first proposals for an optional undergraduate program in the common law as a component of the regular BCL course were mooted.[18] While neither of these documents specifically suggested the creation of a full Bachelor of Laws (LLB) course, evidence that this initiative was on Cohen's mind can be found in his correspondence with the Law Society of Upper Canada in the fall of 1964 concerning course requirements for accreditation of non-Ontario common-law programs.[19]

Nevertheless, Cohen concentrated publicly on arguing for the creation only of those undergraduate courses needed to complement the institute's graduate comparative-law curriculum. To provide the intellectual basis for comparative legal study, Cohen and the newly appointed director of the institute, J.J. Gow, lobbied for separate common-law offerings in core subjects such as property, contract, and torts. Soon it became conventional wisdom in most quarters of the faculty that a successful graduate Institute of Foreign and Comparative Law would require the sustenance of a dynamic undergraduate common-law curriculum (whether accredited as an LLB degree program or not). Moreover, Cohen and Gow (himself a Scots civilian) also believed that the private-law component of the BCL program was in need of revitalization. Without a dynamic North American orientation to the teaching of civil law, they feared that the institute would soon become lop-sided and that the common law would eventually dominate the faculty's undergraduate private-law curriculum.[20]

These two program goals came to direct most institute activity between 1965 and 1968. Notwithstanding its intended use to enhance the faculty's library collection of common-law materials and to bring postdoctoral and visiting comparativist scholars to the institute on a short-term basis, the Ford Foundation grant was used mainly to recruit both common lawyers and civilians as full-time members of the teaching staff.[21] While the faculty was able to attract and retain several common lawyers, just three of the ten new positions created between 1965 and 1968 were filled by professors who taught private civil-law subjects.[22]

Whether by accident or design, it was apparent by early 1967 that the teaching needs of the Institute of Foreign and Comparative Law were to be central to all curricular planning within the faculty.[23] It was also clear that those needs would make major changes to the undergraduate teaching program inevitable. In the 1966–7 academic year, the institute launched three seminars in the common law, and the following year it mounted an extensive series of graduate electives open to undergraduates. The offerings included six advanced comparative-law seminars and eight basic common-law courses: contract, torts, trusts and real property, evidence, family law, personal property, sale of goods, and restitution. Many civil-law colleagues began to become suspicious of the curricular reordering being wrought through the institute and of the changes to the composition of the professoriate which those modifications entailed. Nothing seemed to illustrate the problem with as much poignancy as the faculty's difficulties in recruiting and retaining young civil-law scholars, especially francophones. At the time, few professors seemed to care if this failure were due to Cohen's general orientation towards the aims and methods of legal education in North America rather than in Europe, or to his aggressive recruitment of common lawyers, or to the declining interest in private law generally during the social-activist 1960s. Cohen, his ideas, recruits, and style came, rightly or wrongly, to be seen as a threat to the BCL curriculum.

In part to defuse those criticisms, a research concentration in the civil law, known as the Civil Law Studies Programme, was established in 1966. That concentration, under the direction of Professor Paul-André Crépeau, by then the president of the Province of Quebec's Civil Code Revision Office, was intended to counterbalance the Institute of Foreign and Comparative Law, which had come to be viewed as a Trojan horse for the common law at McGill. Resistance to Cohen's initiatives also came from professors who were members of the Quebec Bar and from the local McGill alumni, who were concerned that, like the initial curricular changes engineered in 1965, the comparative- and common-law renovation of the undergraduate program was occurring prior to the Quebec Bar actually revising its regulations relating to university legal education. Nevertheless, by the spring of 1967 it was an open secret that amendments to the *régime pédagogigue* governing the content of the undergraduate law curriculum were imminent, and this line of criticism began to abate.

For the first twenty years of his McGill career, then, most of Cohen's energy was directed to establishing the conditions for replicating in a Canadian vernacular the great ideas then transforming legal education in the United States. Legal realism, the case method, policy studies, legal theory, international law, and liberal education were the watchwords.[24] The establishment of an undergraduate LLB program with a pan-Canadian student catchment and intellectual focus was to be the vehicle.

THE DREAM REALIZED: THE FORMAL ESTABLISHMENT OF THE NATIONAL PROGRAMME

All the specific curricular developments engineered by Cohen between 1964 and 1966 – the establishment of the Institute of Comparative Law and a resurrected doctoral program, the recruitment of common-law professors, and attempt to reinvigorate the civil law through the Civil Law Studies Programme – laid the intellectual and structural foundations for realizing his dream of a faculty where both the common law and the civil law would be taught side by side at the undergraduate level. To that end, in part to follow up on developments in the Institute of Comparative Law and in part to respond to increasingly vocal dissent within the faculty, an ad hoc Resources Committee chaired by Professor Gerald LeDain was established in November 1966.[25] That committee was formally charged with the tasks of examining what further changes, if any, should be made to the undergraduate curriculum and degree programs, and assessing what additional material and financial resources would be required if the faculty were to launch an accredited LLB degree program. Its report to the faculty in April 1967 (a document of about one hundred pages of text and a like number of pages of appendices covering everything from specific library titles to be acquired to the teaching timetable) unanimously recommended the establishment of a full-fledged undergraduate common-law program. Following its adoption by the Law Faculty Council, this report then served as the basis for Cohen's successful presentation to the university Senate the following month and, after substantial reworking by Cohen himself, to the Board of Governors that autumn. By the spring of 1968 (almost ten years exactly since Cohen began to muse publicly about the creation of a common-law curriculum at McGill), everything seemed to be in place – at least within the university – to launch the main component of what has come to be known as the National Programme.

Yet the establishment of an undergraduate LLB tuition in Quebec of the mid 1960s was seen by almost everyone to have political, social, and financial repercussions far beyond those normally the subject of academic debate within a university. Three of these external factors merit notice. First, there was the uncertain social context. McGill was confronted by projections of an expanded demand for legal education (even from its traditional constituencies) flowing from the postwar baby boom. It was, at the same time, challenged by the political and ideological initiatives of the Quiet Revolution in Quebec. The former stirrings produced, in 1968, the McGill Français movement (hardly congenial to the launching of an English-language common-law program), and the latter, between 1963 and 1966, a Royal Commission Inquiry on Education (the Parent Commission).[26] Some of the commission's recommendations – such as the creation of the postsecondary Collège d'enseignement général et professionnel (CEGEPs) and the direct admission of eighteen-year-old students to legal study – were to challenge the faculty's traditional view of its educational mission. Yet others – such as the recommendation for a withdrawal of the professional corporations from legal education and for a massive infusion of new money into the postsecondary educational system – enabled the faculty to enrich the range of courses offered by increasing its full-time professorial complement from eight to twenty and its first-year student intake from 70 to 150.[27]

A second external element, which was also favourable to the creation of the common-law program, was a changing perception within the Law Society of Upper Canada of the meaning of its decision in 1957 to relinquish its monopoly on legal education in Ontario. By permitting that province's universities to establish accredited law faculties in competition with its own Osgoode Hall Law School, and thereby severing the university education and professional training components of legal education, the Law Society implicitly also accepted that graduates of accredited faculties in other provinces might apply directly for admission to the profession. The affiliation of Osgoode Hall with York University and the recruitment of LeDain as its first academic dean in 1968 happily coincided with Cohen's presentation of McGill's proposal to the Law Society and with the formal recognition of the McGill LLB on 16 February 1968.[28]

The third propitious factor suggesting an opportunity for curricular innovation at McGill was the reorganization of the Professional Training Programme of the Quebec Bar in 1968. Since 1951 the bar-admission course had been given as a fourth year within the law faculties. At a time of increasing enrolments, the presence of an additional eighty fourth-year students taxed both teaching and library resources within the faculty, even after a new library and classroom complex was opened in 1966. Combined with the Quebec Bar's detailed regulation of the undergraduate law program, the bar-admission course also cast an unwelcome careerist and professional shadow over McGill's regular BCL curriculum. As of 1 June 1968, however, the bar reassumed responsibility for the professional training component of legal education and, in conformity with the recommendations of the Parent Commission, relaxed somewhat its controls over the content of the undergraduate teaching program and the admissions requirements of its accredited faculties.[29]

While the external context of Quebec and Canadian legal education in the mid to late 1960s thus presented an excellent occasion for the faculty to reassess its undergraduate curriculum along the lines long advocated by Cohen, that context was not without its immediate challenges to the McGill law program. Two of those challenges seemed particularly threatening to the BCL course as then constituted. The rapid expansion of the French-language law faculties and a renewed Quebec nationalism created a fear that the faculty would have difficulty maintaining its traditional francophone catchment (normally about one-third of the entering class). Further, the social and political uncertainties associated with the Quiet Revolution suggested to many observers that, despite predictions of increased demand for enrolment, the faculty's historical population base in anglophone Quebec would soon be insufficient to sustain a strictly English-language, civil-law faculty. Both those apprehensions played an important role in shaping the deliberations and eventual recommendations of the ad hoc Resources Committee.[30]

In retrospect, it is tempting to conclude, given the conjuncture of circumstances just noted – the academic reasons advanced by Cohen and Gow, the favourable external conditions, and concern about the faculty's capacity to attract qualified students if it simply maintained its traditional BCL program – that the outcome of the ad hoc Resources Committee process was inevitable. Such a conclusion would, however, be a mistake. As the committee's minutes reveal, within the faculty thinly veiled threats, cajoling, compromise, and Cohen's unremitting determination to establish an LLB tuition were needed to see the project through.[31] Indeed, when the LeDain Committee report was presented to the faculty in April 1967, it contained a number of new proposals not anticipated five months earlier when the committee was struck. The report recommended the formal establishment of not only a free-standing three-year common-law course but also a four-year bijuridical tuition (civil law and common law), coupled with a bilingual undergraduate teaching program (especially in the civil law). In furtherance of these recommendations, two major modifications to the existing curriculum were proposed: the creation of a complete common-law program leading to an accredited LLB degree and the establishment of a French-language stream in the BCL curriculum.

In his brief to the McGill Senate dated 17 May 1967, Cohen presented the faculty's case for curricular innovation in the following terms:

As the years go by we will know what student response there will be to these ... [two new] ... programmes, but it is the Faculty's view that without such a programme we would be in danger on two fronts: on the one hand we would be losing English language students to other provinces, and on the other we would remain essentially an English language Civil Law school and losing students as well to the rapidly developing French-speaking law schools, notably Montreal and Laval. Both for reasons of survival and of effective development, the Common Law program and the French language programme are essential. It is the Faculty's belief that the resources are available and that the quite modest price to be paid for this programme will more than justify itself in terms of the contribution that legal education at McGill can make to Canada as a whole, to the scientific development of the law, and in particular to the inter-penetrating of Civil and Common Law which is so much part of the public and commercial life of Quebec.

As this statement reveals, sound theoretical reasons could be advanced to support the two new programs. But the Senate, and presumably also the Board of Governors, were sceptical. Cohen therefore spent a busy summer in 1967 meeting a number of the detailed concerns raised at the May Senate meeting. Almost single-handedly he lobbied every important university official for support of the faculty's proposals. That fall, after a further round of politicking, both the Senate and the Board of Governors approved the two new programs. Nevertheless, despite the opportunity that such approval seemed to present for those on the faculty seeking to exploit the potential of sophisticated comparative study through a single, obligatory, bilingual, four-year program leading to the BCL and LLB degrees for all students, the Faculty Council seemed disinclined to take such a radical step. Perhaps more important, Cohen himself seems to have been unmoved either to seek out or to elaborate the theoretical justification and practical mechanics for any such tuition.[32]

For this reason, the first years of the two new post-1968 teaching ventures could be characterized primarily as a struggle for legitimacy and not as continuing intellectual development, the term National Programme itself having little status (let alone currency) within the university.

The words "National Programme" appear neither in the faculty's presentation to the McGill Senate of May 1967 nor in the accreditation letters exchanged between Cohen and the Law Society of Upper Canada in early 1968. Rather, the term seems to have resulted from the slippage of usage in relation to McGill being a "national" law faculty offering what it came to call "national" courses in public and commercial law.[33] For several years the expression National Programme signalled no particular integrated or unified BCL/LLB program but was simply the code name for the sequential program by which graduates of either the civil-law or common-law course could acquire the second degree upon completing a further year's study. What is more, the three other curricular developments that Cohen had promoted – the graduate and undergraduate programs (including the four-year integrated joint BCL/LLB program) in comparative law offered through the Institute of Foreign and Comparative Law, the Civil Law Studies Programme, and the French-language BCL program – were not seen as central to the National Programme concept.

Neither of the first two of these other innovative components of the McGill curriculum flourished as intended during the remainder of Cohen's deanship. Once the undergraduate LLB program was created, much of the creative energy went out of the Institute of Foreign and Comparative Law. Gow left to practise law in British Columbia, and the recently recruited common-law professors devoted themselves to designing and teaching the new undergraduate curriculum. Only in the late 1970s, with the launching of its International Business Law Programme, did the institute begin to attract large numbers of graduate students, and at this point it was the foreign, not the comparative, law aspect of the endeavour that was predominant.[34] A similar fate befell the Civil Law Studies Programme. Even though Paul-André Crépeau initially was able to use it as a vehicle to recruit young francophone professors to McGill, the demands of the Civil Code Revision Office drew most of the research energy of the faculty's private lawyers. As a result, the program did not develop as a dynamic civil-law research institute until reconstituted under Crépeau's direction as the Quebec Research Centre of Private and Comparative Law after the Civil Code Revision Office completed its work in 1977.³⁵ Even then, however, the teaching of civil law never seemed to elicit the same enthusiasm from students as the theoretically grounded teaching of common-law torts, contracts, and property.

By contrast, the third complementary curricular innovation, and one of the two initiatives approved by the McGill Senate in 1967 was to have a much larger impact on the undergraduate teaching program. In 1968 the faculty decided, as a matter of principle, and where resources permitted, to offer French-language sections of all first-year courses and most basic upper-year subjects in the BCL curriculum, in addition to the regular English-language sections. It was also decided to formalize the practice by which upper-year elective courses and seminars might occasionally be offered in the French language only. While there was some uncertainty within the faculty (especially among common lawyers) about the justification for the French-language program, it is clear from memoranda submitted to the ad hoc Resources Committee that the eventual development of a bilingual curriculum (at least in civil law and federal subjects) was the object that many proponents of the program had in view even in 1968. But despite the momentum given by its approval in the university Senate, the French-language program did not really take immediate root in the faculty, and only during the 1980s were the ambitions stated in 1968 slowly coming to be realized.³⁶

The fourth piece of the curricular plan Cohen put together in the mid 1960s was the establishment of the undergraduate common-law tuition. Given his own longstanding passion for the LLB program, it was to be expected that this component of the new curriculum would become well-established first. For the same reason, it was foreseeable that for many years it alone (and not some coherent combination of all four curricular initiatives of the mid 1960s) would be seen as the leitmotiv of the National Programme. In its initial design, the curriculum of the new undergraduate common-law program was almost symmetrical to that of the existing civil-law program. Apart from a greater number of compulsory private-law courses required of students, the organization and content of the two three-year programs did not differ significantly from those of, say, the University of Toronto or the University of Montreal. Moreover, the fourth year in each program was essentially an intense (and obligatory) exposure to private-law courses in the other program (for example, trusts, wills, restitution, remedies, landlord and tenant, real estate transactions, commercial transactions, and civil procedure for students who initially entered the faculty in the BCL program) rather than a genuinely comparative-law tuition. In Cohen's eyes especially, the primary purpose of the LLB program was to permit students to acquire formal qualifications for membership in various Canadian common-law bars.[37]

Perhaps miraculously, no deep cleavages between civilians and common lawyers, or between anglophone and francophone professors, emerged once this multidimensional National Programme was put into place. A number of reasons, most attributable to Cohen, explain why that feared dissension within the faculty did not develop.[38] Some of those factors were structural. The faculty was not formally divided into two distinct sections with separate deans, admissions procedures, and administrative apparati. Nor was it functionally departmentalized into smaller program units – such as civil law, common law, public law, or commercial law – each with a high degree of autonomy. Professors typically were assigned to teach at least one "national" course as well as one common-law or civil-law course, so that routine pedagogic interaction among most professors was maintained. Undergraduate students in each of the BCL and LLB streams were required to take a minimum of six credits of private-law subjects from the other degree stream, as well as to take all public-law and most commercial-law courses together.

Other reasons for continuing harmony were rhetorical. After 1968 the faculty consciously emphasized in its literature (admissions brochures, calendars, alumni newsletters) the common features of the two streams and stressed its commitment to the idea of the four-year sequential BCL/LLB program which comprised them both. Even though the teaching and research possibilities (and indeed the intellectual ambitions) of a fully integrated undergraduate program were underdeveloped at that time, the public discourse of the faculty towards its student body became increasingly one of bilingualism, comparative study, intellectual endeavour, and public service as nationally trained legal practitioners.

Finally, some of the reasons for ongoing cooperation were personal. Cohen was an enthusiast who was able to sell the possibilities of the National Programme to aspiring young common-law academics. Ideas about the mission of legal education that had appeared so foreign to some commentators and critics just a few years earlier were now seen as self-evident. Cohen was also a social activist, chairing a Royal Commission on Hate Propaganda, consulting widely on matters of international law, and often being away from the faculty for extended periods during his deanship.[39] In his absence, the professoriate began to generate its own consensus about the direction the faculty should be taking and, even though that consensus was sometimes formed as a counterpoint to Cohen's ideas, it provided a coherent focus for debate about matters of curriculum, recruitment, and student admissions policy. A sense of common endeavour in the face of real and imagined external threats also kept the fragile coalition that permitted the launching of the common-law program over the period 1964–8 from disintegrating. When Cohen's five-year term as dean ended in June 1969, he could justifiably say that he had played the major role in transforming the Faculty of Law at McGill into a modern, dynamic, North American institution. He had also given the faculty its undergraduate National Programme, a program which is, in the 1990s, its defining characteristic.

CONCLUSION: MAXWELL COHEN THE ENTHUSIAST

It is now almost twenty-five years since Cohen left the deanship at McGill, but in many ways he has never left. I personally witnessed his continuing interest in the institution and in the National Programme, having benefited between 1984 and 1989 from a stream of ideas and suggestions on ways the faculty should be pursuing its scholarly mission. Legal education today, it is true, is not the legal education of the 1950s and 1960s. Its purveyors, its clientele, and its sense of its appropriate content has, in some places in Canada at least, emerged from the long shadow of the U.S. academy. And the National Programme of 1992 at McGill is not quite the same National Programme that Cohen worked to put into place in 1968. Its theory, its practice, and its ambitions are those of a younger generation. Cohen can, however, continue to derive satisfaction from the fact that his quarter-century of sustained effort contributed mightily to the present flourishing of legal education in Canada and at McGill. The mark of a truly outstanding educator is the ability to recognize and accept that someone else's dream may one day set the curricular and scholarly agenda and yet, however different that dream may be from one's own, to maintain enthusiasm for the challenges and the opportunities of the overall endeavour. On both of these counts Maxwell Cohen surely meets the standard of excellence.

NOTES

Much of the research for this text was undertaken in connection with an earlier study, R.A. Macdonald, "The National Law Programme at McGill: Origins, Establishment, Prospects" (1990), 13 *Dalhousie Law Journal* 211–363. In preparing this revised version, I benefited from several conversations with John Brierley, Paul-André Crépeau, John Durnford, and Ivan Vlasic – each of whom generously shared their memories of Max with me. I am also grateful to Blaine Baker and Nicholas Kasirer for their detailed comments on an earlier version of this article. Obviously, none of those people should be held accountable for anything said here.

1 For a more institutionally focused review of curricular developments at McGill during that period see Macdonald, "The National Law Programme at McGill," 273–318.
2 Cohen's capacity to enthuse is well captured in the tribute by R. St J. Macdonald, "Maxwell Cohen at Eighty: International Lawyer, Educator and Judge" (1989), 27 *Canadian Yearbook of International Law* 3.
3 Basic biographical details about Cohen can be found in K. Simpson, ed., *Canadian Who's Who*, vol. 26 (Toronto: University of Toronto Press 1991), 195, and in the sketch by H. Gutkin, *The Worst of Times, The Best of Times* (Markham: Fitzhenry and Whiteside 1987), 94–108.
4 See, for example, Macdonald, "Maxwell Cohen at Eighty." Given the focus of this text I will not directly discuss Cohen's ideas about pedagogy, legal research, or the meaning of a "liberal legal education," themes that are thoughtfully canvassed in John MacLaren's study in this collection. I do, however, signal where these ideas seem to have informed his "national programme" project.
5 See J.E.C. Brierley, "Quebec Legal Education since 1945: Cultural Paradoxes and Traditional Ambiguities" (1986), 10 *Dalhousie Law Journal* 5, passim, but especially 8–10, 12–14, and 34–6.
6 At the time of his initial appointment (on a limited-term contract), the full-time teaching staff at McGill consisted of Dean Stuart Lemesurier, F.R. Scott, and John P. Humphrey, who was on leave at the United Nations. Cohen acceded to Humphrey's full-time position in 1947, when the latter formally resigned to remain at the United Nations. That same year the faculty hired Louis Baudouin, its first French-trained civilian, who was to prove an important ally of Cohen's on many issues throughout the 1950s.
7 In addition to this flurry of activity within the faculty, Cohen was also busy during the early 1950s on the wider Canadian scene. His pioneering study on law teaching and scholarship, financed by the Social Science Research Council, was published in 1950 as "The Condition of Legal Education in Canada" (1950), 28 *Canadian Bar Review* 267. He was instrumental, along with Frank Scott, in the establishment of what is now the Canadian Association of Law Teachers in 1951. In 1954 he wrote "Objectives and Methods of Legal Education: An Outline" (1954), 32 *Canadian Bar Review* 762, a Canadian adaptation of a

debate about undergraduate legal education then raging in the pages of the *Journal of Legal Education* in the United States.

8 Cohen graduated from the bar-sponsored Manitoba Law School in 1934 and from the LLM program at Northwestern University in 1936. He was a research fellow at the Harvard Law School during the 1937–8 academic year. Brief discussion of formative influences upon him during that period can be found in "Scholar in Residence," *Canadian Lawyer* (Dec. 1981), 16; Macdonald, "Maxwell Cohen at Eighty," 5–6, and in Gutkin, *The Worst of Times*, 101–2. In that third source, Cohen stated that he was greatly influenced by "realists" (presumeably Leon Green and Walter Wheeler Cook, but depending on the degree of precision one attaches to the term, perhaps also Albert Kocourek and John Henry Wigmore) at Northwestern, as well as by Roscoe Pound, Felix Frankfurter, and Thomas Reed Powell at Harvard.

9 For a summary review of McGill's role in the dispute between the teaching faculty at Osgoode Hall Law School and the benchers of the Law Society of Upper Canada see I. Kyer and J. Bickenbach, *The Fiercest Debate* (Toronto: The Osgoode Society 1987), 216 and 271.

10 This impression of the faculty is derived mainly from discussions with current members of the faculty who taught at McGill during the 1950s, as well as from a series of interviews and conversations I have had with, by my estimate, some forty of the approximately two hundred students who graduated from the faculty between 1951 and 1959. Of course, from the perspective of 1992 it is risky to use such charged terms as "trade school" or "liberal education" since their precise content is contingent. What we might deprecate as a trade-school education today, for example, could well have been thought to be the *ne plus ultra* of a liberal legal education in the 1950s. In all events, there seems to be an almost unanimous feeling among those I interviewed that the Faculty of Law in the 1950s was a mediocre and, apart from some excitement about Scott's "big cases" in the Supreme Court of Canada, intellectually sterile institution.

11 See M. Cohen, "Annual Report of the Acting Dean of the Faculty of Law to the Principal, 1960–61," McGill University Archives. It was also around this time that Cohen first began to talk about the possibility of translating the faculty's emerging strength in comparative law into the foundation of a common-law program. The decision of the Law Society of Upper Canada to permit university-based legal education in Ontario, and the foundation of a common-law program at Ottawa, in complement to its civil-law program (which was established in 1953), were no doubt among the factors that directed Cohen's attention to this idea.

12 F.R. Scott, "Annual Report of the Dean of the Faculty of Law to the Principal, 1961–62," McGill University Archives.
13 See, *The Institute of Air and Space Law: A Brief History and Bibliography, 1951–1970* (Montreal: McGill University 1970). Until the late 1950s the institute was essentially directed to training legal officials for the emerging air transportation industry. Given his background in international law and his interest in major policy questions, it is not surprising that Cohen gave the institute a greater focus on theoretical rather than applied research, and on questions of space rather than air law.
14 Three papers published during the early 1960s reveal Cohen's commitment to ideas first expressed in his 1950 study. See M. Cohen, "Lawyers and Lawyering: The Professional and Intellectual Traditions" (1961), 7 *McGill Law Journal* 181; M. Cohen "The Academic Lawyer's Use of Intellect" (1961), 14 *Journal of Legal Education* 141; M. Cohen "The Condition of Legal Education in Canada – Fifteen Years Later" [1964] *Canadian Bar Association Papers* 116. At this same time, Cohen was chairman of the Committee on the Journal of the Association of Canada Law Teachers, and in that quality founded *Canadian Legal Studies*, a Canadian version of the American *Journal of Legal Education*, for the ACLT in 1964. See the Minutes of the Annual Meetings of the ACLT for 1962 and 1963, as reprinted in *Canadian Legal Studies* for those years, pages 59, 113.
15 For a brief review of Scott's ill-fated deanship see S. Djwa, *The Politics of the Imagination: A Life of F.R. Scott* (Toronto: McClelland and Stewart 1987), 365–8. A more detailed assessment of legal education at McGill from 1961 through 1964 is provided in Macdonald, "The National Law Programme," 284–9.
16 See Brierley, "Quebec Legal Education," 18–24, 34–6.
17 See M. Cohen, "Annual Report of the Dean of the Faculty of Law to the Principal, 1964–65," McGill University Archives. While this report clearly states the case for the institute, it does not provide any details as to what exactly "rejoining the vanguard of North American legal education" was meant to signify. Presumably, Cohen had in mind those ideas and proposals mooted in his papers cited in note 14.
18 These memoranda and other documents are collected in the faculty archives relating to the establishment of the National Programme.
19 See the letter to Cohen, dated 30 November 1964, sent by William Howland, chairman of the Legal Education Committee of the Law Society of Upper Canada, in which, responding to Cohen's inquiry, he set out the requirement for accreditation of university law faculties.
20 In view of the prevailing intellectual climate in Quebec, such concerns were not misplaced. See, generally, P. Azard, "L'organisation d'un centre de droit comparé" (1964), 2 *Canadian Legal Studies* 99, who

doubted that such a centre could function without at the same time undermining the integrity of the civil law in Quebec.

21 Not all these positions were financed by the Ford Foundation grant. Based on budgetary difficulties the faculty was to experience during the 1969–70 academic year, it would appear that at least four slots were not fully funded within the faculty's base budget. Among the key professors recruited at this time were Jacob Ziegel, Donovan Waters, William Foster, and Yves Caron.

22 A major part of the difficulty Cohen faced in nurturing the civil-law component of the institute was his lack of exposure to foreign models of civil-law education. While he was able to identify problems with the public- and commercial-law parts of the McGill program (and imagine improvements based on ideas flowing from the United States), he had no such external point of reference by which to evaluate the civil-law program. As a consequence, his considerable energies came increasingly directed to the common-law and public-law components of the curriculum (including the recruitment of professors to teach such subjects), and the civil-law tuition moved further from the mainstream of faculty curricular reform.

23 For a succinct expression of this view see M. Cohen, "Towards Understanding Canada's Two Great Legal Traditions," in "Chancellor Day Hall," a special insert in the *McGill News*, December 1966, which was produced to celebrate the opening of the faculty's new classroom and library block.

24 Of course, each of those "watchwords" could of itself be the subject of an article about Cohen. Let me suggest, briefly and simply by way of identifying key sign-posts, some lines of inquiry: How would Cohen's curricular efforts have been different had his jurisprudential heroes been Lon Fuller and Edwin Patterson, rather than Leon Green and Thomas Reed Powell? How would his view of "modern" pedagogy been different had he done graduate work at Oxford and Cambridge, rather than Northwestern and Harvard? How would his overall view of Canadian law and legal education been different had his primary intellectual extroversions been to the French language and the civil law at Laval and the University of Montreal, rather than to the English-language common-law endeavours at Osgoode Hall and the University of Toronto? In other words, implicit in, and informing all this activity – the scholarship, the teaching, the university administration – was a personal view of the enterprise of legal education, a view very much the product of Cohen's own background, inclinations, and abilities.

25 Besides LeDain, committee members included Professors P.-A. Crépeau and John Durnford, as well as the two institute directors – J.J. Gow (foreign and comparative law) and Edward McWhinney (air and

space law). Marianne Scott, law librarian, and Professor J.E.C. Brierley, chairman of the Library Committee, were also *ex officio* members of the Resources Committee.

26 See *Report of the Royal Commission Inquiry on Education* (Quebec: Queen's Printer 1963–6).

27 Two other fctors that can be seen broadly as related to social context, although their impact at a distance of twenty-five years is more difficult to assess, were the general mood of Canadian patriotism in the lead up to the Centennial year and the increasingly dominating ideology (mythology?) of McGill University as a "national institution" drawing its students from across the country.

28 On the intellectual climate of Ontario legal education at this time see generally H.W. Arthurs, "The Affiliation of Osgoode Hall Law School with York University" (1967), 17 *University of Toronto Law Journal* 194. After Cohen's presentation, the Law Society canvassed the six Ontario law deans for their views of the McGill proposal. One was firmly opposed, one was lukewarm, and four were generally supportive.

29 The official position of the Bar on these questions was set out in "Comité des études universitaires et de formation professionnelle" (1967), 27 *Revue du Barreau* 338, 425, and (1968), 28 *ibid.*, 276, 387. For a detailed review of the 1968 reforms see Brierley, "Quebec Legal Education," 36–7.

30 Whether McGill University's self-perception as a national institution followed or preceded the recognition of the threat to its traditional anglophone catchment is difficult to glean from archival materials. Moreover, whether the law faculty's feared marginalization from Quebec was a product of its own misunderstandings or the misunderstandings of francophone elites (and their children) about McGill is another unanswerable question. Cohen's own orientation at this time, however, was clearly anglophone and pan-Canadian.

31 Scott's bitter opposition to the idea of a common-law program, and the suspicion this opposition nurtured in various other colleagues and among alumni, was only one of the plethora of obstacles that Cohen had to overcome during the period in which the Resources Committee was deliberating.

32 See M. Cohen, "Epilogue," in *Faculty of Law, Special Convocation, January 21, 1967* (Montreal: McGill 1968), a text dated 9 May 1968 and presumably written after both the Senate and the Law Society of Upper Canada had approved the LLB program. In the faculty's presentation to McGill's Senate, the possibility of developing a single bilingual, joint program was not even mooted, although Cohen was at pains to point out that all students would have to take some courses in each stream, and that both BCL and LLB students would be able to acquire the

second degree in one further year's study. In other words, while the possibility of a fully integrated, four-year, bilingual, joint-degree program was not excluded in 1968, it did not form the basis of the faculty's proposal to Senate; nor did the idea appear as a feature of the new program when it was launched that fall.

33 My research indicates that the expression "National Programme" first publicly appeared in a memorandum to all professors drafted by Cohen on 15 August 1967 in which he reported on his efforts to address concerns expressed at the Senate meeting in May, with a view to having the program approved early in the fall. In June 1967 a working document produced for the vice-principal (academic) at McGill refers to the fourth-year tuition as the "Canadian Programme." But this usage seems to have been soon abandoned in favour of the term "National Programme."

34 The faculty's vocation to comparative law at the undergraduate level was not formally realized until the early 1980s when the sequential route to acquiring both BCL and LLB degrees was abolished and students were required to begin a comparative tuition in their second year of studies. At the graduate level, the Institute of Comparative Law began to promote comparative studies as its primary vocation only after 1989, when H. Patrick Glenn became its director. For further details on both these points see Macdonald, "The National Law Programme," 333–46.

35 For a discussion of the influence of the Civil Code Revision Office on civil-law scholarship generally see R.A. Macdonald, "Understanding Civil Law Scholarship in Quebec" (1985), 23 *Osgoode Hall Law Journal* 602–8.

36 A number of explanations – political, financial, and bureaucratic – might be offered for the slow gestation of the French-language program, but they are all highly speculative. Here again, it appears that so much of Max's energy after 1968 was devoted to ensuring the success of the new LLB course that development of the French-language program was essentially left to others, who may not have been able to bring the same enthusiasm to the endeavour as Cohen might have done. There is also the fact that recruitment of francophone civilians was made more difficult by the need, once the Ford Foundation money was exhausted in 1969, to find additional resources within the faculty's base budget to cover the salaries of common-law professors already holding tenure-track positions.

37 Cohen's public articulation of the justification for the LLB appears to have changed somewhat between 1964 and 1969. In the earlier period he consciously sought to emphasize the need to generate understanding of "the two great languages and legal systems of the modern

world," as an intellectual as much as a practical exercise. See M. Cohen, "The Condition of Legal Education in Canada – Fifteen Year Later, 1949–1964" [1964] *Canadian Bar Association Papers* 131; and Cohen, "Towards Understanding," 6–7. By 1969, however, the professional and public service side of a common-law education seemed more dominant in his rhetoric. This change of justification may also help to explain why the comparative-law vocation of the faculty was less prominent in the years immediately after the LLB program was formally established.

38 For an intimation of some of these explanations see H.P. Glenn, "McGill Law School: A Summary of Its Operations" (faculty working paper dated 30 April 1974). See also R.A. Macdonald, "The Theory of the National Programme" (chapter one of the *Self Study Document* prepared for the Cyclical Review of the Faculty of Law, dated April 1988).

39 For a review of these other facets of Cohen's career see the essays by Irwin Cotler and Edward McWhinney in this collection.

Anglophone Quebec and the Quiet Revolution: Maxwell Cohen at McGill University

EDWARD McWHINNEY

I met Maxwell Cohen for the first time in Toronto in the fall of 1955. He had come to the University of Toronto to give the biennial exchange lectures on comparative law that were alternated between the two law schools, Toronto and McGill, and were sponsored with Carnegie Corporation support. Cohen's visit had been arranged by the German *émigré* jurist Wolfgang Friedmann, who had just left Toronto for Columbia University in New York. As Friedmann's successor in teaching comparative law and jurisprudence, I found myself charged with Cohen's lectures. Somewhat unexpectedly, Cohen's chosen theme was public international law, and he delivered the lectures with sparkling wit and a fluid style that bordered on the rococo. I gave the return Carnegie lectures at McGill University in the fall of 1956, lecturing on delictual liability under the French, German, and Soviet civil codes. It was the start of a long-sustained personal and professional association that would include an all too brief period as colleagues on the same faculty, with Cohen as dean.

Contrary to some impressions, Cohen was not Montreal born but had come there only after the war from his native Winnipeg, where he had all his early college and law-school education, followed by graduate work at Northwestern University and at Harvard. Winnipeg in the period of Cohen's youth was certainly the most cosmopolitan, eclectic, and cultured of the Canadian cities outside Quebec, with the first of the opera, ballet, and symphony orchestra groups on a professional, year-round basis in English-speaking Canada. By contrast, the English-speaking community Cohen found in Montreal was somewhat inward-looking, not particularly intellectual, and also monolithic – at least in its elite that dominated the commercial life of the city. These characteristics account for both the success and the problems Cohen encountered in bringing new ideas and a broader intellectual outlook to political problems existing just below the surface during the years he lived in Montreal.

MAXWELL COHEN AND THE LAUNCHING OF THE INTERNATIONAL LAW ASSOCIATION (CANADA)

Cohen was at the core of the intellectual "ginger" group in Montreal in the mid 1950s that launched the Canadian branch of the London-based International Law Association (later incorporated, in its Canadian activities, as the Canadian Society of International Law). He was its first president. The others in the founding group were Louis Bloomfield, an elegant and cultivated leader of the Canadian Jewish Community, whose family roots in Montreal went back to the beginning of the nineteenth century and who had been one of the rare anglophones in the first graduating class of the Faculté de droit of the Université de Montréal in the early 1920s; Gerald FitzGerald, an Irish Canadian from New Brunswick who was, at the time, the permanent general counsel of the International Civil Aviation Organisation in Montreal; and Nicholas Matte, a recent immigrant from Romania who had taken his doctoral degree from the Sorbonne, was one of the pioneers in the newly emerging field of space law, and had just entered on solo legal practice in Montreal. This diverse group of legal intellectuals gave the subject of international law, then hardly recognized in Canadian law schools and graduate schools, a breadth of intellectual outlook and a recognition of the cultural relativism of many of its existing rules and principles that went well beyond the traditional, "classical" international law to be found in most leading textbooks of the Western World.

The Canadian branch, along with branches of nonaligned countries like India and Yugoslavia, persuaded the conservative, London-based headquarters of the International Law Association to include in its agenda for debate at its biennial reunions the concept of peaceful coexistence among different political-ideological systems and the practical implications for international law in the dangerous Cold War era. Prominent jurists from the politically nonaligned countries – Nagendra Singh (later president of the World Court) and Krishna Rao from India and Milan Bartos and Milos Radojkovic from Yugoslavia – joined with the Canadian branch and with

Professor John Hazard, founder of Soviet legal studies in the United States, in launching the project within the ILA. Hazard, together with Manfred Lachs (later president of the World Court) from Poland and Grigory Tunkin, legal adviser to the Soviet Foreign Ministry and a consultant to Secretary Khrushchev from the Soviet Union, added voices of reason in calling for a civilized East-West juridical debate over the political issues that threatened an intercontinental nuclear war. Mᶜ Henri Cochaux of the Brussels bar presided over and directed the activities of the ILA Committee on Peaceful Coexistence from its beginning in the mid 1950s to the successful completion of its mandate a decade and a half later.

The International Law Association provided the first international legal arena for testing and refining, and then consolidating in legal terms, the notion of common legal principles and common orderly processes for law-making between the rival political-military blocs of the Cold War era. The ordinary arenas and processes for communication between East and West, in the United Nations Security Council and General Assembly and in bilateral exchanges between national foreign ministries, had become clogged through Cold War rhetoric and attendant political-military security fears. A neutral, nongovernmental, international scientific-legal arena like the ILA, which government legal advisers could attend in their private capacities without officially involving or committing their governments, could open the door to pragmatic exchanges and possible political compromises. It was at the ILA reunions and its intersessional committee meetings that the first major East-West legal discussions directed to intersystemic accommodation took place. It was here also that a practical *modus vivendi* was worked out between the Soviet campaign for an immediate Codification of Legal Principles of Peaceful Coexistence and Western foreign ministry fears that this would mean an end to "classical" international law. Here was the genesis of that Western-sponsored pragmatic, empirical, problem-oriented, step-by-step approach to international law-making, to be consummated in legal terms in the series of East-West treaties throughout the 1960s and the early 1970s on nuclear and general disarmament and on peacekeeping. This détente process was balanced in doctrinal-legal terms by the initiative of the United Nations General Assembly for codification of high-level or primary legal principles of friendly relations (coexistence), realized eventually in the celebrated General Assembly resolution of October 1970. The authors of this code felt they had created new international law, ranking as *Jus Cogens*, on the nonuse of force and the obligations of peaceful settlement of disputes.

Now that the Cold War has receded into history, it is appropriate to record the role of the Canadian Branch of the ILA and of Cohen, Bloomfield, and their colleagues on the executive. They not only started the East-West legal dialogue in the middle 1950s but insisted on maintaining it on the agenda in spite of pressures exercised on the London-based international executive by timorous national foreign ministries to have the subject dropped as politically too controversial, or as too dangerous to national interests, to analyse in legal terms.

COHEN AND LEGAL EDUCATION: THE NATIONAL PROGRAMME AT MCGILL

At the beginning of 1966 Maxwell Cohen invited me to come to McGill University as director of the Institute of Air and Space Law within the Faculty of Law, where he had recently become dean. The institute had been founded in 1951 and directed by a series of interesting people – some air and transportation specialists like Alfred Rosevear of Canadian National Railways and the first director, the American John Cobb Cooper; others with more varied experience like Eugène Pepin, a Frenchman who had been secretary to Prime Minister Aristide Briand of Kellogg-Briand Pact fame but who was also a pioneer aviator and air lawyer in his own right; Sir Francis Vallat, principal legal adviser to the British Foreign Office, who took over the institute for a year on a sabbatical leave; and Maxwell Cohen himself, who held the post immediately before his deanship. Cohen put the proposal to me on the basis of utilizing my general expertise in Soviet law in the new area of space law, where joint Soviet-Western cooperation would be logical in the development of legal principles and rules; and also as a way of becoming acquainted with the Quiet Revolution and its young francophone jurists in order to further my parallel specialization in federalism and constitutional law. I was, at the time of the McGill offer, already a tenured full professor at the University of Toronto, but the offer was attractive nonetheless.

The University of Toronto, in its constitutional structure at the time, resembled medieval England under the later Norman kings. It had an able and attractive young president, Claude Bissell, but presidential policy-making required a constant battle with entrenched barons in whose hands effective power was still concentrated. The barons were the deans of professional faculties like Law, Medicine, and Engineering, all of whom had been appointed by earlier presidents for life and who claimed and wielded absolute power within their own faculties. The dean of law, Cecil "Caesar" Wright, had been appointed in 1949 by the then president, Sidney Smith (later, and briefly, Canadian foreign minister in the Diefenbaker Conservative government) after Wright had been forced out as dean of the Osgoode Hall Law School (then a nonuniversity-affiliated professional legal school administered by the benchers of the Law Society) less than a year after he had been named to the post. Wright's feud with the Law Society, based originally on his campaign to expel the benchers from control of legal education in Ontario, had gained at least symbolic victory by the end of the 1950s when the benchers, facing the sheer weight of numbers of new students and no doubt wearied from the long battle, voluntarily vacated the entire field of pre-bar examination education. With the end of the internecine hostilities, the original *raison d'être* and justification for Wright's own role in legal education in Ontario tended to disappear also. He did not have any legal philosophy or core of substantive ideas on the goals of law and legal education to offer in its place to provide the intellectual leadership and inspiration for younger faculty and students in a rapidly changing industrial Ontario; rather, he extolled the American system of case law and case-law instruction which he had himself acquired as a graduate student at Harvard in the mid 1920s, and which had already been absorbed in Canadian law school teaching and instruction.

A new vision was needed after the wave of veterans returning from the Second World War had graduated from law school. Friedmann, on leaving Toronto for Columbia after a difficult relationship with Wright, had complained of a medieval fortress mentality in Toronto, one of repelling the invaders (the benchers of the Law Society) but at the same time of keeping out new intellectual ideas. The very able team that Wright had assembled or inherited in the early years of armed combat with the benchers were almost all gone a decade later – Wolfgang Friedmann, Jacob Finkelman, Eugene LaBrie, William Read, David Kilgour, Robert MacKay, A.B. Weston. Bora Laskin, who had come over from Osgoode Hall to Toronto with Wright in 1949 and who had been putative dean-in-waiting to Wright in the years since, had left for the Ontario Court of Appeal in the early 1960s. The arena for testing and developing radically new ideas on the role of law in contemporary society, and the special responsibilities of legal education, seemed to have shifted elsewhere than Toronto. Ironically enough, with Osgoode Hall finally established as a university faculty in its own right with the newly created York University in Toronto, the young Mark MacGuigan, later federal external affairs minister and justice minister, left the Toronto faculty in 1966 to join the new Faculty of Law at Osgoode Hall.

At McGill, meanwhile, Maxwell Cohen had finally become dean of law in 1965. He had voluntarily stood aside from the deanship three years earlier in favour of Frank Scott, who had been passed over for the post several times before by the university administration in apparent fear of adverse reactions from the Quebec government, then as now the principal source of finances for the university. Since the offer of deanship came in his mid fifties, Cohen had the prospect of one, or at most two, five-year terms. He seems to have determined to make something out of the post and to try to effect fundamental changes quickly. The root problems of McGill and its law faculty lay in the decline in effective political power, almost to the point of political irrelevance, of the narrowly Anglo-Saxon economic elite in Montreal which had been its traditional constituency. The political challenges to the economic power of that elite were already presaged with the onset of the Quiet Revolution at the opening of the 1960s and with French-as-language-of-work in industry and commerce that that presaged. In fact, language-of-work became the principal recommendation of Quebec's own Royal Commission on the French Language and Language Rights in Quebec (Commission Gendron) in December 1972, and was quickly embodied in the Bourassa government's Bill 22 of 1974 making French the official language, language of work, and language of education in Quebec. The flight of the Anglo-Saxon economic establishment, in numbers but also in the financial resources they represented, was just over the horizon and capable of being foreseen by intelligent, cool-thinking observers like Cohen.

Cohen's response, from his politically circumscribed post as dean of law, was one of boldness. Instead of joining a crusade against the emerging power of the young francophone intellectual forces of the Quiet Revolution, as did others of the anglophone community of Montreal and some of his university administration colleagues, he developed a positive program with no particular or necessary ethnocultural base. It was nothing less than to make McGill a "national" law school, with a "national programme," offering both the civil law (BCL) degree as before but also a common-law (LLB) degree, with both degrees obtainable in four years of combined study instead of the three years for the BCL degree alone. The hope was that the unique, double-professional degree program would attract able students from all over Canada and establish or re-establish the McGill faculty as a preeminent national educational institution.

At the same time, Cohen wanted to establish an international graduate law centre, drawing students from all over the world with the aid of ample scholarships. The graduate centre was based upon the existing Air and Space Law Institute and a newly founded Centre of Comparative Law. The political and financial dynamic was provided by a generous grant, negotiated by Cohen and Sir Francis Vallat with the Ford Foundation, for international and comparative law studies for an initial three-year period, later extended to five years, and then further extended for an unprecedented (for the Ford Foundation) third term. The financial largesse of the Ford Foundation, which was accompanied by "piggy-back" grants to other McGill activities, overcame the reluctance of the generally inward-looking McGill governors and the law faculty itself, and compelled the legal enactment of the Cohen reforms. The Ford funds, though "soft" (in the sense of not guaranteed as renewable), allowed a considerable diversion of money to recruitment of bright new faculty for the general, undergraduate law programs at salaries well above the national and even competitive u.s. norms, as well as providing the staff for the new graduate centres. With the scholarship facilities, the graduate centres embarked on an ambitious policy of bringing in scholars from all main regions and across the ideological frontiers of the Cold War. Picking up from the earlier initiatives in East-West cooperation by the Canadian branch of the International Law Association, McGill made the first significant allocations among North American universities of funds for scholars from the Communist world. In the late 1960s one-third of the places were reserved for these scholars, in addition to the places reserved each year for Asian, African, and Latin American students.

The Cohen plan for a national law school and international graduate law centre was successful from the beginning, in terms of the quality of students attracted and the reputation and achievements of the faculty recruited to run it. This was reflected both in the Ford Foundation's successive appraisals and ensuing decisions to renew funding, and also in the enrolments in the undergraduate law programs. The new enrolments arrested the haemorrhaging of anglophone students by reaching out to a new national constituency outside the province of Quebec; they also balanced any losses in anglophone registration by bringing in a new francophone constitutency attracted by the possibility of the twin degrees, civil law and common law, and the option of taking the civil-law courses in French as well as English.

The seeds of decay were there, however, along with the success of the innovative new program. The Cohen plan had never had unanimous endorsement or support from the law faculty. Some reacted to its sheer boldness by preferring to retreat into the pre-existing, English-language civil-law program designed for an anglophone

Montreal constituency only, with token graduate offerings at best. They shared reasonable doubts about the continuing financial costs, and also a fear that the Quebec government might view the National Programme, with its common-law LLB component, as a stratagem for assisting the departure of qualified anglophones from Quebec once they had acquired their educational passport to practise in Ontario or other common-law provinces.

The most serious opposition, however, came from within the general university administration, several of the more intransigent academic bureaucrats in particular seeming to resent the stellar billing, within McGill as a whole, given to the Law School by the success of the Cohen plan. One key administrator, determinedly monolingual in practice and in outlook, appeared to confuse a personal opposition to the French fact with a need to oppose the "international" character of the graduate law centres and their courageous openings to Eastern Europe.

It was a time of considerable confusion, self-doubt, and loss of political self-confidence on the part of the anglophone community in Montreal as the intellectual yeastiness and excitement of the Quiet Revolution gave way to the direct political confrontation and occasional violence of 1968 and thereafter. The McGill-based anglophone community had never been part of the Quiet Revolution which, by definition, was French and French-language from the beginning; but the problem of nonparticipation was compounded by the failure to attempt to enter into a dialogue with the younger francophone intellectual leaders of the Quiet Revolution. At that time the McGill community was, to a surprising extent, monolingual. Even functionally bilingual faculty members like Frank Scott were not prepared to venture on political interchange and possible joint action with the francophone leaders of the Quiet Revolution, some of whose objectives were of a general social character and not specifically linguistic, and therefore open to potential accommodation with politically likeminded social democratic thinkers. More important in relation to the Cohen plan, Scott did not lend his own support, either in the law faculty or with the university administration as a whole.

The frustrations of living through an intellectual *Risorgimento* in which McGill was not involved, along with the mounting atmosphere of confrontation between French and English in the province, brought their toll in the departure of some of the exceptional people recruited to staff the Cohen plan. Hamish Gow left for practice in British Columbia (and eventually the BC Supreme Court); Bobby Hahlo for the University of Toronto; Jacob Ziegel for Osgoode Hall; Richard Arens for the United States; Peter Sand for the Food and

Agriculture Organization in Rome; and Gerald LeDain for Osgoode Hall (as dean and eventually to the Supreme Court of Canada).

The art of problem-solving, as Yale Law School professor Harold Lasswell remarked in a brief to Quebec's Commission Gendron, is to attempt solutions while they are still timely and before a situation has become pathological and politically out-of-hand. In historical retrospect, one must conclude there was a failure on the part of the economically dominant Anglo-Saxon establishment in Montreal to comprehend the main social imperatives of the Quiet Revolution in its earlier, formative years and to attempt political bridge-building with the francophone majority in Quebec when the emphasis was still on relatively modest, incremental changes and adjustments within the existing Canadian federal system. Cohen was never intransigent in his own personal approach to the unfolding French fact within Quebec. However, as a Winnipeger he was not part of the anglophone establishment in Montreal; and since he was not fluent in French or functionally bilingual, his ability to deal with the new francophone elements was correspondingly limited. He gravitated, logically and inevitably in terms of his roots and associations, to the federalist liberals in Quebec who found their political expression, from 1968 onwards, in Pierre Trudeau and the federal Liberal Party. That did not, of course, resolve the McGill problems, which were always conditioned by the objective realities of Quebec, provincial government financial underwriting, and by the framework of provincial language, and other laws in which McGill and the francophone universities of Quebec had to operate. It must be a matter of regret that with his obvious skills of intellectual imagination and his powers of communication, Cohen never made the jump into direct political life at the federal level. As it is, however, operating as a jurist within his own academic community, Cohen succeeded in introducing a plan with a national outlook in legal education that was innovatory for its time and that contained within itself a confident, optimistic vision of a plural Canada within a plural world community of the sort first envisaged by the founding group of the Canadian branch of the International Law Association in the 1950s. The ultimate test is that, with Cohen's departure from the deanship at McGill after only a single five-year term, the Cohen plan is still in full working operation a full quarter-century later. It remains one of the most distinctively pan-Canadian contributions to education and an integrating force in professional life in difficult political and constitutional times.

Maxwell Cohen and the Theory and Practice of Canadian Legal Education

J.P.S. McLAREN

My first experience of Maxwell Cohen was at a meeting of the Association of Canadian Teachers of Law (as it then was) in Ottawa in 1967. The organization was engaged in one of its periodic bouts of introspection on legal education. On a humid early summer afternoon the soporific climate of the session was broken by the lively intervention from the audience of a distinguished-looking gentleman who announced himself as Max Cohen. In the space of the next ten minutes he left us in no doubt that, in his opinion, the progressive strains in Canadian legal education came from the United States and that Canadian law graduates who wanted to pursue further legal studies outside the country were well advised to choose an American graduate school. As a recent product of the University of London's graduate program in law and well aware of my own dean's warmth towards Oxford, his alma mater, I was, I suppose, partly offended and in part concerned that others in the room might be feeling as uncomfortable as I. On inquiring who this "assertive" individual was, I was told he was dean of the McGill Law School.

Some seven years later and wiser, with a year of graduate work in the United States behind me, I once again had to consider Cohen's ideas. I was preparing a paper for the International Symposium on Comparative Law held at the University of Ottawa in 1974. The general theme was Recent Trends in Legal Education. My mission was to examine curricular developments in common-law Canada. I had not gone far in my background research in the literature on

Canadian legal education before I began to understand for the first time the importance of Cohen's contribution to both its maturation and its chronicling.

Despite the fact that a rich body of written opinion had developed on legal education in Canada prior to the 1950s, especially in the pages of the *Canadian Bar Review*, no Canadian had ever done an empirical survey of the general state of the country's legal education and law schools. Ironically, the only reports of this type were those of the American scholar, Alfred Z. Reed, in the 1920s studies sponsored by the Carnegie Foundation for the Advancement of Teaching.[1] True, Canadians engaged or interested in legal education were aware that a common curriculum existed, the product of the Canadian Bar Association special committee chaired by Dean Donald MacRae of Dalhousie in the early 1920s.[2] However, with the notable exception of an article on Canadian legal education in 1932 by the dean of the Osgoode Hall Law School, John Falconbridge,[3] much of the writing in the field centred on the seemingly intractable debates between academics and practitioners on the role of legal education in Ontario.[4] There was little or nothing in the way of a national perspective on legal education, let alone any sense of the resources, human and financial, being dedicated to it and the directions it might take in the future. Into this vacuum in the late 1940s walked Max Cohen who, on his return from wartime service, had been persuaded to join the McGill law faculty.[5]

The time was ripe for an analysis and critique of the state of Canadian legal education. Many in the legal profession in Ontario did not appreciate that the "die had been cast" for academic legal education in that province by the resignation of Cecil "Caesar" Wright as dean of the Osgoode Hall Law School early in 1949, along with three of his colleagues.[6] Wright, together with Bora Laskin and John Willis, now constituted the Faculty of Law at the University of Toronto, an avowedly academic law school in competition with Osgoode Hall in the education of potential lawyers in Ontario, although yet to be recognized by the Law Society as a full equal.[7] Elsewhere in the country, British Columbia had recently entered the fold of academic legal education with the founding of the Faculty of Law at the University of British Columbia under the deanship of George Curtis in 1946. After the diminutive classes of the Depression and wartime years, law schools were in the final stages of dealing with the bulge caused by veteran enrolment. Finally, with postwar recovery well under way, money seemed to be available for higher education. It was time both to take stock and to think of charting the course of Canadian legal education.

Cohen's seminal study of the state of Canadian legal education in 1950 was embodied in an article, "The Condition of Legal Education in Canada," published that year in the *Canadian Bar Review*.[8] The article is a remarkable combination of empirical study and reflective scholarship. With research assistance from both McGill and the fledgling Social Science Research Council, Cohen developed an extensive questionnaire which he circulated to the dean of every Canadian law school. Moreover, he travelled to almost all the schools to engage in first-hand observation and to interview deans, faculty members, students, lawyers, and university administrators. The survey ranged widely over student enrolment and fees, faculty numbers, experience, work loads and salaries, physical facilities, including library resources, relations with the legal profession, teaching methodology, course development, and research activity. In his conclusions, Cohen put beyond doubt the parsimony of financial support for legal education in Canada: "Although the number of law students and graduates are now substantially above the average in the period 1925–1939, and the extensive employability of law graduates in the Canadian public service and in corporate enterprise is a recognized fact ... the physical facilities of Canada's eleven law schools do not in themselves suggest that the training of law students is of major concern to government, to business and to the community as a whole."[9] He went on to note the modest salaries of Canadian legal academics and the diminutive size of the country's law faculties in contrast with their American counterparts. The result, he felt, had been a compromise of opportunities for specialization and scholarship. "All this," he said, "means that the resources of the universities and the profession, or, to put it more broadly the resources of the community as a whole, do not seem to have been allocated in any major way to the education and training of the law student."[10]

Although the empirical work behind the paper is interesting historically and was to provide a model for argument in later bids by Canadian law schools for a more equitable share of university funding, the article's more important legacy is the philosophical position it takes on the function and substance of legal education. Influenced by the contrasts in his own legal education at Manitoba and Northwestern and by his work experience as a public servant, Cohen constructed an ideology of legal education that he believed was relevant and adequate to a rapidly changing world in which the demand for those graduating in legal studies was already becoming greater and more diverse.

Although he avoided the fiery words that had marked the acrimonious debate between Wright and his antagonists, Cohen left the reader in no doubt that he thought the place of education for the law was the university. He believed that acceptance of legal education as a university discipline was beneficial to the legal community in general and was recognized as such by many practitioners. In those jurisdictions in Canada in which university legal education was the norm he sensed a greater understanding by the bar of the role of the law teacher, and he pointed to a more cooperative relationship between practitioners and academics.[11]

On the substance of the law-school curriculum, Cohen disputed there was any problem with it encompassing the teaching of skills. While he felt there were matters of technical knowledge of legal practice which were better left to the bar to teach, he saw skills and substance as having a symbiotic relationship which it was necessary to expose and explore in the classroom. "Every course," he opined, "must be explicitly a course in 'skills' as well as a review of the substantive rules in a field. And it is the teacher's task to inculcate this lawyer's kind of thinking and doing at the earliest stage of training." Included within the term skills were, he suggested, "the realistic reading of cases, the understanding of statutes and their creation, the working of the lawyer in counselling, drafting, pleading and his handling of facts in all their complex variety." He had sympathy with the view that an understanding of the common law in particular is an appreciation of its "method."[12]

Legal education in Cohen's view was not exclusively a pursuit of the knowledge of substance and skills. It was important too that students were challenged to develop a sense of the law and legal institutions as part of a broader process of social ordering: "[The] role of [the lawyer] will be made more secure if law students understand the main social and technical forces in society and government that lie behind the legal order, behind those individual 'rules' that are the esoteric concern of lawyers. They will practise law more intelligently and lead the community more responsibly if as lawyers they have some insight into the origin of rules and the impact of social changes on rules, and in turn of rules on social behaviour."[13] These insights, he suggested, could not be supplied by legal educators alone but by the political scientist, economist, sociologist, and criminologist. He was careful in the process to impress upon the bar that this concern with social policy and values was not mere intellectual padding, but was immensely practical in producing lawyers sensitive to political, economic, and social realities and capable of creative use of the law: "Law teachers and practitioners alike therefore must be interested in law training that increasingly understands the complex social order and tries to provide a technical lawyer's equipment that is no less technical because it is maturely social in its view."[14]

There was a necessary connection between these liberal views on the goals of legal education and its substance and methodology. Cohen argued vigorously for the continuing enrichment of the curriculum and for research to provide students with the diversity of experience and range of intellectual insights appropriate to three years of university legal education. He approved of what he perceived to be an increasing commitment to public-law subjects, and at the same time decried the fact that public international law was not receiving the scholarly attention it deserved. In the context of teaching methods, he indicated that he favoured the "case method" of teaching because it challenged the students to use their minds and tested their abilities to apply their knowledge. However, he also recognized that it too could be overdone and become repetitive in the process. The solution, he suggested, was to try other methodologies in the senior years of the degree program.[15]

The themes Cohen developed in his 1950 article were ones he was strongly committed to and not reticent about reaffirming. He returned to them in a paper he presented to the Association of Canadian Law Teachers at its annual meeting in Winnipeg in 1954. In that presentation he developed his view that the study of law should not be confined to a mere statement of principles, rules, and processes, but should consider law and legal theory in a broader social context and cause students to reflect on its effectiveness and how it might be improved. As examples of areas in which a critical, empirical, and reformative approach could and should be employed he cited criminal law, domestic relations, and business law.[16] The correlation of law as a working order and as a system of values and influences was, he suggested, entirely natural: "[N]o legal education can be said to be education about the law that does not provide the student with an awareness of the legal system as a whole. The law is both philosophy and social engineering. The law is art and analysis. The law is history and logic. The law is form and substance – and all these qualities must be communicated to the student."[17]

Cohen reiterated his belief that some elements of practical training had a legitimate place in law school and he commented favourably on the consideration of "clinical experiences" by "forward looking law schools." In his mind, challenge and rigour were necessary in the classroom if student interest was to be piqued, self-reliance fostered, and a maximum of industry encouraged. The law teacher had a duty to create an environment in which the bulk of the class would be inspired to realize their full intellectual potential: "My own experience leads me to believe that the most important method that legal education has developed, faced with large classes in the United States and Canada, is that technique which encourages *pre-class* preparation by the student *and which leads to his greater understanding of, and participation in, the discussion during the class-room hour.* This is a far cry from the note-taking with an occasional relevant or irrelevant question or interjection."[18]

Cohen was to pick up again on the theme that law and legal education necessarily embody both theorizing and pragmatic problem-solving in an article in 1961 on "Lawyers and Learning: The Professional and Intellectual Traditions." In this piece he investigated the relations between the "practitioners" of the law, the lawyers and judges, and the "thinkers," the law teachers, drawing on the experience of both the common-law and civilian traditions in Canada and the legal systems in Britain, the United States, and France. His opening comment was characteristically to the point: "The law has always been at home in both the Academy and the market place. This is not to suggest that the other established disciplines are unaccustomed to bridging the leap, if any, between intellect and 'life.' It is only that law as we understand it in western society has a special quality in this continuing reconciliation between the disciplined, special and often abstract quality of intellectual activity and the more artful, immediate and short-run needs of the day."[19] While recognizing the historical differences in evolution and rationalization between the common-law and the civil-law systems, he stressed that both had a claim to be part of an "intellectual" tradition that enriched and at the same provided a basis for critique of the law in action. "An always fascinating aspect of the law," he claimed, "viewed entire or in the relations of its speculative to its operational side, is this tension between the abstract and the immediate, between idea and implementation, between concept and machinery."[20]

In terms of relationships within the legal profession he viewed that between the judges and academics in Canada as tentative and uncomfortable, lacking the tradition of mutual intellectual inspiration and dialectic which was evident in the United States and even in exalted circles in the United Kingdom. Still more strained had been the connection between the bar and the law schools. This, Cohen believed, was the product of "a colonial and vocational viewpoint" and the "primitive" arrangements for professional training and admission which had been the norm up to the 1920s. Only recently, he suggested, had the bar in any numbers begun to recognize the importance of the obligation of the academic lawyer to scholarship, to progressive development of the law, and to the wider intellectual community.[21]

Tensions, he found, existed within the academy as well and deserved comment. His critique has familiar resonance even today. While finding much that was positive and intellectually challenging in each jurisprudential school, he was obviously concerned that a rigid "party line" could develop which would detract from the richness of theoretical insights important to a broad understanding of law. He found wanting the undue scepticism of the Realists, the compromise of rigorous conceptual analysis involved in sociological jurisprudence, and the esoteric nature of linguistic analysis as applied to law. Each of these views on the nature of law, he felt, could and should inform legal studies, but not to the exclusion of one another.[22]

In 1964, fifteen years after his initial report on the state of Canadian legal education, Cohen revisited the issue by again canvassing the law schools on the questions he had raised earlier.[23] The expansion of and changes in legal education he found encouraging in the main, although the discipline was still treated with parsimony and a frustrating measure of public indifference. Work still needed to be done on refining admissions standards and criteria, strengthening and extending graduate legal education, and improving library facilities and collections.

In Cohen's mind the most significant change had been the almost universal acceptance that the rightful site of legal education was the university campus. However, notwithstanding this desirable development, there was, he sensed, still discomfort within the ranks of the professoriate. He identified in particular the inner turmoil of legal academics seeking both individually and collectively to establish a definable and recognized identity as bridgers of the gap between theory and practice, between critique and analysis. Cohen's reflections suggest that by this time he had shifted from his earlier position of viewing legal education as a grand integrated process of inculcating social theory and values on the one hand and practical knowledge on the other. He was concerned that there was too much introversion in the legal academy as law teachers struggled with issues of role and objectives. While he continued to argue for a process informed by external knowledge from other disciplines, especially the social sciences, he suggested that the law teacher who sought to straddle the roles of "social-critic" and "technician-actor" should give careful thought to what he wanted the students to come away with. The only guidance he felt he could offer was the tension he had experienced and the tentative balance he had achieved:

I suffer ... from this tension of being greedy for all the insights I can get from my peers and my betters in other disciplines. But I am jealous at the same time of just that professional identity which marks me off from the sociologists, the political scientist or economist because I somehow must help students understand and operate a system that, because of its own methods and traditions, has a character and momentum of its own. Knowledge about law must be imparted doubtless as a species of social science knowledge, but even more perhaps as a great and traditional art, with skills and language uniquely related to it. It is this dualism and these dilemmas that excite the modern law teacher as much as frustrate him.[24]

Cohen was quick to add that legal educators should not fall into the trap of becoming mere surrogates for the bar and the educational functions with which it was better equipped to deal. The study ended with the elaboration of a challenging agenda of objectives for Canadian law schools. First, legal education should embrace on the one hand the analytical tools and traditions important to preparation for legal practice and, on the other, new advances in legal thought and in the work of the profession itself. Second, law schools should strive to attract the best students, who all too often were lured into other disciplines, by publicizing more effectively the unique combination of social, intellectual, and practical challenges in legal studies. Third, law schools should commit themselves to training minds for the great range of activities required for "effective lawyership," incorporating into their programs those elements of practical skill development and intellectual and ethical endeavour which coalesced to produce the well-rounded, agile, and socially responsible legal mind. Finally, Cohen suggested, the law school should be "the great home where minds meet to carry that portion of civilization's torch fed by the fuel of law."[25] What he meant by this rhetorical flourish was that a faculty of law should always be striving to expand the boundaries of knowledge, both legal and nonlegal, important to an understanding of law as an intellectual construct and as a practical system of regulation, and to press for reform: "I do suggest that a faculty with a progressive, reforming zeal about itself and about the law, with a critical sense toward the legal order at home and elsewhere, will reflect in its teaching methods and materials both this 'outside' and 'inside view' with the resulting tension producing a more alert, knowledgeable and realistic graduate for the Bar as well as those other institutions in society that will employ this kind of mind and experience."[26]

With the political and social tensions created in Canada by Quebec's Quiet Revolution firmly in mind, Cohen concluded his article by throwing down a particular challenge to Canadian law teachers. They should assist "in the reshaping of our confederation, its tone, its substantive content, its technical design" and sensitize the next generation of lawyers and politicians to be receptive to and understanding of "the two great language and legal systems of the modern world."[27]

Despite the demands of an ever more diverse and vigorous career as an academic administrator, international lawyer and judge, and adviser to government, Maxwell Cohen has never forgotten the challenges of legal education or compromised his own beliefs. The 1980s found him again advocating the importance of an enriched program of legal education which purposively integrated both the intellectual and practical domains. In a response to the eminent American legal academic Willis Reese, Cohen demurred from the view that it is the students who year by year provide the level of excellence upon which the quality and enrichment of legal education depends.[28] Conceding that the leading United States law schools might well be blessed with a cadre of extremely bright and self-motivated students who make the academic and social efforts of the institutions largely superfluous, he went on to suggest that the Canadian law-student body is more diverse, creating greater opportunities for talented and imaginative teachers and their courses to make a mark.

The release of the report of the Consultative Group on Research and Education in Law, *Law and Learning* (the Arthurs Report) in 1983 provided Cohen with an opportunity both to comment on the significance of that document within the ongoing tradition of periodic reappraisals of Canadian legal education and to engage in a retrospective of his own experiences.[29] The report itself had made passing reference to the valuable work he and others had done in charting the history and encouraging the enrichment of Canadian legal education.[30] Cohen's review, while strong in its praise of both the background research carried out by the Consultative Group and its commitment to a strong intellectual strain in legal education and research, proceeds from a rather more optimistic view of the state of the Canadian legal academy than that of Professor Arthurs and his colleagues. In the first place, he hinted that the report was marked by a degree of insularity. He found it odd that, although it purported to emulate United States educational models, there was no reference to the contemporaneous agonizing of some American legal academics, especially Professor Derek Bok, over the state of law and legal formation in that country. While the report's belief in the need to encourage greater efforts within the professoriate in doing "fundamental research" appealed to him, he expressed some difficulty in pinning down exactly what the term meant. Moreover, he expressed reservations about the emphasis the Consultative Group had place on analogies drawn from medical education. Indeed, he called for clearer recognition of the value of the interaction of law as a discipline and site of knowledge with the social sciences, history, and philosophy "for the entire legal educational process and, ultimately for the profession itself." He observed that at least modest experiments of interdisciplinary teaching and research had been underway in several Canadian law schools for some time, and he questioned how accurate a portrayal of the existing state of affairs the report actually provided.[31]

Cohen raised the question whether the "dual stream" approach to legal education and research advocated by the Arthurs group would achieve the stated objective of producing a body of critical knowledge and materials by which the law in action could be both assessed and improved. "What," he asked, "would be the additional benefits over and above the critiques now available from the more sophisticated ongoing scholarship already to be found in the best American, and some of the Canadian law schools?" At the same time as pointing to the value of the report in stressing the "twin missions" of the law and the law schools – scholarship and problem solving, and the need to deploy "all the resources of the intellect ... to help societies fairly fashion and manage their legal orders without which there cannot be workable justice for all" – he pondered whether it had been "bypassed" by the "radical realization" that the legal system itself is now in question in North America.[32]

What has been the contribution of Max Cohen to the evolution and maturation of Canadian legal education? The views expressed in his writing on legal education are by no means original. They drew heavily on the inspiration provided by two generations of American legal academics committed to testing the law by reference to social-science methodology and speculating on and encouraging its use as a form of "social engineering." Moreover, part of his message had already been pressed for several decades in Canada by Caesar Wright. Cohen's singular contribution is that he was able by persuasive advocacy and a nonthreatening posture to establish these ideas firmly within the mainstream of discourse and ideology of Canadian legal education. Although some practitioners and judges still feel that the exclusive role of the law schools is to "train" students for practice, and some academic colleagues see no legitimate role for the law teacher outside inculcating doctrine in the minds of students, there is a more general recognition of the need for legal education to blend intellectual speculation with preparation for practice.

Cohen's role in giving confidence to legal educators interested in experimenting with interdisciplinary approaches, with an enriched range of legal and nonlegal subject matter, with neglected skills and novel teaching methodologies, and in opening the minds of practitioners and judges to the validity of this work should not be underestimated. While he was modest in exposing the degree to which he himself engaged in experimentation, one has the sense from his writing that not only did he believe in what he said but that he had given it substance in the classroom. As Rod Macdonald outlined in his history of McGill's National Programme, the Cohen years were marked by an unyielding commitment to the improvement and enrichment of legal education at that school.[33] Macdonald notes in particular Cohen's mission to liberalize the curriculum and to encourage "polyjurality." On his arrival in 1948 Cohen developed two new courses with a liberal arts flavour, Introduction to Law and another in Jurisprudence. He was a strong supporter of the foundation of the Institute of International Air Law in the early 1950s (he later became its director when it was renamed the Institute of Air and Space Law), and in 1953 he undertook to devise and teach the first optional courses in the curriculum – seminars in The Law and Constitution of the United Nations and Government Control of Business. Both provided opportunities for interdisciplinary experimentation which he eagerly pursued. All this was achieved in an environment that was not openly receptive to new ideas, with a teaching load that would defy the credulity of current law professors, with a vigorous and productive research agenda, and an active and expanding involvement in the community outside the university. During his term as dean, Cohen was able through a combination of vision, personal energy, and a developed capacity for fundraising to strengthen both the graduate and undergraduate programs at McGill. Under his leadership, the Institute of Foreign and Comparative Law was established as a new focus for postgraduate studies, and the foundations of the National Programme, which provides educational opportunity in both the civil and the common law at the undergraduate level, were laid. At the same time the Civil Law Studies Programme was introduced to strengthen the BCL program, to provide instruction in French, and to encourage greater research effort within the civilian tradition.

Cohen's receptiveness to bilingual, bicultural, and comparativist initiatives and his active espousal of them at McGill gave his writing an authority that undoubtedly caused others – teachers, judges, and practitioners – to sit up and take note. Even in the legal educational minefield of Ontario, his views were respected and given serious consideration. The role of stimulating progressive approaches to legal education seems to have come naturally to him and was one in which he felt McGill had particularly valuable insights to bring to debate. In this he was the inheritor of a long-standing McGill tradition that had been established by earlier deans such as Robert W. Lee and Herbert A. Smith, who had supported the cause of academic legal education in Canada in the 1910s and 1920s.[34]

Cohen's writing on legal education has its problems. It gives the impression of someone striving for an ideal that proves elusive, in which he finds the elements difficult to detail. The commitment to an integrative approach to teaching is stated at an abstract level, with little specific guidance on implementation. As the definite, if subtle, tempering of enthusiasm between 1950 and 1964 for his integrative approach suggests, there were difficulties in striking an appropriate balance and in carrying the students through the endeavour. He seems also to have expected that once law teachers recognized the value of combining the intellectual and the practical in legal education and research, a consensus would emerge on the objectives and nature of the enterprises. In his enthusiasm for a liberal educational experience, he accepted as axiomatic that all or most critical perspectives on law were complementary and equally valid, and that progressive law teachers would instinctively recognize the value of appealing to them all. There was, apparently, little or no room in his scheme for diversity in political ideology and the possibility that differences in ideological alignment might well result in legal and constitutional disputation. It is particularly ironic that Cohen's call in 1964 to law teachers to involve themselves in the country's constitutional project has been taken seriously by legal academics across Canada, but with decreasing solidarity in political terms over the shape, substance, and extent of constitutional reform that should take place.

Cohen's educational reflections are more notable for their "grand design" than their specific insights. This observation seems to accord with what we know of his record as a legal educator. Rod Macdonald has suggested that the one area in which Cohen's vision for McGill was wanting was the lack of a clearly worked out "universalist" plan for legal education in which the differences and commonalities of legal systems and cultures were to be explored as a central feature of learning.[35] This shortcoming was reflected in the failure of the comparativist elements of the McGill program to infuse undergraduate education and to create theoretical and ideological bridges between the civil and the common law. Macdonald notes that with the introduction of the National Programme, the work of the Institute of Foreign and Comparative Law became increasingly marginalized.[36] At the same time, the provision of partially overlapping BCL and LLB programs, which demanded that students take some courses in the other system, did little or nothing to look beyond their separate identities to their relative histories, places, and influences within Western legal culture.[37] Like some of the legal scholars who inspired him, perhaps, Cohen too readily accepted that once the battle for change was won and the new design in place, its implementation was largely self-executing.

But this is not the occasion to pick holes. If Maxwell Cohen is to be faulted for an uncritical commitment to a liberal ideology of legal education, his writing nevertheless stands as a unique beacon and inspiration for all those committed to a progressive, interdisciplinary, and reformative agenda in Canadian legal education. Although some of the detail of what he wrote is now dated, his views on legal education have in general a timeless, fresh, and inspirational character which is still capable of exciting enthusiasm for change in the legal academy of the 1990s. The fundamental issues endure. Thanks to Maxwell Cohen, who lit a spark which caught and continues to hold the imagination of others, the quest goes on.

NOTES

1 Alfred Z. Reed, *Present Day Law Schools in the United States and Canada* (New York: Carnegie Foundation Bulletin no. 21 1928).
2 *Proceedings of the Canadian Bar Association*, vol. 5 (1920), 152.
3 John Falconbridge, "Legal Education in Canada" [1932] *Journal of the Society of Public Teachers of Law* 35.
4 John McLaren, "Recent Trends in Legal Education: Curriculum in Common Law Canada," *Proceedings of the Eleventh International Symposium of Comparative Law* (Ottawa: University of Ottawa 1975), 54, 55.
5 On Cohen's education and early career see Ronald St J. MacDonald, "Maxwell Cohen at Eighty: International Lawyer, Educator and Judge" (1989), 27 *Canadian Yearbook of International Law* 3–10.
6 Ian Kyer and Jerome Bickenbach, *The Fiercest Debate: Cecil Wright, the Benchers, and Legal Education in Ontario 1923–1957* (Toronto: Osgoode Society 1987), 201–21.
7 Ibid., 222–40.
8 (1950), 28 *Canadian Bar Review* 267.
9 Ibid., 271; see 295–314 for the tables.
10 Ibid., 274.
11 Ibid., 275, 277–8.
12 Ibid., 285–6.
13 Ibid., 293.

14 Ibid., 294.
15 Ibid., 284–5, 288–9.
16 Maxwell Cohen, "Objectives and Methods of Legal Education: An Outline" (1954), 32 *Canadian Bar Review* 762, 763–4.
17 Ibid., 763. Cohen reiterated this point in a book review he penned in the same year in which he regretted that the theoretical and social perspectives were often lacking in courses in Canadian law schools: "[T]here is missing in Canada a view of the law as an integrated, living social mechanism, a mechanism about which a student should be able to get a whole view before he leaves for the piecemeal, life-time tasks as practitioner, corporate executive or civil servant. If anything is missing in Dean Harno's report that a Canadian searching for guidance might hope to find, it is some indication of how common law courses – and perhaps even the civil law in its own way too – can be given the perspective of unity, of a 'coherent system' of guides for social value and action." Maxwell Cohen, review of Albert J. Harno, *Legal Education in the United States: A Report Prepared for the Survey of the Legal Profession* (San Francisco: Bancroft, Whitney Company 1953), in (1954), 6 *Journal of Legal Education* 416.
18 Kyer and Bickenbach, *The Fiercest Debate*, 767, 768.
19 (1961), 7 *McGill Law Journal*, 181.
20 Ibid., 183, 184.
21 Ibid., 187–8, 189.
22 Ibid., 189–91.
23 Maxwell Cohen, "The Condition of Legal Education in Canada–Fifteen Years Later 1949–1964" [1964] *Canadian Bar Association Papers* 116–31.
24 Ibid., 127.
25 Ibid., 128–30.
26 Ibid., 129–30.
27 Ibid., 130–1.
28 Maxwell Cohen, "What Makes a Law School Great?" (1980), 6 *Dalhousie Law Journal* 351, 353.
29 Maxwell Cohen, review of *Law and Learning: Report to the Social Sciences and Humanities Research Council of Canada* (Ottawa 1983), in (1983), 61 *Canadian Bar Review* 702.
30 Consultative Group of Research and Education in Law, *Law and Learning: Report to the Social Sciences and Humanities Research Council of Canada* (Ottawa: Information Division of SSHRC 1983), 4, 18.
31 Cohen, review of *Law and Learning*, 704–8.
32 Ibid., 710, 712.
33 Roderick Macdonald, "The National Law Programme at McGill: Origins, Establishment, Prospects" (1990), 13 *Dalhousie Law Journal* 274–314.

34 Kyer and Bickenbach, *The Fiercest Debate*, 64–6, 77–8.
35 Macdonald, "The National Law Programme," 314.
36 Ibid., 308–9.
37 Ibid., 310–13.

The Role of the Canadian Institute for the Administration of Justice in the Development of Judicial Education in Canada

DAVID C. McDONALD

I agreed for two reasons to contribute an article to this book describing the role of the Canadian Institute for the Administration of Justice (CIAJ) in the development of judicial education. First, I have known Max Cohen for eighteen years and he and his wife have been good friends, so I am not only honoured but pleased to be able to join in celebrating his life. Second, although Cohen has not been associated with judicial education in Canada, he has been vitally interested in all aspects of legal education and it is thus appropriate to include an article on this particular corner of legal education. My article for the most part describes developments during the decade preceding the establishment of the Canadian Judicial Centre in 1987 (in 1991 renamed the National Judicial Institute), which is the subject of William Stevenson's article in this volume.

I was not one of the founders of the CIAJ, but on the very eve of the first meeting of the Board of Directors I was asked to be its first president. I suppose I was asked because I was a young, newly appointed judge with a demonstrated interest in continuing legal education, and the founders had high hopes of the institute's making an impact on judicial education. I occupied the position for three annual terms, and continued as a director and, more recently, as an honorary director. I continued to be closely associated with the administration of the institute until 1984, and have had a more distant acquaintanceship with its functions since that date.

I was appointed to the Trial Division of the Supreme Court of Alberta effective 1 January 1974. At the time there was no program or seminar for new federally appointed judges other than the annual summer seminars. A week-long summer seminar for superior court judges had been operating since 1968. These seminars were organized at first by the federal government, but after 1971 the Canadian Judicial Council took over the task. The Council consists of the chief justice of Canada and the chief justices of the other federally appointed courts across Canada. The secretary, Pierre Chamberland, administered the seminars, and the first director was Dr Allan Leal, chairman of the Ontario Law Reform Commission. From 1973 onward the council organized similar annual week-long seminars for judges of county and district courts. In the 1980s, when one after another the provincial county or district courts merged with the superior court of the province, the separate county and district court seminars were discontinued.

My own experience enables me to speak of the superior court judges' seminars. I attended the 1975 seminar in July, in Regina. The program was excellent. It consisted of half-day lectures and seminar-type discussions featuring experienced judges and academics. The subjects included criminal law, evidence, family law, judicial ethics, and a perennial favourite – "Was I Right?" – which discussed a number of situations participants had encountered.

The seminars have had important functions apart from the direct benefits flowing from organized programs. Each summer the seminars are held in a different region of Canada, and the most important side-effect has been the opportunity afforded to judges from every province of Canada to meet one another. Many of the recently appointed judges who attended the 1974 seminar from eastern and central Canada, for example, had not previously spent time in the west. Many of the judges, while pursuing their earlier careers as lawyers, had not attended national conventions, whether of the Canadian Bar Association, political parties, or other organizations. For judges from Quebec, the opportunity to mix with judges from the rest of Canada was important, just as it was important for judges from the rest of Canada to meet colleagues from Quebec. The Quebeckers did not mix much with the others, or vice versa, on a social basis, but then the Ontarians and the British Columbians stuck together too – and they did not suffer from "language fatigue" at the end of the day as some of the Quebeckers must have. (The sessions at that time were all in English, without simultaneous translation.) These seminars have enhanced the consciousness among federally appointed judges that they share common problems, both legal and judicial, with judges of diverse backgrounds from other parts of the country. The positive consequences of such contacts may be difficult to identify, but they have been significant.

The conception of what became the CIAJ originated with Professor Stephen Borins, then associate dean of Osgoode Hall Law School at York University. On behalf of the Canadian Judicial Council he served as the second director of the Canadian Judicial Seminar for superior court judges, from 1970 to 1974. In 1972 Chief Justice Gordon Cowan of Nova Scotia, chairman of the council's Education Committee, encouraged Borins to visit the Federal Judicial Center in Washington, DC, to attend a program for recently appointed federal district court judges.

One result of that visit was a decision by Professor Borins and Dean Harry Arthurs, of the same faculty, to develop the concept of the CIAJ as a body which might ultimately evolve into something like the Federal Judicial Center. Despite considerable disfavour among the chief justices who then formed the Canadian Judicial Council, support was forthcoming from Chief Justice Bora Laskin. A major source of encouragement came from Neil McKelvey, QC, of St John, New Brunswick, president of the Canadian Bar Association. (In due course he became one of two initial vice-presidents of the CIAJ).

Arthurs and Borins committed funds from their faculty to the partial financing of the salaries of the director and associate director of the CIAJ, who they anticipated would be law professors. They invited two members of their faculty to accept appointment to those positions on a part-time basis: Allen M. Linden and Sidney J. Lederman, respectively. Arthurs and Borins applied successfully for a grant from the Donner Canadian Foundation: $225,000, which was intended as seed money to finance the first three years of the institute's operations. The proposal they submitted asserted that the judicial system suffered from "serious stresses and strains" and delay, and that judges frequently receive "little or no judicial training or orientation." It added that "court officers and clerks, court registrars" and others who assist the courts in the administration of justice "have had little or no training for their responsibilities." The proposed CIAJ "would function as the educational, planning and research arm of the courts and administrative tribunals throughout Canada." It "should be an independent, but university-housed, non-profit corporation, interdisciplinary in scope, under the patronage of distinguished members of the judiciary, the legal profession, governments and members of the public and governed by a small Board of Directors." Emphasis was placed on the institute not being "a department of any government" and being "free from political constraints and thus able to undertake and to promote projects upon considerations of their respective intrinsic merits."

The proposed functions of the institute were as follows:

1 It would conduct research into the administration of justice in the broadest sense. Such research would be conducted independently pursuant to the approval of the Board of Directors, or would be conducted independently on the basis of contracts obtained from those by whom specific research projects may be requested.
2 It would serve as an advisor to all branches of government and to the legal profession upon request.
3 It would conduct, on a national or regional basis, with regard to general or specific topics, educational programs for members of the judiciary of all levels and for members of administrative tribunals. Such courses and seminars, varying in length, would include courses and seminars for members of courts of specialized jurisdiction, such as, the Family and Juvenile Court, the Surrogate Court, the Bankruptcy Court.
4 The Institute would operate a school, and conduct refresher courses, for Court Executive Officers.
5 The Institute would serve as a central repository for statistical information from all courts and administrative tribunals in Canada.
6 The Institute would establish a Judges-in-Residence program which would involve judges serving as members of the Faculty of the Institute and also as scholars-in-residence at the host university.
7 The research conducted by the Institute would not be confined to administration of justice in any narrow sense. It would include, for example, research with regard to the legal profession such as the delivery of legal services, and research in the area of legal education.

In June 1974 the institute was incorporated under Part 3 of the Canada Corporations Act. The objects, as set forth in the application for incorporation, were as follows:

1 To develop and conduct, directly or by cooperation or consultation with others, programmes of research with regard to the administration of justice in Canada.
2 To be a central repository for statistical and other information from courts and administrative tribunals in Canada.
3 To acquire and assist in the acquisition and dissemination of knowledge with regard to the administration of justice in Canada.
4 To develop and conduct, and assist in the development and conduct, of educational programmes of all types in Canada for members of the judiciary,

for members of administrative tribunals and for those concerned in the administration of courts and administrative tribunals.

The first meeting of the Board of Directors was held in Ottawa in October 1974. It approved the by-laws, which were revised and improved a year later when the advice of a corporate solicitor, Gordon Thompson of Toronto, was obtained. A French version of the by-laws was also adopted in 1975.

At the first meeting, and a second held in Montreal in April 1975, much of the discussion centred on ways in which the institute could develop programs reflecting its objects. Leadership in this regard was furnished most significantly by the executive director, Professor Linden, and the associate director, Professor Lederman. They were particularly enthusiastic about the research functions of the institute, but that aspect falls outside the scope of this article. Suffice it to say that over the years the institute has had some moderate degree of success in organizing and financing research programs relating to such topics as the role of the judiciary, the administration of the courts, and the role of the chief justices.

At an early stage, the institute found that it could be of service to provincial court judges. The initiative came from Judge Sandra Oxner of Nova Scotia, who in 1974 became the first Education Committee chair of the newly formed Canadian Association of Provincial Court Judges. She and her chief judge, Andrew Harrigan, and some other provincial court colleagues met that year with members of the Education Committee of the institute. These members included that committee's chairman, Mr Justice Roy Matas, then a member of the Manitoba Court of Appeal, Chief Judge Fred Hayes of the Provincial Court of Ontario (Criminal Division), who had developed a vigorous education program in his own court, Associate Chief Justice James Hugessen of the Superior Court of Quebec, and Professor Lederman. As a result of that meeting, the CIAJ worked together with the Canadian Association of Provincial Court Judges in organizing a four-day Atlantic region education program, held in June 1975. Judge Oxner, in a recent letter to me, said: "It was a breakthrough in that it was the first time that provincial court judges from different provinces had come together and we felt it contributed a great deal to the uniformity of the administration of justice in Canada." The program included discussion of issues of law reform, social problems, and difficulties sometimes encountered by provincially appointed judges. An example of these problems was that encountered by the Newfoundland magistracy, who were often housed in government accommodation immediately adjoining the offices of RCMP officers, thus adversely affecting the appearance of judicial independence.

The impact of the Atlantic seminar of 1975 on its participants was captured in an extract from the institute's first annual report:

> The Institute, jointly with the Canadian Association of Provincial Court Judges, developed and conducted the first Atlantic regional educational programme for Provincial Court Judges at Mount Saint Vincent University in Halifax, Nova Scotia on June 2–5, 1975. Forty Judges, representing each of the Atlantic provinces, attended the seminar. Separate Criminal and Family Court programmes were conducted. The Judges were divided into small workshops and various topics in the area of Criminal Procedure, Evidence, Sentencing and Post-Conviction matters were considered.
>
> To achieve a total immersion effect, the Judges lived together on campus, in student residences, ate their meals together, and were encouraged to engage in evening discussions in one of the lounges. As a result, a strong spirit of togetherness developed, fostering more active participation in seminar discussions.
>
> The evaluation done at the end of the programme indicated that there was a real need for such a programme, enabling Judges to discuss, in an intensive way, far from the distractions of ordinary life, their everyday problems of judging. These Judges were also brought into contact with law reform commission and parole board personnel and others involved in different aspects of the judicial system, which assisted them to view their own work in a broader context. This is particularly necessary in sentencing, where the Judge must have some knowledge of the facilities and programmes available and the alternatives to sentencing, if he is to make a meaningful disposition. One of the serious problems facing many Provincial Court Judges is the fact of isolation in relatively small communities where they have neither other Judges nor law libraries to turn to for help. The experience of being in residence with forty other Judges for a week-long seminar programme has minimized their feelings of isolation and will assist them to perform their duties in future with more confidence and understanding.

Shortly thereafter a program for provincial court judges from the western provinces was held at Banff, Alberta. Its success was largely due to Chief Judge Allan Cawsey of the Provincial Court of Alberta.

In its first year the institute's potential was also recognized by the district court judges of Alberta, who invited the institute to organize a seminar for them in Red Deer in September 1975. The subject was jury trials; the district court judges had just been granted jurisdiction to preside in jury trials in criminal court cases. Among the speakers were judges from Alberta, British Columbia, Ontario, and Quebec.

Judge Oxner was succeeded as Education Committee chairman of the Canadian Association of Provincial Court Judges by Chief Judge Larry Goulet of the Provincial Court of British Columbia. During his tenure the CIAJ collaborated with him and Judge Oxner (by then president of the association) in organizing the first national seminar for newly appointed provincial court judges. It was a ten-day seminar held in Kingston, Ontario. The program included the first "sensitivity" training to which new Canadian judges were exposed, such as the public's perception of the justice system and the responsibility of judges to visible minority groups.

Thereafter, to the regret of the institute, the Canadian Association of Provincial Court Judges found it was less expensive to use its own volunteers, rather than the institute's personnel, to organize regional and national seminars. However, the institute was happy to have had a part in shaping this type of program for provincial court judges.

During the institute's first year, its only members were its first directors. The directors were initially hesitant to open the door to membership on a broader basis, being uncertain where that might lead. During 1975 and 1976, the institute hosted a series of dinner meetings in Montreal, Toronto, Winnipeg, and Vancouver. The guests were prominent judges, members of the bar, academic lawyers, and lay people interested in the administration of justice. The object was to publicize the purposes and functions of the institute. During the same period, the first of what turned out to be annual national conferences, to coincide with the institute's annual members meetings, was held in February 1976 at Osgoode Hall Law School. These conferences have proved to be among the most successful of the institute's undertakings. The 1976 conference drew unexpectedly large registration: more than 300 people attended, including sixty judges, to consider the subject "The Canadian Judiciary." In 1977 the genuine interest shown by many of those who had attended the previous year's dinners and conference led the directors to open membership in the institute to all persons who applied and who were, in the opinion of the directors, interested in the administration of justice. The directors felt that only by broadening the membership could the goodwill engendered by the institute's activities be properly acknowledged.

The result in the past fifteen years has been that, without actively soliciting memberships on a mass basis, the institute has had a membership of several hundred (1111 in December 1992). Regular members receive a newsletter twice a year, and the regular membership fee is modest ($55). The most important variation in membership status originated in 1980, under the presidency of Judge Oxner. In that year the institute introduced a new category of "subscribing members," for an annual fee of $100 (now $110). The fees of several hundred (now 356) subscribing members have made an important contribution to the financial well-being of the institute, as have the life members (now 82). Many of the subscribing members are federally appointed judges whose fees are reimbursed by the Department of Justice under the provision for incidental allowances that came into effect by amendment to the Judges Act in 1980. Among the members are 578 federally appointed judges, many of whom are subscribing members. There are ninety-three judges who were appointed by provincial or territorial governments. Another important group of subscribing members are members of administrative agencies (now 122), whose interests the institute has served with dramatic success.

Over the years, the dropouts from regular membership have generally been replaced by new members (lawyers, judges, academics, members of administrative agencies, and so on). Members tend to learn of the institute's work through the conferences they attend, because of interest in the subject matter, or through attendance at the seminars for judges and others (especially seminars for members of administrative tribunals). Thus, one way or another, the institute has become an organization with reasonably broad membership support across Canada. A certain trust has developed among a large number of people that when the institute undertakes a project – whether in the field of judicial education or otherwise – it will achieve a high standard of performance.

An outline follows, listing the annual conferences, their locations, and their subjects, as well as a short commentary on the content of each. The attendance of many judges from the Superior Court of Quebec and from the Quebec Court of Appeal has made an important contribution to the maintenance of the institute's genuinely national character. Moreover, the papers delivered at many, but not all, of the conferences were published. For a number of years, publication was managed and supported by Carswell, law publishers, and on several later occasions with the similar support of Les Éditions Yvon Blais.

1976, Toronto, Conference on the Canadian Judiciary
This conference was jointly sponsored by the institute and Osgoode Hall Law School of York University. It was organized by the institute's first executive director, Allen W. Linden, QC. The papers delivered were published by Osgoode Hall Law School in hardback; such

publication was itself no mean undertaking, as the institute's management discovered in regard to the conferences held in subsequent years. The conference presentations covered a number of topics, and are as relevant to today's issues as they were to the judiciary of sixteen years ago: the independence of the judiciary (Professor William R. Lederman of Queen's University), the judge and the adversary system (Professor Neil Brooks of Osgoode Hall Law School), and the judge and court administration (Professor Garry D. Watson of the same law school). Chief Justice Jules Deschênes of the Superior Court of Quebec delivered an excellent paper on "the judge as lawmaker"; its content would be radically different in the era of the Canadian Charter of Rights and Freedoms. Ed Ratushny, then special adviser to the minister of justice of Canada, delivered an informative survey of recent developments in the appointment of federally appointed judges, supplemented by excellent comments by John J. Robinette, QC, of Toronto and Professor William H. Angus of Osgoode Hall Law School; this topic merits early and regular revisiting by the institute. English and American perspectives were brought to this first conference by Professor Gordon Borrie, who had been director of the Institute of Judicial Administration at the University of Birmingham, and by Paul Nejelski, then director of the Institute of Judicial Administration at New York University.

1977, Toronto, Conference on the Canadian Court System
This conference was again co-sponsored by Osgoode Hall Law School. The subjects discussed included the English court system (Dr Ian Scott, who was Professor Borrie's successor at Birmingham), the role of an appeal court (Professor Paul Carrington of the University of Michigan), the administration of the high volume of cases in provincial courts (Dean Frank D. Jones, QC, of the Faculty of Law of the University of Alberta), the role of the Federal Court of Canada in reviewing the decisions of administrative tribunals (Professor David Mullan of Dalhousie University), and "Are We Over-judicialized?" (Mr Justice Antonio Lamer, chairman of the Law Reform Commission of Canada). The concluding speaker, Dr J.A. Corry, former principal of Queen's University, spoke on "The People, the Judges and the Courts," and uttered a plea for greater public education in law as a method of strengthening the independence of the judiciary.

1978, Ottawa, Administrative Justice
This conference, held in January, made 1978 the only year in which two national conferences were held. This subject was chosen in an attempt, repeated in 1982, to demonstrate the institute's concern with

administrative justice. The concern bore more substantial fruit when seminars for members of administrative tribunals were organized on a regional basis in the late 1980s. The organization of such seminars had, by 1991, become a major part of the institute's work.

1978, Edmonton, Conference on Expeditious Justice
This conference was organized by a committee chaired by Mr Justice Matas of the Manitoba Court of Appeal. It looked comprehensively at pre-trial conferences in criminal and civil cases, eliminating or minimizing adjudication, new time-saving technology, efficient court management, improving criminal and civil procedure, expediting appellate justice, and the assumption of responsibility for delay. The proceedings were published. Among the papers was a study by Professor Shimon Shetreet of the Hebrew University of Jerusalem, "The Limits of Expeditious Justice." The sharing of ideas at that conference had some effect on delays across Canada, but many of the points made then could be made again today with much force.

1979, Toronto, Conference on the Cost of Justice
This conference was organized by a committee chaired by Mr Justice Richard E. Holland of the Ontario High Court. It considered alternatives to the formal justice system, whether the adversary system is cost-efficient, the trappings of justice, whether the appellate system is cost-efficient, the public support system, the costs of private delivery of legal services, prepaid legal services, efficiencies in private practice, and the use of computers. The concluding speaker was the Right Honourable Sir Robert E. Megarry, vice-chancellor of England.

1980, Vancouver, Conference on the Trial Process
The chairman of the organizing committee was Mr Justice H.E. Hutcheon of the British Columbia Court of Appeal. The theme was an appreciation of the trial process as a fact-finding process. Time was devoted to the public's perception of the trial process, the future of the rules of evidence, a number of specialized topics, and the psychopathology of the judicial decision-making process. The latter topic presented a double presentation by Judge Borins (by now a member of the County and District Court of Ontario) and his wife, Dr Elaine F. Borins, a psychiatrist. Whereas the 1978 and 1979 conferences had dealt with what might be called "public issues," this conference avowedly placed greater emphasis on matters of practical interest to judges and lawyers. The concluding address was delivered in memorable fashion by the minister of justice, the Honourable Jean Chrétien.

1981, Halifax, Conference on Criminal Justice

The chairperson of the organizing committee was Madam Justice Constance Glube of the Supreme Court of Nova Scotia. This conference attempted an in-depth assessment of contemporary criminal justice in Canada. It considered search, seizure, and arrest; the proposed new Evidence Code (which, as events proved, would be still-born); the role and influence of the prosecutor; the role of the justice of the peace; the role of defence counsel; sentencing; the juvenile trial; the use of the jury trial; pretrial conferences and disclosure; correctional techniques; alternative sentences; defences; and the future directions of criminal law.

1982, Montreal, Judicial Review of Administrative Rulings

The organizing committee was chaired by Mr Justice Marc Beauregard of the Superior Court of Quebec. This conference examined a number of problems of substantive law, including the development of judicial review in the common-law world, the grounds of judicial review, limitations on remedies, and alternative remedies. The speakers were a remarkable group of leading judicial, academic, and practising experts in the field. The concluding speaker was Chief Justice Jules Deschênes of the Superior Court of Quebec, who had been a strong supporter of the institute from its inception.

1983, Winnipeg, The Charter after Eighteen Months

Under the chairmanship of Mr Justice J.E. Wilson of the Court of Queen's Bench of Manitoba, this conference reviewed initial judicial experience with the Canadian Charter of Rights and Freedoms. Emphasis was placed on the emerging principles underlying the rights and freedoms guaranteed by the Charter. The featured speaker was Professor Paul Bender of the University of Pennsylvania, an early and thorough student of the Charter.

1984, Ottawa, Law and Justice beyond 1984

Co-chaired by Judge Rosalie Abella of the Ontario Family Court and Mr Justice Melvin L. Rothman of the Quebec Court of Appeal, the conference was inspired by Orwell's novel. The conference attempted to deal with the relationships between the individual, the state, and the justice system in a democratic tradition. The subjects included several that presented antithetical and sometimes chimerical challenges: the right to speak vs freedom from information; the right to life and death vs freedom from treatment; the right to equality vs freedom from majorities; the right to protection vs freedom from rehabilitation (the criminal law process); the rights of families vs freedom from association. Also considered were the public expectations of justice, information, and accessibility to the public in regard to legal services; barriers to access to justice; and the roles of professionals in the justice system. The featured speaker, novelist Margaret Atwood, delivered an address on Justice in the Literary Tradition.

1985, Toronto, Sentencing
Co-chaired by Brian Crane, QC, of Ottawa and Mr Justice L.W. Houlden of the High Court of Justice of Ontario, this vexing subject was discussed by an outstanding array of speakers, such as Professor David Thomas of the Centre of Criminology at Cambridge University (who had also been on the program in 1981) and Professor Andrew Von Hirsch of the School of Criminal Justice at Rutgers University in New Jersey. The topics included discussion of whether the courts have failed in regard to sentencing, sentencing trends and principles, and sentencing reform in the United States and Canada.

1986, Vancouver, Professional Responsibility
This conference was chaired by Chief Justice Allan McEachern of the Supreme Court of British Columbia. The topics discussed included general trends in liability insurance, trends in professional liability, whether the ability to pay should be a factor in the determination of liability, whether the present state of professional liability in medical cases is contrary to good medical care, whether the courts have gone too far in attaching liability to lawyers and accountants, and whether contingency fees are in the public interest.

1987, Montreal, Justice: Independence and Accountability
Co-chaired by Mr Justice Maurice Lagacé of the Superior Court of Quebec and J. Vincent O'Donnell, QC, of Montreal, this conference focused on a defence of the independence of justice and the accountability of judges and members of administrative tribunals. Specific topics included the independence of courts and administrative tribunals, the status of members of administrative tribunals, and the independence of the lawyer and the notary. In regard to accountability, panels discussed ethics, discipline, quality control, and continuing education. There was also discussion of the increased role of the judiciary because of the Canadian Charter of Rights and Freedoms, the role of the press as critic, and the constitutional guarantee of freedom of the press.

1988, Halifax, Law and the Environment
Co-chaired by Dean Innis Christie of the Faculty of Law, Dalhousie University, and Mr Justice R. Macleod Rogers of the Supreme Court of Nova Scotia (Trial Division), this seminar faced the prospect that the present involvement of the courts and other legal processes in the regulation of activities which create a risk of harm to the environment may be expected to increase in the future. The specific topics were based on a hypothetical scenario involving the transportation of a hazardous substance by sea to Canada, its transshipment by rail or truck to a central Canadian manufacturing plant, its processing as a pesticide, and its release into a forest. Panelists addressed environmental legislation, common-law remedies and decision-makers, the management of toxic and hazardous risks, the judicial function in relation to transport at sea and on land, civil and criminal remedies after chemical spills, environmental impact assessments and judicial review, regulatory and civil issues in controlling herbicide and pesticide, and the role of the courts in Canada, the United States, and Great Britain. Dr David Williams (now Sir David), president of Wolfson College, Cambridge University, who had been among the speakers at the conference on Judicial Review of Administrative Rulings in 1982, spoke for Great Britain in the last session.

1989, Kananaskis (Alberta), Discrimination in the Law and the Administration of Justice
Chaired by Mr Justice John D. Bracco of the Court of Appeal of Alberta, this conference was held four years after the equality rights section of the Canadian Charter of Rights and Freedoms came into effect. The speakers included government officials, personnel from human rights commissions, lawyers, doctors, professors of law and other disciplines, and judges. The topics discussed included the history of discrimination in Canada, a critical survey of human rights legislation and commissions, the jurisdiction and effectiveness of remedies at the disposition of human rights commissions, issues related to litigation of discrimination cases, the definition of equality rights, and discrimination in a number of areas of the law – municipal and public utilities, remote and isolated communities, age discrimination, pay equity, gender discrimination, electoral laws, the disabled, health care, and visible minorities.

1990, Toronto, Health Care, Ethics, and Law
Co-chaired by Mr Justice Horace Krever of the Ontario Court of Appeal and Professor Bernard Dickens of the Faculty of Law and

Medicine, University of Toronto, this outstanding program featured medical practitioners and health-care experts. The topics discussed included ethical and legal implications of the allocation of resources; psychiatry, law, and the Charter; health care and the needs of the physically disabled and the elderly; health care and AIDS; legal implications of scientific and technological innovation in medical science – scientific uncertainty and legal proof; the effect of court judgments on the quality of medical practice; hospitals and the law; reforms of compensation for medical negligence; the law and the right to health care.

1991, St Andrews-by-the-Sea, Work, Unemployment, and Justice
Co-chaired by Madam Justice Margaret Larlee of the Court of Queen's Bench of New Brunswick and Michel Bastarache, president and CEO of Assumption Mutual Life Insurance Company, Moncton, the subject was appropriate to a time of mass unemployment in Canada. The speakers included government officials, members of administrative tribunals, professors of law and industrial relations, lawyers and judges. The topics discussed included the constitutional distribution of powers in relation to labour law, the economic and social impacts of discrimination, employment equity, wrongful dismissal, mandatory retirement, the Charter of Rights and employment, damages in employment and labour law, labour tribunals and judicial review, labour codes and standards, the duties of former employees, and free trade and deregulation.

1992, Montreal, Culture, Justice and Law
Chaired by Judge Michèle Rivet, president, Tribunal des Droits de la Personne, Quebec. Papers were presented on a diversity of subjects: historical, sociological, and anthropological dimensions of culture in Canada ("Lord Durham Revisited: The Struggle of Nations and Peoples for Survival within the Canadian State" and "Tendencies of Social Change in Canada"); the development of two distinct Canadian legal cultures ("Code Civil, Droit Commun?" and "Culture and the Common Law"); the constitutional protection of multiculturalism in Canada; cultural minorities and the administration of justice (their treatment in the media, faculties of law, policing, and administrative tribunals); arts and culture, including television and Canadian content; aboriginal legal culture and other issues relating to the administration of justice involving aboriginal peoples ("Cultural Considerations in Evidence and Decision-Making" and "Community Circle Sentencing").

Although these annual conferences have been designed not only for judges but for others interested in the administration of justice, the planners have always borne in mind that a substantial number of judges, particularly federally appointed judges, would be in attendance. Attendance by federally appointed judges has been encouraged by the Canadian Judicial Council's annual designation of the conference as one that is approved pursuant to section 22(2) of the Judges Act as "promoting efficiency, uniformity or improvement of the quality of judicial service in the courts." This has meant that the expenses of those federally appointed judges desiring to attend have been paid by the federal government. Such designation has not been automatic in recent years. The substance of the proposed program must be such as to satisfy the Canadian Judicial Council that the agenda will be of educational value to judges. Consequently, in considering the record of the Institute in the field of judicial education, these conferences must be taken into account along with the seminars that the institute has organized for judges exclusively.

Once the institute was under way, its Education Committee decided that, for both federally and provincially appointed judges, the existing annual seminars left something to be desired in terms of the needs of those persons who had been appointed only a matter of months. Moreover, these seminars were intended to satisfy a different need: that of judges who had at least a few years of judicial experience and could benefit from the opportunity to review principles and practice with "instructors" and colleagues who were also experienced. There was a need to devise a program cast at a level and with a perspective that would correspond to the sense of uncertainty and even discouragement felt by many new judges. These characteristics are not unusual in the case of new judges, especially those whose practice as lawyers has not taken them to court very much or, in some cases, not at all. A variation of the problem is that many newly appointed judges have had some or even a good deal of experience in civil litigation but none in criminal cases. New judges are also often faced with practical and ethical problems that arise from the transformation from lawyer to judge. They find it difficult to cope with the sudden sense of isolation they experience in comparison with the hurly-burly of the practice of law. No longer do they deal daily with the often intense and fast-flowing problems of clients, the administration of a law office, community activities, and responsible positions in the organizations of the profession. Frequently they find it difficult to come to terms with the increased social circumspection necessitated by the dignity and standards of judicial office.

And, however helpful the new judge's judicial "elders" may try to be, he or she is often sitting in court away from home for a week at a time in a smaller centre, where there is no other judge from whom to seek advice about the problems facing the new judge. Even the experience, usually quite new to the judge, of eating three meals a day alone and being alone in a hotel for a week can contribute to the "culture shock." It was felt, and experience has borne this out, that seminars for newly appointed judges would enable those from across the country to share their experiences and to carry out their duties more effectively in consequence.

The first such seminar was organized in 1976 by the institute on behalf of the Canadian Association of Provincial Court Judges. It was considered to be a success and was repeated in subsequent years, but without the assistance of the institute. In this instance, therefore, the institute served as an instrument for getting a judicial education program successfully under way and then, with some regret, having its "client" develop its own "in-house" means of carrying on with the program.

Meanwhile, Professor Linden was discussing with Chief Justice Nathan Nemetz of British Columbia, chairman of a special subcommittee of the Canadian Judicial Council, the feasibility of a seminar for new federally appointed trial judges. A study showed that there was definitely a need: as of August 1975, 34 per cent (thirty-nine judges) of the judges appointed by the federal government between 1 January 1973 and May 1975 had not yet attended one of the summer sessions. As for the remaining seventy-five judges who did attend a summer seminar, the average delay from time of appointment to attendance at a seminar was 11.27 months for superior court judges and 12.31 months for county and district court judges. Although Nemetz's subcommittee supported the initiation of such a seminar, he was unable to secure the approval of the Canadian Judicial Council as a whole. In a bold personal move, he asked the institute to organize a seminar in British Columbia for newly appointed judges in that province, and he invited newly appointed judges from other provinces to attend if they wished. As a result, such a seminar was held in Victoria in March 1976. It was attended by new judges from British Columbia and from other western provinces, as well as two from Ontario. Contemporaneously, a similar seminar was held for new French-speaking judges, under the auspices of the Superior Court of Quebec. In both cases the institute acted as the organizing agent. The success of these seminars was such that the Canadian Judicial Council, in its chairman's report dated 15 December 1976, claimed to have sponsored them. By the time that report was prepared, the council had decided it would establish such a seminar nationally, using the institute as its instrument for the organization and administration of the seminars. The first was held in 1977, and seminars have been held annually since then. The institute has continued to act as the organizing instrument on behalf of the Canadian Judicial Council, even since the creation of the Canadian Judicial Centre. In recent years the chairman of the institute's Education Committee, Mr Justice James Carnwath of the Ontario Court (General Division), has been heavily involved in organizing these seminars. The Canadian Judicial Centre has itself organized regional seminars to provide assistance to judges who are appointed shortly after the annual national seminar has been held.

In 1980 the institute persuaded the Canadian Judicial Council that a need existed for a seminar designed to enhance the facility of federally appointed judges in the preparation of written judgments and to improve the quality of such judgments. The first Judgment Writing Seminar was held in July 1981, and such seminars have been held each July since then. The institute has continued to act as the organizing instrument of the seminars on behalf of the Canadian Judicial Council. The chairman of the institute's Judicial Education Committee, Mr Justice William A. Stevenson of the Court of Appeal of Alberta (a member of the Supreme Court of Canada 1990–2), led the organization of the first seminar and was largely responsible for its evolution in subsequent years. The "faculty" for these seminars in their early years consisted of American professors of English who had been involved in similar programs for American judges. From 1982 until the present, there has been a bilingual component of the program under the direction of Madame la juge Louise Mailhot, now of the Quebec Court of Appeal. With the passage of years, other Canadians were added to the list of instructors until Canadian "faculty" members assumed half of the instructional duties.

At the beginning of the 1980s the institute decided to launch a new series of seminars intended for both judges and lawyers. It was hoped to attract those who would be attending the annual conventions of the Canadian Bar Association held in August, and therefore the seminars were held immediately after the bar conventions. Attendance was not limited to those persons, and the composition of attendees has varied according to the subject matter but judges have always been among those attending. In the earlier years these two-day seminars tended to focus on law in a manner of direct value to the practising needs of lawyers and the duties of judges. More recently both the subject matter and the approaches to them have been of a more general scope. The precise function of these seminars is constantly under review. The August seminars have been on the following topics.

1981, Family Law
Chaired by Judge Rosalie Abella, Provincial Court Family Division, Ontario. There were nineteen papers by eight judges and eleven academic lawyers and medical and other experts. The topics included alternatives to litigation, financial support, custody of children, and matrimonial property.

1982, Evidence
Chaired by the present author. There were fourteen papers by twelve judges, one lawyer, and the president of the Law Reform Commission of Canada (F.C. Muldoon, QC). The topics included character evidence, hearsay, evidence in sexual cases, eyewitness identification, issues in cross-examination, conspiracy trials, confessions, Crown privilege, voir dires, alibi evidence, and expert opinion evidence.

1983, Criminal Law
Chaired by Mr Justice Jacques Ducros, of the Superior Court of Quebec. There were seven papers by practising and academic lawyers. The topics included the Canadian Charter of Rights and Freedoms, evidence of electronic eavesdropping, and defences.

1984, Remedies
There were twenty papers by thirteen judges and six practising and academic lawyers.

1985, Family Law
Co-chaired by Mr Justice Guy H. Boisvert of the Court of Queen's Bench of New Brunswick and Judge Paul S. Niedermayer of the Family Court of Nova Scotia. There were twenty-four papers by nine judges, nine practising and academic lawyers, and four social workers.

1986, The Art of Judging
The co-chairmen were Mr Justice Allan Cawsey and Mr Justice Tellex W. Gallant, both of the Court of Queen's Bench of Alberta, and Associate Chief Judge Walder White of the Provincial Court of Alberta. The seven papers by four judges and three academic lawyers considered "A Look to the Future," "A Critical View of the Art of Judging," "The Art of Pre-trial," "The Art of Listening/Observation," and "The Art of Creating Law (Judicial Legislation)."

1987, Legislative Drafting and Interpretation
There were ten papers by one judge, five government lawyers, and the chairman of the Canadian Human Rights Commission.

1988, The Future Role of Appellate Courts
Co-chaired by Mr Justice Louis Lebel of the Quebec Court of Appeal and Professor André Tremblay of the Faculté de Droit, Université de Montréal. Panels of judges and lawyers considered the nature and function of a right of appeal, the organization and working of some Canadian appellate courts, the role of intermediate appellate courts in giving direction to the law, restrictions on the right of appeal to the Supreme Court of Canada, structural reform of superior courts, the creation of a national appellate court, the evolution of the role of appellate courts in criminal and sentencing matters, and access to appellate courts.

1989, Technology, Law, and the Courts
Co-chaired by Dean Peter V. Burns, QC, of the Faculty of Law at the University of British Columbia and Mr Justice Kenneth M. Lysyk of the Supreme Court of British Columbia. Panels of law professors, government officials, lawyers, and judges considered technology and the law of evidence and in the courtroom, legal and ethical issues, the use and misuse of computers, and the impact of computers on intellectual property laws. There were also demonstrations of many uses of computers and other technological advances.

1990, Courts, Media, and the Law
Co-chaired by Mr Justice Michel Monnin of the Court of Queen's Bench of Manitoba and Dean Roland W. Penner, QC, of the Faculty of Law, University of Manitoba. There were panels of media personnel, lawyers, law professors, and judges on freedom of expression and the right to privacy, fair trial vs the public's right to know, media coverage of judicial inquiries, and the tasks and role of a spokesperson for the courts.

1991, Police, the Community, and the Administration of Justice
Co-chaired by Mr Justice Del W. Perras of the Court of Queen's Bench of Alberta and Professor Patrick J. Knoll of the Faculty of Law at the University of Calgary. The seminar was attended by many senior police officers from forces across Canada, as well as a few judges, lawyers, and government officials. The topics discussed included the future of policing, policing family violence, minorities

and the police, aboriginal justice, the police and the Charter, the civil liability of the police, and street gangs.

The Canadian Charter of Rights and Freedoms became part of Canada's Constitution on 17 April 1982. Even before that date the institute began to plan a series of seminars on the Charter for federally appointed judges. The lead in this initiative was taken by Mr Justice Matas of the Manitoba Court of Appeal, who had been a member of the board since the institute's inception. He was assisted by a vigorous committee, among whose most active members were Professor Gerald Gall of the University of Alberta and Professor Dale Gibson of the University of Manitoba. An academic advisory committee was chaired by Professor Walter S. Tarnopolsky. After obtaining the endorsement of the Canadian Judicial Council, twenty-five judicial seminars were held across Canada during the autumn of 1982. They included four provincial court meetings (national, regional, and provincial) outside Quebec, and one seminar for each of the four divisions of the Provincial Court of Quebec. The institute also provided Charter programs for lawyers' meetings in four provinces and territories. Some of those who prepared papers and lectured appeared as lecturers at many of the seminars, at considerable personal inconvenience. These seminars performed an important service in giving the Canadian judiciary a reasonably informed appreciation of the Charter as a constitutional instrument and of many of its detailed provisions, particularly in regard to legal rights, that would soon become difficult issues in criminal trials.

The institute's temporary focus on the Charter was reinforced by the planning for the 1982 annual conference held in October in Winnipeg. The title of the program was "The Charter after Eighteen Months," and Mr Justice Matas again chaired the organizing committee.

Section 15 of the Charter, which guarantees equality rights, came into effect on 18 April 1985. Once again the institute met the special need created by this development by conducting a series of seminars for federally appointed judges in most of the provinces. The planning of these seminars was carried out by Mr Justice Charles Gonthier of the Superior Court of Quebec, as chairman of the Judicial Education Committee, and Madame la juge Alice Desjardins of the same court. Among the seminars were one for Atlantic provinces superior court and appellate judges, another for the Atlantic provinces provincial court judges, one for the judges of Quebec and French-speaking judges from Ontario, and seminars in each of the western provinces. As was the case with some other judicial education projects of the institute, particularly those relating to the Charter, the financial support of the federal Department of Justice was of vital importance. It is worth noting that as early as February 1984 the seminars for recently appointed federal-appointed judges, organized by the institute on behalf of the Canadian Judicial Council, included a half-day component on the Charter.

In 1980 the institute organized a small claims court seminar, in keeping with its constant exploration of new constituencies for judicial education. The topics considered included the jurisdiction of such courts, experiments with diversion in Canada and the United States, the nature of the hearing (inquisitorial or adversarial), the applicability of the rules of evidence, limits on legal representation, appeal procedures, and execution and enforcement. A second such seminar was held in 1982. It was co-sponsored by the Canadian Association of Provincial Court Judges. The organizing chairman was Judge E. O'Donnell of British Columbia.

The objects of the institute, in referring to educational programs, specifically mentioned not only members of the judiciary but also "members of administrative tribunals." The development of programs for such persons was on the agenda of the institute once it had the foregoing programs for judges underway. The directors, like the framers of the objects of the institute, recognized that the network of federal and provincial administrative tribunals constituted an important domain in which the rights of citizens were determined. In time, as the possibility of developing such programs was explored, it became apparent that there had never been any occasion for members of federally appointed tribunals and agencies to meet to compare ways of doing things and the principles of procedure and conduct. Not even residents of Ottawa had done so. The same was true at the level of the provincial governments. A pilot project was carried out in the early 1980s on the initiative of Judge Sandra Oxner as president of the institute and with the assistance of Professor Innis Christie of Dalhousie University. After that, some time elapsed before a breakthrough occurred at both the federal and the provincial levels. The seminars held have been as follows, each for one day.

April 1987, Hull, chaired by Judge Rosalie Abella, by then chairperson of the Ontario Labour Relations Board. It was attended by members of thirteen federal tribunals.

June 1987, Toronto, for members of fifteen provincial tribunals.

December 1987, the Maritimes, for members of sixteen tribunals.

January 1988, Alberta and NWT, for thirty-one persons from fifteen provincial boards.

February 1988, Manitoba, for thirty-seven persons from seven provincial boards and four federal boards.

April 1988, Saskatchewan, for twenty-eight persons from fifteen provincial boards.

Another area in which the institute has been innovative relates to the process of drafting legislation and its interpretation. Judges, of course, are directly interested in the latter. There have been judges in attendance at the Conference on Legislation, organized for the institute by Professor Jean-Louis Baudoin in 1982, and at a series of seminars on legislative drafting and interpretation. The first of these, chaired by Mr Justice Hugessen (by then a member of the Federal Court of Appeal), was held in Ottawa in 1987. It was attended by 120 persons, including draft persons from the federal government and the governments of all provinces and territories. In 1989, again in Ottawa, 130 persons attended, including twenty-five municipal government lawyers who were attracted by a component on the drafting of municipal by-laws. In 1990, again in Ottawa, more than one hundred persons were in attendance. In 1991 a one-day seminar was held in each province for municipal government lawyers. In 1992 the institute sponsored a national seminar on "Legislative Drafting: International Perspectives."

Throughout its history, the institute has adhered to its original intention to be housed in a university. While the institute began its life at Osgoode Hall Law School of York University in Toronto, the board from the start recognized that that location might not be permanent. In response to an attractive invitation from Dean Frank D. Jones of the Faculty of Law at the University of Alberta, the institute's offices moved to Edmonton in 1978 and remained there until 1986. Then, in response to another generous initiative by the Faculty of Law at the Université de Montréal, supported by the Bar and the Notaries of Quebec, the institute moved its office to that university, where it is still housed. In each case the host university has supported the work of the institute by freeing faculty members from certain of their regular duties so they might devote part of their time to the institute's work.

Financing of the institute's judicial education endeavours has usually been through registration fees covering essentially break-even budgets which have included a small component dedicated to the institute's overhead. The remainder of the overhead, after the first three years when the funding by the Donner Canadian Foundation was available, has been covered by similar overhead components in other activities including research grants, as well as by membership fees and grants by the federal Department of Justice, the Department of the Secretary of State, and other governmental and private sources. Financing of a nongovernmental organization such as the institute demands constantly changing and imaginative responses to genuine needs. The task of meeting those needs has not been easy.

CONCLUSION

Much credit for the introduction of judicial education must be given to the Canadian Judicial Council and the Canadian Association of Provincial Court Judges. Not long after they had entered the field, the CIAJ – a voluntary, nongovernmental organization – appeared on the scene. Its objects included judicial education, and its founders thought that much more could be done in this area in Canada. Their initiatives eventually evoked a warm and supportive response, in particular from the Canadian Judicial Council, on whose behalf the CIAJ served as the agent for the development and implementation of new and creative programs. The vital role of the CIAJ in judicial education, achieved by the early 1980s, helped it to establish its presence and relevance throughout the country. This reputation in turn enabled it to organize its research programs with greater confidence, in that it understood the "justice community" in Canada.

In regard to the education of judges in the strict sense (that is, leaving administrative tribunals aside), the institute has in a sense been a victim of its own success. One has the curious feeling that in the early 1980s some of the members of the Canadian Judicial Council, even those who had been closely connected with the institute's programs, became uneasy or restless about leaving so much development and administration in the hands of a voluntary society that had an independent Board of Directors not subject to the control of the Canadian Judicial Council. No matter how genuinely the institute reiterated in words and deeds that it was always the servant of the Canadian Judicial Council and respected its wishes in the content of seminars and conferences, there was a view among some of the chief justices that it would ultimately be better if some programs were created and undertaken by a body more directly responsible to the Canadian Judicial Council, or at least more governmental in nature. Perhaps it was felt that government financing, by both federal and provincial governments, would be more forthcoming if programs were directly created and organized by an agency that was in some real sense a creature of cooperative parenting by the federal and provincial governments.

I am not qualified to comment on the decision that was taken to establish the Canadian Judicial Centre. Nor am I qualified to comment on the directions that have been taken by the centre since its creation. Let me nonetheless conclude with several points.

First, when judges are excited by the potential for judicial education, it is not surprising that some of them should be keen to develop a new mechanism for the delivery of services to their own constituency, without having to go through some extrinsic organization. This temptation is likely to be enhanced if the new mechanism appears to be able to attract greater government funding than was previously the case.

Second, there has in the past been a tendency in Canadian governments to prefer to have public service functions performed by government departments or agencies which are entirely subject to Treasury Board scrutiny and public audit. Public servants tend to be uneasy when functions they think could perfectly well be carried out by government departments or agencies are carried out instead by a private agency, even a non-profit one. These tendencies are currently being questioned in some political circles, but they have had an effect on recent developments in judicial education.

Third, when we are concerned about community service endeavours such as judicial education, the means to achieve such ends should be as far removed as possible from the atmosphere of government. A central agency such as the Canadian Judicial Centre, if it is established with the cooperation of all levels of government but is governed essentially by judges who themselves have security of tenure, may have the necessary distance between the agency and the government. The possibility remains, however, that such an agency may become too much like a government department: permanence and the assurance of perennial financial support, together with traditions of public service security of employment or, even if staff serve on fixed-term contracts, a sense of obligation on the part of management to renew such contracts in the absence of misbehaviour by the staff, may lead to stagnation and loss of creativity as the years go by. Contracting the execution of such community needs out to a private nonprofit agency is much less likely to run those risks.

Fourth, in a federal state such as ours it is a matter of concern if a voluntary national community service society such as the CIAJ has failed to secure support from one level of court – specifically, the provincial courts. Perhaps that failure occurred because, among provincial court judges, there was a sense that federally appointed judges had too much influence in the direction of the CIAJ. Whatever the reason for the failure, it may be that to secure the cooperation and participation of all levels of court in the development of programs of judicial education that are of countrywide importance (criminal law and procedure, family law, the Canadian Charter of Rights and Freedoms, and gender issues, for example), a fresh start was required by the creation of a central agency in which all levels of courts and both levels of government would feel they have an equitable share in decision-making and execution of functions. Perhaps that is the price that must be paid in a federal country where jurisdictions are guarded jealously.

Finally, there is no doubt that, by whatever means may be effective, it is desirable to enhance the degree of cooperation among various bodies which are involved in judicial education. If coordination and the satisfaction of other imperatives can be achieved only through some body such as the Canadian Judicial Centre, so be it. But that should not cause our society to ignore the value of voluntary initiatives or to forget the impressive history of such organizations as the CIAJ in the development of judicial education.

The wide variety of educational functions the institute has performed could scarcely have been anticipated by its founders. Perhaps the past is prologue. If so, the future holds promise of still more constituencies to serve and services to perform in the interest of enhancing the administration of justice by education of those whose functions place them at its centre.

NOTE

I wish to express my thanks in particular to Mr Justice Stephen Borins, Judge Sandra Oxner, Mr Justice Kenneth Lysyk, and Mr Justice James Carnwath.

1 The presidents of the institute have been:

  1974–77   Mr Justice D.C. McDonald (Alberta)
  1977–78   Mr Justice R.J. Matas (Manitoba)
  1978–80   Mr Justice R.E. Holland (Ontario)
  1980–82   Judge Sandra Oxner (Nova Scotia)
  1982–83   Mr Justice Jacques Dugas (Quebec)
  1983–85   Mr Justice W.A. Stevenson (Alberta)
  1985–87   Mr Justice Charles Gonthier (Quebec)

1987–89   Mr Justice Horace Krever (Ontario)
1989–91   Mr Justice K.M. Lysyk (British Columbia)
1991–92   Mr Justice Robert Wells (Newfoundland)

The executive directors have been:

1974–78   Professor Allen M. Linden
          Professor Sidney J. Lederman (associate)
1978–79   Professor Lyndon Irwin
1979–82   Professor Gerald Gall
1983–85   Professor Peter J. Lown
1985–86   Professor Pierre-André Côté
          Professor Jean-Louis Baudoin (associate)
1987–88   Hélène Dumont
1988–   Joyce Whitman

Assistants to the executive director have been Madeleine Smith (1974–78), Mariette Kathol (Dufresne) (1978–86), Claudette Racette (1986–88), and Christine Huglo-Robertson (1988–).

The Founding of the Canadian Judicial Centre

WILLIAM STEVENSON

"Among the more narcissistic of professional behavioural patterns in Canada ... are the frequent (perhaps 'chronic') reappraisals by the legal profession of its training."[1]

Maxwell Cohen prefaced his review of *Law and Learning* with that observation, remarking on the excessive tendency of Canadian law teachers to gaze at their navels. No such comment could be directed towards the study of judicial training in Canada. Unfortunately, "Judge" Maxwell Cohen did not have the opportunity to direct the impressive talents of "Dean" Maxwell Cohen to the subject of judicial education.

That subject has only recently been recognized as justifying any appraisal, let alone reappraisal. The first institution designed exclusively for the development of judicial education, the Canadian Judicial Centre, was established in December 1987 and housed at the University of Ottawa in December 1988. The writer's 1986 report recommended the creation of such a centre.[2]

This article will look at three aspects of the subject of judicial education: the need for training, the nature of the response to that need before the establishment of the Canadian Judicial Centre, and the development of the Canadian Judicial Centre as a vehicle for meeting the need, with some thoughts about the challenges to that centre.

Like law school education, judicial education embraces both the development of skills and the learning of substantive law. Like law teachers, the teachers of judges must today concern themselves with the development of a greater understanding of the contributions of other disciplines and the encouragement of a sensitivity towards the special problems of those who may be the victims of discrimination. But unlike law teachers, judicial educators face an argument that their services are not needed at all.

Ambivalence about the need for judicial education does not rest solely with judges. The bar, custodian of an adversary system, is rightly anxious that the judges remain open to education by counsel appearing before them, in the context of the particular case. The bar fears that judges, fresh from a new educational program, will not permit a challenge to their expertise. Worse, it fears that judges may apply that expertise without giving the lawyers appearing before them an adequate opportunity to challenge it. A judge, or court, that claims ownership of a subject is not an ideal tribunal. Paradoxically, the bar will often endorse suggestions that there be judicial specialization (implying specialized expertise) without so much as a thought to the implications for the adversary system. The demands of the adversary system are not to be ignored. Counsel who has lost on a point not taken, or who has been defeated by an authority not cited, has legitimate concerns. The judge must not only be open to persuasion but must be ready, willing, and able to expose any knowledge which predisposes him or her to a conclusion in the particular case.

The attitude of the bench and bar here is mirrored in the attitude towards judicial education found in sister common-law jurisdictions. While the United States has educational programs extending through virtually every state to the national level, in the United Kingdom, programs for judges of the superior courts are almost unknown. Programs for judges of other courts are not extensive, and are largely oriented towards criminal practice and the sentencing process. In its 1983–7 report, the United Kingdom's Judicial Studies Board observed that in the past it had been thought that some exception might be taken to words like "train" and "instruct" when applied to professional judges who had gone to the bench after many years as successful advocates.[3] Indeed, it is only recently that the Judicial Studies Board extended its activities beyond the criminal law into family law.

Proposals for an educational program in Australia similarly met with mixed response. Some senior members of the judiciary pointed out that training programs were unnecessary for skilled members of the bar appointed to the bench. In his comment on the Australian scene ("Training for Judges?"), Mr Justice Kennedy discusses the opposition; he identifies that opposition as coming from those who perceive no benefit to Australian judges with their experience and background, who see an adverse effect upon the public standing of judges, or who fear an attack upon judicial independence.[4] Moreover, in all such jurisdictions, there may be some risk that special interest groups, or government itself, could use the availability of educational programs to espouse views in circumstances where no adversary is available to expose error.

The challenge is to identify and fill the needs while recognizing and addressing the legitimate concerns that give rise to opposition. Judicial educators must weigh and accommodate the interests of the public, reflected by the bar that serves it. These kinds of concerns have convinced the Canadian judiciary of one essential requirement: that educational programs must be administered by the judiciary itself as the only effective means of insuring balanced presentations sensitive to the legitimate demands of an adversary system and free of illegitimate pressures.

Let me turn to those who say there is no need. They could be answered by pointing to the results of judicial surveys in this country, or by looking at the demands made on the Canadian Judicial Centre. The critic, however, may be best persuaded by some reflection on the kinds of programs that are offered to judges.

Even the harshest critic, the most hardened sceptic, may usually be persuaded that some form of orientation program is probably needed. That sceptic may also be persuaded that knowledge of basic rules of evidence and criminal law is essential in a jurisdiction which recognizes the obligation of the court to intervene to protect the interests of the criminal accused. After all, the accused is not to suffer the full rigours of the adversary system. That sceptic or critic will probably also accept the benefit of some training in such subjects as writing, ethics, and courtroom decorum.

Are not, the sceptic may ask, the adversaries to teach substantive law? Our system increasingly demands legally trained judges. But what level of expertise do the adversaries assume exists? They cannot assume that experienced judges bring only their formal law school training to the bench. The sceptic may then accept that some form of "refresher" in the nature of continuing legal education is desirable, at least to ensure that the judges have the opportunity to develop a uniform level of training.

One might face more scepticism with the suggestion that judges should be given some opportunity to learn about economics, philosophy, statistics, medicine, history, or anthropology. The critic should accept the need for some study of the Canadian Charter, because very few of Canada's judges have had an opportunity to study the

Charter as a law school subject. And if judges are to learn anything about the implementation of section 1, or its application, disciplines other than the law are bound to intrude themselves.

Simon Lee in his recent book, *Judging Judges*, quotes Learned Hand:

> I venture to believe that it is as important to a judge called upon to pass on a question of constitutional law, to have a bowing acquaintance with Acton and Maitland, with Thucydides, Gibbon, and Carlyle, with Homer, Dante, Shakespeare, and Milton, with Machiavelli, Montaigne, and Rabelais, with Plato, Bacon, Hume and Kant as with books that have been specifically written on the subject. For in such matters everything turns upon the spirit in which he approaches the question before him. The words he must construe are empty vessels into which he can pour nearly everything he will. Men do not gather figs of thistles, nor supply institutions from judges whose outlook is limited by parish or class. They must be aware that there are before them more than verbal problems; more than final solutions cast in generalizations of universal applicability. They must be aware of the changing social tensions in every society which make it an organism; which demand new schemata of adaptation; which will disrupt it, if rigidly confined.[5]

Lee notes that the job description shows the enormous power of judges who act as constitutional guardians, the role of u.s. judges, and, increasingly, I must say, of our judges.

Maxwell Cohen recognized this educational gap in a comment in 1970 when discussing the implications of a Bill of Rights:

> Will the next generation of Canadian judges, and will the Canadian Bar functioning within its established and technical adversary tradition, be able to meet, constructively, these new challenges to having them play ever more sophisticated informational and interpretative roles in the management of Canadian federalism? Some preliminary doubts may be raised about expectations here. Much depends upon the quality of the men involved and upon the character of legal education itself and the willingness of the Bench to relate the new roles to the kind of informational input, or sources of authority, which heretofore cautious Canadian Courts have been reluctant to accept – sources now to be supplied by government documents and the behavioural sciences. It is highly probable, however, that once given the fact of constitutional change and that such a new role must be played, there would be reason to expect that the Courts, the Bar and the Universities will respond accordingly. But there may be a period of at least a decade or more within which Canadian judges, and more particularly the final 'constitutional' tribunal, will be feeling their way toward the appropriate balance to

be found in performing these new and often more direct policy-making functions. Moreover, once such doctrinal changes take place in the key areas referred to, decisions on them will likely have pervasive effects throughout the whole of the constitutional process.[6]

Surely, also, the judge must have some understanding of the special problems of victims of discrimination. Expressed public concerns about statements which seem to reflect at least insensitivity to the problems of racial minorities or betray unacceptable gender bias demand the availability of some forum in which these concerns may be analysed and addressed.

In the last analysis, the sceptic must agree with the observation of the Judicial Studies Board in its 1983–7 report when it says that no competent and conscientious occupant of any post would suggest that his or her performance is incapable of being improved. The critics of judicial education must either accept a thesis of perfection or acknowledge the desirability of providing an effective means for helping those who can only strive for perfection.

Even without a formal educational centre, some form of training program invariably develops. What develops, without some organization, is an ad hoc unstructured response to the most pressing needs.

Before the advent of the Canadian Judicial Centre, many courts had developed some in-house programs which certainly fell within the rubric of "education." These programs ranged from nothing more sophisticated than the provision of handouts (perhaps "bench books") to orientation and mentor programs; from annual meetings where changes in law and practice were discussed to one- or two-day intense seminars.

These programs were not uniform and they were invariably underfunded. They were frequently the products of duplicated efforts, without any sharing of resources or experiences. They were put together by people who had many other duties and responsibilities and, all too often, did so without any appreciation of the techniques which ought to apply in the delivery of adult education.

Before the establishment of the Canadian Judicial Centre, most judicial education in Canada consisted of programs which were the result of independent initiatives. At the provincial court level what was done was largely court-based, with provincial associations of the provincial court judges taking a significant part in some provinces while exercising little influence in others. Funding was largely provided through the court's budget and administered by the chief judges. The funding support in many jurisdictions was wholly inadequate to provide any substantial program. One sustained program, a new judges program, and some occasional national programs were produced through the efforts of the Canadian Association of Provincial Court Judges. The funding of these activities has largely been dependent on chief judges arranging funding for their individual judges with some assistance from the federal Department of Justice and other funding agencies. In recent years, an energetic regional operation, the Western Judicial Education Centre, supported by the chief judges of the western provinces and territories and sponsored by the Canadian Association of Provincial Court Judges has been providing more extensive programs presented on a regional basis.

The Canadian Judicial Council, established in 1971, was given a mandate to provide judicial education for federally appointed judges. Its early activities centred on the presentation of an annual refresher course – one for county and district court judges and one for superior court judges. It later established, through sponsorship, programs developed by other groups and organizations. A number of the section 96 courts also provided their own programs. The principal independent suppliers of judicial education programs are the Canadian Institute for the Administration of Justice and the Institute of Advanced Legal Studies. These organizations sponsor a number of programs, most designed to meet the interests and needs of federally and provincially appointed judges. Programs provided by the bar through continuing legal education exercises also provide some educational experiences for judges. Funding for the attendance of provincially appointed judges has been, and continues to be, a special concern.

The source of funding is the main problem. Courts can neither increase their programming nor improve the methods of delivery because of the absence of an adequate budgetary base. So long as courts were able to provide programs by using judges to administer and give the training, and were satisfied with "in-house" programs, budget demands were modest and were, for the most part, met out of unspecified general funds. The recognition that more and better programs were needed, and that more resources had to be found, coincided with budgetary restraints – restraints administered by treasury officials requiring proof of cost benefit.

This observation does not gainsay the importance of cost-benefit analysis, but what is of great concern (in this and many other fields) is the absence of a mechanism arithmetically demonstrating the benefit. Chief judges could, of course, point out that it did not make much sense to have well-paid judges carrying out administrative and

487 The Founding of the Canadian Judicial Centre

teaching tasks which could be done by others. More importantly, they could point out the serious cost, in more than just financial terms, of errors which could be reduced by effective training programs. Every new trial in a criminal case results, presumptively, from a trial judge's error. The cost of one or two significant criminal trials per year would satisfy a modest judicial education budget in any province. The conduct of efficient trials, the promotion of settlements, and the elimination of delay all contribute substantial savings to the administration of justice. Yet measurement, establishing the "bottom line," was, and remains, an elusive task.

I concluded in my 1986 report that judicial education in Canada was an uncoordinated patchwork of programs suffering from unnecessary duplication and, at the same time, significant gaps. Perhaps the Canadian judicial education scene could be best described, prior to the establishment of the Canadian Judicial Centre, as an exercise in the "ad hoc." Earlier commentators, notably Chief Justices Hugessen and Howland had reached similar conclusions in reports for the Canadian Judicial Council. Other agencies such as the Canadian Institute for the Administration of Justice and the Canadian Association of Provincial Court Judges had also demonstrated the need for some coordinated new initiative. Not only was there no coordination with little cooperation, but little attention could be given to questions of "pedagogy" or to resources developed in other jurisdictions. The programs that were offered were largely responses to pressing situations. There were some exceptions, which largely served to emphasize the value of coordination – the Canadian Institute for the Administration of Justice programs in judicial writing and on the Canadian Charter being good examples. These programs, offered in cooperation with the Canadian Judicial Council, provided impetus to the movement towards a new method of developing and offering education programs in this country.

The "idea" of a Canadian Judicial Centre, then, was to be converted into an institution responding to the needs of the judiciary. What kind of centre could best fill the needs?

To rationalize judicial education, there was an obvious need for some central and coordinating organization. At the same time, the establishment of an agency providing all judicial education in Canada was clearly not practicable. Individual courts, individual chief justices or chief judges, and individual judges demand a measure of independence. With limited funds at their disposal, those responsible for the disposition of those funds (primarily chief judges and chief justices) must seek maximum benefit for their education dollars. In some circumstances, a court might decide that available resources should all be spent on intensive programs available to all the judges of that province. In other circumstances, national or regional programs would best fulfil the needs of the judiciary.

The constitutional division of responsibility over judges must also be accommodated. The federal government accepts a significant obligation to support educational programs for federally appointed judges. It has also made significant contributions to programs for provincially appointed judges, recognizing the fact that these judges are heavily involved in the administration of federal law. At the same time, provincial attorneys-general and chief judges are anxious to ensure that not only is a certain measure of provincial independence preserved, but that provincially appointed judges are not, and do not appear to be, given roles subordinate to the federally appointed judiciary.

The most significant deficiency prior to the establishment of the Canadian Judicial Centre was the absence of any comprehensive professional resource. Yet, in times of restraint, governments could not be expected to look with enthusiasm at a vastly expanded new structure.

A paramount consideration had to be the independence of the judiciary. The judiciary could not accept, and will not accept, either government or private interest groups dictating the curriculum. The bilingual and bijuridical nature of the country also had to be accommodated. The solution required some mechanism which would establish a partnership that did not sacrifice independence. These concerns focused on two features: the financing and governance of an educational centre.

Both the federal and provincial governments were expected to provide financial support and to control the global budget. The governance would be in the hands of the various judicial constituencies. Accordingly, the individual governors have been selected by the four primary constituents: the chief justices (federally appointed), the chief judges (provincially appointed), the federally appointed puisne judges, and the provincially appointed puisne judges. The president was to be the chief justice of Canada, seen to represent all the Canadian judiciary.

The object was to make the Canadian Judicial Centre a facility controlled by and responding to the needs of all judges. The executive director is a federally appointed judge, and the associate executive directors are provincially appointed judges. These roles may change – indeed it is confidently expected that they will – although American experience tends to show that the day-to-day executive administration need not be performed by a judge.

It is to the credit of Canada's governments – federal, provincial, and territorial – that they have supported the Canadian Judicial Centre. It is financed by joint contributions, supplemented by the secondment of some of the judges engaged in the centre's operations. The centre's services are available to all levels of courts, and to all regions and provinces. The joint cost-sharing arrangement is extremely important. It establishes a commitment to the provision of a needed service. It enables the centre, in turn, to commit itself to all levels of court. No court, no level of judiciary, owns the service. Importantly, no government owns the service.

An important element in the establishment of the centre was that it not be a central school facility. It is to be a service that can design educational programs for use on a national, regional, or local basis. It is to assist judges in self-improvement and courts in developing their own programs, and yet recognize the diversity of needs and resources. It is not to usurp the whole field of judicial education but to leave room for other initiatives, by courts and other agencies. For those reasons it was designed as a resource centre. Any program it initiates is available for use by the judiciary, but the actual delivery is financed by those using it.

The centre is now in place. It is assured long-term financing for the exercise of its resource functions. As it develops expertise in the delivery of programs it may well expand its activities on a self-financing basis.

Success will breed one major problem. As the centre develops new training programs, the judiciary will respond by asking for those programs. Courts will invariably find need for more funds to subscribe to or provide those programs and there will be a need to convince treasury boards of the value of that budget allocation. It should, however, no longer be necessary to convince those administrators of the need for judicial education. What remains, perhaps, is a new initiative in measuring the level of service required. Success will breed problems, but not insoluble ones. If Canada's governments were to fail to respond to the legitimate needs of the judiciary, demands would develop for greater fiscal independence of the judiciary. The Canadian Judicial Centre is evidence that Canada's governments are sensitive to the need to provide the funding necessary to discharge their responsibilities to fund the administration of justice.

This comment began with a reference to the functions of Canada's law schools. The analogy to the Canadian education program is, of course, imperfect, but there is much in common. In common is the need for effective curriculum development responding to needs but forecasting, also, future demands. The centre shares with the law schools the desire to develop the most effective means of adult education. The centre, like the law schools, must be prepared to experiment. It, too, must find effective means of introducing the fruits of other disciplines – a task particularly important in Charter studies. Both must maintain independence from the agencies that fund them.

There remains one very important distinction. Judicial education is not engaged in navel gazing; rather, it is still studying its umbilical cord. In that task it will benefit from the experiences of the legal educators who developed Canada's law schools from their infancy.

NOTES

1 Maxwell Cohen, review, *Law and Learning – le droit et le savoir: Report to the Social Sciences and Humanities Research Council of Canada* (1983), 61 *Canadian Bar Review* 702.
2 Canadian Judicial Centre Project Report, 1986.
3 Judicial Studies Board, *Report for 1983–87* (London: HMSO 1988).
4 Kennedy, "Training for Judges" (1987), 10 *University of New South Wales Law Journal* 47.
5 Simon Lee, *Judging Judges* (New York: Faber and Faber 1989).
6 Maxwell Cohen, "The Judicial Process and National Policy" (1970), 16 *McGill Law Journal* 297.

Bibliography

Maxwell Cohen: An Overview of His Publications

Compiled by ANNEMIEKE HOLTHUIS

This bibliography of Maxwell Cohen's work, while not exhaustive, presents an overview of the different areas of law Cohen has examined in his legal scholarship and to which he made significant contributions.

GOVERNMENT REPORTS, ROYAL COMMISSIONS, AND RELATED DOCUMENTS

Canada. Advisory Committee on Reconstruction. *Governmental Machinery of Wartime Controls and Its Relation to Postwar Problems.* Ottawa 1942

Report on the McGill Senate and University Government. Montreal, Jan. 1959

Canada, Royal Commission on Government Organization, vol. 4, Report 21 (background investigation by M. Cohen). Ottawa: Queen's Printer 1962–3

– Department of External Affairs. *The Columbia River Treaty and Protocol: A Presentation* Background Study by M. Cohen (Ottawa: Queen's Printer, 1964)

– *Report of the Special Joint Committee on Hate Propaganda.* M. Cohen, chairman. Ottawa: Queen's Printer 1966

Report of the Committee on Manpower Problems in the Unloading of Grain Vessels, Port of Montreal. Montreal 1968

New Brunswick. Constitutional Conference 1968. *Views of the Government of New Brunswick with respect of the Prime Minister's Five Steps in Implementing Linguistic Rights.* Ottawa 1968

New Brunswick. Constitutional Conference, Dec. 1969. *Comments on the Judicial Process and National Policy in a Federal State.* Ottawa: Constitutional Conference, Continuing Committee of Officials 1969

Newfoundland. *Report of the Royal Commission on Labour Legislation in Newfoundland and Labrador.* M. Cohen, chairman. St John's: Queen's Printer 1972

Canada. Environment Canada. *Report on Outside Review and Public Participation.* Second Report of the PCB Board of Review. M. Cohen, chairman. Ottawa: Government of Canada, Environment Canada 1980

BOOKS, ARTICLES, POLICY PAPERS

"The Immigration Act and Limitations on Judicial Power: Bail" (1936), 14 *Canadian Bar Review* 405

"Some Considerations on the Origins of Habeas Corpus" (1937), 16 *Canadian Bar Review* 92.

"The Canadian Anti-Trust Law–Doctrinal and Legislative Beginnings" (1938), 16 *Canadian Bar Review* 439

"Habeas Corpus Cum Causa – The Emergence of the Modern Writ: I" (1940), 18 *Canadian Bar Review* 10

"Habeas Corpus Cum Causa – The Emergence of the Modern Writ: II" (1940), 8 *Canadian Bar Review* 172

The Dominion Provincial Conference: Some Basic Issues. Toronto: Ryerson Press 1945

"Some Pending Constitutional Issues" (1945), 17 *Manitoba Bar News* 1

"Can 'Trust-Busting' Preserve Competition?" (Dec. 1947), 11 *Public Affairs* 6

"Espionage and Immunity: Some Recent Problems and Developments" (1948), 25 *British Yearbook of International Law* 404

"The Condition of Legal Education in Canada" (1950), 28 *Canadian Bar Review* 267

"The Role of Law and Lawyers in Industrial Relations" (1950) McGill Industrial Relations Centre; (1951), 11 *Revue du Barreau* 477; (1952), 3 *Labor Law Journal* 276

"Communists – Labour Law – Public Policy – Certification and Decertification – Certiorari – Interpretation of Statutes." Comment on *Re Labour Relations Board of Nova Scotia* (1952), 30 *Canadian Bar Review* 408

"The MacQuarrie Report and the Reform of Combines Legislation – The Background, Main Features and Problems" (1952), 30 *Canadian Bar Review* 551

"Communist China – To Recognize or Not to Recognize" (1952–3), 8 *International Journal* 266

"The United States and the United Nations Secretariat: A Preliminary Appraisal" (1953), 1 *McGill Law Journal* 169

"Objectives and Methods of Legal Education: An Outline" (1954), 32 *Canadian Bar Review* 762

"The United Nations Secretariat and the Eighth General Assembly" (1954) Proceedings of the Annual Meeting of the International Law Association, American Branch

"Some International Law Problems of Interest to Canada and to Canadian Lawyers" (1955), 33 *Canadian Bar Review* 389

"The United Nations Secretariat – Some Constitutional and Administrative Developments" (1955), 49 *American Journal of International Law* 295

"International Legal Problems of the Columbia River" [1957] *Canadian Bar Association Papers* 99

"The United Nations Emergency Force: A Preliminary View" (1957), 12 *International Journal* 109

"International Law and Canadian Practice." In E. McWhinney, ed. *Canadian Jurisprudence: The Civil and Common Law in Canada.* Toronto: Carswell 1958. At 316.

"Some Legal and Policy Aspects of the Columbia River Dispute" (1958), 36 *Canadian Bar Review* 25

"Bill C-60 and International Law – The United Nations Charter – Declaration of Human Rights" (1959), 37 *Canadian Bar Review* 228

"From diversity to Unity: International Law in a Bipolar World" [1959] American Society of International Law, *Proceedings* 98

"The Law Governing the Use of International Rivers," Address at the Round Table, Inter-American Bar Association, 11th Conference, 1959

"Non-Navigational Uses of International River Basins," International Law Association, Committee on Law of Waters of International River Basins and Canals, 1959

"Some Bibliographic Problems of Public International Law" (1959–60), 6 *McGill Law Journal* 277

With G. Nadeau. "The Legal Framework of the St. Lawrence Seaway." In P.O. Proehl, ed. *Legal Problems of International Trade.* Urbana: University of Illinois Press 1959. At 29; University of Illinois Law Forum 1959

"The Columbia River Problem: Canadian Aims" (1960), 2 University of Windsor Seminar on Canadian-American Relations, *Proceedings* 88

"Reflections on Law and the United Nations System" (1960), 54 American Society of International Law, *Proceedings* 243

"The Rule of Law in a Divided World." In *This Divided World,* [1960] Conference on World Affairs 91

"Are Quebec Arbitration Procedures Obsolete?" (1961), 7 *McGill Law Journal* 255

"Lawyers and Learning: The Professional and Intellectual Traditions" (1961), 7 *McGill Law Journal* 181

"The Columbia River Treaty – A Comment" (1961), 8 *McGill Law Journal* 212

"Basic Principles of International Law" (1963) *World Peace Through Law* 759

"Canada–United States Treaty Relations: Trends and Future Problems." In D.R. Deener, ed. *Canada–United States Treaty Relations*. Durham, NC: Duke University Press 1963. At 185

"Some Main Directions of International Law: A Canadian Perspective" (1963), 1 *Canadian Yearbook of International Law* 15

"The 'Freedom' of Outer Space – Comments, from the Conference on the Law of Space and Satellite Communications" [1963] American Society of International Law, *Proceedings* 49

"Towards a Legal Regime in Space" (1963), 1 *Manitoba Law Society Journal* 147

"Towards Reconsideration in Anti-Combines Law and Policy" (1963), 9 *McGill Law Journal* 81

"'Basic Principles' of International Law – A Revaluation" (1964), 42 *Canadian Bar Review* 449

"Canada and the United States: Framework for the Future" (1964) 58 A.S.I.L. Proceedings 225.

"Canada and the United States: A Legal Framework for the Future" (1964) 10 *McGill Law Journal* 233

"The Condition of Legal Education in Canada – Fifteen Years Later 1949–1964" [1964] *Canadian Bar Association Papers* 116

"An Outside View." In H.C.L. Merrillat, ed. *Legal Advisers and Foreign Affairs*. New York: Oceana Publications 1964. At 43

ed. *First McGill Conference on the Law of Outer Space: Proceedings* 1963 (Leicester: Leicester University Press, 1964).

"Expanding Structure of International Law: Peacekeeping, General Principles and International Organizations" (1965) *World Peace Through Law* 565

"Foreword," (1965), 1 *Yearbook of Air and Space Law*

"The New Federalism: Comments in the Dark." In P.A. Crepeau and C.B. MacPherson, eds. *The Future of Canadian Federalism*. Toronto: University of Toronto Press 1965. At 173

"Canada in a Changing World: A Background Paper on Canadian Foreign Policy". Paper prepared for the National Meeting and Liberal Party Congress, 10–12 Oct. 1966

The Future of Canadian Federalism. Toronto: University of Toronto Press, mimeograph no. 41, 17 Nov. 1966

"Mergers and Joint Ventures – A Canadian-American Perspective and Comparison" (1966), 32 *American Bar Association Antitrust Law Journal* 156

"An Approach to Criminal Justice" (1967), 15 *Chitty's Law Journal* 239

"A Canadian Looks at American Law and Justice" (1967), 36 *Bar Examiner* 35

"The Demise of the U.N.E.F." (1967–8), 23 *International Journal* 18

"Canada and Quebec in North America: A Pattern for Fulfillment" (1968), 75 *Queen's Quarterly* 389

"The Canadian Federal Dilemma" (1968), 14 *McGill Law Journal* 357

"Human Rights: Programme or Catchall? A Canadian Rationale" (1968), 46 *Canadian Bar Review* 554

"Can Canada Have an Independent Foreign Policy" [1968–9] Empire Club Addresses 148

"Civil Disobedience, Dissent and Violence – A Canadian Perspective" (1969), 10 *William and Mary Law Review* 631

"Just Policies and the National Interest." Paper presented to the Harrison Liberal Conference, Harrison Hot Springs, BC, 21–23 Nov. 1969. Ottawa: National Liberal Federation 1969

"The Search for a Viable Federalism" (1969), 3 *Manitoba Law Journal* 1

"The Individual and International Law." In A. Gotlieb, ed. *Human Rights, Federalism and Minorities*. Toronto: Canadian Institute of International Affairs 1970. At 111

"The Judicial Process and National Policy: A Problem for Canadian Federalism" (1970), 16 *McGill Law Journal* 297

"A Just Foreign Policy and the National Interest." In A.M. Linden, ed. *Living in the Seventies* (Toronto: Peter Martin Associates 1970). At 225

"The Arctic and the National Interest" (1970–1), 26 *International Journal* 52

"The Hate Propaganda Amendments: Reflections on a Controversy" (1971), 9 *Alberta Law Review* 103

"Human Rights and Hate Propaganda: Controversial Canadian Experiment." In Shlomo Shoham, ed. *Of Law and Man: Essays in Honour of Mr. Justice Haim Cohn, Supreme Court of Israel*. Tel Aviv: University of Tel Aviv Press 1971. At 59

"The Individual and International Law." In Institut international des droits de l'homme, *René Cassin, Amicorum Disciplorumque Liber III*. Paris: Éditions A. Pedone 1971

"Canada and the United States – Possibilities for the Future" (1973), 12 *Columbia Journal of Transnational Law* 196

The Problem of Essential Services in Industrial Relations. McGill Industrial Relations Centre, 28 March 1973

"The Quebec Advisory Council on the Administration of Justice: Le conseil consultatif de Justice" (1973), 1 *Dalhousie Law Journal* 349

"Canada and the International Legal Order: An Inside Perspective." In R. St J. Macdonald et al., eds. *Canadian Perspectives on International Law and Organization*. Toronto: University of Toronto Press 1974. At 3

"The International Joint Commission: United States – Canada" (1974), 68 American Society of International Law, *Proceedings* 236

"Reflections on the Comparative Law Element of Public International Law." In Adrian Popivici, ed. *Problèmes de droit contemporain: Mélanges Louis Baudouin*. Montreal: Presses de l'Université de Montréal 1974. At 485

"Secrecy in Law and Policy: The Canadian Experience and International Relations." In T.M. Franck and E. Weisband, eds. *Secrecy and Foreign Policy.* New York: Oxford University Press 1974. At 53

The Regime of Boundary Waters – The Canadian–US Experience. The Hague Academy Lectures. Leyden: A.W. Sijthoff 1975; *Recueil des Cours: Collected Courses of the Hague Academy of International Law* 1975, vol. III, 1977 at 219

"Canada and United States: Dispute Settlement and the International Joint Commission – Can This Experience Be Applied to Law of the Sea Issues?" (1976), 8 *Case Western Reserve Journal of International Law* 69

Closing addresses (1976) McGill Air and Space Conference 161

"The Pattern of Settlement – Canada, the United States and the International Joint Commission." Paper presented to Canada–United States Relations Conference of the Conference Board of Canada, Toronto, 9 Nov. 1976

"Refections on International Rivers." In M.K. Nawaz, ed. *Essays on International Law in Honour of Krishna Rao.* Leyden: Sijthoff 1976. At 141

With A.F.W. Plumptre. "Canada/US Relations: The International Joint Commission – North American Cultures." Taped interview (cassette or reel) by Robert Reford. Canadian contemporary issues on tape. Toronto: Ontario Institute for Studies in Education 1976

"Penal Sanctions in Labour Law" (1977), 115 *International Labour Review* 11

"Thou Shalt Not Pollute: The International Joint Commission at 70" (1978), 1 *Report on Confederation* 19

"Canada – the United States and Water Issues" (1979) 4 *Canadian Water Resources Journal* 40

A Round Table from Sea to Sea ... the Order of Canada. Ottawa: Honours Secretariat, Government House 1979

"The Canada–United States Boundary Waters Treaty and the International Joint Commission" (1980), 11 *Etudes Internationales* 375

"Reagan Presidency: Constants and Variables in Canada–United States Relations" (Nov.–Dec. 1980) *International Perspectives* 3

"What Makes a Law School Great?" (1980), 6 *Dalhousie Law Journal* 350

"The Commission from the Inside." In R. Spencer et al., eds. *The International Joint Commission Seventy Years On.* Toronto: Centre for International Studies 1981. At 106

"Constantes et variables dans les relations canado-américaines" (hiv. 1981) *Perspectives Internationales* 9

With J. Reiskind. "Toward a Responsible Use of Nuclear Power in Outer Space – The Canadian Initiative in the United Nations" (1981), 6 *Annals of Air and Space Law* 461

"River Basin Planning: Observations from International and Canada–United States Experience" (1982) 6 *Natural Resources Forum* 247

"The Canadian Legal Profession and International Law" (1983), 13 *Manitoba Law Journal* 201

Foreword. J. Carroll. *Environmental Diplomacy*. Ann Arbor: University of Michigan Press 1983

Remarks. [1983] *Proceedings of the American Society of International Law* 17

With A.F. Bayefsky. "The Canadian Charter of Rights and Freedoms and Public International Law" (1983), 61 *Canadian Bar Review* 265

"Canada and the US – New Approaches to Undeadly Quarrels" (March–April 1985) *International Perspectives* 16

"The Lawyer and Nuclear Weapons" (1985), 14 Canadian Council of International Law, *Proceedings* 194

"Convergence, Global Equilibrium and Disorder – The Environmental Priority" (1986), 16 *Environmental Policy and Law* 106

"International Law and the Global Environment" (Sept.–Oct. 1986) *International Perspectives* 3

Preface, Great Lakes Legal Seminar: Diversion and Consumptive Use (1986), 18 *Case Western Reserve Journal of International Law* 1

"Towards a Paradigm of Theory and Practice: The Canadian Charter of Rights and Freedoms – International Law Influences and Interactions" (1986), 3 *Canadian Human Rights Yearbook* 47

"The Canadian Yearbook and International Law in Canada after Twenty-five Years" (1987), 25 *Canadian Yearbook of International Law* 3

With M.E. Gouin, *Lawyers and the Nuclear Debate: Proceedings of the Canadian Conference on Nuclear Weapons and the Law*. Ottawa: University of Ottawa Press 1988

BOOK REVIEWS

N.H. Moller, *Law of Civil Aviation* (London: Sweet & Maxwell 1936), in (1937), 15 *Canadian Bar Review* 388

G. Glen, *The Army and the Law* (New York: Columbia University Press 1943), in (1943), 21 *Canadian Bar Review* 773

L.J. Hobbs, *Police Manual of Arrests and Searches* (Toronto: Carswell 1946), in (1946), 24 *Canadian Bar Review* 739

P. Calvocoressi, *Nuremberg: The Facts, the Law and the Consequences* (London: Chatto and Windus 1947), in (1948), 26 *Canadian Bar Review* 744

L.M. Jones, *Full Powers and Ratification; A Study in the Development of Treaty-making Procedure* (Toronto: Macmillan 1946), in (1947), 25 *Canadian Bar Review* 555

H. Lauterpacht, *Recognition in International Law* (Cambridge: Cambridge University Press 1947), in (1948), 26 *Canadian Bar Review* 479

G. Schwarzenberger, *Manual of International Law* (London: Stevens and Sons 1947), in (1948), 26 *Canadian Bar Review* 898

G. Schwarzenberger, *International Law*, vol. 1: *International Law as Applied by International Courts and Tribunals*, 2d ed. (London: Stevens and Sons 1949), in (1950), 8 *University of Toronto Law Journal* 428

A.J. Harno, *Legal Education in the United States 1953*, in (1954), 6 *Journal of Legal Education* 416

Report of the Director of Investigation and Research, Combines Investigation Act, for the fiscal year ended 31 March (Ottawa: Dept of Justice 1955), in (1955), 33 *Canadian Bar Review* 1198

Antitrust Laws: A Comparative Symposium, University of Toronto Faculty of Law Comparative Law Series, vol. 3, ed. Friedmann (Toronto: Carswell 1956), in (1956), 34 *Canadian Bar Review* 1094

L. Oppenheim, *International Law: A Treatise,* vol. 1: *Peace,* 8th ed. H. Lauterpacht (Toronto: Longmans, Green and Co. 1955), in (1956), 34 *Canadian Bar Review* 236

A.J. Peaslee, *International Governmental Organizations: Constitutional Documents,* 2 vols. (The Hague: Martinus Nijhoff 1956) in (1957), 35 *Canadian Bar Review* 1237

L.B. Sohn, *Cases on United Nations Law* (Brooklyn: The Foundation Press 1956), in (1958), 36 *Canadian Bar Review* 122

P. Weis, *Nationality and Statelessness in International Law* (London: Institute of World Affairs; Stevens and Sons 1956), in (1957), 3 *McGill Law Journal* 230

S.N. Whitney, *Antitrust Policies: American Experience in Twenty Industries,* 2 vols. (The 20th Century Fund 1958), in (1959), 5 *McGill Law Journal* 204

H.R. Hahlo, J.G. Smith, and R.W. Wright, eds., *Nationalism and Multinational Enterprise – Legal, Economic, and Managerial Aspects,* (Dodds Ferry, NY: Oceana Publications 1973), in (1974), 20 *McGill Law Journal* 330

Independent Africa – Challenge to the Legal Profession, in (1978), 13 *Journal of Asian and African Studies* 136

C. Campbell and G.J. Szablowski, *The Superbureaucrats: Structure and Behaviour in Central Agencies* (Toronto: Macmillan 1979), in (1980), 58 *Canadian Bar Review* 809

S.A. Williams and A.L.C. de Mestral, *An Introduction to International Law* (Toronto: Butterworths 1979), in (1980), 25 *McGill Law Journal* 632

R. St J. Macdonald, D.M. Johnston, and G. Morris, *The International Law and Policy of Human Welfare,* in (1981), 59 *Canadian Bar Review* 613

Report of the Joint Committee of the American Bar Association and the Canadian Bar Association on the Settlement of International Disputes between Canada and the United States of America (Ottawa: Canadian Bar Association 1979), in (1982), 60 *Canadian Bar Review* 224

R.J. Roberts, *Anti Combines and Antitrust: The Competition Law of Canada and the Antitrust Law of the United States* (Toronto: Butterworths 1980), in (1982), 27 *McGill Law Journal* 387

Law and Learning – le droit et le savoir: Report to the Social Sciences and Humanities Research Council of Canada by Consultative Group on Research and Education in Law (Ottawa 1983), in (1983), 61 *Canadian Bar Review* 702

Hugh Kindred et al., *International Law: Chiefly as Interpreted and Applied in Canada*, 4th ed. (Toronto: Emond Montgomery 1987), in (1987–8), 33 *McGill Law Journal* 444

MAGAZINE ARTICLES

Over the years, Cohen has written articles on matters of politics, foreign policy, and international law for a variety of newspapers and magazines. In particular, he was a contributing editor for foreign affairs from 1957 to 1961 at *Saturday Night* magazine. Selected articles are listed below.

"Which Way Canada?" *The New Republic*, 16 March 1938
"Couchiching," *Canadian Forum*, Oct. 1940
"Canada and the Total War" *Canadian Forum*, Dec. 1941
"Newfoundland: Atlantic Rampart," *The Yale Review*, March 1943
"Canada Stands Pat," *The Nation*, 23 June 1945
"Premiers Conference Has Many Problems," *Saturday Night*, 28 July 1945
"Dominions Proposal Make 1945 Sense," *Saturday Night*, 18 Aug. 1945
"New Responsibility in Foreign Policy," *Saturday Night*, 19 Jan. 1957
"Eisenhower Doctrine: Containment by Ambiguity," *Saturday Night*, 2 Feb. 1957
"World Disarmament, the Minuet of Diplomacy," *Saturday Night*, 16 Feb. 1957
"Competitive Coexistence," *Saturday Night*, 30 March 1957
"Empire to Commonwealth: Commonwealth to What?" *Saturday Night*, 13 April 1957
"NATO: An Alliance Seeking a Reason," *Saturday Night*, 11 May 1957
"Foreign Policy and the Election," *Saturday Night*, 25 May 1957
"Algeria: Pride without Prejudice," *Saturday Night*, 22 June 1957
"Our New Direction in Foreign Policy," *Saturday Night*, 6 July 1957
"Russian Revolution Devours Its Young," *Saturday Night*, 3 Aug. 1957
"Peace Is Not Inevitable," *Saturday Night*, 31 Aug. 1957
"Agenda for Mankind: UN's Twelfth Assembly," *Saturday Night*, 14 Sept. 1957
"The Columbia River: An Asset and an Irritation," *Saturday Night*, 28 Sept. 1957
"The United Nations Emergency Force: World Policeman with a Future," *Saturday Night*, 12 Oct. 1957
"Canada, Britain and the Common Market," *Saturday Night*, 26 Oct. 1957
"Who Makes the Traffic Laws in Space," *Saturday Night*, 9 Nov. 1957
"Coexistence Tito-style," *Saturday Night*, 23 Nov. 1957
"Foreign Aid: The New Warfare," *Saturday Night*, 7 Dec. 1957

"America's Burden of World Leadership," *Saturday Night*, 21 Dec. 1957
"Partnership Problems for Canada and the United States," *Saturday Night*, 4 Jan. 1958
"Give and Take at the Summit," *Saturday Night*, 18 Jan. 1958
"Middle East: Dangerous Playground," *Saturday Night*, 1 Feb. 1958
"Kennnan Thesis: New Cold War Debate," *Saturday Night*, 15 Feb. 1958
"Revival of Freedom in Latin America," *Saturday Night*, 1 March 1958
"The Diminishing High Seas," *Saturday Night*, 15 March 1958
"National Politics and Foreign Affairs," *Saturday Night*, 29 March 1958
"Fusion and Confusion: The Dilemma of Diplomacy," *Saturday Night*, 26 April 1958
"Diefenbaker and Our Future Abroad," *Saturday Night*, 10 May 1958
"Global Triple Play: Ike to Dag to Mr. K," *Saturday Night*, 24 May 1958
"Leadership and Ideas on Trial," *Saturday Night*, 21 June 1958
"NORAD, NATO and the National Interest," *Saturday Night*, 19 July 1958
"Nasser and the West: From Crisis to Force," *Saturday Night*, 2 Aug. 1958
"Polar Ice and Arctic Sovereignty," *Saturday Night*, 30 Aug. 1958
"Commonwealth Conference Surveys the Family Fortunes," *Saturday Night*, 13 Sept. 1958
"A China Policy for Canada," *Saturday Night*, 11 Oct. 1958
"Items and Atoms on UN Agenda," *Saturday Night*, 25 Oct. 1958
"The British West Indies: Federation and Friend," *Saturday Night*, 22 Nov. 1958
"Towards Universal Human Rights," *Saturday Night*, 6 Dec. 1958
"Scholarship of the Press," *Saturday Night*, 20 Dec. 1958
"Wanted Now: A Defence Policy," *Saturday Night*, 3 Jan. 1959
"U.S. Supreme Court versus Canadian Freedom," *Saturday Night*, 28 Feb. 1959
"Berlin – The Showdown," *Saturday Night*, 14 March 1959
"Neutralism: The Canadian Flirtation," *Saturday Night*, 11 April 1959
"Changing Mood in Washington – from Dulles to Herter," *Saturday Night*, 6 June 1959
"Nehru the Titan and His India," *Saturday Night*, 18 July 1959
"Howard Green and the Direction of Canadian Foreign Policy," *Saturday Night*, 15 Aug. 1959
"Mr. K. Comes to Town," *Saturday Night*, 12 Sept. 1959
"Parliament of Man: The 14th UN Assembly," *Saturday Night*, 29 Sept. 1959
"The U.N.: Toward a World Government," *Saturday Night*, 20 Feb. 1960
"A Method or How to Act in Ottawa," *The Globe and Mail*, 7 Jan. 1966
"Are Canadians Drifting into Provincial 'Cults'?" *London Free Press*, 7 April 1966
"Johnson and Lesage – Part One," *Montreal Gazette*, 19 July 1966; "Part Two," 20 July 1966
"Marginal Victories Reflect Indecision," *Windsor Star*, 21 July 1966

"The Search for the Centre," *Winnipeg Free Press*, 21 July 1966
"Quiet Revolution and Mr. Johnson," *Windsor Star*, 22 July 1966
"Three Tests for Mr. Johnson," *Winnipeg Free Press*, 23 July 1966
"Continentalism and Canadians," *Globe and Mail*, 29 Dec. 1966
"Issues and Options," Part One, *Montreal Gazette*, 29 Dec. 1966; Part 2, 30 Dec. 1966
"Vietnam Again," *Montreal Gazette*, 15 March 1967
"Foreign Policy, a Centennial View," Part 1, *Montreal Gazette*, 24 April 1967; Part 2, 25 April 1967
"Canada and Quebec: The Shape of Things to Come," *Orah*, vol. 6, April 1967
"Israel, Arabs and the United Nations," *Montreal Gazette*, 1 June 1967
"The Search for a Viable Canada," *Viewpoints*, vol. 1 no. 1
"From Ceasefire to Peace," *Montreal Gazette*, 15 June 1967
"Nation and Province: De Gaulle," *Montreal Gazette*, 24 July 1967
"The Constitutional Crisis," *Montreal Gazette*, 3 Oct. 1967
"Charter and the Constitution," *Montreal Gazette*, 9 and 20 Feb. 1968
"Confederation: A Balance Sheet for a New Leader," *Montreal Gazette*, 3 April 1968
"More than a Fair Chance for Trudeau to Save a Dual Canada"; digest of address, *Financial Post*, 22 March 1969
"Students Deny the Taming of Power"; excerpts from address, *Financial Post*, 22 March 1969